BLACKS AND THEIR CONTRIBUTIONS TO THE AMERICAN WEST;

A Bibliography and Union List of Library Holdings Through 1970

Compiled by
JAMES de T. ABAJIAN

For the Friends of the
San Francisco Public Library

In cooperation with the American Library Association

G. K. HALL & CO., 70 LINCOLN STREET, BOSTON, MASS. 1974

Library of Congress Cataloging in Publication Data

Abajian, James.
    Blacks in the American West.

    1. Negroes--The West--Bibliography--Union lists.
2. Catalogs, Union--The West. 3. Catalogs, Union--
California. I. San Francisco. Public Library.
Friends. II. Title.
Z1361.N39A27   016.9178'06'96073   74-8695
ISBN 0-8161-1139-1

TO MY MOTHER, ELIZABETH,
whose continuous community
involvement for 64 years
has brought much pleasure
to both of us.

Preface

Blacks and Their Contributions to the American West; a Bibliography and
Union List of Library Holdings through 1970 was launched in 1969 with the
approval of Phyllis Dalton, then President of the California Library Association. Press releases describing the project and its aims were mailed to
nearly 800 newspaper publications and wire services throughout the western
United States. Requests for specific cooperation were made to 438 library
institutions. Returns from these libraries were almost universally enthusiastic though uneven in results. The largest of the university, public, and
research libraries found it unfeasible, due to their large size, to sift out
items relating to the black experience in the American West. Few, if any,
library bibliographers were able to determine western black authorship or institutions in their collections. Fortunately, it was possible for the compiler to spend considerable time in the largest of the California libraries
and to have in his possession a large card catalog of miscellaneous black
name and subject information as an aid in properly identifying materials for
inclusion in the present work.

The reader will be aware frequently that the present bibliography is not
the product of a lifetime of dedication and careful devotion such as that
which have produced such outstanding achievements as Monroe N. Work's A Bibliography of the Negro in Africa and America, originally issued in 1928 and
reprinted in 1965, and George L. Belkanp's highly refined bibliographical
masterpiece, Oregon Imprints, 1845-1870 (University of Oregon, 1968).

The preponderance of titles in the bibliography which relate to California
is due to California's long history and proportionately larger black population. The scattered nature of black settlers in many of the outlying western
areas was expressed poignantly in 1926 by Anita Scott Coleman when she wrote:
"They are as sparse as rose bushes upon the prairies." The proliferation of
California titles is also due to the outburst of scholarly and other analyses
of the 1965 Watts riot which far exceeded that of the 1943 zoot-suit riots in
the same approximate area; however, the bibliography does not attempt a complete coverage of the tremendous quantity of literature describing the 1965
riot, the Black Panthers, and black power generally.

The southern peace marches, new civil rights legislation, and the Watts
Riot brought a rapid expansion in library funds budgeted first for black and
later for ethnic titles which flowed quickly from both publishing and reprint
houses. Among these, scarcely a single title does not address itself to the
West in some small way; therefore, for purposes of limiting the size of this
bibliography, such general titles have been excluded from this volume.

It became academically popular to establish black or ethnic studies collections in every campus library. These collections concentrated on developing secondary source materials and consequently there is in the West no adequately supported and staffed library collection charged with the acquisition of primary source materials and other scarce items describing the black experience in the United States. There have been several ambitious programs, but even the largest institutions have failed to guarantee the long-term support necessary for successful continuity of collection and service. There seems to be little inter-agency cooperation among those few agencies performing even the smallest amount of tape recording and original source collecting.

A few of the largest and oldest library collections have acquired black materials of importance through their sheer accidental size and age. An administrator of one of these important library collections wrote to the compiler stating that it had "probably considerable material but scattered through files not indexed." The value of such a collection is diminished unless there is some means of retrieval and access. The preparation of added catalog entries for black materials was often ignored in the past, and thus analysis of scarce or unusual items will require a strenuous effort and commitment for some years to come.

Little attention has been given to continuous acquisition of local and regional imprints and original sources. For this reason, the present bibliography has placed considerable emphasis on local imprints, including periodicals and newspapers. The specific has been stressed over the general and the obscure over the well-known in the knowledge that general bibliographies of black literature have fulfilled the opposite functions. The large number of index entries for individual names and for business and social organizations enables this bibliography to fulfill a research as well as a reference function.

Questionable items have been included in the hope that thorough access to such materials might suggest new avenues of investigation and offer new resources for the researcher.

All titles of known, western black authorship have been included except for the large area of scholarly effort in African studies. However, the bibliography occasionally does include works relating to African-American relations and other titles of nonwestern interest, particularly educational studies produced in the West but relating to the South and to other sections of the United States and the Americas.

Blacks and Their Contribution to the American West is not a definitive bibliography, yet it is a foundation on which future reference works can be built as aids to those working in black studies. If future literature evidences a broader and more resourceful approach, due in some part to the present work, then our labors will have been justified.

Acknowledgments

This bibliography owes its inception to a citizens' committee chaired by Mrs. Cecil F. Poole, member of the Advisory Council of the Friends of the San Francisco Public Library. The membership of this short-lived committee was a happy combination of leaders in San Francisco's black community and library friends and administrators.

The Friends of the San Francisco Public Library assisted the committee with an initial gift of $1,000 in memory of the late Dr. Martin Luther King, Jr., while Joseph Staples and others began to sound out further sources of financial support for a bibliography of black activities in the American West, which all committee members considered a primary need in aid of regional library collection and black studies.

The Committee, the Friends of the San Francisco Public Library, and the compiler are all indebted to the enthusiastic support given over a two-year period by the San Francisco Foundation, the Mary A. Crocker Trust, the Hearst Foundation, the Richard N. Goldman Trust, William Matson Roth, the William Randolph Hearst Foundation, Mrs. Ansley K. Salz, and the Women's Press Club. Without their financial support, this bibliography would have remained but a well-intentioned resolution spread upon the pages of the committee's minutes.

The San Francisco Public Library provided the secretarial services of Maxine Smith whose efficiency and interest contributed immeasurably to the project and also enabled the project to use office space and furniture at the library.

Several special acknowledgments appear at the beginnings of the bibliography subject sections entitled "Art and Architecture" and "Periodicals and Newspapers."

In the matter of individual credits, there is the frustrating danger of omission. Whereas the proofreading services of Elizabeth L. Parker and Leslie Winant are of very recent recollection, it is more difficult to credit everyone who was of assistance to the present project or who has contributed in some way during the past fifteen years to the compiler's general information files.

During the project's period of greatest activity, 1969-71, foremost thanks are due Henry M. Bowles for his interest in the success of the bibliography, a devotion which went far beyond his responsibility as an officer of the Friends of the San Francisco Public Library and continued to the day of actual publication.

ACKNOWLEDGMENTS

The compiler is indebted surely to an array of distinguished bibliographers both for his early training and for the encouragement and experience gained as a working member on several cooperative projects. The enthusiasm of the late Douglas C. McMurtrie kindled the bibliographic interests of hundreds of librarians who came in contact, as the present writer did, with his absolutely boundless enthusiasm. The more quiet perserverance of Margaret Miller Rocq's eleven-year dedication in compiling her monumental California Local History was an almost daily joy to observe. In the latter case, the essential mechanics were learned which serve as the foundation for the present bibliography.

Although it is not possible to list here the large number of cooperating librarians, the names of their institutions can be found by consulting the list of Library Location Symbols in this volume.

The compiler recalls with pleasure the long hours of search spent in many of California's great library collections. It was a delight to encounter the thoughtful and erudite staff members of the California State Archives, Sacramento; the University of California's Bancroft Library, Berkeley; and the Henry E. Huntington Library, San Marino. Generous privileges were given by Peter Evans, Librarian of the California Historical Society, and by his assistant, Maude K. Swingle, who has directed my attention to a continuous flow of queries, book notices, and other relevant information.

Miriam Matthews, recently retired from her position as an administrator in the Los Angeles Public Library system, has been a foremost authority on California black bibliography since her own annotated work was completed at the University of Southern California in 1945. Consistent with her enthusiastic dedication to her professional field, Miss Matthews twice opened her impressive personal library for the compiler's use and also made available to the project the results of her own bibliographical collecting.

Ethel Ray Nance of San Francisco's African American Historical and Cultural Society has been a constant source of advice and assistance, for her personal experience in the black area extends from the Harlem Renaissance to the present day and includes association with both W. E. B. Du Bois and Charles Spurgeon Johnson. The Society's own publication program, unique in the West, has long been the recipient of her interest and guidance.

Mr. and Mrs. Eugene P. Lasartemay, Berkeley, made available their own library collection as well as that of the East Bay Negro Historical Society.

Julian Richardson, proprietor of Marcus Books, San Francisco, kept watch several years for current imprints of black authors.

George N. Belknap gave his permission to quote from his Oregon Imprints, 1845-1870. Permission also was received from the Washington State Library, Olympia, to quote from The Negro in the State of Washington, 1788-1967; a Bibliography of Published Source Materials on the Life and Achievements of the Negro in the Evergreen State (Olympia, 1967) and from its revised edition published in 1970.

The bibliography also is indebted to the following persons for their response to a variety of requests: Patricia Adler, Hilda Grayson Finney,

ACKNOWLEDGMENTS

E. Peter Mauk, Dr. Doyce B. Nunis, and Dr. W. Sherman Savage, Los Angeles; Mrs. Robert B. Flippin, Catherine Harroun, Robert J. Harvey, M.D., the Reverend Eugene H. Huffman, Margaret Garner Joseph, Lawton Kennedy, Printer, and Ruth Teiser, San Francisco; Lavola J. Bakken, Idlewyld Park, Oregon; Bert M. Fireman, Arizona Historical Foundation, Phoenix; Michael Harrison, Sacramento; Dr. Rudolph M. Lapp, College of San Mateo, San Mateo; Rudecinda Lo Buglio, Janesville; Dr. Dorothy B. Porter, Howard University Library, Washington, D. C.; Helen Sayre, Mill Valley; De Witt Smith, Oakland; Enid Thompson, Colorado State Historical Society, Denver; Lucille Smith Thompson, Montana State University Library, Bozeman; Eckard V. Toy, Jr., University of Wyoming Library, Laramie; and the late Lee H. Watkins, University of California, Davis.

For general advice and very kind assistance, I wish to thank the descendants of the following mid-nineteenth century Californians: John Hanson Butler, Barney Fletcher, Robert Coleman Francis, Capt. John Jones, Robert Tilghman, and Thomas Towns.

Contents

Explanatory Notes   xiii
Abbreviations   xv
References   xvii
Library Location Symbols   xix

                                                        Entries

Africa (as it relates to the U.S.)   **1-22**   1
Armed Services   23-68   3
Art and Architecture   7
   Exhibit Catalogs; Art History and Criticism;
   General Works   69-117   7
   Artists Represented in Permanent Museum
   Collections   118-144   12
Bibliographies and Finding Aids   145-274   16
Biography   29
   Individual Biographies and Autobiographies   275-449   29
   Collected Biography   450-481   46
   Original Sources   482-555   49
Black Movement and Racial Dissent   56
   Black Muslims (Nation of Islam)   556-564   56
   Black Panther Party   565-639   57
   Black Student Unions   639a-649   62
   National Association for the
   Advancement of Colored People   650-667   63
   Watts and the Watts Riot   668-829   65
   General Works   830-925   77
Business and Industry; Cooperatives   926-996   86
Caribbean, Hispanic America, Brazil   997-1015   93
Civil Rights   1016-1157   95
Colonization, Migration, and Population Statistics   1158-1228   109
Cookbooks, Food   1229-1235   115
Directories, Census Records, etc.   1236-1300   116
Education   124
   Counseling and Guidance   1301-1320   124
   Segregation and Desegregation   1321-1470   126
   Southern U. S.   1471-1509   138
   Primary and Pre-School   1510-1573   141
   Secondary   1574-1614   148

Contents

	Entries	
College and University	1615–1670	152
General Works	1671–1831	157
Employment and Unemployment; Occupations	1832–1947	171
Entertainment: Motion Pictures, Stage, and Radio	1948–2004	182
History and Historiography	2005–2130	187
Housing, Restrictive Covenants, and Urban Redevelopment	2131–2263	200
Journalism	2264–2297	213
Juvenile Literature	2298–2353	216
Labor	2354–2403	221
Language and Language Instruction	2404–2426	226
Law and Order, Correctional Institutions, etc.	2427–2488	228
Literature		235
Anthologies	2489–2508	235
Folklore	2509–2513	237
History and Criticism	2514–2553	237
Drama	2554–2573	240
Essays and Speeches	2574–2590	242
Fiction	2591–2686	244
Poetry and Proverbs	2687–2757	252
Medicine and Health	2758–2781	257
Miscegenation and Passing	2782–2795	260
Music and Dance	2796–2865	261
Politics, Government, and Suffrage	2866–2955	266
Race Relations, Discrimination, and Prejudice	2956–3164	275
Ranch Life, Including Cowboys	3165–3172	294
Religion and Philosophy	3173–3340	294
Slavery and Anti-Slavery		310
California and the West	3341–3429	310
Elsewhere in the U. S.	3430–3456	320
Social and Service Organizations		323
Community Service	3457–3507	323
Fraternal	3508–3544	327
Social and Benevolent	3545–3569	331
Women's Clubs	3570–3580	333
Sociology	3581–3635	334
Sports	3636–3680	339
Urban Life and History	3681–3826	343
Miscellaneous	3827–3883	356
Periodicals	3884–4048	362
Newspapers	4049–4302	375
Index		397

Explanatory Notes

If specific page numbers are not given for material of black interest, it may be assumed the entire work relates to black activities in the West.

It is important to note that all materials in the bibliography refer to black activities or authorship even though it is not stated in the entry.

An asterisk has been used to identify all known black authors and institutions in an effort to provide black studies with an in-field corpus. If any author has been misidentified, the compiler would be glad to receive correct information.

"American West" refers to the thirteen states farthest west, beginning with the Mountain States. These are: Montana, Wyoming, New Mexico, Idaho, Colorado, Utah, Nevada, Arizona, Washington, Oregon, California, Alaska, and Hawaii.

The state designation is not used after any California place name nor is it used after place names of obvious location, e.g., Albuquerque, Denver, Seattle.

The terminology used by reporting libraries in describing manuscript collections has been generally retained.

Nearly every printed work concerned with the early history of California and San Francisco describes the activities of William A. Leidesdorff, a black United States Vice-Consul under Mexican rule and later a city official. Therefore, no attempt has been made to list each work describing his career.

Whenever an individual title has been reported by thirty or more libraries, the statement "Available in many libraries," or a variation thereof, is used.

When no library location symbol is shown, it may be assumed the title was held in a private collection at the time of its examination. In the case of titles in periodical publications, the library location may be obtained by consulting the Union List of Serials in the Libraries of the United States and Canada. A few eastern United States library locations are shown for occasional works not found in a western library.

Because all academic dissertations and theses require the inclusion of bibliographies, the reader may assume that such a section exists even though no separate pagination is shown. Most of these dissertations and theses are available in photocopy by purchase from University Microfilms, 300 North Zeb Road, Ann Arbor, Michigan 48106.

Each title is entered only once; however, cross references and the index facilitate subject locations.

Both the San Francisco Examiner and the Stockton Record reported library holdings of "clippings and picture files," which "are not open for use by the general public."

In the present day, authors as well as entertainers and athletes have become increasingly peripatetic workers. Black entertainers and athletes have mainly been omitted, and the listing of works of authors generated during their western residence, e.g., Wallace Thurman, Ed Bullins, Chester B. Himes, is presented with only moderate success.

Some attempt has been made to investigate individual resources in the California State Archives, Sacramento, although an examination has been made only of the bare tip of an incredible mass of source material. It has neither been possible to locate nor describe black materials in the other federal, state, county, local, and business archives. This is but another indication of the indescribable possibilities for research in black studies both for the lay as well as the professional worker.

Articles of a popular nature have been generally excluded, as well as stories in news magazines. No effort has been made to duplicate listings found in the Index to Periodical Articles By and About Negroes, although occasionally selected entries have been included when content of sufficient merit warranted. The reader is also advised to use the Readers' Guide to Periodical Literature as well as the other indices found in the reference areas of all large public and academic libraries.

This bibliography identifies holdings as entered in the card catalog of the libraries surveyed; occasionally although items are listed in card catalogs, the actual titles are missing. The California State Library's union catalog of statewide holdings has been used sparingly to report otherwise unknown library locations. The researcher is advised to use this and other union catalogs with care.

Abbreviations

A. L. S.	autography letter(s) signed	ℓ.	leaf, leaves
assoc.	association	L. A.	Los Angeles
ave.	avenue	ltd.	limited
b.	born	m.	month, monthly
bet.	between	mimeo.	mimeographed
bk.	book	min.	minutes
bro., bros.	brother, brothers	ms., mss.	manuscript, manuscripts
c.	copyright	n.d.	no date of publication
ca.	about	n.p.	no place of publication
ch.	chapter	neg.	negative
co., cos.	company, companies	no., nos.	number, numbers
col., cols.	column, columns	off.	office
coll.	collection, collections	p., pp.	page, pages
comp.	compiled, compiler	pam.	pamphlets
corp.	corporation	photos.	photographs
d.	died	port., ports.	portrait, portraits
dept.	department	pref.	preface
diagrs.	diagrams	print.	printed, printer, printing
dist.	district		
div.	division	pseud.	pseudonym
e.g.	for example	pts.	parts
ed., eds.	edition, editor, editors	pub.	public, published, publisher, publication
enl.	enlarged	pubs.	publishers, publications
est.	established	q.	quarterly
facsim.	facsimile	reprint.	reprinted
ff.	following	rev.	revised
fold.	folded	S. F.	San Francisco
front.	frontispiece	ser.	series
govt.	government	sess.	session
i.e.	that is	sr.	senior
illus.	illustrated, illustrations, illustrator	supt.	superintendent
		t. p.	title page
inc.	incorporated	typew.	typewritten
incl.	including	univ.	university
ins.	insurance	unp.	unpaged
introd.	introduction	v.	volume, volumes
ir.	irregular	v.d.	various dates
jr.	junior	v.p.	various paging
		w.	weekly

References

BAIRD   Baird, Newton D. <u>An annotated bibliography of California fiction, 1664–1970</u>, by Newton D. Baird and Robert Greenwood. Georgetown, Talisman literary research, inc., 1971.

BEASLEY   Beasley, Delilah Leontium. <u>The Negro trail blazers of California: a compilation of records from the California archives in the Bancroft library at the University of California; and from the diaries, old papers and conversations of old pioneers in the state of California. It is a true record of facts as they pertain to the history of the pioneer and present-day Negroes of California</u>. L. A. [Times mirror printing and binding house] 1919.

DRURY   Drury, Clifford Merrill. <u>California imprints, 1846–1876, pertaining to social, educational, and religious subjects. A bibliography of 1099 titles: books, pamphlets, broadsides, periodicals, newspapers, and manuscripts; each described, annotated, and located</u>, by Clifford Merrill Drury ... [Pasadena] Privately printed, 1970.

GREENWOOD   Greenwood, Robert. <u>California imprints, 1833–1862; a bibliography</u>. Compiled by Seiko June Suzuki & Marjorie Pulliam and the Historical records survey. Los Gatos, Talisman press, 1961.

HATCH   Hatch, James V. <u>Black image on the American stage; a bibliography of plays and musicals 1770–1970</u>, by James V. Hatch. N. Y., Drama book specialists, inc., 1970.

NUC   Library of Congress and national union catalog. Use of this symbol refers to works issued or in process of being issued in 1970, <u>e.g.</u>, <u>Author lists, 1942–1962: a master accumulation</u> and <u>The National union catalog pre-1956 imprints</u>.

ROCQ   Rocq, Margaret (Miller), ed. <u>California local history, a bibliography and union list of library holdings</u>. Second ed., rev. and enl. Stanford, Stanford univ. press, 1970.

SPEAR   Spear, Dorothea N. <u>Bibliography of American directories through 1860</u>. Worcester, Mass., American antiquarian society, 1961.

References

WEST   West, Earle H.   A bibliography of doctoral research on the Negro, 1933-1966, compiled by Earle H. West ... [Ann Arbor, Mich.] University microfilms, 1969.

WORK   Work, Monroe Nathan.   A bibliography of the Negro in Africa and America, compiled by Monroe N. Work ... N. Y., The H. W. Wilson co., 1928.

Library Location Symbols

Az	Department of Library and Archives, State of Arizona, Phoenix
AzTeS	Arizona State University Library, Tempe
AzU	University of Arizona Library, Tucson
C	California State Library, Sacramento
C-ArS	California State Archives, Sacramento
C-S	California State Library, Sutro Branch, San Francisco
CAna	Anaheim Public Library
CAuP	Placer County Free Library, Auburn
CB	Berkeley Public Library
CBBD	Berkeley Baptist Divinity School Library
CBGTU	Graduate Theological Union Library, Berkeley
CBPac	Pacific School of Religion Library, Berkeley
CBSK	Starr King School for the Ministry Library, Berkeley
CBaK	Kern County Library, Bakersfield
CBb	Burbank Public Library
CBea	Beaumont District Library, Beaumont
CBloCM	San Bernardino County Museum Library, Bloomington
CBu	Burlingame Public Library
CCC	Claremont College Library
CChiS	California State University Library, Chico
CColu	Colusa County Free Library, Colusa
CCotS	California State College Library, Rohnert Park (Former address: Cotati)
CCovB	American Baptist Seminary of the West Library, Covina
CDc	Daly City Public Library
CEH	Humboldt County Library, Eureka
CEcaC	El Camino College Library, El Camino
CEs	El Segundo Public Library
CF	Fresno County Free Library, Fresno
CFS	California State University Library, Fresno
CFa	Solano County Free Library, Fairfield
CFlS	California State University Library, Fullerton
CGl	Glendale Public Library
CHC	Chabot College Library, Hayward
CHCL	Alameda County Library, Hayward
CHS	California State University Library, Hayward
CHanK	Kings County Library, Hanford
CHe	Healdsburg Public Library
CHem	Hemet Public Library
CHi	California Historical Society Library, San Francisco
CHu	Huntington Beach Public Library
CKenM	College of Marin Library, Kentfield
CL	Los Angeles Public Library

CLAF	Anna Freud Research Library, Reiss-Davis Child Study Center, Los Angeles
CLAMP	Academy of Motion Picture Arts and Sciences Library, Los Angeles
CLCM-A	Los Angeles County Museum of Art Library, Los Angeles
CLCo	Los Angeles County Public Library, Los Angeles
CLGPC	George Pepperdine College Library, Los Angeles
*CLGS	Golden State Mutual Life Insurance Company Library, Los Angeles
CLM	Los Angeles County Museum of Natural History Library, Los Angeles
CLMSm	Mount St. Mary's College Library, Los Angeles
CLS	California State University Library, Los Angeles
CLSU	University of Southern California Library, Los Angeles
CLU	University of California Library, Los Angeles
CLU-C	William Andrews Clark Memorial Library, University of California, Los Angeles
CLob	Long Beach Public Library
CLobS	California State University Library, Long Beach
CLod	Lodi Public Library
CLom	Lompoc Public Library
CMS	Stanislaus County Free Library, Modesto
CMa	Madera County Free Library, Madera
CMary	Marysville City Library
CMerCL	Merced County Free Library, Merced
CMl	Mill Valley Public Library
CMlG	Golden Gate Baptist Theological Seminary Library, Mill Valley
CMp	Menlo Park Public Library
CMpS	McKeon Memorial Library, St. Patrick's Seminary, Menlo Park
CMv	Mountain View Public Library
CNF	Napa County Free Library, Napa
CNoS	San Fernando Valley State University Library, Northridge
CO	Oakland Public Library
*COEB	East Bay Negro Historical Society Library, Oakland
COHN	College of the Holy Names Library, Oakland
COM	Merritt College Library, Oakland
COMC	Mills College Library, Oakland
COrCL	Orange County Free Library, Orange
COro	Oroville Public Library
COroB	Butte County Library, Oroville
CP	Pasadena Public Library
CPa	Palo Alto Public Library
CPhCL	Contra Costa County Library, Pleasant Hill
CPhD	Diablo Valley College Library, Pleasant Hill
CPl	Placentia District Library, Placentia
CPla	El Dorado County Free Library, Placerville
CPom	Pomona Public Library
CPomCP	California State Polytechnic College, Kellogg-Voorhis Campus Library, Pomona
CQCL	Plumas County Free Library, Quincy
CRbCL	Tehama County Free Library, Red Bluff
CRcS	San Mateo County Free Library, Belmont (formerly in Redwood City)
CRedCL	Shasta County Library, Redding
CRic	Richmond Public Library
CRiv	Riverside County Library, Riverside
CS	Sacramento City-County Library
CSS	California State University Library, Sacramento
CSalCL	Monterey County Library, Salinas

CSaT	San Francisco Theological Seminary Library, San Anselmo
CSb	San Bernardino Public Library
CSbCL	San Bernardino County Library, San Bernardino
CSbS	California State College Library, San Bernardino
CSd	San Diego Public Library
CSdCiC	San Diego City College Library
CSdHi	San Diego Historical Society Library
CSdS	California State University Library, San Diego
CSea	California Public School Libraries, Seaside
CSf	San Francisco Public Library
*CSfAA	San Francisco African American Historical and Cultural Society Library
CSfCP	The Society of California Pioneers Library, San Francisco
CSfCiC	City College of San Francisco Library
CSfGG	Golden Gate University Library, San Francisco
CSfL	San Francisco Law Library
CSfSt	California State University Library, San Francisco
CSfU	University of San Francisco Library
CSj	San Jose Public Library
CSjC	California State University Library, San Jose
CSjCL	Santa Clara County Free Library, San Jose
CSjCi	San Jose City College Library
CSlu	San Luis Obispo Public Library
CSluCL	San Luis Obispo County Free Library, San Luis Obispo
CSluSP	California State Polytechnic College Library, San Luis Obispo
CSmH	The Henry E. Huntington Library, San Marino
CSmarP	Palomar College Library, San Marcos
CSmatC	College of San Mateo Library, San Mateo
CSoS	South San Francisco Public Library
CSp	South Pasadena Public Library
CSrCL	Marin County Free Library, San Rafael
CSt	Stanford University Library, Stanford
CSt-H	Hoover Institution on War, Revolution and Peace Library, Stanford University, Stanford
CSt-Law	Stanford University School of Law Library, Stanford
CStaB	Charles W. Bowers Memorial Museum Library, Santa Ana
CStb	Santa Barbara Free Public Library
CStcrCL	Santa Cruz County Public Library
CStma	Santa Maria Public Library
CStmo	Santa Monica Public Library
CSto	Public Library, Stockton-San Joaquin County, Stockton
CStoC	University of the Pacific Library, Stockton
CStoPM	Pioneer Museum & Haggin Galleries Library, Stockton
CStp	Dean Hobbs Blanchard Memorial Library, Santa Paula
CStrCL	Sonoma County Free Library, Santa Rosa
CSuLas	Lassen County Free Library, Susanville
CTul	Tulare Free Public Library
CTur	Turlock Public Library
CTurS	Stanislaus State College Library, Turlock
CU	University of California Library, Berkeley
CU-A	University of California Library, Davis
CU-B	Bancroft Library, University of California, Berkeley
CU-I	University of California Library, Irvine
CU-M	University of California Medical Center Library, San Francisco
CU-SB	University of California Library, Santa Barbara

CU–SC	University of California Library, Santa Cruz
CUn	Universal City Studios, Research Department Library, Universal City
CUpl	Upland Public Library
CViCL	Tulare County Free Library, Visalia
CVt	Ventura Public Library
CVtCL	Ventura County Free Library, Ventura
CWM	Mount San Antonio College Library, Walnut
CWh	Whittier Public Library
CWiwCL	Glenn County Free Library, Willows
CWoY	Yolo County Free Library, Woodland
CYcCL	Sutter County Free Library, Yuba City
CoHi	State Historical Society of Colorado Library, Denver
*DHU	Howard University Library, Washington, D. C.
DLC	Library of Congress, Washington, D. C.
KHi	Kansas State Historical Society Library, Topeka
MtGf	Great Falls Public Library, Great Falls, Montana
MtH	Helena Public Library, Helena, Montana
MtHi	Montana Historical Society Library, Helena
MWA	American Antiquarian Society Library, Worcester, Mass.
*NN	Arthur A. Schomburg Collection, New York Public Library, New York
NmU	University of New Mexico Library, Albuquerque
NvHi	Nevada Historical Society Library, Reno
Or	Oregon State Library, Salem
Or–Ar	Oregon State Archives, Salem
OrFP	Pacific University Library, Forest Grove, Oregon
OrHi	Oregon Historical Society Library, Portland
OrMcL	Linfield College Library, McMinnville, Oregon
OrP	Library Association of Portland, Portland, Oregon
OrU	University of Oregon Library, Eugene
WHi	State Historical Society of Wisconsin Library, Madison
Wa	Washington State Library, Olympia
WaPu	Puyallup Public Library, Puyallup, Washington
WaPlP	Pacific Lutheran University Library, Parkland, Washington
WaPS	Washington State College Library, Pullman
WaSp	Spokane Public Library, Spokane, Washington
WaT	Tacoma Public Library, Tacoma, Washington
WaTC	Tacoma Community College Library, Tacoma, Washington
WaTP	University of Puget Sound Library, Tacoma, Washington
WaU	University of Washington Library, Seattle
Wy	Wyoming State Archives and Historical Department Library, Cheyenne
WyU	University of Wyoming Library, Laramie

*The library of a black institution.

*Refers only to known black authors and black organizations.
Obviously, many other black authors are not so designated
because of lack of information.
If no library location for a book or pamphlet title is shown,
and no other source of information is given, the reader
may assume that the title was held in a private collection
at the time of this bibliography's compilation.

AFRICA (as it relates to the U. S.)

1. *Afro-American institute. Malcolm X unity house. Black man speaks;
organ of the Afro-American institute, Malcolm X unity house –
1553 Fulton St., S. F. [S. F., 1970]. 60 p. port. (cover).
   Consists mainly of essays on various African countries.

2. BARNETT, DON. With the guerrillas in Angola, by Don Barnett.
[Seattle] Liberation support movement [information center, 1970].
34 p. illus., ports., map.

3. BERKES, ROSS N. "African affairs," a lecture given Feb. 11, 1966
for "Perspectives on the Negro in our affluent society," a lecture
series sponsored by the Associated students of Palomar college,
San Marcos. CSmarP (tape, 1200 feet).
   Relates problems of the Negro in the U. S., with problems which
exist in other countries including the new African nations.

4. California. University. African studies. African studies at
U. C. L. A. L. A., Univ. of Calif. [n.d.]. 30 p. CLU.

5. CLENDENEN, CLARENCE CLEMENS. Americans in Africa, 1865–1900 [by]
Clarence Clendenen, Robert Collins [and] Peter Duignan. Stanford,
Stanford univ., 1966. 130 p. CSt-H.

6. _____. Americans in black Africa up to 1865 [by] Clarence C.
Clendenen and Peter Duignan. Stanford [Stanford univ.], 1964. 109p.
CSt-H.

7. COLLINS, ROBERT. Americans in Africa; a preliminary guide to
American missionary archives and library manuscript collections on
Africa, by Robert Collins and Peter Duignan. [Stanford] Stanford
univ., 1963. 96 p. CSt-H.

Africa

8. DAVIDSON, BASIL. Can we write African history? L. A., Univ. of Calif. African studies center [1965]. 19 p. Occasional papers no. 1. CLU.

9. DUIGNAN, PETER JAMES, 1926– . African and Afro-American studies; notes on reference tools. [Stanford, Hoover institution on war, revolution and peace, 1969]. 44 p. CSt, CSt-H.
   A bibliographical study authored by the curator, Africa collections, the Hoover institution.

10. _____. The United States and the African slave trade, 1619–1862, by Peter Duignan and Clarence Clendenen. [Stanford]. Hoover institution on war, revolution, and peace, Stanford univ., 1963. vii, 72 p. Bibliography: pp. 63–72. CFS, CNoS, CSt-H.

11. HARVEY, ROY. People's war in Angola; report on the first eastern regional conference of the MPLA, by Roy Harvey. [Seattle, Liberation support movement information center, 1970]. 28 p. illus., ports., map.

12. Liberation support movement. Interview on Angola [with] commander and member of MPLA comité director, Spartacus Monimambu. Movimento popular de libertação de Angola. [Seattle, Liberation support movement information center, 1970]. 34 p. ports., map.

13. _____. Interview [with] George Nyandoro, general secretary, Zimbabwe African people's union (ZAPU). [Seattle, Liberation support movement information center, 1970]. 12 p. illus., map.

14. _____. Interview [with] member of MPLA comité director, Daniel Chipenda. Movimento popular de libertação de Angola. [Seattle Liberation support movement information center, 1970]. 22 p. port., map.

15. _____. Memorandum of activities of Medical assistance services (S. A. M.) of the Popular movement for the liberation of Angola (MPLA) in the liberated regions of the eastern front - region III. Interview with Dr. Americo Boavida ... [Seattle, Liberation support movement information center, 1970]. 27 p. illus., ports.
   Includes poetry.

16. _____. MPLA 1970; Movimento popular de libertação de Angola. [Seattle] Liberation support movement information center [1970]. 30 p. illus., ports., maps. 2nd ed.
   A survey of progress issued on the 9th anniversary of the struggle to free Angola from Portuguese rule. Includes poetry.

17. *MAGUBANE, BERNARD, 1930– . The American Negro's conception of Africa: a study in the ideology of pride and prejudice. Doctoral dissertation, Univ. of Calif., Los Angeles, 1967. 385 ℓ.

18. *MIDDLETON, WILLIAM J. "Pan-Africanism, a historical analysis and critique," in The black scholar, v. 1, Jan.-Feb., 1970, pp. 58–64.
   Author is a doctoral candidate, Univ. of Calif., Berkeley.

Africa

19. *PITTMAN, JOHN.   "Africa against the axis," in <u>Negro quarterly</u>,
    v. 1, Fall, 1942, pp. 207-18.
       By the foreign ed. of the Los Angeles <u>Peoples world</u>.

20. *SCOTT, HORATIO L.   The truth of Africa, agricultural-mineral; a
    short history of the present conditions of Central and South Africa.
    Its mountains, rivers, lakes, climate and climatic changes in all
    sections. Oakland, William H. Day, 1901. DHU (no pagination given).
       Authored by a native of San Francisco.

21. TAKAKI, RONALD TOSHIYUKI. A pro-slavery crusade: the movement to
    reopen the African slave trade. Doctoral dissertation, Univ. of Calif.,
    Berkeley, 1967. 248 ℓ.

22. VEATCH, LAURELYN LOVETT. African students in the United States:
    their political attitudes and the influence of the United States on
    those attitudes. Master's thesis, Univ. of Calif., Berkeley, 1968.
    iii, 188 ℓ.

ARMED SERVICES

23. ADKINS, W. B. The Buffalo soldiers. [Stockton, n.d.]. 10 p.
    Mimeo. CStoC.

24. BARROW, WILLIAM. "The Buffalo soldiers; the Negro cavalry in the
    West, 1866-1891," in <u>Black world</u>, v. 16, July, 1967, pp. 34-37, 89.

25. *BATTEAU, ELGIE ADELAIDE.   A study of the Negro soldier in the
    United States from the American revolution to 1900. Master's thesis,
    Univ. of Arizona, Tucson, 1944. 151 ℓ.

26. BIGELOW, JOHN, 1854-1936. On the bloody trail of Geronimo [by]
    Lt. John Bigelow, Jr. With the original illustrations of Hooper,
    McDougall, Chapin, Hatfield, and Frederic Remington. Foreword, introd.
    and notes, by Arthur Woodward. L. A., Westernlore press, 1968. xxv,
    237 p. illus., map (on lining papers), ports. Bibliographical refer-
    ences included in "Notes": pp. 225-31. CSj, CSt.
       Military operations of the 10th U. S. cavalry in Ariz., N. Mex., &
    Sonora.

27. "Brief history of troop 'K', tenth U. S. cavalry," in <u>Colored</u>
    <u>American magazine</u>, v. 7, Dec., 1904, pp. 730-33.
       Describes operations in Arizona and Montana.

28. BROWN, EARL and GEORGE R. LEIGHTON. The Negro and the war. N. Y.,
    Public affairs pamphlet no. 71. 1941. 32 p.
       Includes the Ninth and Tenth cavalry which fought the Indians on
    the plains of the West.

29. CASHIN, HERSHEL V. Under fire. With the tenth U. S. cavalry. Being
    a brief, comprehensive view of the Negro's participation in the wars of

Armed Services

the United States. Especially showing the valor and heroism of the
Negro soldiers of the ninth and tenth cavalries, and the twenty-fourth
and twenty-fifth infantries ... Famous Indian campaigns and their
results ... By Hershel V. Cashin ... Charles Alexander [and others].
N. Y., F. T. Neely [c1899]. xv, 361 p. illus., ports. NUC, ante-1956.

30. _____. Same. N. Y., Arno press, 1969. CNoS.

31. CORNISH, DUDLEY T. Negro troops in the Union army, 1861-1865.
Doctoral dissertation, Univ. of Colorado, Boulder, 1950.

32. DOUGLAS, HELEN GAHAGAN, 1900- . The Negro soldier, a partial
record of Negro devotion and heroism in the cause of freedom gathered
from the files of the War and Navy departments [by] Helen Gahagan
Douglas, 14 district, California, House of representatives ... appearing
in the Congressional record, January 22, 24, 25, 28, 29, 30, 31, and
February 1, 1946. [n.p., 1946]. 54 ℓ. CLU.

33. FINLEY, LEIGHTON, 1856-1894. Notebooks and photographs pertaining
to his service as a lieutenant with the 10th cavalry, U. S. army in
Texas and Arizona during the Indian wars. AzU.

34. FISHER, BARBARA ESTER, 1939- . Forrestine Cooper Hooker's notes
and memoirs on army life in the West, 1871-1876. Master's thesis,
Univ. of Arizona, Tucson, 1963.

35. [GLASS, EDWARD L. N.], 1890- , ed. The history of the tenth cavalry,
1866-1921. [Tucson, Acme printing co., 1921]. 141 p. illus. AzTeS,
AzU, CLGS. "Compiled and edited by Major E. L. N. Glass, 10th cav."

36. GOOD, DONNIE D. "The buffalo soldier," in American scene, v. 10,
no. 4, 1970.

37. HANFORD, CORNELIUS HOLGATE, 1849- , ed. Seattle and environs;
1852-1924. Hon. C. H. Hanford, editor. Chicago, Pioneer historical
pub. co., 1924. 3 v. (fold.) map, plates, ports. CSf, CSmH, Wa.
    Contains a list of Negroes who served in World war I, p. 664.

38. JACKSON, JAMES W. The black man and military mobilization in the
United States: 1916-1919. Master's thesis, Calif. state univ.,
Hayward, 1970. iii, 176 ℓ.

39. LECKIE, WILLIAM H. The buffalo soldiers; a narrative of the Negro
cavalry in the West. Norman, Univ. of Oklahoma press [c1967]. xiv,
290 p. illus., maps, ports. Bibliography: pp. 262-76.
    Pertains mainly to Arizona, New Mexico, and Texas.
    Available in many libraries.

40. *LEE, CHAUNCEY. "USO camp shows and the soldier," in Crisis,
v. 51, Feb., 1944, pp. 50 and 61.
    By the civilian coordinator of shows at Fort Huachuca, Ariz.

Armed Services

41. *LEE, IRVIN H., 1932- . Negro medal of honor men, by Irvin H. Lee.
Illus. with photographs. Second ed., enl. N. Y., Dodd, Mead & co.
[c1967]. xii, 142 p. illus., ports. Bibliography: pp. 131-32. C,
CEcaC, CSbCL, CSbS, CSfCiC, CSj, CSp, CSt, CU-A, WaT.
    Includes accounts of members of the 9th and 10th U. S. cavalry units
in Arizona and New Mexico.

42. _____. Same. 3rd ed. N. Y., Dodd, Mead & co., 1969. CNoS.

43. LEE, ULYSSES GRANT. United States army in World war II. Special
studies: the employment of Negro troops. Washington, D. C., Office
of the Chief of military history, United States army, 1966. xix, 740 p.
illus., maps (fold.), ports, tables. CFS, CNoS, CSt, CU-SB.
    Describes activities of army units and of camps and forts throughout
the West.

44. MANDELBAUM, DAVID GOODMAN, 1911- . Soldier groups and Negro
soldiers. Berkeley, Univ. of Calif. press, 1952. viii, 142 p.
Bibliography: pp. 133-38. CFS, CHS, CLSU, CNoS, CPhD, CSbS, CSdS,
CSf, CSluSP, CSt, CU, CU-A, CU-SB, CU-SC, CWM.

45. MARSHALL, OTTO MILLER. The Wham paymaster robbery. Sponsored and
distributed by the Pima Chamber of commerce. [Pima, Ariz.?]. c1967.
iii, 79 [10] p. illus., ports., map.
    Describes the as yet unsolved robbery of a U. S. Army paymaster,
Maj. Joseph W. Wham, of $29,000 in Howard County in 1889. The major's
escort were members of the 10th Cavalry, eight of whom were wounded.

46. MULLER, WILLIAM G. The twenty-fourth infantry, past and present;
a brief history of the regiment compiled from officials records, under
the direction of the regimental commander. By William G. Muller ...
[n.p.], 1923. [128] p. illus., ports. Lettered on cover: 1869. 1922.
CSt-H.

47. MURRAY, ROBERT A. "The United States army in the aftermath of the
Johnson county invasion: April through November, 1892," in Annals of
Wyoming, v. 38, Apr., 1966, pp. 59-75.
    Concerns the all-black cavalry units operating there.

48. NANKIVELL, JOHN H., 1884- . The history of the twenty-fifth
regiment, United States infantry, 1869-1926, comp. and ed. by John H.
Nankivell ... [Denver, Smith-Brooks printing co., c1927]. xvii, 212
[21] p. illus., ports. Bibliography: p. [233]. DLC.

49. *NELSON, DENNIS DENMARK, 1907- . The integration of the Negro into
the United States navy, 1776-1947, with a brief historical introd.
[Washington, D. C.], 1948. v. p. illus., ports. Bibliography:
pp. 209-12.

50. _____. Same. N. Y., Farrar, Straus and Young [1951], xv, 238 p.
CCotS, CHS, CL, CLCo, CRic, CSdS, CSf.
    Authored by a San Diego resident. Based upon his Master's thesis,
Howard univ., Washington, D. C.

Armed Services

51. *PITTS, LUCIA MAE.   One Negro WAC's story [by] Lucia M. Pitts.
L. A., Privately printed, c1968. 22 p.
     Autobiography of Los Angeles resident. Includes experience at
Fort Huachuca, Ariz.

52. REEVE, FRANK D., ed. "Frederick E. Phelps: a soldier's memoirs,"
in New Mexico historical review, v. 25, Apr., 1950, pp. 187-221.
     This portion of Phelps' memoirs describes some actions of Negro
army units.

53. REMINGTON, FREDERIC, 1861-1909. "Artist rides with 10th U. S.
Cavalry, a scout with the Buffalo-Soldiers, famous Negro dragoons,"
in Butterfield express; historical newspaper of the Southwest, v. 4,
Aug.-Sept., 1966.

54. _____. "A scout with the buffalo-soldiers. Written and illustrated
by Frederic Remington," in Century magazine, v. 37, Apr., 1889,
pp. 899-912.
     Reprinted in Pacific historian, v. 12, Spring, 1968, pp. 25-39.

55. Seattle-King county health and welfare council. Committee on
intergroup relations. A report on recreational facilities and services
for Negro servicemen in the Seattle area. [Seattle], 1950. Wa.

56. STILLMAN, RICHARD JOSEPH. Integration of the Negro in the U. S.
armed forces [by] Richard J. Stillman, II. N. Y., Frederic A. Praeger
[c1968]. xii, 167 p. "Bibliographical essay": pp. 157-67. CNoS,
CSdS, CSt.
     Contains occasional information about the West.

57. THOMPSON, ERWIN NORMORE. The Negro regiments of the U. S. regular
army, 1866-1900. Master's thesis, Univ. of Calif., Davis, 1966. 175 ℓ.

58. _____. "The Negro soldiers on the frontier: a Fort Davis study,"
in Journal of the West, v. 7, Apr., 1968, pp. 217-35.
     Includes activities in New Mexico and Arizona.

59. U. S. Adjutant general's office. The Negro in the military service
of the United States; a compilation of official records, state papers,
historical extracts, etc. relating to his military status and service,
from the date of his introduction into the British North American
colonies. Prepared under the direction of Brigadier general Richard C.
Drum, Adjutant general, U. S. army, by Elon A. Woodward. 1888. Positive
film. Reel 1, 1639-1862; reel 2, 1863; reel 3, 1864; reel 4, 1865-77;
and reel 5, 1862-65; 1866-86. CHS, CLU.

60. _____. Army. Military division of the Missouri. Correspondence
and related materials, 1878-1880 ... concerning Capt. Nichols Nolan,
10th Cavalry, U. S. army. AzU (xerox copies of original Mss. in the
Ft. Huachuca museum).

61. WARD, C. H. "A trip to the cavalry camps in southern Arizona,"
in Cosmopolitan, v. 2, Oct., 1886, pp. 109-14.
     Includes activities of black soldiers.

Armed Services

62. WHARFIELD, HAROLD B. "The affair at Carrizal," in <u>Montana, magazine</u>
<u>of western history</u>, v. 18, Autumn, 1968, pp. 24-39.
     Describes 10th Cavalry operations in New Mexico and Mexico.

63. _____. 10th cavalry & border fights, by H. B. (Dave) Wharfield.
[El Cajon?, Calif., 1965]. vii, 114 p. illus., maps, ports. AzTeS,
AzU, CU.

64. _____. With scouts and cavalry at Fort Apache. Ed. by John
Alexander Carroll. Tucson, Arizona pioneer historical society [1965].
xii, 124 p. illus., ports., map (on lining papers). AzU, CU.

65. *WILKINS, ROY, 1901- . "Nurses go to war," in <u>Crisis</u>, v. 50,
Feb., 1943, pp. 42-44.
     Nurses at Station hospital no. 1, Fort Huachuca, Ariz.

66. _____. "The West in wartime," in <u>Crisis</u>, v. 50, May, 1943, pp. 142
and 153.
     Describes treatment of black soldiers in California; Ogden, Utah;
Denver; Cheyenne; and Fort Huachuca, Ariz.

67. WILSON, CHARLES HENRY. The American Negro's part in the world's
war. Master's thesis, Univ. of southern Calif., Los Angeles, 1929.
vi, 97 ℓ.

68. YOUNG, KARL. "A fight that could have meant war," in <u>American west</u>,
v. 3, Spring, 1966, pp. 17-23, 90.
     Describes the military activities of the 10th Cavalry against Pancho
Villa units on the New Mexico border and in Mexico.

ART AND ARCHITECTURE

EXHIBIT CATALOGS; ART HISTORY AND CRITICISM; GENERAL WORKS

69. Arrowhead allied arts council. Arrowhead allied arts council presents
festival of arts, May 2-12, 1968. Afro-American art exhibit (exhibit
at the San Bernardino women's club), May 4-5, 1968, sponsored by
Social-lites social & charitable club. [San Bernardino, 1968].
[24] ℓ. illus.
     Includes catalog of exhibits and 16 biographical accounts.

70. ARVEY, VERNA. "By her own bootstraps," in <u>Opportunity</u>, v. 22, Jan.-
Mar., 1944, pp. 17 and 42.
     A biographical account of Mrs. Beulah E. Woodard, Los Angeles
sculptor.

71. _____. "Sargent Johnson," in <u>Opportunity</u>, v. 17, July, 1939,
pp. 213-14.

Exhibit Catalogs; Art History and Criticism; General Works

72. *Blackman's art gallery, San Francisco. Blackman's art gallery;
dedicated to black culture ... 619 Haight street, San Francisco.
[S. F., Golden printers, 1970]. [15] p. illus., ports.
A descriptive brochure also containing biographical information.

73. California. University. Berkeley. Robert H. Lowie museum of
anthropology. African arts; an exhibition of the Robert H. Lowie
museum of anthropology of the University of California, Berkeley,
April 6/October 22, 1967. Presented with the support of the California
alumni foundation and the Committee for arts and lectures. Catalogue
by William Bascom. [Berkeley, 1967]. 70 p. illus. maps (on end
papers). Bibliography: pp. 89-90. CU.

74. _____. _____. Los Angeles. Art galleries. The Negro in American
art; an exhibition co-sponsored by the California arts commission.
UCLA art galleries, September 11 to October 16, 1966; University of
California, Davis, November 1 to December 15, 1966; Fine arts gallery
of San Diego, January 6 to February 12, 1967; Oakland art museum,
February 24 to March 19, 1967. [L. A., 1966]. 63 p. illus. CHi,
CLU, CNoS, CP, CSf, CU-A.

75. *CLARK, CLAUDE. A black art perspective (a black teacher's guide
to a black visual art curriculum) prepared by Claude Clark, painter &
instructor in African and Afro-American art, Merritt college, Oakland,
California 94609. Oakland, c1970. 136 p. illus.
"Drawings by Claude Lockhart Clark."

76. Contemporary black artists. N. Y., Ruder and Finn fine arts, c1969.
[40] p. illus. CSf.
Catalog of a traveling exhibit which included in its 1970 itinerary
the San Francisco museum of art and the Art galleries, Univ. of Calif.,
Santa Barbara. California and western artists represented were Marvin
Harden, Betye Saar, Raymond Saunders, and Earl Miller.

77. *Cultural exchange center of Los Angeles.* Prints by American Negro
artists. Second ed. L. A., 1967. 51 p. plates. COM, CSdS, CSf.
"Volume one of the series 'Contemporary American artists'."

78. DOVER, CEDRIC. American Negro art. [Greenwich, Conn.] N. Y.
graphic society [1960]. 186 p. illus., plates, ports. "Bibliography by
Maureen Dover": pp. 57-60. C, CCovB, CFS, CKenM, CNoS, CSdS, CSf,
CSj, CSjCi, CU-SC, CWM.
Western artists represented include Sargent C. Johnson, Guy Miller,
Charles White, J. Eugene Grigsby, Claude Rockingham Clark, Leonard
Cooper, and James Washington.

79. _____. Same. N. Y. graphic society, 1962. COM.

80. _____. Same. N. Y. graphic society, 1965. CSfCiC.

81. *Family savings and loan association, pub. Gallery of Negro-American
pioneers ... [L. A., 1969?]. [20] p. ports.
Showing portraits painted by Alice (Taylor) Gafford, Los Angeles.

Exhibit Catalogs; Art History and Criticisms; General Works

82. *FAX, ELTON CLAY, 1909- . "Four rebels in art," in Freedomways, v. 4,
Spring, 1964, pp. 215-25.
    Includes Charles White.

83. *FULLER, HOYT WILLIAM, 1928- . "Charles White, artist," in Black world,
v. 12, July, 1963, pp. 40-45.

84. GARRISON, LILLIAN JOY. An oil painting depicting a group of Negro
workers. Master's thesis, Univ. of southern Calif., Los Angeles, 1951.
21 ℓ. mounted photos.

85. [Golden state mutual life insurance company].* GSM's Negro art
collection. [L. A., 196-?]. [38] ℓ. plates, ports. CHi, CLCM-A,
CLGS.
    "Includes 35 plates with commentary and four pages of biographical
notes." - Dorothy B. Porter.

86. _____. Historical murals: the contribution of the Negro to the
growth of California from exploration and colonization through settlement and development is portrayed in these murals. [L. A., 1965].
15 p. illus., port. CHi, CLCM-A, CLGS, CU-B.

87. _____. Selected pieces from [the] Golden state mutual life insurance
co. Afro-American art collection. L. A. [196-?]. [16] p. illus.,
ports. CLGS, CSfAA.
    Also contains biographical accounts of artists.

88. HERSKOVITS, MELVILLE JEAN, 1895-1963. The backgrounds of African
art, by Melville J. Herskovits. Three lectures given on the Cooke-
Daniels lecture foundation, in conjunction with an exhibition of African
art assembled by the Denver art museum, January and February, 1945.
[Denver, 1945]. 64 p. illus. (incl. map). "Suggested readings":
pp. 63-64. CU.

89. _____. Same. Ann Arbor, Mich., Univ. microfilms, 1966. CSt.

90. HOWELL, JOHN BERNARD. A study of an elementary school art enrichment
program through sculpture for gifted children who lived in a culturally
deprived area. Master's thesis, Calif. state univ., San Francisco,
1965. 111 ℓ.
    "A description of an art enrichment program for 'culturally
deprived', gifted children at San Francisco's Starr King elementary
school. Sculpting was employed to help students discover and evaluate
the relationship between self-expression and the role of the arts in
society."

91. "Images of dignity: the drawings of Charles White," in Black world,
v. 16, June, 1967, pp. 40-48.

92. *JOHNSON, MARIE EDWARDS. Blackness: a focal point, a project in
painting. Master's thesis, Calif. state univ., San Jose, 1968. 18 ℓ.
col. illus.

Exhibit Catalogs; Art History and Criticism; General Works

93. KERR, ADELAIDE. "A record-breaking exhibit (library) by a group of
artists (black)," in Wilson library bulletin, v. 43, Apr., 1969,
pp. 756-59.
An exhibit at the Inglewood public library.

94. La Jolla. Art center. The sculpture of Negro Africa. [Exhibition
organized by the Art center in La Jolla and arranged by the Stolper
galleries of primitive arts, New York and Los Angeles, to be shown ...
May 1960 through March 1961. La Jolla, 1960]. [27] p. illus. NUC,
1942-1962.

95. *LEWIS, SAMELLA S., ed. Black artists on art, volume 1. [Ed. by]
Samella S. Lewis and Ruth G. Waddy. L. A., Contemporary crafts, c1969.
xi, 132 p. illus., ports. Biographies of artists: pp. 122-32. CCotS,
CHS, CNoS, CRic, CSf, CSfSt, CSfU, CSjC, CSt, CStb.
Shows works of mainly Los Angeles and San Francisco bay area artists.

96. Los Angeles county museum of art, Los Angeles. Five younger artists.
Exhibition, Nov. 26-Dec. 26, 1965. L. A., 1965. CLCM-A.
Exhibit catalog.

97. Los Angeles county museum of natural history, Los Angeles. An
exhibition of America's black heritage at the Los Angeles county museum
of natural history, December 3, 1969 through February 15, 1970. Russell
E. Belous, editor; William M. Mason [and] Burton A. Reiner, associate
editors. L. A., 1969. 64 p. illus., ports., facsims. C, CLM, CSf,
CSfAA.
"History division Bulletin no. 5."
"The Los Angeles black community, 1781-1940": pp. 40-64.

98. MCLEAN, SANDRA. Some contemporary Negro artists in Los Angeles,
background and development. Research paper, Univ. of Calif. extension
class, Los Angeles county museum of art, 1967. 71 p. CLCM-A.
Part I: Bibliographical study; Part II: Biographical questionnaires
returned by the artists.

99. MANN, MARGERY. "Can whitey do a beautiful black picture show?", in
Popular photography, v. 64, May, 1969, p. 82ff.
A review of the exhibit of photographs taken of San Francisco bay
area Black Panthers by Pirkle Jones and Ruth-Marion Baruch.

100. M. H. de Young memorial museum, San Francisco. African Negro sculpture [by] Paul S. Wingert. A loan exhibition. September 24-November 19,
1948. S. F., 1948. v, 26 [99] p. plates, map. CSfSt, CU, CU-A.

101. MONTESANO, PHILIP MICHAEL, 1941- . "The mystery of the San Jose
statues," in Urban west, v. 1, Mar.-Apr., 1968, pp. 25-27.
Describes three of Edmonia Lewis' sculptures held by the San Jose
public library.

102. MORRILL, SIBLEY S. "Negro artists of the bay area," in Alameda
county weekender, Sept. 10, 1966, pp. 1-12.

Exhibit Catalogs ; Art History and Criticism; General Works

103. Oakland museum. Art division. Art-west associated/north, inc.,
     presents new perspectives in black art ... Kaiser center gallery,
     October 5–October 26, 1968, Oakland, California. [Oakland, 1968].
     24 p. illus. CLSU, CSfCiC.

104. Paramount pictures corporation, Los Angeles.
         "Our collection is devoted mainly to art, architecture, costume,
     and history of the world. In addition to the books and periodicals we
     have a large file of photographs and clippings. Within this collection
     there are some photographs and text referring to Afro-Americans in the
     West, also African contributions in the fields of sculpture, art, and
     design."

105. PARROTT, WANDA SUE. "Studio Watts workshop," in Arts in society,
     v. 5, Fall–winter, 1968, pp. 510–19.
         The story of an arts workshop established in 1965 mainly for the
     integration of school dropouts into society.

106. "Paul R. Williams," in Opportunity, v. 6, Mar., 1928, p. 81.
         A biographical account with illus. of Los Angeles area buildings
     designed by him.

107. ROELOF-LANNER, T. V., ed. Prints by American Negro artists. L. A.,
     Cultural exchange center of Los Angeles [c1965]. [57] ℓ. (chiefly
     illus.) CCotS, CFS, CGl, CHS, CNoS, CP, CSf, CSfSt, CSfU, CSjC, CStb,
     CU-SB, CU-SC.

108. Scripps college. Lang art gallery. Benny, Bernie, Betye, Noah, &
     John ... 16 Dec. 70–12 Feb. 71. Claremont [1970]. [20] p. illus.,
     ports.
         "This exhibition curated by Samella Lewis, associate professor of
     art, Scripps college and Black studies center, Claremont colleges."
         Art exhibit catalog of works of Benny Andrews, Bernie Casey, Betye
     Saar, Noah Purifoy, and John Outterbridge.

109. SIEBER, ROY, and ARNOLD RUBIN. Sculpture of black Africa. The Paul
     Tishman collection. Los Angeles county museum of art. [L. A.], 1968.
     150 p. illus. CLCM-A.

110. TEILHET, JEHANNE, ed. Dimensions of black, La Jolla museum of art,
     February 15–March 29, 1970. [La Jolla, Univ. of Calif., San Diego,
     1970]. vii, 154 p. illus. Bibliography: pp. 150–53. CLU.

111. *THOMPSON, NOAH DAVIS,   -1933. [Biographical account of Paul Revere
     Williams, Los Angeles architect], in Opportunity, v. 2, Dec., 1924,
     pp. 380–81.

112. WATKINS, APRIL JOHNSON. Art and the black child: a study of the
     relationship between black children's drawings and their conversation.
     Master's thesis, Calif. state univ., San Francisco, 1968. 114 ℓ.
     illus.
         Records the art activities and conversations of 18 black children
     during their participation in a Haight-Ashbury settlement house art class

taught by the author. Discusses the relationships between conversations and art work and the children's greater awareness of themselves and others.

113. *WHITE, CHARLES WILBERT, 1918- . Images of dignity; the drawings of Charles White. Foreword by Harry Belafonte. Introduction by James Porter. Commentary by Benjamin Horowitz. [L. A.] Ward Ritchie press [c1967]. vi, 121 p. illus., ports. CEcaC, CG1, CLGS, CNoS, COM, CP, CSf, CSt, CWM, WaT.
     Issued by the Golden state mutual life insurance co., Los Angeles.

114. _____. 10 Charles White [drawings]. Preface by Harry Belafonte. Hollywood, Carlton Moss, 1962. 10 plates (in portfolio), port. DHU.

115. *WILLIAMS, PAUL REVERE, 1894- . New homes for today, by Paul R. Williams, A. I. A. Hollywood, Murray & Gee, inc., 1946. 95 p. illus., plans. On cover: Remodeling interiors, duplexes, ranch houses. WaPu. Also available in many California libraries according to the Calif. state library's union catalog.
     "Drawings, plans, and text on modern home architecture."

116. _____. The small home of tomorrow, by Paul R. Williams, A. I. A. Hollywood, Murray & Gee, inc., 1945. 95 p. illus., ports., plan.
     Available in many California libraries according to the Calif. state library's union catalog.

117. WOLFE, EVELYN. "Charles White, painter of black dignity," in Urban west, v. 3, Dec., 1969, pp. 21-23.

ARTISTS REPRESENTED IN PERMANENT MUSEUM COLLECTIONS

     Credit is due to the late James A. Porter who suggested that the following section be included in this bibliography as encouragement to black artists and to museums' collection programs. Much of the information about holdings of museums was secured by Mrs. Evangeline J. Montgomery of the Oakland museum's Art section.

118. *African American historical and cultural society, San Francisco.
     Carraway, Arthur

119. California. State univ. San Jose.
     Epting, Marion

120. _____. University. Berkeley.
     Bearden, Romare
     Harden, Marvin
     Lawrence, Jacob
     White, Charles Wilbert
     (Acquired by the Committee for the acquisition of Afro-American art).

Artists Represented in Permanent Museum Collections

121. _____. _____. Los Angeles.
     Epting, Marion A.

122. California college of arts and crafts, Oakland.
     Saunders, Raymond

123. California historical society, San Francisco.
     Brown, Grafton Tyler

124. Charles W. Bowers memorial museum, Santa Ana.
     Gafford, Alice (Taylor)

125. Fine art patrons of Newport harbor, Newport Beach.
     Haynie, Wilbur

126. Fine arts gallery of San Diego.
     Johnson, Sargent Claude

127. *Golden state mutual life insurance co., Los Angeles.
     Adams, Ron
     Alston, Charles
     Barthé, Richmond
     Boghossian, Alexander
     Carter, William
     Gafford, Alice (Taylor)
     Green, Rose
     Hunt, Richard
     Johnson, Daniel
     Jordan, Jack
     Lee-Smith, Hughie
     Mills, P'lla
     White, Charles Wilbert
     Woodard, Beulah E.
     Woodruff, Hale

128. *Howard university, Washington, D. C.
     Johnson, Sargent Claude

129. La Jolla museum of art.
     Andrews, Benny

130. Long Beach museum of art.
     White, Charles Wilbert

131. Los Angeles county museum of art, Los Angeles.
     Edwards, Mel
     Pippin, Horace
     Saar, Betye
     Sills, Thomas
     Tanner, Henry Ossawa
     Washington, Timothy
     White, Charles Wilbert

Artists Represented in Permanent Museum Collections

132. New Mexico. University.
        Britt, Arthur L.

133. Oakland museum.
        Akolo, J. B.
        Amos, Emma
        Arnold, Ralph
        Bellow, Cleveland
        Branch, Harrison
        Brandon, Brumsic
        Britton, Sylvester
        Brown, Grafton Tyler
        Burkes, Eugene Alexander
        Burnett, Calvin
        Burns, Eugene A.
        Burroughs, Margaret
        Cadoo, Foyer
        Carraway, Arthur
        Carter, Yvonne
        Cheltenham, Eugene
        Clark, Claude
        Coleman, Hoyd W.
        Cremer, Marva
        Dunn, Eugenia V.
        Eubanks, Jonathan
        Eversley, Fredric
        Ferguson, Charles
        Forman, Doyle
        Glover, Robert
        Gordon, Russell T.
        Greene, Donald
        Greene, Michael
        Hammers, Ronald
        Hammons, David
        Harrell, Hugh
        Harris, Scotland
        Hawkins, Eugene
        Hayden, Palmer
        Hazard, Ben
        Henderson, Leroy W.
        Henderson, William Mike
        Hicks, Leon
        Hooper, Elvoyce
        Howell, Raymond
        Humphrey, Margo
        Hunt, Richard
        Jackson, William
        James, Wilmer
        Johns, William N.
        Johnson, Marie
        Johnson, Melvin G.
        Johnson, Milton
        Johnson, Sargent Claude

Artists Represented in Permanent Museum Collections

133. (cont.)
    Johnson, William H.
    Jordan, Jack
    Kinney, Richard
    Lane, Doyle
    Lenard
    Lewis, Samella S.
    McCullough, G.
    McNeil, James
    McNeil, William
    Macklin, Anderson
    Mason, Phillip Lindsay
    Meo, Yvonne
    Montgomery, Evangeline J.
    Morgan, Norma
    Outterbridge, John Wilfred
    Overstreet, Joe
    Parker, Leroy
    Pope, Alvin
    Price, Leslie
    Purifoy, Noah
    Pusey, Mavis
    Pyburn, Don
    Riddle, John
    Rogers, Charles D.
    Rollins, Henry
    Saar, Betye
    Satchell, Ernest
    Sekoto, C.
    Slater, Van
    Smith, Frank E.
    Smith, William E.
    Snowden, Sylvia
    Soares, Laura
    Tessema Memo
    Vaughn, Royce H.
    Waddy, Ruth G.
    Walker, Larry
    Washington, James
    White, Charles Wilbert
    Wilson, Fred R.
    Yates, Charles E.
    Yeargans, Hartwell

134. Otis art institute, Los Angeles.
    Epting, Marion A.
    Haynie, Wilbur

135. Palm Springs desert museum.
    Casey, Bernie

136. Pasadena art museum.
    Haynie, Wilbur

Artists Represented in Permanent Museum Collections

137. Phoenix art museum.
       Sills, Thomas

138. San Diego Jewish community center.
       Harden, Marvin

139. San Francisco maritime museum.
       Johnson, Sargent Claude

140. San Francisco museum of art.
       Johnson, Sargent Claude

141. San Jose public library.
       Lewis, Edmonia

142. Santa Clara univ., Santa Clara. de Saisset art gallery & museum.
       Monroe, Arthur

143. Society of California pioneers, San Francisco.
       Brown, Grafton Tyler

144. Westside Jewish community center, Los Angeles.
       Harden, Marvin

BIBLIOGRAPHIES AND FINDING AIDS

145. ADDISON (WALLACE), books, Los Angeles. [Sales catalog no. 1].
     Negro literature - biography - sociology. [L. A., 1964?]. [8] p.
     Mimeo.

146. _____. List no. 2. Negro literature, history, biography, slavery,
     etc. [L. A., 1964?]. [17] p. Mimeo.

147. _____. Supplement to List no. 2. [L. A., 1964?]. [6] p. Mimeo.

148. _____. List no. 3. Negro literature, history, biography, slavery,
     etc. [L. A., 1965]. [26] p. Mimeo.

149. _____. Catalogue no. 4. [L. A., 1966]. [34] ℓ. Mimeo. CHi.

150. ADLER, PATRICIA. Ethnic and political minorities in the Los Angeles
     area: a bibliography of doctoral dissertations and master's theses at
     the University of southern California, 1912-1969. Prepared by Patricia
     Adler, M. A., under the direction of Professor Doyce B. Nunis, Jr.
     L. A., Dept. of history, Univ. of southern Calif., 1970. 25 p. Mimeo.
     Negro studies, pp. 16-20.

151. *African bibliographic center. Black history viewpoints; a selected
     bibliographical guide to resources for Afro-American and African history:
     1968. N. Y., Negro universities press [1969]. CLSU, CNoS.

Bibliographies and Finding Aids

152. Alta California bookstore, Albany. Catalogue 28. Unusual books,
manuscripts, broadsides & pamphlets relating to the American Negro.
[Berkeley, 1965]. [22] p. CHi.

153. American river college library. Afro-Americans. Sacramento, 1969.
18 p. C.
    A bibliography of holdings.

154. BAIRD, NEWTON D. An annotated bibliography of California fiction,
1664-1970, by Newton D. Baird and Robert Greenwood. Georgetown, Talisman
literary research, inc., 1971. xvi, 521 p. facsims.
    The index entry "Negroes" conveys the reader to numerous descriptions
of novels having a black relevance.

155. BELKNAP, GEORGE NICHOLAS, 1905- . Oregon imprints, 1845-1870 [by]
George N. Belknap. Eugene, Univ. of Oregon books [c1968]. 305 p.
illus. (facsims.). CHi, CSmH, OrU.
    Describes 24 imprints relating to Negroes and slavery, most of which
are listed in the present bibliography.

156. BOOTH, ROBERT E. Culturally disadvantaged; a bibliography and
keyword-out-of-context (KWOC) index [by] Robert E. Booth [and others].
Detroit, Wayne state univ. press, 1967. 803 p. CSt.
    Contains California and western materials throughout. Many of the
items listed are held by the Educational research information center of
the U. S. office of education, Washington, D. C., and may be ordered on
microfiche from Bell & Howell co., Cleveland.

157. BROWN, WARREN HENRY, 1905- . Check list of Negro newspapers in the
United States (1827-1946), by Warren Brown. Jefferson City, Mo.,
School of journalism, Lincoln univ., 1946. 37 p. CLSU, CNoS, CSt-H,
CU-SB.
    Includes newspapers pub. in the West. Shows library holdings when
available.

158. BROWNELL, JEAN B. Negroes in Oregon before the Civil war. Bibliography. 25 p. Typew. OrHi.

159. California. State univ. Fresno. Afro- and Mexican-Americana; books
and other materials in the library of Fresno state college relating to
the history, culture, and problems of Afro-Americans and Mexican-Americans.
Fresno, 1969. 109 p. CFS, CHS, CSfU, CSjC, CSt, CU-A.

160. _____. _____. Hayward. Black bibliography. [Hayward, 1969].
143 p. CCotS, CHS, CSf, CSfSt, CSfU, CSjC.
    "The principal work of compiling and organizing this bibliography
was done by Inso Chung."
    A bibliography of the college library's holdings.

161. _____. _____. Long Beach. Black bibliography; a selected list of
books on Africa, Africans, and Afro-Americans. Long Beach, California
state college, 1969. 88 p. CCotS, CHS, CNoS, CSdS, CSjC, CU-SB.
    A bibliography of the college library's holdings.

Bibliographies and Finding Aids

162. _____. _____. Los Angeles. A library guide to Afro-American studies, John F. Kennedy memorial library, California state college, Los Angeles. [L. A., 1969]. 13 p. CHS, CLS, CLSU, CSdS, CSjC.

163. _____. _____. Northridge. Black brown bibliography [of holdings in the San Fernando valley state college library. Compiled by Dennis C. Bakewell. Northridge, 1968]. 86 p. CBGTU, CChiS, CHS, CLSU, CNoS, CSdS, CSjC.

164. _____. _____. _____. The black experience in the United States; a bibliography based on collections of the San Fernando valley state college library. Dennis C. Bakewell, compiler. Northridge, San Fernando valley state college foundation, 1970. viii, 162 p. ports., facsims. CNoS, CSS, CSfU, CSjC.

165. _____. _____. Sacramento. The black man in America, a bibliography. Compiled by Leah Freeman. Bibliographic series #4. Sacramento, Sacramento state college library, 1969. 13 p. CChiS, CHS, CSf, CSS, CU-SB.
    Consists of bibliographies, general reference works, newspapers, magazines, and "selected subject headings used in main catalog."

166. _____. _____. _____. Black music; a selected discography. Sacramento, Sacramento state college library, 1971. 35 p. Mimeo. CSS.
    "Lists selected recordings from the Sacramento State College Library's phonorecord collection."

167. _____. _____. San Bernardino. Black and brown bibliography: history. A selected list of books relating to the history of Afro-Americans and Mexican-Americans. San Bernardino, California state college library, 1970. 39 p. Mimeo. CSbS.

168. _____. _____. _____. Black and brown bibliography: literature, art, music, [and] theatre. A selected list of books relating to the culture of Afro-Americans and Mexican-Americans. San Bernardino, California state college library, 1970. 16 p. CSbS.

169. _____. _____. _____. Black and brown bibliography: philosophy, social sciences, political science, [and] education. A selected list of books relating to the culture of Afro-Americans and Mexican-Americans. San Bernardino, California state college library, 1970. 13 p. CSbS.

170. _____. _____. San Diego. Afro-American bibliography; list of the books, documents and periodicals on black-American culture located in San Diego state college library. Comp. by Andrew Szabo. [San Diego], San Diego state college library, 1970. iii, 327 p. C, CSdS, CSf, CSfU, CSjC.

171. _____. _____. San Jose. Bibliography of minorities, black and Mexican-American. [San Jose] 1968. 29 ℓ. CSt-H.

172. _____. _____. _____. Minorities in America; a list of books on blacks and Mexican-Americans in the San Jose state college library.

Bibliographies and Finding Aids

Compiled by Kathleen Thorne [and others]. San Jose, 1969. 151 p. CCotS, CHS.

173. _____. State library. Administrative-legislative reference service. Social and psychiatric treatment approaches with minority groups, especially Negroes in the United States. Selected material. [Sacramento, 1964]. 7 ℓ. C.
"Includes periodical articles and books from 1914 to date."

174. _____. _____. Law library. Selected bibliography on discrimination in housing. [Sacramento], 1964. 9 ℓ. C, CSt-Law.

175. _____. State polytechnic college. San Luis Obispo. Afro-American and Mexican-American bibliography; a selected guide to materials in the California state polytechnic college library. San Luis Obispo, 1969. ii, 155 p. CSjC, CSluSP.

176. _____. University. Davis. Black sojourn; a bibliography by Sherri Kirk and Glenda Peace. University of California at Davis. Collection development section, Ethnic studies unit, University library. Davis, Pub. by the University library, 1969. [12], 95 p. C, CSf, CU-A, CU-SB.

177. _____. _____. Santa Barbara. Black studies in the United States; a selective guide to research materials in the UCSB library. Rev. ed. Santa Barbara, University library reference department, Univ. of Calif., 1970. v, 40 p. CSf, CU-SB.

178. California historical society. Index to California historical society quarterly, volumes one to forty, 1922-1961. S. F., The Society, 1965. 483 p.
There are numerous entries under Negroes, William Alexander Leidesdorff, James Pierson Beckwourth, Allen B. Light, and possibly other names. An annual index for the years after 1961 can be found in each December Quarterly.

179. California library association. Young adult librarians round table. The American Negro in contemporary society; an annotated booklist. Berkeley, The association [1966]. 26 p. CChiS, CLSU, CMp, CSS, CSfSt, CSjC, CStcrCL, CU-SB.

180. Chabot college library. From Africa to America; a list of materials in the Chabot college library relating to the history of black people in America. [Hayward, 1969]. 18 p. CHC.

181. CHAPMAN, ABRAHAM. The Negro in American literature and a bibliography of literature by and about Negro Americans. Stevens Point, Wisconsin state univ., 1966. 135 p. CSt.
Contains some western authors.

182. Colorado. Adams state college. Alamosa. Knowing and educating the disadvantaged; an annotated bibliography. Alamosa, 1965. 460 p. CSdS.

Bibliographies and Finding Aids

183. COLVIG, RICHARD, comp. Black music; a checklist of books. Oakland, Oakland public library [1969]. [20] p. CHS, CLSU, CO.
    "A bibliography of monographs in the English language ... dealing ... with the music of the Negro in Africa and North America."

184. COWAN, ROBERT GRANNISS. The admission of the 31st state by the 31st Congress; an annotated bibliography of congressional speeches upon the admission of California. L. A. [Torrez press], 1962. 139 p. facsim. CFS, CHS, CHi, CLSU, CNoS, CSf, CS1uSP, CSmH.
    Lists the speeches of approximately 175 Congressmen, about one-fifth of whom spoke more than once in relation to the territory recently acquired from Mexico and the establishment of slavery in it. In all, about 155 of these speeches were imprinted separately during the period in which they were given, July 26, 1848–Sept. 7, 1850.

185. *CROUCHETT, LAURENCE.   The Negro in United States history; a bibliography of books, pamphlets, periodicals, and articles. Concord, Diablo valley college, 1965. 35 p. CLSU, CSdS, CSf, CSt, CU-A.
    Contains a special appendix of western U. S. materials.

185a. *DAVIS, LENWOOD G., 1939- . Blacks in the state of Oregon, 1788-1971; a bibliography of published works and of unpublished source materials in the life and achievement of black people in the beaver state. [Monticello, Ill., Council of planning librarians, 1971]. 54 ℓ. CU-B.

186. Deutsch & Shea, inc. A guide to Negro media: magazines, newspapers, radio and college. N. Y., 1968. 38 p. C.
    "... updates 'A guide to Negro publications and colleges' issued ... in 1967."

187. Diablo valley college library. Afro-American books in the Diablo college library. [Pleasant Hill, 1969?]. 30 p. CHS, CPhD, CSf.

188. Directory of U. S. Negro newspapers, magazines & periodicals in 42 states. [N. Y., U. S. Negro world], 196 . CLU (1967), CSdS (1966), CSt (1967).
    Lists California and western states publications.

189. DRURY, CLIFFORD MERRILL, 1897- . California imprints, 1846-1876, pertaining to social, educational, and religious subjects. A bibliography of 1099 titles: books, pamphlets, broadsides, periodicals, newspapers, and manuscripts; each described, annotated, and located, by Clifford Merrill Drury ... [Pasadena], Privately printed, 1970. 220 p. CHi.
    Contains occasional items of Afro-American interest.

190. DUIGNAN, PETER JAMES, 1926- . Handbook of American resources for African studies [by] Peter Duignan. [Stanford], Stanford univ., Hoover institution on war, revolution and peace, 1967. 218 p. (Hoover institution bibliographical studies, 29). CSt-H.
    Describes holdings of about 300 U. S. public and private collections. Includes Univ. of Ariz., Tucson; Arizona Pioneers' historical society, Tucson; Univ. of Calif., Berkeley and Los Angeles; California institute

Bibliographies and Finding Aids

of technology, Pasadena; Sutro branch of the California state library, San Francisco; Huntington library and art gallery, San Marino; Univ. of Oregon, Eugene; Pacific school of religion, Berkeley; Stanford univ., Stanford; Church of Jesus Christ of the latter-day saints, Salt Lake City; Military aviation fellowship, Fullerton; Oriental missionary society, Los Angeles; World missions, inc., Long Beach; Arizona state museum, Tucson; Denver art museum, Denver; La Jolla art center, La Jolla; and the Los Angeles county museum of art, Los Angeles.

191. *Ebony. The Negro handbook, comp. by the editors of Ebony. Chicago, Johnson pub. co., 1966. 535 p. tables.
     Contains California and Western materials throughout.
     Available in many libraries.

192. El Camino college library. Afro-American resources of the El Camino college library. [El Camino, 1969]. 55 p. CEcaC.

193. FLESHER, LORNA. American minorities; a checklist of bibliographies published by government agencies, 1960-1970. Sacramento, California state library, 1970. 7 p. C.

194. FULLER, JUANITA BOYKIN. An annotated bibliography of biographies and autobiographies of Negroes, 1839-1961. Master's thesis, Atlanta univ., 1962. iii, 62 ℓ. CSdS, CU (microcard).

195. HATCH, JAMES VERNON, 1928- . Black image on the American stage: a bibliography of plays and musicals 1770-1970, by James V. Hatch. N. Y., Drama book specialists pubs., 1970. xiii, 162 p. Bibliography: pp. 119-21. CHS, CSfSt, CSfU, CSjC, CU-SB.
     Contains occasional entries with a California and western significance.

196. HELLER, PAUL. An annotated bibliography of black history. [S. F., Human rights commission, 1969?]. [12] ℓ. Mimeo. CSf.

197. *Howard university. Library. Dictionary catalog of the Jesse E. Moorland collection of Negro life and history, Howard university library, Washington, D. C. Boston, G. K. Hall & co., 1970. 9 v. CSfU, CU.
     Contains some California and western materials throughout.

198. _____. _____. Dictionary catalog of the Arthur B. Spingarn collection of Negro authors, Howard Univ. library, Washington, D. C. Boston, G. K. Hall & co., 1970. 2 v. CU.
     Contains some California and western materials throughout.

199. HUMPHREY, DWIGHT H. An annotated bibliography of the slavery collection in Doheny library of the University of southern California. Master's thesis, Univ. of southern Calif., Los Angeles, 1951. iv, 170 ℓ.

200. ILIFF, JOHN G. Where to read up on racism and human rights. S. F., Northern California branch, American civil liberties union, 1954. 79 p. CMp, CSfSt, CSt.
     An annotated guide to publications of the Northern California branch

Bibliographies and Finding Aids

and the West coast regional office of the National association for the advancement of colored people.

201. *Index to selected periodicals. 1950+. Boston, G. K. Hall & co., 1961+. Indexing by the staff of the Hallie Q. Brown library, Central state univ., Wilberforce, Ohio, 1950-59. 1960 - includes periodicals indexed by the staff of the Schomburg collection, New York public library. Continued as Index to periodicals by and about Negroes, v. 17- . 1966 - Contains citations to California and western materials throughout. CCotS, CHS, CLSU, CLU, CSaT, CSdS, CSf, CSjC, CSluSP (1950-66), CSt, CU, CU-SB.

202. Institute of labor and industrial relations. (Univ. of Michigan-Wayne state univ.). Research division. Equal employment opportunity commission. Document and reference text; an index to minority group employment information. Prepared by the research division of the Institute of labor and industrial relations, the University of Michigan-Wayne state university. Produced under contract with the Equal employment opportunity commission, 1967. [Ann Arbor], 1967. viii, 602, 8, 17, 5 p. CSt.
    An extensive bibliography listing many items of California and western interest.

203. *JACKSON, MILES MERRILL, 1929- , comp. A bibliography of Negro history and culture for young readers. Miles M. Jackson, Jr., comp. and ed., assisted by Mary W. Cleaves and Alma L. Gray. Pittsburgh, Pub. for Atlanta univ. by the Univ. of Pittsburgh press [c1968]. xxxi, 134 p. CNoS.

204. KELLEY, ESTELLE F. Negro literature, by Estelle F. Kelley, while working on Project 1-F1-44, in the Curriculum division of the Los Angeles county superintendent of schools office, Lorraine Miller Sherer, director. L. A., 1935. 106 p. Typew.
    Contains annotated and unannotated lists of poetry, drama, fiction, and non-fiction. Contains very little if any western material.

205. LEWINSON, PAUL, comp. A guide to documents in the National archives: for Negro studies. Compiled by Paul Lewinson for the Committee on Negro studies of the American council of learned societies. Washington, D. C., The American council, 1947. x, 28 p. Committee on Negro studies. Publications no. 1. CSt.

206. Los Angeles. Public library. Democracy unlimited for America's minorities. L. A., 1944. [8] p. CU-B (California federation for civic unity collection).
    A selected book list.

207. _____. _____. Municipal reference library. The prevention and control of race riots: a bibliography for police officers. L. A., 1944. 12 p. Mimeo. CL.

208. MCLATCHY, PATRICK, comp. Montana, the magazine of western history. Index to volumes I-X, 1951-1960 ... Helena, The historical society of Montana [1961?]. 71 p.
    See entries under Negroes, etc.

Bibliographies and Finding Aids

209. *MATTHEWS, MIRIAM, 1905- . The Negro in California from 1781-1910, an annotated bibliography. Graduate paper, Univ. of southern Calif., Los Angeles, 1944. xxv, 52 p. CU-B (photocopy also containing: a copy of her Guide to the collection of source materials in Negro history, 1 ℓ., and a Citizen's guide to collection of source materials in Negro history, 5 ℓ.).

210. Merritt college library. Merritt college library guide for Afro-American studies. [Oakland, 1969]. 33 p. "2nd printing, January, 1969." COM, CSf.

211. MESSNER, STEPHEN D. Minority groups and housing; a selected bibliography, 1950-67. Selected and edited under the direction of Stephen D. Messner. [Storrs, Center for real estate and urban economic studies, Univ. of Connecticut, 1968]. 60 p. CNoS, CSfSt.

212. MILLER, ELIZABETH W. The Negro in America: a bibliography. Compiled by Elizabeth W. Miller for the American academy of arts and sciences. With a foreword by Thomas F. Pettigrew. Cambridge, Mass., Harvard univ. press, 1966. xvixi, 190 p. CCovB, CEcaC, CFS, CLSU, CLU, CNoS, COM, CPhD, CSaT, CSb, CSdS, CSf, CSfCiC, CSfGG, CSjCi, CSt, CU, CU-A, CU-I, Wa.
　　Contains California and western materials throughout.

213. *More book store. Catalog of books available at the More book store, 1413 Fillmore street, San Francisco ... S. F., 1968. 30 p. illus.
　　A catalog of newly-published titles.

214. Mt. San Antonio college library. Bibliography part I: the black American. [Walnut, 1969?]. 17, 9, 2 p. CSf, CWM.

215. *Negro handbook ... N. Y., W. Malliet and co., 1942-49. C Complete; CFS 1942; CHS 1942, 1944, 1947; CLGS 1944, 1947, 1949; CLSU Complete; CLU 1942, 1944, 1947, 1949; CSf Complete; CSluSP 1942- ; CSmH Complete; CSt 1944-49; CStcrCL 1947, 1949; CU-A Complete; CU-SB 1946/47.
　　Contains California and western material throughout.

216. *The Negro in print. Washington, D. C. My, 1965+. b-m. Pub. by the Negro bibliographic and research center. At head of title, May 1965-Mar. 1968: Bibliographic survey. CHS 1965+; CLU 1965+; CNoS 1965+; CSdS 1965+; CSf 1965+; CSjC 1965+; CSt 1965+.
　　"An annotated list of fiction and nonfiction, paperbacks, and books for young readers, with occasional periodical articles and references on poetry and art." - Dorothy B. Porter.

217. *Negro year book, an annual encyclopedia of the Negro ... 1912-1952. Tuskegee Institute, Ala., Negro year book pub. co., c1912-52. C 1916/17, 1918/19, 1921/22, 1925/26, 1931/32, 1937/38, 1947 (1941-46); CHS 1912, 1918/19, 1925/26, 1947 (1941-46), 1952; CLGS 1921/22, 1922/23, 1924/25, 1931/32, 1933/34, 1947 (1941-46); CLSU 1918/19, 1921/22, 1925/26, 1931/32, 1937/38, 1947 (1941-46), 1952 (v. 11); CLU 1918/19, 1925/26, 1931/32, 1937/38, 1947 (1941-46), 1952; CLobS 1931/32; CNoS Complete; CSdS Complete; CSf 1916/17, 1925/26, 1931/32, 1937/38, 1947 (1941-46), 1952

23

Bibliographies and Finding Aids

(v.11); CSmH 1947 (1941–46); CU Complete; WaTP 1914/15–1952.
No editions were pub. for 1920/21, 1923/24, 1927/28–1929/30. Title
varies slightly. Contains California and western material throughout.

218. New York City. Public library. Schomburg collection of Negro
literature. Dictionary catalog of the Schomburg collection of Negro
literature and history. Boston, G. K. Hall, 1962. 9 v. CFS, CHS, CL,
CLSU, CLU, CNoS, COM, CSdS, CSf, CSfSt, CSluSP, CSt, CU, CU–A, CU–I,
CU–SB.
Contains some California and western materials throughout.

219. _____. _____. _____. Same. First supplement, 1967. 2 v. CHS, CL,
CLSU, CLU, CNoS, CSf, CU, CU–A, CU–I.

220. New York times index, 1851– . A subject index to the articles
appearing in the New York times newspaper. CL, CLU, CSf, CSmH, CU, CU–SB.
An indispensable source for news stories and the dating thereof.
Available in most large libraries. Title varies slightly.

221. NICHOLS, MARGARET S. Multicultural educational materials; bibliography of a demonstration collection assembled by Margaret S. Nichols
for all ages and reading abilities largely in the areas of black and
Mexican-American cultures. Menlo Park, Menlo Park library, 1970. 53 ℓ.
CSS.

222. Oakland. Public library. His house below: books from the black
struggle. Oakland [1969]. 6 p. CLSU, CO.

223. _____. _____. The Negro literature collection: books of Negro
authorship to be found in the Oakland free library. List revised for
Negro history week, February, 1937. [Oakland, 1937]. 11 p. Mimeo. CO.

224. _____. _____. Young adult division. The Negro in America. Oakland,
1967. 8 p. CO.

225. _____. _____. _____. Same. 1969 ed. 10 p. CO, CSS.

226. _____. Public schools. Cultural diversity: library and audio
visual materials for in-service education, prepared by Helen Cyr,
Barbara Baker, and George Noone. Oakland, 1964. 2 v. Bibliography.
CO.

227. _____. _____. Resource guide for teaching contributions of minorities
to American cultures (for use with secondary school students).
[Oakland], 1966. 121 p. CSf, CSfSt.

228. OEHLERTS, DONALD E., comp. Guide to Colorado newspapers, 1859–1963.
Denver, Bibliographical center for research, Rocky mountain region, inc.,
1964. x, 184 p. map. CHi, CoHi.
Lists Negro newspapers and the locations of some files.

229. Oregon historical society. Oregon historical quarterly index,
volumes I to XL, 1900–1939. Portland, The Society, 1941. 834 p.

Bibliographies and Finding Aids

230. _____. Oregon historical quarterly index, 1940-1960, volumes XLI-LXI. Josephine Baumgartner, compiler. Portland, The Society, 1967. 711 p.
  Both indexes contain extensive references to Negroes, slavery, the U.S. 14th and 15th constitutional amendments, George W. Bush, and perhaps other individuals' names.

231. Oregon spectator. Oregon spectator index, 1846-1854 ... Prepared by W. P. A. newspaper index project ... Sponsored by city of Portland [and] Oregon historical society [Portland?], 1941. 2 v. Mimeo. CHi, OrHi.
  Index contains entries for Negroes, slavery, secession movement, etc., and for individuals such as Winslow Anderson and George Bush.

232. Pasadena public library. Afro-Americans in the U. S., a selected list. [Pasadena?], 1939. [6] p. (folder). CSmH.

233. PLOSKI, HARRY A. The Negro almanac, compiled and edited by Harry A. Ploski and Roscoe C. Brown, Jr. N. Y., Bellwether pub. co., [1967]. xi, 1,012 p. illus., maps, ports. Bibliography: pp. 946-65.
  Contains California and western materials throughout.
  Available in many libraries.

234. *PORTER, DOROTHY (BURNETT), 1905- . The Negro in the United States, a selective bibliography. Compiled by Dorothy B. Porter, librarian of the Negro collection, Howard univ., Washington, D. C., Library of Congress, 1970. x, 313 p. CHS, CSS, CSfSt, CSjC.
  Contains some California and western materials throughout.

235. _____. North American Negro poets, a bibliographical checklist of their writings, 1760-1944, by Dorothy B. Porter. Hattiesburg, Miss., Book farm, 1945. 90 p. [Heartman's historical series no. 70]. CNoS, CSmH, CU.
  "An expansion of the Schomburg checklist."
  Contains listings for California poets.

236. _____. Same. N. Y., Burt Franklin, 1963. CSdS.

237. _____. A working bibliography on the Negro in the United States, compiled by Dorothy B. Porter. [Ann Arbor, Mich.], University microfilms, 1969. 202 p. C, CCotS, CNoS, CSS, CSdS, CSfSt, CU.
  Contains some California and western materials throughout.

238. POTTS, ALFRED M. Knowing and educating the disadvantaged; an annotated bibliography. Alamosa, Colo., Adams state college center for cultural studies, 1965. vii, 460 p. DHU.

239. Ravenswood city school district instructional materials center. Library materials written by or about Negroes; including African and island history. [n.p.], 1968. 6 p. CMp.
  A bibliography.

240. *REARDON, WILLIAM R., ed. The black teacher and the dramatic arts; a dialogue, bibliography, and anthology. William R. Reardon and Thomas

Bibliographies and Finding Aids

    D. Pawley, eds. Westport, Conn., Negro universities press [c1970].
xviii, 487 p. illus., ports. CCotS, CHS, CSf, CSfU, CSjC, CU-SB.
    Reardon is professor of dramatic art, Univ. of Calif., Santa Barbara.

241. REVITT, PAUL JOSEPH, 1923- . The George Pullen Jackson collection
of Southern hymnology; a bibliography, comp. with an introd. by Paul J.
Revitt. L. A., Univ. of Calif. library, 1964. 26 p. CLU.

242. RHODEHAMEL, JOSEPHINE (DE WITT). The black man's point of view; a
list of references to material in the Oakland free library, compiled by
Josephine De Witt at a suggestion from Delilah L. Beasley. Oakland,
California, Oakland free library, 1930. 30 p. CO.

243. RICHARDS, MARION, comp. Black and brown; bibliography. In
collaboration with Robert Dees. San Jose, Spartan bookstore, 1969.
67 p. CSjC.

244. ROCQ, MARGARET (MILLER). California local history; a bibliography
and union list of library holdings. Second ed., rev. and enl. Ed. by
Margaret Miller Rocq for the California library assoc. Stanford,
Stanford univ. press, 1970. xv, 611 p. map. CHi, CLU, CSf, CSt, CU.
    The most extensive Californiana bibliography issued to date contains
17,261 entries including occasional Afro-American titles.

245. ROSS, FRANK ALEXANDER, 1888- . A bibliography of Negro migration,
by Frank Alexander Ross and Louise Venable Kennedy. N. Y., Columbia
univ. press, 1935. 251 p. CNoS.
    Contains California and Colorado references.

246. _____. Same. N. Y., Burt Franklin [1969].
    Available in many libraries.

247. San Diego. City schools. Curriculum services division. Bibliography
of black art, prepared by Archie Taylor. [San Diego, 196-?]. 6 ℓ.
CSjC.

248. San Francisco. Public library. Office of adult services. Negro
interest list, January, 1969 ... [S. F., 1969]. 20 p. Mimeo. CSf.
    A bibliography.

249. San Mateo county library system. A time to listen, a time to act.
Belmont [n.d.]. Flyer. CMp.
    A bibliography.

250. San Mateo school district. Our American heritage; a suggested book
list. San Mateo [n.d.]. 5 p. CMp.

251. SCHATZ, WALTER, ed. Directory of Afro-American resources. Ed. by
Walter Schatz, Race relations information center. N. Y., R. R. Bowker
co. [c1970]. xv, 485 p. Bibliography: pp. 347-56.
    A reference work of considerable importance which locates many re-
sources in all western states except Montana and Idaho. Emphasizes
holdings of primary source materials but seldom reports holdings of
newspaper and serial publications.

Bibliographies and Finding Aids

252. *SCHOMBURG, ARTHUR ALFONSO, 1874–1938. A bibliographical check list
of American Negro poetry compiled by Arthur A. Schomburg. N. Y., C. F.
Heartman, 1916. 57 p. CSmH.
    Contains listings of California poets.

253. Seattle public schools. Books transcend barriers; a bibliography of
books about Negroes for elementary school children. [Seattle], 1967.
53 p. Wa.

254. Sonoma county. Office of education. The minority experience; a
basic bibliography of American ethnic studies. Compiled by Ron Caselli
and the Sonoma county ethnic studies curriculum committee. Santa Rosa,
1970. 70 p. CCotS.

255. State historical society of Colorado. Index to The Colorado magazine,
volume I to XXV (1923–1948). Denver, 1950. 296 p.

256. _____. The Colorado magazine index, 1949/1960, volumes XXVI/XXXV.
[Denver], 1964. 267 p.
    There are numerous entries under blacks in both volumes which are also
available in the larger libraries outside of Colorado.

257. Stockton and San Joaquin county public library. Afro–American
heritage. [Stockton, 1969]. 21 p. CSf.
    A list of library holdings "compiled by Tobin Clarke of the library
staff."

258. Tacoma area urban coalition. Education task force project. A bibliography of Afro–American print and non–print resources in libraries of
Pierce county, Washington. Tacoma area urban coalition, Education task
force project in cooperation with Pierce county libraries. Tacoma,
Tacoma community college library, 1969. iv, 104 p., 105–16 ℓ. Bibliography: ℓ. 114–16. CNoS, CSS, CSjC, WaTC.

259. *THOMPSON, LUCILLE (SMITH). The Negro in Montana, 1800–1945; a
selective bibliography by Lucille Smith Thompson and Alma Smith Jacobs.
Helena, Montana state library, 1970. 23 p. port. (cover). CU–B,
MtGf, MtH, MtHi.

260. U. S. General services administration. National archives and records
service. Federal population censuses, 1790–1890; a catalog of microfilm
copies of the schedules. Washington, D. C., 1971. vii, 90 p.
    Lists the cost of individual rolls of microfilm available from the
General services administration, Washington, D. C. 20408. Includes
individual cities and counties in California and other western states.
Available in the larger libraries.

261. _____. Works progress administration. California. Bibliography of
California fiction, poetry, drama ... prepared under the direction of
Edgar J. Hinkel, M. A., editor, William E. McCann, M. A., assistant
editor, Marie Holden, cataloguer. Oakland, 1938. 3 v. Mimeo. C, CHi,
CL, CLU, CO, CSmH.
    Contains occasional information about black authors.

Bibliographies and Finding Aids

262. Universal books, Hollywood. Antiquarian bookseller's catalogs.
    Sales list, Oct., 1967; List no. 107, Jan., 1968; List no. 109, Mar. 1,
    1968; List no. 112, 1968; List no. 117, July 12, 1968; List no. 119,
    Oct., 1968; List no. 121, Feb., 1969; List no. 121, Suppl. A, 1969;
    Catalog no. 152, July, 1970. CHi; List no. 112; List no. 121, Suppl. A.
        Titles vary: "The Negro in America and Africa, a choice collection
    of books by or about the black man," "Black America," etc. Catalogs
    contain from several hundred to more than 2,000 entries each.

263. University of southern Calif., Los Angeles. Library. An introduction
    to materials for ethnic studies in the University of southern California
    library. L. A., Univ. of southern Calif. library, 1970. ii, 198 p.
    CLSU, CSf.
        The library's holdings of works about Negro Americans appear on
    pp. 19-110.

264. Washington state library, Olympia. Minorities and discrimination in
    the United States with particular reference to employment practices:
    a selective bibliography of books in the Washington state library ...
    [Olympia, Wash., 1968?]. 8 p. CFS, CU-SB, Wa.

265. _____. The Negro in the state of Washington, 1788-1967; a biblio-
    graphy of published works and of unpublished source materials on the
    life and achievements of the Negro in the evergreen state. Compiled by
    the Washington state library. Olympia, 1968. ii, 14 p. maps (covers).
    CFS, CSf, CU-B, CU-SB, Wa.

266. _____. Same. Rev. ed. Olympia, 1970. ii, 21 p. maps (covers).
    CSf, Wa.

267. WEINBERG, MEYER, 1920- , ed. School integration; a comprehensive
    classified bibliography of 3,100 references. Ed. by Meyer Weinberg.
    Chicago, Integrated education associates, 1967. iv, 137 p. CFS, CLSU,
    CNoS, CSaT, CSdS, CSf, CU-A.
        Contains references to California and western materials throughout.

268. WELSCH, ERWIN K. Negro in the United States; a research guide, by
    Erwin K. Welsch. Bloomington, Indiana univ. press, 1965. xiii, 142 p.
    Bibliographies: pp. 94-142. CCovB, CEcaC, CFS, CLSU, CNoS, COM, CPhD,
    CSaT, CSb, CSdS, CSf, CSto, CU-A, CU-I, CU-SC, Wa.
        A very good general work of some western interest.

269. *WEST, EARLE H., comp. A bibliography of doctoral research on the
    Negro, 1933-1966, compiled by Earle H. West, associate professor of
    education, Howard univ. [Ann Arbor, Mich.], University microfilms,
    1969. vii, 134 p. CCotS, CHS, CNoS, CSdS, CSfU, CSjC, CSt.
        Contains many listings of theses having an obvious relevance to the
    West, and these are listed in the present bibliography. Other theses,
    which cover general subjects, are not listed but should be investigated
    by those performing appropriate research.

270. WHITEMAN, MAXWELL. A century of fiction by American Negroes, 1853-
    1952; a descriptive bibliography. Philadelphia, 1955. 64 p. CCotS,

Bibliographies and Finding Aids

CHS, CNoS, CSfSt, CSjC, CS1uSP, CU-SB, CU-SC.
Contains listings of works by California and Nevada residents.

271. _____. Same. Philadelphia, A. Saifer, 1968. CSdS.

272. *WORK, MONROE NATHAN, 1866-1945, comp. A bibliography of the Negro in Africa and America, compiled by Monroe N. Work ... N. Y., The H. W. Wilson co., 1928. xxi, [1], 698 p.

273. _____. Same. N. Y., Octagon books, 1965.
Available in many libraries.

274. _____. Same. N. Y., Argosy-antiquarian, ltd., 1965.

BIOGRAPHY

INDIVIDUAL BIOGRAPHIES AND AUTOBIOGRAPHIES

275. *ADAMS, ELIZABETH LAURA, 1909- . Dark symphony, by Elizabeth Laura Adams. N. Y., Sheed & Ward, 1942. 194 p. CFa, CL, CLCo, CLob, CPhCL, CViCL, WaT.
Autobiographical.

276. _____. Same. London, Sheed & Ward, 1943. DLC.

277. _____. Same. Symphonie in't donker. Brussels, Sheed & Ward, 1946. DLC.
A translation.

278. *ALEXANDER, CHARLES, 1868-1923. Battles & victories of Allen Allensworth, A. M., Ph.D., lieutenant-colonel, retired, U. S. army, by Charles Alexander. Boston, Sherman, French & co. [1914]. 429 p. port. CHi, CL, CLSU, CNoS, CSfAA (photocopy), CSmH, CViCL, NUC, pre-1956.
A biography of the Army chaplain, Allen Allensworth (1842-1914), who founded the colony of Allensworth, Tulare county.

279. *ANDERSON, ROSA CLAUDETTE. River, face homeward (Suten dan wani hwe fie); an Afro-American woman in Ghana. N. Y., Exposition press [c1966]. 120 p. CNoS.
Autobiographical account of a Los Angeles resident's experiences in Ghana.

280. *ANGELOU, MAYA, 1928- . I know why the caged bird sings [by] Maya Angelou. N. Y., Random house [c1969]. 281 p. C, CNoS, CRic, CSf.
An autobiography by a former Arkansas and San Francisco resident.

281. ARVEY, VERNA, 1910- . "Librarian stimulates community thought," in Opportunity, v. 25, Apr.-June, 1947, p. 82.
The career of Miriam Matthews, head librarian of a Los Angeles branch library.

Individual Biographies and Autobiographies

282. AYER, JOHN EDWIN. "George Bush, the voyageur," in Pacific northwest quarterly, v. 7, Jan., 1916, pp. 40-45.

283. BARTLETT, VIRGINIA STIVERS. "Uncle Nate of Palomar; the entertaining story of the carefree life of Nathaniel Harrison, a Negro, but known as the first white man to live on Palomar Mountain," in Westways, Oct., 1931, pp. 22-25.

284. BATTU, ZOE A. "Cornelia Jones Robertson," in The bystander, v. 1, Sept. 15, 1930, pp. 12-13.

285. *BECKWOURTH, JAMES PIERSON, 1798-1866. Life and adventures of James P. Beckwourth, mountaineer, scout, and pioneer, and chief of the Crow nation. With illustrations. Written from his own dictation by T. D. Bonner. N. Y., Harper & brother, 1856. 537 p. illus., ports. Available in many libraries. NUC, pre-1956.
    This work has appeared in many subsequent editions and condensations, both in the U. S., and in other countries. The French translation of 1860 was issued under the title of Le chasseur.

286. BELL, HORACE. Reminiscences of a ranger: or early times in southern California. Santa Barbara, Wallace Hebberd, 1927. 499 p. illus. Available in many libraries. Rocq 2788-90.
    An account of Peter Biggs can be found on pp. 22-27, 69, and 94. "The author's brief references to the Negro are condescending in tone." - Miriam Matthews.
    Other editions appeared in 1881 and 1933.

287. *BENJAMIN, ROBERT CHARLES O'HARA, 1855-1900. [Biographical account] in Negro history bulletin, v. 5, Jan., 1942, pp. 92-93.
    Note: year of death is established by a news story of Benjamin's murder in the Seattle Republican, Oct. 19, 1900, p. 3, col. 4-5.

288. _____. Life of Toussaint L'Ouverture, warrior and statesman. With an historical survey of the island of San Domingo from the discovery of the island by Christopher Columbus in 1492 to the death of Toussaint in 1803. By R. C. O. Benjamin. Accompanied with a map. [L. A., Evening express co., print, c1888]. ix, 109 p. port., map. DLC, NN, NUC, pre-1956.

289. BERGMAN, G. M. "The other pathfinder: Jacob Dodson," in Black world, v. 14, Aug., 1965, pp. 72-75.

290. BLANK, DENNIS M. "Anatomy of a Negro cartoonist," in Black world, v. 15, Apr., 1966, pp. 45-48.
    About Morrie Turner, Berkeley.

291. BLANKENSHIP, GEORGIANA (MITCHELL), 1860- , comp. Early history of Thurston county, Washington, together with biographies and reminiscences of those identified with pioneer days; comp. and ed. by Mrs. George E. Blankenship. Olympia, 1914. 392 p. plates, ports. CLU, CSmH, Wa.
    The George W. Bush family's activities are described, pp. 320-24.

Individual Biographies and Autobiographies

292. *BONTEMPS, ARNA WENDELL, 1902-1973. We have tomorrow, by Arna Bontemps, illustrated with photographs by Marian Palfi. Boston, Houghton, Mifflin co., 1945. vi, 131 p. ports. CBea, CEs, CHS, CLSU, CLobS, COM, CPhD, CRic, CSdS, CSuLas, CU, CU-A, Wa.
    Contains an account and portrait of Horace R. Cayton, Jr., pp. 26-33.

293. _____. Same. Boston, Houghton, Mifflin, 1960. CNoS.

294. BRISTOL, SHERLOCK, 1815- . The pioneer preacher; incidents of interests, and experience in the author's life ... illustrated by Isabelle Blood. Chicago [etc.], Fleming H. Revell co., 1898 [c1887]. 336 p. port. CHi, CSf, Rocq 15715.
    Isaac Isaacs, Downieville boxing champion, pp. 172-75.

295. BRODERICK, FRANCIS L. W. E. B. Du Bois, Negro leader in a time of crisis. Stanford, Stanford univ. press, 1959. 259 p. Includes bibliography. CBGTU, CEcaC, CFS, CHS, CKenM, CLSU, CLobS, CM1G, CNoS, COM, CPhD, CSdS, CSf, CSjCi, CSluSP, CSto, CU, CU-A.

296. _____. Same. 1967 ed. CBGTU, CU.

297. BROOKS, JACQUELINE. "This is the pass that Beckwourth found," in National motorist, v. 16, Aug., 1939, pp. 7-8, 17.
    Contains a biographical account of Beckwourth.

298. BRUYN, KATHLEEN, 1903- . "Aunt" Clara Brown; story of a black pioneer, by Kathleen Bruyn ... Boulder, Colo., Pruett pub. co. [c1970]. xv, 206 p. illus., ports., facsim. Bibliography: pp. [194]-202. CHS, CSS, CSfAA, CSfU, CSjC.
    A biography of Mrs. Clara Brown (1800?-1885), Colorado pioneer of 1859 and a resident of Central City.

299. BRYANT, EDWIN, 1805-1869. What I saw in California, being the journal of a tour by the emigrant route and south pass of the Rocky mountains across the continent of North America, the great desert basin, and through California in the years 1846, 1847 ... By Edwin Bryant ... Santa Ana, Fine arts press, 1936. xxiv, 481 p. plates, map, facsim.
    For accounts of William A. Leidesdorff and a description of his home, see pp. 301-03, 308, 310, and 413.
    Many editions of this title have appeared since its first publication in 1848.
    Available in many libraries.

300. BUCKBEE, EDNA BRYAN. "The 'boys' called her 'Mammy' Pleasant," in The pony express, v. 20, Oct., 1953, pp. 3-4, 13-14.

301. *BUNCHE, RALPH JOHNSON, 1904-1971. "My most unforgettable character," in Reader's digest, v. 95, Sept., 1969, pp. 45-49.
    An account of his living conditions and schooling in Los Angeles, 1917ff.

Individual Biographies and Autobiographies

302. California. Legislature. Senate. <u>Sixth session</u>. Journal of the
sixth session of the Legislature ... Sacramento, State print., 1855.
970 p. C, C-ArS, CLU, CSf, CSmH, CU, NUC, pre-1956.
   Contains the message of Gov. John Bigler relative to the William A.
Leidesdorff estate, pp. 324-26.

303. California. World's fair commission. Literary and other exercises
in California state building, World's Columbian exposition, Chicago,
1893. Chicago, Rand, McNally, 1893. 96 p. C, CU-B.
   Frederick Douglass' speech and his physical appearance are both
described, pp. 26-27.

304. CATLIN, AMOS PARMALEE, 1823-1900. Rancho "Rio de los Americanos,"
granted to William A. Leidesdorff, by Governor Micheltorena; finally
confirmed to the executors of Joseph L. Folsom, deceased. Surveyed by
Surveyor general John C. Hays, and approved by the U. S. District court
for the northern district of California, 25th June, 1862 ... [S. F.,
B. F. Sterett, 1862]. iv, 71 p. fold. map. CSmH, CU-B.

305. *CAYTON, HORACE ROSCOE, 1903-1970. Long old road. N. Y., Trident
press, 1965 [c1964]. 402 p. CEcaC, CHS, CHi, CKenM, CLobS, CNoS,
CPhD, CSdS, CSt, Wa, WaT.
   Cayton's autobiography in which his early life in Seattle and in
Alaska is described, pp. 1-174.

306. Cayton's year book; Seattle's colored citizens. Seattle, H. R.
Cayton and son, 19- . illus., incl. ports. NN (1923).

307. CLARK, C. "Tootsie: belle of Alaska," in <u>Black world</u>, v. 12, Mar.,
1963, pp. 46-49.
   About Tootsie Wade.

308. *CLEAVER, ELDRIDGE, 1935- . Soul on ice. With an introduction by
Maxwell Geismar. N. Y., McGraw-Hill, c1968. xv, 210 p. Available in
many California libraries and WaPu, WaT, WaTC.
   "In a collection of essays and open letters written from
California's Folsom state prison, the author, an Afro-American now on
the staff of <u>Ramparts</u>, writes about the forces which shaped his life." -
Dorothy B. Porter.

308a.*COFFEY, ALVIN AARON, 1822-1902. Biographical account of a
California 1849er and the only black member of the Society of California
pioneers. 2 p. Typew. CSfCP.

309. *Congress of racial equality. Seattle branch. Washington's Negro
pioneer: George Washington Bush. [Seattle, 1967]. 8 p. illus., maps.
CSfAA, CU-B, Wa.

310. CONNER, VEDA N. "There's a big we in New Mexico," in <u>Crisis</u>, v. 61,
Jan., 1954, pp. 5-8, 62.
   Biography of Herbert La Grone, Albuquerque.

Individual Biographies and Autobiographies

311. *COVINGTON, FLOYD C.   1901- . "Democracy at work; the story of
Reginald L. Jones," in Opportunity, v. 22, Oct.-Dec., 1944, pp. 162-63.
     Biography of a Monrovia native and personnel representative,
Lockheed aircraft corp., Burbank.

312. ____. "Ethiopia spreads her wings," in Opportunity, v. 8, Sept.,
1930, pp. 276-77.
     Biography of Jay Howard Montgomery, Colorado, Arizona, and
California mining and aeronautical engineer and inventor.

313. ____. "Greene of Los Angeles," in Crisis, v. 40, Mar., 1933,
pp. 57-58.
     An account of Y. M. C. A. secretary, Thomas Augustus Greene.

314. CRANE, WARREN EUGENE. "Interesting westerners," in Sunset, v. 45,
Dec., 1920, p. 48.
     Concerns John Cragwell, Seattle barber, friend of numerous celebrities.

315. *CRUMBLY, FLOYD H.   "A Los Angeles citizen," in Colored American
magazine, v. 9, Sept., 1905, pp. 482-85.
     An account of Robert Curry Owens.

316. Daughters of the American revolution. "Family records of Washington
pioneers prior to 1891." v. 8, 1938. Typescript. Wa.
     Contains biographical information on W. O. Bush, son of George W.
Bush, contributed by John S. Bush, pp. 388-89.

317. *DAVIS, ELIZABETH LINDSAY.   Lifting as they climb. [Chicago], 1933.
424 p. ports. DHU.
     Contains a biography of Delilah L. Beasley, pp. 107, 188-95.

318. DAVIS, SAMUEL POST, 1850-1918. "'Mammy' Pleasant; memoirs and autobiography," in Pandex of the press, v. 1, Jan., 1902, pp. 1-6. CU-B.
     A 3-paged promotional insert in front of this issue describes the
extensive nature of the Memoirs. However, the Feb., 1902 issue, p. 94,
states that the "Memoirs of 'Mammy' Pleasant" have been discontinued
owing to a misunderstanding between the author and the editor.

319. DAVY, MARGUERITE ROSS. "Novel concessionaire; the story of Arthur L.
Reese, who developed for himself an unusual occupation," in Opportunity,
v. 22, Apr.-June, 1944, pp. 58-59.
     Biography of a Venice decorator for festivals and expositions.

320. *DEAN, HARRY, 1864- . The Pedro Gorino; the adventures of a Negro
sea captain in Africa and on the seven seas in his attempts to found an
Ethiopian empire. An autobiographical narrative by Captain Harry Dean
written with the assistance of Sterling North. Boston, Houghton Mifflin
co., 1929. xvi, 262 p. WaTP.
     A descendant of Paul Cuffe describes his San Francisco experiences
in the 1870's, pp. 37-43.
     London edition (Harrap, 1929) has title: Umbala.

Individual Biographies and Autobiographies

321. DE FORD, MIRIAM ALLEN. "Who was Leidesdorff?" in Westways, v. 45,
Mar., 1953, pp. 18-19.

322. DELANO, ALONZO, 1806-1874. Life on the plains and among the diggings
... Auburn, N. Y., Miller, Orton & Mulligan, 1854. 384 p. illus. C,
CHi, CL, CLSU, CLU, CO, CP, CSd, CSf, CSfCP, CSmH, CU-B, Rocq 6041.
  Includes an incident in the life of James P. Beckwourth, pp. 327-30.

323. ____. Across the plains and among the diggings ... a reprint of
the original edition ... N. Y., Wilson-Erickson, 1936. 192 p. illus.
Available in many California libraries. Rocq 6042.

324. DOBIE, CHARLES CALDWELL, 1881-1943. San Francisco; a pageant, by
Charles Caldwell Dobie; illus. by E. H. Suydam. N. Y., D. Appleton-
Century co., 1939. xiii, 440 p. illus., plates. Available in many
California libraries. Rocq 9175.
  "The house of mystery," pp. 316-23 describes the career of Mary Ellen
Pleasant and her relationship with Thomas and Teresa Bell, all of whom
were residents of the house at 1661 Octavia St.

325. DOUGLAS, PATRICK. "The family of two revolutions," in Seattle
magazine, v. 6, Jan., 1969, pp. 21-25, 28-29, 38-39.
  Concerns the Gayton family resident in Seattle for 80 years.

326. DOYLE, HELEN (MACKNIGHT), 1872- . A child went forth; the autobiography of Dr. Helen MacKnight Doyle; with a foreword by Mary Austin.
N. Y., Gotham house, 1934. 364 p. Available in many California
libraries.
  A folklore account is given of the heroic death of Charles Summers
for whom Charley's Butte near Owensville is named, pp. 157-58. A more
authentic account of Summers, one of California's earliest cowboys and
the only black resident of the Owens river valley at that time, is given
in the San Francisco Pacific appeal, May 30 and June 13, 1863.

327. DRAKE, CISCO. "How Pico boulevard got its name," in The message
magazine, Mar.-Apr., 1970, pp. 32-33.
  Biographical information on California governor Pío Pico (1801-1894)
in a Seventh day adventist publication.

328. EAMES, NINETTA. "Staging in the Mendocino redwoods," in Overland
monthly, v. 20 (ser. 2), Sept., 1892.
  Contains an account and a portrait of Nathaniel Smith, a California
pioneer of 1852, pp. 270 and 274-76.

329. EGE, ROBERT J. "Custer's Negro interpreter," in Black world, v. 14,
Feb., 1965, pp. 29-35.
  Relates activity of Isaiah Dorman.

330. *EVERS, MYRLIE. For us, the living, by Mrs. Medgar Evers with
William Peters. Garden City, N. Y., Doubleday, 1967. 378 p. CFS,
CKenM, CLSU, CNoS, CO, CPhD, CSdS, CSf, CS1uSP, WaPu, WaT, WaTC.
  The California widow of Medgar Wiley Evers recounts her own and her
husband's lives.

Individual Biographies and Autobiographies

331. _____. "Mrs. King and Mrs. Kennedy," in Ladies home journal, v. 85, June, 1968, p. 32.

332. EWING, BELLE C. "Adventure was his name," in California highway patrolman, v. 30, June, 1966, pp. 57, 101-03.
    Concerns James P. Beckwourth.

333. FABRE, MICHEL. "Report from Paris; the last quest of Horace Cayton," in Black world, v. 19, May, 1970, pp. 41-45, 95-97.
    Cayton's death.

334. *FERGUSON, IRA LUNAN, 1904- . I dug graves at night to attend college by day; the story of a West Indian Negro-American's first 30 years in the United States; an autobiography. Brooklyn, N. Y., Theo Gaus' sons, inc. [c1968-70]. 3 v. ports., facsims. CSf, CSt (v. 1).
    Authored by a San Francisco psychologist.

335. *FLEMING, GEORGE JAMES, 1904- . "Preacher-at-large to universities," in Crisis, v. 46, Aug., 1939, pp. 233, 251, and 253.
    About the Rev. Howard Thurman.

336. *FLIPPER, HENRY OSSIAN, 1856-1940. Negro frontiersman; the western memoirs of Henry O. Flipper, first Negro graduate of West Point. Edited with an introduction by Theodore D. Harris. El Paso, Texas western college press, 1963. x, 54 p. ports. AzU, CBb, CLU, CLobS, CSj, CSmH, CSt, CU-B.
    "Sequel to ... The colored cadet at West Point ... published in 1878."

337. *FLORY, ISHMAEL P. "Walter Arthur Gordon, a biographical sketch," in Opportunity, v. 10, Sept., 1932, pp. 283-84, 292.
    Account of a Univ. of Calif. (Berkeley) athlete by a Los Angeles resident.

338. FURGATCH, LEON. "Juanita Terry: Congressional secretary," in Crisis, v. 58, Jan., 1951, pp. 14-16.
    The career of the secretary to California Representative, Helen Gahagan Douglas.

339. *GIBBS, MIFFLIN WISTAR, 1823-1915. Shadow and light; an autobiography with reminiscences of the last and present century, by Mifflin Wistar Gibbs. With an introduction by Booker T. Washington ... Washington, D. C., 1902. xv, 372 p. ports. C, CHS, CHi, CSmH, WaTC.
    The author describes his early life as a merchant in gold rush San Francisco and later in Victoria, B. C.

340. _____. Same. N. Y., Arno press, 1968. CHi, CLobS, CNoS, CSbS, CSd, CSdS, CSfSt, CSjC, CU-B.

341. *GOODWIN, RUBY (BERKLEY), 1903- . It's good to be black. Garden City, N. Y., Doubleday [c1953]. 256 p. Available in many California libraries and WaPu, WaT.
    Her autobiography.

Individual Biographies and Autobiographies

342. *GORDON, TAYLOR, 1893- . The man who built the stone castle. White
    Sulphur Springs, Mont., Meaher county news, 1967. 46 p. McBC.
        Biography of Byron Roger Sherman, pioneer white developer of White
    Sulphur Springs, written for the County's centennial.

343. GRAVES, JACKSON ALPHEUS, 1852-1933. My seventy years in California,
    1857-1927 ... L. A., Times-mirror press, 1927. 478 p. illus. Available
    in many libraries. Rocq 3857.
        Includes a portrait of and information about an employee, George
    Edmonds, pp. 234-35, 389-92, and 401. "Patronizing in tone." - Miriam
    Matthews.

344. HAFEN, LEROY R., ed. The mountain men and the fur trade of the far
    west; biographical sketches of the participants by scholars of the
    subject ... under the editorial supervision of LeRoy R. Hafen ... Glen-
    dale, Arthur H. Clark co., 1965-71. 8 v. illus., maps. C, CHi, CL,
    CLU, CMary, CSbCL, CSmH, CU-B.
        The following biographies may be found: Jacques Clamorgan, v. 2,
    pp. 81-94; Moses ("Black") Harris, v. 4, pp. 103-17; and James P.
    Beckwourth, v. 6, pp. 37-60.

345. HARRIS, MARK. "The legend of Black Mary," in Black world, v. 8, Aug.,
    1950, pp. 84-87.
        Describes activities of Mary Fields also known as "Black Mary."

346. *HARRISON, NATHANIEL. [Biographical file]. 16 p. ports. CSdHi.

347. *HENDERSON, LENNEAL J. "W. E. B. Du Bois, black scholar and prophet,"
    in Black scholar, v. 1, Jan.-Feb., 1970, pp. 48-57.
        By a faculty member at St. Mary's college, Moraga.

348. HENRY, FRANCIS. "George Bush," in Oregon pioneer association trans-
    actions, Fifteenth annual reunion, Portland, June 15, 1887, pp. 68-69.
        Francis Henry of Olympia was a friend of the Bush family.

349. *HICKS, ESTELLE BELLE. The golden apples; memoirs of a retired
    teacher, by Estelle Belle Hicks. N. Y., Exposition press [c1959]. 75 p.
        Autobiography of a Los Angeles resident and retired Mobile, Ala.
    teacher.

350. HILL, LAURENCE LANDRETH. La reina; Los Angeles in three centuries;
    a volume commemorating the fortieth anniversary of the founding of the
    Security trust & savings bank of Los Angeles, February 11, 1889 ...
    [L. A.] Security trust & savings bank, 1929. 208 p. illus., ports.

351. _____. _____. 4th ed., 1931. Editions are available in many
    California libraries. Rocq 3882-83.
        Information about Peter Johnson is given, p. 74.

352. HINES, HARVEY K., 1828-1902. An illustrated history of the state of
    Washington, containing ... biographical mention of ... its pioneers and
    prominent citizens ... By Rev. H. K. Hines ... Chicago, Lewis pub.
    co., 1893. xii, 933 p. illus., plates, ports. CSmH, CU, Wa.
        Biographical sketch of Bush family, pp. 378-79.

Individual Biographies and Autobiographies

353. HOLDREDGE, HELEN (O'DONNELL). Mammy Pleasant. N. Y., Putnam's, c1953. 311 p. illus., ports. Bibliography: pp. 310-11. Available in many California libraries.
A biography of Mrs. Mary Ellen Pleasant (1812-1904).

354. _____. Same. Index ... compiled by San Francisco public library. Reference department. S. F., 1954. unp. CSf.

355. _____. Mammy Pleasant's partner. N. Y., Putnam's [1954]. 300 p. illus., ports. Bibliographies: pp. 295-300. CBb, CHC, CHi, CLU, CLobS, COroB, CSd, CSf, CSj, CSlu, CSmH, CStmo, CU-B, CViCL, Rocq 9840.
This sequel to the author's biography of Mrs. Mary Ellen Pleasant relates the latter's business connections with the San Francisco capitalist, Thomas Bell.

356. HOLLOWELL, ELLIS CHANDLER. John Roy Lynch, Negro congressman from Mississippi. Master's thesis, Univ. of Calif., Berkeley, 1951. iii, 114 ℓ.

357. HUTCHINSON, WILLIAM H. "Mountain man of color," in Westways, v. 41, July, 1949, pp. 16-17.
Concerns James P. Beckwourth.

358. Illustrated atlas and history of Yolo county, Cal., containing a history of California from 1513 to 1850, a history of Yolo county from 1825 to 1880, with ... portraits of well-known citizens, and the official county map. S. F., De Pue & co., 1879. 105 p. illus., ports., maps. C, CHi, CO, CSf, CSfCP, CSmH, CU-A, CU-B, CWoY, Rocq 15537.
A biography of Basil Campbell (b. 1823) and his brother, Elijah Jennings (b. 1834), may be found on pp. 84-85 and 90, respectively.

359. JACKSON, SAMETTA WALLACE. "Mifflin Wistar Gibbs," in Negro history bulletin, v. 4, May, 1941, pp. 175-76.
A biography of Gibbs, pioneer San Francisco shoe merchant of the 1850's.

360. "Jacob Dodson, the Negro who rode with Frémont the pathfinder from Los Angeles to Monterey, California in 1847," in Negro history bulletin, v. 28, Nov., 1964, pp. 31-32.

361. JAMES, LAURA M. "Palomar's friendly hermit," in San Diego historical society quarterly, v. 4, Jan., 1958, pp. 5-8.
An account of Nathaniel Harrison (1819-1920).

362. "Jim Beckwourth and Ina Coolbrith," in Pony express, v. 14, July, 1947, p. 9.

363. *JOHNSON, JAMES WELDON, 1871-1938. Along this way; the autobiography of James Weldon Johnson. N. Y., Viking press, 1934. 418 p. plates, ports., facsims. CHS, CHi, CKenM, CNoS, COM, CSaT, CSdS, CSf, CSjCi, CSluSP.
His experiences in San Francisco are described, pp. 204-09.

Individual Biographies and Autobiographies

364. _____. ... Black Manhattan. N. Y., A. A. Knopf, 1930. xvii, 284, xxxiv p. ports., maps, facsim. CFS, CNoS.
    Garland Anderson, pp. 203-05. Also contains a chapter on Egbert Austin Williams, famous New York stage entertainer from San Francisco and Riverside.

365. _____. "Robert C. Owens, a Pacific coast successful Negro; adapted from notes furnished by James W. Johnson," in Colored American magazine, v. 9, July, 1905, pp. 391-93.
    An illus. account of a Los Angeles resident, Robert Curry Owens (b. 1859).

366. KAROLEVITZ, B. "Northwest city builder: George Washington," in Black world, v. 12, Sept., 1963, pp. 70-75.
    About the founder of Centralia, Washington.

367. KEEN, HAROLD. "Bert Ritchey and Negro responsibility," in San Diego and Point magazine, v. 18, Nov., 1965, pp. 64-66, 131-34.

368. LAPP, RUDOLPH MATTHEW, 1915- . "Jeremiah B. Sanderson: early California Negro leader," in Journal of Negro history, v. 53, Oct., 1968, pp. 321-33.

369. LEE, DANIEL, 1806-1895. Ten years in Oregon. By D. Lee and J. H. Frost ... N. Y., Pub. for the authors, J. Collord, Printer, 1844. 344 p. front., fold. map. CU-B.

370. _____. Same. Fairfield, Washington, Ye Galleon press, 1968. Wa.
    Information concerning George Washington, a Negro river pilot from Vancouver, pp. 224-25.

371. LEIGHTON, AMANDA. "The Collins family," in Immigration and race problems, 1954, pp. 336-43. Oakland, Mills college Dept. of economics and sociology, 1954. COMC.

372. LEWIS, OSCAR, 1893- . Bonanza inn; America's first luxury hotel, by Oscar Lewis & Carroll D. Hall. N. Y., A. A. Knopf, 1939. 346, xii, p. plates, ports., facsims. Available in many California libraries. Rocq 10215.
    Information about Mary Ellen Pleasant, pp. 151-54, 157-58, 160, 165-67, 205, 209-13.

373. *LIGHT, ALLEN B. [Biographical file]. 2 p. CSdHi.
    Light arrived in southern California in 1835.

374. *LOGAN, RAYFORD W. "Estevanico, Negro discoverer of the Southwest: a critical re-examination," in Phylon, v. 1, 4th quarter, 1940, pp. 305-14.

375. "Loren Miller, January 30, 1903-July 14, 1967," in Crisis, v. 74, Aug.-Sept., 1967, p. 345.
    Tribute to a Los Angeles jurist and journalist.

Individual Biographies and Autobiographies

376. "Loren Miller's contributions," in <u>Crisis</u>, v. 74, Aug.-Sept., 1967, p. 336.

377. *LOVE, NAT, 1854- . The life and adventures of Nat Love, better known in the cattle country as "Deadwood Dick." By himself. A true story of slavery days, life on the great cattle ranges and on the plains of the "wild and woolly" West based on facts and personal experiences of the author. L. A., Author [1907]. 162 p. ports. CNoS, CoHi, CSf, CSmH, WaTC.

378. _____. Same. N. Y., Arno press, 1968. CAuP, CEH, CEcaC, CLCo, CMS, CNoS, CRbCL, CRcS, CS, CSalCL, CSd, CSdS, CSjCi, CSrCL, CStaB, CStb, CSto, CTurS.

379. *LOVINGOOD, PENMAN. A Negro seer: the life and work of Dr. R. S. Lovingood, educator, churchman [and] race leader, by Penman Lovingood. Compton, The Lovingood co. [c1963]. 111 p. ports. DHU.
    Biography of Reuben Shannon Lovingood, Wiley college educator, Marshall, Texas.

380. MC CLURE, GALEN. "James P. Beckwourth - trail blazer of the Sierra," in <u>California highway patrolman</u>, v. 13, Feb., 1950, pp. 12, 101-02, 104-05.

381. MC CONNELL, ROLAND C. "Isaiah Dorman and the Custer expedition," in <u>Journal of Negro history</u>, v. 33, July, 1948, pp. 344-52.
    An account of an army guide and interpreter who was killed shortly after the battle of the Little Big Horn.

382. MC CULLOCH, SAMUEL CLYDE, 1916- . The life and times of Dr. Thomas Bray (1656-1730): a study in humanitarianism. Doctoral dissertation, Univ. of Calif., Los Angeles, 1944. v, 316 ℓ.

383. *MC DONALD, EMANUEL B., 1884- . "Sam" McDonald's farm; Stanford reminiscences by Emanuel B. "Sam" McDonald. Stanford, Stanford univ. press [c1954]. ix, 422 p. illus. (lining papers). C, CO, CPa, CRcS, CSd, CU-B.

384. *MC DONALD, VERNON SUGG. "The pioneer Sugg family," in the Quarterly of the <u>Tuolumne county historical society</u>, v. 4, July-Sept., 1964, pp. 97-98.
    History of a Sonora family which has resided in the same home since 1855.

385. MC GUE, D. B. "John Taylor -- slave-born Colorado pioneer," in <u>Colorado magazine</u>, v. 18, Sept., 1941, pp. 161-68.

386. MC MILLIAN, CECILLE VANDEL. "The Benjamin Joiner family," in <u>Las Calaveras</u>, v. 17, July, 1969, pp. [1-2].
    Publication of the Calaveras county historical society, San Andreas.

387. MANNING, JAMES FRANCIS. William A. Leidesdorff's career in California. Master's thesis, Univ. of Calif., Berkeley, 1941. iii, 141 ℓ.

Individual Biographies and Autobiographies

388. MATTHEWS, JIM, ed. Five dark days in history; biography of a nonviolent warrior. [L. A., Creative advertising media, c1968]. 1 v.
(unp.), illus. CSf.
    Biography of Martin Luther King, Jr.

389. MEEKER, EZRA, 1836-1928. The busy life of eighty-five years of Ezra
Meeker; ventures and adventures. Seattle, 1916. 299 p. illus. CSf,
CSmH, Wa.
    Describes "A great pioneer - George Bush, the voyager," pp. 107-15.

390. A memorial and biographical history of northern California, illustrated. Containing a history ... and biographical mention of many of
its pioneers ... Chicago, Lewis pub. co., 1891. 834 p. illus., ports.
C, CBb, CHi, CL, CLU, CMary, CO, CSf, CSmH, CU-B, CU-SB, Rocq 15952.
    Biographical account of Basil Campbell (b. 1823), Yolo county,
pp. 323-24.

391. A memorial and biographical history of the counties of Fresno,
Tulare, and Kern, California ... Chicago, Lewis pub. co. [1891]. 822 p.
illus., ports. C, CBaK, CCC, CF, CFS, CHanK, CHi, CLSU, CLU, CO, CSf,
CSfCP, CSj, CSmH, CU-B, CViCL, Rocq 1839.
    Page 288 contains a biography of Wiley Hinds (b. 1836) who settled
in Tulare county in 1858.

392. *MOON, HENRY LEE. "Loren Miller, legal scholar," in Crisis, v. 74,
Aug.-Sept., 1967, pp. 346-47.

393. MORGAN, CHARLES. "Huckster on horseback," in Westways, v. 60, Nov.,
1968, pp. 39-40.
    Concerns James P. Beckwourth.

394. MORGAN, JOHN EDWARD. Comparison study of the lives of William
Alexander Leidesdorff and Joseph Libby Folsom ... Copies presented to
The Oakland Park Negro museum and library; the California room,
California state library. Rev., May 1966. [20] l. Typew. CU-B.

395. "Mrs. Mary Ray, celebrant of 101st birthday," in Colored American
magazine, v. 14, Apr., 1908, pp. 174-75.
    Illus. biography of Seattle resident, Mrs. Mary (Johnson) (Dosier)
Ray.

396. MUMEY, NOLIE, 1891- . James Pierson Beckwourth, 1856-1866, an
enigmatic figure of the West. A history of the latter years of his
life. Denver, F. A. Rosenstock, Old West pub. co., 1957. 188 p.
illus., ports., fold. map, facsims. Bibliographical footnotes.
"Edition limited to five hundred numbered and signed copies." CMary,
CSmH, CU-B.

397. "Negro founder of Centralia, Washington," in Negro history bulletin,
v. 27, Nov., 1963, pp. 44-47.
    About George Washington.

Individual Biographies and Autobiographies

398. "A Negro pioneer in the West," in <u>Journal of Negro history</u>, v. 8,
July, 1923, pp. 333-35.
Tells of George Bush and his son, W. O. Bush, Washington pioneers.

399. NEIN, ROBERT M. "Don't be fooled by this lady's laughter - white man,
she'll pin your tail to the wall," in <u>Seattle magazine</u>, v. 3, Dec., 1966,
pp. 59-62.
An account of Roberta Byrd Barr.

400. NIDEVER, GEORGE, 1802-1883. The life and adventures of George
Nidever ... ed. by William Henry Ellison. Berkeley, Univ. of Calif.
press, 1937. xi, 128 p. port., facsim. Available in many California
libraries. Rocq 13636.
Information on the otter hunter, Allen B. Light, also known as the
"Black steward," pp. 39-62 <u>passim.</u>, and pp. 108-09.

401. NYGREEN, GLEN T. "Bruce Frederick Rowell of Seattle, Washington,"
in <u>Opportunity</u>, v. 25, Apr.-June, 1947, p. 63.
Biography of a service station manager.

402. O'BRIEN, ROBERT W. "George Washington, founder of Centralia," in
<u>Negro history bulletin</u>, v. 5, June, 1942, pp. 194, 197, and 215.

403. OGDEN, ADELE. The California sea otter trade, 1784-1848, by Adele
Ogden. Berkeley, Univ. of Calif. press, 1941. xi, 251 p. illus.
CHi, CU-B, Rocq 15989.
The author's doctoral dissertation, Univ. of Calif., Berkeley, 1938.
For information about the career of Allen B. Light, 1835ff., see index.

404. *OWEN, CHANDLER. "Dr. Eugene Curry Nelson, a professional and business
man of a new type among Negroes," in <u>Messenger</u>, v. 6, Oct., 1924,
pp. 316-22.
An illus. biography of a Los Angeles resident.

405. PARKHILL, FORBES, 1892- . Mister Barney Ford; a portrait in bistre
[by] Forbes Parkhill. Denver, Sage books [c1963]. 218 p. illus.
Bibliography: pp. 213-16. CFS, CHi, CNoS, CSluSP, CoHi, WyU.
Biography of a Wyoming and Colorado hotel owner.

405a.*PATTERSON, WILLIAM LORENZO, 1891- . The man who cried genocide;
an autobiography, by William L. Patterson. N. Y., International pubs.
[c1971]. 223 p. illus., ports. CU.
A San Francisco native describes his own and his forebears'
California experiences, pp. 17-46.

406. *PINKNEY, WILLIAM HENRY 1872- . Interview with William Henry
Pinkney, May 22, 1951," by Richard C. Bailey, in <u>Historic Kern</u> (pub. of
the Kern county historical society), v. 3, Oct., 1951, pp. 1-3.
Pinkney arrived in Kern county from South Carolina, 1884.

407. "A pioneer's lonely path; setting his sights on suburbia, he made it
to Bellevue the hard way," in <u>Seattle magazine</u>, v. 1, Apr., 1964,
pp. 22-23, 35.

Individual Biographies and Autobiographies

408. PLEASANT, MARY ELLEN, 1812-1904. Memorial services in honor of
Mary Ellen Pleasant, 1812-1904, mother of civil rights in California,
friend of John Brown, Friday, February 12, 1965, 2 o'clock P. M.,
Tulocay [i.e., Tucolay] cemetery, Coombsville road and Silverado trail,
Napa ... [S. F.] San Francisco Negro historical and cultural society
[1965]. [3] p. CSfAA.

409. POTTER, ELIZABETH (GRAY). San Francisco skyline, by Elizabeth Gray
Potter; with illus. from photographs by the author and by Gabriel Moulin,
and maps. N. Y., Dodd, Mead, & co., 1939. xvi, 284 p. illus., maps
(part fold.). Available in many California libraries. Rocq 11026.
    See index for information on William A. Leidesdorff's career in
California.

410. PROSSER, WILLIAM FARRAND. A history of the Puget sound country; its
resources, its commerce and its people. N. Y., Lewis pub. co., 1903.
2 v. Wa.
    Life of George Washington, founder of Centralia, v. 2, pp. 325-26.

411. RAUCH, LAWRENCE LEE. "Triple-threat artist," in Opportunity, v. 17,
Sept., 1939, pp. 275-76.
    An account of Clarence Muse, Los Angeles musician and actor.

412. *RAY, EMMA J. (SMITH), 1859- . Twice sold, twice ransomed; autobiography of Mr. and Mrs. L. P. Ray; introduction by Rev. C. E.
McReynolds. Chicago, Free Methodist publishing house [c1926]. 320 p.
front., plates, ports. CSmH, Wa.
    The Rays were social and mission workers in Seattle in the late 19th
and early 20th centuries.

413. RICE, HALLIE EVELYN. Pío Pico, last Mexican governor of California.
Master's thesis, Univ. of Calif., Berkeley, 1933. ii, 201 l. ports.
    A study of Pico's term as governor, 1845-48, but also includes
general biographical material, 1801-94.

414. ROTHE, ANNA, ed. Current biography; who's news and why; 1946. N. Y.,
H. W. Wilson co., 1946. Wa.
    Biography and portrait of Horace R. Cayton, Jr., pp. 103-06.

415. *SAMS, JESSIE (BENNETT). White mother, by Jessie Bennett Sams.
McGraw-Hill book co. [c1957]. 241 p. CL, CNoS.
    An autobiographical account of twin Negro girls raised in Florida
by a white woman. Authored by a Los Angeles school teacher.

416. *SAVAGE, WILLIAM SHERMAN, 1890- . "George Washington of Centralia,
Washington," in Negro history bulletin, v. 27, Nov., 1963, pp. 44-47.
    About George Washington Bush.

417. _____. "The influence of William Alexander Leidesdorff on the history
of California," in Journal of Negro history, v. 38, July, 1953, pp. 322-
31.

Individual Biographies and Autobiographies

418. _____. "Intrigue in California (1846)," in Midwest journal, v. 2,
Winter, 1949, pp. 63-68.
    Two letters from William A. Leidesdorff to Thomas Oliver Larkin,
U. S. consul in California, Monterey.

419. *SCRUGGS, BAXTER S.   A man in our community; the biography of L. G.
Robinson of Los Angeles, California. Gardena, The Institute press,
1937. 134 p. illus., ports., facsim. CHi, CNoS, Rocq 4372.
    About Louis George Robinson, Los Angeles county civil servant, who
migrated from Georgia in 1904.

420. SHEPARD, BETTY, ed. Mountain man, Indian chief: the life and adventures of Jim Beckwourth. N. Y., Harcourt, Brace & World, 1968. 184 p.

421. SIMPSON, ALICE FISHER. "Folsom, city of history," in California
highway patrolman, v. 16, Jan., 1953, pp. 17-19, 85-88.
    Information on William Alexander Leidesdorff.

422. SMALL, KATHLEEN EDWARDS. History of Tulare county by Kathleen Edwards
Small. Chicago, S. J. Clarke pub. co., 1926. 2 v. illus., map, ports.
C, CCC, CHanK, CHi, CL, CSf, CSmH, CViCL, Rocq 15170.
    Contains a biography and portraits of Lieut. Col. and Mrs. Allen
Allensworth, v. 2, pp. 454-59.

423. *SMALLWOOD, WILLIAM.   "They made good in the movie capital," in
Opportunity, v. 19, Mar., 1941, pp. 76-77.
    The Los Angeles careers of Mrs. Hazel Washington, leatherwork artist,
and Mildred Blount, hat designer.

424. SMITH, HERNDON. Centralia, the first fifty years, 1845-1900.
Centralia, 1941. Wa.
    Contains a section on George Washington, the founder of Centralia,
by Dorothy Mae Rigg, pp. 193-233.

425. SMITH, MARIAN ELIZABETH. Pío Pico, ranchero and politician. Master's
thesis, Univ. of Calif., Berkeley, 1928. 218 ℓ. port., facsims.
    A biography, 1801-45.

426. *SOMERVILLE, JOHN ALEXANDER, 1881-1973. Man of color, an autobiography,
by J. Alexander Somerville; a factual report on the status of the
American Negro today. L. A., Lorrin L. Morrison [c1949]. 170 p. front.
(col. port.) C, CHS, CHi, CL, CLGS, CLM, CLobS, CNoS, CSS, CSbS, CSf,
CSluSP, CStcrCL, CU.
    Somerville arrived in Los Angeles at "the turn of the century" and
was the first Negro to receive a degree in dentistry from the Univ. of
southern California.

427. _____. Same. Kingston, Jamaica [1951]. Title varies slightly.
CLSU, CSt.

428. STAUFFER, HENRY. "A young lawyer," in Crisis, v. 36, Dec., 1929,
pp. 410 and 426-27.
    A biographical account of George M. Johnson of San Bernardino and
Berkeley.

Individual Biographies and Autobiographies

429. *STILL, WILLIAM. The underground rail road. A record of facts,
authentic narratives, letters &c., narrating the hardships, hair-breadth
escapes, and death struggles of the slaves in their efforts for freedom
... Philadelphia, Porter & Coates, 1872. 780 p. illus., ports. CHi,
CSmH, CSt.

430. _____. Same. N. Y., Arno press, 1968. CEcaC, CHS, CSdS, CSf.
Includes a biographical account and portrait of San Francisco
resident, Samuel D. Burris, a well-known underground railroad conductor
in Delaware and Maryland, pp. 746-47.

431. STRUNK, GORDON B. "Robert B. Pitts - statistician," in Opportunity,
v. 25, Apr.-June, 1947, p. 64.
Account of an employee of the Washington state dept. of health.

432. TERRELL, JOHN UPTON. Estevanico the black. L. A., Westernlore press,
1968. 155 p. illus. Bibliography: pp. 147-51. CNoS, COroB, CP,
CSbCL.
In 1539, Estevanico the Moor preceded Fray Marcos of Nice, and thus
was the first foreign explorer to enter Arizona and New Mexico.

433. THOMAS, PAUL F. George Bush. Master's thesis, Univ. of Washington,
Seattle, 1965. 126 p.

434. THOMPSON, NANETTE C. "Old Uncle Nate," in California herald, v. 8,
July, 1961, p. 3.
Information about Nathaniel Harrison, Palomar.

435. THOMPSON, VIRGINIA. George Nidever: a pioneer of California.
Master's thesis [n.p., n.d.]. iii, 222 p. illus., maps, ports. CHi.
Contains occasional information about Allen B. Light, known as the
Black steward.

436. TOWNSEND, CHAUNCEY. "Out of the kitchen," in Crisis, v. 42, Jan.,
1935, pp. 15 and 29.
A biographical account of Louise Beavers of Los Angeles and Pasadena.
Authored by a Los Angeles journalist.

437. TRUMAN, BEN CUMMINGS, 1835-1916. "The passing of a Sierra knight,"
in Overland monthly, v. 42, July, 1903, pp. 33-39.
Describes the career and death of George Monroe, an expert stage
driver who drove President U. S. Grant on a three-team coach along the
tortuous roads into Yosemite Valley in 1879. The name of Monroe Meadow
in today's Park honors his family.

438. TYLER, HELEN. "The family of Pico," in Southern California quarterly,
v. 25, Sept., 1953, pp. 221-38.

439. U. S. Congress. The Congressional globe ... of the second session of
the thirty-third congress. Volume XXX ... Washington, D. C., Printed
at the office of John C. Rives, 1855. 1,190 p. CSf, CU, WaU.
Passage of the bill on Feb. 7, 1855 for the relief of George Bush,
confirming his claim to 640 acres of land as requested by the Washington
territorial legislature in a memorial to Congress.

Individual Biographies and Autobiographies

440. *VAN PEEBLES, MELVIN, 1932?- . The big heart by Melvin Van. Photography [by] Ruth Bernhard. [S. F., Fearon pubs., c1957]. 77 p. illus. CHi, CSf.
     The author describes his feelings and experiences as a San Francisco cable car grip man.

441. *[WAGONER, HENRY OSCAR,   -1902]. "Henry Oscar Wagoner, 'The Douglass of Colorado'; a sketch of his life and work," in Colored American magazine, v. 5, July, 1902, pp. 188-92.

442. Washington (territory). Legislative assembly. House of representatives. Journal ... first session ... begun February 27, 1854. Olympia, 1855. WaU.
     Memorial praying Congress to confirm to George Bush, a free mulatto, and his heirs, a section of land, pp. 157-58.

443. WHEELER, GERALD EVERETT, 1924- . Hiram R. Revels, Negro educator and statesman. Master's thesis, Univ. of Calif., Berkeley, 1949. 80 ℓ. illus.

444. *WILLIAMS, JAMES, 1825- . Life and adventures of James Williams, a fugitive slave, with a full description of the underground railroad. Sacramento, 1873. 48 p. Preface signed: John Thomas Evans (formerly) now James Williams. CHi, CLU, CSaT, CSf, CSmH, CU-B, Rocq 12843.

445. ____. Same. Third ed. S. F., Women's union print., 1874. 124 p. CHi, CO, CU-B.
     Describes his 1851 voyage from New York to California and subsequent experiences in Sacramento, Nevada, San Francisco, and the mining regions. On p. 101ff., Williams states his opposition to U. S. actions in the Modoc war, 1873. Underground railroad activities in the East are related, pp. 66-99 only.

446. ____. Same. 5th ed. Philadelphia, A. H. Sickler & co., 1893. 130 p. NN.

447. ____. Same. Reprint of third ed. S. F., R & E research associates, 1969. C, CAuP, CF, CNoS, CSalCL, CSd, CSfAA, CSto.

448. WOOD, CATHERINE M. Palomar from tepee to telescope [by] Catherine M. Wood; art work by May H. Negley. [San Diego, Printed by Frye & Smith, ltd., c1937]. 149 p. illus., map, port. C, CHi, CL, CLU, CO, CSd, CSdHi, CSdS, CSf, CSmH, CStmo, CU-B, Rocq 7624.
     "The first white man on the mountain," pp. 39-42 being "about Nathanial Harrison of Palomar Mountain." -- San Diego Historical Society.

449. *WRIGHT, RICHARD ROBERT, 1878- . "Negro companions of the Spanish explorers," in Phylon, v. 2, 4th quarter, 1941, pp. 325-33. "Notes on R. R. Wright's 'Negro companions of the Spanish explorers'," by Rayford W. Logan, pp. 334-36.
     Describes especially the activities of Estevanico.

COLLECTED BIOGRAPHY

450. BANCROFT, HUBERT HOWE, 1832-1918. Register of pioneer inhabitants of
California, 1542 to 1848, and index to information concerning them in
Bancroft's History of California, volumes I-V. L. A., Dawson's book
shop, 1964. 683-795, 733-92, 688-786, 687-784 p. Cover title: Pioneer
register. C, CHi, CSf, CU.

451. _____. Same. Baltimore, Regional pub. co., 1964. 392 p.
Both editions are reprints from volumes 2, 3, 4, and 5 of Bancroft's
History of California pub. in San Francisco, 1885-86, and held by many
libraries. Included are biographical accounts of all of the then known
Afro-American residents of California before 1848.

452. BARTON, REBECCA (CHALMERS), 1905- . Witnesses for freedom; Negro
Americans in autobiography, by Rebecca Chalmers Barton ... foreword by
Alain Locke. N. Y., Harper & brother [c1948]. xiii, 294 p. CNoS.
Contains information on William J. Powell and Taylor Gordon.

453. BEATTIE, GEORGE WILLIAM. Heritage of the valley; San Bernardino's
first century, by George William Beattie and Helen Pruitt Beattie ...
Pasadena, San Pasqual press, 1939. 459 p. illus., ports., maps. "List
of references": pp. 427-39. C, CBea, CBu, CCC, CF, CFS, CGl, CHi, CL,
CLSU, CLU, CO, CP, CPom, CRcS, CSbCL, CSdS, CSf, CSfCP, CSmH, CStb,
CStmo, CU-B, CViCL, CYcCL, Rocq 7049.
Information about the Embers and Flake families, San Bernardino
emigrants from Salt Lake City in the 1850's, p. 186.

454. _____. Same. Oakland, Biobooks, 1951. 459 p. illus., ports., maps.
C, CHi, CLU, CRcS, CSd, CStcrCL, CSto, Rocq 7050.

455. *BRAWLEY, BENJAMIN GRIFFITH, 1882-1939. The Negro genius; a new
appraisal of the achievement of the American Negro in literature and
the fine arts ... N. Y., Biblo and Tannen, 1966 [c1937]. xiii, 366 p.
illus., ports. Bibliography: pp. 331-50. CFS, CKenM, CLobS, CNoS,
COM, CSdS, CSf, CSjCi, CSluSP, CU-SB, CU-SC, WaPu, WaT, WaTC.
Contains biographical information on James Madison Bell, James
Monroe Whitfield, Sargent C. Johnson, Egbert Austin Williams, Paul R.
Williams, William Grant Still, and others.

456. BUCKBEE, EDNA BRYAN. The saga of old Tuolumne ... N. Y., Press of
the pioneers, 1935. x, 526 p. illus. Available in many California
libraries. Rocq 15342.
Describes the gold rush activities of Tom Gilman, pp. 308-10, and
Moses Dinks, p. 329.

457. BURT, MC KINLEY. Black inventors of America [by] McKinley Burt, Jr.
Portland, Ore., National book co. [c1969]. 143 p. illus., ports. CCotS.
Biographies accompanied by descriptions of inventions. Included is
a biography of Richard B. Spikes, Los Angeles and San Francisco, inventor of the automatic gear shift, and descriptions of the activities
of the Watts industrial park, Los Angeles, and The Albina corporation,
Portland.

Collected Biography

458. DANNETT, SYLVIA G. L., 1909- . Profiles of Negro womanhood. Illus.:
Horace Varela. Roll of honor ports.: Tom Feelings. Yonkers, N. Y.,
Educational heritage [c1964, c1966]. 2 v. illus., ports., facsims.
(Negro heritage library). Available in many libraries.
    Contents. -v. 1. 1619-1900; -v. 2. 1900-1965. v.1 - biographical
accounts of Delilah L. Beasley and the Hyers sisters; v. 2 - account of
Mrs. Namahyoke (Sockum) Curtis.

459. *DE COY, ROBERT H.   Robert H. de Coy's This is progress; the blue
book manual of Nigritian history. American descendants of African
origin: textbook, reference, study guide, encyclopedia. Collaboration
by Roselle Kahn. [L. A.]   Nigritian, inc. [c1969]. xiii, 257 p. CHS,
CL.
    A biographical directory.

460. *DELANY, MARTIN ROBISON, 1812-1885. The condition, elevation, emigration, and destiny of the colored people of the United States politically
considered. Philadelphia, Privately printed, 1852. 214 p. DLC.

461. _____. Same. N. Y., Arno press, 1968. CNoS, CSf.
    Contains biographical accounts of California residents Philip A.
Bell, pp. 102-03, Henry M. Collins, pp. 104-05, Robert Banks, pp. 139-40,
and Henry Knight, pp. 140-41; also Portland resident, Abner Hunt Francis,
p. 139.

462. DELANY, WILLIAM, 1824-1899. Biographical sketches of William Delany,
Cassandria McKoin Delany, and Rachel Belden or Delany, slave of Daniel
Delany. Ms. OrHi.

463. *DOWNS, KARL E.,   -1948. Meet the Negro [by] Karl E. Downs. L. A.,
Methodist youth fellowship, southern California-Arizona annual conference
[1943]. xvi, 179 p. ports. CBb, CHCL, CHS, CL, CLS, CLSU, CLU, CNoS,
CP, CPa, CSaT, CSd, CSf, CU-SC, NUC, pre-1956.
    Contains 67 biographical sketches including Californians William
Nickerson, Jr., Floyd C. Covington, Paul R. Williams, William Grant
Still, Bill Smallwood, Hazel Washington, Mildred Blount, M. Earl Grant,
and Calvin Bailey.

464. DROTNING, PHILLIP T. Black heroes in our nation's history; a tribute
to those who helped shape America, by Phillip T. Drotning. N. Y.,
Cowles book co. [c1969]. xii, 242 p. illus., ports. Bibliography:
pp. [225]-30. C, CHS, CLSU, CNoS, COro, CSdS, CSf, CSfGG, CSluSP, CSt,
CU, CU-SB.
    Some Californians and Westerners are described in "Taming the
western wilderness," pp. 52-72.

465. *HILL, ROY L. Who's who in the American Negro press. Dallas, Royal
pub. co. [1960]. 80 p. Bibliography: p. 70. CU-A.

466. *JENNESS, MARY. Twelve Negro Americans, by Mary Jenness ... N. Y.,
Friendship press, 1936. x, 180 p. CL, CSaT, CSf, CSt.
    Contains "A leader of students," an account of Howard Thurman,
pp. 145-60.

Collected Biography

467. _____. Same. Freeport, N. Y., Books for libraries press [1969].
CSjC.

468. Negro who's who in California.* 1948 ed. [Edited by Commodore Wynn].
[L. A.?] Negro who's who in California pub. co., 1948. 133 p. ports.
C, CLGS, CLM, CNoS, CSf, CSj, CSmH, CU-B.
Only year published.

469. *POWELL, WILLIAM J. Black wings [by] Lieut. William J. Powell.
L. A., Ivan Deach, Jr., 1934. 218 p. ports. C (photocopy), CHi,
CLCo, CLM, CSf, CU, Rocq 4317.
Activities of early California and U. S. aeronauts.

470. REASONS, GEORGE. They had a dream, by George Reasons and Sam Patrick.
L. A., Los Angeles times syndicate [c1969]. 64 p. ports. CSf.
Contains biographical accounts of 53 persons including James P.
Beckwourth, John Roosevelt Robinson, George Washington, Egbert Austin
Williams, York, William A. Leidesdorff, George Jordan, Bose Ikard, Mary
Fields, Esteban, Jacob Dodson, Alvin A. Coffey, and George Washington
Bush.

471. _____. Same. Volume II. L. A. [c1970]. CSf.
Contains biographical accounts of 52 persons including Isaiah Dorman,
Barney Ford, Mifflin W. Gibbs, George Monroe, William Grant Still, and
Paul R. Williams.

472. *ROBINSON, WILHELMINA S. Historical Negro biographies, by Wilhelmina
S. Robinson. N. Y., Publishers co. [c1967]. xii, 291 p. ports.
(International library of Negro life and history, v. 1). Bibliography:
pp. 271-81. CBGTU, CBea, CEcaC, CFS, CLSU, CNoS, CO, CSdS, CSf, CSjCi,
CSt, CU-A, CU-SB, CU-SC.
Contains California and western materials throughout.

473. * Searchlight pub. co. Who's who in religious, fraternal, social,
civic and commercial life on the Pacific coast, state of Washington.
[Samuel P. De Bow and Edward A. Pitter, eds. and compilers.] Pub. by
the authority of the Searchlight pub. co., Seattle, Washington, 1926-27.
Seattle, 1926. 253 p. illus., map, ports. Wa.
Essentially a biographical directory for the state of Washington.
Includes membership lists for Pacific coast labor, religious, and
fraternal organizations.

474. *SIMMONS, WILLIAM J., 1849- . Men of mark: eminent, progressive
and rising ... With an introductory sketch of the author by Henry M.
Turner ... Cleveland, G. M. Rewell & co., 1887. 1,138 p. front.,
ports. CL, CSmH.
Contains a number of biographical accounts of persons who spent a
portion of their lives in California and the West including Mifflin W.
Gibbs, Allen Allensworth, and Robert Charles O'Hara Benjamin.

475. _____. Same. N. Y., Arno press, 1968. CEcaC, CLobS, CNoS, CSS,
CSbS, CSdS, CSjC, CSluSP, CSt, CU-A.

Collected Biography

476. STONE, IRVING, 1903– . There was light. Autobiography of a university, Berkeley: 1868–1968. Ed. and with an introd. by Irving Stone.
Garden City, N. Y., Doubleday, 1970. 454 p. CU.
    "Personal reminiscences [of] thirty-nine notable alumni." Included
are the statements of Ida L. Jackson, teacher at El Centro and Oakland's
first black teacher, pp. 249–66, and William Byron Rumford, Berkeley
pharmacist and California state assemblyman, pp. 403–09.

477. *WATKINS, GEORGE E.   A souvenir of distinguished Afro-Americans of
the Pacific coast. [n.p., 189–?]. pam.
    Unlocated title, see in Beasley, p. 256.

478. Who's who in colored America; an illustrated biographical directory
of notable living persons of African descent in the United States. Ed.
by G. James Fleming and Christian E. Burckel ... Yonkers-on-Hudson,
N. Y., Christian E. Burckel & associates, 1950. 7th ed. (Six other
eds. appeared in 1927, 1928, 1930, 1933, 1938, and 1941.) C 1927, 1928,
1950; CHS 1927; CL 1927, 1928, 1930, 1938, 1941, 1950; CLGS 1950; CLSU
1927, 1928, 1938, 1941, 1950; CNoS 1927+; CSbS 1927; CSdS 1928–1929 [sic];
CSf 1927, 1938, 1950; CStcrCL 1927; CU 1927, 1928, 1950; CU-A 1928, 1950;
CU-I 1950; CU-SB 1927, 1950; CU-SC 1927.
    Contains the biographical accounts of 122 persons in seven of the
western states but who resided chiefly in Los Angeles, San Francisco,
and Denver. This does not include the biographical accounts of scores
of musicians, composers, and artists whose works received public exposure
in the West, especially in California.

479. Who's who of the colored race; a general biographical dictionary of
men and women of African descent. Chicago, 1915. 296 p. illus. DLC.

480. *WILLIAMS, ETHEL L., 1909– . Biographical dictionary of Negro ministers
by Ethel L. Williams. N. Y. and London, Scarecrow press, inc., 1965. xi,
421 p. Bibliography: pp. 407–12. CFS, CLSU, CLU, CNoS, CSf, CSjC.

481. *WRIGHT, RICHARD ROBERT, 1878– , ed. The encyclopaedia of the
African Methodist Episcopal church, containing principally the biographies
of the men and women, both ministers and laymen, whose labors during a
hundred and sixty years, helped make the AME church what it is; also
short historical sketches of annual conferences, educational institutions,
general departments, missionary societies ... 2d ed. Philadelphia, 1947
[i.e., 1948]. 688 p. illus., ports., maps. First ed., 1916 has title:
Centennial encyclopaedia of the African Methodist Episcopal church. CU.

    Contains occasional information about California and western churches
and clergymen.

ORIGINAL SOURCES

482. *ADAMS, MARY ELIZABETH. Her scrapbooks, 1860–1947, containing
material of general interest but emphasizing Seattle and vicinity. WaU.

Original Sources

483. *ALEXANDER, JAMES MILO.   Papers, 1848–1939, including 35 items relating to his son, Titus, Los Angeles, 1924–39, and a pocket notebook of another son, John Hanks Alexander, containing a 41-page itinerary of a march of Co. M, 9th U. S. cavalry, from Ft. Washakie, Wyo., to Ft. Du Chesne, Utah, 1888. CSmH.

484. *ARMSTRONG, CALVIN.   Tape-recorded interview of this Seattle resident, 1968. WaU.

485. *ASBERRY, NETTIE J., 1865–1968. Correspondence, reports, minutes, and related items concerning Tacoma National association for the advancement of colored people and Colored women's federation of Washington, 1889–1966; also containing a journal, certificates, photographs, and Prismatic charts, 1886–1952. 5 inches. WaU.

486. *ATKINS, JAMES A., 1890–1968. Papers and correspondence, 1920–68. 62 boxes (ca. 30,000 items). CoHi.
    Geographical coverage includes the South, 1920–50, and Colorado, 1950–68. Subjects include adult education, housing, biography and autobiography, police brutality, race relations, employment, and labor. Correspondents include George Brown and Harry Moon. An important collection of large scope.

487. *BARNETT, POWELL S., 1883– . Reminiscences, ephemera, clippings, and a recorded interview of this Washington state resident, 1960–67. 19 items. WaU.

488. *BEASLEY, DELILAH LEONTIUM, 1871–1934. Five letters and three cards, Dec. 27, 1920, Nov. 5, 1922, and [n.d.] describing personal matters and the sales of her The Negro trail blazers of California in the Middle West. In the Francis B. Loomis Papers. CSt.

489. *BURTON, PHILIP L.   Correspondence and related items concerning work with the NAACP, the Washington state board against discrimination, and other organizations, 1950–62. About 1,000 items. WaU.

490. *CARTER, RANDOLPH WARREN.   Interview, minutes, correspondence, reports, and agreements concerning his work with the Model cities program and the Washington state board against discrimination, 1964–69. WaU.

491. *COOPER, BELLA TAYLOR.   Reports, clippings, and one letter of this Washington state resident, 1947–61. WaU.

492. *COOPER, FELIX B.   Correspondence, financial records, ephemera, scrapbooks, and clippings of this Washington state resident, 1929–61. WaU.

493. *CRISTOBAL, JUAN.   Baptismal statement, Aug. 16, 1819. No. 522 in the Santa Barbara Presidio register for non-Indian baptisms. Mission Santa Barbara Archives, Santa Barbara.
    "A slave of Captain [William?] Smith of an Anglo-American ship which arrived within this jurisdiction; Smith left the Negro under the care of Capt. José de la Guerra y Noriega. The Negro was about 20 years old

Original Sources

and a native of Africa. He had asked for baptism repeatedly and after giving him the proper instruction Fr. [Antonio] Ripoll baptized him at the Mission." - Doyce B. Nunis, Jr.

494. *DE BOW, SAMUEL P. Scrapbooks, 1915-36, containing letters, photo-graphs, leaflets, and clippings of a Washington state resident. WaU.

495. *DELLUMS, COTTRELL LAURENCE, 1900- . Interview of this Oakland resident was in process 1971 under the auspices of the Univ. of Calif. Oral history program, Berkeley.

496. _____. Correspondence and other papers, ca. 1934-60, of an inter-national vice president of the Brotherhood of sleeping car porters and an Oakland resident. ca. 43 cartons. CU-B (Unprocessed in 1971. Con-sult Head, Manuscript division).

497. *DIXON, WILLIAM H. Family papers consisting of correspondence, reminiscences, and ephemera concerning Negroes in Washington and mainly emphasizing the career of his grandfather, William Gross, sometimes William Grose. WaU.

498. FITCH, HENRY DELANO, 1799-1849. Papers, 1827-58. CU-B.
    Contain a Feb. 5, 1846 promissory note (in Spanish) signed by
Allen B. Light.

499. *FLOWERS, ALLEN ELMER, 1847-1934. Family memorabilia, including a scrapbook of clippings pertaining to the Flowers family and other early Portland Negroes. Ms. OrHi.

500. *FRASER, CLARA. Tape-recorded interview of this Seattle resident, 1970. WaU.

501. *GAYTON, JOHN THOMAS Clippings, ephemera, and memorabilia collected by the Gayton family concerning Negroes in Washington, ca. 1900-60; also includes interviews with Mr. and Mrs. Gayton, 1968. 6 inches. WaU.

502. *GOODLETT, CARLTON BENJAMIN, 1914- . Papers and correspondence, 1942 and 1946-47, of a San Francisco publisher and physician. WHi.

503. *GOODWIN, TERENZ. Tape-recorded interview of this Seattle resident, 1968. WaU.

504. *GORDON, WALTER ARTHUR, 1894- . Interview of this Berkeley resident was in process 1971 under the auspices of the Univ. of Calif. Oral history program, Berkeley.

505. *GRIMES, LEOLA. Tape-recorded interview of this Seattle resident, 1968. WaU.

506. *GRIMKE, FRANCIS JAMES, 1850-1937. Funeral eulogy delivered for Frederick G. Barbadoes, a California civil rights leader in the 1850's. Ms., Washington, D. C., Mar. 10, 1899. 4 p. DHU.

Original Sources

507. *GROSS, WILLIAM,   -1898. Family papers, including memories of the Seattle fire, letters, newspapers, and other items. About 5 folders. WaU.

508. *HART, BEULA.   Tape-recorded interview of this Seattle resident, 1968. WaU.

509. *HEARST, BENNIE.   Tape-recorded interview of this Seattle resident, 1968. WaU.

510. HOLDREDGE, HELEN (O'DONNELL). Research notes and other materials relating to the career of Mrs. Mary Ellen Pleasant and used in the preparation of Mrs. Holdredge's two biographies, Mammy Pleasant and Mammy Pleasant's partner. About 550 items. CSf.

511. *HUNSAKER, JANE CHANDLER.   Papers and photographs, 1936-37, of this Washington state resident. WaU.

512. *[LEE, ARCHY, 1837?-]. Petition for writ of habeas corpus, Jan. 8, 1858, sought for Lee by Charles W. Parker through his attorneys, Edwin Bryant Crocker and John H. McKune in the Sacramento county court. Ms. [1] ℓ. C-ArS.

513. *LEIDESDORFF, WILLIAM ALEXANDER, 1810-1848. Papers and correspondence, 1840-67, mainly dealing with business and social affairs in and around San Francisco and, as U. S. vice-consul in San Francisco, touching on political events. In English, Spanish, and German. Mss. 502 pieces. CSmH.

514. _____. Papers and correspondence, 1846-57, relating to his service as a pioneer California merchant and U. S. vice-consul (89 pieces) and to his estate (82 pieces). Contains "Quantity of hides received and delivered, 1843" (3 p.); "Account of goods taken up, 1843" (6 p.); "Indian accounts" [1847] (59 p.), being financial records with Indians at his "Fishing rancho"; "Canaca book," 1847 (10 p.), showing accounts with Hawaiian seamen; Account book, 1847-48 (50 p.), of the City hotel, San Francisco, various crew members, and the schooner Tonitta and other vessels; account book, 1844-47, showing records of laborers and seamen employed by Leidesdorff; and other business ephemera. Includes correspondence located in other collections, viz., the Stephen Smith papers, the Joseph Libby Folsom papers, and in "Early San Francisco letters, documents, etc." Mss. CHi.

515. _____. Three letters, Feb. 9, Apr. 13, 1846, and May 25, 1847. Mss. C.

516. * LEWIS, JOHN.   His affidavit given in the Sacramento district court, Aug. 21, 1850, that $200 in gold dirt and coin was stolen from Robert Forman, deceased. Ms. [1] ℓ. C-ArS.

517. * LEWIS, JUNIUS R., 1842-1938. Correspondence, legal papers, mining deeds and patents, tax receipts, lease agreements, and various miscellaneous items relating to his mining activities in Boulder county, Colorado, 1907-38. Mss. 99 pieces. CoHi.

Original Sources

517a. *LIGHT, ALLEN B. Letter to Light, Santa Barbara, Jan. 27, 1839. Ms.
Mission Santa Barbara Archives, Santa Barbara.

518. *MC ADOO, BENJAMIN. Correspondence and ephemera, 1952-66. WaU.

519. *MC CABE, ELIZA. Correspondence of a Washington state resident, also
including reports, magazines, journals, and organizational materials,
1909-66. WaU.

520. *MONROE, PEARLEY. Recollections of a Coloma resident given before
the Placerville Pioneer Club. CPla.
    Tape recording owned by the Friends of the Placerville public library.
The author, whose name is sometimes given as Perly Munro, owned the site
of Sutter's mill at which gold was discovered early in 1848. See
California historical society quarterly, v. 26, June, 1947, p. 129.

521. *MORGAN, EARNEST. Transcribed interview from tape. 6 p. Typew.
CSdHi.
    "An early settler" of San Diego county.

522. *OWENS, ROBERT CURRY, 1859- . Autobiography, Los Angeles, 1930,
also containing a biographical account of Robert Owens, Sr. (1806?-1865).
Ms. 9 p. CLGS.

523. *PATTERSON, EDGAR JAMES. Interview of this Sacramento resident was
in progress 1971 under the auspices of the Univ. of Calif. Oral history
program, Berkeley.

524. PHELAN, JAMES DUVAL, 1861-1930. Correspondence and papers of a U. S.
senator and San Francisco mayor, ca. 1880-1930. 131 boxes, 29 cartons,
103 volumes. CU-B.
    Contains occasional letters from black people regarding Democratic
party politics including two from J. Gordon McPherson, editor of the
Bakersfield Colored citizen, Sept. 22 and Oct. 24, 1914, and one from
Titus Alexander, chairman, Colored Democratic league of southern
California, May 1, 1924.

525. *Pico Family. Papers of this pre-gold rush California family are
widely scattered, although concentrations are located in the Bancroft
library, Univ. of California, Berkeley, the California historical society,
San Francisco, the Henry E. Huntington library, San Marino, the
California state library, Sacramento, and probably in other collections
of Californiana, both in the state and elsewhere in the nation. The
largest group of correspondence, located at the Bancroft library, documents the career of the family's most distinguished member, California
governor, Pío Pico (1810-1894). This library also holds manuscript
sources concerning Antonio María (1808-1869), José de Jesús (b. 1807),
José Ramón, José Dolores (b. 1827), Fernando, Francisco, Andrés (1810-
1876), and José Antonio Bernardino Pico (1794-1871).

526. *PITTMAN, TAREA (HALL). Interview of this Oakland resident was in
process 1971 under the auspices of the Univ. of Calif. Oral history
program, Berkeley.

Original Sources

527. *PLEASANT, MARY ELLEN, 1812–1904. Two letters to James Grasses, San Francisco, 1896. A calling card is included. Mss. CU-B.

528. ROLPH, JAMES, 1869–1934. Correspondence and papers, 1911–1930, mainly while serving as mayor of San Francisco. 111 boxes, 35 v. CHi.
Contains letters from S. L. Mash, Mar. 27, 1915, as president of the Colored non-partisan league of California; Garland Anderson, New York City, Apr. 12, 1925; and probably other persons.

529. *ROSTON, JAMES A., JR. Tape-recorded interview of this Seattle resident concerning his father, 1969. WaU.

530. *ROSTON, JAMES A., 1864–1924. Scrapbook of this Seattle resident containing letters, documents, clippings, and ephemera, ca. 1897–1924. WaU.

531. *RUSSELL, CHARLES. Tape-recorded interview of this Seattle resident, 1968. WaU.

532. San Francisco. [San Francisco town journal, 1847–1848]. Ms. 12 p. CHi.

533. _____. San Francisco town journal, 1847–1848. William A. Leidesdorff, treasurer, October 7, 1847 to May 2, 1848 ... S. F., Albert Dressler [1926]. 12 p. Facsim. C, CHi, CLU, CO, COEB, CSf, CSfAA, CSmH, CU-B, Rocq 11271.

534. *SAUNDERS, CORNELIA. Tape-recorded interview of this Seattle resident, 1968. WaU.

535. *SAUNDERS, ROBERT. Tape-recorded interview of this Seattle resident, 1968. WaU.

536. *SHOREY, WILLIAM T., 1855–1919. [His license as master of steam vessels], U. S. dept. of commerce, San Francisco, 1918. Ms. [1] ℓ. CHi (photocopy).

537. *SMITH, EDWARD. Tape-recorded interview of this Ellensburg, Washington resident, 1968. WaU.

538. *SOMERVILLE, JOHN ALEXANDER, 1881–1973. Tape-recorded interview of Mr. and Mrs. Somerville, Los Angeles, June, 1968. Elapsed time: about 90 minutes. CLSU.
Dr. Somerville describes his experiences while a student at the Univ. of southern Calif., 1903–07, and his living arrangements in Los Angeles during this period; as a Los Angeles dentist; in seeking an officer's commission during World War I; in Los Angeles politics and especially as a member of the Los Angeles police commission. Mrs. Vada J. Somerville, also a School of dentistry graduate at the Univ. of southern Calif., describes her education, marriage in 1912, and her political and social life in Los Angeles. Both relate their attitudes toward events and activists of the 1960's.

Original Sources

539. *SPEARMAN, ELIHU E., 1892-   . Tape-recorded interview of this Seattle resident, 1968. WaU.

540. *SPEARMAN, VIVIAN. Tape-recorded interview of Mrs. Elihu E. Spearman, Seattle resident, 1968. WaU.

540a.*STEWART, THOMAS MC CANTS, 1853-1923. DHU.
      Correspondence and memorabilia, portions of which relate to his career as an attorney in Hawaii, ca. 1900-10, and the activities of his children, Carlotta, teacher on the island of Kauai; McCants, Portland and San Francisco attorney; and Gilchrist, New York attorney. This large collection also illustrates the activities of associated family members, Mrs. Victoria S. (Dickinson) Weir, San Francisco, ca. 1920-30, and Robert Browning Flippin, ca. 1925-63, pioneer administrator of the Booker T. Washington community service center, in San Francisco public housing, and of the Northern California assoc. of Alcoholics anonymous, especially of its San Quentin prison chapter.

541. STONE, IRVING, 1903-   . "There was light." Original manuscripts, correspondence, galleys. 2 boxes. CU-B.
      Includes the manuscript of Ida Louise Jackson's memoir (43 ℓ., typew.), with manuscript emendations by Stone, and two letters, Feb. 4 and Apr. 10, 1969 to Stone.

542. *STRONG, EVA.   Tape-recorded interview of this Seattle resident, 1968. WaU.

543. *TAYLOR, CHARLES.   Tape-recorded interview of this Seattle resident, 1968. WaU.

544. THOMAS, PAUL F. Correspondence, interviews, and other material collected while doing research for his Master's thesis on George Bush, Univ. of Washington, Seattle, 1965. About 6 folders. WaU.

545. *UNDERWOOD, WILLIAM H.   Papers, 1914-57, of Washington state resident, including correspondence, minutes, reports, clippings, and ephemera [n.d.]. WaU.

546. *VENABLE, ELIZABETH (LANDEWAY), 1856-   . Her letter, Oakland, Sept. 4, 1930, giving a short history of the John R. Landeway family in California, 1852ff. Ms. 2 p. CHi.

547. *WARE, WAYMON.   Tape-recorded interview of this Seattle resident, 1970. WaU.

548. *WASHINGTON, JAMES.   Scrapbook of this Washington state resident [n.d.]. WaU.

549. *WELLS, GERALD.   Correspondence and memoirs of this Washington state resident, 1959. WaU.

550. *WHITE, ERNST.   Tape-recorded interview of this Seattle resident, 1968. WaU.

Original Sources

551. *WOFFERT, LIOLA.   Tape-recorded interview of this Seattle resident,
     1968. WaU.

552. *WOOD, THOMAS ALEXANDER, 1837-1904. Autobiographical notes made by
     a Methodist Episcopal preacher and real estate salesman. Includes an
     account of his church work and a paper entitled, "First admission of
     collored [sic] children to the Portland public schools." Mss. 1 folder.
     OrHi.

553. *WOODSON, FRED PATTERSON.   Papers including clippings, photographs,
     ephemera, and a tape-recorded interview concerning Negroes in Seattle,
     1912-68. 1 foot. WaU.

554. *WRIGHT, GEORGE.   Tape-recorded interview of this Seattle resident,
     1968. WaU.

555. Writers' program. Colorado. Negro pioneers - interviews. [Denver,
     1940]. Typew. Ms. CoHi.

                    BLACK MOVEMENT AND RACIAL DISSENT

                    BLACK MUSLIMS (Nation of Islam)

556. *Afro-American institute.   Malcolm X unity house. Black man speaks;
     an organ of the Afro-American institute, Malcolm X unity house. [S. F.,
     1970]. [5] ℓ. Mimeo.
        Promotional brochure describing aims, language classes, and a
     Summer camp.

557. "Allah be praised," in Seattle magazine, v. 2, Dec., 1965, pp. 15-17.
     Describes Black Muslim movement in Seattle.

558. California. Bureau of criminal identification and investigation.
     Para-military organizations in California. [Sacramento, State print.,
     1965]. v.p. CNoS, CSt.
        Includes the Black Muslims.

559. HOWARD, JOHN ROBERT. Becoming a Black Muslim: a study of commitment
     processes in a deviant political organization. Doctoral dissertation,
     Stanford univ., Stanford, 1965. iii, 234 ℓ.

560. JARRETTE, ALFRED Q. Muslim's black metropolis; an authentic report
     on the Black Muslim movement in the United States containing actual
     documents and photographs [some of which appeared in the Herald-Dispatch.
     L. A., Great western book pub.], c1962. 40 p. illus., ports. CL.

561. *LINCOLN, CHARLES ERIC, 1924- . The Black Muslims in America. Fore-
     word by Gordon W. Allport. Boston, Beacon press [1964, c1961]. xi, 276 p.
     Bibliographical notes. Available in many libraries.
        Contains some information about Los Angeles activities and the Los

Black Muslims

Angeles <u>Herald-Dispatch</u> which in 1959-60 had "become in effect the official Muslim organ."

562. *LOMAX, ALMENA (DAVIS).   "The Muslim trial in Los Angeles," in <u>Frontier</u>, v. 14, July, 1963, pp. 5-7.

563.   [TEISER, RUTH].   "Black muslims turn to baking," in <u>Bakers weekly</u>, v. 216, Jan. 13, 1969, pp. 26-28.
        Describes the activities of the Universal bakery, Richmond.

564. *WHITE, MILTON.   "Malcolm X in the military," in <u>The black scholar</u>, v. 1, May, 1970, pp. 31-35.
        The establishment of a Malcolm X organization at the Vandenberg air force base, Lompoc.

BLACK PANTHER PARTY

565. *ADAMS, OVID P.   ... Adventures of black Eldridge, the panther. [S. F., Marcus books, c1970].   [24] p. illus.
        Concerns the wounding of the artist, Metégo [Sohan], in Utah and the death of the Mormon clergyman, S. J. Holyoke, 1970.

566. ANDERSON, JERVIS. "Race, rage & Eldridge Cleaver," in <u>Commentary</u>, v. 46, Dec., 1968, pp. 63-69.

567. *ANTHONY, EARL LEON, 1941- . Picking up the gun; a report on the Black panthers. N. Y., Dial press, 1970. ix, 160 p. C, CBGTU, CSjC, CStb, CU-B.

568.   "Background information relating to the Cleaver controversy," in <u>California digest</u>, v. 1, Dec., 1968, p. 121.

569.   BAKUNIN, MIKHAIL ALEXANDROVICH, 1814-1876. The catechism of the revolutionist by Mikhail Alexandrovich Bakunin. Introduction by [Eldridge Cleaver] Minister of information, Black panther party for self defense. Perspectives in black liberation #1. Cover design by revolutionary black artist Emory [Douglass]. Oakland, The Party [196-?]. [13] p. illus.

570.   BARUCH, RUTH-MARION. The vanguard; a photographic essay on the Black panthers, by Ruth-Marion Baruch and Pirkle Jones. With an introd. by William Worthy. Boston, Beacon press [c1970]. 127 p. illus., ports. C, CBGTU, CNoS, CSjC.

571.   BAZAAR, MONA, ed. The trial of Huey Newton, edited by Mona Bazaar. [L. A.?, 196-?]. unp. illus. CSfAA.

572.   BERRIGAN, PHILIP F. "Berrigan from jail: 'truth creates its own room'," in <u>Commonweal</u>, v. 89, Dec. 6, 1968, pp. 333-34.
        An imprisoned Jesuit writes about Eldridge Cleaver.

Black Panther Party

573. *Black panther party   Rules. [Oakland, 1968?]. 2 p. CU-B.

574. "The Black panther party: toward liberation of the colony," in
New left review, no. 56, July-Aug., 1969, pp. 40-43.

575. "Black panther ten-point program," in North American review, v. 5,
July, 1968, pp. 16-17.

576. "Black panthers: the Afro-Americans' challenge," in Tricontinental,
Jan.-Feb., 1969, pp. 96-111.
    An interview with George Murray and John Major Ford.

577. BUCKLEY, WILLIAM F. "Cleaver for president," in National review,
v. 20, Dec. 3, 1968, p. 1,237.

578. _____. "Total confrontation," in National review, v. 21, Nov. 18,
1969, pp. 1,157-58.

579. CANNON, TERRY. All power to the people; the story of the Black
panther party. [S. F., People's press, 1970]. 45 p. illus. CU-B.

580. *CLEAVER, ELDRIDGE, 1935- . Dig; Eldridge Cleaver recorded at
Syracuse. [S. F.]. More record co. [c1968]. 2 sides.
    Recording of Cleaver's speech before the Peace and freedom party
at Syracuse, July 28, 1968.

581. _____. "Education and revolution," in The black scholar, v. 1,
Nov., 1969, pp. 44-52.

582. _____. Eldridge Cleaver; post-prison writings and speeches. Edited
and with an appraisal by Robert Scheer. N. Y., Random house [1968].
xxxiii, 211 p. Available in many California libraries.

583. _____. "The fire now; field nigger power takes over the black
movement," in Commonweal, v. 88, June 14, 1968, pp. 375-77. Reply by
J. Pius Barbour, v. 88, July 12, 1968, pp. 478-79.

584. _____. "Introduction to selections from the biography of Huey P.
Newton with an aside to Ronald Reagan," in Ramparts, v. 7, Oct. 26, 1968,
pp. 22-24.

585. _____. "Land question," in Ramparts, v. 6, May, 1968, pp. 51-53.

586. _____. "Letter from jail," in Ramparts, v. 6, June 15, 1968, pp. 17-
21.

587. _____. "My father & Stokely Carmichael," in Ramparts, v. 5, Apr.,
1967, pp. 10-14.

588. _____. On the ideology of the Black panther party, by Eldridge
Cleaver. Part I. [S. F.?, 1970?]. 11 [3] p.

Black Panther Party

589. _____. "Requiem for nonviolence," in Ramparts, v. 6, May, 1968, pp. 48-49.

590. _____. Revolution and education by Eldridge Cleaver, Minister of information. [n.p.] Black panther party [196-?]. [8] p.

591. _____. "Revolution in the white mother country and national liberation in the black colony," in North American review, v. 5, July, 1968, pp. 13-15.

592. _____. "Tears for the pigs," in Humanist, v. 29, Mar.-Apr., 1969, pp. 5, 8-10.

593. _____. "Three notes from exile," in Ramparts, v. 8, Sept., 1969, pp. 29-35.

594. COLES, ROBERT. "Black anger," in Atlantic, v. 221, June, 1968, pp. 106-07.
    About Eldridge Cleaver.

595. COVER, ROBERT. "A year of harassment," in Nation, v. 210, Feb. 2, 1970, pp. 110-13.

596. COYNE, JOHN R. "Cleaver compromise," in National review, v. 20, Nov. 5, 1968, pp. 1,115-16ff.
    About Eldridge Cleaver.

597. DIDION, JOAN. "Black panther," in Saturday evening post, v. 241, May 4, 1968, p. 20.

598. DOUGLAS, PATRICK. "Black panthers on the prowl," in Seattle magazine, v. 5, Oct., 1968, pp. 36-47, 57-61.

599. FONER, PHILIP SHELDON, 1910- , ed. The Black panthers peak, ed. by Philip S. Foner. Philadelphia, J. B. Lippincott co. [c1970]. xxx, 274 p. Cover title: "The Black panthers speak; the manifesto of the party: the first complete documentary record of the Panthers' program." CU-B.

600. GARDNER, DAVID P. "Some marginal notes on the Berkeley-Eldridge Cleaver affair," in California digest, v. 1, Dec., 1968, pp. 121-23, 142.

601. HARRIS, MICHAEL. "Black panthers: the cornered cats," in Nation, v. 207, July 8, 1968, pp. 15-18; Aug. 26, 1968, p. 148.

602. HAUGHEY, JOHN C. "Those Black panthers," in America, v. 122, Jan. 17, 1970, pp. 43-44.

603. "Hitch for Cleaver," in Economist, v. 228, Sept. 28, 1968, p. 43.
    Univ. of California's president Charles Hitch's attitude toward lectures by Cleaver before students at Berkeley.

Black Panther Party

604. JACOBS, PAUL. "Bobby Seale and the Chicago 8," in Urban west, v. 3, Dec., 1969, p. 17.

605. KEVELI, HAMAJI UDUMU. "Black panthers vs. the police," in Liberator, v. 9, Feb., 1969, pp. 9-11.

606. LEARY, MARY ELLEN. "Uproar over Cleaver," in New republic, v. 159, Nov. 30, 1968, pp. 21-24.

607. LOCKWOOD, LEE. Conversation with Eldridge Cleaver, Algiers, by Lee Lockwood. [N. Y., Dell pub. co., c1970]. 131 p. CNoS, CRic, CSt.

608. LOVDJIEFF, CRIST. "Guru of San Quentin," in Esquire, v. 67, Apr., 1967, p. 88ff.
Concerns Eldridge Cleaver.

609. LUCE, PHILLIP ABBOTT, 1938- . "Funeral with guns," in National review, Sept. 10, 1968, p. 890.

610. MARINE, GENE. The Black panthers. [N. Y.] New American library [c1969]. 224 p. illus., ports. CL, CSf, CSjC, CU-B.
Relates mainly to the leadership of the Black panther party in California.

611. _____. "Getting Eldridge Cleaver," in Ramparts, v. 6, May, 1968, pp. 49-50.

612. _____. "Persecution and assassination of the Black panthers as performed by the Oakland police under the direction of Chief Charles R. Gain, Mayor John Reading, et al.," in Ramparts, v. 6, June 29, 1968, pp. 37-47.

613. _____. "Shooting Panthers is easy," in Commonweal, v. 88, May 10, 1968, pp. 223-24.

614. "Marked for extinction," in Nation, v. 209, Dec. 22, 1969, p. 684.

615. *MAYFIELD, JULIAN, 1928- . "New mainstream," in Nation, v. 206, May 13, 1968, pp. 638ff.
About Eldridge Cleaver.

616. MONTESANO, RANDY and PAULETTE SCHWARTZ. "The Black panther party." 20 p. Typescript. Term paper, Univ. of San Francisco, 1969. CSf (photocopy).

617. MULHERIN, KATHY. "Stalking the Panthers," in Commonweal, v. 89, Oct. 11, 1968, pp. 58-62.

618. *NEWTON, HUEY P., 1942- . Essays from the Minister of defense. [Oakland?, 1968]. 23 p. CNoS, CSS.
Newton writes as an official of the Black panther party. An introduction is written by George Murray, Minister of information. Taken from the author's column in the Black panther entitled "In defense of self defense."

Black Panther Party

619. _____. Huey Newton talks to The movement about the Black panther
party, cultural nationalism, SNCC, liberals and white revolutionaries.
[S. F., The movement, 1969]. 14 p. illus. CU-A.
    "Huey Newton interview originally published in The Movement,
August 1968."

620. "New breed of blacks," in Economist, v. 228, Aug. 31, 1968, pp. 22-23.

621. PACION, STANLEY. "Still soul on ice? The talent and troubles of
Eldridge Cleaver," in Dissent, v. 16, July-Aug., 1969.

622. ROGERS, RAY. "Panthers and tribesmen: black guns on campus," in
Nation, v. 208, May 5, 1969, pp. 558-60.
    The Black panthers and Ron Karenga's US at the Univ. of Calif.,
Los Angeles.

623. ROSEBURY, CELIA. Black liberation on trial: the case of Huey Newton.
Reprinted from articles originally appearing during the summer of 1968
in the People's world. Berkeley, Bay area committee to defend political
freedom, 1968. 19 p. port. (cover). CU-B.

624. SAMUELS, GERTRUDE. "Sexual response of hatred," in Saturday review,
v. 51, Mar. 9, 1968, p. 31.
    About Eldridge Cleaver.

625. SAYRE, NORA. "Black panthers," in Progressive, v. 33, July, 1969,
pp. 20-23.

626. _____. "The Black panthers are coming: America on the eve of race
revolution," in New statesman, v. 77, May 2, 1969, pp. 613-16.

627. SCHANCHE, DON A., 1926- . "Burn the mother down," in Saturday
evening post, v. 241, Nov. 16, 1968, pp. 30-32ff.
    About Eldridge Cleaver.

628. _____. The Panther paradox: a liberal's dilemma, by Don A. Schanche.
N. Y., David McKay co. [c1970]. xx, 231 p. C, CU-B.

629. SCHOLEFIELD, HARRY B. The Black panthers I; a sermon delivered by the
Reverend Harry B. Scholefield, D. D., First Unitarian church of San
Francisco. S. F. [1970]. 8 p. Mimeo.

630. _____. The Black panthers II; a sermon delivered by the Reverend
Harry B. Scholefield, D. D., First Unitarian church of San Francisco.
S. F. [1970]. 8 p. Mimeo.

631. *SEALE, BOBBY, 1936- . "A rap from Bobby Seale," in University
review, Feb., 1970, p. 13.

632. _____. "Revolutionary action on campus and community; an appeal from
prison," in Black scholar, v. 1, Dec., 1969, pp. 4-7.
    Written while in a San Francisco jail.

Black Panther Party

633. _____. Seize the time; the story of the Black panther party and
Huey P. Newton. N. Y., Random house [1970]. xi, 429 p. CBGTU, CSf,
CSjC.

634. _____. The "trial" of Bobby Seale. With special contributions by
Julian Bond, Norman Dorsen [and] Charles Rembar and a personal statement
by Bobby Seale. N. Y., Prima books [c1970]. 128 p.

635. "Selections from the biography of Huey P. Newton; with introd. by
E. Cleaver, B. Seale," in Ramparts, v. 7, Oct. 26, 1968, pp. 21-34 and
Nov. 17, 1968, p. 8ff.

636. STEEL, RONALD. "Letter from Oakland: the Panthers," in New York
review of books, v. 13, Sept. 11, 1969, pp. 14-23.

637. SWAIM, LAWRENCE. "Eldridge Cleaver," in North American review, v. 5,
July, 1968, pp. 18-21.

638. _____. "Interview with a Black panther," in North American review,
v. 5, July, 1968, pp. 27-34.

639. SZANTO, GEORGE H. "Soul crystallized," in Catholic world, v. 207,
Sept., 1968, p. 280.
About Eldridge Cleaver.

BLACK STUDENT UNIONS

639a.*Black student union, Univ. of California, Riverside. Black students
at UC Riverside. [Riverside?, 1969?]. [12] p. CU-I.

639b. Concerned citizens of northern California, eds. and pubs. Black
strike - shut it down! San Francisco state college. [S. F.?, 1969].
[32] p. illus., ports. CMp.
A pictorial history of the strike in which the demands and the gains
of the Black students union are set forth.

640. *EDWARDS, HARRY, 1942- . Black students [by] Harry Edwards. N. Y.,
The free press [c1970]. 234 p. illus., ports., tables. CBGTU, CCotS,
CHS, CNoS, CSfSt, CSfU.
A study of the U. S. black student revolt, including California and
the West. Gives curricula outlines of black studies programs.

641. HARRIS, SHELDON. "San Fernando's black revolt," in Commonweal, v. 89,
Jan. 31, 1969, pp. 549-52.
The revolt at Calif. state univ., Northridge.

642. MCEVOY, JAMES, comp. Black power and student rebellion. Ed. by James
McEvoy & Abraham Miller. Belmont, Wadsworth pub. co. [c1969]. xiii,
440 p. Includes bibliographies. C, CBGTU, CLSU, CNoS, CSbS, CSf, CSjC.
Pertains mainly to conditions at Calif. state univ., San Francisco,
Stanford univ., and the Univ. of Calif., Berkeley.

Black Student Unions

643. "San Francisco's state," in Economist, v. 229, Dec. 28, 1968, pp. 23-
     24.
          Mentions conflicts and friction among blacks and whites, Black
     students union, Third world liberation front, and the Black panther party
     at Calif. state univ., San Francisco.

644. "Statement of representatives of Black students union: California
     state college, Los Angeles," in California digest, v. 1, Dec., 1968,
     pp. 123-27, 142.

645. SWANSTON, DAVID. "How to wreck a campus," in Nation, v. 206, Jan. 8,
     1968, pp. 38-41.
          Calif. state univ., San Francisco.

646. THOMAS, ARIEL EATON. "The black students: they have their dream
     too," in Mills quarterly, v. 41, May, 1969, pp. 10-18.
          Discussion of the Black students union protests at Mills college.

647. U. S. National commission on the causes and prevention of violence.
     Shut it down! A college in crisis. San Francisco state college,
     October, 1968-April, 1969. Staff report to the Commission prepared by
     William H. Orrick, Jr. Washington, D. C., 1969. 172 p. CNoS, CU-I.

648. WERT, ROBERT J. A special report from President Robert J. Wert of
     Mills College, April 9, 1969, to the parents of students, the alumnae
     and friends ... [Mills College, 1969]. 12 p.
          Report on "the actions taken last week by the Board of trustees in
     relation to the demands of the College's black students, which have been
     under discussion since February 17."

649. WOODRING, P. "Struggle for black identity," in Saturday review,
     v. 52, Jan. 18, 1969, p. 62.
          Calif. state univ., San Francisco.

          NATIONAL ASSOCIATION FOR THE ADVANCEMENT OF COLORED PEOPLE

650. BECK, NICHOLAS. "N. A. A. C. P. in Los Angeles," in California sun
     magazine, v. 11, Fall & Winter, 1959-60, pp. 38, 93-94.

651. "California calls," in Crisis, v. 49, May, 1942, pp. 152-57.
          Illus. article describing the 33rd annual meeting of the
     N. A. A. C. P., in Los Angeles, July 14-19, 1942.

652. *DU BOIS, WILLIAM EDWARD BURGHARDT, 1868-1963. "The California con-
     ference," in Crisis, v. 35, Sept., 1928, pp. 311-12.
          Describes the 19th annual convention of the N. A. A. C. P. in Los
     Angeles and especially the city itself and the Hotel Somerville, later
     the Dunbar hotel.

653. ELLIS, MARGRETTA. "The Negro enemy," in Crisis, v. 58, Nov., 1951,
     pp. 575-77.

N. A. A. C. P.

The secretary of the Albuquerque N. A. A. C. P. branch describes the problem of Blacks and Whites working together for a common purpose.

654. HARRELL, JERRY D. "The fight for recognition," in Crisis, v. 61, Mar., 1954, pp. 133-35 and 188.
The establishment of an N. A. A. C. P. branch at the Univ. of Oregon, Eugene.

655. HARRISON, GLORIA. The National association for the advancement of colored people in California. Master's thesis, Stanford univ., Stanford, 1949. 93 p.

656. LAMPKIN, DAISY E.* "California campaigns for the N. A. A. C. P.," in Crisis, v. 41, July, 1934, pp. 210-11.
Membership campaigns in Los Angeles, Pasadena, Santa Monica, San Diego, Monrovia, Vallejo, and the San Francisco bay area.

657. National association for the advancement of colored people.* 1969 N. A. A. C. P. life membership committee dinner [program, menu, etc., S. F., 1969]. [16] p. ports.

658. _____. Nineteenth annual conference, the National association for the advancement of colored people at Los Angeles, California, June 27-July 3, 1928 ... [N. Y., Herald-Nathan press], 1928. 23p. CU-B.

659. _____. Berkeley. Annual awards dinner program. COEB 1965.

660. _____. Los Angeles. Branch files [of correspondence, etc.] 1913-39. CLU (film).

661. _____. Northern California branch. Yearbook of the Northern California branch of the National association for the advancement of colored people. [Oakland?, 1919?]. 26 [4] p. ports.

662. _____. Oakland. [Souvenir program]. Freedom fund banquet. COEB 1966.

663. _____. Seattle. Correspondence, minutes, reports, ephemera, and related items, 1935-66. About 3 feet. WaU.

664. _____. Vancouver, Wash. Correspondence, reports, minutes, and ephemera, 1945-69. WaU.

665. _____. West coast region. NAACP civil rights program, including NAACP legislative score board ... [Oakland, Tilghman press, 1960]. 12 p. ports. COEB.

666. _____. _____. West coast regional annual conference, September 19, 20, 21, 1969, Pacific Grove, California ... [Oakland, Tilghman press, 1969]. 21 p. ports.
Gives a history of the West coast region, a detailed program, and a list of recently deceased members.

N. A. A. C. P.

667. "Willkie speech in Los Angeles," in Crisis, v. 49, Sept., 1942,
pp. 296 and 301.
Wendell Willkie's speech before the 33rd annual meeting of the
N. A. A. C. P., Los Angeles.

WATTS AND THE WATTS RIOT

668. "The abandonment of the Watts line," in Headlights, v. 21, Dec., 1959,
p. 5.
The trolley car line from downtown Los Angeles to Watts.

669. ADLER, PATRICIA. "Watts: a legacy of lines," in Westways, v. 58,
Aug., 1966, pp. 22-24.

670. "After the blood bath," in Newsweek, v. 66, Aug. 30, 1965, pp. 13-18,
50-51.

671. AINSWORTH, EDWARD MADDIN, 1902-1968. Maverick mayor, a biography of
Sam Yorty of Los Angeles. Garden City, N. Y., Doubleday [c1966]. viii,
256 p. illus., ports. Bibliography: pp. 254-56. CSf.
Contains information on the 1965 Los Angeles riot.

672. ALLEN, GARY. "The plan to burn Los Angeles," in American opinion,
v. 10, May, 1967, pp. 31-40.
Describes the "Watts rebellion" as a Communist conspiracy.

673. American civil liberties union. Southern California branch. Police
malpractice and the Watts riot: a report. [L. A.?, 1966?]. 67 p.
CNoS, CSt.

674. APTHEKER, HERBERT. "The Watts ghetto uprising," in Political affairs,
v. 44, Oct., 1965, pp. 16-29, and Nov., 1965, pp. 28-44.

675. "Bad mass transit a factor in Watts riot," in American city, v. 81,
Nov., 1966, p. 32ff.

676. BERKELEY, ELLEN P. "Workshop in Watts," in Architectural forum,
v. 130, Jan.-Feb., 1969, pp. 58-63.
About the Urban workshop, a group of black architects and planners.

677. BIANCHI, EUGENE C. "Los Angeles tragedy: and opportunity," in
America, v. 113, Sept. 11, 1965, pp. 260-61.

678. "Black ghetto in revolt," in Economist, v. 216, Aug. 21, 1965,
pp. 692-93.

679. BLAUNER, ROBERT. "Whitewash over Watts," in Trans-action, v. 3,
Mar.-Apr., 1966, pp. 3-9, 54.

680. BOSKIN, JOSEPH. "Violence in the ghettos," in New Mexico quarterly,
v. 37, Winter, 1968, pp. 317-34.
In part, concerns the Watts troubles.

Watts and the Watts Riot

681. _____., ed. Urban racial violence in the twentieth century. Beverly Hills, Glencoe press [1969]. xii, 148 p. Bibliographical footnotes. C, CBGTU, CLSU, CNoS, CSt.
   Authored by a Univ. of southern California professor of history who includes Watts in his study.

682. _____., and VICTOR PILSON. "The Los Angeles riot of 1965: a medical profile of an urban crisis," in Pacific historical review, v. 39, Aug., 1970, pp. 353-65.

683. BOYD, MALCOLM. "Violence in Los Angeles," in Christian century, v. 82, Sept. 8, 1965, pp. 1,083-95.

684. *BUGGS, JOHN A. "Report from Los Angeles," in Journal of intergroup relations, v. 5, Autumn, 1966, pp. 27-40.

685. *BULLOCK, PAUL, 1924- . "Fighting poverty: the view from Watts." CSmarP.
   Reprinted from the Proceedings of the 19th annual meeting of the Industrial relations research association, Univ. of Calif., Los Angeles, 1967.

686. _____. "Poverty in the ghetto; a program to get at the heart of the problem in Los Angeles," in Frontier, v. 16, Oct., 1965, pp. 5-7.
   Pertains mainly to the Watts area.

687. _____., ed. Watts: the aftermath, an inside view of the ghetto, by the people of Watts. Ed. with an introd., notes, and a concluding chapter, by Paul Bullock. N. Y., Grove press [1969]. 285 p. Bibliographical footnotes. CCotS, CNoS, CSf, CSjC, CSp, CSt, CU.
   Interviews of Watts residents.

688. California. Bureau of criminal statistics. Watts riot arrests, Los Angeles, August 1965; final disposition. A statistical accounting as of June 30, 1966 of the procedures followed in completing actions initiated by the arrest of participants in the Watts riots of August 1965. [Sacramento] 1966. 46 p. tables. CL, CO, CSdCiC, CSf, CSt, CU.

689. _____. Governor's commission on the Los Angeles riots. Report on education submitted by Kenneth A. Martyn, California state college at Los Angeles. Washington, D. C., 1965. 131 p. C.
   Reports, in disadvantaged areas, the level of pupil achievement; the progress of schools in creating equal opportunity; and immediate needs to improve the educational level.

690. _____. _____. Staff report of actions taken to implement the recommendations in the Commission's report. August 17, 1966-August 18, 1967. [L. A., 1966-67]. 2 v. (Its Status report, no. 1-2.) C (v. 2), CL, CLSU (v. 1), CO, CPomCP, CSdCL (v. 2), CSf, CU.

691. _____. _____. Transcripts, depositions, consultants reports and selected documents. L. A., 1965. 18 v. illus., maps. John A. McCone, Chairman. CFS, CHS (film), CL (film), CLGPC (photocopy), CLS, CLSU, CNoS,

Watts and the Watts Riot

      CSdS (film), CSf, CSj, CSt, CU (photocopy), CU-A, CU-I (film).

692. _____. _____. Violence in the city -- an end or a beginning? A
report, December 2, 1965. [L. A., 1965]. iii, 101 p. illus., map (in
pocket). Available in many libraries.
    A summary of the original 18-volume report.

693. _____. Insurance industry committee. The insurance business and the
south central Los Angeles area; a report by the Insurance industry committee for the special problems in the south central Los Angeles area.
[n.p., 196-]. [8] ℓ. CSt (photocopy).
    The 1965 riot.

694. _____. National guard. Military support of law enforcement during
civil disturbances; a report concerning the California national guard's
part in suppressing the Los Angeles riot, August 1965. [Sacramento,
State print., 1966]. 63 p. illus. CSf, CSt-H.

695. *COBBS, PRICE MASHAW   "Journeys to black identity: Selma and Watts,"
in Black world, v. 16, July, 1967, pp. 16-20 and 64-74.

696. COHEN, JERRY. Burn, baby, burn! The Los Angeles race riot, August,
1965 by Jerry Cohen and William S. Murphy. Introduction by Robert Kirsch.
N. Y., Dutton, 1966. 318 p. illus., ports. Available in many libraries.

697. COHEN, NATHAN EDWARD. The context of the curfew area. L. A., Univ.
of Calif. institute of govt. and public affairs, c1967. 41 p. Bibliographic footnotes. Los Angeles riot study, MR-94. C, CLSU, CLU, CSaT,
CSd, CSt, CSt-Law.

698. _____. "The Los Angeles riot study," in Social work, v. 12, Oct.,
1967, pp. 14-21.

699. _____. The Los Angeles riot study (LARS) [by] Nathan E. Cohen, Study
co-ordinator [and others]. [L. A.] Univ. of Calif. institute of govt.
and public affairs, 1967. 20 ℓ. CLSU, CO, CSS.

700. _____., ed. The Los Angeles riots; a socio-psychological study. Ed.
by Nathan Cohen. Pub. in cooperation with the Institute of government
and public affairs, University of California, Los Angeles. N. Y.,
Praeger [1970]. xxxii, 742 p. Includes bibliographies. C, CL, CLU,
CNoS, CSt, CU-B.

701. Columbia broadcasting system, inc. CBS news. Los Angeles, Watts
riot; CBS and NBC television networks, August 12, 20, 1965. [n.p., n.d.]
1 v. (v.p.). C.
    Includes CBS evening news with Walter Cronkhite, Aug. 12-13, 16-19;
CBS news special report, Aug. 15; and NBC scripts for newscasters Tom
Pettit and Richard Hunt, Aug. 12-20, 1965.

702. _____. CBS television. CBS reports "Watts: riot or revolt?"
as broadcast over the CBS television network, Tuesday, Dec. 7, 1965,

Watts and the Watts Riot

10:00–11:00 P.M., EST. Reporter: Bill Stout. Producer: Jack Beck. [n.p., 1965]. 34 ℓ. CU-B (photocopy).

703. CONOT, ROBERT E. Rivers of blood, years of darkness, by Robert Conot. Toronto, New York, Bantam books [1967]. x, 497 p. Bibliography: pp. 493-97. Available in many California libraries.

704. _____. Same. N. Y., Morrow, 1968 [1967]. Available in many California libraries.
An hour-by-hour account which probes into the lives of the people involved and describes the events leading up to and during the Los Angeles riot of 1965.

705. COSTAIN, DAVE, ed. Anarchy. Los Angeles. L. A., 1965. Unp.

706. CRABB, RILEY HANSARD. "Long hot week in Los Angeles," in Round robin, the journal of borderland research, v. 21, Sept., 1965, pp. 1-5.

707. CRUMP, SPENCER. Black riot in Los Angeles; the story of the Watts tragedy. L. A., Trans-Anglo books [1966]. 160 p. illus., facsims., maps, ports. Bibliography: p. 155. "Appendix: the text of the McCone commission report": pp. 125-54. Available in many California libraries.

708. Decline & the fall of the "spectacular" commodity-economy. [n.p.], Frontier press [1966?]. 10 p.
"Frontier pamphlet number one."
An analysis of the 1965 riot.

709. "Does anyone really care? Negroes who rioted in Los Angeles," in Christian century, v. 82, Sept. 22, 1965, p. 1,148.
The causes of the riot.

710. DUNNE, JOHN GREGORY. "T. V.'s riot squad," in New republic, v. 153, Sept. 11, 1965, pp. 27-29.
Describes bias in news coverage especially during the Watts riot.

711. _____. "The ugly mood of Watts: militant leaders in Los Angeles' Negro ghetto are trying to win power by threatening whites with violence -- and behind their threats lies hatred," in Saturday evening post, v. 239, July 16, 1966, pp. 83-87.

712. "The fire that time," in New south, v. 20, Nov., 1965, pp. 2-10.
The 1965 riot, pp. 3-5.

713. FOGELSON, ROBERT M. "White on black: a critique of the McCone commission report on the Los Angeles riots," in Political science quarterly, v. 82, Sept., 1967, pp. 337-67.

714. _____., comp. The Los Angeles riots, compiled by Robert M. Fogelson. N. Y., Arno press, 1969. xviii, 187 p. illus., map (fold.), ports, tables. C, CHi, CSS.
Includes Violence in the city - and end or a beginning? A report,

Watts and the Watts Riot

by the Governor's commission on the Los Angeles riots; White on black:
a critique of the McCone commission report on the Los Angeles riots, by
Robert M. Fogelson; The Watts manifesto and the McCone report, by Bayard
Rustin; Whitewash over Watts: the failure of the McCone commission
report, by R. Blauner.

715. FRANKLIN, RUTH. Study of the services needed and/or available to
Negro newcomer families; a study of perceptions of eleven health and
welfare agencies serving the community of Watts. Master's thesis, Univ.
of southern Calif., Los Angeles, 1962. iii, 104 ℓ. illus.

716. FRITCHMAN, STEPHEN HOLE, 1902- . The crisis in Watts is not over.
L. A., First Unitarian church of Los Angeles [1965]. 13 p. Mimeo. CHi.

717. *GLASGOW, DOUGLAS GRAHAM. The sons of Watts improvement association.
"The sons of Watts": analysis of mobility aspirations and life-styles
in the aftermath of the Watts riot, 1965. Doctoral dissertation, Univ.
of southern Calif., Los Angeles, 1968. ix, 294 ℓ. illus., tables.
CNoS (photocopy).

718. GOODMAN, GEORGE W. "Watts, U. S. A.: a post mortem," in Crisis,
v. 72, Oct., 1965, pp. 487-92, 532.

719. HACKER, FREDERICK J. "What the McCone commission didn't see," in
Frontier, v. 17, Mar., 1966, pp. 10-15.
     The effect of the riot upon black Los Angeles residents.

720. HANNON, MICHAEL. "Behind the Watts revolt," in New politics, v. 4,
Summer, 1965, pp. 36-40.
     States that the causes essentially were economic impoverishment and
suggests some solutions.

721. HENEHAN, ANNE. "On-the-spot in Watts ... facing the problems of
minority ghettos in today's cities," in Senior scholastic (teacher ed.),
v. 89, Jan. 20, 1967, pp. 9-12.

722. HERBERG, WILL. "Who are the guilty ones?" in National review, v. 17,
Sept. 7, 1965, pp. 769-70.

723. HERMAN, MELVIN, and FLORA RHETA SCHREIBER. "Psychiatrists analyze the
Los Angeles riots," in Science digest, v. 58, Nov., 1965, pp. 33-37.

724. "The insurrection," in Frontier, v. 16, Sept., 1965, pp. 3-4.

725. ISENBERG, IRWIN, ed. The city in crisis. N. Y., 1968. 246 p.
     Contains "Watts -- 'remarkably the same'," by John C. Waugh, pp. 50-
54, and "On-the-spot in Watts," by Anne Henehan, pp. 54-63.

726. JACKSON, M. B. The second civil war commentary as broadcast on KMPC
Radio and KTLA Channel 5 [by] M. B. Jackson. Hollywood, Golden west
broadcasters, 1965. 10 p. C.

Watts and the Watts Riot

727. JONES, JACK. The view from Watts. [n.p., 1965]. [28] p. illus.
C, CL.
    A series of articles originally appearing in the Los Angeles Times,
Oct. 10-17, 1965.

728. _____. The view from Watts today. [n.p., 1967?]. CPomCP.
    A series of articles reprinted from the Los Angeles Times, July,
1967.

729. "Karl Fleming of Newsweek is beaten up getting a story in Watts," in
New south, v. 21, Summer, 1966, pp. 85-86.

730. KERBY, PHIL. "The report on the McCone commission report on Watts,"
in Frontier, v. 17, Feb., 1966, p. 4.

731. _____. "Riding shotgun in Watts," in Nation, v. 207, Sept. 2, 1968,
pp. 166-67.

732. Kimtex corp., pub. Anarchy Los Angeles. L. A., c1965. [65] p.
illus., ports. CHi, CLU (Spec. Coll.).
    Mainly an illus. description of the Los Angeles riot. Cover title:
"... shocking photos of the most terrifying race riot in history ..."

733. *KING, MARTIN LUTHER, 1929-1968, and M. L. SCHWARTZ. "Beyond the
Los Angeles riots," in Saturday review, Nov. 13, 1965, pp. 33-37.

734. KIRSCHMAN, RICHARD. "Actors 'On cue' for Watts workshop," in Urban
west, v. 2, Feb., 1969, pp. 13, 26-27.
    Interviews with Sidney Poitier, Greg Morris, and Talmadge Sprott
concerning the Douglass house foundation.

735. KOPKIND, ANDREW. "Lesson of Watts," in New statesman, v. 70, Dec. 17,
1965, pp. 960-61.

736. _____. "The spectre of Watts returns," in New statesman, v. 71,
June 3, 1966, pp. 799-800.

737. _____. "Watts, waiting for D-day," in New republic, v. 154, June 11,
1966, pp. 15-17.

738. "Learn, baby, learn," in Los Angeles magazine, v. 10, Oct., 1965,
pp. 24-28.

739. "Lesson of Los Angeles," in New statesman, v. 70, Aug. 20, 1965,
p. 237.

740. LEWIS, EDNA. Black men in Watts, 1967: an exploratory study of Negro
males' willingness to accept social workers in a ghetto area. Master's
thesis, Calif. state univ., Fresno, 1968.

741. LOREN, EUGENE L. Economic background - the Los Angeles riot study.
L. A., Univ. of Calif. institute of govt. and public affairs, c1967.
48 ℓ. CSt-Law.

Watts and the Watts Riot

742. Los Angeles. City council. Police, fire and civil defense committee. Report on Los Angeles riot. Council files nos. 125, 342 and 125, 343. [L. A., 1967?]. 26, xxi ℓ. CL, CO.

743. _____. City planning commission. Watts community plan. [L. A., 1966]. [6] 40 [8] p. maps.
 A plan for the physical development of the Watts and the southeast Los Angeles area.

744. "Los Angeles; a civil revolt," in Liberation, v. 10, Oct., 1965, pp. 5-7ff.

745. Los Angeles county. District attorney's office. The District attorney's report to the Governor's commission on the Los Angeles riot, October 28, 1965. L. A., Los Angeles daily journal, 1965. 24 p. CL.

746. _____. Probation dept. Riot participant study: juvenile offenders. [L. A.], 1965. 33 p. illus., maps, tables. CL, CO.

747. "Los Angeles en feu," in Paris match, Aug. 28, 1965, pp. 18-45.

748. "Los Angeles riot," in Crisis, v. 72, Aug.-Sept., 1965, pp. 414-16.

749. "Los Angeles riot heaps Nisei business with $1 million loss," in Pacific citizen, v. 61, Aug. 20, 1965, p. 1.

750. "Los Angeles searches for answer to riots," in Business world, Aug. 21, 1965, pp. 28-29.

751. Los Angeles Times. The McCone report; its content and significance. [n.p., 1965?]. 38 p. illus. C.
 Articles reprinted from the Los Angeles Times, Dec., 1965.

752. MCCORD, WILLIAM M. "'Burn, baby, burn!'", in The new leader, v. 48, Aug., 1965, pp. 3-5.
 Explains the causes of the 1965 riot.

753. MCGRORY, MARY. "A new outburst in Watts," in America, v. 114, Apr. 2, 1966, p. 437.

754. MCWILLIAMS, CAREY, 1905- . "Watts: the forgotten slum," in Nation, v. 201, Aug. 30, 1965, pp. 89-90.

755. MARX, WESLEY. "Watkins of Watts: what one man can do," in Reporter, v. 38, Jan. 25, 1968, pp. 36-38.
 About Ted Watkins.

756. MASTRONARDE, LINDA. "Watts - a colonial situation," in Community, v. 27, Sept., 1967, pp. 4-7.

757. *MERIWETHER, LOUISE M. "What the people of Watts say," in Frontier, v. 16, Oct., 1965, pp. 7-9.
 Quotations from residents.

Watts and the Watts Riot

758. MOORE, E. T. "Library burns in the Los Angeles riot: Willowbrook branch," in ALA bulletin, v. 59, Dec., 1965, pp. 983-86.

759. MORRIS, RICHARD THACKER. The white reaction study [by] Richard T. Morris and Vincent Jeffries. L. A., Univ. of Calif. institute of govt. and public affairs, c1967. 71, 43 p. map, tables. Los Angeles riot study, MR-84. C, CLSU, CLU, CSaT, CSt-Law, CU-B.

760. _____., and VINCENT JEFFRIES. "Violence next door," in Social forces, v. 46, Mar., 1968, pp. 352-58.

761. MURPHY, RAYMOND JOHN, 1926- . The structure of discontent: the relationship between social structure, grievance, and support for the Los Angeles riot [by] Raymond J. Murphy and James M. Watson. L. A., Univ. of Calif. institute of govt. and public affairs, c1967. 115 p. map, tables. Bibliographical footnotes. Los Angeles riot study, MR-92. C, CLSU, CLU, CSaT, CSt-Law, CU-B, CU-I.

762. MUSE, BENJAMIN. The American Negro revolution; from non-violence to black power, 1963-1967. Bloomington, Indiana univ. press [c1968]. xii, 345 p. CFS, CKenM, CNoS, CSaT, CSbS, CSdS, CSf, CSfCiC, CSluSP, CSto, CU-A, CU-I.
    The Watts riot is described, pp. 204-17.

763. NEVINS, ALLAN, 1890-1971. "Dateline Watts: from the ashes, a solution," in Saturday review, v. 50, Sept. 23, 1967, p. 79.
    Discusses Budd Schulberg's From the ashes.

764. "New hope for Watts," in IUD agenda, v. 3, Feb., 1967, pp. 13-15ff.

765. "No busing for Watts," in Nation, v. 206, Mar. 18, 1968, pp. 365-66.

766. "Not just America," in Economist, v. 216, Aug. 21, 1965, pp. 673-75.

767. OBERSCHALL, ANTHONY R. "Los Angeles riot of August, 1965," in Social problems, v. 15, Winter, 1968, pp. 322-41.

768. "Objective and dispassionate study? [McCone report on violence in Watts]," in Social service review, v. 40, Mar., 1966, pp. 86-87; Reply by F. L. Feldman, in June, 1966, pp. 216-20.

769. ORPAZ, YITSHAK. "Judgment day in Los Angeles," in Atlas, v. 11, Apr., 1966, pp. 240-41.

770. Our community Watts; originally called Tajuata, 1850-1941. Compilation: October 1941, of information collected by various classes, committees, and individuals, 1937-1941. [L. A.] Copied [by] Los Angeles city planning dept., 1965. CL.

771. PAGE, DONALD. "Watts -- one year later," in Employment service review, v. 3, Aug., 1966, pp. 21-22ff.
    Relates action taken by the state government.

Watts and the Watts Riot

772. PARKER, MICHAEL. "Watts: the liberal response," in New politics,
      v. 4, Summer, 1965, pp. 41-49.

773. PARROTT, WANDA SUE. "Studio Watts workshop," in Arts and society,
      v. 5, Fall-Winter, 1968, pp. 510-19.
         The story of an arts workshop established in 1965 mainly for the
      integration of school dropouts into society.

774. POE, ELIZABETH. "Watts," in Frontier, v. 16, Sept., 1965, pp. 5-7.

775. RAINE, WALTER JEROME, 1923- . The ghetto merchant survey. L. A.,
      Univ. of Calif. institute of govt. and public affairs, c1967. 34 p.
      tables. Los Angeles riot study, MR-98. C, CLSU, CLU, CSt-Law, CU-B.

776. _____. The perception of police brutality in south central Los
      Angeles. L. A., Univ. of Calif. institute of govt. and public affairs,
      c1967. 33 p. tables. Los Angeles riot study, MR-109. CLSU, CLU, CSaT,
      CSt-Law.

777. RANSFORD, HARRY EDWARD, 1936- . "Isolation, powerless, and violence:
      a study of attitudes and participation in the Watts riot," in American
      journal of sociology, v. 73, Mar., 1968, pp. 581-91.

778. "Report from Los Angeles, the Watts riot of 1965," in Journal of
      intergroup relations, v. 5, Autumn, 1966, pp. 27-40.

779. "Riot and premise protection," in Security world, v. 2, Sept., 1965,
      pp. 10-14.

780. ROBERTS, MYRON. "A whitey's tour of Watts," in Los Angeles, v. 13,
      June, 1968, p. 27ff.

781. *ROBINSON, LOUIE. "This would never have happened ... if they hadn't
      kicked that man: police action ignites fiery L. A. riot," in Ebony,
      v. 20, Oct., 1965, pp. 114-24.

782. ROBISON, JOSEPH. "Ghettos, property rights and myths," in Frontier,
      v. 15, June, 1964, pp. 5-8.

783. ROSSA, DELLA. Why Watts exploded: how the ghetto fought back.
      [L. A., Los Angeles local, Socialist workers party, 1966]. 21 p.
      illus. CNoS, CU-B.

784. *RUSTIN, BAYARD, 1910- . "Some lessons from Watts," in Journal of
      intergroup relations, v. 5, Autumn, 1966, pp. 41-48.

785. _____. "The Watts 'manifesto'," in New America, Sept. 17, 1965.

786. _____. "The Watts manifesto and the McCone report," in Commentary,
      v. 41, Mar., 1966, pp. 29-35.

Watts and the Watts Riot

787. _____. The Watts "Manifesto" & the McCone report. A commentary
report with study guide and letters. N. Y., Commentary, c1966. 11 p.
CSd.

788. _____., and others. "The Negro revolution in 1965." Santa Barbara,
Center for the study of democratic institutions [196-?]. Tape. 1 hour.

789. "Sam of Watts," in Arts and architecture, v. 68, July, 1951, pp. 23-25.
About Simon Rodia, builder of the Watts towers, Los Angeles.

790. *SANDERS, STANLEY. "The other alternative," in Black world, v. 15,
May, 1966, pp. 24-30.
Reprinted from Nation.

791. _____. "Riot as a weapon: the language of Watts," in Nation, v. 201,
Dec. 20, 1965, pp. 490-93.

792. SAYRE, NORA. "Conversations in Watts," in New statesman, v. 75,
Feb. 2, 1968, pp. 137-38.

793. SCHREIBER, FLORA RHETA, and MELVIN HERMAN. "Psychiatrists analyze
the Los Angeles riots," in Science digest, v. 58, Nov., 1965, pp. 18-22.

794. SCHULBERG, BUDD. "The angry voices of Watts," in Los Angeles, v. 11,
June, 1966, pp. 32-34, 66-67.

795. SCOBLE, HARRY M. "McCone commission and social science," in Phylon,
v. 29, Summer, 1968, pp. 167-81.

796. _____. Negro politics in Los Angeles: the quest for power. L. A.,
Univ. of Calif. institute of govt. and public affairs, c1967. 40 p.
"References": p. 40. Los Angeles riot study, MR-89. C, CLSU, CLU, CP,
CSS, CSaT, CSt, CSt-Law, CU-B, CU-I.

797. "Search for why's," in Senior scholastic, v. 87, Sept. 23, 1965,
pp. 23-24.

798. SEARS, DAVID O. "Black attitudes toward the political system in the
aftermath of the Watts insurrection," in Midwest journal of political
science, v. 13, Nov., 1969, pp. 515-44.

799. _____. Political attitudes of Los Angeles Negroes. L. A., Univ. of
Calif. institute of govt. and public affairs, c1967. 28 p. tables.
Bibliographical footnotes. Los Angeles riot study, MR-96. C, CLSU, CLU,
CSS, CSt-Law, CU-B.

800. _____. The politics of discontent: blocked mechanisms of grievance
redress and the psychology of the new urban black man [by] David O. Sears
and John B. McConahay. L. A., Univ. of Calif. institute of govt. and
public affairs, c1967. 75 p. tables. Bibliographical footnotes.
Los Angeles riot study, MR-117. CLU, CSt, CSt-Law.

Watts and the Watts Riot

801. _____. Riot participation [by] David O. Sears and John B. McConahay. L. A., Univ. of Calif. institute of govt. and public affairs, c1967. 27 p. tables. Bibliographical footnotes. Los Angeles riot study, MR-99. CLSU, CLU, CSaT, CU-B.

802. _____., and JOHN B. MC CONAHAY. "Participation in the Los Angeles riot," in Social problems, v. 17, Summer, 1969, pp. 3-20.

803. _____., and TOMMY MACK TOMLINSON. "Riot ideology in Los Angeles: a study of Negro attitudes," in Social science quarterly, v. 49, Dec., 1968, pp. 485-503.

804. SELBY, EARL, and ANNE SELBY. "Watts: where welfare bred violence," in Reader's digest, v. 88, May, 1966, pp. 67-71.

805. Sepia. The issue of Nov. 1965 is devoted almost entirely to Los Angeles and the Watts area riot. Subjects covered include employment, police brutality, politics, race relations, recreation, religion, education, athletics, and Samuel William Yorty.

806. SHERMAN, JIMMIE. "From the ashes: a personal reaction to the revolt of Watts," in Antioch review, v. 27, Fall, 1967, pp. 285-93.

807. SILBERMAN, CHARLES ELIOT, 1925- . "The deepening crisis in metropolis," in Journal of intergroup relations, v. 4, Summer, 1965, pp. 119-31.
    Anticipates the Los Angeles riot.

808. SOLLEN, ROBERT H. "The insurrection," in Frontier, v. 16, Sept., 1965, p. 1ff.

809. "Symposium on Watts 1965," in Law in transition quarterly, v. 3, Summer, 1966, pp. 174-96.
    Includes "Arrests and trials," "Analysis and statistics," and "Attitudes of Negroes toward the Los Angeles riots."

810. TAYLOR, WILLIAM C. "Storm over Los Angeles," in Political affairs, v. 44, Oct., 1965, pp. 8-15.

811. "Terror in Los Angeles: interview with a policeman assigned to the Watts area," in National review, v. 17, Sept. 7, 1965, pp. 773-74.

812. TOMLINSON, TOMMY MACK, 1931- . Ideological foundations for Negro action: a comparative analysis of militant and non-militant views of the Los Angeles riot. L. A., Univ. of Calif. institute of govt. and public affairs, c1967. 56 p. tables. Los Angeles riot study, MR-116. CLU, CSt, CSt-Law.

813. _____. Method: Negro reaction survey [by] T. M. Tomlinson and Diana L. Ten Houten. L. A., Univ. of Calif. institute of govt. and public affairs, c1967. 13 p. Los Angeles riot study, MR-95. CLSU, CLU, CSt, CSt-Law.
    "This report provides a detailed description of the data-gathering

Watts and the Watts Riot

and data-analysis procedures for the sample of Negro respondents interviewed ..."

814. _____. Negro attitudes toward the riot [by] T. M. Tomlinson and
David O. Sears. L. A., Univ. of Calif. institute of govt. and public
affairs, c1967. 37 p. tables. Los Angeles riot study, MR-97. CLSU,
CLU, CSaT, CSt, CSt-Law, CU-B.

815. "Trouble from Los Angeles," in Economist, v. 218, Mar. 19, 1966,
p. 1,128.

816. U. S. Commission on civil rights. California advisory commission.
An analysis of the McCone commission report. [n.p.], 1966. iv, 18 ℓ.
CL, CO.

817. *VERNON, ROBERT. Watts and Harlem; the rising revolt in the black
ghettos. By Robert Vernon and George Novack. [N. Y.] Pioneer pub.
[1965]. 15 p. illus.
    Contains "Birmingham, Harlem and Watts," by Robert Vernon, pp. 3-5,
and "Meaning of the Los Angeles ghetto rebellion," by George Novack,
pp. 5-9.

818. Watts advertiser-review. A picture of Watts in 1913 and history of
its growth until that time. [n.p., 1965]. 10 ℓ. Reprinted from the
Watts advertiser-review, Apr., 1938. CL.

819. "Watts and the 'War on Poverty'," in Political affairs, v. 44, Oct.,
1965, pp. 1-7.

820. "Watts revisited," in Economist, v. 220, Aug. 13, 1966, p. 645.

821. "Watts: the forgotten slum," in The nation, v. 201, Aug. 30, 1965,
pp. 89-90.

822. WEBSTER, ARGOW. "Formula for explosion," in Frontier, v. 16, Oct.,
1965, pp. 12-15.

823. "What for Watts?" in Economist, v. 217, Dec. 11, 1965, pp. 1,203-04.

824. *WHEELDIN, DONALD. "The situation in Watts today," in Freedomways,
v. 7, Winter, 1967, pp. 54-59.

825. WILKINSON, FRANK. "And now the bill comes due," in Frontier, v. 16,
Oct., 1965, pp. 10-12.

826. WILLIFORD, STANLEY O. "Watts - five years later," in Black politician,
v. 2, Oct., 1970, pp. 20-23.

827. WILSON, JOYCE R. "Why the Watts festival failed," in Urban west,
v. 3, Oct., 1969, p. 15.

828. *WORK, LENA BROWN. "A different view of Watts; follow-up report,"
in Harper's magazine, v. 234, May, 1967, p. 38.

Watts and the Watts Riot

    Lists Jordan high school graduates who have attended college and developed successful careers.

829. "The year of the rebels ... and the riots," in Los Angeles, v. 10, Sept., 1965, pp. 30-31.
    Concerns the Los Angeles riot and the Hell's angels.

GENERAL WORKS

830. *African communities league. Articles of incorporation, Los Angeles, 1931. [3] p. Typew. C-ArS.
    Devoted to the advancement of Negroes throughout the world. "All persons of Negro blood and African decent [sic] are regarded as members ..." The universal Negro improvement association and African communities league was an associated but unincorporated body having burial insurance features. Directors were Philip Declair, Foster Hydes, and Charles H. Small.

831. *African descendants nationalist independence partition party. African descendants manifesto ... self-determination and national independence by 1973. [S. F., 1967?]. 63 p. illus., ports.
    Also known as the AD NIP party and headed by Nasser Ahmad Shabazz.

832. *African mission and industrial association of Los Angeles, California. Articles of incorporation, Watts, 1923. 4 p. Typew. C-ArS.
    To advance status of Negroes generally and to conduct missionary work in Africa. Directors were Preston Robinson, Compton; and Henry Reneau, J. H. Andrews, H. Robinson, G. Gail, M. Reneau, Ida Robinson, and Mrs. J. H. Andrews, Watts.

833. *Afro-American league. First meeting of the Afro-American congress of California, California hall, 620 Bush St., San Francisco, Cal., July 30 to August 3, 1895. [S. F., 1895]. [28] p. port. C, C-S, CHi (photocopy), CSfCP.
    Contains a detailed program of activities and "A brief history of the Afro-American league of San Francisco."

834. *Afro-American league [of San Francisco]. Souvenir programme for the emancipation celebration. [S. F., 1902]. 16 p. illus., ports. CHi.
    Includes "A brief history of the Afro-American league of San Francisco, with some reference to its objects and what it has accomplished."

835. *Afro-American state league of California. Articles of incorporation, Oakland, 1900. [6] p. Printed form filled in. C-ArS.
    To unite all persons of the Negro race; to conduct a general merchandise business; and to educate its members and to advance their political interests. Directors were J. A. Derrick and John C. Rivers, San Francisco; and Dr. G. B. H. Rutherford, George Ingraham, J. F. Summers, I. Beal, George Seguie, E. H. Barrett, George R. Cashen, J. K.

General Works

Dickinson, and William Tipton, Oakland. J. A. Hackett, F. F. White, and C. P. Duncan also were listed as shareholders.

836. ALLEN, GARY. "Black power; American opinion goes to a Berkeley rally," in American opinion, v. 10, Jan., 1967, pp. 1-14.
Reports a three-day Black power conference held at the Univ. of Calif.

837. _____. Communist revolution in the streets, by Gary Allen with the editors of Western islands. Introd. by W. Clean Skousen. Boston and L. A., Western islands, 1967. 115 p. illus., map, ports. CSf.
Troubles in Watts, Delano, Berkeley, and elsewhere are described by an opponent of Martin Luther King, Jr.

838. American civil liberties union. Southern California branch. Day of protest, night of violence, the Century City peace march; a report of the American civil liberties union of southern California. [L. A.] Sawyer press, 1967. 46 p. illus. CSt.
Report of events resulting from a Vietnam war protest.

839. *BANKS, HENRY A. "Black consciousness: a student survey," in The black scholar, v. 2, Sept., 1970, pp. 44-51.
Based upon a study of students at Abraham Lincoln high school and the City college of San Francisco and Tamalpais high school and the College of Marin, Marin county.

840. *BARRETT, SAMUEL. The need of unity and cooperation among colored Americans; a book discussing the problems of unity and co-operation among American Negroes in those matters concerning their betterment. Sixth ed., enlarged and rev. [Oakland, Voice pub. co., c1946]. 140 p. port. COEB, CSto, NUC, pre-1956.

841. _____. "A plea for unity," in Colored American magazine, v. 7, Jan., 1940, pp. 46-51.

842. _____. A plea for unity among American Negroes; a book dealing with the problem of unity and cooperation among Negroes in the United States in those matters concerning their uplift and advancement, a solution of many of their problems. 5th ed. [Oakland, Printed by Harrington-McInnis, c1943]. 96 p. port. CL, CLGS, NUC, pre-1956.

843. _____. A plea for unity among American Negroes and the Negroes of the world; a book dealing with one of the phases of the Negro problem as it effects the Negroes themselves. By Dr. Samuel Barrett ... (3d ed. - enl. and rev.). [Cedar Falls, Ia., Woolverton print. co., c1926]. 67 p. DLC, NUC, pre-1956.

844. _____. The significance of leaders in Afro-American progress, a book dealing with the principles underlying permanent and successful leadership in the progress of the Afro-Americans, by the Rev. Samuel Barrett ... Newburgh, N. Y., The News co., 1909. 28 p. port. DLC, NUC, pre-1956.

845. BATTISTA, DANIEL JOSEPH. Negro social action organizations and the civil rights movement. Master's thesis, Calif. state univ., Sacramento, 1969. 147 ℓ.

General Works

846. BAZAAR, MONA, ed. Black fury, by Mona Bazaar. L. A., Open city
[1968?]. [71] ℓ. illus. CHS, CSfAA.
Essays mainly pertaining to the black revolutionary movement.

847. Berkeley conference on black power and its challenges. ... [Speech
of] Stokely Carmichael (chairman of SNCC). Conference convened by campus
SDS. [Berkeley, 196-]. 12 p. CU-B.

848. BERNSTEIN, SAUL, 1905- . Alternatives to violence: alienated youth
and riots, race, and poverty. N. Y., Association press [1968, c1967].
192 p. Bibliography: pp. 187-92. CNoS, CSf, CU.
A study of disturbances in various U. S. cities including Los Angeles
and San Francisco.

849. BEVEL, JAMES. James Bevel on black power. Berkeley, Pacifica tape
library A2148, 1966. [Phonotape]. Duration: 42 min. CSS.
A speech given at the Conference on black power sponsored by the
Students for a democratic society at the Univ. of Calif., Berkeley,
Oct. 29, 1966. Introduction by James Shaw.

850. BLEVINS, CLIFTON and WALLACE HOMITZ. "What the San Diego Negro is
thinking," in San Diego magazine, v. 17, Sept., 1965, pp. 44-46, 106-08.

851. BOSKIN, JOSEPH. "The revolt of the urban ghettos, 1964-1967," in
Annals of the American academy of political and social science, v. 382,
Mar., 1969, pp. 1-14.
Authored by a Univ. of southern California educator.

852. *BRACEY, JOHN H., ed., 1941- . Black nationalism in America. Ed. by
John H. Bracey, Jr., August Meier [and] Elliott Rudwick. Indianapolis
and N. Y., Bobbs-Merrill co. [c1970]. lxx, 568 p. CCotS, CNoS, CSt.
Contains "A California newspaper looks at the National Negro business
league," an editorial from the Oakland Sunshine, Sept. 4, 1915; "We must
create a national black intelligencia in order to survive," by Askia
Muhammad Touré (Rolland Snellings), from the Journal of black poetry,
Spring, 1968; and "Political power comes through the barrel of a gun,"
being "The Black panther party program," 1968, and "An interview with
Huey P. Newton," 1968.

853. BRACY, JAMES. The psychological implications of the current revolution. Master's thesis, Sonoma state college, Rohnert Park [1970?]. 20 ℓ.

854. BRADFORD, AMORY. Oakland's not for burning. N. Y., David McKay co.
[c1968]. vii, 248 p. C, CKenM, CLod, CNoS, COroB, CP, CRic, CSaT,
CSfCiC, CSrCL, CStmo, CTur, CU-B.
How positive social action prevented a threatened racial explosion
in Oakland similar to the earlier trouble in Watts.

855. BRELL, HARRY. Black militancy: a case study in ego politics.
Doctoral dissertation, Univ. of Calif., Berkeley, 1969. vi, 325 ℓ.

856. BUDDRESS, LOREN A. N. Black power and the black concept. Master's
thesis, Calif. state univ., San Jose, 1970. vi, 73 ℓ.

General Works

857. California. State fair employment practice commission. Observations on recent San Francisco disturbance and the community's response, by Edward Howden. [Sacramento?]. 1966. 5 p. C.
The San Francisco riot, 1966.

858. CERVANTES, ALFONSO J. "To prevent a chain of super-Watts," in Harvard business review, v. 45, Sept., 1967, pp. 55-65.

859. *CHRISMAN, ROBERT. "The formation of a revolutionary black culture," in The black scholar, v. 1, June, 1970, pp. 2-9.

860. *COLE, JOHNNETTA B. "Culture: Negro, black and nigger," in The black scholar, v. 1, June, 1970, pp. 40-44.
Authored by the Director of black studies, Washington state univ., Pullman.

861. *Colored workers' association. Articles of incorporation, Los Angeles, 1922. [4] p. Typew. C-ArS.
"To foster and advance anything that may help persons of the Negro race ..." Directors were Sophie Ann Hoard, William Davis, Emma Johnson, Texas Cook, and Jessie D. Hoard.

862. Congress of racial equality. Western regional office. Papers, 1948-67, including correspondence and subject files on administration, education, employment, housing, and reference materials. WHi.

863. *DAVIS, ANGELA YVONNE, 1944- . Lectures on liberation, by Angela Davis. [L. A.? Printed by the Peace press, 1970?]. 8 p.

864. EASON, CHARLES LEWIS. An analysis of the social attitudes and casual factors of Negro problem boys of the Los Angeles city schools. Master's thesis, Univ. of southern Calif., Los Angeles, 1936. iii, 96 ℓ. diagrs., tables.

865. "An eloquent epitaph for Ed Pratt - spoken in his own words," in Seattle magazine, v. 6, Mar., 1969, p. 50.
Concerns a Seattle civil rights leader, murdered Jan. 26, 1969.

866. FOGELSON, ROBERT M. "From resentment to confrontation: the police, the Negroes, and the outbreak of the nineteen-sixties riots," in Political science quarterly, v. 83, June, 1968, pp. 217-47.
Also appeared in Social action, v. 35, Feb., 1969, pp. 6-33. Includes statements and attitudes of western blacks.

867. _____. "Violence as protest," in Academy of political science proceedings, v. 29, July, 1968, pp. 25-41.

868. *FRANCOIS, TERRY ARTHUR, 1921- . "A black man looks at black racism," in Reader's digest, v. 95, Sept., 1969, pp. 209-14.
By a San Francisco city supervisor.

869. GLICK, RONALD. Protest organizations of the urban poor. Master's thesis, Univ. of Calif., Berkeley, 1968. 169 ℓ.

General Works

870. _____. Southern community and new left organizers: a cultural
meeting. Doctoral dissertation, Univ. of Calif., Berkeley, 1969. 250 ℓ.

871. *HARE, NATHAN. "The challenge of a black scholar," in The black
scholar, v. 1, Dec., 1969, pp. 58-63.

872. *HEWITT, MARY JANE C., 1934- . Negro social protest, 1919-1925.
Master's thesis, Univ. of southern Calif., Los Angeles, 1966. v, 193 ℓ.

873. *HILL, ROY L., ed. Rhetoric of racial revolt. Denver, Golden bell
press, 1964. 378 p. CCotS, CEcaC, CFS, CHS, CLSU, CLobS, CPhD, CSbS,
CSdS, CSf, CSjCi, CU, CU-A, CU-SC, WaTP.
By a faculty member, Dept. of speech, Univ. of Denver. National
in coverage. Contains "Good news for the underprivileged," by Howard
Thurman, pp. 258-65.

874. *HIMES, CHESTER BOMAR, 1909- . "Negro martyrs are needed," in Crisis,
v. 51, May, 1944, pp. 159 and 174.
An argument for revolution and leaders in the tradition of Nat
Turner.

875. _____. "Zoot riots are race riots," in Crisis, v. 50, July, 1943,
pp. 200-01 and 222.
Author's eye-witness account of riots and the conditions which led
up to them.

876. HOLISI, CLYDE, and JAMES MTUME, eds. The quotable Karenga. L. A.,
US organization [c1967]. iii, 30 p.

876a.*HUFFMAN, EUGENE HENRY. "Where there is no vision the people perish"
... [S. F.] United African appeal, inc. [196-?]. [7] p.
Describes the aims of the United African appeal, a nationalist and
pan-African movement.

877. JUSTICE, DAVID BLAIR. An inquiry into Negro identity and a method-
ology for investigating potential racial violence. Doctoral dissertation,
Rice univ., Houston, 1966. 284 p.
"The investigation was given impetus by the Watts riot, with authorities in Houston requesting that findings on the level of racial tension
be presented so steps could be taken to head off the widespread rumors
of impending racial violence locally." -- Dissertation abstracts, v. 27,
Nov.-Dec., 1966.

878. KENNEDY, T. H. "Racial tensions among Negroes in the intermountain
northwest," in Phylon, v. 7, 4th quarter, 1946, pp. 358-64.
A general study based upon data from questionnaires circulated in
the area between the Rocky Mountains and the Cascades, north of the
California-Nevada state line.

879. LUCE, PHILIP ABBOTT, 1938- . Road to revolution: communist guer-
rilla warfare in the U. S. A. San Diego, Viewpoint books [c1967].
174 p. CL, CSt.

General Works

880. MC WILLIAMS, CAREY, 1905-. "The zoot-suit riots," in New republic,
      v. 108, June 21, 1943, pp. 818-20.

881. MASOTTI, LOUIS H. and DON R. BOWEN, eds. Riots and rebellion; civil
      violence in the urban community. Beverly Hills, Sage pubs. [c1968].
      459 p. CLSU, CNoS, CSaT, CSdS, CU-A, CU-I.
          Includes William McCord and John Howard, "Negro opinions in three
      riot cities" [Houston, Los Angeles, Oakland], and T. M. Tomlinson, "Riot
      ideology among urban Negroes," based on data from a study of the Los
      Angeles riot of 1965.

882. MEISTER, DICK. "Black nationalism in San Francisco ghetto," in
      Frontier, v. 14, Jan., 1963, pp. 5-7.

883. _____. "The new militancy for freedom now," in Frontier, v. 15,
      Apr., 1964, pp. 9-10.

884. MILLER, MAGGIE ULLERY. A study of the movement for the advancement of
      Negroes in Oklahoma ... Master's thesis, Univ. of southern Calif.,
      Los Angeles, 1947. iii, 68 ℓ. tables.

885. MOSS, PHOEBE ELEANOR. Garveyism as an expression of American Negro
      Pan-Africanism. Master's thesis, Univ. of Calif., Berkeley, 1959. iv,
      153 ℓ.

886. MURPHY, RAYMOND JOHN, 1926- , ed. Problems & prospects of the Negro
      movement, ed. by Raymond J. Murphy and Howard Elinson. Belmont,
      Wadsworth pub. co. [c1966]. 440 p. illus. Bibliography: pp. 437-40.
      C, CEcaC, CGS, CHS, CL, CLSU, CNoS, CPhD, CSaT, CSbS, CSdS, CSf, CSluSP,
      CSt, CU-A, CU-SC.
          Contains 32 articles on the current movement. "The protest against
      housing segregation," by Loren Miller, pp. 159-66.

887. National committee to free Angela Davis, Los Angeles. A political
      biography of Angela Davis. [L. A., 1970?]. 8 p.

888. *National Negro congress. Los Angeles council. Jim crow in national
      defense. [L. A., 1940?]. 27 p. facsim. C, CHi, CU, Rocq 3214.

889. *Negro citizens and taxpayers league. 1946, the status of Negroes in
      Portland, and program of the Negro citizens and taxpayers league.
      Portland, Ore., 1946. 8 p. OrU.

890. News & letters. The free speech movement and the Negro revolution,
      by Mario Savio, Eugene Walker [and] Raya Dunayevskaya. Includes also:
      Robert Moses on education in the South and inside Sproul hall: an eye-
      witness account of the arrest of 800 students, by Joel L. Pimsleur.
      Detroit, 1965. 53 p. illus., ports. DHU.
          "A News & letters pamphlet."

891. PARDEE, GOERGE COOPER, 1857-1941. Correspondence and papers, 1890-
      1941, of a California governor. 117 boxes, 11 cartons, 58 volumes,
      portfolio. CU-B.

General Works

     Contains 16 letters, 1902-06, from the Afro-American congress and one letter from Giles B. Jackson of the Negro development and exposition co. of the U. S., May 20, 1904.

892. "The path of Angela Davis; from promising childhood to desperate flight," in Life, v. 69, Sept. 11, 1970, pp. 20D-27.
     A biographical account of a one-time Univ. of Calif., Los Angeles, educator.

893. *PETERS, GENE RAYMOND. Prime thoughts for black folks [by] Gene Raymond Peters. Rev. fourth international printing ... Edited by O[rganization of] A[fro-] A[merican] U[nity] - West coast. [Encanto?]. c1968. [12] p. port.

894. POWELL, INGEBORG BREITNER. Ideology and strategy of direct action: a study of the Congress of racial equality. Doctoral dissertation, Univ. of Calif., Berkeley, 1965. vi, 367 ℓ.
     "The ideology of the Congress of Racial Equality, contrasted with Gandhian, Quaker and other ideologies." - West, p. 92.

895. RANSFORD, HARRY EDWARD, 1936- . Negro participation in civil rights activity and violence. Doctoral dissertation, Univ. of Calif., Los Angeles, 1966. xiv, 262 ℓ. tables.
     Based upon 400 interviews in two sections of Los Angeles. Includes the 1965 riot.

896. RAWITSCHER, AUDREY, comp. Riots in the city; an addencum [sic] to the McCone commission report. L. A., National assoc. of social workers, Los Angeles area chapter [1967]. vi, 73 p. Bibliography: pp. 23-24. CLAF, CLSU.
     Contents: "A history of urban racial conflicts in the twentieth century," by J. Boskin; "Public welfare: despondency, despair, and opportunity," by F. L. Feldman; and "Epilogue," by A. Rawitscher.

897. RECORD, WILSON, 1916- . The role of the Negro intellectuals in contemporary radical movements. Doctoral dissertation, Univ. of Calif., Berkeley, 1953. ii, 3, vi, 325 ℓ. tables.

898. REICH, KENNETH. "Angela Davis - is she more red than black?" in Black politician, v. 1, Jan., 1970, pp. 25-27.

899. ROBERTS, MYRON. "The Angela heresy," in Los Angeles, v. 14, Nov., 1969, pp. 30-33ff.
     Angela Davis at the Univ. of Calif., Los Angeles.

900. ROBERTS, S. V. "Russians are coming at UCLA: the firing of A. Davis," in Commonweal, v. 91, Nov., 1969, pp. 174-75.

901. SCHWAB, HEIDI. "Four black activists speak: what we want from the white establishment," in Puget soundings, Jan., 1969, pp. 10-11, 27-29.

902. *SOLIMAN, ABD ELLATIF. The past, present and future of the Negro. L. A., California eagle pub. co. [c1926]. 324 [2] p. Bibliography: pp. 321-24. CL, CU.

General Works

903. STEINFIELD, MELVIN. "In San Diego, new evidence of growing black
power and black unity," in San Diego and Point magazine, v. 19, Jan.,
1967, pp. 64-65.

904. TEODORI, MASSIMO, ed. The new left: a documentary history, ed. by
Massimo Teodori. Indianapolis, Bobbs-Merrill co. [c1969]. 501 p.
Includes bibliography. CSf.
    For information on the black left in California, see pp. 275-96.

905. THORNE, RICHARD. "Integration or black nationalism: which route
will Negroes choose?" in Black world, v. 12, Aug., 1963, pp. 36-47.
    A Californian advocates nationalism.

906. *THURMAN, HOWARD, 1899- . Disciplines of the spirit. N. Y., Harper
& Row [c1963]. 127 p. CL, CSf, WaTC.
    "The technique of nonviolence in the revolutionary struggle of the
Negro." - Elizabeth W. Miller.

907. TOMLINSON, TOMMY MACK, 1931- . "The development of a riot ideology
among urban Negroes," in American behavioral scientist, v. 11, Mar.-Apr.,
1968, pp. 27-31.

908. U. S. Commission on civil rights. A time to listen, a time to act;
voices from the ghettos of the nation's cities. Washington, D. C.,
1967. vii, 133 p. CU.

909. _____. National advisory commission on civil disorders. Report
[Otto Kerner, chairman. Washington, D. C., Govt. print., 1968]. 425 p.
illus., ports., charts. CHS, CL, CLGS, CNoS, CSf, CSlu, CStb, CU-I,
CU-SC.
    Contains information about disorders in several western states.

910. _____. _____. Same. Introduction by Tom Wicker; illus. with photos.
[Chairman: Otto Kerner.] The New York Times edition. N. Y., Dutton,
c1968. 609 [49] p. illus., charts. CEcaC, CHS, CL, CLSU, CP1, CSdS,
CSfCiC, CSt, CU-SC.

911. _____. _____. Same. Special introduction by Tom Wicker; with 32
pages of selected photos. [Chairman: Otto Kerner.] N. Y., Bantam,
c1968. 609 [49] p. illus., charts. CKenM, CL, CO, CSbS, CSluSP,
CU-A, CWM.

912. _____. _____. Supplemental studies for the National advisory commission on civil disorders [conducted independently of the Commission].
Washington, D. C., Govt. print., 1968. 248 p. forms. CL, CSf.

913. _____. _____. Same. N. Y., Praeger [1968]. viii, 248 p. tables.
CHS, CL, CLSU, CSdS.
    Based upon studies made in a group of U. S. cities including San
Francisco and, to a lesser extent, Los Angeles and Phoenix.

914. *Universal Negro improvement association. Local no. 188. Articles
of incorporation, Oakland, 1927. 6 p. Typew. C-ArS.

General Works

      Directors were C. A. Davis, M. Hodge, David E. Vassel, Ella King, William Jackson, J. C. Cook, Felix Beckford, Joseph Johnson, and James H. Pon[ti]flet.

915. *Universal Negro improvement association and African communities league. Designation of representative in the state of California, 1921. [5] p. Typew. C-ArS.
      Designation of D. J. Henderson, Los Angeles, as attorney for the New York state organization. Signed by Marcus Garvey, President. A copy of the New York state articles of incorporation is included.

916. "The violence," in Nation, v. 205, Aug. 14, 1967, pp. 101-07.
      Racial disorders in four cities including Los Angeles.

917. *W. E. B. Du Bois clubs of America. Culture and education; convention report. [S. F., 1964?] 24 p. illus. CU-B.
      "Report and resolutions on culture and education adopted at the founding convention, San Francisco, 21 June 1964."

918. WAGNER, HARR, 1857-1936, ed. Notable speeches by notable speakers of the greater West ... S. F., Whitaker and Ray co., 1902. 430 p. ports. CSf.
      Included, pp. 323-29, is "The improvement of the colored race," a speech delivered by T. B. Morton "as his annual address as state president of the Afro-American Leagues of California ... Fresno, July 20, 1897." Also included is a short biographical account and Morton's portrait.

919. WAGSTAFF, THOMAS, comp. Black power: the radical response to white America. Beverly Hills, Glencoe press [1969]. 150 p. Bibliographical footnotes. CSt.

920. Washington. State commission on the causes and prevention of civil disorders. Race and violence in Washington state; report of the commission on the causes and prevention of civil disorder. Olympia, 1969. 63 p. Wa.

921. WELLMAN, DAVID THOMAS. Negro leadership in San Francisco. Master's thesis, Univ. of Calif., Berkeley, 1966. ii, 181 ℓ.

922. "Who's who: Noah D. Thompson," in Messenger, v. 4, Aug., 1922, pp. 466-67.
      The actions of Thompson of Los Angeles in exposing Marcus Garvey and the Universal Negro improvement association.

923. WILSON, JOYCE R. "Black congress," in Urban west, v. 2, Dec., 1968, p. 19.
      Describes the Los Angeles Black congress of 72 organizations and its Deputy administrator, Roygene Robinson.

924. WRIGHT, JEROME WENDELL. Negritude: an example of reaction against the acculturation process. Master's thesis, Calif. state univ., San Francisco, 1969. iii, 84 ℓ.

General Works

925. YODER, EDWIN M. "Voices from burning slums," in Saturday review,
      v. 50, Aug. 26, 1967, pp. 28-29.
         Conditions in Los Angeles.

                  BUSINESS AND INDUSTRY; COOPERATIVES

926. *Afro-American co-operative association. Articles of incorporation,
     San Francisco, 1901. 5 p. Typew. C-ArS.
        "... to conduct a general mercantile manufacturing and contracting
     business ..." Directors were John C. Rivers, William F. Ford, Thaddeus
     A. Brown, T. B. Morton, A. L. Dennis, John A. Wylley, Joseph R. Sands,
     Israel C. Wilson, and the Rev. J. H. Kelley, San Francisco; Capt. W. T.
     Shorey, Oakland; and A. Strather, Alameda. Twenty-eight shareholders
     were listed.

927. *Afro-American cooperative cleaning and dyeing plant. Articles of
     incorporation, Los Angeles, 1925. 4 p. Typew. C-ArS.
        Directors were Joseph M. Walker, L. G. Robinson, W. T. Martin, A. L.
     Potts, and L. K. Beeks.

928. *Afro-American cooperative laundry company. Articles of incorporation,
     Ocean Park, 1906. 6 p. Typew. C-ArS.
        Directors were Charles E. A. Bronson, Mrs. Annie Woods, Mrs. Joseph
     Cross, Mrs. Mary E. Collier, Lewis W. Bronson, Henry Sample, and Emmet
     Carter, Ocean Park; Miss Susie E. Edmonds and J. L. Edmonds, Santa
     Monica; and Dr. Joseph W. Ball and Dr. James J. Leggett, Los Angeles.
     Twenty-two shareholders were also listed.

929. *Afro-American council commercial company. Articles of incorporation,
     Los Angeles, 1909. 4 p. Typew. C-ArS.
        To engage in real estate, insurance, and employment enterprises.
     Directors were Willis Jackson, James A. Thomas, James H. Clark, Henry
     Batie, O. E. Brookings, J. M. Alexander, P. J. Anderson, G. W. Whitley,
     H. A. Reeves, A. Osborne, and Joseph Bronson.

930. *Afro-American investment company. Articles of incorporation, Watts,
     1921. 2 p. Typew. C-ArS.
        To engage in general business operations. Directors were James R.
     Skinner, Thomas J. Duckett, James C. Lampkin, John W. McElroy, and
     Thomas Adams, Los Angeles; and William D. Jordan, Edward Douglas Owens,
     Frank F. Screen, E. A. Doram, Robert Stanton, and W. H. Britton, Watts.

931. *Afro-American real estate association and employment bureau of
     California. Articles of incorporation, Oakland, 1908. [5] p. Typew.
     C-ArS.
        Directors were J. B. Wilson, J. F. Summers, A. Strather, and S. W.
     Hawkins, Oakland; J. A. Dennis and Arthur P. Lee, San Francisco; David
     Holden, Berkeley; and William Tipton and C. C. X. Laws, Sacramento.

932. Allensworth city water company. Articles of incorporation, Alpaugh,
      1908. 3 [1] p. Typew. C-ArS.

Business and Industry; Cooperatives

A Tulare county irrigation company, the directors of which were
W. H. O'Bryan, Lenwood Abbott, R. P. Gage, J. W. Palmer, and Harry
Mitchell, Los Angeles.

933. Allensworth land company. Articles of incorporation, Merced, 1914.
[4] p. Typew. C-ArS.
"To carry on a general land and real estate business." Directors
were H. K. Huls, Merced; L. E. Grimm, Oakland; and G. Canevaro, Snelling.
The Allensworth Justice of the Peace stated with regard to the
company: "It is in no way connected with Allensworth, and the lands it
is offering for sale should be investigated ... The Negro agents who
have been employed will do well to ascertain their position before any
sales are undertaken." Los Angeles California eagle, Dec. 5, 1914, p. 8,
col. 3.

933a. _____. Order for dissolution, 1919. [4] p. C-ArS.

934. Allensworth rural water company. Articles of incorporation, Alpaugh,
1908. 3 [1] p. Typew. C-ArS.
A Tulare county irrigation company, the directors of which were
W. H. O'Bryan, Lenwood Abbott, R. P. Gage, J. W. Palmer, and Harry
Mitchell, Los Angeles.

935. *ANDERSON, TALMADGE. "Black economic liberation under capitalism,"
in The black scholar, v. 2, Oct., 1970, pp. 11-14.
Authored by the Director of black studies, Washington state univ.,
Pullman.

936. *Bay cities investment company. Articles of incorporation, Oakland,
1917. 3 p. Typew. C-ArS.
Directors were A. L. Allen, Reno, and R. L. Williams, Andrew S.
Duggar, E. B. Gray, Aide L. Dawson, Joseph F. Carroll, Willis P. Taylor,
Walter Gentry, and Carl A. Kent, Oakland.

937. *Booker T. luncheon club. Articles of incorporation, Richmond, 1945.
[4] p. Printed form filled in. C-ArS.
"To buy and sell real estate and merchandise... Specifically - to
promote the (legal) business ideas of one, Mr. A. J. Gardner of Richmond."
Directors were Gardner, Bertha Ward, and Andrew Ross.

938. *Booker T. Washington apts., inc. Articles of incorporation, Los
Angeles, 1947. 3 p. Typew. C-ArS.
Directors were Marvin G. Wagner, Alvin W. Glass, and Charles D.
Wagner.

939. *Bookertee film company. Articles of incorporation, Los Angeles,
1920. [5] p. Typew. C-ArS.
A motion picture company, the directors of which were Sidney P. Dones,
William H. Browning, D. D. S., and G. W. Wickliffe.

940. BULLEN, MARION PROSPER. Golden state mutual life insurance company.
[Term paper]. Univ. of southern California, Los Angeles, 1948. CLGS.

Business and Industry; Cooperatives

941. *California cocoanut pulverizing company.   Articles of incorporation,
   1874. Ms. [4] p. C-ArS.
      This San Francisco firm extracted cocoanut oil for the manufacture of
   soap and other toilet articles which were exhibited at the U. S. centennial commission's International exhibition at Philadelphia, 1876. Its
   officers were Alexander P. Ashburne, Jesse Slaughter, Thomas L. Williams,
   Claiborne H. Harris, and Robert J. Fletcher of Sacramento, and James
   Richard Phillips and William M. Smith of San Francisco.

942. *CANDEE, BEATRICE.   "Women in defense industry," in Opportunity,
   v. 21, Apr., 1943, pp. 46-49 and 86-87.
      Authored by a social psychologist then conducting studies in Portland.

943. *COKER, GEORGE CICERO.   Study of the proposed consolidation of the
   Pennsylvania railroad under the 1929 plan of the Interstate commerce
   commission. Master's thesis, Univ. of southern Calif., Los Angeles,
   1931. 121 ℓ.

944. *Colored business men's association of Stockton.   Articles of incorporation, 1944. 10 p. Typew. C-ArS.
      Organized to enter into various types of business, issue stock, and
   "to strive for the future economic security of the colored people in
   San Joaquin county and to prepare them for post war economic security."
   Signed by Roy Parker, Howard Harris, George R. Miller, Thomas E. Carter,
   and Sam Bryant.

945. *Colored workers association.   Articles of incorporation, Los Angeles,
   1933. 4 p. Typew. C-ArS.
      Organized to operate a real estate business and to secure employment
   for its members. Directors were Mamie V. White, Minnie Slaten, Marie
   Chinn, Max Du Valliere, and James Hill.

946. *Commercial council of Los Angeles.   Articles of incorporation, 1924.
   3 p. Typew. C-ArS.
      Devoted to the promotion of business, manufacturing, and immigration.
   Directors: Eugene C. Nelson, Albert E. Duncan, V. M. Cole, S. B. W. May,
   Lewis K. Beeks, Mrs. B. E. Prentice, P. D. Buck, C. T. Jones, Joseph
   Blackburn Bass, Charles E. Pearl, Noah Davis Thompson, A. L. Johnston,
   A. Hartley Jones, Paul Revere Williams, George Grant, Norman Oliver
   Houston, Titus Alexander, Grant Smith, Elijah Cooper, G. W. City,
   Charles S. Darden, and B. H. Graham.

947. COOK, J. E. "Black capitalism - by the time it gets to Phoenix the
   hard core will be softer," in Arizona, Mar. 30, 1969, pp. 8-15.

948. *EASON, NEWELL D.   The Negro in American industry. Master's thesis,
   Univ. of southern Calif., Los Angeles, 1932.

949. *East bay cosmetologists association.   The East bay cosmetologists
   association present their third annual heritage hair-dos fashion show,
   dance, and crowning of Miss East east [sic] bay cosmetologist for 1969
   ... [Oakland, California voice pub. co., 1969]. 19 p. ports.
      A short history of the organization is given together with biographi-
   cal accounts of contestants.

Business and Industry; Cooperatives

950. *Elevator silver mining co., San Francisco. Articles of incorporation
executed by Henry M. Collins, John C. Mortimer, H. H. Pearson, John E.
Ince, and C. E. Pearson, 1869, for a company to engage in mining in
White Pine county, Nevada. Ms. [3] p. C-ArS.

951. *Enterprise Rochedale company, Oakland. Articles of cooperative
association and incorporation, 1901. Ms. [5] p. C-ArS.
    A general merchandise cooperative, the directors of which were Capt.
William T. Shorey, George R. Cashen, Enoch H. Barrett, James F. Summers,
James Alexander Hackett, J. K. Dickinson, George Ingraham, J. T. Callender,
and Sylvester R. Hackett.

952. *Ethiopia co-operative business association, Oakland. Articles of
incorporation, March, 1928. 3 p. Typew. C-ArS.
    A loan company. Directors: C. H. Rice, Thomas J. Jefferson, E. R.
Green, Charles S. Truehill, James R. Ross, Walden Banks, Henry M. Smith,
Claude J. Davis, and Bertrand Chrisman.

953. *Ethiopia credit union, Oakland. Articles of incorporation, May, 1928.
4 p. Typew. C-ArS.
    Apparently succeeded the Ethiopia co-operative business association.
The directors were the same with the addition of Robert Green and W. J. D.
Thompson.

954. FERRELL, DENNIS. The organization and development of the Negro insurance business in the United States. Master's thesis, Univ. of
southern Calif., Los Angeles, 1957. v, 104 ℓ.

955. FINNIE, RICHARD, comp. and ed. Marinship; the history of a wartime
shipyard, told by some of the people who helped build the ships,
Sausalito, Calif., 1942-45. S. F., Taylor & Taylor, 1947. 403 p.
illus., ports., maps. C, CHi, CL, CLSU, CO, CRcS, CSdS, CSf, CSfCP,
CSrCL, CU-B, Rocq 4974.
    This large industry attracted many black Southerners who settled
at adjacent Marin City.

956. FLOWERS, CHARLES E. Negro insurance companies ... and why ...
Term paper, Los Angeles city college, Los Angeles [n.d.]. CLGS.

957. *FRANCIS, ROBERT COLEMAN. A survey of Negro business in the San
Francisco bay region. Master's thesis, Univ. of Calif., Berkeley, 1928.
104 ℓ.

958. *Frederick Douglass cooperative realty company of San Francisco.
Articles of incorporation, 1911. Ms. 5 p. C-ArS.
    Directors: W. E. De Claybrook, Miles Beasley, and John Taylor.

959. *GORDON, WALTER ARTHUR, 1894- . The stockholder's right to inspect
books and records of the corporation. Doctoral dissertation (J. D.),
Univ. of Calif., Berkeley, 1922. 28 ℓ.

960. GRANBERG, W. J. "Dream's end," in Crisis, v. 54, Oct., 1947, pp. 298-
300 and 317.

Business and Industry; Cooperatives

The Robert Leonard family moves from San Francisco to Seattle to find success in truck farming.

961. KEEN, HAROLD. "Rochester, Skippy Smith and company; production that knows no color line," in Survey graphic, v. 31, Sept., 1942, pp. 379-82.
"Negro-owned parachute factory in San Diego operated on an interracial basis" - Miriam Matthews.

962. *Lincoln motion picture company. Articles of incorporation, Los Angeles, 1917. 6 p. Typew. C-ArS.
Directors were J. Thomas Smith, Noble M. Johnson, Clarence A. Brooks, Harry Gant, Dudley A. Brooks, and George P. Johnson.

963. *Lower California Mexican land & development co., Los Angeles. Articles of incorporation, 1927. 3 p. Typew. C-ArS.
Directors: Theodore W. Troy, J. N. Littlejohn, Robert W. Head, Hugh E. Macbeth, Andrew J. Roberts, E. Waller, and John R. Scott.

964. Million dollar productions, inc. Articles of incorporation, Los Angeles, 1937. 5 p. Typew. C-ArS.
An interracial motion picture company, the directors of which were Harry M., Leo C., and Frances Popkin, and Ralph Cooper.

965. *Negro alliance grocery company. Articles of incorporation, San Francisco, 1912. [4] p. Printed form filled in. C-ArS.
Directors were John A. Wylley, C. W. H. Nelson, George W. Dorsey, Allen Davis, Walter Freeman, J. M. Thompson, Robert A. Macon, John A. Francis, and Oliver Fountain. The signatures of Kazan Lange, S. E. Barrett, and W. T. Knowles were deleted.

966. *Negro America transcribed, inc. Articles of incorporation, Alameda county, 1949. 4 [2] p. Typew. C-ArS.
To conduct a musical recording business. Directors were Curtis N. Hunt and Enoch A. Woods, Oakland; Woodrow Young, and Ollie T. Hunt, San Francisco; and Thomas L. Berkley, Berkeley.

967. *Negro business association. Articles of incorporation, Los Angeles, 1937. 4 p. Typew. C-ArS.
To promote the business community, civic strength, and "to train and educate Negroes along business and professional lines ..." Directors were B. L. McDowell, S. D. Patterson, Owendell Jackmon, B. L. Hester, George Moore, Leo Draper, Harold Russell, G. E. Bryant, and F. S. Patterson.

968. *Negro business league. Articles of incorporation, Oakland, 1919. 3 p. Typew. C-ArS.
A branch of the National Negro business league. Directors were E. Marshall, J. M. Bridges, H. H. Godfrey, Mrs. Nettie Modeste, L. M. Hudson, Nelson Henderson, Mrs. Ellen Marshall, Mrs. Tobe Williams, H. H. Modeste, W. L. Howard, and S. W. Hawkins.

969. *Negro business men's association of southern California. Articles of incorporation, Los Angeles, 1951. C-ArS.

Business and Industry; Cooperatives

    Directors were Olen Hayes, Jack Lauderdale, D. C. Settle, Herman Hill, Charles Latimore, Ben C. Waller, and Jack Hightower.

970. *Negro consumers' agency.   Articles of incorporation, Los Angeles, 1947. 3 p. Typew. C-ArS.
    "To engage in business as mercantile agents ..." Directors were Caleb Peterson, Leon Hardwick, and John L. Rau.

971. *Negro consumer's and producer's association.   Articles of incorporation, Los Angeles, 1942. 3 p. Typew. C-ArS.
    "To promote the economic welfare of its members by utilizing their united funds ..." Directors were the Rev. Clayton D. Russell, Celestus King, Isaiah Robinson, Theodore Albritton, and Crispus A. Wright.

972. *Negro national political and protective league.   Articles of incorporation, Oakland [192-?]. [3] p. Typew. C-ArS.
    Purposes "are the counseling and advising of business activities among the Negro race... to secure justice ..." Directors were E. Marshall, J. H. Kirk, W. W. Purnell, A. Perry, H. Attaway, Charles Baker, B. F. Harris, H. L. Richardson, B. Marion Jones, and C. Rotero.

973. *Nil desperandum mining co., San Francisco.   Articles of incorporation executed by R. H. Minor, Frederick G. Barbadoes, Richard T. Houston, Robert George Gross, and James P. Dyer, 1863, for a company to engage in mining at Lancha Plana, Amador county. Ms. [4] p. C-ArS.

974. *Pacific coast appeal, pub.   Souvenir guide and reference book, 1904. [S. F.?, 1904]. [25] ℓ. illus., ports.
    Gives some description of business enterprises in the Sacramento and San Joaquin valleys.

975. *People's auditorium co., Los Angeles.   Articles of incorporation, 1916. 3 p. Typew. C-ArS.
    To operate "a public auditorium, office building and moving picture show-house." Directors: William L. Fields, Oliver S. Thomas, Nathaniel R. Harding, Robert M. Mitchell, James H. Eades, Caesar Powell, and Alfred C. Williams.

976. PIERCE, JOSEPH. "Black business in the city," in San Francisco business, v. 4, Apr., 1969, pp. 33-35.

977. Plan of action for challenging times, inc., pub. Black business in San Francisco; the problems and the solutions. S. F., 1968. 63 ℓ. tables. CO.

978. *PORTER, KENNETH WIGGINS. "Negroes and the fur trade," in Minnesota history, v. 15, Dec., 1934, pp. 421-33.
    Activities of York, Edward Rose, James P. Beckwourth, François Duchouquette, John Brazear, Andrew and Dick Green, Cadet Chevallier, and others.

979. Prince Hall bay counties credit union, Alameda county. Articles of incorporation, 1953. Ms. 4 p. C-ArS.

Business and Industry; Cooperatives

Directors: Walter J. Taylor, Harvey Chisom, Dero J. Howard, Joseph Simmons, Clarence White, Charles D. Robinson, and Wilson D. Pitts.

980. *Prince Hall credit union, Riverside. Articles of incorporation, 1952. Ms. 4 p. C-ArS.
     Directors: Starling J. Hopkins, Du Bois McGee, Stanley Y. Beverley, Calvin Edwards, Walter L. McDonald, Ralph H. Johnson, Earl L. Mitchell.

981. *Prince Hall #2 credit union, Los Angeles. Articles of incorporation, 1952. Ms. 4 p. C-ArS.
     Directors: Ellsworth C. Harris, Junior Beane, John Narcisse, Wm. H. Davis, Philip B. Vaughner, Edward A. McCoy, and Joseph E. Dow.

982. *Prince Hall #3 credit union, Vallejo. Articles of incorporation, 1954. Ms. 4 p. C-ArS.
     Directors included Peter Larieau and Lloyd Murray.

983. *Prince Hall #5 credit union, Bakersfield. Articles of incorporation, 1955. Ms. 4 p. C-ArS.
     Directors included William McKinley Wilkerson and Harold Lloyd Matlock, Bakersfield; Verl McGaughy and Edward Antonine St. James, Fresno; and Otis Straughter, Tulare.

984. *Rare ripe gold and silver mining co. Articles of incorporation, Marysville, 1864. Ms. [5] p. C-ArS.
     Directors were Fitz James Vosburg, John R. Johnson, John B. Johnson, J. M. Wiley, and Anderson Devers.

985. "Self-help program stirs a Negro slum; operation bootstrap," in Business week, Mar. 25, 1967, pp. 67-68ff.
     Operation bootstrap, Watts.

986. *SMITH, J. ROBERT. "Vegetable merchant," in Crisis, v. 52, Feb., 1945, pp. 47-48.
     Biography of Edwin Louis Petty, owner of the Petty produce co., Los Angeles.

987. SMITH, WILLIAM THOMAS. "Golden state mutual steps forward," in Crisis, v. 49, May, 1942, pp. 164-65.
     Progress of the Golden state mutual life insurance co., Los Angeles.

988. "A successful business venture," in Colored American magazine, v. 13, Oct., 1907, pp. 269-72.
     An illus. account of the restaurant of William L. Vance and Simon A. Dedrick, Oakland.

989. *THOMPSON, NOAH DAVIS,   -1933. "California: the horn of plenty," in Messenger, v. 6, July, 1924, pp. 215-17 and 220-21.
     Almost entirely about blacks in Los Angeles.

990. THORNDALE, C. WILLIAM. Washington's Green river coal company: 1880-1930. Master's thesis, Univ. of Washington, Seattle, 1965. 168 p.

Business and Industry; Cooperatives

991. "Trans-Bay federal savings and loan association," in <u>Crisis</u>, v. 56, July, 1949, pp. 212 and 220-21.
       The opening of the Association in San Francisco.

992. *United hall assoc., Oakland.   Articles of incorporation, 1914. Application for and decree of dissolution, 1918. Mss. [10] p. C-ArS.
       To erect a meeting hall. Among the 25 directors listed are Geraldine Withers, J. Lincoln Derrick, Hettie B. Tilghman, W. A. Butler, J. M. Bridges, W. W. Dewson, Lawrence Sledge, and William T. Boliver.

993. "An up-to-date haberdasher," in <u>Colored American magazine,</u> v. 14, Apr., 1908, pp. 223-24.
       Illus. article on the men's furnishings store of Henry W. Jones, Oakland.

993a. Washington mining company, Hornitos. [Records, 1869-82]. 2 v., and 1 portfolio. CU-B.
       Consists of financial accounts of a gold and silver mining company in Mariposa county. Moses L. Rogers was superintendent of the mine.

994. *West side investment association, Los Angeles.   Articles of incorporation, 1920. 3 p. Typew. C-ArS.
       Members: George W. Whitley, Susan D. Biggs, Hattie D. Brown, Jesse William Walker, Samuel A. Coffin, Annie H. Taylor, Susie E. Poal, Callie D. Jackson, Minans H. Fletcher, Samuel H. Pool, James A. Ryan, Clara Nelson, Carrie W. Jones, Wilhelmina Anderson, Henry T. Nelson, Elizabeth Harris, Elijah Shamley, Lewis Shamley, Maggie J. Whitley, and Bessie B. Coffin.

995. WILLIAMS, WILLIAM JAMES. Attacking poverty in the Watts area: small business development under the Economic opportunity act of 1964. Doctoral dissertation, Univ. of southern Calif., Los Angeles, 1966. vii, 273 ℓ. illus. (part fold.).

996. *Workingmens' [sic] joint stock association of Portland, Oregon. Articles of incorporation, 1869. Ms. [4] p.
       Organized to operate a real estate business with a capital stock of $50,000 by George P. Riley, Mark A. Bell, William Brown, and Edward S. Simmons.
       Located in Corporation div., Dept. of commerce, Salem, 1967.

CARIBBEAN, HISPANIC AMERICA, BRAZIL

997. BELL, WENDELL. Jamaican leaders; political attitudes in a new nation. Berkeley, Univ. of Calif. press, 1964. xii, 229 p. illus., map, ports. Bibliographical references included in "Notes" (pp. 211-24). CLU, CSf, CU.
       Authored by the director of the Study of elites and nationalism in the West Indies, Univ. of Calif., Los Angeles.

Caribbean, Hispanic America, Brazil

998. BENNETT, J. HARRY, 1911- . The slaves on the Codrington plantations
of Barbados, 1710-1834. Doctoral dissertation, Univ. of Calif., Los
Angeles, 1948. 291 ℓ.

999. BOWSER, FREDERICK PARK. Negro slavery in colonial Peru, 1529-1650.
Doctoral dissertation, Univ. of Calif., Berkeley, 1967. iv, 520 ℓ.

1000. BUNIFF, EGBERT D. N. La historia del Negro en Costa Rica. Master's
thesis, Univ. of southern Calif., Los Angeles, 1951. x, 90 ℓ. map.

1001. DONNER, CHRISTOPHER SILVESTER. The abolition of Negro slavery in
Brazil. Master's thesis, Stanford univ., Stanford, 1940. iv, 180 ℓ.

1002. FARRELL, JOSEPH RICHARD. Nicolas Guillen: poet in search of Cubani-
dad. Thesis, Univ. of southern Calif., Los Angeles, 1968. iii, 255 ℓ.
Blacks in Cuba.

1003. FERGUSON, XENOPHON F. The old plantation regime in Jamaica, 1655-
1834. Master's thesis, Univ. of Calif., Berkeley, 1933. 271 ℓ. illus.,
fold. map.

1004. FRANKEL, BENJAMIN ADAM. Bolívar and the colored castes in Venezuelan
independence. Master's thesis, Univ. of Calif., Berkeley, 1948. iv,
159 ℓ.

1005. GRAY, ELIZABETH BAYNE. The establishment of the Haitian state, 1789-
1820. Master's thesis, Univ. of Calif., Berkeley, 1934.

1006. HELWIG, ADELAIDE BERTA, 1900- . The early history of Barbados and
her influence upon the development of South Carolina. Doctoral dissertation, Univ. of Calif., Berkeley, 1931. xvi, 388 ℓ.

1007. *HUGHES, LLOYD HARRIS. The laws of reform in Mexico, 1856-1859.
Master's thesis, Univ. of Calif., Berkeley, 1936. iii, 224 ℓ.

1008. JOHNSON, LAURENCE. The upward extension of the Canal Zone schools
for native colored children. Doctoral dissertation, Stanford univ.,
Stanford, 1949. 293 ℓ. fold. plans.

1009. KING, JAMES FERGUSON, 1913- . Negro slavery in the viceroyalty of
New Granada. Doctoral dissertation, Univ. of Calif., Berkeley, 1940.
vii, 291 ℓ. map, facsims.

1010. KLINGBERG, FRANK JOSEPH, 1883- , ed. Codrington chronicle; an experiment in Anglican altruism on a Barbados plantation, 1710-1834, ed.
by Frank J. Klingberg. Berkeley, Univ. of Calif. press, 1949. vii,
157 p. front. (Univ. of Calif. publications in history, v. 37). Bibliographical footnotes. CLU, CSf, CU.
     A work produced mainly by staff members of the Univ. of Calif.,
Los Angeles.

1011. ROWLAND, DONALD WINSLOW, 1898- . The Cuban race war of 1912. Master's thesis, Univ. of Calif., Berkeley, 1926. 110 ℓ.

Caribbean, Hispanic America, Brazil

1012. SMITH, ROBERT WORTHINGTON, 1915- . The conflict between planter and
       parliament over the slave laws of Jamaica. Doctoral dissertation, Univ.
       of Calif., Los Angeles, 1942. 318 ℓ.

1013. Sonora, Mexico. Sonora 18th and 19th century parish archival records.
       Occasional references were made to the baptism, marriage, and burial of
       Negro slaves. AzU (microfilm no. 811).

1014. U. S. Works progress administration. California. Slavery in the
       West Indies. The slave colonies of Great Britain or a picture of Negro
       slavery drawn by the colonists themselves. S. F., 1940. 149 p. In 2
       parts. Sutro branch, California state library. Occasional papers.
       Reprint series no. 22. ... P. Radin, ed. C-S, CHi, CSf.

1015. WHITACRE, ROBERT HUNTLEY. The United States and Haiti, 1798-1864.
       Master's thesis, Univ. of Calif., Berkeley, 1936. 93, viii ℓ.

                              CIVIL RIGHTS

1016. ALLEN, ROBERT LEE. A resource unit on civil rights. Master's thesis,
       Univ. of southern Calif., Los Angeles, 1965. ii, 71 ℓ.

1017. American civil liberties union. Northern California branch. ACLU
       1963-66. S. F. [n.d.]. 92 p. CMp.

1018. _____. _____. Annual report. CSt 1944/45; 1948/49-1950/51; 1954/56-
       1963/66.

1019. BABOW, IRVING PAUL, 1913- . A civil rights inventory of San Fran-
       cisco; a study conducted under the auspices of the Council for civic
       unity of San Francisco, with the assistance of a grant from the Columbia
       foundation. Daniel E. Koshland, chairman, Committee on civil rights in-
       ventory. S. F., 1958- . 2 v. CLO, CSd, CSf, CSt, Rocq 8154.
           Part 1. Employment, by Irving Babow and Edward Howden.
           Part 2. San Francisco's housing market--open or closed.

1020. _____. "Discreet discrimination," in Frontier, v. 13, Feb., 1962,
       pp. 7-10.

1021. _____. "Discrimination in places of public accommodation: findings
       of the San Francisco civil rights inventory," in Journal of intergroup
       relations, v. 2, Fall, 1961, pp. 332-41.

1022. _____. "Restrictive practices in public accommodations in a northern
       community," in Phylon, v. 24, Spring, 1963, pp. 5-12.
           Concerns San Francisco.

1023. BAILEY, WILLIAM, and others. "Discrimination is not always overt,"
       in California sun magazine, v. 11, Fall & Winter, 1959-60, pp. 41-44,
       92-93.

Civil Rights

1024. BARTLING, PETER RALPH. The unfinished revolution: the civil rights
movement from 1955 to 1965. Master's thesis, Univ. of southern Calif.,
Los Angeles, 1966. v, 216 ℓ.

1025. BATTISTA, DANIEL JOSEPH. Negro social action organizations and the
civil rights movement. Master's thesis, Sacramento state univ., 1969.
147 ℓ.

1026. Bay area council against discrimination, San Francisco. Council presents plan to end discrimination. [S. F.?, 194-]. [4] p. CU-B.
Plan presented to the San Francisco board of supervisors offered a
program in the areas of police relations, news reporting, education,
employment, housing, and allied fields.

1027. BEAN, BENJAMIN W., vs. Charles, man of color, servant of Lieut. May,
U. S. Navy. Ms. [1] ℓ. C-ArS.
Suit for garnishment in the Sacramento District court, Oct., 1849.

1028. *BELL, HOWARD HOLMAN, 1913- . "Some reform interests of the Negro
during the 1850's as reflected in state conventions," in Phylon, v. 21,
Summer, 1960.
Includes the California conventions.

1029. _____. A survey of the Negro convention movement, 1830-1861 [by]
Howard Holman Bell. N. Y., Arno press and the New York times, 1969.
vii, 298 p. Bibliography: pp. 279-98. CSt.
The author's doctoral dissertation, Northwestern univ., 1953. The
1855 and 1856 California conventions are described, pp. 199-200, 203-04.
Emigration of Californians to Haiti, pp. 251-52.

1030. *BENJAMIN, ROBERT CHARLES O'HARA, 1855-1903. Southern outrages; a
statistical record of lawless doings, by R. C. O. Benjamin ... [L. A.?
c. 1894]. 64 p. DLC.

1031. BERWANGER, EUGENE HARLEY. "The 'black law' question in ante-bellum
California," in Journal of the West, v. 6, Apr., 1967, pp. 205-20.
Concerns the legislation which attempted to prevent Negro residence
in California.

1032. BINDER, CAROL TIMBERLAKE. The theoretical basis of non-violence in
the civil rights movement: Martin Luther King, Jr. Master's thesis,
Univ. of southern Calif., Los Angeles, 1965. iii, 174 ℓ.

1033. BLOUNT, GEORGE WINFIELD. Legislation in the South that has tended to
defeat the purpose of the 15th amendment. Master's thesis, Univ. of
southern Calif., Los Angeles, 1914. 87 p.

1034. *BOND, HORACE MANN, 1904- . "What the San Francisco conference means
to the Negro," in Journal of Negro education, v. 14, Fall, 1945, pp. 627-
30.
The United nations conference.

Civil Rights

1035. BRADEN, ANNE, 1924- . House un-American activities committee: bulwark of segregation. [L. A., National committee to abolish the House un-American activities committee, 1964.] 49 p. illus. C, CHS, CLSU, CSS.

    Charges that the Committee and its counterparts are the fountainheads of charges of subversion against integration movement leaders.

1036. *BROWN, CHARLOTTE L., plaintiff, vs. The North Beach and Mission railroad company, appellant. Mss. 18 pieces, 1 clipping. CHi.

    A successful suit brought before the 12th District court of California charging an ejectment, Apr. 17, 1863. Contains testimony of Mrs. James E. Brown and her daughter, Charlotte L. Brown, later Mrs. James H. Riker, and lists the names of jurors.

1037. *BURDETT, SAMUEL. [A test of lynch law; an expose of mob violence and the courts of hell. Seattle, 1901.]

    The title is taken from the publication announcement at 25¢ in the Seattle Republican, Oct. 11, 1901, p. 3, columns 3-4. In a review, Oct. 18, 1901, p. 1, column 4, the author is described as a retired U. S. veterinary surgeon, and the booklet comprising "a hundred or more pages" is entitled "Lynchings exposed." Although the author's name is given as Burdette, all other available sources show it as Burdett.

1038. CALDWELL, WALLACE F. Use of the administrative process by states to secure civil rights. Doctoral dissertation, Univ. of Washington, Seattle, 1965.

    "The extent to which states have used regulatory and nonregulatory activities to prohibit discrimination." - West, p. 90.

1039. *California. Colored citizens. Proceedings of the California state convention of colored citizens held in Sacramento the 25th, 26th, 27th, & 28th of October, 1865. S. F., Printed at the office of "The Elevator," 1865. 28 p. C, CHi (photocopy), CU-B.

    This fourth state convention, of which Frederick G. Barbadoes was President, requested the franchise, equal citizenship, and educational advantages.

1040. _____. _____. Proceedings of the first state convention of the colored citizens of the state of California. Held at Sacramento, Nov. 20th, 21st, and 22d, in the Colored Methodist church. Sacramento, Democratic state journal print, 1855. 27 p. CHi (photocopy), CU-B (photocopy), NN.

1041. _____. _____. Proceedings of the first state convention[s] of the colored citizens of the State of California, 1855, 1856, [and] 1865. S. F. [R & E research associates, 1969]. 100 p. CLS, CSd, CSS.

    A reprint of the original convention proceedings which were printed separately.

1042. _____. _____. Proceedings of the second annual convention of the colored citizens of the state of California. Held in the city of Sacramento, Dec. 9th, 10th, 11th, and 12th. S. F., J. H. Udell and W. Randall, printers, 1856. 44 p. C, CHi (photocopy), CLU, CSaT (photocopy), CSmH, CU-B.

Civil Rights

1043. California. Dept. of justice. Equal rights under the law; providing
for equal treatment for all citizens regardless of race, religion, color,
national origin or ancestry. [Issued by] Constitutional rights section.
[Sacramento? n.d.]. CFS.

1044. _____. Laws, statutes, etc. The general laws of the state of
California from 1850-1864, inclusive. Compiled by Theodore H. Hittell.
S. F., H. H. Bancroft and co., 1865. 2 v. C, CU.
    Slavery: prohibited by constitution, i, 28 (Article I, 102 of the
State constitution, 1862); not allowed in California, i, 460 (Article I,
3177 of the State constitution, 1862). Mulattoes: marriages between
whites and mulattoes void, ii, 650 (Paragraph 4462, section 3). Negroes:
marriages between whites and Negroes void, ii, 998 (Paragraph 6733,
section 68).

1045. _____. Legislature. Third session.
    To the honorable senate and assembly of the state of California: the
undersigned residents of the county of San Francisco, state of California,
pray your honorable body to repeal so much of the third paragraph ...
of an act entitled "An act to regulate proceedings in civil cases in the
courts of justice in this state, passed April 29, 1851, as relates to
Negroes." Also, to repeal ... "An act concerning crimes and punishments,
passed April 16, 1850, as relates to Negroes and Mulattoes ..." C-ArS.
    Ms. petition received Mar. 10, 1852. 15 p. Two columns of signa-
tures, mainly of white people.
    Ms. petition received Mar. 22, 1852. 9 p. Two columns of signatures,
mainly of black people, including Henry C. Cornish, Mark J. Matheson,
Garrett A. Cantine, William H. Byrd, J. Thomas Ricks, William Queen,
William Wright, Aaron White, Benjamin W. Judah, H. R. Holland, James M.
Reese, Michael Howard, Daniel Seales, James Riker, William Gross,
Solomon Peneton, Robert Tilghman, Aaron Cisco, William H. Hamilton,
George M. Wysham, Marshall Sedgwick, Wellington Delaney Moses, William H.
Harper, Griffin Dobson, Riley Fields, John Cromwell, William Washington,
Samuel D. Burris, John G. Pallier, William Gordon, Marcus A. Bell, and
many others.
    Concerns testimony in judicial cases.

1046. _____. _____. Eighth session. [Petition from Amador county residents advocating the right of Negro testimony in judicial cases.] Ms.
[6] p. Two columns of signatures. C-ArS.
    Petition received Feb. 26, 1857.

1047. _____. _____. _____. [Petition from Butte county residents advocating the right of Negro testimony in judicial cases.] Ms. [6] p.
Two columns of signatures. C-ArS.
    Petition received Feb. 18, 1857.

1048. _____. _____. _____. [Petition from Sacramento county residents
advocating the right of Negro testimony in judicial cases.] Ms. [11] p.
Two columns of signatures. C-ArS.
    Petition received Feb. 18, 1857.

Civil Rights

1049. ____. ____. ____. [Petition from Shasta county residents advo-
cating the right of Negro testimony in judicial cases.] Ms. [8] p.
Two columns of signatures. C-ArS.
   Petition received Feb. 18, 1857.

1050. ____. ____. ____. [Petition from Siskiyou county residents ad-
vocating the right of Negro testimony in judicial cases.] Ms. [2] p.
Two columns of signatures. C-ArS.
   Petition received Feb. 25, 1857.

1051. ____. ____. ____. [Petition from Yuba county residents advocating
the right of Negro testimony in judicial cases.] Ms. [7] p. Two
columns of Caucasian and black signatures. C-ArS.
   Petition received Feb. 26, 1857.

1052. ____. ____. ____. [Petition from Amador county residents advo-
cating the right of Negro testimony in judicial cases.] Ms. [7] p.
One column of signatures. C-ArS.
   Petition received Feb. 1, 1858.

1053. ____. ____. ____. [Petition from El Dorado county residents ad-
vocating the right of Negro testimony in judicial cases.] Ms. [8] p.
Two columns of signatures. C-ArS.
   Petition received Feb. 3, 1858.

1054. ____. ____. ____. [Petition from Mariposa county residents ad-
vocating the right of Negro testimony in judicial cases.] Ms. [4] p.
Two columns of signatures. C-Ars.
   Petition received Feb. 1, 1858.

1055. ____. ____. ____. [Petition from Nevada county residents advo-
cating the right of Negro testimony in judicial cases.] Ms. [5] p.
Two columns of signatures. C-ArS.
   Petition received Feb. 19, 1858.
   Contains signatures of E. G. Waite, Simon Rosenthal, David Belden,
James Churchman, Alonzo Delano, A. B. Dibble, Warren B. Ewer, Josiah
Royce, W. P. Goldsmith, and many others.

1056. ____. ____. ____. [Petition from Placer county residents advo-
cating the right of Negro testimony in judicial cases.] Ms. [3] p.
Two columns of signatures. C-ArS.
   Petition received Feb. 2, 1858.

1057. ____. ____. ____. [Petition from Sacramento county residents
advocating the right of Negro testimony in judicial cases.] Ms. [8] p.
Two columns of signatures. C-ArS.
   Petition received Feb. 19, 1858.
   Contains signatures of B. F. Folger, W. P. Fuller, C. H. Holbrook,
George W. Swinerton, Jacob Shew, John F. Morse, N. A. Haven Ball, Samuel
Kyburz, George Cadwalader, Leland Stanford, Abraham D. Starr, and others.

1058. ____. ____. ____. [Petition from San Francisco residents advocating the right of Negro testimony in judicial cases.] Ms. [18] p.

Civil Rights

Two columns of mainly Caucasian signatures. C-ArS.
Petition received Feb. 19, 1858.
Contains signatures of John H. Titcomb, Henry P. Coon, Francis J.
Lippett, David O. Shattuck, William Hooper, Ferdinand Vassault, Julius K.
Rose, Epes Ellery, John H. Still, Matthias Gray, Milo Calkin, William
Neely Thompson, Daniel Gibb, Alexander Forbes, John Archbald, Henry L.
Dodge, Thomas Day, Annis Merrill, Daniel Norcross, H. Channing Beals,
Edward Bosqui, Edward Vischer, William Tecumseh Sherman, Frederick
Billings, Frederick A. Woodworth, James N. Olney, Bolton, Barron &
company, Fletcher M. Haight, Henry Gibbons, William L. Duncan, Thomas
Sim King, Louis McLane, Albert G. Randall, James Laidley, Christian O.
Gerberding, Jacob Bacon, Theodore H., and John S. Hittell, Abel Whitton,
Macondray & company, Jacob Underhill, Levi Parsons, John H. Brodt, William
Rabé, George C. Lawrence, Thomas Houseworth, Hiram G. Bloomer, Joseph
Haine, Charles T. Blake, James J. Ayers, Albert Miller, Horace W. Car-
pentier, William F. Herrick, David Burbank, George A. Snook, Charles E.
Holbrook, Charles F. Robbins, J. B. Bidleman, Peter W. Cassey, Peter
Lester, Frank M. Pixley, Stanford Brothers, and many others.

1059. _____. _____. _____. [Petition from Sierra county residents advo-
cating the right of Negro testimony in judicial cases.] Ms. [3] p.
One column of signatures. C-ArS.
Petition received Feb. 1, 1858.

1060. _____. _____. _____. [Petition from Yuba county residents advocating
the right of Negro testimony in judicial cases.] Ms. [2] p. Two
columns of signatures. C-ArS.
Petition received Feb. 1, 1858.

1061. _____. _____. Assembly. Eighth session. Bill no. 240, "An act
concerning the testimony of children and other than white persons,"
1857. Ms. [4] p. C-ArS.
"Negroes or persons having one-third or more of African blood ...
shall be admissable as witnesses in any action when it shall appeal to
the satisfaction of the court that they comprehend the responsibility of
an oath and the crime of perjury, and that they are of capable mind ...
but their testimony shall not be received as conclusive evidence ...
except so far as the same may be confirmed by circumstantial evidence or
corroborated by the testimony of other witnesses ..."

1062. _____. _____. Senate. Eighth session. Bill no. 31, "An act concerning the testimony of children and other than white persons," 1857.
Ms. [2] p. C-ArS.

1063. _____. _____. _____. _____. Judiciary committee. Report on "a
petition from the citizens of El Dorado county relative to the repeal of
all laws in this state prohibiting Negros [sic] and Mulattos [sic] from
giving testimony against white persons," 1858. Ms. [2] p. C-ArS.

1064. _____. _____. _____. Eighteenth session. Journal of the Senate
during the eighteenth session ... Sacramento, State print., 1870.
904 p. C, C-ArS, CLU, CSf, CSmH, CU, NUC, pre-1956.
Concurrent and joint resolutions opposing adoption of the fifteenth

Civil Rights

U. S. constitutional amendment, pp. 184, 198-99. Introduced by John S. Hager and William M. Gwin.

1065. CASAL, JAMES. Telephone study of discrimination in accommodation within the San Diego area, by James Casal, Jr. and others, under the direction of Thomas O. McJunkins. San Diego, Dept. of sociology, San Diego state univ., 1967. 65 ℓ. CSd, CSdS.

1066. CAUGHEY, LAREE. "Los Angeles: no Birmingham west," in Frontier, v. 14, July, 1963, pp. 3-4.

1067. "Civil rights roundtable," in Seattle magazine, v. 3, Nov., 1966, pp. 12-16, 47-51.
Panel discussion by James C. Meredith and West coast civil-rights advocates, mainly concerning Seattle.

1068. CLARKE, MAXINE ADAMS. A survey of social right literature pertaining to civil rights for Negroes. Master's thesis, Univ. of southern Calif., Los Angeles, 1963. 106 ℓ.

1069. Communist party of the United States of America. California. Memorandum [on] the struggle for Negro rights and the struggle against white chauvinism. S. F., 1948. 8 ℓ. Mimeo. CU-B.

1070. _____. _____. State educational commission. The struggle against white chauvinism. S. F., 1947. 6 p. CU-B.

1071. _____. _____. State Negro commission. State conference on Negro work and fight for Negro rights; main report (Prepared by State Negro commission). [n.p., 1948]. 3 [2] p. Mimeo. CU-B.

1072. _____. San Francisco. Education dept. An introduction to the Communist party; outline for new members' class. S. F., 1949. 1 v. (v.p.). CU-B.
Places occasional emphasis on Negro rights.

1073. "Congressional authority to restrict the use of literacy tests," in California law review, v. 50, May, 1962, pp. 265-82.

1074. "Discrimination in places of public accommodation: finding of the San Francisco civil rights inventory," in Journal of intergroup relations, v. 2, Autumn, 1961, pp. 332-41.

1075. DRAPER, HAROLD. Jim crow in Los Angeles. [L. A.] Workers party [1946]. 22 p. illus. DHU, NN.

1076. ELLIS, JUDITH, 1938- . The attitudes of white liberals to the Negro movement for civil rights. Doctoral dissertation, Univ. of Calif., Los Angeles, 1969.

1077. ENDORE, SAMUEL GUY, 1901- . A walk in Alabama [by] Guy Endore; a talk given on April 6, 1965 to the School of library science, UCLA. [L. A., Univ. of Calif., 1965]. [17] ℓ. Mimeo. CLU (Spec. Coll.).
The Selma freedom march.

Civil Rights

1078. *FISHER, JAMES ADOLPHUS. "The struggle for Negro testimony in California, 1851-1863," in Southern California quarterly, v. 51, Dec., 1969, pp. 313-24.

1079. FLEISHMAN, STANLEY, and SAM ROSENWEIN. The new civil rights act: what it means to you! L. A., Blackstone book co., 1964. 191 p. DLC.

1080. FRIIS, LEO J. "At the bar: 'segregation'," in California herald, v. 12, Mar., 1965, pp. 2, 15.

1081. GERNER, HENRY L. A study of the Freedom riders with particular emphasis upon three dimensions: dogmatism, value-orientation, and religiosity. Doctoral dissertation, Pacific school of religion, Berkeley, 1963.

1082. GOODWIN, CARDINAL LEONIDAS. The establishment of state government in California, 1846-1850. N. Y., Macmillan, 1914. 359 p. CHi, CSd, CSf, CU-B, CU-SB, Rocq 5699.
    The free Negro question in the Constitutional convention, 1849, pp. 110-32; in Peter H. Burnett's annual message as first governor, pp. 266-67, and in the first legislature, pp. 318-23.

1083. HAGER, JOHN SHARPENSTEIN, 1818-1890. Fifteenth amendment to Constitution. Speech of Hon. John S. Hager, of San Francisco, in the Senate of California, January 28th, 1870, on Senator Hager's joint resolution to reject the fifteenth amendment to the Constitution of the United States. [n.p., 1870]. 14 p. CU.

1084. *HENINGBURG, ALPHONSE M. "What the Urban league expects for all races as a result of the San Francisco conference," in Opportunity, v. 23, July-Sept., 1945, p. 123.
    The United nations conference.

1085. HOPKINS, DONALD. "Reflections on 'civil rights in a cracker barrel'," in San Francisco, v. 8, Nov., 1966, pp. 43, 67.

1086. *HUBBARD, JOHN PURLEY. Why lynching must go, by J. P. Hubbard, minister, Beth Eden Baptist church, Oakland, California ... [Oakland?, 193-?]. 8 p. port. COEB.

1087. HUGHES, RUTH CAROL. Education implications of civil rights practices with minority groups in a local community. Master's thesis, Stanford univ., Stanford, 1948. 127 ℓ. tables.

1088. KEEN, HAROLD. "De facto segregation in San Diego," in San Diego and Point magazine, v. 18, Aug., 1966, pp. 53-54.

1089. KONVITZ, MILTON RIDVAS, 1908- . A century of civil rights by Milton R. Konvitz. With a study of state law against discrimination, by Theodore Leskes. N. Y., Columbia univ. press, 1961. viii, 293 p. "Table of statutes": pp. [278]-80. Bibliographic footnotes. CCovB, CFS, CKenM, CNoS, CSbS, CSdS, CSfGG, CSto, CU-SC.
    Describes civil rights statutes in California, Colorado, Oregon and Washington.

Civil Rights

1090. LANEY, L. M. "State segregation laws and judicial courage," in
   Arizona law review, v. 1, Spring, 1959, p. 102.

1091. LAPP, RUDOLPH MATTHEW, 1915- . "Negro rights activities in gold rush
   California." [n.p., 1964]. 29 ℓ. Bibliographical notes. CU-B.
      Photocopy of typescript.

1092. _____. "Negro rights activities in gold rush California," in
   California historical society quarterly, v. 45, Mar., 1966, pp. 3-20.

1093. LLOYD, KENT MURDOCK. State FEPC public education program; a comparative civil rights study, by Kent M. Lloyd. Prepared under the supervision of Prof. Nathan Grundstein. Olympia, State research council,
   1957. 200 ℓ. tables. Bibliography: ℓ. 192-200. CSt.

1094. LONG, GEORGE. "How Albuquerque got its civil rights ordinance," in
   Crisis, v. 60, Nov., 1953, pp. 521-24.

1095. Los Angeles committee for fair play in bowling. American bowling
   congress drops Caucasian rule. [L. A., 1950]. 7 p. Mimeo. CU-B.
   (California federation for civic unity collection).
      A history of the fight to eliminate racial discrimination from
   bowling.

1096. MC CULLOUGH, JOHN G. Letter to George S. Evans, Adjutant general of
   California, Dec. 20, 1864. Ms. [6] p. C-ArS.
      McCullough, as Attorney general of California, gives his opinion that
   "cooks of African descent ... are entitled to receive from the State the
   same bounties as white volunteers." He also states that "While the
   American of Caucasian descent is fighting for the preservation of our
   national life and the maintenance of republican liberty, the Africo-
   American is fighting for that national life and for both political and
   personal freedom."

1097. MC NICHOLS, STEVEN E., 1939- . The Houston freedom ride. L. A.,
   1964. v, 404 ℓ. Typew. CLU.
      Transcript of an interview completed under the auspices of the UCLA
   Oral history program. UCLA student Steven McNichols discusses his participation in the 1961 Houston freedom ride, conditions in Texas, and the
   CORE movement in general.

1098. _____. Houston in retrospect. L. A., 1965. iii, 43 ℓ. Typew. CLU.
      Transcript of an interview completed under the auspices of the UCLA
   Oral history program. Reflections of McNichols concerning his return to
   Houston in 1962, after his participation in the 1961 freedom ride to
   Houston.

1099. Marin county. Board of supervisors. Resolution no. 7893: resolution
   establishing a Human rights commission; providing the responsibilities
   thereof and appointing initial members thereto. [San Rafael?] 1964.
   2 ℓ. CO.

Civil Rights

1100. *MILLER, LOREN R., 1903-1967. The petitioners; the story of the
Supreme court of the United States and the Negro. N. Y., Random house,
c1966. xv, 461 p. Bibliographical references included in "Notes":
pp. [435]-55. Available in many libraries.
  "This is a full chronicle of what the Supreme court has said and done
in respect of the rights of Negroes, slave and free, between 1789 and
1965 ..." The author was a prominent Los Angeles jurist and publisher.

1101. MINKE, KARL ALFRED. Negro discrimination in Stockton. [Stockton,
ca. 1960]. 15 p. Typew. CSto.

1102. Modesto. Human rights commission. Final report. Modesto, 1964.
25 p. CO.

1103. MOTHERSHEAD, HARMON. "Negro rights in Colorado territory, 1859-1867,"
in Colorado magazine, v. 40, 1963, pp. 212-23.

1104. National association for the advancement of colored people. Portland
branch. Civil rights bill for the state of Oregon: equal rights in
places of public accommodation, resort or amusement, and in the employment of labor. [Portland?]. 1945. 3 p. CLSU.

1105. _____. _____. Facts in the Robert Folkes case. [n.p., n.d.] 30 p.
CLSU.

1106. "Northern California, Jim Crow or cosmopolitan?", in Black world,
v. 9, Feb., 1951, pp. 94-97.

1107. Oregon. Legislative assembly. House. [House bills. Fourth regular
session. Salem, State print., 1866]. 2 p. Or-Ar, OrU (photocopy),
Belknap 884.
  No. 27. To amend ... "An act relating to poll tax of Negroes,
Chinamen, Kanakas and Mulattoes ..."

1108. PARSONS, EDGAR W. "California faces crucial civil rights test," in
Phi delta kappan, Oct., 1964.

1109. PECK, JAMES. "The proof of the pudding," in Crisis, v. 56, Nov.,
1949, pp. 292-94 and 355.
  The Committee of racial equality fights Jim Crow at the Bimini baths,
Los Angeles.

1110. People of the state of California, appellants, vs. George Washington,
respondent. Mss. [13] p. C-ArS.
  Washington, a native of Virginia, was charged with the robbery of a
Chinese in Nevada City, Nov. 8, 1867. He was there discharged on the
basis of his free U. S. birth as opposed to the witnesses against him
who were foreign-born Chinese. Appealed to the California Supreme court.

1111. _____. Brief for the people. Jo Hamilton, attorney general. Sacramento, State print.. 1867. No. 1531 in the Supreme court of the state
of California. 16 p. C-ArS.

Civil Rights

1112. People vs. James Howard, appellant. On appeal to the Supreme court
from the Court of sessions of the county of Sacramento. C. Cole,
District attorney, for respondents; J. W. Coffroth, for appellant. Ms.
[13] ℓ. Supreme court case no. 2906, 1860. C-ArS.
   Howard, a Caucasian, was charged with stealing a gold watch in 1859
from Albert Grubbs, a Negro, and was sentenced to two years in prison.
The sentence was set aside on the grounds that Grubbs was a Negro which
made his testimony inadmissable.

1113. People vs. Louis Raines, alias Dutch Louie, for assault on Jackson
Jourdan, 1850. Ms. [3] p. C-ArS.
   The defendant was arrested on July 20, 1850, brought before the
Sacramento Justice's court, but the complainant and his witness being
black, the defendant was "discharged for want of witnesses."

1114. People vs. William H. Potter in Sacramento dist. court. Charge of
grand larceny by Sarah Carroll, 1850. Ms., 4 p. C-ArS.
   "Defendant discharged, he proving himself a white man & none but
colored testimony against him. Charles Sackett, Judge."

1115. *Pleasant, John J., and Mary E., his wife, respondents, vs. The North
Beach and mission rail road company, appellant. Ms. [15] p. C-ArS.

1116. *Pleasants [i.e., Pleasant], John J., and Mary E. (his wife),
respondents, vs. the North Beach and mission rail road co., appellant.
Appellant's point in reply. [S. F.?], 1868. C-ArS.
   Broadside.

1117. _____. Brief for the appellant. J. G. McCullough, of counsel for
the appellant. S. F., Wade & co., printers [1867]. 19 p. Case no. 1380
in the Supreme court of the state of California. C-ArS.
   The appellant refused to stop upon twice being summoned by the
plaintiff to do so. The plaintiff, then in the company of Mrs. Selim E.
Woodworth, charged that employees of the defendant were required to
refuse to stop the cars to allow Negroes to board and therefore sued for
$500 damages.

1118. _____. Brief of respondents. Geo. W. Tyler, attorney for respondents.
S. F., Geo. W. Stevens, printer [1868?]. 7 p. C-ArS.

1119. _____. Transcript on appeal. W. W. Crane, Jr., for appellant. G. W.
Tyler, for respondents. S. F., Alta California printing house, 1867.
28 p. C-ArS.

1120. RECORD, WILSON, 1916-   , ed. Little Rock, U. S. A.; selected and
edited by Wilson Record and Jane Cassels Record. S. F., Chandler pub.
co. [1960]. 338 p. illus. CFS, CHS, CLSU, CNoS, CSbS, CSdS, CSluSP,
CSmH, CU, CU-A.

1121. Regan, John T., plaintiff, vs. Cameron King, registrar of the city
and county of San Francisco, defendant. Oral argument of U. S. Webb ...
[of] Webb, Webb & Olds ... attorneys for plaintiff. [S. F., Pernau-Walsh

Civil Rights

print. co., 193-?]. 23 p. CU-B.
    At head of title: In the Southern division of the United States district court in and for the Northern district of California, no. 22, 178. CU-B.
    Involves the 14th amendment and the citizenship of non-whites born in the United States.

1122. RIGBY, GERALD. Little Rock and desegregation: an analysis of the political implementation of legal decision. Doctoral dissertation, Univ. of Calif., Los Angeles, 1960. 472 ℓ.

1123. San Francisco. Human rights commission. Annual report. 1965 - . CO.

1124. _____. _____. A point of acceleration, the San Francisco situation: an action inventory. S. F., 1968. 10 ℓ. CO, CSf.

1125. "San Francisco, California, hotels," in Crisis, v. 63, May, 1956, pp. 270-72.

1126. San Francisco theological seminary, San Anselmo. [Documents related to the participation of the San Francisco theological seminary in the Selma, Ala. march in March, 1965]. San Anselmo, 1965. CSaT.

1127. SCHEVILLE, JAMES. "Notes on a march up Market street," in Review of general semantics, v. 21, June, 1964, pp. 202-10.
    A San Francisco state univ. poet describes a civil rights march.

1128. SHERWOOD, FRANK PERSONS, 1920- . The mayor and the fire chief; the fight over integrating the Los Angeles fire department [by] Frank P. Sherwood and Beatrice Markey. University, Ala., Pub. for the I[nter-university] C[ase] P[rogram] by the Univ. of Alabama press [c1959]. 24 p. illus. CLSU, CNoS, CSfSt, CSmH, CU, Rocq 4384.

1129. SILK, KENNETH R. "Application of exhaustion of state remedies to anti-NAACP legislation," in Southern California law review, v. 33, Fall, 1959, pp. 82-87.

1130. SNYDER, DAVID L. Negro civil rights in California: 1850. [Sacramento] Sacramento book collectors club, 1969. [6] ℓ. illus., facsims. "Special publication no. 10. Three hundred copies were printed by Roger Levenson at the Tamalpais press ..." CHi, CSS.

    The case of People vs. W[illiam] H. Potter before a Sacramento county Justice's court in which the complainant, Sarah J. Carroll, accused the defendant of grand larceny. The case was dismissed on the grounds that "Defendant discharged, he proving himself a white man & none but Colored testimony against him."

1131. SOBEL, LESTER A., ed. Civil rights, 1960-66, ed. by Lester A. Sobel. N. Y., Facts on file, inc. [1967]. xii, 504 p. CNoS, CSf, CU-I.
    Contains information about conditions in various California cities.

Civil Rights

1132. STEFFGEN, KENT H. The bondage of the free, by Kent H. Steffgen. Berkeley, Vanguard books [1966]. CSt, NUC, 1963-67.

1133. *Turner, Emma Jane, respondent, vs. North beach and mission railroad company, appellant. Appellant's brief in reply. [S. F.?, 1867]. 2 p. "No. 1379 in the Supreme court of the state of California." C-ArS.
    An ejectment case.

1134. ____. Brief for appellant. W. W. Crane, Jr., for appellant. S. F., Alta California printing house, 1867. 17 p. C-ArS.

1135. ____. [Statement of respondent] W. C. Burnett, attorney for respondent. S. F., Towne & Bacon, 1867. 5 p. C-ArS.

1136. ____. Transcript on appeal. W. W. Crane, Jr., for appellant. W. C. Burnett, for respondent. S. F., Alta California printing house, 1867. 40 p. C-ArS.

1137. U. S. Commission on civil rights. The 50 states report submitted to the Commission on civil rights by the State advisory committees, 1961. [Washington, D. C., Govt. print., 1961]. vi, 687 p. illus., maps. CEcaC, CFS, CKenM, CL, CLSU, CSdS, CSf, CS1uSP, CU-A.
    Reports on the rights of minority groups as they existed in each of the states.

1138. ____. ____. Hearings before the United States commission on civil rights. Hearings held in Los Angeles, California, January 25, 1960, January 26, 1960; San Francisco, California, January 27, 1960, January 28, 1960. Washington, D. C., Govt. print., 1960. v, 902 p. illus., maps (part fold.), ports. CL, CLSU, CNoS, CU.

1139. ____. ____. Hearings before the United States commission on civil rights. Hearing held in San Francisco, California, May 1-3, 1967 and Oakland, California, May 4-6, 1967. [Washington, D. C., Govt. print., 1967]. vi, 1,090 p. illus. CFS, CL, CLSU, CNoS, CSaT, CSfCiC, CS1uSP.

1140. ____. ____. Hearings before the United States commission on civil rights, Phoenix, Arizona, Feb. 3, 1962. [Washington, D. C., Govt. print., 1962]. 149 p. fold. map. AzU, CFS, CL.

1141. ____. ____. State advisory committees division. Reports on apprenticeship by the Advisory committees to the United States commission on civil rights in California, Connecticut, District of Columbia, Florida, Maryland, New Jersey, New York, Tennessee, and Wisconsin. [Washington, D. C.?] 1964. CFS.

1142. ____. ____. California advisory committee. Report. Washington, D. C. [196-?]. CL (1961, 1963).

1143. VINES, DWIGHT DELBERT. The impact of Title VII of the 1964 Civil rights law on personnel policies and practices. Doctoral dissertation, Univ. of Colorado, Boulder, 1967. 408 ℓ.

Civil Rights

1144. *WALTON, SIDNEY F., 1934- . "Census 70: blueprint for repression,"
in The black scholar, v. 1, Mar., 1970, pp. 28-34.
Authored by a San Francisco bay area educator.

1145. Washington. State board against discrimination. [Annual] report.
1949- . CSt-Law 1949+; CU 1950-57, 1961-62+; Wa 1949+; WaU 1953-62,
1966-67.
Some volumes also have distinctive titles: 1957, A new era; equal
opportunity for all.-1958, Ten years of civil rights. 1963-65 not published.

1146. _____. _____. Digest of the Washington state law against discrimination. 1961. Wa.

1147. _____. _____. Hats in the ring. [Olympia?, 1952]. 20 p. WaU.

1148. _____. _____. Semi-annual report. CU Je, 1950-Ja, 1954 (2d-9th);
WaU 1949-53.

1149. _____. _____. Your rights are protected by the state of Washington.
1967. Wa.

1150. Washington (territory). Legislative assembly. House of representatives. Journal ... second session ... begun December 4, 1854. Olympia,
1855. WaU.
Act to prevent Negroes and mulattoes from living in Washington
territory indefinitely postponed, p. 44.

1151. _____. _____. _____. Journal ... eighth session ... begun December
30, 1860. Olympia, 1861. WaU.
House memorial to allow Jackson Jordan, a free mulatto, the benefit
of the pre-emption law, p. 352.

1152. WEAVER, VALERIE WHITTEMORE. The Civil rights act of 1875: reactions
and enforcement. Master's thesis, Univ. of Calif., Berkeley, 1966.
86 ℓ.

1153. WEINBERGER, ANDREW D. Freedom and protection. S. F., Chandler pub.
co., 1962. 180 p.
"A study of the Bill of rights in the form of abridged legal opinions
describing its status and wide application." - Journal of Negro education.

1154. WESTIN, ALAN F. Freedom now! The civil rights struggle in America.
N. Y., Basic books, 1964. 346 p. C.
An anthology which includes "Freedom now -- but what then?" and
"Negroes and the police in Los Angeles," by Loren Miller. Also contains
"A selected bibliography of the civil rights struggle."

1155. *WILLIAMS, FRANKLIN H "California's new civil rights tool," in
Christian century, v. 77, June 15, 1960, pp. 720-21.
Constitutional rights section in State justice department.

Civil Rights

1156. *WITHERS, ZACHARY. Our inheritance. By Z. Withers, author of "Slavery days." Oakland, Tribune pub. co., 1909. 104 p. port. CHi, CU-B.
     "This essay ... argues for the rights of my people before an unbiased and just American public."

1157. ZIMPEL, LLOYD. "Where civil rights start," in Frontier, v. 16, Nov., 1964, pp. 20-21.

COLONIZATION, MIGRATION AND POPULATION STATISTICS

1158. ADKINS, W. B. The role of black men and women in Americanizing the western frontier. Term paper, Univ. of the Pacific, Stockton [n.d.]. CStoC.

1159. Afro-American colonization company of Mexico.* Articles of incorporation, San Diego, 1891. [4] p. Typew. C-ArS.
     A colonization company, the directors of which were James M. Fowler, M. D. Allen, Samuel Edmonston, James Johnson, L. Montgomery, Benjamin Caddle, Alexander Cox, W. H. Hamilton, and Thomas Grigly, San Diego; and Ed. Wilson, Coronado Beach.

1160. [Allensworth], in Tulares, June, 1956, p. 4.
     A short description of the black settlement at Allensworth in the publication of the Tulare county historical society, Visalia.

1161. The Allensworth story; souvenir program celebration and dedication, October 6, 1968. [Allensworth?, 1968]. [19] ℓ. illus. Mimeo. CViCL.

1162. BOYD, WILLIS DOLMOND, 1924- . Negro colonization in the national crisis, 1860-1870. Doctoral dissertation, Univ. of Calif., Los Angeles, 1953. 513 ℓ.

1163. California. Legislature. Second session. Journals of the legislature of the State of California at its second session held at the city of San Jose ... [San Jose] State print., 1851. 1,865 p. C, C-ArS, CLU, CSmH, CU, NUC, pre-1956.
     Contains the annual message of Gov. Peter Burnett which advocates the exclusion of free Negroes from California, pp. 19-21.

1164. _____. _____. Assembly. Eighth session. Bill no. 411, "An act to restrict and prevent the emigration to and residence in this state by Negroes and Mulattoes," 1857. Ms. [16] p. C-ArS.

1165. _____. _____. _____. Eighth session. Journal of the eighth session of the Assembly ... Sacramento, State print., 1857. 992 p. C, C-ArS, CLU, CSf, CSmH, CU, NUC, pre-1956.
     Contains a resolution concerning the immigration of Negroes and mulattoes to California, p. 720.

Colonization, Migration and Population Statistics

1166. _____. _____. _____. Ninth session. Bill no. 395, "An act to restrict and prevent the immigration to and residence in this state of Negroes and Mulattoes," 1858. Ms. 14 p. C-ArS.

1167. _____. _____. _____. Tenth session. Journal of the House of assembly of California ... Sacramento, State print., 1859. 914 p. C, C-ArS, CLU, CSf, CSmH, CU, NUC, pre-1956.
    A resolution tabled concerning prevention of immigration of Chinese, Mongolians, and free Negroes into California, pp. 154-55.

1168. _____. _____. Senate. Fourth session. Document no. 14 ... Governor's message; and report of the Secretary of state on the census of 1852, of the state of California. 58 p. C, CLU, CSf, CSfL, CSmH, CU, NUC, pre-1956.
    Lists Negro population totals by county. This Document is usually bound as an Appendix to the Journal of the Senate, 1853.

1169. _____. _____. _____. 1970. Resolution relative to the town of Allensworth, by Mervyn M. Dymally of the twenty-ninth senatorial district. [Sacramento, 1970]. Broadside.

    "Senate resolution no. 100 read and unanimously adopted March 9, 1970." Concerns the establishment of Allensworth as a state historic park.

1170. California commission of immigration and housing. Community survey made in Los Angeles city. S. F. [1919?]. 74 p. tables. NN (film).

1171. CARLSON, OLIVER, 1899- . "The Negro moves west," in Fortnight, v. 17, Oct. 6, 1954, pp. 23-26.

1172. CLAWSON, MARION. "What it means to be a Californian," in California historical society quarterly, v. 24, June, 1945, pp. 139-61.
    Describes migration to California, 1870-1945, and contains information on racial groups.

1173. *COLBERT, ROBERT E. "The attitude of older Negro residents toward recent Negro migrants in the Pacific northwest," in Journal of Negro education, v. 15, Fall, 1946, pp. 695-703.

1174. *Colored colonization association of Fresno county, California. Articles of incorporation, 1891. Ms. [5] p. C-ArS.
    Organized to purchase land for purposes of subdivision. Directors were A. F. Holland, Oakland; Frank A. Alexander, San Francisco; E. H. Brown, and J. G. Sanford, Fresno; and A. J. Wallace, Anthony Lilly, and Simon Williams, Waco, Texas.

1175. *Colored colonization company. Articles of incorporation, San Diego, 1893. Ms. [4] p. C-ArS.
    Organized to acquire and operate farm lands, to enter into any other remunerative activity thereon, and to enter into trade with Mexico, Central America, and other countries. Signed by Ed Wilson, M. D. Allen, Benjamin Caddle, James M. Fowler, A. L. Allen, A. B. Hollowdyce, Alex Cox, L. Montgomery, James Johnson, Solomon Johnson, and Samuel Edmoston.

Colonization, Migration and Population Statistics

1176. *Colored Mexican colonization company. Articles of incorporation, San Diego, 1891. Ms. [4] p. C-ArS.
Organized to acquire, colonize, and operate farming lands in Mexico and to do whatever else may be thought necessary. Signed by M. D. Allen, Samuel Edmoston, Benjamin Caddle, James M. Fowler, Thomas Gregory, Walker Davis, James Johnson, W. H. Hamilton, A. L. Allen, and L. Montgomery.

1177. COX, EARNEST SEVIER. Lincoln's Negro policy. [2d ed.] L. A., Noontide press, 1968. 64 p. illus., ports. CL, CNoS.
A reprint of the 1938 ed. as a memorial to the author. The first ed. of 36 p. is held by the New York public library's Schomburg collection.

1178. "Deerfield, Colorado, a Negro ghost town in Weed county," in Negro history bulletin, v. 27, Nov., 1963, pp. 38-39.

1179. DE GRAAF, LAWRENCE BROOKS. Negro migration to Los Angeles, 1930 to 1950. Doctoral dissertation, Univ. of Calif., Los Angeles, 1962. 358 ℓ. illus.

1180. DOUGLAS, JESSE S. "Origins of the population of Oregon in 1850," in Pacific northwest quarterly, v. 41, Apr., 1950, pp. 95-108.
Contains tables showing number of Negro residents by Oregon county and by state of birth.

1181. DUNIWAY, DAVID CUSHING. The relation of the United States government to the origin and foundation of Liberia. Master's thesis, Univ. of Calif., Berkeley, 1934. 161 ℓ.

1181a. Federal writers' project. Oakland. [Monographs prepared for a Documentary history of migratory farm labor], 1938. 1 box containing 17 monographs. CU-B.
Includes one monograph on "Negroes in California agriculture."

1182. FOLEY, JAMES. The Allensworth story, by James Foley, in Souvenir program, celebration & dedication, Oct. 6, 1968, of the Allensworth water system, Allensworth membership water co. 20 p. Typew. CViCL.

1183. *FRANCE, EDWARD EVERETT. Some aspects of the migration of the Negro to the San Francisco bay area since 1940. Doctoral dissertation, Univ. of Calif., Berkeley, 1962. v, 191 ℓ. maps. CNoS (photocopy).

1184. HART, JOHN FRASER. "The changing distribution of the American Negro," in Annals of the association of American geographers, v. 50, Sept., 1960, pp. 242-66.

1185. HENDERSON, ARCHIE MAREE. Introduction of the Negroes into the Pacific northwest, 1788-1842. Master's thesis, Univ. of Washington, Seattle, 1949. 43 p.

1186. HOWAY, FREDERIC WILLIAM, 1867- . "The Negro immigration into Vancouver Island in 1858," in British Columbia historical quarterly, v. 3,

Colonization, Migration and Population Statistics

Apr., 1939, pp. 101-13.
Describes the first settlement there of California Negroes.

1187. _____. "Negro migration to Vancouver Island in 1858," in Transactions of the Royal society of Canada, 1935, sec. 2, pp. 147-56.

1188. *HUFFMAN, EUGENE HENRY. Voice in the wilderness, by Rev. Eugene Henry Huffman. S. F., Africano pubs., c1959. 82 p. CHi, CU-I, NUC, 1942-62.
"Addressed to the people of Black African descent" and encouraging them to return to Africa.

1189. KILBOURN, CHARLOTTE. Factors conductive to the migration to and from Vanport City. Master's thesis, Reed college, Portland, 1944.

1190. KILLICK, VICTOR W., 1889- . Changes in California population status, July 16, 1945. Sacramento, Dept. of motor vehicles, Bureau of statistics, 1945.
Gives statistics on the increase in Negro population in certain California cities.

1191. LEARD, ROBERT BENSON. Civil war attempts at Negro colonization. Master's thesis, Univ. of Calif., Berkeley, 1948. 98 ℓ.

1192. MCINTOSH, MARY SUSAN. The lack of Negro migration in the United States before 1915. Master's thesis, Univ. of Calif., Berkeley, 1962. iv, 109 ℓ. tables.

1193. MITCHELL, MARILYN. "The migrant Negro in San Francisco," in Problems of American communities, 1945, v. 1, pp. 125-40. Oakland, Mills college Dept. of economics and sociology, 1945. COMC.

1194. MONTESANO, PHILIP MICHAEL, 1941- . "A black pioneer's trip to California," in Pacific historian, v. 13, Winter, 1969, pp. 58-62.
Describes, through the use of original sources, the 1849 overland trip of Alvin Aaron Coffey (1822-1902) from Missouri to California.

1195. MOORMAN, MADISON BERRYMAN. The journal of Madison Berryman Moorman, 1850-1851. Ed., with notes and an introduction by Irene D. Paden, together with a biographical sketch of the author by his granddaughter, Louise Parker Banes. S. F., California historical society, 1948. ix, 150 p. port., map (fold.). CB, CBb, CChiS, CHi, CSd, Rocq 15971.
Contains a description of an overland journey on which Richard Rapier, brother of U. S. Congressman James T. Rapier, and two other Negroes were party members.

1196. NAKAYAMA, ANTONIO. "California pioneers from Sinaloa, Mexico," in Pacific historian, v. 13, Spring, 1969, pp. 66-69.
A discussion of the racial background of California's first Mexican settlers.

1197. "Nineteen hundred and sixty census shows Negroes leaving south for western and northern industrial centers," in Interracial review, v. 34, May, 1961, pp. 120-21.

Colonization, Migration and Population Statistics

1198. O'BRIEN, ROBERT W. "Victoria's Negro colonists -- 1858-1866," in
Phylon, v. 3, 1942, 1st quarter, pp. 15-18.
Describes the first settlement there of California Negroes.

1199. Oregon. Secretary of state. Proposed constitutional amendments and
measures (with arguments) to be submitted to the voters of Oregon at the
general election ... November 2, 1926.
Repeal of section of state constitution forbidding free Negroes and
mulattoes coming into, residing, or being in the state of Oregon, or
having any civil rights therein, pp. 8-9.

1200. Pacific farming company. Articles of incorporation, Alpaugh, 1908.
3 [2] p. Typew. C-ArS.
To purchase rural lands; to lay out town sites; etc. Directors were
Willifam Loftus, Fullerton, and J. R. Treat and W. H. O'Bryan, Los
Angeles.

1201. _____. Same. Amendment, 1914. 4 p. C-ArS.

1202. _____. A birdseye view of the colony, tract and surrounding country
of activity, Tulare co., California ... [and] map showing lots in town
of Allensworth. [L. A.?, 191-?].
Broadsheet.

1203. PILTON, JAMES WILLIAM. Netro settlement in British Columbia, 1858-
1871. Master's thesis, Univ. of British Columbia, Vancouver, 1951.
247 p. CHi (film), WaU (photocopy).
The history of the colony of California Negroes. Close contact was
retained with their former home, and many of the colonists eventually
returned to California.

1204. POTTS, E. DANIEL. "The Negro and the Australian gold rushes, 1852-
1857," by E. Daniel and Annette Potts, in Pacific historical review,
v. 37, Nov., 1968, pp. 381-89.
California civil rights conditions are described. It appears probable
that a number of the Australians listed had arrived there from California.

1205. RECORD, WILSON, 1916- . "Willie Stokes at the Golden Gate," in
Crisis, v. 56, June, 1949, pp. 175-79, 187-88.
Describes the plight of migrants to the San Francisco bay area during
the World War II years and after.

1206. *RICHARDS, EUGENE SCOTT. A census study of the Negro in California.
Research report, Univ. of Calif., Los Angeles, 1940. x, 95 ℓ.
"A statistical picture of the Negro in California from 1850-1930." -
Miriam Matthews.

1207. _____. "Culture change due to migration; study of Negro migration to
California," in Sociology and social research, v. 26, Mar., 1942,
pp. 334-45.

1208. _____. The effects of the Negro's migration to southern California
since 1920 upon his sociocultural patterns. Doctoral dissertation, Univ.
of southern Calif., Los Angeles, 1941. ix, 309 ℓ. tables.

Colonization, Migration and Population Statistics

1209. *ROBINSON, LOUIE. "Death threatens western town," in Ebony, v. 22, June, 1967, pp. 60-62, 64, 66.
    Describes the problem of arsenic in the water supply of Allensworth.

1210. *SAVAGE, WILLIAM SHERMAN, 1890- . "The Negro in the history of the Pacific northwest," in Journal of Negro history, v. 13, July, 1928, pp. 255-64.
    Mainly concerns early residents of Oregon and residential restrictions there.

1211. _____. "The Negro in the westward movement," in Journal of Negro history, v. 25, Oct., 1940, pp. 531-39.
    Includes biographical accounts of Biddy Mason, Moses Rodgers, John Fisher, and George W. Bush.

1212. SCHMID, CALVIN FISHER, 1901- , and WAYNE W. MCVEY. Growth and distribution of minority races in Seattle, Washington. Seattle, Seattle public schools, 1964. 62 p. CO, Wa.

1213. The sentiment maker, May 15, 1912. [L. A.?, 1912]. 8 p. illus., ports. CTul.
    A promotional brochure of newspaper size which describes the Allensworth colony, Tulare county.

1214. SIEGEL, JAY. Intrametropolitan migration of white and minority group households. Doctoral dissertation, Stanford univ., Stanford, 1970. v, 113 ℓ.

1215. SMITH, THOMAS LYNN. "Redistribution of the Negro population of the United States, 1910-1960," in Journal of Negro history, v. 51, July, 1966, pp. 155-73.
    Includes Negro migration to the West, pp. 166-67.

1216. *STARKEY, JAMES RYLANDER, 1821-1870. "Documents" [six letters, 1848-50, written at New Bern, N. C., to the American colonization society regarding possible migration to Liberia], in Journal of Negro history, v. 10, Apr., 1925, pp. 229-34.
    Starkey arrived in California, 1853, and remained there until his death.

1217. SWETT, H. Negro migration during the war period. Master's thesis, Reed college, Portland, 1944.

1218. THACKER, M. EVA. "California's Dixie land," in California history nugget, v. 5, Mar., 1938, pp. 174-81.
    "Discusses James Gadsden's plan to bring Negro slaves to California to start a cotton plantation system ... in 1851 ... failure of the Cotton grower's association project in 1871 ... and the unsuccessful effort of 1884 when several thousand Negroes imported from the South left the fields ..." -- Miriam Matthews.

1219. THOMPSON, WARREN SIMPSON, 1887- . Growth and changes in California's population, by Warren S. Thompson, with chapters by Varden Fuller and

Colonization, Migration and Population Statistics

    Richard C. Singleton. L. A., Haynes foundation [c1955]. xxx, 377 p. maps, tables, diagrs. CLU, CU.

1220. U. S. Bureau of the census. Negro population, 1790-1915. Washington, D. C., Govt. print., 1918. 844 p. maps, tables, diagrs. CFS, CNoS, CPhD, CSf, CSt, CU-SB.

1221. _____. _____. Same. N. Y., Arno press, 1968. CSbS, CSdS, CU-A, CU-I.
    An indispensible and detailed source of information compiled from published and unpublished sources. Provides a wealth of information on every facet of life susceptible to statistical study.

1222. _____. _____. ... Negroes in the United States, 1920-32. Prepared under the supervision of Z. R. Pettet, chief statistician for agriculture, by Charles E. Hall, specialist in Negro statistics. Washington, D. C., Govt. print., 1935. xvi, 845 p. maps, tables, diagrs. CFS, CSf, CSj.

1223. _____. _____. Same. N. Y., Arno press, 1969. CNoS, CSbS, CSf, CSluSP, CU-SB.

1224. _____. District court. Oregon. [Documents concerning the case of Theophilus Magruder vs. Jacob Vanderpool, 1851.] Mss. (photocopy). 1 folder with 6 documents. OrU.
    Pertains to the trial of Vanderpool, a Negro, and his deportation from Oregon.

1225. *WAGONER, HENRY OSCAR, -1902. "From the Pike's peak gold region," in Douglass' monthly, v. 4, Apr., 1861, p. 439.
    His letter from Denver, Feb. 22, 1861.

1226. *WILLIAMS, ROBERT L. "The Negro's migration to Los Angeles, 1900-1946," in Negro history bulletin, v. 19, Feb., 1956, p. 102ff.

1227. WOOLFOLK, GEORGE RUBLE. "Turner's safety-valve and free Negro westward migration," in Journal of Negro history, v. 50, July, 1965, pp. 185-97.

1228. _____. "Turner's safety valve and free Negro westward migration," in Pacific northwest quarterly, v. 56, July, 1965, pp. 125-30.

COOKBOOKS; FOOD

1229. *HARWOOD, JIM. Soul food cook book. [By] Jim Harwood [and] Ed Callahan. Concord, Nitty gritty productions, c1969. 210 p. illus.

1230. HOLDREDGE, HELEN (O'DONNELL), comp. Mammy Pleasant's cookbook. Comp. and ed. by Helen Holdredge. Illus. by James Beauchamp Alexander. S. F., 101 productions [c1970]. 157 p. illus. CHi, CSfAA.
    Contains considerable biographical information about Mrs. Mary Ellen Pleasant.

Cookbooks; Food

1231. *JACKSON, LILLIE. "Soulin'," in Synergy, Oct./Nov., 1969, pp. 7-8.
San Francisco public library publication describes soul food and
restaurants in the San Francisco bay area.

1232. KUFFMAN, DOROTHY, ed. West Oakland soul food cook book. [Oakland,
Peter Maurin neighborhood house? 1968?]. 47 p. illus. CO, CU-A.

1233. *Negro culinary art club of Los Angeles. Eliza's cook book; favorite
recipes, compiled by Negro culinary art club of Los Angeles. L. A.,
Wetzel pub. co. [c1936]. 101 p. DLC.

1234. *Students of Ravenswood high school. Soul power cook book, by the
Students of Ravenswood high school, East Palo Alto, California ... Menlo
Park, Pub. in cooperation with Lane magazine & book co., c1970. 64 p.
illus. CSfAA.

1235. *THURMAN, SUE (BAILEY), comp. and ed. The historical cookbook of the
American Negro. Published under the auspices of the National council of
Negro women, Archives and museum dept. Washington, D. C., Corporate
press, c1958. 144 p. illus. CSf, CSt.

DIRECTORIES, CENSUS RECORDS, ETC.

1236. *BASS, JOSEPH BLACKBURN, and J. W. DUNCAN, pubs. [Directory -
Butte's colored organizations; churches, lodges, business concerns, etc.,
Helena, Mont., 1906.]
Publication announced in Helena Montana plaindealer, Jan. 4, 1907,
p. 1.

1237. BEAN, EDWIN F., comp. Bean's history and directory of Nevada county,
California. Containing a complete history of the county, with sketches
of the various towns and mining camps ... also, full statistics of
mining and all other industrial resources ... Nevada [City], Print. at
the Daily gazette bk. & job off., 1867. 424 p. C, CHi, CL, CLU, CSf,
CSmH, CU-B, Rocq 5956.
Designates Afro-Americans.

1238. *Black business directory. v. 1, no. 1, 1969- . Los Angeles,
1969- .
Pub. by E. M. Cavin, John L. Hathman, F. J. Brown, and R. H. Ferguson.

1239. *Black business in San Diego directory. [San Diego, W. L. Morrow,
196-?]. [8] p. C.

1240. BYRNE, WILLIAM S. Directory of Grass Valley township for 1865; con-
taining a historical sketch of Grass Valley, of Allison ranch, and Forest
Springs; also a description of the principal mines ... S. F., Charles F.
Robbins & co., 1865. 144 p. C, CHi, CLU, CSfCP, CSmH, CU-B, Rocq 6035.
Designates Afro-Americans.

Directories, Census Records, etc.

1241. California. Census. 1852. Ms. C-ArS.
Opened for public use in 1971. A typed copy was prepared earlier in this century by the Daughters of the American revolution. Later, this unalphabetized copy was issued by the D. A. R. on positive microfilm. Some errors and omissions in transcription make use of the original census advisable. Because portions of the 1850 U. S. census for California were destroyed shortly after preparation, including the San Francisco section, the 1852 State census assumes a greater importance. Contains names of black and mulatto residents and gives previous place of non-California residence in addition to age, occupation, and birthplace.

1242. *California eagle publishing co., pub. Los Angeles Negro directory and who's who, 1930-1931 ... published annually. [L. A., 1930]. 135 p. illus., ports.

1243. *Center on urban and minority affairs, Los Angeles. National roster of black elected officials. [L. A., 1969]. 137 p. Preface signed: Mervyn M. Dymally. CL, CSS, CU.

1244. COLLINS, CHARLES, comp. Mercantile guide and directory for Virginia City, Gold Hill, Silver City and American City, comprising a general business and resident directory for those cities ... Virginia [City], Printed by Agnew & Deffebach, S. F. [1864]. 386 p. C, CHi, CSmH, CU-B, NvHi.
Designates Afro-Americans.

1245. *Colored directory of the leading cities of northern California, 1916-1917 [Ed. and pub. by Tilghman printing co., Oakland.] [Oakland, 1916]. 140 p. illus., ports. COEB.
Introduction: "Glance at the last page of our 1915 Directory and these words you will see 'Watch this directory grow ... From seventy-six pages it has grown to one hundred and forty'."

1246. *Colored people's business directory, v. 1, 1925- . San Diego. [City print. co., 1925?-]. CSmH, v. 2, 1926.
"The colored directory of San Diego for 1930-1931" has been issued by Eugene Lucas. Los Angeles California news, Dec. 25, 1930, p. 1, col. 2.

1247. Community health workers, Health center 2. Community resources in [the] Western addition; a survey of resources done in the Summer of 1968 by Community health workers, Health center 2 ... [S. F., 1969]. [8] ℓ. map.
A directory of schools, health agencies, and service, recreational, and cultural centers.

1248. *East bay colored business directory, 1930 ... Created by W. J. D. Thompson, designed by Kelly Williams. Oakland, W. J. D. Thompson [and] Kelly Williams, pubs.; printed by California voice press, 1930. 32 p. illus., ports. CU-B.

1249. GILLIS, WILLIAM ROBERT, 1840-1929, comp. The Nevada directory, for 1868-9: containing a full list of the residents, mining and business men

Directories, Census Records, etc.

of Virginia, Gold Hill, Silver City, Carson, Washoe, Dayton, Empire City, Reno and Genoa; with a historical sketch of the principal places ... Compiled and pub. by William R. Gillis, Virginia [City]. S. F., M. D. Carr & co., 1868. xxviii, 309 p. CU-B.
Designates Afro-Americans.

1250. *History and guide of the Pacific coast. [L. A.] A. D. Griffin, c1892. 24 p. illus. CNoS.
"Lists 103 families and 19 Pullman porters for whom Los Angeles was home base." - Patricia Adler.

1251. Interracial council for business opportunity. Minority vendors guide, southern California. L. A., 1971. 81 p. 2nd ed. CSS.

1252. KELLY, J. WELLS, comp. First directory of Nevada territory, containing the names of residents in the principal towns ... Compiled from the most recent and authentic sources by J. Wells Kelly. S. F., Commercial steam presses: Valentine & co., 1862. 266 p. C, CSmH, NvHi, NvU.
Designates Afro-Americans.

1253. _____. Same. Los Gatos, Talisman press, 1962. C, CHi, CLU, CU-B.

1254. _____. Second directory of Nevada territory; embracing a general directory of residents of all the principal towns ... compiled from the most recent and authentic sources, by J. Wells Kelly. Virginia [City], Printed by Valentine & co., S. F., 1863. viii, 486 p. CHi, CSmH, CU-B, NvHi, NvU.
Designates Afro-Americans.

1255. MCCORMICK, STEPHEN J., comp. and pub. The Portland directory, for the year commencing January, 1867; embracing a general directory of residents ... fifth year of publication. Portland, A. G. Walling & co., printer, 1867. 120, 18 p. CHi.
Designates Afro-Americans.

1256. _____. Same. Portland, 1869. CHi.
Also designates Afro-Americans. It has not been possible to examine other Portland directories for the same information.

1257. Marysville. City council. The Marysville city library reports that the Council Minutes have been carefully indexed at the library. "Many Negroes owned property or worked for the city, etc., but in most cases we must know their names to check for material on them except where there is a voter list of Negroes."

1258. Marysville. Directories. 1855. Colville, Samuel, comp. Colville's Marysville directory for the year commencing November 1, 1855 ... together with a history sketch of Marysville. S. F., Monson & Valentine, 1855. 96 p. C, CHi, CLU, CMary, CSmH, CU-B, Rocq 15583, Spear, p. 186.
Designates Afro-Americans.

Directories, Census Records, etc.

1259. _____. _____. 1856. Amy, George Sturtevant, and O. Amy, comp.
G. and O. Amy's Marysville directory for the year commencing November 1,
1856 ... together with an historical sketch of Marysville ... S. F.,
Commercial bk. & job steam print., 1856. 128 p. C, CHi (photocopy),
CMary, CSmH, CU-B, Rocq 15584, Spear, p. 186.
Designates Afro-Americans.

1261. _____. _____. 1858. Smith, Mix, and G. Amy, comp. Amy's Marysville
directory, for the year commencing June 1858 ... prefaced by a history
of the county of Yuba ... Marysville, Daily news bk. & job off., 1858.
108 p. C, CHi (photocopy), CMary, CSfCP, CSmH, CU-B, Rocq 15585, Spear,
p. 186.
Designates Afro-Americans.

1262. _____. _____. 1861. Brown, W. C., pub. Brown's Marysville directory
for the year commencing March, 1861 ... prefaced by historical sketches
of industrial enterprises, benevolent and charitable organizations, etc.
Marysville, Daily California express, 1861. 115 p. CHi, CMary, CSmH,
CU-B, Rocq 15586.
Designates Afro-Americans.

1263. _____. _____. 1870. Kelley, John G., comp. The Marysville, Yuba
City and Colusa directory for the year commencing August 1, 1870 ...
[Sacramento, H. S. Crocker, 1870]. 421, v. p. CHi, CMary.
Designates Afro-Americans.

1264. *National association of Negro business and professional women's
clubs, inc. East bay area club. Directory, Alameda, Contra Costa and
Solano counties, Calif. [Oakland?, 1967]. 44 p. CSfAA.
Lists business, social, professional, religious, and community
service organizations.

1265. *Negro directory of the bay cities. Oakland, Tilghman press, 1915.
Notice of publication appears in the Oakland Western outlook, May 22,
1915, p. 2. Apparently this is the first ed. of Colored directory of
the leading cities of northern California, 1916-1917.

1266. *Negro social register, inc. Articles of incorporation, Los Angeles,
1953. 8 p. Typew. C-ArS.
Directors were Dorothy H. Salata, Sylvia Koenigsberg, and Marlene
Gurian, Los Angeles; and Charlene Ross, Sherman Oaks.

1267. *New age publishing co., comp. and pub. ... The official California
Negro directory and classified buyers' guide; a west coast directory ...
L. A. [1939?-]. CL (1940), COEB (1942).
Title varies. In 1940: The official Central avenue district

Directories, Census Records, etc.

directory ... The 1942 ed. stated "Vol. 4, no. 1 ... This is the 3rd [sic] anniversary of our publication and the first issue to cover the state of California. Our first directory contained 84 pages ..." The 1941 ed. contained 96 pages, while the 1942 ed. of 238 pages supplied directory information for Los Angeles, Bakersfield, Oakland, San Francisco, Berkeley, El Centro, Fresno, Long Beach, Pasadena, Riverside, Sacramento, San Bernardino, San Diego, San Mateo, Santa Barbara, Santa Monica, Venice, Vallejo, Oregon, and Washington.

1268. OWENS, G., comp. and pub. Salt Lake City directory, including a business directory of Provo, Springville, and Ogden, Utah territory ... [n.p.] 1867. 135 p. CHi (photocopy).
Designates Afro-Americans. No examination has been made of other Utah directories.

1269. OWENS, GEORGE. A general directory and business guide of the principal towns east of the Cascade mountains for the year 1865 ... San Francisco, Towne and Bacon, 1865. 210 p. map. CHi (photocopy).
Designates Afro-Americans.

1270. Placerville. Directories. 1862. Fitch, Thomas, and co., pub. Directory of the city of Placerville, and towns of Upper Placerville, El Dorado, Georgetown, and Coloma, containing a history of these places ... [Placerville] Placerville republican print., 1862. 128 p. C, CHi, CLU, CSmH, CU-B, Rocq 1822.
Designates Afro-Americans.

1271. *Plan of action for challenging times, inc., pub. Directory of black businesses in San Francisco. [S. F., 1969]. iv, 46 p. "Publication no. 104." C, CHi, CSf, CSfU.

1272. *RAINEY, DOUGLAS L. Directory of minority contractors and black businesses in the bay area, prepared by Douglas L. Rainey and David J. Venediger. S. F., Coro foundation [1970]. 79 p. C.

1272a. _____., & associates ... Where it's at (a Bay area urban inventory) ... [S. F., c1971]. 393 p. illus., ports.
A directory of community organizations, churches, schools, minority businesses, cooperatives, poverty programs, news media, medical and legal facilities, labor and political organizations, and federal and local government departments.

1273. RASMUSSEN, LOUIS J. San Francisco ship passenger lists, by Louis J. Rasmussen ... Colma, San Francisco historic records [c1965-   ]. v. Contents: v. 1 - 1850-75; v. 2 - 1850-51; v. 3 - 1851-52; v. 4 - [c1970] -1852-53. CHi (v. 1, 2, and 3), CSf (v. 4), CSmH (v. 1 and 3).

These detailed lists contain some names of Negro passengers.

1274. Sacramento. Directories. [185-?]-1856/57. Colville, Samuel, pub. Colville's Sacramento directory. Sacramento [185-?]-1856. Title varies. C 1853/54-1855/56; CCC 1855/56; CHi 1854/55 (photocopy), 1855/56 (photo-

Directories, Census Records, etc.

  copy), 1856/57; CLU 1854/55-1856/57; CS 1853/54-1855/56; CSfCP 1855/56-1856/57; CSmH 1853/54-1856/57; CU-B 1854/55-1856/57; Rocq 6522; Spear, p. 327.
   Designates Afro-Americans.

1275. _____. _____. 1857/58. Irwin, I. N., comp. Sacramento directory and gazetteer, for the years 1857 and 1858. By I. N. Irwin, collator and publisher ... S. F., Printed by S. D. Valentine & son, 1857. 106 p. C, CHi, CLU, CS, CSfCP, CSmH, CU-B, Rocq 6524, Spear, p. 328.
   Designates Afro-Americans.

1276. _____. _____. 1860. Cutter, D. S., & co., comp. & pub. Sacramento city directory, for the year A. D. 1860; being a complete general and business directory of the entire city ... also containing correct statistics of all the churches, Sunday schools, societies, courts, schools, fire departments ... Sacramento, H. S. Crocker & co., book and job printers, 1859. 128 p. C, CHi (photocopy), CS, CSmH, CU-B, Rocq 6526, Spear, p. 328.
   Designates Afro-Americans.

1277. _____. _____. 1861/62. Bidleman, H. J., comp. The Sacramento directory for the years 1861 and 1862 ... Sacramento, John J. Murphy, 1861. xxv, 168 p. C, CS, CU-B.
   Designates Afro-Americans.

1278. _____. _____. 1863/64. Mears, Leonard, comp. Mears' Sacramento directory ... Sacramento, Printed by A. Badlam, 1863. 142 p. C, CS, CU-B, Rocq 6528.
   Designates Afro-Americans.

1279. _____. _____. 1866, 1868-69. Draper, Robert E., comp. and pub. Sacramento directories ... Sacramento, H. S. Crocker, print., 1866-69. 3 v. 1868-69 includes Sacramento county. C 1866, 1868-69; CHi 1866, 1868-69; CLU 1868-69; CS 1866, 1868-69; CSmH 1866, 1868-69; CU-B 1866, 1868-69; Rocq 6515 and 6529.
   Designates Afro-Americans.

1280. _____. _____. 1870. McKenney, L. M., comp. & pub. McKenney's Sacramento directory, for the year 1870 ... together with statistics, historical references and a large amount of general information appertaining to the city ... Sacramento, Russell & Winterburn, steam bk. & job print. [n.d.]. 332 p. C, CHi, CL, CS, CU-B, Rocq 6530.
   Designates Afro-Americans.

1281. _____. _____. 1871. Crocker, Henry Smith, pub. The Sacramento directory for the year commencing January, 1871 ... Sacramento, 1871. 432 p. C, CHi, CLU, CS, CSmH, CU-B, Rocq 6531.
   Designates Afro-Americans.

1282. Sacramento county. Index to the Great register of the county of Sacramento, 1866- . Ms. 1 v. C-ArS.
   Note: These manuscript Great registers are located usually in the archives of the appropriate counties.

Directories, Census Records, etc.

A folio register of voters arranged chronologically under each letter
of the alphabet. Numerous names of new black voters appear during April,
1870. Age, occupation, and other information are given.

1283. *Sacramento observer, pub. Who's who in the Negro community of
Sacramento, California: the people in business, the institutions, and
organizations. Sacramento Negro directory. Sacramento, 1965. 14 p. CS.

1284. San Francisco. Directories. 1852. Morgan, A. W., and co., pub.
A. W. Morgan and co.'s San Francisco city directory, September, 1852 ...
S. F., F. A. Bonnard, print., 1852. 174 p. (Pagination varies). C,
CHi, CLU, CSfCP, CSmH, CU-B, Rocq 7982, Spear, p. 337.
Designates Afro-Americans.

1285. _____. _____. 1852. Parker, James M., pub. The San Francisco
directory, for the year 1852-53 ... First publication. S. F., Monson,
Haswell & co., print., 1852. 145 p. map. C, CCC, CHi, CLU, CS, CSfCP,
CSmH, CU-B, Rocq 7983, Spear, p. 337.
Designates Afro-Americans.

1286. _____. _____. 1856. Colville, Samuel, comp. Colville's San Francisco directory, vol. 1. For the year commencing October, 1856; being
a gazetteer of the city ... S. F., 1856. 307 p. map. C, CHi, CLU,
CSfCP, CSmH, CU-B, Rocq 7986, Spear, p. 338.
Designates Afro-Americans.

1287. _____. _____. 1856. Harris, Bogardus and Labatt, comp. and pub.
San Francisco city directory, for the year commencing October, 1856.
Containing a general directory of citizens, a street directory, and an
appendix of all useful and general information pertaining to the city
... S. F., Whitton, Towne & co., print., 1856. 138 p. C, CHi (imper-
fect), CSfCP, CSmH, CU-A, CU-B (imperfect), Rocq 7987, Spear, p. 338.
Designates Afro-Americans.

1288. _____. _____. 1858/75. Langley, Henry G., pub. Langley's San
Francisco directory, 1858-75. C 1858-75; CHi 1858-75; CL 1859-65, 1867-
69, 1871-74; CLU 1858-62, 1864-71, 1873-75; CO 1860-75; CSf 1858-75;
CSfCP 1858-75; CSmH 1858-75; CU-B 1858-65, 1867-69, 1871-75; Rocq 7988.
These annual directories designate Afro-Americans and give descriptive listings for many Afro-American religious, fraternal, benevolent,
and military organizations. Afro-Americans are not designated separately
after 1875.

1289. San Jose. Directories. 1870. Colahan, W. J., and Julian Pomeroy,
comps. San Jose city directory and business guide of Santa Clara co.
for the year commencing January 1, 1870 ... S. F., Bacon & co., print.,
1870. 242 p. C, CHi, CLU, CSmH, CU-B, Rocq 13739.
Designates Afro-Americans.

1290. SATTERWHITE, FRANK J. California directory of Afro-American educators.
Compilers: Frank Satterwhite [and] Betty S. Satterwhite. [L. A.,
1970?]. iii, 36 p. CSfSt.

Directories, Census Records, etc.

1291. SIRACUSA, ERNEST V. "Black '49ers"; the Negro in the California gold
       rush, 1848-1861. Research paper, Univ. of Calif., Santa Barbara, 1969.
       iv, 227 p. illus. CHi (photocopy), CU-B (photocopy).
           Essentially a directory of black residents, 1850-67 [sic].

1292. Stockton. Directories. 1852. The Stockton directory and emigrant's
       guide to the Southern mines. Published semi-annually. Stockton, "San
       Joaquin republican" off., 1852. 140 p. map. CHi (photocopy), CLU,
       CSmH, Rocq 12978, Spear, p. 350.
           Designates Afro-Americans.

1293. _____. _____. 1856. Harris, Joseph & co., pub. Stockton city
       directory, for the year 1856 ... Together with a historical sketch of
       Stockton, by J. P. Bogardus. S. F., Whitton, Towne & co., 1856. 96 p.
       C, CHi, CSmH, CSto, CU-B, Rocq 12979, Spear, p. 350.
           Designates Afro-Americans. No examination has been made of later
       Stockton directories.

1294. *Success publishing co., pub. The success directory, 1959 edition ...
       sponsored by the Committee for community solidarity, inc. S. F., 1959.
       80 p. illus., ports. C, CSf, CU-B.
           A listing of San Francisco business firms in which Afro-Americans
       either participated in the profits, held executive positions, or were
       employed as salesmen on a commission basis. Only year published.

1295. U. S. Bureau of the census. 1850. Census of the city and county of
       Los Angeles, California for the year 1850 together with an analysis and
       an appendix ... L. A., Times-mirror press, 1929. 139 p. illus., ports.,
       map. Available in many libraries. Rocq 3330.
           Contains the names of at least 15 black people.

1296. _____. _____. 1850-1880.
           Microfilm copies of the original decennial population schedules for
       California, New Mexico, Oregon, and Utah are available in a few of the
       larger libraries and in genealogical centers. They are also available
       by purchase from the General services administration, Washington, D. C.
       Information about individual black and mulatto names is given in each of
       the censuses. A portion of the 1850 California census, including San
       Francisco, was accidently destroyed.

1297. _____. _____. _____. [Records for California.] C, CHi (film),
       CU-B (film).
           Includes deaths for the years ending June 1, 1850 [i.e., 1851],
       June 1, 1860, June 1, 1870, and May 31, 1880; descriptive listings for
       individual miners and business firms under "Products of industry";
       descriptive listings for individual farming and ranch operations under
       "Products of agriculture"; and "Social statistics" listing churches, etc.

1298. _____. _____. 1860-1880.
           Microfilm copies of the original decennial population schedules for
       Washington are also available in a few of the larger libraries and in
       genealogical centers.

Directories, Census Records, etc.

1299. _____. _____. 1870-1880.
      Microfilm copies of the original decennial population schedules for
   Arizona, Colorado, Idaho, Montana, Nevada, and Wyoming are also available
   in a few of the larger libraries and genealogical centers.

1300. Watts-Compton city directory. 1914/15- . Publisher and title vary.
   CL 1914/15, 1919, 1921, 1922/23, 1925, 1927/28, 1932; CLCo 1914/15.

EDUCATION

COUNSELING AND GUIDANCE

1301. *ADAMS, JOHN QUINCY.   A handbook for guidance personnel at Douglas
   junior high school. Master's project report, Univ. of southern Calif.,
   Los Angeles, 1951. v, 74 ℓ. illus.

1302. BJORKLUND, JAUNITA H.   A comparative study of the need structure of
   Negro graduate students enrolled in a counselor education program.
   Master's thesis, Calif. state univ., Hayward, 1969. viii, 65 ℓ.

1303. BROWN, REBECCA DANICE.   Attitudes of black junior college students
   toward counseling services. Master's thesis, Calif. state univ.,
   Hayward, 1970. viii, 83 ℓ. charts.

1304. *CURRY, WILLA CLOTHILDE.   Educational and vocational guidance of
   Negroes. Master's thesis, Univ. of Calif., Los Angeles, 1939. 119 ℓ.
   tables, diagrs.

1305. *East bay guidance council.   An educational assist from the East bay
   guidance council. The 1958 revision of "Neighbor to neighbor talk."
   [Oakland], 1958. 34 p.
      Essentially authored by Harold P. Jones, columnist of the Oakland
   California voice.

1306. _____. Neighbor to neighbor talk from the East bay guidance council.
   [Oakland?, 1956?]. 46 p. COEB.
      A child guidance handbook.

1307. EKBERG, DENNIS, and CLAUDE URY.   "'Education for what?' - a report on
   an M. D. T. A. program," in Journal of Negro education, v. 37, Winter,
   1968, pp. 15-22.
      The Management development training act program in West Oakland.

1308. GRAHAM, LUELVA BROUSSARD.   A survey of counseling needs as reported
   by Negro female students in the twelfth grade of the Los Angeles area.
   Master's thesis, Univ. of Calif., Los Angeles, 1967. x, 76 ℓ.

1309. HANNAH, HELEN WALLIS.   A study of guidance procedure for dealing with
   problems of Negro youth in a period of transition in education. Master's

Counseling and Guidance

project report, Univ. of southern Calif., Los Angeles, 1956. iii, 45 ℓ.

1310. HEFFERNON, ANDREW WILLIAM. The effect of race and assumed professional status of male lay counselors upon eighth grade black males' perceptions of and reactions to the counseling process. Doctoral dissertation, Univ. of Calif., Berkeley, 1969. ix, 118 ℓ.

1311. JACKSON, JOSEPH SYLVESTER. What to tell them; a booklet designed to be of special service to counselors, guidance workers and agencies with reference to Negro girls and boys in Seattle; and for the use of students themselves. Seattle, Seattle Urban league, 1938. 34 p. Publication no. 1. Wa.

1312. JONES, ALVIN HENRY. An investigation of self concept using group counseling with Afro-American male ninth-grade students. Doctoral dissertation, Ariz. state univ., Tempe, 1971. 148 ℓ. illus.

1313. *JONES, MARTIN H., and MARTIN C. JONES. "The neglected client," in Black scholar, v. 1, Mar., 1970, pp. 35-42.
     The authors, father and son, describe their attitudes toward black counseling in which capacity they are employed at Calif. state univ., San Francisco.

1314. *LOVE, RUTH B. "Counseling the disadvantaged youth," in California teachers association journal, v. 61, Mar., 1965, pp. 32-34.

1315. _____. "Expanding opportunities for all youth through counseling," in California education, v. 3, Apr., 1966, pp. 15-16.

1316. _____. "Some answers to administrators' questions on counseling minority youth," in California education, v. 2, Feb., 1965, pp. 23-24.

1317. MINOR, BILLY J. Black students' relationship with counselors: a comparison of counselor perceptions and characteristics. Master's thesis, Calif. state univ., Hayward, 1969. 94 ℓ. tables.

1318. NICE, EVERT C. A survey of some racial prejudice factors having implications for high school guidance and counseling. Research paper, Calif. state univ., Fresno, 1959.

1319. RECORD, WILSON, 1916- . "Counseling and color: crisis and conscience," in Integrated education, v. 4, Aug.-Sept., 1966, pp. 34-41.
     Authored by a professor of sociology, Portland state college.

1320. TURCHIN, LEAH LILLIAN. The role of the counselor in the guidance of Negro students. Master's project report, Univ. of southern Calif., Los Angeles, 1964. ii, 51 ℓ.

SEGREGATION AND DESEGREGATION

1321. Affirmative school integration; efforts to overcome de facto segrega-
tion in urban schools. Edited by Roscoe Hill and Malcolm Feeley. With
a foreword by James S. Coleman and an introd. by Richard D. Schwartz.
Pub. in cooperation with the Law and society association. Beverly Hills,
Sage pubs. [1968]. 172 p. Bibliography: pp. 151-65. CBGTU, CNoS,
CSdS, CSf, CSt.
    First appeared in Law and society review, v. 11, Nov., 1967.

1322. AGGER, ROBERT E., and CLYDE EDWARD DE BARRY. "School and race in
Portland," in Integrated education, v. 3, Apr.-May, 1965, pp. 11-27.

1323. American civil liberties union. Southern California branch. A call
for integrated schools. [L. A., 1963?]. 23 p. CHi.
    Relates mainly to Los Angeles.

1324. ANDERSON, DONALD GEORGE. Some characteristics of Negro open enroll-
ment transferees. Doctoral dissertation, Univ. of Calif., Berkeley,
1967. vii, 258 ℓ.

1325. Arizona council for civic unity. Close the breach [a study of school
segregation in Arizona. Phoenix, 1949?]. AzU.

1326. ARMSTRONG, VERNON LEE, 1920- . A comparison of intelligence and
achievement scores between children in the Sacramento city unified school
district program of school integration and children not presently involved. Master's thesis, Sacramento state univ., 1969. 155 ℓ.

1327. BARNES, MEDILL MCCORMICK. "The neighborhood school comes to Denver,"
in Integrator, v. 2, Fall, 1969, pp. 22-23.

1328. BENET, JAMES. "Busing in Berkeley proves to be neither calamity nor
cure-all," in City, v. 4, June-July, 1970, pp. 17-20.

1329. Berkeley. Board of education. Integration; a plan for Berkeley.
[Berkeley, 1967]. 29 p. C.

1330. _____. _____. Committee to study certain interracial problems in the
Berkeley schools and their effect upon education. Interracial problems
and their effect on education in the public schools of Berkeley,
California. Report to the Board of education by an advisory committee
of citizens. [Berkeley] 1959. 36 p. tables, diagrs. Bibliography:
p. 36. C, CO, COEB, CU.

1331. _____. _____. De facto segregation study committee. Report.
Berkeley, 1963. 108 ℓ. maps, tables. Bibliography: pp. 104-05.
CChiS, CO, COEB, CU.

1332. _____. Educational park study. Integrated quality education. A
study of educational parks and other alternatives for urban needs.
Berkeley, 1968. 80 p. illus., maps, tables.

Segregation and Desegregation

1333. _____. Unified school district. Co-sponsored workshop in interracial gains and goals, Mar. 10 and 11, 1961. Longfellow school. Berkeley, 1961. 31 ℓ. CO.

1334. _____. _____. Desegregation of the Berkeley public schools, its feasibility and implementation. Superintendent's report of a staff task group study [to the Board of education]. [Berkeley] 1964. iv, (v.p.) tables. CO (photocopy), CU.

1335. _____. _____. Integration of the Berkeley elementary schools; a report to the superintendent, by the Summer staff task force. Berkeley, 1967. 67 ℓ. CU.

1336. [Berkeley] citizens committee. "School segregation in Berkeley," in Integrated education, v. 2, Apr.-May, 1964, pp. 43-46.

1337. BLACKMAN, ALAN. "Planning and the neighborhood school," in Integrated education, v. 2, Aug.-Sept., 1964, pp. 49-57.
    An expansion of a talk given before the Northern California chapter, American institute of planners.

1338. California. Dept. of education. California laws and policies relating to equal opportunities in education. Sacramento, 1966. 18 p. CChiS, CFS, CStb, CSt-Law.

1339. _____. _____. Procedures to correct racial and ethnic imbalance in school districts. California administrative code, title 5, Education, sections 2010 and 2011. Sacramento, 1969. vi, 25 p. CLSU, CStb.

1340. _____. _____. Commission on equal opportunities in education. Annual report to the California state board of education. [Sacramento?] 1959- . CFS.

1341. _____. _____. _____. Equal educational opportunities in a changing society; report of a conference March 16-18, 1965. Sacramento [1965]. 50, 16 p. (2 pts.) C, CSt-Law.
    Includes addresses: "Equal educational opportunities in a changing society," by John Hope Franklin; "De facto segregation and the neighborhood school," by Dan W. Dodson; and "The basis in law," by Richard Mayers.

1342. _____. _____. _____. Recommendations to the Oakland Board of education on certain ethnic problems in the Oakland city unified school district. [Oakland] 1964. 21 ℓ. CO (photocopy).

1343. _____. _____. Office of compensatory education. The effect of integration on the achievement of elementary pupils; progress report of McAteer project M7-14. Riverside, 1967. 30 ℓ. C.

1344. _____. _____. _____. A study of desegregation in the public schools, Riverside, California, final progress report, McAteer project no. M7-14, 1967-68. [Riverside?] 1968. CFS.

Segregation and Desegregation

1345. _____. University. Berkeley. Survey research center. Educational consequences of segregation in a California community [by] Alan B. Wilson. Berkeley, 1966. 119 p. C, CU.
   A study of Richmond. An abbreviated version with the same title was pub. in Racial isolation in the public schools, v. 2, 1967.

1346. California current review of human resources. Desegregating California schools. S. F., League of women voters, 1969. 31 p. C.

1347. CARTER, THOMAS P., and NATHANIEL HICKERSON. "A California citizens' committee studies its schools and de facto segregation," in Journal of Negro education, v. 37, Spring, 1968, pp. 98-105.

1348. "The case against de facto segregated education in the North and West: a contemporary case study," in Journal of Negro education, v. 33, Fall, 1964, pp. 371-81.

1349. CAUGHEY, JOHN WALTON, 1902- . School segregation on our doorstep; the Los Angeles story. By John and LaRee Caughey ... L. A., Quail books [c1966]. vii, 103 p. illus., maps. C, CChiS, CFS, CHS, CKenM, CL, CLSU, CNoS, CP, CSaT, CSbCL, CSbS, CSdS, CSmH, CU-A, CU-B.

1350. _____. Segregation blights our schools; an analysis based on the 1966 official report on racial and ethnic distribution school by school throughout the Los Angeles system. L. A., Quail books, 1967. 20 p.

1351. _____. "Segregation increases in Los Angeles," in CTA journal, Oct., 1968, pp. 39-41.

1352. _____., and LAREE. "Decentralization of the Los Angeles schools; front for segregation," in Integrated education, v. 41, 1969, pp. 48-51.

1353. CHAMBERS, R. L. "The Negro in New Mexico," in Crisis, v. 59, Mar., 1952, pp. 145-50 and 196-97.
   Racial discrimination mainly as it affects schools.

1354. CHRISTY, WILFORD L. A proposed plan for integration of Ascension parish public schools. Master's thesis, Univ. of southern Calif., Los Angeles, 1955. vii, 88 ℓ.

1355. Citizens' advisory committee on Oakland school needs. Report of Equal educational opportunities committee of the Citizens' advisory committee on Oakland school needs. [Oakland] 1964. 214 p. diagrs., maps, tables. CO, CSf.
   Reports on racial composition of teachers and students, physical facilities, relation of racial composition to other school characteristics, and other associated areas.

1356. CLARK, ALICE M. "De facto integration in Bel Air," in Saturday review, v. 49, Jan. 15, 1966, pp. 72-73.

1357. COHEN, DAVID K. "Defining racial equality in education," in UCLA law review, v. 16, Feb., 1969, pp. 255-80.

Segregation and Desegregation

An analysis of progress since the Brown vs. Board of education decision.

1358. *Congress of racial equality, Los Angeles. Education committee. Segregated schools in Los Angeles. Prepared by Education committee, Los Angeles CORE, Kenneth B. Fry, chairman. [L. A.] c1963. 29 p. CLU (Spec. Coll.).

1359. CORBO, JAMES. A study of the effects of integration upon achievement, self-concept and adjustment. Research paper, Calif. state univ., Fresno, 1966.

1360. COWDERY, JABEZ FRANKLIN, 1834-1914. The word "white" in the California school laws. Speech of Hon. J. F. Cowdery, of San Francisco, in the house of assembly, Sacramento, Cal., January 30, 1874. [Printed for the executive committee of the California state convention of colored citizens.] [Sacramento. 1874?]. 8 p. Brackets are used on the title page. CHi, CU-B.

1361. CRAIN, ROBERT L. The politics of school desegregation; comparative case studies of community structure and policy making, by Robert L. Crain. With the assistance of Morton Inger, Gerald A. McWorter, [and] James J. Vanecko. Chicago, Aldine pub. co., [c1968]. xviii, 390 p. illus., tables. "References": pp. 373-77. CEcaC, CFS, CHC, CLSU, CSaT, CSbS, CSdS, CSf, CSfCiC, CSt.
   Uses as examples eight northern cities including San Francisco.

1362. *DAUTERIVE, VERNA BLANCHE. Historical legal development of integration in public schools. Doctoral dissertation, Univ. of southern Calif., Los Angeles, 1966. xii, 382 ℓ.
   "Narrative summary of judicial decisions and educational developments relative to integration and segregation in the public schools of the U. S."

1363. Denver. Superintendent of schools. Planning quality education; a proposal for integrating the Denver public schools. [Denver], 1968. 131 ℓ. maps, tables. CO.

1364. "Desegregation. 10 blueprints for action," in School management, Oct., 1966.
   Includes educational desegregation at Riverside.

1365. DODSON, DAN W. "Does school integration conflict with quality education?", in Integrated education, v. 4, Apr.-May, 1966, pp. 11-18.
   Text of an "address to the San Francisco civic unity committee."

1366. DUNCAN, T. ROGER. "Does California have 'segregated' schools?", in California teachers association journal, v. 61, Mar., 1965, pp. 22-25.

1367. DYCK, HENRY OTTO. An analysis of the changes in attitudes regarding desegregation of the public schools in the seventeen southern states during the twenty-one months following the United States Supreme court opinion of May 17, 1954. Master's thesis, Univ. of southern Calif., Los Angeles, 1956. xxii, 466 ℓ.

Segregation and Desegregation

1368. *DYMALLY, MERVYN MALCOLM, ⊥926- , and ALBERT S. RODDA. "Memo on segregation and busing in the schools," in Black politician, v. 2, July, 1970, pp. 22-26.
   Authored by two Calif. state senators and relates mainly to California.

1369. EDWARDS, THOMAS BENTLEY, 1906- . School desegregation in the North; the challenge and the experience. Ed. by T. Bentley Edwards and Frederick M. Wirt. S. F., Chandler pub. co. [1968, c1967]. viii, 352 p. illus., maps. Bibliographical references included in "Notes," pp. 331-52. CHS, CLSU, CNoS, CSaT, CSbS, CSdS, CSt-Law.
   "The California experience," pp. 49-152, describes desegregation at Berkeley, Sacramento, Riverside, San Bernardino, Sausalito, and Mill Valley.

1370. Equal education opportunity. Prepared by the editorial board of the Harvard educational review. Cambridge, Mass., Harvard univ. press, 1969. 273 p. CNoS, CSf.
   "An expanded version of the Winter 1968 special issue of the Harvard Educational Review." Contains "Compensation and integration: the Berkeley experience," by Neil V. Sullivan, pp. 220-27.

1371. *FAVORS, KATHRYNE. De facto segregation and its effect on children, by Kathryne Favors. [Berkeley, 1962]. iii, 36 p. COEB.

1372. FORT, EDWARD BERNARD. A case study of the struggle to secure an administrative plan for eliminating de facto segregation in the junior high schools in Sacramento, California. Doctoral dissertation, Univ. of Calif., Berkeley, 1964. 413 ℓ. maps, tables.

1373. FOSTER, G. W. "The north and west have problems, too," in Saturday review, v. 46, Apr. 20, 1963, pp. 69-72.
   Relates to educational integration.

1374. FREUDENTHAL, DANIEL K. "How Berkeley came to grips with de facto segregation," in Phi delta kappan, v. 46, Dec., 1964, pp. 184-87.

1375. GILES, HERMANN HARRY, 1901- . The integrated classroom. N. Y., Basic books [1959]. xii, 338 p. CNoS, CSt.
   Includes New Mexico in a report on 13 states.

1376. GITELSON, ALFRED E. "The power and duty to integrate," in Integrated education, v. 8, May-June, 1970, pp. 10-15.
   Los Angeles court bans segregation.

1377. GRIFFIN, PLES ANDREW. The administrative problems of segregation and desegregation of public schools in southern California. Master's project report, Univ. of southern Calif., Los Angeles, 1964. iii, 55 ℓ.

1378. GUNSKY, FREDERIC R. "Racial and ethnic survey of California public schools," in Integrated education, v. 5, June-July, 1967, pp. 44-46.

Segregation and Desegregation

1379. HADSELL, VIRGINIA T. Equal start; a new school, a new chance. Photographs by Helen Nestor. Text by Virginia T. Hadsell and Grethel C.
Newcom. Designed by Marion Skinner. S. F., Glide urban center, c1968.
52 p. illus., ports. C.
    Foreword by Neil V. Sullivan, Sup't., Berkeley unified school district.
    Relates the experience of integrating Berkeley's primary schools
through busing.

1380. HAGER, DON J. "Equal opportunity; schools are responsible," in
Integrated education, v. 1, Apr., 1963, pp. 36-37.
    Speech delivered before the Los Angeles county teachers institute by
a professor of sociology, California state college, Los Angeles.

1381. HALEY, FRED T. "Tacoma faces school segregation," in Integrated
education, v. 2, Apr.-May, 1964, pp. 24-29.
    Authored by the chairman of the Tacoma Board of education.

1382. HALPERN, RAY. "Tactics for integration," in Saturday review, v. 51,
Dec. 21, 1968, pp. 47-49ff.
    Berkeley educational plan.

1383. _____., and BETTY HALPERN. "Integration in Berkeley: the city that
went to school," in Nation, v. 206, May 13, 1968, pp. 632-36.

1384. HAMPTON, CLAUDIA HUDLEY. The effects of desegregation on the
scholastic achievement of relatively advantaged Negro children. Doctoral
dissertation, Univ. of southern Calif., Los Angeles, 1970. iii, 77 ℓ.

1385. HELIX, DANIEL CLARE. The legal effects of Brown versus Board of
education, 1954-1964. Master's thesis, Calif. state univ., San Francisco,
1965. 130 ℓ.

1386. HENDRICK, IRVING G. The development of a school integration plan in
Riverside, California: a history and perspective, by Irving G. Hendrick.
Riverside ... a joint project of the Riverside unified school district
and the University of California, Riverside. Riverside, 1968. viii,
264 p. maps, tables. Bibliography: pp. 226-37. C, CHi.

1387. HICKERSON, NATHANIEL. "Some aspects of school integration in a
California high school," in Journal of Negro education, v. 34, Winter,
1965, pp. 130-37.
    School located in the San Francisco bay area.

1388. HILL, ROSCOE, ed. Affirmative school integration; efforts to overcome
de facto segregation in urban schools. Ed. by Roscoe Hill and Malcolm
Feeley. With a foreword by James S. Coleman and an introd. by Richard D.
Schwartz. Beverly Hills, Sage publications [c1968]. 172 p. Biblio-
graphy: pp. 151-65. CBGTU, CNoS, CSdS, CSf, CSt.
    "First appeared as an issue of Law and society review, v. 2, no. 1,
November 1967."
    Includes writings by California educators William Cohen, Ira Michaels
Heyman, Harold Horowitz, John Kaplan, and Meyer Weinberg. Among the
eight cities studied are Berkeley, Pasadena, and San Francisco.

Segregation and Desegregation

1389. HODGE, JACQUELINE G. "Ask, seek, knock - desegregate," in _Crisis_,
v. 70, Dec., 1963, pp. 581-84.
Desegregation in Fresno.

1390. HOHN, F. R. "Wat's happening? Project APEX, Los Angeles," in
Journal of secondary education, v. 42, Nov., 1967, pp. 334-36.
Describes a voluntary busing program aimed at desegregation.

1391. *INGHRAM, DOROTHY. "An experiment in intercultural education," in
California journal of elementary education, v. 22, Nov., 1953, pp. 88-94.
Concerns Mill school, San Bernardino.

1392. JENSEN, ARTHUR ROBERT. Parent and teacher attitudes toward integration
and busing, by Arthur R. Jensen. Burlingame, California advisory council
on educational research of the California teachers association, 1970.
48 p. (California state advisory council on educational research. Research resume, no. 43). C.
Based upon a Berkeley questionnaire.

1393. KERBY, PHIL. Minorities oppose Los Angeles school system: persistent
segregation," in _Christian century_, v. 85, Sept. 4, 1968, pp. 1,119-22;
Discussion, in v. 85, Oct. 16, p. 1,310 and Nov. 20, 1968, p. 1,482.

1394. KERIDT, LEONARD. "The schools and the people must work for integration," in _California teachers association journal_, Mar., 1964.

1395. KOSSOW, HENRY H. "An integration success story," in _American school
board journal_, July, 1965.
A study of Sacramento's Del Paso Heights school district.

1396. "The law, the mob, and desegregation," in _California law review_, v. 47,
Mar., 1959, p. 126.
"Includes examination of possible legal remedies against school of-
ficials, individuals, and state officials." - Elizabeth W. Miller.

1397. Los Angeles. Board of education. Report of the Ad hoc committee on
equal educational opportunity, Sept. 12, 1963 [and actions taken by the
Board of education on the report of the Ad hoc committee on equal edu-
cational opportunity, during the period May 20, 1963-Dec. 23, 1963].
Committee members: Georgiana Hardy, chairman; Arthur F. Gardner and
Hugh C. Willett. [L. A., 1963]. 2 v. in 1. CL.

1398. MCATEER, J. EUGENE. "Equality of opportunity must be real," in
California teachers association, v. 60, Mar., 1964, pp. 14-15.

1399. _____. "Law for compensatory education," in _Integrated education_,
v. 1, June, 1963, p. 48.

1400. MCKENNEY, J. WILSON. "California equalizes opportunity; school districts struggle with educational problems," in _California teachers association journal_, v. 61, Mar., 1965, pp. 8-12.
Pertains mainly to segregation.

Segregation and Desegregation

1401. *MAJOR, REGINALD W.   "Integration for excellence," in Nation,
      Sept. 12, 1966.
           A study of San Francisco schools.

1402. MARASCUILO, LEONARD A. Attitudes toward de facto segregation in a
      northern city, 1964-1965 [by] Leonard A. Marascuilo. Berkeley, Univ. of
      Calif. [1967]. v.p. CU-B.
           A study of educational segregation in Berkeley.

1403. _____., and KATHLEEN PENFIELD. "A northern urban community's attitudes
      toward racial imbalance in schools and classrooms," in School review,
      Winter, 1966.
           A study of Berkeley schools.

1404. MARSHALL, RACHELLE. "Concrete curtain - the East Palo Alto story," in
      Crisis, v. 64, Nov., 1957, pp. 543-48.
           The problem of school integration in a community separated by a
      freeway.

1405. MECKLER, ZANE. "De facto segregation in California," in California
      teachers association journal, v. 58, Jan., 1963, pp. 26-28.

1406. METZ, WILLIAM. "Negro segregation in Los Angeles - Does it exist?",
      in California sun magazine, v. 12, Fall and Winter, 1960-61, pp. 49-52.

1407. NEFF, TED. "What do we know about desegregation?", in California
      education, v. 2, Mar., 1965, pp. 13-14.

1408. Oakland. Interagency project. A bold venture; integration in depth
      with student populations. [Oakland] 1965. 14 l. CO (photocopy).

1409. _____. Public schools. Progress report of study and action related
      to civil rights problems and compensatory education programs. [Oakland]
      1964. 32 l. CO (photocopy).

1410. OLSON, E. "APEX, an area concept," in Journal of secondary education,
      v. 43, Nov., 1968, pp. 309-12.
           A Los Angeles plan for desegregation through voluntary busing.

1411. PASNICK, RAY. "School segregation -- North and West," in American
      federationist, v. 70, July, 1963, pp. 23-24.

1412. PLATT, WILLIAM J. Racial balance in the San Francisco unified school
      district -- phase I ... by William J. Platt [and others]. Menlo Park,
      Stanford research institute, 1966. v.p. tables. CSf, CSt.
           "Interim report, July 1966" prepared for the San Francisco unified
      school district, by the Stanford research institute (S. R. I. project
      1-6018).

1413. POE, ELIZABETH. "Segregation in the Los Angeles schools," in
      Frontier, v. 13, Oct., 1962, pp. 12-13.

Segregation and Desegregation

1414. POLOS, NICHOLAS C. "Segregation and John Swett," in Southern
California quarterly, v. 46, Mar., 1964, pp. 64-82.
Educational segregation in California, 1850's and 1860's.

1415. Portland. Committee on race and education. Race and equal educational
opportunity in Portland's public schools; a report to the Board of education, Multnomah school district no. 1. Portland, Metropolitan print
1964. 24 p. tables. Bibliography. CO, OrU.

1416. QUINN, ALFRED THOMAS. Persistent patterns and problems peculiar to
selected schools and communities in racial transition. Doctoral dissertation, Univ. of Calif., Los Angeles, 1964. 127 ℓ.
Identified and codified 53 persistent patterns and problems faced by
schools, based on examination of 7 cities in various stages of racial
transition.

1417. RECORD, WILSON, 1916- . "Board members and integration," in
California teachers association journal, v. 61, Mar., 1965, pp. 18-21.

1418. _____. Discrimination-fact. [Vista, P. Chacon, 1962?]. 25 ℓ. C.
A series of five articles on discrimination in education reprinted
from Teacher, Sept., and Nov., 1961; Jan., Mar., and May, 1962.

1419. _____. "Promised land; school board and Negro teacher in California,"
in Integrated education, v. 1, Apr., 1963, pp. 20-24.
Authored by a professor of sociology, Sacramento state college. Reprinted in part from The teacher, March, 1962.

1420. _____. "Racial integration in California schools," in Journal of
Negro education, v. 27, Winter, 1958, pp. 17-23.

1421. *RILES, WILSON CAMANZA, 1917- . "Equal educational opportunities in
a changing society - conference report," in California education, v. 2,
June, 1965, pp. 11-13, 15.
Authored by the Chief, Bureau of intergroup relations, California
state department of education.

1422. _____. "Integrating the desegregated school," in California teacher
association journal, v. 61, Mar., 1965, pp. 13-16.

1423. _____. "School boards and 'de facto' segregation," in California
education, v. 1, Nov., 1963, pp. 7-8.

1424. ROBINSON, W. A. "The functions of libraries in newly integrated
schools," in School review, Oct., 1955.
Concerns Phoenix schools.

1425. ROESER, VERONICA A. "De facto school segregation and the law: focus
San Diego," in San Diego law review, v. 5, Jan., 1968, pp. 57-82.

1426. "Roundup report: How schools meet desegregation challenges," in
Nation's schools, v. 78, Nov., 1966, pp. 62-72.
Includes schools in Pasadena, San Mateo, Los Angeles, Oakland,
Denver, and Seattle.

Segregation and Desegregation

1427. ROWE, ROBERT N. "Is Berkeley school integration successful?", in American school board journal, Dec., 1965.

1428. San Diego. City schools. We the people; official report of the three-year program of the intercultural project of the San Diego city schools, summarizing practices and recommending future activities for improving human relations. [San Diego, 1949]. 178 p. illus. Bibliography: pp. 177-78. CU.

1429. "San Diego parents sue to end segregation," in Classroom teacher, v. 10, Dec., 1967, p. 1.

1430. San Francisco. Board of education. Report of the Ad hoc committee of the Board of education to study ethnic factors in the San Francisco public schools. S. F., 1963. 27 p. CO.

1431. _____. Unified school district. Selected data for study in the challenge to effect a better racial balance in the San Francisco public schools, 1967-1968. S. F., 1968. 14 p. Tables only.

1432. "School progress in San Bernardino - documents," in Integrated education, v. 5, Apr.-May, 1967, pp. 22-35.
   The results of a complaint to the California state department of education by the N. A. A. C. P., C. O. R. E., and other groups.

1433. "School segregation in Berkeley," in Integrated education, v. 2, Apr.-May, 1964, pp. 43-46.

1434. SCHWARTZ, RUTH EVELYN. A descriptive analysis of oral argument before the United States supreme court in the school desegregation cases, 1952-1953. Thesis, Univ. of southern Calif., Los Angeles, 1966 [c1967]. v, 545 ℓ.

1435. *SCOTT, JOHNIE. "How it is -- my home is Watts," in Harper's magazine, v. 233, Oct., 1966, pp. 47-48.
   School integration.

1436. Seattle public schools. A report of racial distribution among pupils and employees. Seattle, 1968. Wa.

1437. _____. The report of the Citizens' advisory committee for equal educational opportunity. Seattle, 1964. Wa.

1438. _____. Research office. Racial distribution; distribution and change among pupils and employees of the Seattle public schools, Seattle, Washington, 1957 to 1966. Seattle, 1966. 49 p. Wa.

1439. "Segregation," in Southern California law review, v. 36, no. 3, 1963, pp. 493-96.
   "In the case of Jackson v. Pasadena City school district, the court, while acknowledging the school board's right of discretion, equated abuse of discretion with the establishment of segregation." - Elizabeth W. Miller.

Segregation and Desegregation

1440. SEIDENBAUM, ART. "Los Angeles: private integration of the public
schools," in Integrated education, Nov.-Dec., 1968, pp. 14-18.
The activities of the Transport a child foundation.

1441. SINGER, HARRY, and IRVING G. HENDRICK. "Total school integration:
an experiment in social reconstruction," in Phi Delta Kappan, v. 49,
Nov., 1967, pp. 143-47.
Pasadena.

1442. SMITH, STAN. "Compton ... a case study in gradual integration," in
California sun magazine, v. 12, Fall & Winter, 1960-61, pp. 53-56.

1443. SODERSTROM, MARY MC GOWAN. The dissemination of information in the
Berkeley school desegregation decision. Master's thesis, Univ. of Calif.,
Berkeley, 1969. 150 ℓ.

1444. SOLOMON, BENJAMIN. "Integration and the educators," in Integrated
education, v. 1, Aug., 1963, pp. 18-26.
"Tactics, strategies, and goals of Northern and Western school integration movements." - Elizabeth W. Miller.

1445. SPARROW, GLEN. "Like Eisenhower, like Nixon - school desegregation
revisited," in Black politician, v. 1, Jan., 1970, pp. 30-35.
By an intern in the California state Assembly.

1446. Stanford research institute. Analysis of alternative methods of improving racial balance in the San Francisco unified school district; a
proposal for research. Menlo Park, 1966. 19 ℓ. CSt-Law.

1447. _____. Racial balance in the San Francisco unified school district --
phase 1; interim report, by William J. Platt [and others]. Menlo Park,
1966. 37 ℓ. CSt-Law.
"Prepared for San Francisco unified school district, San Francisco,
California."

1448. STOCKER, J. "Segregation's last stand; the prospective victory over
discrimination in Arizona's schools ..." in Frontier, v. 2, Apr., 1957,
pp. 10-12.

1449. SULLIVAN, NEIL VINCENT. "A case study in achieving equal educational
opportunity," in Journal of Negro education, v. 34, Summer, 1965,
pp. 319-26.
The Superintendent of schools, Berkeley, uses the Free schools in
Prince Edward County, Virginia as his example and documents "those
things which must be done if we are to achieve equal educational opportunity for all our children."

1450. _____. "The eye of the hurricane," in Integrated education, v. 3,
Aug.-Nov., 1965, pp. 13-19.
School desegregation in Berkeley.

1451. _____. "Ghetto schools? close 'em!", in Nation, v. 206, May 27,
1968, pp. 694-96.

Segregation and Desegregation

1452. _____. Integration; a plan for Berkeley. A report to the Berkeley board of education. [Berkeley] 1967. 29 p. illus. CMp, CO.

1453. _____. "Make freedom live," in Integrated education, v. 4, Aug.-Sept., 1966, pp. 55-59.
   A lecture delivered before the Intergroup education project, Berkeley unified school district.

1454. _____. "Myths and gaps in school integration," in Today's education, v. 57, Sept., 1968, pp. 38-41.
   Berkeley.

1455. _____. Now is the time; integration in the Berkeley schools, by Neil V. Sullivan, with Evelyn S. Stewart. Foreword by Martin Luther King, Jr. Bloomington, Indiana univ. press [1970, c1969]. xvii, 205 p. CBGTU, CNoS, CSf, CStb, CU-B.

1456. _____. "The right to read -- a straight path to integration," in Integrated education, v. 5, Feb.-Mar., 1967, pp. 41-47.

1457. _____., and THOMAS D. WOGAMAN. "Berkeley: anatomy of community change," in Public management, v. 51, May, 1969, pp. 4-6.
   Berkeley's experience in school desegregation.

1458. THORNSLEY, JEROME RUSSELL. The superintendent's leadership techniques for intergroup racial and ethnic relations in desegregated public schools. Doctoral dissertation, Univ. of southern Calif., Los Angeles, 1969. ix, 266 ℓ. illus.

1459. U. S. Commission on civil rights. Racial isolation in the public schools. Washington, D. C., Govt. print. [1967]. 2 v. in 1. CNoS, CSdS, CSf.
   Although national in scope, some information is given about 9 city school systems in California and in Denver, Reno, Portland, Salt Lake City, and Seattle.

1460. VALLEAU, JOHN. "The school board is alive and listening; first break-through in de facto segregation," in San Diego magazine, v. 20, July, 1968, pp. 50-53, 84, 90.

1461. Vallejo. Unified school district. The findings of a survey to develop an inventory of problems and practices regarding ethnic imbalances in California schools ... Vallejo, 1965. 58 p. C.

1462. *WARDEN, DONALD. "Walk in dignity," in Congressional record, May 18, 1964, A2575-2577.
   Address by the president of the Afro-American association, Oakland, relative to educational integration.

1463. *WEBSTER, STATEN WENTFORD. "The influence of interracial contact on social acceptance in a newly integrated school," in Journal of educational psychology, v. 52, Dec., 1961.
   San Francisco.

Segregation and Desegregation

1464. _____., and MARIE KROGER. "A comparative study of selected perceptions and feelings of Negro adolescents with and without white friends in integrated schools," in Journal of Negro education, Winter, 1966.

1465. WEINBERG, MEYER, comp. Integrated education, a reader. Beverly Hills, Glencoe press [1968]. 376 p. illus., maps. CNoS, CSdS, CSf.
"Consists of selections from the magazine, Integrated education. Includes bibliographies."

1466. WIGGINS, SAMUEL PAUL, 1919- . The desegregation era in higher education. Berkeley, McCutchan pub. corp., 1966. xiv, 106 p. Includes bibliographical references. CFS, CLSU, CNoS, CSdS, CSfCiC, CSluSP, CU-A.

1467. WILLIAMS, ROBIN MURPHY, 1914- , ed. Schools in transition; community experiences in desegregation, ed. by Robin M. Williams, Jr., and Margaret W. Ryan. Chapel Hill, Univ. of North Carolina press [c1954]. xiii, 272 p. tables. Bibliography: pp. 263-64. CFS, CNoS, CSdS, CSf.
Includes experience in Arizona and New Mexico.

1468. WILSON, ALAN BOND. The consequences of segregation: academic achievement in a northern community. Berkeley, Univ. of Calif. [1969]. viii, 92 p. "Works cited": pp. 88-92. CBGTU, CNoS.

A detailed study of segregation in the Richmond school district.

1469. WOGAMAN, THOMAS D. "The Berkeley story: desegregation under the Ramsey plan," in California education, v. 3, Dec., 1965, pp. 4-6.

1470. Workshop on interracial gains and goals, Longfellow school, Berkeley, 1961. Berkeley unified school district [and] Council of social planning, Berkeley area: co-sponsored workshop on interracial gains and goals, March 10 and 11, 1961, Longfellow school. [Berkeley] 1961. 31 ℓ. tables. CU.
Racial discrimination in education.

SOUTHERN UNITED STATES

1471. ALEXANDER, EMMET GERALD. State education of the Negro in the South. Master's thesis, Univ. of Calif., Berkeley, 1907. xiv, 107 ℓ.

1472. AUSTIN, LETTIE JANE. Programs of English in representative Negro high schools in Texas. Doctoral dissertation, Stanford univ., Stanford, 1952. 129 ℓ.

1473. BLACKMON, BERNARD H. An occupational survey of the students and their parents of Lincoln high school, Dallas, Texas. Master's project report, Univ. of southern Calif., Los Angeles, 1960. viii, 71 ℓ. illus.

1474. BROWN, REUBEN HENRY. Problems in the democratic administration of an elementary school ... Master's thesis, Univ. of southern Calif., Los

Southern U. S.

   Angeles, 1945. vii, 84 ℓ. tables, diagrs., forms.
      Based upon a study of the Attucks school, Kansas City, Mo.

1475. BRYANT, IRA BABINGTON, 1908- . Administration of vocational education in Negro high schools in Texas. Doctoral dissertation, Univ. of
   southern Calif., Los Angeles, 1948. xi, 248 ℓ. maps, tables, diagrs.

1476. COBB, WILLIE LENOX, 1910- . Provisions for vocational education for
   Negroes in the high schools of Texas. Master's thesis, Univ. of southern
   Calif., Los Angeles, 1940. viii, 91 ℓ. tables.

1477. DOTSON, ALPORTA. An analysis of Negro pupils' responses to a social
   competence test. Master's thesis, Univ. of southern Calif., Los Angeles,
   1943. xiii, 183 [1] ℓ., 15 [4] p.
      Concerns the Hoffman and Wicker schools, New Orleans, La.

1478. DOVE, PEARLIE C. A study of the relationship of certain selected
   criteria and success in the student teaching program at Clark College,
   Atlanta, Georgia. Doctoral dissertation, Univ. of Colorado, Boulder,
   1959.
      Developed criteria for a selective admission plan in a predominantly
   Negro college.

1479. ECHOLS, JACK W. Criteria for evaluating teacher education in the
   Negro colleges of Texas. Doctoral dissertation, Univ. of Denver, Denver,
   1955.

1480. EL-SAYEH, HUSSEIN BAYOUMI. Booker T. Washington; a study of his
   educational experiments in Tuskegee normal and industrial institute.
   Master's thesis, Calif. state univ., Fresno, 1964.

1481. FAULK, HENRY DANIEL. A comparative study of occupational interests
   and opportunities of Negro rural high school students in Louisiana ...
   Master's thesis, Univ. of southern Calif., 1947. viii, 107 ℓ. map,
   tables, diagr.

1482. GOODEN, JOHN EDDIE. Negro participation in civil government with
   emphasis on public education in Texas. Doctoral dissertation, Univ. of
   southern Calif., Los Angeles, 1949. viii, 226 ℓ.

1483. GRAY, WILLIAM THEODORE. A handbook for the instructor of industrial
   arts in the Negro rural schools of Macon county, Alabama. Master's
   thesis, Univ. of southern Calif., Los Angeles, 1949. ii, 69 ℓ. illus.

1484. HENDRICKS, HARRY G. The full-time Negro principalship in Texas.
   Doctoral dissertation, Univ. of Colorado, Boulder, 1960.

1485. *HORNE, FRANK SMITH. The present status of Negro education in certain
   of the southern states, particularly Georgia. Master's thesis, Univ. of
   southern Calif., Los Angeles, 1932. vii, 231 ℓ. tables.

1486. JOHNSTON, WILLIAM E. A study of the registrar in state-supported colleges for Negroes. Doctoral dissertation, Univ. of Oregon, Eugene, 1952.

Southern U. S.

1487. KNIGHT, CHARLES L. A study of student personnel programs in Negro
colleges accredited by the Southern association. Doctoral dissertation,
Univ. of Denver, Denver, 1951.

1488. LANE, H. B. The present status of secondary education for Negroes in
Texas. Master's thesis, Univ. of southern Calif., Los Angeles, 1932.
iv, 95 ℓ. forms, tables.

1489. LANIER, RAPHAEL O'HARA. The history of Negro education in Florida.
Master's thesis, Stanford univ., Stanford, 1928.

1490. LOTT, MABEL SMITH, 1917- . The extra-curricular activities program:
a case study of Booker T. Washington high school, Houston, Texas. Doctoral dissertation, Univ. of Calif., Berkeley, 1953. ix, 191 ℓ. diagrs.,
tables.

1491. MC CALL, OLALEE. Deficiencies found in elementary urban Negro schools
of the South with a suggested program for their elimination. Master's
thesis, Univ. of southern Calif., Los Angeles, 1941. viii, 176 p.
tables, forms, diagrs.

1492. MC DONALD, JACK ARTHUR. Higher education for Negroes in Texas.
Master's project report, Univ. of southern Calif., Los Angeles, 1947.
iv, 50 ℓ.

1493. MANLEY, ALBERT EDMOND. An evaluative study of ten secondary schools
for Negroes in North Carolina. Doctoral dissertation, Stanford univ.,
Stanford, 1946. xi, 324, 192 ℓ. maps, forms, tables.

1494. MILLER, MAGGIE ULLERY. A study of the movement for the advancement of
Negroes in Oklahoma ... Master's thesis, Univ. of southern Calif., Los
Angeles, 1947. iii, 68 ℓ. tables.

1495. NEEDHAM, WALTER E. Intellectual, personality, and biographical
characteristics of southern Negro and white students. Doctoral dissertation, Univ. of Utah, Salt Lake City, 1966.
"Similarities and differences in southern Negro and white college
students with emphasis on creativity."

1496. NICHOLS, RUBY MARION. An appraisal of the educational program of
selected consolidated rural high schools for Negroes in Texas. Master's
thesis, Univ. of southern Calif., Los Angeles, 1948. vii, 100 ℓ.
tables, forms.

1497. PERPENER, JOHN O. The effects of the Gilmer-Aikin laws upon fifteen
schools in Texas that have Negro superintendents or supervising principals. Doctoral dissertation, Univ. of Colorado, Boulder, 1953.

1498. REITNOUER, MINNIE GRAGE. A comparative study of the achievements of
New Orleans' tenth grade colored pupils in reading comprehension, vo-
cabulary, and spelling. Thesis, Univ. of southern Calif., Los Angeles,
1928. xi, 100 ℓ. diagrs., tables.

Southern U. S.

1499. ROBERSON, ALBERTA CARL. A survey of certain aspects of the Negro
high schools in Leon county, Texas. Master's thesis, Univ. of southern
Calif., Los Angeles, 1941. iv, 77 ℓ.

1500. SANDERS, CHARLES D. Student personnel service in Negro colleges of
the south Atlantic states. Doctoral dissertation, Univ. of Oregon,
Eugene, 1963.

1501. SANDFORD, PAUL L. The origins and development of higher education for
Negroes in South Carolina to 1920. Doctoral dissertation, Univ. of New
Mexico, Albuquerque, 1965.

1502. SMITH, L. B. A survey of Negro schools in Wood county, Texas.
Master's thesis, Univ. of southern Calif., Los Angeles, 1936.

1503. SUMMERSETTE, JOHN FRED. The structure of the Atlanta university
center. Doctoral dissertation, Stanford univ., Stanford, 1952. 139 ℓ.

1504. THORNTON, PETER B. Analysis of the counselor-training program at
Texas southern university. Doctoral dissertation, Colorado state college,
Greeley, 1963.
    Data collected from university graduates, 1951-60.

1505. WATKINS, JOCELYN HENDERSON. The history and development of the
Colored state teachers' association of Texas. Master's thesis, Univ. of
southern Calif., Los Angeles, 1941. iv, 117 [2] ℓ.

1506. WATKINS, PAULINE MELONEE. An investigation of Negro elementary schools
in the state of Texas. Master's thesis, Univ. of southern Calif., Los
Angeles, 1937. ix, 132 ℓ. map, tables, form.

1507. WIGGINS, SAMUEL PAUL, 1919- . Higher education in the South [by]
Sam P. Wiggins. Berkeley, McCutchan pub. corp. [1966]. xx, 358 p.
illus., maps. CFS, CHS, CLSU, CNoS, CSdS, CSfCiC, CSluSP, CU-A.
    Discusses segregation in southern education.

1508. WILLIAMS, JAMES HENRY, 1905- . Equalization of school support in
Texas, by James Henry Williams. L. A., Univ. of southern Calif. press
[c1944]. xii, 90 p. (Univ. of southern Calif. education monographs,
no. 13). Bibliography: pp. [81]-90. CLSU, CSdS.

1509. _____. Equalization of school support in Texas. Doctoral dissertation, Univ. of southern Calif., Los Angeles, 1943. vii, 143 ℓ. tables,
diagr.

PRIMARY AND PRE-SCHOOL

1510. AMETJIAN, ARMISTRE. The effects of a pre-school program upon the
intellectual development and social competency of lower-class children.
Doctoral dissertation, Stanford univ., 1966. 127 ℓ. tables.
    Reported that early intervention can produce significant differences
in mental age, social competence and language development.

Primary and Pre-School

1511. BLAKE, DUDLEY ARTHUR. Racial and social-class differences as perceived by seventh-grade children through binocular rivalry. Doctoral
dissertation, Univ. of southern Calif., Los Angeles, 1965. v, 122 ℓ.
"Devised a binocular presentation of disparate pairs of slides depicting racial and class difference as a means of determining the influence of race and social class upon children's perceptions."

1512. BOYD, G. F. "The levels of aspiration of white and Negro children in
a non-segregated elementary school," in Journal of social psychology,
v. 36, 1952.
Study of a Portland school.

1513. BOYDSTON, ELEANOR RUTH HERTZ. Concepts of "good" and "bad" behavior
of Negro and white kindergarten children and their parents. Master's
thesis, Univ. of Calif., Berkeley, 1958. iv, 90 ℓ. diagrs., forms.

1514. BRADFORD, JAMES LOVELLE. Low self-concept and low achievement of
Negro children in the elementary school. Master's thesis, Calif. state
univ., Hayward, 1970. iv, 59 ℓ.

1515. BRAND, LILLIAN. "I teach colored children," in Opportunity, v. 15,
Feb., 1937, pp. 54-57.
A white teacher's impressions of a black primary school class in
Los Angeles.

1516. BRINKER, LEOLA ELIZABETH. A comparative study of the achievement
motivation of black fifth grade males in schools having three differing
racial balances. Master's thesis, Calif. state univ., San Jose, 1970.
76 ℓ. illus.

1517. BROMWICH, ROSE MEYER, 1923- . Some correlates of stimulus-bound
versus stimulus-free verbal responses to pictures by young Negro boys.
Doctoral dissertation, Univ. of Calif., Los Angeles, 1967. xii, 235 p.
tables.

1518. *BUFORD, CURTYCINE J. Zero difficulties in grade III. Master's
project report, Univ. of southern Calif., Los Angeles, 1948. iii, 57 ℓ.

1519. BUSH, ROBERT L. A study of the culturally disadvantaged students of
Cacheville elementary school. Master's thesis, Calif. state univ.,
Sacramento, 1968. 101 ℓ. illus.

1520. CAPPELLUZZO, EMMA M. Ethnic distance as it appears in teachers from
three elementary schools of differing ethnic composition. Doctoral dissertation, Univ. of Arizona, Tucson, 1965.
No discriminating data were obtained from scales of social distance
and dogmatism, but distinct patterns emerged from open-ended interviews.

1521. CAROLLO, DOROTHY B. Developing curriculum procedures for introducing
science concepts to culturally disadvantaged pre-school children.
Master's thesis, Calif. state univ., San Francisco, 1968. 89 ℓ.
"includes 15 sample curriculum units and a list of science books
for children."

Primary and Pre-School

1522. DU PONT, PHYLLIS MC LEAN. A determination by a projective technique of
young children's responses to persons of different skin color, using
fifty white five-year-old children of upper socio-economic status.
Master's thesis, Univ. of Calif., Berkeley, 1949. 37 ℓ. illus., tables.

1523. ELIOFF, IONE HILL. Reactions of parents from diverse social backgrounds to their experience in a parent participation preschool program.
Master's thesis, Calif. state univ., San Francisco, 1968. 90 ℓ.
     "In 1966/67, three co-ordinated projects at 22 Berkeley, California
schools offered nursery school programs in which parent participation
was expected. The parents, of diverse racial and social backgrounds,
answered questionnaires about their experiences for this study."

1524. "An experiment that uses computers to teach concept rather than merely
monitoring basic skills," in Southern education report, v. 2, Dec., 1966,
pp. 15-19.
     Brentwood Elementary School, East Palo Alto.

1525. FRENCH, GERALD DEAN. Racial self-perception in the black child: a
factor of the self-concept and an indicator of social competency.
Master's thesis, Calif. state univ., San Francisco, 1969. v, 58 ℓ.

1526. GOLDSTEIN, LILLIAN FAIDAR. A comparison of the auditory discrimination
ability of lower-class Negro and Mexican-American children in kindergarten and first grade. Master's thesis, Univ. of Calif., Los Angeles,
1967. viii, 48 ℓ. tables.

1527. *GOODLETT, CARLTON BENJAMIN, 1914- . The mental abilities of twenty-
nine deaf and partially deaf Negro children, by Carlton B. Goodlett and
Vivian R. Greene (with a foreword by Harry W. Greene) ... [Charleston,
W. Va., Jarrett print. co., 1940]. 23 p. illus., tables, diagr.
(West Virginia state college bulletin ... Ser. no. 4, June, 1940). CU.
     Authored by a San Francisco physician and publisher.

1528. GRANT, DORIS. A comparison of the self-concept of two groups of
culturally disadvantaged kindergarten children. Master's thesis, Calif.
state univ., San Francisco, 1966. 62 ℓ.
     "Determines the effectiveness of a Palo Alto head start program on
the self concept of six of its pupils as compared to the self concept of
six culturally disadvantaged children who did not attend head start ...''

1529. GRUNWALD, JOAN H. A study of the play patterns of a certain class
of low income four year old children. Master's thesis, Calif. state
univ., San Francisco, 1968. 88 ℓ.
     "A study of 25 four year olds, the majority Negro, enrolled in the
compensatory education program of the Bell Haven pre-school in East
Menlo Park ...''

1530. HOWISON, VICTORINNE HALL. "We like our Negro teacher," in Opportunity,
v. 23, July-Sept., 1945, p. 149.
     Account of Blossom Lorraine Van Lowe, first black teacher hired in
San Diego, 1942.

Primary and Pre-School

1531. HULTGREN, RUTH DAVIS. Changes in non-cognitive school readiness be-
havions shown by rural head start children as related to educational
impact of the head start program upon the children's parents. Master's
thesis, Calif. state univ., San Francisco, 1968. 129 ℓ.
"This study has a dual purpose: 'By innovative methods to measure
changes over a sixteen week period in selected non-cognitive school
readiness behaviors of sixteen children attending the full year head
start program in Morgan Hill ...'"

1532. JOHNSON, BARBARA CHILD. A comparison of three and five-year-old
Negroes' responses to persons of different skin colors. Master's thesis,
Univ. of Calif., Berkeley, 1951. iv, 40 ℓ. tables.

1533. JOHNSTON, ANDREW V. An investigation of elementary school teachers
information concepts and generalizations about races, cultures and
nations. Doctoral dissertation, Univ. of Oregon, Eugene, 1963.
A study of factors influencing the extent of knowledge possessed by
elementary school teachers about races and their international understanding.

1534. KATZ, LILIAN GONSHAW. A study of the changes in behavior of children
enrolled in two types of head start classes. Doctoral dissertation,
Stanford univ., Stanford, 1968. viii, 144 ℓ.

1535. KERRIGAN, JEAN M. A community resource guidebook for Bay view elementary school, San Francisco. Master's thesis, Calif. state univ.,
San Francisco, 1955. 70 ℓ.
"A 1955 directory of firms and service agencies in the Hunters Point
area which co-operate with school teachers in organizing field trips and
classroom presentations."

1536. KIEVMAN, ELAINE LARSON, 1917- . A pilot study designed to expand
the linguistic versatility of socially disadvantaged kindergarten Negro
children. Doctoral dissertation, Univ. of Calif., Los Angeles, 1968.
xii, 207 ℓ. illus.

1537. *KING, LOUIS DEVOID. Industrial arts made easy for your elementary
pupils: a handbook for elementary teachers. Master's project report,
Univ. of southern Calif., Los Angeles, 1951. v, 85 ℓ. illus.

1538. KUSMA, KAY JUDEEN, 1941- . The effects of three preschool inter-
vention programs on the development of autonomy in Mexican-American and
Negro children. Doctoral dissertation, Univ. of Calif., Los Angeles,
1970.

1539. LEWIS, MARY S. Development of an intake interview schedule; an in-
strument to assess change in families participating in a cross-cultural
nursery school. Master's thesis, Calif. state univ., San Francisco,
1966. 59 ℓ.
"Describes the formulation of interview questions to be used as a
major data collecting device in the measurement of the positive effects
of a cross-cultural nursery school. The school studied was established

Primary and Pre-School

in 1966 in San Francisco's Western addition under a National institute of mental health grant."

1540.   MC CLELLAN, WILLIAM CIRCE. The status and function of Negro men teachers in the public elementary school of Arizona. Master's thesis, Ariz. state univ., Tempe, 1948. 94 ℓ. illus.

1541.   MARSHAK, MARIANNE. Teachers evaluate the progress of the head start child. L. A., Economic and youth opportunities agency, Training dept. [c1966]. 55 p. Bibliography: p. 53. CU.

1542.   MATZEN, STANLEY PAUL. The relationship between racial composition and scholastic achievement in elementary school classrooms. Doctoral dissertation, Stanford univ., Stanford, 1965. 138 ℓ. forms, tables.
     "Studied the relation between the percentage of Negroes in a classroom and mean scholastic achievement of 5th- and 7th-grade classes; concluded that the relationship is largely a function of school grouping practices." - West, p. 66.

1543.   MONGET, PATRICIA ANN. A resource unit on the American Negro for seventh grade social studies. Master's thesis, Univ. of Calif., Los Angeles, 1968. viii, 157 ℓ. illus.

1544.   MORAN, JAMES ANNE (religious). An examination of the need for family-centered nursery schools for culturally disadvantaged children. Master's thesis, Calif. state univ., San Francisco, 1968. 58 ℓ.
     "Examines the need for family involvement in nursery schools for culturally disadvantaged children. Interviews with the staff of Nurseries in cross-cultural education project in San Francisco's Western addition, questionnaires completed by nursery school teachers in San Francisco and Chicago, and a review of the literature constituted the research method."

1545.   *Mothers for equal education bookstore, pub. Day school E[ast] P[alo] A[lto], by day school people. East Palo Alto, c1970. 88 p. illus., ports.
     Mainly essays by teachers and students describing the aims and activities of the school and its personnel.

1546.   NEWMAN, KATHRYN LEAH. An investigation of the effects of cultural differences in relation to preschool dependency behavior in a cross-cultural nursery school. Master's thesis, Calif. state univ., San Francisco, 1967. 101 ℓ.
     "Investigates how cultural differences in beliefs, attitudes, and customs affect the dependency behavior of pre-schoolers, and how such behavior is changed after five months' attendance in the N. I. C. E. project, School of education, San Francisco state college (Nurseries in cross-cultural education)."

1547.   NORTH, GEORGE E., and O. LEE BUCHANAN. "Maternal attitudes in a poverty area," in Journal of Negro education, v. 37, Fall, 1968, pp. 418-25.
     Pre-school and kindergarten children in Phoenix.

Primary and Pre-School

1548. PAYNE, EILEEN. A study to examine the effect of the experience of a one-year head start program on the development of the child's self-concept. Master's thesis, Calif. state univ., San Francisco, 1968. 56 ℓ.

"The development of self-concept (as measured by psychological tests) in 10 San Mateo kindergarten head start graduates as compared to that of a group of 10 kindergarteners with no head start experience."

1549. PLATT, ELIZABETH FRAZIER. Young children's response to differences in skin color. Master's thesis, Univ. of Calif., Berkeley, 1950. 39 ℓ. diagrs., tables.

1550. PORTUGUES, STEPHEN HOWARD. The effects of positive and negative styles on imitation in Negro and white boys and girls. Master's thesis, Univ. of Calif., Los Angeles, 1968. vii, 44 ℓ.

1551. POZOVICH, GREGORY J. A comparative investigation of the differences between Negro and Mexican-American fifth graders in ability and school achievement. Master's thesis, Calif. state univ., Fresno, 1968.

1552. RACHIELE, LEO D. A comparative analysis of ten year old Negro and white performance on the Wechsler intelligence scale for children. Doctoral dissertation, Univ. of Denver, Denver, 1953.

1553. RADER, TONJA EVETTS. A creative dance and body movement experience and its effect upon the self-concept of disadvantaged nursery school children. Master's thesis, Calif. state univ., San Francisco, 1968. 61 ℓ.

"A study of Negro children (in attendance at Potrero Hill A[ssembly] B[ill] 1330 nursery school project in San Francisco, California) to investigate their self concept and to measure whether a creative dance and body movement experience altered or improved their self concept."

1554. RANDALS, EDWYNA HENRIETTA. A comparative study of the intelligence test results of Mexican and Negro children in two elementary schools. Master's thesis, Univ. of southern Calif., Los Angeles, 1929. v, 65 ℓ. diagrs., tables.

1555. ROGERS, WANDA J. The Negro child's recognition of his skin color; a survey of family portraits made by primary grade children in four selected schools. Master's thesis, Calif. state univ., Fresno, 1959.

1556. San Francisco. Unified school district, pub. Introductory teaching guide for black studies in elementary schools, March, 1969. S. F., 1969. 61 p.

1557. SHIKOMBA, MADELINE. A suggested method to develop a positive self-image in black children. Master's thesis, Calif. state univ., San Francisco, 1968. iv, 102 ℓ. illus.

1558. SILBERSTEIN, RUTH LEIBOWITZ. Risk-taking behavior in preschool children from three ethnic backgrounds. Master's thesis, Univ. of Calif., Los Angeles, 1969. ix, 43 ℓ.

Primary and Pre-School

1559. SIMONDS, OLIVE B. A language arts curriculum for disadvantaged Negro kindergarten children. Master's thesis, Calif. state univ., Los Angeles, 1968.

1560. TABACHNICK, BENJAMIN ROBERT. Some correlates of prejudice toward Negroes in elementary age children; satisfaction with self and academic achievement. Doctoral dissertation, Stanford univ., Stanford, 1959. 70 ℓ. forms, tables.
  "Found that satisfaction with self in 8 categories of Self-Concept Inventory is related to prejudice." - West, p. 28.

1561. *TAYLOR, ETHEL ALEXANDRIE. A guide for arithmetic experience in the second grade. Master's project report, Univ. of southern Calif., Los Angeles, 1950. iv, 113 ℓ.

1562. TYRRELL, FRANK EDWARD. Administrative policies and practices of programs for the culturally disadvantaged in elementary schools of the U. S. Doctoral dissertation, Univ. of southern Calif., Los Angeles, 1965.
  Reports on 136 elementary school districts with programs for culturally disadvantaged children.

1563. U. S. Dept. of health, education and welfare. Office of education. Preschool program, Fresno, California; one of a series of successful compensatory education programs. Washington, D. C., Govt. print., 1969. 16 p. CMp.

1564. *Ward, Mary Frances, by A. J. Ward, her guardian ad litem, plaintiff, vs. Noah F. Flood, principal of the Broadway grammar school, in the city and county of San Francisco, defendant. Ms. 4 p., 1872 and 1874. Case no. 3532 in the Supreme court of the state of California. See also Cal. 36. C-ArS.

1565. _____. Answer of the defendant. Williams & Thornton, attorneys for defendant. S. F., B. F. Sterett, 1872. 5 p. C-ArS.
  Plaintiff sued to gain admission to the Broadway grammar school, San Francisco.

1566. _____. Application for mandate. John W. Dwinelle, for plaintiff. S. F., Bacon & co., 1872. 6 p. C-ArS (contains Ms. amendations).

1567. _____. Brief of plaintiff on the right of colored children to be admitted to the public schools. John W. Dwinelle, of counsel for plaintiff. S. F., Bacon & co., 1872. 25 p. C-ArS.

1568. _____. Statement of the case. [Argument of Mr. John W. Dwinelle on the right of colored children to be admitted to the public schools. S. F., Bacon & co., printers, 1872?]. 26 p. CHi, CU.

1569. WASSERMAN, SUSAN ARNESTY, 1931- . Expressed "humanitarian" and "success" values of four-year-old Mexican-American, Negro, and Anglo

Primary and Pre-School

blue-collar and white-collar children. Doctoral dissertation, Univ. of Calif., Los Angeles, 1969. xiv, 179 ℓ. plates, tables.

1570. WILLIAMS, CHARLOTTE ANNE. Testing for conformity among black-American and Mexican-American elementary school children. Master's thesis, Calif. state univ., Hayward, 1970. viii, 64 ℓ. charts.

1571. *WILLIAMS, JOSEPH JOHNSON. Methods of teaching figure drawing in the upper elementary grades. Master's thesis, Univ. of southern Calif., Los Angeles, 1951. iv, 100 ℓ. illus.

1572. YABLON, ROBERTA SEIFERT. Sharing behavior of Negro children as it is affected by Negro and Caucasian models. Master's thesis, Calif. state univ., Sacramento, 1970. 41 ℓ.

1573. YABROFF, LAWRENCE JONAS. The effect of personalized instructional material on the comprehension and retention of the culturally disadvantaged child. Master's thesis, Calif. state univ., San Francisco, 1968. 53 ℓ.
     "A study of thirty-nine third graders in Central public school, Sausalito, California, testing the hypothesis that individualized instructional materials aid learning and retention."

SECONDARY

1574. ALEXANDER, RUTH. Racial characteristics and conditions of the student population at Watsonville union high school. Master's thesis, Stanford univ., Stanford, 1940. 138 ℓ.

1575. *CAGLE, MABELLE CLAIR. A course of study for ninth grade social living classes. Master's project report, Univ. of southern Calif., Los Angeles, 1951. viii, 102 ℓ.

1576. California. University. Berkeley. School of education. McClymonds: a problem in urban redevelopment; unofficial working papers [prepared by] University of California, Berkeley, School of education, Oakland redevelopment agency [and] Oakland school board. [Berkeley, 1966]. 305 ℓ. CU.
     A study of McClymonds high school, Oakland.

1577. _____. _____. _____. _____. McClymonds: a search for environmental and educational excellence. [By] University of California, Berkeley, School of education, Oakland redevelopment agency [and] Oakland unified school district. [Berkeley, 1966]. 88 p. CU-B.
     A study of McClymonds high school, Oakland.

1578. COBB, WILLIE LENOX, 1910- . Vocational interests of white and Negro pupils at the secondary level. Doctoral dissertation, Univ. of Calif., Berkeley, 1949. 176 ℓ. tables.

Secondary

1579. CRUMAL, GLENA. "Tulare's attempt to reduce dropouts," in California education, v. 2, Nov., 1964, pp. 27-28.
     A project undertaken by the Inter-racial advisory council of Tulare.

1580. DANIELS, HAZEL BURTON, 1906- . A Negro high school in Tucson, Arizona. Master's thesis, Univ. of Arizona, Tucson, 1941.

1581. EPPS, EDGAR G. "Socioeconomic status, race, level of aspiration and juvenile delinquency: a limited empirical test of Merton's conception of deviation," in Phylon, Spring, 1967.
     Study based upon a Seattle high school.

1582. FRELOW, ROBERT DEAN. Intergroup associations at an East bay junior high school. Master's thesis, Calif. state univ., San Francisco, 1964. viii, 93 ℓ. tables.

1583. HANCOCK, ALLEN C. A study of the programs for professional preparation of secondary school teachers in the Negro publicly supported colleges. Doctoral dissertation, Univ. of Colorado, Boulder, 1952.

1584. HARRIS, FLORENCE. The adjustment of the Negro in a California junior high school. Master's thesis, Stanford univ., Stanford, 1949. 180 ℓ. tables.

1585. HATCH, ROBERT H. A study of the leadership ability of Negro high school principals. Doctoral dissertation, Colorado state college, Greeley, 1964.
     Behavioral characteristics that distinguish effective from less effective leaders in a group of Negro principals.

1586. HELTSLEY, DIANE VICTORIA. A description of multi-racial drama programs in selected bay area high schools. Master's thesis, Calif. state univ., San Francisco, 1966. 96 ℓ.
     "A survey of approaches to drama programs in eight San Francisco bay area multi-racial high schools. Practice rather than theory is emphasized ..."

1587. *HERNDON, JAMES. "The way it 'spozed to be," in Harper's, v. 231, Sept., 1965, pp. 79-87.

1588. _____. The way it 'spozed to be: a report on the classroom war behind the crisis in our schools. N. Y., Simon & Schuster, 1965 [c1968]. 188 p. C, CHC, CNoS, CSf, CStcrCL, CSto.
     The author's report about a year spent teaching in a Negro junior high school in San Diego.

1589. HICKERSON, NATHANIEL. Comparisons between Negro and non-Negro students in participation in the formal and informal activities of a California school. Doctoral dissertation, Univ. of Calif., Berkeley, 1962. viii, 122 ℓ.
     Comparisons between Negro, Filipino, and white high school students in a San Francisco bay area school.

Secondary

1590. _____. "Some aspects of school integration in a California high
    school," in Journal of Negro education, v. 34, Spring, 1965, pp. 130-37.
        A summary of his doctoral dissertation.

1591. HOHN, F. R. "What's happening? Council of black administrators,"
    in Journal of secondary education, v. 44, Feb., 1969, p. 96.
        Los Angeles.

1592. KAHL, SUE ANN. An evaluation of the interdepartmental African studies
    unit at Lowell junior high school in Oakland. Master's thesis, Calif.
    state univ., San Francisco, 1968. 70 ℓ.
        "An evaluation of an 11 week, interdepartmental African studies unit
    presented at Oakland's Lowell junior high school in the Spring of
    1968."

1593. KEEN, HAROLD. "What can we learn from the hard lesson of Lincoln
    High," in San Diego magazine, v. 21, July, 1969, pp. 46-49, 73-77.

1594. KURTH, MYRTLE. A study of four racial groups in a Pasadena junior
    high school. Master's thesis, Univ. of southern Calif., Los Angeles,
    1941. 143 p.
        McKinley junior high school.

1595. LARSEN, CECIL EVVA. "Control patterns in an interracial school; the
    Thomas Jefferson high school in east Los Angeles," in Sociology and
    social research, v. 30, May, 1946, pp. 383-90.

1596. *LAWRENCE, PAUL FREDERICK. The vocational aspirations of Negro youth
    in secondary schools of California. Doctoral dissertation, Stanford
    univ., Stanford, 1948. 162 ℓ. forms, tables.

1597. MC CREARY, EUGENE. "Learning to teach deprived children," in
    Integrated education, v. 1, Apr., 1963, pp. 38-40.
        Authored by the Supervisor of secondary education, Berkeley.

1598. *MC DOWELL, LEONA BABER. A critical study of high school social studies
    textbooks for matter tending to foster racial prejudice. Master's
    thesis, Univ. of southern Calif., Los Angeles, 1955. 61 ℓ.

1599. MEZZ, SHEILA MAYERS. Effects of a "Black Cultural Positives" program
    on the self concepts and attitudes of black junior high students.
    Doctoral dissertation, Ariz. state univ., Tempe, 1971. 197 ℓ. illus.

1600. *MURPHY, S. JACKSON. A survey of Woodland rural high school building
    to determine its fitness for utilization in a rural community. Master's
    thesis, Univ. of southern Calif., 1928. 78 ℓ. tables.

1601. Oakland. Public schools. McClymonds, a search for environmental and
    educational excellence. Oakland, 1966. 88 p. illus., maps, tables. CO.

1602. OSTROV, GORDON I. Family solidarity and school dropouts: a compara-
    tive study of adolescents from Negro ethnic group families, city of

Secondary

Fresno, California, dichotomized by dropouts and graduates from high
school. Master's thesis, Calif. state univ., Fresno, 1968.

1603. PARKER, PAULINE E. Relationship of deferred gratification to attitudes and performance of minority groups in one high school. Master's
thesis, Calif. state univ., Sacramento, 1963. 129 ℓ.

1604. PENN, NOLAN. Occupational choices of tenth grade students and the
influences of racial and socio-economic factors upon them. Master's
thesis, Univ. of southern Calif., Los Angeles, 1952. viii, 102 ℓ.

1605. _____. "Racial influence on vocational choice," in Journal of Negro
education, v. 35, Winter, 1966, pp. 88-89.
A study of 75 students in a junior high school in Compton.

1606. PITTS, J. C. The organization and administration of school clubs in
the Jefferson high school of Los Angeles, California. Master's thesis,
Univ. of southern Calif., Los Angeles, 1941.

1607. RATTERMAN, BREEN. Guidance practices for Negro youth in selected
California secondary schools. Master's thesis, Stanford univ., Stanford,
1948. 89 ℓ. forms.

1608. RICHARDSON, ADELINE (CLAFF). A follow-up study of Negro girl graduates
of a Los Angeles high school. Master's thesis, Univ. of southern Calif.,
Los Angeles, 1941. 105 ℓ. tables, forms.
Relates to Thomas Jefferson high school graduates.

1609. Seattle public schools. Research dept. The Garfield Leaver study.
Seattle public schools, April 1950. [Seattle, 1950]. Wa.
A study of Negro dropouts from Garfield high school.

1610. SILVERTHORN, WILLIAM A. The development of a racial attitude scale
for secondary school students. Master's thesis, Univ. of southern
Calif., Los Angeles, 1952. iii, 87 ℓ.

1611. *WALKER, OLIVE. "The Windsor Hills school story," in Integrated
education, v. 8, May-June, 1970, pp. 4-9.
The high rating of a Los Angeles school.

1612. *WEBSTER, STATEN WENTFORD. Correlates and effects of ethnic group
identification; a study of Negro adolescents in urban high schools, by
Staten W. Webster and Marie N. Kroger. Berkeley, Univ. of Calif., 1963.
94 ℓ. illus. Bibliography: ℓ. 92-94. CU.

1613. WHITMAN, WINSLOW, and ISABELLE G. ROSENFELS. Study and evaluation of
racial tension at Pasco high school. Olympia, Washington state board
against discrimination, 1969. 44 p. Wa.

1614. *WILLIAMS, GEORGIA MAE. A study of the adaptation of the curriculum
to Negro pupils in public secondary schools. Master's thesis, Univ. of
southern Calif., Los Angeles, 1938. 95 ℓ. tables, form.

COLLEGE AND UNIVERSITY

1615. *ALLEN, LA MAR.   A proposed program of intramurals for Arkansas state agricultural, mechanical and normal college. Master's project report, Univ. of southern Calif., Los Angeles, 1951. vii, 91 l.

1616.   American association of university professors. University of Oregon chapter. Research council. The Negro and higher education in Oregon. Eugene, Ore., 1964. 14 l. OrU.

1617.   BELANGER, LAURENCE L.   "Educational opportunities program at UCLA," in California education, v. 3, Oct., 1965, p. 16.

1618. *BILLINGSLEY, ANDREW, DOUGLAS DAVIDSON, and THERESA LOYA.   "Ethnic studies at Berkeley," in California monthly, v. 80, June-July, 1970, pp. 12-20.

1619.   BLOSSOM, HERBERT HENRY.   Some factors influencing high school graduates' attendance at different types of colleges. Doctoral disser- tation, Univ. of Calif., Berkeley, 1966. xi, 159 l.
       Factors considered included race, academic ability, socio-economic level, sex, and motivation.

1620.   BOLTON, INA ALEXANDER.   The problems of Negro college women. Doctoral dissertation, Univ. of southern Calif., Los Angeles, 1949. xii, 258 l.

1621.   BOONE, F. THERESSA.   Higher education for the Negro. Master's thesis, Univ. of southern Calif., Los Angeles, 1925. 92 p.

1622.   BOYKIN, CYNTHIA ANN.   "Merritt college, a pivot of social change," in Urban west, v. 2, Apr., 1969, pp. 13, 24.
       Interview with Norvell Smith, Oakland college president.

1623. *BRADFORD, VIOLA.   "Letter from Arizona," in Southern courier, June 24, 1967.
       A Negro student reflects on her first year at the Univ. of Arizona.

1624.   BRANN, JAMES.   "San Jose: the bullhorn message," in Nation, v. 205, Nov. 6, 1967, pp. 465-67.
       Conditions at California state univ., San Jose.

1625. *BUNCHE, RALPH JOHNSON, 1904-1971. UCLA Bunche hall ceremony, Friday, 23 May, 1969, 3:30 p. m. Remarks by Ralph J. Bunche (Dr. Bunche has pre- sented the manuscript of his remarks — with emendations and interpolations — to the UCLA library) ... [L. A., Univ. of Calif., 1969]. 4 p. Mimeo. CLU, CSf.

1626.   BUNZEL, JOHN H.   "Black studies at San Francisco state," in Public interest, Fall, 1968, pp. 22-38.

1627.   BURTON, MARY LILLIAN.   A survey of guidance problems in four-year Negro colleges and universities. Master's thesis, Univ. of southern Calif., Los Angeles, 1952. iii, 64 l. illus. (part fold.).

College and University

1628. California. Coordinating council for higher education. California higher education and the disadvantaged; a status report. [Sacramento] 1968. iii, 68 p. tables. CLS, CSf, CSluSP.
    Gives recommendations based upon evaluations of existing programs in California colleges and universities.

1629. CAMPA, ARTHUR LEON, ed. Discrimination in higher education in the Mountain states region, proceedings of a conference sponsored by the Mountain states committee on discrimination in higher education of the American council on education, held at Denver, Colorado, Feb. 10, 1951. Denver, The committee, 1951. vii, 37 p. CL, CSdS.
    An examination of discrimination mainly against Jews, Negroes, and Italians in Colorado, Utah, New Mexico, and Wyoming.

1630. CLARK, SANDRA JEAN, 1938- . An exploratory analysis of Educational opportunity program (EOP) women students in a UCLA residence hall. Doctoral dissertation, Univ. of Calif., Los Angeles, 1969. xii, 211 ℓ.

1631. College and university self-study institute, Univ. of Calif., 1970. The minority student on the campus: expectations and possibilities. Ed. by Robert A. Altman and Patricia O. Snyder. [Boulder, Colo.] Western interstate commission for higher education, 1970. x, 219 p. CHS.
    "Papers from the 12th annual College and University Self-Study Institute, July 6-9, 1970, University of California, Berkeley ..."

1632. CUMMINS, THOMAS J. "Chaos on the campus," in New republic, v. 158, Jan. 6, 1968, pp. 14-15.
    Calif. state univ., San Francisco.

1633. *DERBIGNY, IRVING ANTONY, 1900- . General education in the Negro college, by Irving A. Derbigny. Stanford, Stanford univ. press [c1947]. ix, 255 p. Bibliography: pp. 245-49. CHS, CLobS, CSS, CSjC, CU, CU-A.

1634. DERBYSHIRE, ROBERT L. "Identity conflict in Negro college students," in Integrated education, v. 4, June-July, 1966, pp. 12-21.
    Authored by a psychiatrist at the Univ. of Calif., Los Angeles.

1635. DIDION, JOAN. "Revolution games," in Saturday evening post, v. 242, Jan. 25, 1969, p. 20.
    Calif. state univ., San Francisco.

1636. EGERTON, JOHN. State universities and black Americans; an inquiry into desegregation and equity -- for Negroes in 100 public institutions. Atlanta, Southern education foundation, 1969. 96 p. illus. CHS.
    Contains "UCLA: suburbia meets the urban crisis."

1637. FREEDMAN, MERVIN B. "Urban campus prototype," in Nation, v. 208, Jan. 13, 1969, pp. 38-42.
    Calif. state univ., San Francisco.

1638. *Golden state mutual life insurance company. Destination: tomorrow; education's part in your child's future. [L. A., 196-?]. [8] p. illus.

College and University

CLGS.
Explains the advantages and the costs of a college education.

1639. GRANBERG, W. J. "Appreciation from knowledge," in Crisis, v. 56, Aug.-Sept., 1949, p. 237.
Describes a course in Afro-American history taught by Ralph Johnston at the Univ. of Puget Sound, Tacoma.

1640. *HARE, NATHAN, and S. J. WRIGHT. "Black students and Negro colleges," in Saturday review, v. 51, July 20, 1968, pp. 44-46ff. Discussion, in v. 51, Aug. 17, 1968, p. 40.

1641. HARRIS, MORGAN. Closed doors; a report on certain cases of unfair discrimination among students applying for admission to publicly tax supported institutions of higher education in California. [n.p., 1957?]. 27 p. C.

1642. HUMISTON, THOMAS FREDERIC. Participation of ethnic groups in student activities at a junior college. Doctoral dissertation, Stanford univ., Stanford, 1959. 139 ℓ. forms, tables.
"Minority-group students showed differences from dominant group in nature and extent of extracurricular participation." - West, p. 45.

1643. Immaculate heart college, Los Angeles. On the move, Fall, 1969 ... Editors: Erin Hennessey [and] Mary Helen Pendel ... L. A., c1969. [14] ℓ. illus., ports. CSf.
Describes the Black students union, a Chicano studies program, and the change in the philosophy of education at the College.

1644. JONES, ARLYNNE L. An investigation of the response patterns which differentiate the performance of selected Negro and white freshmen on SCAT. Doctoral dissertation, Univ. of Colorado, Boulder, 1960.
Strength of positive relationship between sentence understandings and word meaning differentiated Negro and white performance at both upper and lower levels.

1645. KHAN, TAKI MOHAMMAD. Ethnic prejudice among Negro and foreign students. Master's thesis, Calif. state univ., Sacramento, 1969. 179 ℓ. illus.

1646. KIRSCHMAN, RICHARD. "Dean on a troubled campus," in Urban west, v. 2, Feb., 1969, pp. 15, 31.
An interview with Joseph White, Dean of undergraduate studies, California state univ., San Francisco.

1647. *KNOX, ELLIS ONEAL. The trend of progress in the light of new educational concepts in a group of American colleges dominated by religious influences. Doctoral dissertation, Univ. of southern Calif., Los Angeles, 1931. vii, 290 ℓ. tables.

1648. MANNING, HARVEY. "This social tragedy"; Part I: "It couldn't happen here, could it?" Part II: "What is the university doing about it?" in

College and University

Alumnus; a publication of the University of Washington alumni association, Winter, Spring, 1968, pp. 16-24, 12-17.

1649. MARTYN, KENNETH A. Increasing opportunities in higher education for disadvantaged students. A report prepared for the coordinating council for higher education by Dr. Kenneth A. Martyn ... Sacramento [State print.] 1966. 74 p. tables. CSf.
      A study of programs in California state and private colleges.

1650. MAY, HENRY F. "Living with crisis: a view from Berkeley," in American scholar, v. 38, Autumn, 1969.

1651. *MILLER, LOREN R., 1903-1967. "College," in Crisis, v. 33, Jan., 1927, pp. 138-40.

1652. *MUMFORD, ARNETT WILLIAM, 1898- . The present status of health and physical education programs in Negro senior colleges ... Master's thesis, Univ. of southern Calif., Los Angeles, 1947. xii, 150 [5] ℓ. tables, form, diagrs.
      Also pub. under same title in Research quarterly, Oct., 1948.

1653. *National association for African-American education. Black university, new black perspectives, and creative black solutions. Atlanta, Georgia, Aug. 20-24, 1969 ... [Palo Alto?, 1969]. [4] p. illus.
      Prospectus and announcement of Atlanta meeting issued by Sidney F. Walton, Jr., Palo Alto.

1654. Oakland city college workshop on cultural diversity, Univ. of Calif., 1963. Oakland city college workshop on cultural diversity [report] written under the direction of Joseph D. Lohman. Berkeley, Univ. of Calif., School of criminology, 1964. 71, 51 ℓ. Includes bibliography. CU.

1655. *OLAYINKA, MOSES SIYANBOLA, 1932- . Effectiveness of two modes of counseling in assisting African students to adjust to the general university environment. Doctoral dissertation, Univ. of Calif., Los Angeles, 1970. xvii, 193 ℓ.

1656. "139X," in National review, v. 20, Oct. 8, 1968, p. 996.
      About Eldridge Cleaver's course, Social analysis 139X, taught at the Univ. of Calif., Berkeley.

1657. ORRICK, WILLIAM H. College in crisis, a report to the National commission on the causes and prevention of violence [by] William H. Orrick, Jr., Director, San Francisco state college study team. Nashville, Aurora publishers, inc., 1970. ix, 180 p. illus., map, ports.
      Preface by S. I. Hayakawa.
      Describes the campus strike as it related to the San Francisco black community, the college Black student union and black studies program.

1658. Pepsi-cola scholarship board. College primer for Negro students. Palo Alto [1948]. 59 p. CLSU.
      Prepared by Paul Frederick Lawrence.

College and University

1659. PERRY, MARY ELLEN. "The prizefighter-professor heads a black curriculum," in Urban west, v. 1, Aug., 1968, pp. 20-21.
    Nathan Hare at California state college, San Francisco.

1660. PETERSON, CARL DANIEL, 1943- . An exploratory analysis of the development and achievement of E. O. P. (Equal opportunity program)
students. Doctoral dissertation, Univ. of Calif., Los Angeles, 1970.
xii, 127 ℓ.

1661. PETRAS, JAMES. "Politics of bureaucracy," in Liberation, v. 11, Feb.,
1967, pp. 21-26.
    Univ. of Calif., Berkeley.

1662. ROCHELLE, CHARLES EDWARD, 1895- . Graduate and professional
education for Negroes. Doctoral dissertation, Univ. of Calif., Berkeley,
1942. ix, 276 ℓ. tables.

1663. San Mateo. College of San Mateo. A profile of students in the
college readiness programs at College of San Mateo. [San Mateo, 1968].
[33] ℓ. CSjC.

1664. SATTERWHITE, MILDRED MC KINLEY, 1915- . Vocational interests of
Negro teachers college students. Doctoral dissertation, Univ. of Calif.,
Berkeley, 1949. 79 ℓ. diagrs., tables.

1665. SOMERVILLE, BILL. "Can selective colleges accommodate the disadvantaged? Berkeley says 'yes'," in College board review, v. 65, Fall,
1967, pp. 5-10.

1666. *THURMAN, HOWARD, 1899- . "The new heaven and the new faith: an
interpretation of certain aspects of the American Negroes' encounter
with higher education," in Journal of Negro education, v. 27, Spring,
1958, pp. 115-19.
    Equal rights in education.

1667. VOLLMER, HOWARD MASON. Variations in parental preferences of Negro
and white college students. Master's thesis, Stanford univ., Stanford,
1951. iv, 68 ℓ. tables.

1668. WALKER, PAUL. Court decisions dealing with legal relationships
between American colleges and universities and their students. Doctoral
dissertation, Univ. of southern Calif., Los Angeles, 1961. vii, 368 ℓ.
    Most frequently litigated question was attempted discrimination
against Negroes.

1669. Western interstate commission for higher education. Urban and
minority centered programs in western colleges and universities, 1969-70.
Report of a WICHE staff survey made in the Spring, 1969. Compiled by
Robert H. Kroepsch and Ian M. Thompson. Boulder, Colo., 1969. 72 p. C.

1670. YOUNG, KENNETH EVANS. Who can and should go to what kind of college?
Doctoral dissertation, Stanford univ., Stanford, 1953. 209 ℓ.

College and University

"Race was one of 8 variables in this temporal study of college admission requirements; notes effect of depression and war." - West, p. 52.

GENERAL WORKS

1671. ARMSTRONG, HUBERT C. "Educational opportunity and the Negro," in California journal of secondary education, v. 18, Oct., 1943, pp. 331-37.

1672. *BANNING, MAGNOLIA LOWE. The contribution of the Julius Rosenwald fund to Negro education and better race relations. Master's thesis, Univ. of Arizona, Tucson, 1945. 47 ℓ.

1673. *BECNEL, MILTON JOSEPH. Procedures for organizing and administering an effective health program in a small school district. Master's project report, Univ. of southern Calif., Los Angeles, 1949. 36 ℓ.

1674. Berkeley. Unified school district. The intergroup education project, 1963-64. [Berkeley, 1964]. 54 p. C.
A transcript containing lectures as well as panel discussion and audience reaction to major racial issues involving education.

1675. *BERRY, EDWIN C. "Intercultural education in Portland," in Opportunity, v. 24, Oct.-Dec., 1946, pp. 175-77 and 183.

1676. BOLNER, JAMES. "Defining racial imbalance in public educational institutions," in Journal of Negro education, v. 37, Spring, 1968, pp. 114-26.
Includes California.

1677. BOND, MARJORIE H. "Teenage attitudes and attitude change as measured by the Q-technique," in Journal of educational sociology, v. 36, Sept., 1962, pp. 10-15.
Concerns Brotherhood, U. S. A., an interracial workshop for southern California youth.

1678. BOYKIN, LEANDER L. Differentials in Negro education. Doctoral dissertation, Stanford univ., Stanford, 1948. 292 ℓ. tables.

1679. BROWN, MINTA (PALMER). Black power and education: a comparative study of student-administrator views. Doctoral dissertation, Univ. of southern Calif., Los Angeles, 1970. iv, 166 ℓ.

1680. *BULLOCK, JAMES, and LANNY BERRY, eds. Marin City, U. S. A. [Sausalito, Graphic arts of Marin, inc., 1970]. [50] p. illus., ports. CKenM.
"Marin City, USA has emerged from the work of black students in Project break-through. This project is part of the educational program of the Tamalpais union high school district, with funding from the federal government."

General Works

1681. *BULLOCK, PAUL, and ROBERT SINGLETON. "Some problems of minority-group education in the Los Angeles public schools," in Journal of Negro education, v. 32, Spring, 1963, pp. 137-45.

1682. BUSKIN, MARTIN. "How schoolmen are handling the hot ones: integration, innovation, and negotiation," in School management, v. 11, June, 1967, pp. 59-69, 72-76, 81, 83.
    Concerns Inglewood and other schools.

1683. BUTLER, JOHN HAROLD, 1897- . An historical account of the John F. Slater fund and the Anna T. Jeans foundation. Doctoral dissertation, Univ. of Calif., Berkeley, 1932. ix, 502 ℓ. tables.
    Relates to Negro education.

1684. BUTLER, VIVIAN LEOLA. The disadvantaged American Negro urban school child. Master's thesis, Calif. state college, Los Angeles, 1968.

1685. California. Commission on discrimination in teacher employment. Report. [1st-   Sacramento], 1959- . C (1959-64), CChiS (1960-62), CLSU (1959-64), CStb (1963).

1686. _____. Dept. of education. The commission on discrimination in teacher employment; services, policies, principles, statutes. [Sacramento?] 1960. CFS.

1687. _____. _____. Fifth biennial report ... for the school years 1872 and 1873. Sacramento, State print., 1873. 366 p. C, CSf, CSmH, CU, NUC, pre-1956.
    Lists number of black children by county who attended public and private schools or no school, 1872-73. Information is given on age, sex, and number of children under five years. See pp. 5, 140-42, 145-48, and 193. Subsequent biennial reports contain similar information about black schools and children of school age.

1688. _____. _____. Thirteenth annual report of the Superintendent of public instruction of the state of California for the year 1863. [Sacramento, State print., 1864]. 214 p. CSf.
    "Mongolian, Indian, and Negro children": pp. 67-68.
    Lists schools for black children in San Francisco, Sacramento, Marysville, San Jose, and Stockton.
    Other Annual reports, 1850-63, contain occasional information about black schools and children of school age.

1689. _____. _____. Office of compensatory education. An analysis of comparative data from schools in predominantly Negro, Mexican-American, and privileged sections of Los Angeles; final report of research project sponsored by Compensatory education commission under grant M-522 and M-622. [Sacramento?] 1967. 1 v. (v.p.). C.

1690. _____. _____. _____. A training demonstration and research program for the remediation of learning disorders in culturally disadvantaged youth. [Sacramento?, 1967]. 35 ℓ. C.

General Works

1691. _____. _____. _____. Bureau of intergroup relations. Northern
California conference on intergroup education [a report]; a conference
for school superintendents and school board members of northern
California, March 22, 1967. Oakland, 1967. 32 p. C.

1692. _____. _____. _____. _____. Racial and ethnic survey of California
public schools. [Sacramento, 1967]. 2 v. illus. C, CFS (v. 2), CLS,
CSt.

1693. _____. Legislature. Assembly. Tenth session. Appendix to the
journal of Assembly ... Sacramento, State print., 1859. C, CLU, CSf,
CSmH, CU, NUC, pre-1956.
    Contains the Annual report of the State superintendent of public
instruction in which appears his report on "Negroes in the public
schools," pp. 14-15.

1694. _____. State fair employment practice commission. Report on Oakland
schools; an investigation under Section 1421 of the California labor
code of the Oakland unified school district, 1962-1963. [Report by
C. L. Dellums, assigned commissioner. S. F., 1964]. 31 ℓ. illus.
CLSU, CS1uSP, CSt-Law, CU (photocopy).

1695. _____. University. Berkeley. School of education. Field service
center. Report of re-survey of school building needs, Berkeley unified
school district; presented to the Board of education, October 1956;
prepared by the Field service center, School of education, University
of California. Berkeley [1956]. 38 p. CU.

1696. California elementary school principals' association. Education for
cultural unity ... [L. A.] 1945. 156 p. (Its Seventeenth yearbook).
NN.
    Contents: "The minority side of intercultural education [by] Alain
Locke," pp. 60-64; "Langston Hughes tours high schools, a new approach
to interracial understanding [by] M. Margaret Anderson," pp. 103-05; and
"General survey of the literature and teaching aids in the field of
intercultural education," pp. 110-40.

1697. "California law on teaching Negro history; document," in Integrated
education, v. 4, Apr.-May, 1966, pp. 34-35.
    Text of amendments to the state Education code originally introduced
by Senator Mervyn Dymally, Los Angeles.

1698. "California's law on Negro history," in Black world, v. 30, Feb.,
1967, pp. 21-22.

1699. CLARK, WILLIAM RICHARD. The assimilation of the Negro teacher in
Massachusetts. Thesis, Colo. state college, Greeley, 1967. xv, 194 ℓ.
illus., map, tables. CSjC (photocopy).

1700. *CLEAVER, LOWELL HENRY. A study of the causes and methods of combating truancy. Master's thesis, Univ. of southern Calif., Los Angeles,
1951. iii, 88 ℓ.

General Works

1701. COLEMAN, JAMES S., and others. Equality of educational opportunity ... [Washington, D. C.] U. S. office of education [1966]. vi, 737 p. tables, charts. CSt.
"A publication of the National center for educational statistics."
Gives regional information in areas variously described as the "West," "Southwest," "Far West," "Rocky Mountains," and combinations thereof.

1702. COOPER, ELIZABETH KEYSER. Attitudes of children and teachers toward Mexican, Negro and Jewish minorities. Master's thesis, Univ. of Calif., Los Angeles, 1945. 91 [i.e., 94] ℓ. tables, diagrs.

1703. CORSARO, RICHARD J. Student activities: a means of developing self-image in Negro youth. Research paper, Calif. state univ., Fresno, 1968.

1704. CRAIGHILL, KARILYN (FRAMPTON). The effect of I. Q. instruction versus non-I. Q. instruction on digit symbol coding scores of culturally different black children. Master's thesis, Calif. state univ., Hayward, 1970. vii, 61 ℓ.

1705. DAWSON, HELAINE. On the outskirts of hope; educating youth from poverty areas. N. Y., McGraw-Hill [1967, c1968]. xiv, 329 p. illus. CSf, CSfCiC.
Based upon experience gained working in the Youth opportunities center in Hunter's Point, San Francisco.

1706. DEAN, CORINNE COLOYTHA. A study of the performance of Negro children on the Leiter international performance scale. Master's thesis, Univ. of southern Calif., Los Angeles, 1941. viii [62] ℓ. tables, diagrs.

1707. DE BARRY, CLYDE EDWARD. A study of attitudes toward equal educational opportunities and of community decision-making. Doctoral dissertation, Univ. of Oregon, Eugene, 1967. 373 p.

1708. DELLEFIELD, CALVIN J. Aspirations of low socio-economic status adults and implications for adult education. Doctoral dissertation, Univ. of Calif., Los Angeles, 1965.
Aspirations related mainly to obtaining jobs and producing adequate income, and to education for their children rather than for themselves.

1709. DICKEY, LLOYD DUQUESNE. Adult education in Phoenix, Arizona, with special reference to Negro adults. Master's thesis, Ariz. state univ., Tempe, 1943. 72 ℓ. illus.

1710. DUNNAWAY, EDWIN E., and others. "Affirmative discrimination: I. Schools and housing." Santa Barbara, Center for the study of democratic institutions [196-?]. Tape. 50 minutes.

1711. EASON, CHARLES LEWIS. An analysis of the social attitudes and casual factors of Negro problem boys of the Los Angeles city schools. Master's thesis, Univ. of southern Calif., Los Angeles, 1936. iii, 96 ℓ. diagrs., tables.

General Works

1712. ELLIOTT, MERLE HUGH, and ALDEN W. BADAL. "Achievement and racial composition of schools," in California journal of educational research, v. 16, Sept., 1965, pp. 158-66.
    Concerns Oakland schools.

1713. ELLIS, WILLIAM RUSSELL, 1935- . Operation bootstrap: a case study in ideology and institutionalization of protest. Doctoral dissertation, Univ. of Calif., Los Angeles, 1969. 436 l.
    Describes a self-help job training organization.

1714. *ESSIEN, JOSEPH EFIONG. Science curriculum and behavioral objectives (chemistry). Master's thesis, Univ. of Calif., Los Angeles, 1965. 128 l.

1715. FARMER, GEORGE LUTHER. Education: the dilemma of the Afro-American, by George L. Farmer. [L. A.] School of education, Univ. of southern Calif., 1969. ii, 110 l. tables, graphs, charts. Bibliography: l. 108-10. CLSU.
    Relates to education in the West.

1716. _____. A panorama of the Negro in the United States; a syllabus, by George L. Farmer. [L. A.] School of education, Univ. of southern Calif., 1968. ii, 40 l. Bibliography: l. 17-40. CLSU.

1717. FAVORS-CURTIS, JUANITA GWENDOLYN. A study of the conditions of the Negro rural schools in Maricopa county. Master's thesis, Ariz. state univ., Tempe, 1944. 78 l. illus., maps.

1718. FERRIER, WILLIAM WARREN, 1855-1945. Ninety years of education in California, 1846-1936; a presentation of educational movements and their outcome in education today, by William Warren Ferrier. Berkeley, Sather gate book shop [c1937]. xv, 413 p. CHi, CRbCL, CSd, CSdS, CU.
    "Schools for Negroes": pp. 97-102.

1719. "First Negro history class in Los Angeles city schools at Dorsey adult school," in Negro history bulletin, v. 25, Oct., 1961, pp. 18-19, 22.

1720. FORBES, JACK DOUGLAS, 1934- . The education of the culturally different; a multi-cultural approach. [A handbook for educators, by] Jack D. Forbes. [Berkeley, Far West laboratory for educational research and development [1967]. 35 p. "Bibliographical essay": pp. 27-35. C, CSt.
    A general work.

1721. _____. _____. Rev. ed. Washington, D. C., U. S. Health services and mental health administration, 1969. 63 p. C.

1722. FRANK, FRANK HILLEL, 1940- . On-the-job-training for minorities: an internal study. Doctoral dissertation, Univ. of Calif., Los Angeles, 1969.

General Works

1723. Fresno. City schools. Compensatory education evaluation booklet for
   1964-65. [Fresno city unified school district, 1965]. 83 ℓ. CSjC.

1724. GRANT, EVA H., ed. PTA guide to What's happening in education.
   Selections from the PTA magazine, Eva H. Grant, ed. N. Y., Scholastic
   book services [c1965]. v, 312 p. Bibliography: pp. 305-[11].
      Contains "Help for 'children without'," by James E. Stratten,
   president, San Francisco board of education, pp. 184-94.

1725. GROFF, PATRICK J. "Teaching the CD child: teacher turnover," in
   California journal of educational research, v. 18, Mar., 1967, pp. 91-95.
      A teacher-opinion study of teaching the culturally deprived.

1726. GUNSKY, FREDERIC R. "Problems and opportunities in intergroup relations," in California journal for instructional improvement, Oct., 1966.

1727. HACKETT, MATTIE (NANCE). A survey of the living conditions of girls
   in the Negro schools of Phoenix, Arizona. Master's thesis, Ariz. state
   univ., Tempe, 1939. 50 ℓ. illus.

1728. HAYS, MITZI PITTS. A study of white standards and models of achievement and their application to black students. Master's thesis, Calif.
   state univ., San Jose, 1970. vi, 59 ℓ. illus.

1729. HEYMAN, IRA MICHAELS. Civil rights, U. S. A., public schools, cities
   in the North and West, 1963: Oakland. Staff report submitted to the
   United States commission on civil rights. [Washington, 1963]. vi,
   74 p. maps, tables. CO.

1730. HILL, BEATRICE M., and NELSON S. BURKE. "Some disadvantaged youths
   look at their schools," in Journal of Negro education, v. 37, Spring,
   1968, pp. 135-39.
      Neighborhood youth corps program members' attitude toward schools in
   California.

1731. HUGHES, WILLIAM EDWARD. Lower socio-economic class Negro children's
   perceptions of their teachers' feelings toward them related to self-
   perception, school achievement, and behavior. Master's thesis, Calif.
   state univ., San Francisco, 1968. 35 ℓ.
      "The title topic is investigated in 'a relatively small northern
   California public school system. The system had desegregated two years
   previously'."

1732. *JACKSON, IDA LOUISE, 1902- . Rate of development of Negro
   children in relation to education. Master's thesis, Univ. of Calif.,
   Berkeley, 1923. 78 ℓ. diagrs.

1733. *JACKSON, JOHN HENRY, 1850- . History of education from the Greeks
   to the present time. Denver, Western newspaper union, 1903. 223 p.
   illus., port. DHU, NN.
      Authored by a resident of Colorado Springs.

General Works

1734. _____. History of education from the Greeks to the present time, by
John H. Jackson ... 2d ed. Denver, Western newspaper union, 1905. 304 p.
illus., ports. DLC.
Education of the Negroes: pp. 159-304.

1735. JACKSON, THOMAS CONRAD, 1914- . Negro education in Arizona. Master's
thesis, Univ. of Arizona, Tucson, 1941.

1736. *JACKSON, WILFRED P. An exploratory course in vocational music.
Master's project report, Univ. of southern Calif., Los Angeles, 1950.
ix, 104 ℓ.

1737. JARRARD, RAYMOND DENNIS. Minority pupils and their needs in a suburban school district. Master's project report, Univ. of southern Calif.,
Los Angeles, 1965. iv, 63 ℓ.

1738. *JOHNSON, DOROTHY P. (VENA). Methods for directing children's racial
attitude through literature with reference to the Negro. Master's
thesis, Univ. of southern Calif., Los Angeles, 1942. iii, 80 ℓ.

1739. JOHNSON, HYCINTHIA L. The negative self concept of the culturally
deprived Negro and school success. Research paper, Calif. state univ.,
Fresno, 1966.

1740. JOHNSON, MAYME EVELYN LAWLAH. The educational needs of Negro youth.
Doctoral dissertation, Stanford univ., Stanford, 1951. 382 ℓ.

1741. JOHNSON, MILO PERRY. The trade and industrial education of Negroes
in the Los Angeles area. Master's thesis, Univ. of Calif., Los Angeles,
1945. 86 ℓ.

1742. JONES, BOBBY. A study of the educational system of the Nation of
Islam in the San Joaquin Valley, California. Research paper, Calif.
state univ., Fresno, 1967.

1743. JUAREZ, LYNNE MARIE. An investigation of the self-image of some
black children. Master's thesis, Calif. state univ., San Francisco,
1970. iv, 65 ℓ. illus.

1744. KEELER, KATHLEEN F. R. Post-school adjustment of educable mentally
retarded youth educated in San Francisco. Doctoral dissertation,
Colorado state college, Greeley, 1963.
"Recommends training in homemaking skills as being of special importance for the Negro and the Mexican-American group." - West, p. 54.

1745. KENDALL, ROBERT. Never say nigger. [London] Library 33 [1966].
223 p. CSfSt, CSjC.
Originally published as White teacher in a black school in which a
teacher relates his two years' experience in a Los Angeles school.

1746. _____. White teacher in a black school. N. Y., Devin-Adair [c1964].
241 p.
Available in many libraries.

General Works

1747. KNAPP, DALE L. "The educationally disadvantaged: teaching beyond the stereotype," in <u>California journal of instructional improvement</u>, Dec., 1964.

1748. LAMOREAUX, LILLIAN A. "There's work to be done," in <u>Opportunity</u>, v. 19, Dec., 1941, pp. 366-67.
Describes an effective, temporary race relations program in the Santa Barbara city schools.

1749. LANGER, LEONARD H. A comparison of twelve-year-old white and Negro boys on the Rorschach test. Master's thesis, Univ. of southern Calif., Los Angeles, 1951. 26 ℓ.

1750. LASKEY, ROBERT LEMUEL. The function of educational technology in teaching the educationally deprived. Master's thesis, Calif. state univ., San Francisco, 1968. 83 ℓ.
"The study surveys educational technology available for use with the educationally deprived, the use of selected media, and teacher training programs involving their use. S. T. E. P. (Sausalito teacher education project), a co-operative teacher training project involving San Francisco state college student teachers, the residents of Marin City, and the Sausalito school district, is described as an example."

1751. LAURENCE, PAUL. "Education," a lecutre given Mar. 18, 1966 for "Perspectives on the Negro in our affluent society," a lecture series sponsored by the Associated students of Palomar college, San Marcos. CSmarP (tape, 1200 feet).

1752. *LAWRENCE, PAUL FREDERICK. "New credential proposals," in <u>California education</u>, v. 1, Feb., 1964, pp. 15-16.
Authored by the Associate superintendent of public instruction and Chief, Div. of higher education, State dept. of education.

1753. LAYNE, JANICE L. Prejudice and discrimination in the public schools. Master's thesis, Univ. of Calif., Los Angeles, 1967. ix, 105 ℓ. illus.

1754. LEE, DOUGLAS WILLIAM. An analysis of the underprivileged intermediate child in a metropolitan area. Master's thesis, Calif. state univ., San Francisco, 1963. 41 ℓ. tables.

1755. LOHMAN, JOSEPH DEAN, 1909-1968. Operation fair chance; report on the first year operation; produced under the direction of Joseph D. Lohman and Paul T. Takagi. [Berkeley] Univ. of Calif., School of criminology, 1967. vi, 115 ℓ. Bibliographical footnotes. CU.
A study of socially handicapped children funded by the U. S. office of education.

1756. _____. Teacher education and parent-teacher aides in a culturally different community. Produced under the direction of Joseph D. Lohman and Paul T. Takagi. [Berkeley] 1967. 2 v. CU.
"Funded by Office of economic opportunity ... under sub-contract with Berkeley unified school district."

General Works

1757. ____., comp. Cultural patterns in urban schools; a manual for
teachers, counselors, and administrators. Written under the direction
of Joseph D. Lohman. Berkeley, Univ. of Calif. press, 1967. xix, 210 p.
Bibliographical footnotes. CSdS, CSf, CU.
"Joint project of the School of criminology and the School of education, University of California, Berkeley."

1758. LONG, JOHN CORNELIUS. The Disciples of Christ and Negro education.
Doctoral dissertation, Univ. of southern Calif., Los Angeles, 1960.
v, 286 ℓ.
By 1955, 10 schools had been established but only 2 remained in
operation.

1759. LOPEZ, LEO. "Compensatory education in California: a progress
report," in California education, v. 2, Jan., 1965, pp. 13-14.
Defines methods of encouraging disadvantaged children to remain in
school until graduation. A program funded by the McAteer act.

1760. Los Angeles. Board of education. Annual report ... 1880/81. L. A.,
Mirror printing and binding house, 1882. 40 p.
Lists number of Negro children of school age and not of school age,
pp. 14-15.

1761. ____. ____. Annual report ... 1883/84. L. A., Marley and
Freeman, 1885. 72 p.
Lists number of Negro children in and out of school, p. 15.

1762. ____. ____. Annual report ... 1884/85. L. A., Times-mirror co.,
1886. 60 p.
Lists number of Negro children of school age, 1876-85, p. 25.

1763. Los Angeles city school district. Negro and California history.
[L. A., 1935?]. 26 p. Mimeo. CSmH.
At head of p. [1]: "Los Angeles city board of education emergency
education program."
Relates the history of education in the city and county of Los
Angeles.

1764. MC CONE, JOHN A. "Break the spiral of failure," in Integrated
education, v. 5, Feb.-Mar., 1967, pp. 10-18.
A general report authored by the chairman of the California Governor's
commission on the Los Angeles riots.

1765. MC CORD, WILLIAM M. Life styles in the black ghetto [by] William
McCord [and others]. N. Y., W. W. Norton & co. [c1969]. 334 p.
Bibliography: pp. [297]-302. CNoS, CSS, CSf.
Contains "Watts: the revolt and after," by John Howard and William
McCord. Urban life and dissent in Oakland, San Francisco, San Diego,
Compton, and Los Angeles.

1766. ____., and JOHN HOWARD. "Negro opinions in three riot cities," in
American behavioral scientist, v. 11, Mar., 1968, pp. 24-27.
Includes Los Angeles and Oakland.

General Works

1767. MC DONALD, FRANKLIN RANDOLPH. The effect of differential cultural pressures on projective test performances of Negroes. Doctoral dissertation, Univ. of southern Calif., Los Angeles, 1952. x, 144 ℓ.

1768. *MABSON, BERLINDA (DAVISON). Educational status of the Negro in the San Francisco bay region. Master's thesis, Univ. of Calif., Berkeley, 1921. xxiv, 80 ℓ. tables, diagrs.

1769. *MADKIN, NORMA HILLARY. Modifying a reading program to meet the needs of Spanish-speaking children. Master's project report, Univ. of southern Calif., Los Angeles, 1950. ii, 64 ℓ.

1770. [Material collected by John Kaplan about the San Francisco school system for the U. S. commission on civil rights. v.p., v.d.]. 3 portfolios. CSt-Law.

1771. MAYER, MARTIN. "The good slum schools," in Harper's, v. 222, Apr., 1961, pp. 46-52.
    Includes a program in Tucson.

1772. MECKLER, ZANE. "The challenge of the educationally disadvantaged child," in California teachers association journal, v. 60, Mar., 1964, pp. 31, 33-34, 58-60.

1773. MINGORI, LYNN BOSLEY. The history of Negro education in California, 1850-1890. Master's thesis, Univ. of Calif., Los Angeles, 1971. 115 ℓ.

1774. MOSS, JEFFERY ALAN. Discernible effects attendant to de facto segregation in public schools. Master's thesis, Univ. of southern Calif., Los Angeles, 1970. iii, 180 ℓ.

1775. *[NELSON, LONDON, 1800-1860]. "London Nelson," in News and notes, no. 2, Apr., 1955, p. 2.
    The publication of the Santa Cruz historical society contains an account of London [Loudon?] Nelson whose name and bequest to local schools are honored annually on May 30.

1776. "New compensatory education project established by McAteer act," in California education, v. 1, Dec., 1963, pp. 17-18.
    A two-year study to determine the best use of public schools by culturally disadvantaged pupils.

1777. Oakland. Public schools. Citizens advisory committee on Oakland school needs. Equal opportunities report. [Oakland] 1964. 214 p. tables. CSf.

1778. _____. _____. Cultural diversity; library and audio-visual materials for in-service education. [Prepared by] Helen Cyr, Barbara Baker [and] George Noone. [Oakland] 1964. 39 p. DHU.

1779. O'BRIEN, KENNETH BOSTWICK. The Supreme court and education. Doctoral dissertation, Stanford univ., Stanford, 1956. xiii, 316 ℓ.
    "Traces influence of court decisions on educational leaders." - West, p. 38.

General Works

1780. O'BRIEN, WILLIAM JESS, 1924- . An experimental use of modified group therapy in a public school setting with delinquent adolescent males. Doctoral dissertation, Univ. of Calif., Berkeley, 1963. 110 ℓ. illus.
    Based on results from a group therapy program using Negro and Caucasian delinquent boys.

1781. OHLES, JOHN F. "Watts, the schools, and citizenship education," in School and society, v. 95, Apr. 15, 1967, p. 256.

1782. OWENS, CHRISTOPHER COLUMBUS. A study of church schools for Negroes to determine their usefulness in Negro education. Master's thesis, Univ. of southern Calif., Los Angeles, 1933. 79 ℓ. tables.

1783. PARMEE, LEILA K., 1929- . Perception of personal-social problems by students of different ethnic backgrounds. Doctoral dissertation, Univ. of Arizona, Tucson, 1965.
    "More areas of the Mooney problem check list reflected general adolescent concerns than ethnic differences, but the most apparent differences were in personality and self-concept."

1784. PETERSON, MOZART ERNEST. Obstacles to Negro education in the United States. Master's thesis, Univ. of southern Calif., Los Angeles, 1931. vi, 102 ℓ. tables.

1785. *PHILLIPS, HILTON ALONZO. Analyzing some teacher, student and community activities toward establishing intergroup harmony. Master's project report, Univ. of southern Calif., Los Angeles, 1952. iv, 81 ℓ.

1786. PRICE, RITA M. Problems related to the interpretation of individual mental test scores for Negro children. Master's thesis, Calif. state univ., Hayward, 1969. 65 ℓ.

1787. RECORD, WILSON, 1916- . "Racial diversity in California public schools," in Journal of Negro education, v. 28, Winter, 1959, pp. 15-25.

1788. RELLER, THEODORE LEE. Problems of public education in the San Francisco bay area. Berkeley, Institute of governmental studies, 1963. 33 p. tables, charts. CSf, CU.

1789. *RICHARDS, EUGENE SCOTT. A study of material dealing with race educational problems. Master's thesis, Univ. of southern Calif., Los Angeles, 1931. 79 ℓ. table.

1790. RIORDAN, MARGUERITE. "Tolerance goes to school in Denver - 'with liberty and justice for all'," in Opportunity, v. 25, Jan.-Mar., 1947, pp. 6-8.

1791. ROBERTSON, FLORENCE (KEENEY). Problems in training adult Negroes in Los Angeles. Master's thesis, Univ. of southern Calif., Los Angeles, 1929. vi, 95 ℓ.
    "Racial attitudes of Negroes in Los Angeles." - Miriam Matthews.

General Works

1792. ROSENBERG, HARRY E. Administrative problems in hiring Negro teachers. Master's thesis, Calif. state univ., Fresno, 1965.

1793. ROUSSEVE, RONALD J. "A Negro American's reflections on some aspects of education," in Washington education, v. 77, Oct., 1965, pp. 14-17.

1794. RUST, BEN. "Racial discrimination and the teacher shortage in California," in Frontier, v. 8, May, 1957, pp. 15-16.

1795. San Francisco. Board of education. Educational equality/quality. Report no. 1 ... program alternatives. S. F., 1967. 108 p. tables. CO.

1796. _____. Unified school district. The Negro in American life and history; a resource book for teachers. [S. F., 1965]. 367 p. Bibliography: pp. 359-67. CHS, CSluSP, CSfAA, CU.
    "Preliminary edition."

1797. _____. Same. 1967 ed. CHS, CSS, CSluSP.

1798. SAVAGE, WILLIAM SHERMAN, 1890- . "Early Negro education in the Pacific coast states," in Journal of Negro education, v. 15, Winter, 1946, pp. 134-39.

1799. SHIKOMBA, MADELINE. A suggested method to develop a positive self-image in black children. Master's thesis, Calif. state univ., San Francisco, 1968. 102 ℓ. illus.
    "Discusses the development of reading materials to enhance reading interest and self esteem in Afro-American children. The author presents two original illustrated stories (with glossary and teachers guide) whose plot and vocabulary reflect the experience of many black children in the San Francisco bay area."

1800. SHIPPEY, MERVYN G. A short history of the Visalia colored school ... [by] Mervyn G. Shippey. [n.p., n.d.] [19] ℓ. maps (fold.), plans, facsims. Typew. C.
    Includes a discussion of the California supreme court case of Wysinger vs. Cruikshank which resulted in the termination of segregation in the Visalia public schools in 1890.

1801. _____. Same. S. F., R and E research associates, 1970.

1802. Simril-Curry-Moore scholarship foundation.* [Souvenir program.] Annual banquet. COEB. 6th (1969).

1803. SINGH, SURENDRA PRATAP, 1937- . A comparison between privileged Negroes, under-privileged Negroes, privileged whites, and under-privileged whites, and under-privileged white children on a test of creativity. Doctoral dissertation, Univ. of Calif., Los Angeles, 1967. xiii, 157 ℓ. tables, forms.

1804. SINGLETON, ROBERT. Some problems in minority group education in the Los Angeles public schools [by] Robert Singleton and Paul Bullock.

General Works

[Washington, D. C., Howard univ. press] 1963. 137-45 p.
   Includes bibliographical footnotes.
   A separate from the Journal of Negro education, v. 32, Spring,
1963.

1805. "Small staff does big job for disadvantaged students," in American
school board journal, v. 155, June, 1968, pp. 20-21.
   Los Angeles.

1806. *SMITH, ANNIE ISABELLE.   A critique of some Negro intelligence tests'
results. Master's thesis, Univ. of southern Calif., Los Angeles, 1928.
iv, 86 ℓ. tables.

1807. SMITH, BRENDA JOYCE. The motor and rhythmic proficiency of young
black stutterers as measured by the Oseretsky tests and rhythmic tasks.
Master's thesis, Calif., state univ., San Jose, 1970. 39 ℓ. illus.

1808. "Some problems in minority group education in the Los Angeles public
schools," in Journal of Negro education, v. 32, Spring, 1963, pp. 137-45.

1809. SPEARS, HAROLD, and ISADORE PIVNICK. "How an urban school system
identifies its disadvantaged," in Journal of Negro education, v. 33,
Summer, 1964, pp. 245-53.
   Authored by San Francisco unified school district administrators.

1810. SPINDLER, GEORGE D. "Our changing culture, creativity, and the
schools," in California journal for instructional improvement, May,
1966.

1811. *SPRAINGS, VIOLET E.   "The educationally handicapped pupil as seen
by an educational psychologist," in California education, v. 3, pp. 19-20.
   Authored by the Director, Psychological and educational services
school for cerebral palsied children, northern California.

1812. *SPRIGGS, HAROLDIE K.   Minority group education in New Mexico prior
to 1954. Master's thesis, Howard univ., Washington, D. C., 1967. 64 ℓ.

1813. [SWETT, JOHN, 1830-1913]. Have Negroes been taught and classed on
terms of equality in a public school under the charge of Mr. John Swett?
[S. F.?, 1862]. Broadside. CU-B.

1814. _____. History of public school system in California. By John Swett.
A. L. Bancrof and co., 1876. 246 p. illus. C, CHi, CL, CLSU, CLU, CO,
CSS, CSf, CSmH, CU-B, Rocq 12416.
   Includes special laws governing the education of ethnic groups.

1815. TARQUINIO, CHERYL. "Black culture instruction program lags in San
Diego schools," in Classroom teacher, v. 10, Apr., 1968, pp. 1, 7.

1816. *TATE, MERZE. "The Sandwich Island missionaries lay the foundation
for a system of public instruction in Hawaii," in Journal of Negro
education, v. 30, Fall, 1961, pp. 396-405.

General Works

1817. THOMPSON, AMELIA ELLEN (BROWN). Home environment and school achievement. Master's thesis, Ariz. state univ., Tempe, 1939. 53 ℓ. illus.

1818. *TOWNSEND, JONAS HOLLAND,   -1872. "American caste and common
schools," in Anglo-African magazine, v. 1, Mar., 1859, pp. 80-83.
    Describes efforts of Grass Valley, Sacramento, and San Francisco
residents to secure public educational opportunities for their children,
1854-59, pp. 81-83.

1819. TRETTEN, RUDIE WEBER. Changing status space in Negro teacher-pupil
interaction. Doctoral dissertation, Stanford univ., Stanford, 1970.
viii, 95 ℓ.

1820. TRILLINGHAM, C. C. "Lesson from Watts; it can happen here," in PTA
magazine, v. 61, Oct., 1966, pp. 12-14.

1821. U. S. Commission on civil rights. Civil rights U. S. A.: public
schools, cities in the North and West 1963, Oakland. By Ira Michaels
Heyman. [Washington, D. C., 1963]. 74 p. (Its Staff report [no. 5]).
    CFS, CHS, CO, CSt-Law.

1822. _____. Dept. of health, education and welfare. Office of education.
Project R-3 San Jose, California; one of a series of successful compensatory education programs. Washington, D. C., Govt. print., 1969.
16 p. CMp.

1823. WALDIE, HELEN BULLOCK. Education in San Francisco, 1850-1860: a
study of frontier attitudes. Master's thesis, Stanford univ., Stanford,
1953. 155 ℓ.
    Includes "provision for facilities; establishment of schools; evalua-
tion of system; aims; development of high school program, of female
education, of industrial schools, of adult education, of Negro education,
of the state university."

1824. *WALTON, SIDNEY F., 1934- . The black curriculum; developing a
program in Afro-American studies, by Sidney F. Walton, Jr. Palo Alto,
Black liberation pubs. [c1969]. xv, 522 p. illus., facsims., port.
CHS, CNoS.

1825. _____. Excerpts from the book The black curriculum; developing a
program in Afro-American studies. Oakland, Black liberation pubs.,
1968. 23 p. CSdS.

1826. "War on illiteracy in Los Angeles; an excerpt from a proposal for
funds under title II-B of the Economic opportunity act of 1964," in
California education, v. 2, Apr., 1965, pp. 23-24.

1827. WEINBERG, CARL. Education level and perceptions of Los Angeles
Negroes of educational conditions in a riot area," in Journal of Negro
education, v. 36, Fall, 1967, pp. 377-84.

1828. The western student movement, Los Angeles. The western structure
movement: a prospectus, April 10, 1964. [L. A., 1964]. 16 p. Mimeo.

General Works

CLU (Spec. Coll.).
To set up a tutorial program in Los Angeles ghetto areas.

1829. *WHITAKER, HAZEL GOTTSCHALK. A study of gifted Negro children in the Los Angeles city schools. Master's thesis, Univ. of southern Calif., Los Angeles, 1931. v, 86 ℓ. tables.

1830. ZANDERS, IDA O. WILLIAMS, 1915- . Negro education in Tucson, Arizona. Master's thesis, Univ. of Arizona, Tucson, 1946.

1831. ZIMBLEMAN, ERNEST AUGUST, 1926- . The influences in the intellectual development of Negro American students. Doctoral dissertation, Univ. of Oregon, Eugene, 1965. 218 ℓ. CSjC (photocopy).
"Considers such categories as the socialization processes, religion, socio-economic status, work opportunity, self and racial attitudes."

EMPLOYMENT AND UNEMPLOYMENT; OCCUPATIONS

1832. ANDERSON, BERNARD E. Negro employment in public utilities; a study of racial policies in the electric power, gas, and telephone industries. Philadelphia, Wharton school of finance, Univ. of Pennsylvania [1970]. 261 p. Studies of Negro employment, v. 3. CSS.

1833. _____. The Negro in the public utilities industries, by Bernard E. Anderson. Philadelphia, Wharton school of finance, Univ. of Pennsylvania [1970]. xix, 261 p. Racial policies of American industry. Report no. 10. CSS.

1834. Bank of America national trust and savings association. Bank of America and the Congress of racial equality; a report on the public relations activities of Bank of America during its dispute with CORE. [S. F.?], 1964. 1 v. (v.p.). CSt-Law.

1835. *Bay area urban league, inc. ... On-the-job training; final reports on contract #057-308-0000, San Francisco office, and contract #057-351-3000, Oakland office, October 1, 1966 through April 30, 1969. [n.p., 1969?]. 73 p. CSf.
A detailed report listing individual companies, type of job, etc.

1836. Berkeley. Personnel dept. Employment of minority group persons in the Berkeley fire department and in the Berkeley police department. Berkeley, 1964. 27 ℓ. tables. C, CO.

1837. BETTER, NORMAN MICHAEL, 1935- . Discrimination in educational employment. Doctoral dissertation, Univ. of Calif., Los Angeles, 1966. xvi, 177 ℓ.
"Race and age differentiated successful and unsuccessful applicants for secondary school positions." - West, p. 33.

Employment and Unemployment; Occupations

1838. BLAUNER, ROBERT. New careers and the person, by Robert Blauner and Anatole Shaffer. [Walnut Creek, Contra Costa council of community services, 1967]. 57 ℓ. (A series of technical monographs, no. 16). CU.
A study of employment in Richmond.

1839. *BRIMMER, ANDREW FELTON. Some economic aspects of fair employment. Master's thesis, Univ. of Washington, Seattle, 1951.

1840. *BULLOCK, PAUL, 1924- . "Combating discrimination in employment," in California management review, v. 3, Summer, 1961, pp. 18-32.

1841. _____. Equal opportunity in employment. Ed. by Irving Bernstein. Drawings by Marvin Rubin. L. A., Institute of industrial relations, Univ. of Calif. [1966]. vii, 114 p. illus. Bibliography: pp. 110-14. CLU, CSt, CU, Wa.
Discrimination in employment since 1960.

1842. _____. Merit employment: nondiscrimination in industry. Ed. by Irving Bernstein. Drawings by Marvin Rubin. L. A., Institute of industrial relations, Univ. of Calif. [1960]. 101 p. illus. CLU, CSfSt, CU.

1843. *BURCH, EDWARD ALEXANDER, 1912- . Attitudes of employers engaged in manufacturing in the Los Angeles area relative to the employment of Negroes. Master's thesis, Univ. of southern Calif., Los Angeles, 1948. vi, 101, 3, 3 ℓ. map, tables, forms.

1844. California. Dept. of employment. Human relations agency. How the California state employment service helps the minority job applicant. Sacramento, 1968. 19 p. CMp.

1845. _____. Governor, 1958-1966. (Edmund G. Brown). Ethnic survey of employment and promotion in state government. Report. Sacramento. 1st, 1963- . CLS, CSt-Law.

1846. _____. _____. _____. Report to Governor Edmund G. Brown: second ethnic survey of employment and promotion in state government, from William L. Becker. [Sacramento?], 1965. [19] ℓ. C, CFS, Wa.

1847. _____. _____. _____. Negroes and Mexican-Americans in the California state government; a cooperative project conducted by the office of the Governor Edmund G. Brown, selected California newspaper publishers, and the State personnel board. [Sacramento], 1965. [96] ℓ. illus., ports. C, CFS, CHS, CL, CLS, CMS, CNoS, CP, CSb, CSf, CSj, CSt-Law, CStb, CStmo, CU, CU-A, CWM, Wa.
A reprinting of articles about 70 occupationally different state employees which appeared in 36 publications whose participation was requested.

1848. _____. _____. Same. 1966 ed. CStcrCL.

1849. _____. Legislature. Assembly. Interim committee on governmental efficiency and economy.

Employment and Unemployment; Occupations

Transcript of hearing on employment practices of state and local public agencies, San Francisco, November 1, 1967. [Sacramento, 1967]. 151 ℓ. CSt-Law.

1850. _____. State board of cosmotology.
Applications for licenses, examinations, and photographs of cosmotologists, 1928-54. 4 cu. ft. C-ArS. Includes Afro-Americans.

1851. _____. State fair employment practice commission. [Annual] report. 1st-   [Sacramento] 1959/60- . CChiS 1959/60+; CFS 1959/60+; CLS 1959/60+; CLSU 1959/60+; CSdS 1959/60+; CS1uSP 1963/64-1965/66; CStb 1961-69; CSt-Law 1959/60+; CU 1959/60-1964/65.

1852. _____. _____. Bank of America employment practices; first report by California FEPC in the course of an affirmative action of the Fair employment practice commission. [Sacramento, 1964]. 1 v. (v.p.). CSt-Law.

1853. _____. _____. California's Negro citizens and the work they do. [Sacramento?] 1967. Folder. ports. CFS, CMS, CMp, CO, CSb, CStmo.

1854. _____. _____. Employment practices, city of Pasadena; an investigation under Section 1421 of the California labor code, 1963-65. [Sacramento?] 1965. CFS.

1855. _____. _____. Employment practices, city of San Diego; an investigation under section 1421 of the California labor code, 1963-1964. [Sacramento, 1964]. 8 p. tables. CSt.

1856. _____. _____. Informational memo no. 1-5. [Sacramento?] 1962-1963. 1 v. CSt-Law.
Issued under the name of Division of fair employment practices.

1857. _____. _____. Memo to management re: employment on merit under law. [Sacramento?] 1960. CFS.

1858. _____. _____. Negro Californians; population, employment, income, education. S. F., 1963. 34 p. tables. Available in many libraries.
"Derived principally from the 1960 Census of population, the statistical tables were compiled by the California Division of Labor Statistics and Research."

1859. _____. _____. Supplement, Dec., 1965. 15 p. CB, CO, CP, CSt, CStma, CU, CViCL.

1860. _____. _____. Reprint, 1967. 34 p.

1861. _____. _____. Promoting equal job opportunity, a guide for employers. [Sacramento?, n.d.]. CFS.

1862. _____. _____. State of California fair employment practice act; guide to pre-employment inquiries. Sacramento, 1964. 27 p. CMp.

Employment and Unemployment; Occupations

1863. _____. _____. Two years of progress; Fair employment practice commission reports: 1961 and 1962. Sacramento, 1962. 39 p. CSmarP.

1864. _____. State personnel board. Ethnic census of examination competi-
tors; report of examinations given July through December 1965, summary.
March 1966. [Sacramento] 1966. [15] ℓ. C.
    A comparison between black, white, and Mexican-American participation
and success in testing programs.

1865. _____. Technical advisory committee on testing. Fair employment
practices equal good employment practices; guidelines for testing and
selecting minority job applicants. [S. F.?] Technical advisory committee on testing, Fair employment practice commission, 1966. 16 p.
CSt-Law.

1866. _____. University. Berkeley. Institute of governmental studies.
Selected list of references on minority group employment in the public
service. Compiled by Dorothy Simpson and Barbara Hudson. [Berkeley]
1964. 34 ℓ. CO, CSt.

1867. _____. _____. _____. Survey research center. Tables on employment
and unemployment from the 701 household survey of Oakland. Berkeley,
1968. 33 ℓ. maps, tables. CO.
    Including unemployment and labor force by color.

1868. _____. _____. Los Angeles. Institute of industrial relations.
Combating discrimination in employment. L. A., 1961. [14] p. CO.

1869. _____. _____. _____. _____. Hard-core unemployment and poverty in
Los Angeles. Prepared by the staff of the Institute ... under a contract
with the Area redevelopment administration. [Washington, D. C.] Dept.
of commerce, Area redevelopment administration, 1965. 1 v. (v.p.).
maps, tables. CNoS.

1870. CALVERT, ROBERT. How to recruit minority group college graduates;
its problems, its techniques, its sources, [and] its opportunities. By
Robert Calvert, Jr., manager, Student and alumni placement center, University of California at Berkeley. Swarthmore, Pa., The personnel
journal, inc., c1963. 41 p. table. Bibliography: pp. 40-41. CSf.

1871. CHAMBERLAIN, RODERICK. Employment aspirations of male Negro youths.
Master's thesis, Calif. state univ., Fresno, 1968.

1872. Citizens interracial committee, San Diego. Directory of opportunities
in San Diego: employment opportunities, student financial aid, work experience programs, vocational services, E. O. A. training programs.
Compiled by Citizens interracial committee. San Diego, The committee
[1966]. 38 p. CSd.

1873. Colorado committee for equal employment opportunities. Taking stock;
a final report on the campaign for a fair employment practices law for
Colorado. Denver [1951]. 89 p. CO.

Employment and Unemployment; Occupations

1874. *Colored-American employees' association. Articles of incorporation,
San Francisco, 1918. 5 p. Typew. C-ArS.
    An organization established for benevolent and employment purposes.
Directors were William E. Collins, Leon Dawson, William Patterson,
LePage Williams, and Leland Hawkins.

1875. COOPER, CLARE C. Unemployment and minority groups in California, by
Clare C. Cooper. Berkeley, Univ. of Calif. Center for planning and development research, 1965. 536 p. C.
    Mainly relates to the alleviation of unemployment among minorities
and young people.

1876. Coro foundation internship in public affairs. Minority unemployment,
San Francisco. Prepared for the California job training and placement
council. [n.p.] 1968. 81 p. C.

1877. Council of social planning - Berkeley area. ... Wasted man power -
Berkeley challenge and opportunity. [Berkeley] 1963. [27] ℓ. tables.
CFS, CO.

1878. CRAINE, JAMES FORRESTER. A comparison of the occupational aspirations
of Negroes and whites. Doctoral dissertation, Univ. of southern Calif.,
Los Angeles, 1953. viii, 121 ℓ.

1879. DIZARD, JAN E. Patterns of unemployment in Berkeley, California.
[Berkeley] Univ. of Calif. survey research center, 1968. v, 149 ℓ.
CU-B.

1880. DRAKE, E. MAYLON. Employment of Negro teachers. Doctoral dissertation, Univ. of southern Calif., Los Angeles, 1963. v, 235 ℓ. tables.
    Analyzes changes in the employment of Negro teachers by Los Angeles
county school districts following enactment in 1959 of Fair employment
practices act legislation.

1881. DUFFY, JOHN F. State organization for fair employment practices.
Berkeley, Univ. of Calif., Bureau of public administration, 1944. 25 ℓ.
"Selected reading list": pp. 24-25. CSfSt.

1882. FLETCHER, F. MARION. The Negro in the drug manufacturing industry,
by F. Marion Fletcher ... Philadelphia, Wharton school of finance,
Univ. of Pennsylvania [c1970]. xi, 149 p. illus. Racial policies of
American industry. Report no. 21. CSS, CSjC.
    Contains information on the far West, especially Los Angeles.

1883. FLETCHER, LINDA PICKTHORNE. The Negro in the insurance industry, by
Linda Pickthorne Fletcher. Philadelphia, Wharton school of finance,
Univ. of Pennsylvania [c1970]. xii, 178 p. Includes bibliographical
references. Racial policies of American industry. Report no. 11. CSS,
CSjC.

1884. FOGEL, WALTER A. The Negro in the meat industry, by Walter A. Fogel.
Philadelphia, Wharton school of finance, Univ. of Pennsylvania [c1970].

Employment and Unemployment; Occupations

x, 146 p. Includes bibliographies. Racial policies of American industry.
Report no. 12. CSS, CSjC.

Includes western states. By a faculty member, Univ. of Calif.,
Los Angeles.

1885. *FRANCIS, ROBERT COLEMAN.   "Should the 'Forgotten men of the sea'
stay ashore?", in Opportunity, v. 14, July, 1936, pp. 211-12.
Francis, a Berkeley resident, replies to an earlier article in
Opportunity, "Forgotten men of the sea," and advises them to remain
ashore.

1886. GRISSOM, THOMAS WILLIAM. Occupational opportunities and vocational
education for Negroes in Oklahoma. Master's thesis, Ariz. state univ.,
Tempe, 1940. 50 ℓ. illus.

1887. GWYNN, DOUGLAS BRUCE. Communalism: a study of its effects on job
success. Master's thesis, Ariz. state univ., Tempe, 1971. 102 ℓ.
illus., maps.

1888. *HAWKINS, LELAND STANFORD.   "Boulder dam," in Crisis, v. 41, Mar.,
1934, pp. 77-78.
A San Francisco attorney writes of the efforts of Walter Hamilton,
Las Vegas, to secure employment of Blacks.

1889. HOWARD, JOHN C. The Negro in the lumber industry, by John C. Howard.
Philadelphia, Wharton school of finance, Univ. of Pennsylvania [c1970].
ix, 97 p. Racial policies of American industry. Report no. 19. CSjC.
Includes Arizona, California, Idaho, Montana, Oregon, and
Washington.

1890. JACOBS, PAUL. "The lower depths in Los Angeles," in Midstream, v. 13,
May, 1967, pp. 14-23.
Employment agencies and the unemployed.

1891. *JONES, HENRY LEON, 1900- . The Negro's opportunity [by] Henry L.
Jones ... A job for you! A career! Own your own business! Choose
your own career! Select the business you like! Choose your own location!
L. A., H. L. Jones and co., c1940. 208 p. Mimeo. CHi, CL.

1892. JONES, JAMES L. An investigation of the agent selection and sales
training activities of the Golden state mutual life insurance company.
Master's thesis, Univ. of southern Calif., Los Angeles, 1956. vii,
136 p.

1893. JONES, LILLIAN. "Charles Henry Fletcher, welder," in Opportunity,
v. 22, Jan.-Mar., 1944, pp. 20-21.
An account of the success of an employee of Moore dry dock co.,
Oakland.

1894. KING, CARL B. The Negro in the petroleum industry, by Carl B. King
and Howard W. Risher, Jr. Philadelphia, Wharton school of finance and

Employment and Unemployment; Occupations

commerce, Univ. of Pennsylvania [c1969]. viii, 96 p. Bibliographical
footnotes. CNoS, CSf, CSt.
   Gives some information about operations in California with emphasis
on oil refining.

1895. KOZIARA, EDWARD C. The Negro in the hotel industry, by Edward C.
Koziara and Karen S. Koziara. Philadelphia, Wharton school of finance
and commerce, Univ. of Pennsylvania [c1968]. vii, 74 p. tables. Racial
policies of American industry. Report no. 4. CLU, CNoS, CSS, CSdS, CSf,
CSfGG, CSt.
   Among the cities examined are San Francisco and Los Angeles.

1896. League of California cities. Survey of racial background of applicants
for civil service examinations in 29 California cities. Jan. 1, 1966-
Dec. 31, 1966. [n.p.] 1967. [11] ℓ. C.

1897. LEON, WILMER JOSEPH. The Negro contractor in Oakland, California, and
adjacent cities. Master's thesis, Univ. of Calif., Berkeley, 1954. iv,
96 ℓ. tables.

1898. LLOYD, KENT MURDOCK. Solving an American dilemma. The role of the
FEPC official: comparative study of state Civil rights commissions.
Doctoral dissertation, Stanford univ., Stanford, 1964. xiv, 303 ℓ.
   "The role of the FEPC in four widely separated states." - West,
p. 35.

1899. Los Angeles. Council of social agencies. Preliminary review and
recommendations regarding employment problems of minorities during the
reconversion period, August 1944. [L. A., 1944?]. 7 p. Mimeo.

1900. Los Angeles county. Ordinances. Equal employment opportunities
ordinance. [Draft submitted by Office of the county counsel]. L. A.,
1958. 16 ℓ. CSt-Law.

1901. LOUIE, JAMES W. Ethnic group differences in ability, temperament,
and vocational aspirations. Doctoral dissertation. Univ. of southern
Calif., Los Angeles, 1955. xi, 195 ℓ. illus.

1902. MARKEY, BEATRICE. Minority problems in public employment with special
reference to the Negro. Master's thesis, Univ. of southern Calif.,
Los Angeles, 1952. vi, 117 ℓ.

1903. *MILLER, LOREN R., 1903-1967. "The Negro faces the machine," in
Opportunity, v. 8, Oct., 1930, pp. 297-99.

1904. "Minority worker hiring and referral in San Francisco," in Monthly
labor review, v. 81, Oct., 1958, pp. 1,131-36.

1905. MITCHELL, JAMES P. "Employers must hire 'qualifiable Negroes' and
train them, says James P. Mitchell," in The commonwealth, v. 40, June 15,
1964, p. 163.

Employment and Unemployment; Occupations

1906. MOYNIHAN, DANIEL PATRICK. "Behind Los Angeles: jobless Negroes and the boom," in Reporter, v. 33, Sept. 9, 1965, p. 31.

1907. "Negroes win city jobs in Los Angeles," in American city, v. 82, Oct., 1967, p. 89.

1908. "1969, year of involvement; a report on B[ank] of A[merica]'s progress in its minority commitment," in Bankamerican, v. 40, Apr., 1969, pp. 1-6.

1909. "No Negro workers wanted," in Crisis, v. 41, Nov., 1934, pp. 334 and 340.
        The non-employment of blacks at Boulder dam.

1910. NORTHRUP, HERBERT ROOF, 1918- . "The Negro in aerospace work," in California management review, v. 11, Summer, 1969, pp. 11-25.

1911. _____. The Negro in the aerospace industry, by Herbert R. Northrup. Philadelphia, Wharton school of finance, Univ. of Pennsylvania [c1968]. ix, 90 p. illus. Racial policies of American industry. Report no. 2. CLSU, CNoS, CSdS, CSjC, CSt.
        Describes industrial policies in effect in California and Washington. Emphasis is placed upon southern California.

1912. _____. The Negro in the paper industry, by Herbert R. Northrup. Philadelphia, Wharton school of finance, Univ. of Pennsylvania [c1969]. viii, 96 p. Bibliographical footnotes. Racial policies of American industry. Report no. 8. C, CSS, CSjC, CSt, CU.

1913. _____. The Negro in the rubber tire industry, by Herbert R. Northrup ... with the assistance of Alan B. Batchelder ... Philadelphia, Wharton school of finance, Univ. of Pennsylvania [c1969]. viii, 134 p. tables. Bibliographical footnotes. Racial policies of American industry. Report no. 6. C, CSf, CSfGG, CSjC.

        Contains information about the industry in the cities of Hanford, Los Angeles, and Salinas.

1914. Opportunities industrialization center west, Menlo Park. The Menlo Park public library reports holding a small collection of ephemera describing job training, employment, volunteer, and health programs of the Center.

1915. ORR, SAMUEL MARSHALL. Cultural bias and the Armed forces qualification test. Master's thesis, Calif. state univ., San Francisco, 1969. v, 87 ℓ. tables, forms, graphs.
        Test used as a hiring device.

1916. PENN, NOLAN. "Racial influence in vocational choice," in Journal of Negro education, v. 35, Winter, 1966, pp. 88-89.
        A Compton study.

Employment and Unemployment; Occupations

1917. *PITTMAN, JOHN.   "The battle of San Francisco, March 6-8, 1964," in
      Freedomways, v. 4, Fall, 1964, pp. 489-502.
          Concerns drive for equal employment.

1918. QUAY, WILLIAM HOWARD. The Negro in the chemical industry, by William
      Howard Quay, Jr., with the assistance of Marjorie C. Denison. Phila-
      delphia, Wharton school of finance, Univ. of Pennsylvania [c1969]. xi,
      110 p. Includes bibliographical references. Racial policies of American
      industry. Report no. 7. CSS, CSjC.

          Contains information on the west coast and specifically in Los
      Angeles and Long Beach.

1919. REYNOLDS, WILLIAM H.   Experience of Los Angeles employers with
      minority group employees, by William H. Reynolds. [L. A.]   Univ. of
      southern Calif., research institute for business and economics [1967].
      54 p. CLSU.

1920. RICHMOND, ALEXANDER, 1913- . Ten years; the story of a people's
      newspaper, by Al Richmond, executive editor. S. F., Daily people's
      world. 1948. 31 p. illus., ports., facsims. CU-B.
          "Jobs and Jim Crow," pp. 15-17, describes employment discrimination
      on San Francisco municipal railways.

1921. RIKER, SAMUEL. The effects of training in test taking techniques on
      minority group job applicants. Master's thesis, Calif. state univ.,
      San Francisco, 1966. 102 ℓ. illus., tables.
          "Investigates the hypothesis that low scores on job screening tests
      may be test taking-ability related rather than job-ability related.
      Subjects were Spanish-American and Negro recruits in a San Francisco
      urban league program aimed at placing unemployed workers in on-the-job
      training projects in the electronic business machine repair industry."

1922. ROSS, ARTHUR MAX,   -1970, ed. Employment, race and poverty. Edited
      by Arthur M. Ross and Herbert Hill. [N. Y., Harcourt, Brace & World,
      1967]. ix, 598 p. tables. Bibliographical notes. CFS, CHS, CKenM,
      CLSU, CLobS, CNoS, COrob, CPhD, CSdS, CSf, CSfCiC, CSfGG, CSluSP, CSto,
      CU-A, CU-SC, CWM, Wa.
          Chapter 4, pp. 107-37, contains Paul Jacobs' "Bringin' up the rear"
      which narrates the lives of three San Francisco bay area men in relation
      to their employment, race, and poverty in the 1960's. Chapter 10,
      pp. 261-89, contains George Strauss' "How management views its race re-
      lations responsibilities" as correlated mainly with the San Francisco
      scene in the middle 1960's.

1923. ROWAN, RICHARD L. The Negro in the steel industry, by Richard L.
      Rowan. Philadelphia, Wharton school of finance, Univ. of Pennsylvania
      [c1968]. xi, 148 p. Bibliographical footnotes. Racial policies of
      American industry. Report no. 3. C, CNoS, CSdS, CSf, CSfGG, CSjC, CSt.

          Includes the steel industry in Colorado, Utah, Arizona, Washington,
      Oregon, California, and Hawaii.

Employment and Unemployment; Occupations

1924. RUCHAMES, LOUS, 1917- . Race, jobs and politics: the story of the
FEPC. N. Y., Columbia univ. press, 1953. xi, 255 p. Bibliographical
references included in "Notes": pp. [215]-40. CFS, CNoS, CSdS, CU-I,
CU-SC.
    Includes material on Los Angeles hearings of FEPC.

1925. RUSMORE, JAY THEODORE. Psychological tests and fair employment; a
study of employment testing in the San Francisco bay area [by] Jay T.
Rusmore. [Sacramento] Fair employment practice commission, 1967.
58 p. CLSU, CSaT, CSt, CU-A.

1926. RUTLEDGE, AARON L. Nineteen Negro men; personality & manpower re-
training [by] Aaron L. Rutledge & Gertrude Zemon Gass. S. F., Jossey-
Bass, 1967. xv, 109 p. CFS, CHS, CLSU, CLobS, CNoS, CSaT, CSdS, CSf,
CSfGG, CSjCi, CSluSP, CSt, CU-A, CU-SC, Wa.
    Employment and occupational retraining.

1927. San Francisco. Board of supervisors. Fair employment practices
ordinance. [S. F., 1957]. 23 p. CO.

1928. _____. Commission on equal employment opportunity. Final report
of the commission on equal employment opportunity of the City and county
of San Francisco. [S. F.] 1960. 30 p. illus., ports. CO, CSfSt.

1929. _____. Human rights commission. Racial and ethnic employment pattern
survey of the city and county of San Francisco government; departmental
analysis. S. F., 1965. 98 ℓ. tables. CO.

1930. _____. Ordinances, etc. Fair employment practices ordinance: City
and county of San Francisco. [S. F.] Pub. under the authority of the
Board of supervisors [n.d.]. 22 p. CSfSt.

1931. *SAVAGE, WILLIAM SHERMAN, 1890- . "The Negro on the mining frontier,"
in Journal of Negro history, v. 30, Jan., 1945, pp. 30-46.
    Mining activities in California and to a smaller extent in Colorado
and Utah.

1932. *Seattle urban league. Who's available? A listing of black college
students in the state of Washington. Seattle, 1969. 256 p. Wa.

1933. SMITH, GARRET. How to keep a job ... and how to turn it into a better
one, by Garret Smith. L. A., Golden state mutual life ins. co. [1939].
7 p. COEB.
    Reprinted from the Feb. 26, 1939 issue of This week magazine, Los
Angeles Times.

1934. SMITH, STANLEY HUGH. Freedom to work. N. Y., Vantage press [1955].
217 p. illus. CSt-Law.
    "Taken in part from ... [the author's] doctoral dissertation sub-
mitted at the State College of Washington, 1953."
    Describes employment discrimination in Washington.

Employment and Unemployment; Occupations

1935. South central and east Los Angeles transportation-employment project. Interim final report; a research project to determine and test the relationship between a public transportation system and job and other opportunities of low income groups. [L. A.], 1970. xiii, 116 p. maps (part fold.). CU.
Motor bus lines and employment discrimination.

1936. _____. Progress report. CU, No. 5-13 (0, 1967-69).

1937. Southern Pacific company. General instructions covering service by dining car waiters, August 15, 1928. [S. F., 1928]. ix, 20 p.

1938. Stanford research institute. Human resources for Oakland: problems and policies. [Menlo Park] 1968. 65 p. tables. CO.
Tables showing labor force and unemployment by age, color, sex.

1939. THIEBLOT, ARMAND J. The Negro in the banking industry, by Armand J. Thieblot, Jr. ... Philadelphia, Wharton school of finance, Univ. of Pennsylvania [c1970]. xiii, 211 p. Includes bibliographical references. Racial policies of American industry. Report no. 9. CSS, CSjC.
Includes banking practices in the West and specifically in Denver, Los Angeles, Phoenix, San Francisco, and Seattle.

1940. TOBRINER, MICHAEL CHARLES. The California fair employment practices commission: its history, accomplishments, and limitations. Master's thesis, Stanford univ., Stanford, 1963. iv, 118 ℓ.

1941. U. S. Dept. of commerce. Area redevelopment administration. Hard-core unemployment and poverty in Los Angeles. Prepared by the staff of the Institute of industrial relations at the Univ. of Calif., Los Angeles, under a contract with the Area redevelopment administration ... Washington, D. C., Govt. print., 1965. v.p., tables.

1942. VAN DYKE, DUANE JOHN. Role perceptions of the California state F[air] E[mployment] P[ractice] C[ommission] staff consultant. Master's thesis, Univ. of southern Calif., Los Angeles, 1964. viii, 97 ℓ.

1943. Washington. State board against discrimination. Annual survey of non-white employment by state agencies. Reports for the years 1964 and 1965. Wa.

1944. _____. _____. Pre-employment inquiry guide. 1967. Wa.

1945. _____. University. Institute of labor economics. Job opportunities for racial minorities in the Seattle area. Seattle, Univ. of Washington press [1948]. 30 p. tables. CLSU, Wa.
"Study ... conducted ... at the request of the Civic unity committee."

1946. WELLMAN, DAVID. "The wrong way to find jobs for Negroes; the case history of an employment program that turned into a fiasco," in Trans-action, v. 5, Apr., 1968, pp. 9-18.
"The program was known as TIDE. It was run by the California

181

Employment and Unemployment; Occupations

department of employment, and classes were held five days a week in the Youth opportunities center of West Oakland."

1947. Workshop on wasted manpower. 3d, Berkeley, Calif., 1963. Berkeley unified school district-Council of social planning, Berkeley area co-sponsored Workshop on wasted manpower, Berkeley challenge and opportunity, Mar. 15 and 16, 1963, Willard school. [Berkeley?], 1963. 24 ℓ. C.

ENTERTAINMENT: MOTION PICTURES, STAGE, AND RADIO

1948. *ANDERSON, GARLAND. The how's and why's of your success, by Garland Anderson. Definitely outlining how he raised $15,000. [S. F., 1927?]. 30 p. port. C, CHi, CU-B, NUC, pre-1956.
  Cover title: From newsboy and bellhop to playwright.
  San Francisco playwright's account of the New York City production of his "Appearances."

1949. _____. My experiences in writing and having "Appearances" produced. [n.p., n.d.] 19 p. DHU.

1950. *BEAVERS, LOUISE. "My biggest break," in Black world, v. 8, Dec., 1949, pp. 21-22.

1951. *BULLINS, ED, 1935- . "An interview with Ed Bullins ... conducted by Marvin X," in Black world, v. 18, Apr., 1969, pp. 9-16.
  Contains autobiographical information about Bullins' theatrical experiences in San Francisco.

1952. BURKE, WILLIAM LEE. The presentation of the American Negro in Hollywood films, 1946-1961: analysis of a selected sample of feature films. Doctoral dissertation, Northwestern univ., Evanston, Ill., 1965. 379 p.

1953. *CARTER, PHIL. "It's only make-believe," in Crisis, v. 53, Feb., 1946, pp. 44-45 and 61.
  Suggests means by which blacks can secure employment in other than menial positions in the motion picture industry.

1954. CHUDHURI, ARUN K. A study of the Negro problem in motion pictures. Master's thesis, Univ. of southern Calif., Los Angeles, 1951. iii, 107 ℓ.

1955. *COVINGTON, FLOYD C., 1901- . "The Negro invades Hollywood," in Opportunity, v. 7, Apr., 1929, pp. 111-13, 131.
  The motion picture industry and especially the activities of Charles E. Butler and the Central casting corp.

1956. CRIPPS, THOMAS R. "The death of Rastus: Negroes in American films since 1945," in Phylon, v. 28, Fall, 1967, pp. 267-75.

Entertainment: Motion Pictures, Stage, and Radio

1957. CROSBY, HARRY LILLIS "BING," 1904- . "What show business owes the
     Negro," in Black world, Aug., 1951, pp. 3-6.

1958. *DANDRIDGE, DOROTHY,   -1965, and EARL CONRAD. Everything and
     nothing: the Dorothy Dandridge tragedy. N. Y., Abelard-Schuman, 1970.
     224 p. illus. CU.

1959. *DAVIS, SAMMY, 1925- . Yes, I can; [the story of Sammy Davis, Jr.,
     by Sammy Davis, Jr., and Jane and Burt Boyar. N. Y., Farrar, Straus &
     Giroux, 1965]. 612 p. ports. CEcaC, CFS, CHS, CKenM, CLSU, CLod,
     CNoS, CO, CPhD, CSbCL, CSbS, CSluSP, CSto, CU-A, WaT, WaTC.
          Relates experiences in Las Vegas, Los Angeles, and San Francisco.

1960. "Do you remember Stepin Fetchit?", in Black world, v. 9, Nov., 1950,
     pp. 42-43.

1961. EDMERSON, ESTELLE. A descriptive study of the American Negro in
     United States professional radio, 1922-1953. Master's thesis, Univ. of
     Calif., Los Angeles, 1954. 442 ℓ.

1962. ELLIS, ROBERT. "A Hollywood director speaks out," in Black world,
     v. 9, Jan., 1951, pp. 42-44.

1963. FRIEDMAN, RALPH. "The Negro in Hollywood," in Frontier, v. 9, July,
     1958, pp. 15-19.

1964. GARFIELD, JOHN. "How Hollywood can better race relations," in Black
     world, v. 6, Nov., 1947, pp. 4-8.

1965. * HALLIBURTON, CECIL D.   "Hollywood presents us; the movies and racial
     attitudes," in Opportunity, v. 13, Oct., 1935, pp. 296-97.

1966. HALPIN, JAMES. "You gotta have soul," in Seattle magazine, v. 4,
     Sept., 1967, pp. 60-61.
          Concerns Station KYAC, a Negro radio station.

1967. "Hollywood what now?", in Black world, v. 14, Dec., 1964, pp. 72-78.

1968. *HUGHES, LANGSTON, 1902-1967. Black magic; a pictorial history of
     the Negro in American entertainment [by] Langston Hughes [and] Milton
     Meltzer. Englewood Cliffs, N. J., Prentice-Hall [1968, c1967]. 375 p.
     illus., ports.
          Contains a chapter on "The Negro in films," pp. 298-307, and also
     information on Egbert Austin (Bert) Williams, Garland Anderson, and the
     San Francisco mime troupe.
          Available in many libraries.

1969. _____. "Is Hollywood fair to Negroes?", in Black World, v. 1, Apr.,
     1943, pp. 16-21.

1970. HUNTER, ROBERT G. "Hollywood and the Negro," in Black world, v. 15,
     May, 1966, pp. 37-41.
          Discrimination in motion pictures.

Entertainment: Motion Pictures, Stage, and Radio

1971. ISAACS, EDITH JULIET (RICH), 1878- . The Negro in the American
    theatre. N. Y., Theatre arts, 1947. 143 p. illus. CEcaC, CFS, CLU,
    CNoS, CSbS, CSdS, CSf, CSjCi, CSluSP, CU, CU-SB, CU-SC.
        Contains accounts of Egbert Austin Williams, pp. 32-42, and other
    figures of the U. S. stage some of whom had west coast connections.

1972. JEROME, VICTOR JEREMY, 1896- . The Negro in Hollywood films. N. Y.,
    Masses & mainstream [1950]. 64 p. CO, CSbS, CSfSt, CSt, CU, CU-A.
        "The text of this booklet is an expansion of a lecture, 'The Negro
    in Hollywood films,' delivered at a public forum held under the auspices
    of the Marxist cultural magazine, Masses & Mainstream, at the Hotel
    Capitol, New York, on February 3, 1950."

1973. _____. "Third printing, January, 1952." CHS, CU-SB.

1974. JOHNSON, BROOKS. "In the wake of Gregory, Cosby becomes a star," in
    Black world, v. 15, Oct., 1966, pp. 39-42.

1975. *JOHNSON, GEORGE PERRY, 1885- . Collector of Negro film history.
    L. A., 1970. xiii, 322 (i.e., 323) ℓ. port. Typew. CLU, CU-B (photo-
    copy).
        Transcript of an interview completed under the auspices of the UCLA
    Oral history program. Johnson reminisces about boyhood in Colorado
    Springs, Colo. and his careers as general booking manager of the Lincoln
    motion picture co., owner of the Pacific coast news bureau, and collector
    of materials on the Negro in motion pictures since 1916.

1976. _____.
        The George P. Johnson Negro film collection is housed in the Dept. of
    special collections, Univ. of Calif., Los Angeles, and reflects the early
    involvement of Negroes in the moving picture industry. Mr. Johnson's
    first contact with the industry was in 1916 as General booking manager of
    the Lincoln motion picture company when his brother, Noble Johnson, was
    a leading actor in motion pictures. Correspondence, playbills, adver-
    tising materials, still photographs, and records of Negro movie theatres
    of this period form a part of the collection. Materials on more than
    100 firms and corporations which produced Negro films, such as the
    Bookertee film co., Los Angeles, and the Million dollar production co.,
    Hollywood, are included.
        Pamphlets, newspaper and magazine clippings and miscellaneous papers
    of Mr. Johnson are also in the collection. There are listings of some
    1,400 Negro film actors and actresses, with some of their roles, and
    other listings of Negroes prominent in adjacent entertainment fields.
    Materials were being added to the collection in 1970. One day's advance
    notice must be given to use materials in the Johnson collection. **13 boxes.**
    CLU.
1977. *JOHNSON, JAMES WELDON, 1871-1938. Black Manhattan. N. Y., Alfred A.
    Knopf, 1930. 284 p. CFS, CNoS.
        Contains a chapter on Bert Williams, famous New York stage entertainer
    from San Francisco and Riverside. Also Garland Anderson, pp. 203-05.

1978. JONES, ROBERT. "How Hollywood feels about Negroes," in Black world,
    v. 5, Aug., 1947, pp. 4-8.

Entertainment: Motion Pictures, Stage, and Radio

1979. *KILLENS, JOHN OLIVER, 1916- . "Hollywood in black and white," in
Nation, v. 201, Sept. 20, 1965, pp. 157-60.

1980. LASH, JOHN S. "The Negro in motion pictures," in Negro history
bulletin, v. 8, Oct., 1944, pp. 7-8, 17-18.

1981. LEWIS, LLOYD. "Life with Uncle Eggs," in Black world, v. 4, July,
1946, pp. 19-22.
About Egbert Austin Williams.

1982. MC MANUS, JOHN T., and LOUIS KRONENBERGER. "Motion pictures, the
theatre, and race relations," in The annals of the American academy of
political and social science, v. 244, Mar., 1946, pp. 152-58.
Describes, in part, the place of Negroes in Hollywood films.

1983. *MILLER, LOREN R., 1903-1967. "Hollywood's new Negro films," in
Crisis, v. 45, Jan., 1938, pp. 8-9.

1984. _____. "Uncle Tom in Hollywood," in Crisis, v. 41, Nov., 1934,
pp. 329 and 336.

1985. *MUSE, CLARENCE E., 1889- . The dilemma of the Negro actor. L. A.
[1934]. 26 ℓ. CLSU.

1986. _____. Way down south, by Clarence Muse and David Arlen; wood cuts by
Blanding Sloan. Hollywood, D. G. Fischer [c1932]. 145 p. illus.,
plates. CHS, CLSU, CNoS, CU.
"The first edition ... consists of one thousand copies, signed by
the author and numbered."
The story of a Negro vaudeville troupe.

1987. "NAACP sticks to Hollywood deadline: no set quota for Negroes in
production crews," in Broadcasting, v. 32, Sept. 16, 1963, p. 84.

1988. "NAACP vs. The birth of a nation," in Crisis, v. 72, Feb., 1965,
pp. 96-97, 102.

1989. *Negro art theatre. Articles of incorporation, Los Angeles, 1950.
[3] p. Typew. C-ArS.
To provide opportunities primarily for actors and theater craftsmen.
Directors were Joel Fluellen, Camille Cannady, and Leo Branton, Jr.

1990. *Negro pageant movement. Articles of incorporation, Los Angeles,
1938. 3 p. Typew. C-ArS.
"To ascertain, determine, explore, display and exhibit at various
places, the progress and accomplishments of the Negro race through
pageants and otherwise." Directors were Claude C. Honeybuss, Ethel
Thomas, and Lew Payton.

1991. NOBLE, PETER, 1917- . The Negro in films, by Peter Noble. London,
Skelton Robinson [1948]. 288 p. plates, ports. Bibliography:
pp. 241-54. CFS, CL, CLAMP, CLU, CLobS, CNoS, CSbS (1937 ed.), CSf,
CSjC, CSt, CU, CU-A, CU-SB, CU-SC.

Entertainment: Motion Pictures, Stage, and Radio

"List of films, 1902–1948, featuring Negroes or containing important racial themes": pp. 255–73.

1992. _____. Same. Reprint. Port Washington, N. Y., Kennikat, 1969. CHS, CSS.

1993. *ROLLINS, CHARLEMAE HILL, 1897- . Famous Negro entertainers of stage, screen, and TV. N. Y., Dodd, Mead [1967]. 122 p. ports. CNoS, CSdS.
    Includes Nat "King" Cole, Sammy Davis, Jr., Sidney Poitier, Egbert Austin Williams, and others.

1994. ROWLAND, MABEL, ed. Bert Williams, son of laughter; a symposium of tribute to the man and to his work, by his friends and associates with a preface by David Belasco. N. Y., The English crafters [c1923]. xvii, 218 p. illus., ports., facsims. DLC.
    Tributes by George M. Cohan, Heywood Broun, Ring Lardner, W. E. B. Du Bois, Leon Erroll, Jessie Fauset, W. C. Fields, and others. Brief information on his California life.

1995. SHAW, ARNOLD. Belafonte, an unauthorized biography. Philadelphia, Chilton co. book division [c1960]. xiv, 338 p. ports. CHS, CNoS, CSf.
    Includes experiences in California and Nevada.

1996. SMITH, WILLIAM THOMAS. "Hollywood report," in Phylon, v. 6, 1st quarter, 1945, pp. 13–16.
    Lists film industry employees and states that racist policies remain unchanged.

1997. SPINKS, WILLIAM C. "Bert Williams: brokenhearted comedian," in Phylon, v. 11, 1st quarter, 1950, pp. 59–65.

1998. *STILL, WILLIAM GRANT, 1895- . "How do we stand in Hollywood?", in Opportunity, v. 23, Apr.–June, 1945, pp. 74–77.
    Mainly relates to music in the motion picture industry.

1999. "'Sunshine Sammy' (Ernest Morrison)," in Crisis, v. 36, Jan., 1929, pp. 10 and 26–27.
    Describes Morrison's motion picture and vaudeville career.

2000. THEODORE, TERRY. The Negro in Hollywood; a critical study of entertainment films containing Negro themes. Master's thesis, Univ. of southern Calif., Los Angeles, 1962. iii, 173 ℓ.

2001. *TRUMBO, DALTON. "Blackface, Hollywood style," in Crisis, v. 50, Dec., 1943, pp. 365–67 and 378.
    Authored by a resident of Stauffer and a native of Denver.

2002. U. S. Works progress administration. California. San Francisco theatre research. Volume 17 ... Minstrelsy. S. F., 1939. 298 p. illus., ports. Mimeo. C, CBb, CFS, CHi, CL, CLSU, CO, CSS, CSdS, CSf, CSmH, CStmo, CSto, CU-B, Rocq 12643.
    Appearances in San Francisco of Callender's minstrels, 1882–83, pp. 146–50, and Mme. Sissieretta Jones and her Colored troubadors, p. 207. Biographical account of Egbert Austin Williams, pp. 217–18.

Entertainment: Motion Pictures, Stage, and Radio

2003. *WALKER, GEORGE W.,   -1909. "The Negro on the American stage," in
     Colored American magazine, v. 11, Oct., 1906, pp. 243-48.
          Describes his first stage experience in San Francisco with Egbert
     Austin (Bert) Williams.

2004. *WITHERS, ZACHARY. "The Negro and the stage," in Half-century
     magazine, v. 4, June, 1918, pp. 9 and 13.
          The New York stage by an Oakland resident.

                         HISTORY AND HISTORIOGRAPHY

2005. AGUIRRE BELTRAN, GONZALO. ... La población negra de México, 1519-
     1810; estudio, etnohistórico. Portada por Juan Alberto Barragán.
     México, D. F., Ediciones Fuente cultural [c1946]. x, 347 p. maps,
     diagrs. CL, CU-B.
          Important as a basis for understanding the probable ethnic ratio of
     the Southwest before U. S. occupation. An ethnic separation is shown
     for Alta California in 1793, p. 230.

2006. American freedman's union commission. No. 3. The work commenced.
     The great meeting at San Francisco Jan. 29, 1866. Speeches of Hon.
     Cornelius Cole and Fred'k. Billings. Letters from Governor Low and
     twenty-two other eminent citizens. [S. F.], 1866. 16 p. CHi, NUC,
     pre-1956.
          This report describes a public meeting and gives statements of
     interested persons including John J. Moore, Horatio Stebbins, Cornelius
     Cole, and Frederick Billings.

2007. American missionary association.
          Its archives, numbering 300,000 items, are available on microfilm
     from the Amistad research center, Dillard univ., New Orleans. The
     California and Colorado section appears on one roll and consists of
     letters mainly from California clergymen, 1865-78, and Colorado corres-
     pondents, 1873-75, relating to the Freedmen's missionary committee of
     California, southern freedmen, and freedmen's schools. The California
     section contains some peripheral information on race relations.

2008. American oil company, pub. American traveler's guide to Negro history.
     [n.p., n.d.]. 30 p. CHi.
          Second edition. Describes historic events and sites in western
     states.

2009. _____. 3rd ed. Chicago, 1965. 58 p. CChiS, CHi, CU-I.

2010. [ANGEL, MYRON, ed.]. History of Nevada with illustrations and bio-
     graphical sketches of its prominent men and pioneers. Oakland, Thompson
     & West, 1881. xiv, 680 p. illus., ports. CHi, CU-B.
          Carson City Freemasons, p. 242; churches, pp. 209 and 217; admission
     to schools, p. 230; and homicides, p. 345ff.

History and Historiography

2011. _____. Same. Berkeley, Howell-North, 1958. k, xiv, 680 p. illus., ports. CHi, CU-B.

2012. _____. Index to ... by Helen J. Poulton. Reno, Univ. of Nevada press, 1966. 148 p. CHi, CU-B.

2013. APTHEKER, HERBERT, 1915- , ed. A documentary history of the Negro people in the United States. Pref. by W. E. B. Du Bois. [1st] N. Y., Citadel press [1951]. xvi, 942 p. Available in many libraries.
    This title has been reprinted numerous times in two volumes with the original pagination.
    Included are "First California Negro convention, 1855," pp. 373-76; letter of Mifflin W. Gibbs and John [i.e., Peter] Lester objecting to payment of a poll tax without right of franchise, San Francisco, 1857, p. 395; letter of Jonas Holland Townsend, San Francisco, in the Anglo-African magazine, Mar., 1859, concerning "California schools and the Negro," pp. 416-18; and "California Negroes fight Jim Crow schools," from an editorial appearing in the San Francisco Elevator, May 4, 1872, p. 624.

2014. ASHLEY, WILLIAM H. The west of William H. Ashley; the international struggle for the fur trade of the Missouri, the Rocky mountains, and the Columbia, with explorations beyond the continental divide, recorded in the diaries and letters of William H. Ashley and his contemporaries, 1822-1838. Ed. by Dale L. Morgan. Denver, Fred Rosenstock, Old west pub. co., 1964. liv, 341 p. illus., ports., maps, facsims. CHi, CLU, CU.
    Contains numerous references to James P. Beckwourth and occasional references to other persons without the use of surnames.

2015. *Association for the study of Negro life and history. Los Angeles branch. Our authors study club. Negro history week in Los Angeles. 1st, 1949- . C 12th-15th (1960-63), 17th-21st (1965-69); CLGS 17th.

2016. BEAN, WALTON ELBERT. California; an interpretive history [by] Walton Bean. N. Y., McGraw-Hill [1968]. xvi, 576 p. illus., maps, ports. CHi, CP, CSbCL.
    Various facets of Negro history such as civil rights, work as agricultural laborers, slavery, segregation, in Los Angeles, free Negroes, and population.

2017. *BEASLEY, DELILAH LEONTIUM, 1871-1934. The Negro trail blazers of California: a compilation of records from the California archives in the Bancroft library at the University of California; and from the diaries, old papers and conversations of old pioneers in the state of California. It is a true record of facts as they pertain to the history of the pioneer and present-day Negroes of California. L. A. [Times mirror printing and binding house], 1919. 317 p. ports., front.
    Foreword by Charlotte [i.e., Charlotta] A. Bass.
    Available in many libraries. Bound in Stanford university's copy is Miss Beasley's presentation ALS to Mary White Ovington.

History and Historiography

2018. _____. Same. S. F., R and E Research associates, 1968.
Available in many libraries.

2019. _____. Same. N. Y., Negro universities press [1969]. CCotS.

2020. BELL, HORACE. On the old west coast: being further reminiscences of
a ranger. Edited by Lanier Bartlett. N. Y., Morrow and co., 1930.
336 p. Available in many libraries. Rocq 2791.
References to Peter Biggs can be found on pp. 75-76, and to Harry,
a young Arkansas slave in California, pp. 21, 22, and 27.

2021. *BELL, HOWARD HOLMAN, 1913- . "Negroes in California, 1849-1859,"
in Phylon, v. 28, Summer, 1967, pp. 151-60.
Based on original sources secured mainly from copies of the Rochester
(N. Y.) Frederick Douglass' paper and the New York City weekly Anglo-
African.

2022. BERGMAN, PETER M. The chronological history of the Negro in America,
by Peter M. Bergman assisted by a staff of compilers under the direction
of Mort N. Bergman. N. Y., A Bergman book pub. in association with
Harper & Row [c1969]. 698 p. port. CNoS, CSf.
See Index, pp. 625-98, for references to California and western
materials especially after 1950.

2023. Berkeley interracial committee, pub. Achievements of the Negro in
California; a supplement to be used with Achievements of the Negro in
Chicago published by Board of education, City of Chicago. Berkeley,
1945. 21 p. C, CB, CO, CU.
"Prepared by M. C. Claiborne, member Berkeley interracial committee.
The text relies heavily upon Delilah L. Beasley's The Negro trail
blazers of California ... L. A., 1919.

2024. BREWER, WILLIAM HENRY. Up and down California in 1860-1864. Edited
by Francis P. Farquhar. New Haven, Yale univ. press, 1930. 601 p.
illus., ports., map. C, CHi, CL, CLU, CSf, CSmH, CU.
Mexican Negroes gain U. S. citizenship through Treaty of Guadalupe
Hildalgo, 1848, p. 45; activities of Millerton hotel waiter, p. 395.

2025. BRUFF, JOSEPH GOLDSBOROUGH, 1804-1889. Gold rush; the journals,
drawings, and other papers of J. Goldsborough Bruff, captain, Washington
city and California mining association, April 2, 1849-July 20, 1851. Ed.
by Georgia Willis Read and Ruth Gaines. With a foreword by F. W. Hodge.
N. Y., Columbia univ. press, 1944. 2 v. illus., plates, maps, plans,
facsims. Available in many California libraries. Rocq 15724.

2026. _____. Same. Calif. centennial ed. N. Y., Columbia univ. press,
1949. 794 p. illus., maps. Available in many California libraries.
Rocq 15725.
See 32 entries in the index under "Negroes." Surnames are not given.

2027. BURCH, PAULINE, comp. Documents concerning the families and decend-
ants of Nathanial Ford and Samuel Townsend Burch, 1799-1952. Mss.
4 pieces, typed documents, 1953. OrHi.

History and Historiography

Includes excerpts from the family Bibles of Ford and Burch; also a statement of Burch concerning Negroes with the Ford family and surveying in southern Oregon.

2028. BURNETT, PETER HARDEMAN, 1807-1895. Recollections and opinions of an old pioneer, by Peter H. Burnett, the first governor of the state of California. N. Y., D. Appleton and co., 1880. vii, 448 p. CHi, CP, CSdS, CSf, CStmo, CU-B, Rocq 8471.
 Burnett writes of a black man's experience with a grizzly bear, pp. 162-63; of Black Harris, p. 155; and describes the anti-Negro attitude of the Oregon territorial legislature, 1844, pp. 212-33.

2029. _____. Same, with title: An old California pioneer ... Oakland, Biobooks, 1946. 287 p. illus., maps, facsims. Available in many libraries. Rocq 8473.

2030. California. Dept. of parks and recreation. Allensworth state historic park study. [Sacramento?, 1970?]. viii, 20 p. port., maps (1 fold.). COEB.
 Stamped: "Preliminary subject to revision."

2031. _____. University. Berkeley. Dept. of history. The Negro in American history textbooks; a report of a study of the treatment of Negroes in American history textbooks used in grades five and eight and in the high schools of California's public schools. [Prepared by a panel of historians from the University of California, Kenneth M. Stampp, chairman]. Sacramento, Calif. state dept. of education, 1964. iv, 25 p. Bibliographical footnotes. Available in many California libraries.

2032. CARROLL, WILLIAM. ALS, June 3, 1860, Salmon Falls. Ms. CSmH.
 Mentions expelling of mulatto boy from local school due to objection of southerners. Also states that no one knows the writer to be a Black Republican since they "are very unpopular here."

2033. CARTER, KATE B. The Negro pioneer. [Salt Lake City, Utah printing co., c1965]. 84 p. illus., ports., facsim. CNoS, CP.
 A history of Utah pioneers, 1848-1964.

2034. CASTLES, JEAN I. "The West: crucible of the Negro," in Montana, magazine of western history, v. 19, Winter, 1969, pp. 83-85.

2035. CHAMBERLIN, WILLIAM HENRY, and HARRY LAURENZ WELLS. History of Yuba county, California ... Oakland, Thompson & West, 1879. 150 p. illus., ports., maps. C, CCC, CHi, CL, CLSU, CLU, CMary, CO, CSS, CSf, CSfCP, CSmH, CSt, CU-B, CYcCL, Rocq 15577.
 Contains biographical information on early Afro-American clergymen and residents, pp. 54-55.

2036. CHEEK, WILLIAM F., 1933- . Black resistance before the Civil war. Beverly Hills, Glencoe press [1970]. vi, 161 p.
 Includes bibliographies.
 Authored by a California educator.

History and Historiography

2037. COLE, MARTIN. "Pio Pico mansion: fact, fiction and supposition," in
Journal of the West, v. 2, 1963, pp. 281-304.

2038. Cole family. Papers, 1833-1943. 57 boxes and 4 packages. CLU (Spec.
Coll.).
    Correspondence, documents, clippings, and family memorabilia concern-
ing the public and private career of a U. S. Senator from California,
Cornelius Cole, and his family.
    Material on Negro slaves, freedmen, and the 13th amendment may be
found in 7 folders, 1 envelope, and 1 scrapbook, 1865-70.

2039. COY, OWEN COCHRAN, 1884-   . In the diggings in 'forty-nine, by Owen
C. Coy ... L. A., Calif. state historical assoc., 1948. xi, 132 p.
illus., port., maps. Available in many California libraries. Rocq 15764.
    Attitude toward Negro miners, p. 38.

2040. *CURETON, MINNIE EDITH, 1910-1951. The history of the criticism of
the Turner thesis. Doctoral dissertation, Stanford univ., Stanford,
1949. 139 ℓ.

2041. DALE, HARRISON CLIFFORD, ed. The Ashley-Smith explorations and the
discovery of a central route to the Pacific, 1822-1829, with the original
journal ed. by Harrison Clifford Dale. Rev. ed. Glendale, Arthur H.
Clark co., 1941. 360 p. maps. CHi.
    Contains information about Peter Ranne, member of Jedediah Smith's
expedition to California, 1826, and about James P. Beckwourth.

2042. DECKER, PETER, 1822-1888. The diaries of Peter Decker; overland to
California in 1849 and life in the mines, 1850-1851 ... Edited by Helen
S. Giffen. Georgetown, Talisman press, 1966. 338 p. port., maps.
CHi, CSfCP.
    Contains occasional references to mainly unidentified black California
pioneers.

2043. DIETRICH, Dr. The German emmigrants; or Frederick Wohlgemuth's voyage
to California, by Dr. Dietrich. Translated by Leopold Wray [pseud.]
Guben, F. Fechner [1852?]. 39 p. illus. CLSU, CLU, CU-B, NUC, pre-
1956, Baird 663.
    The adventures of a small group including one black in the
California mines.

2044. _____. Same. [Stanford] J. L. Delkin, 1949. 47 p. illus. CLU,
CSt, CU-B, NUC, pre-1956.

2045. DOWNIE, WILLIAM, 1819-1894. Hunting for gold; reminiscences [sic] of
personal experience and research in the early days of the Pacific coast
from Alaska to Panama. By William Downie ... S. F., Press of the
California pub. co., 1893. 407 p. illus., port. Available in many
California libraries.
    Contains information on the early mining activities of blacks in-
cluding Albert Callis and Charles Wilkins.

History and Historiography

2046. _____. Same. Index ... Joseph Gaer, ed. ... [S. F., 1935]. 29 ℓ.
CHi, CP, CSdS, CSf, Rocq 14508.

2047. DROTNING, PHILLIP T. A guide to Negro history in America. Garden
City, N. Y., Doubleday, 1968. xiv 247 p. C, CHS, CKenM, CLSU, CLom,
CNoS, COroB, CSaT, CSbS, CSdS, CSfCiC, CSj, CSlu, CSt, CStb, CStma, CU,
CU-A, CU-I, CU-SB, CVt.
　　The author lists historic areas in each of the 13 western states,
including Alaska and Hawaii, and relates their significance to Afro-
American history. For California, see pp. 16-24.

2048. *DYMALLY, MERVYN MALCOLM, 1926- . "The struggle for the inclusion
of Negro history in our text-books ... a California experience," in
Negro history bulletin, v. 33, Dec., 1970, pp. 188-91.

2049. Federal writers' project. California. The story of the Negro in
Los Angeles county. Compiled by Federal writers' project of the Works
progress administration, under the supervision of Hugh Harlan. [L. A.?],
1936. 68 ℓ. Typew. C.
　　A work not without error and therefore to be used with care.

2050. _____. _____. Same. S. F., R and E research associates, 1970.

2051. _____. Colorado. Colorado Negroes. [Denver, 1940?]. Typew. Mss.
CoHi.

2052. *FISHER, JAMES ADOLPHUS. A social history of Negroes in California,
1860-1900. Master's thesis, Calif. state univ., Sacramento, 1966.
187 p. tables.

2053. FORBES, JACK DOUGLAS, 1934- . "California's black pioneers," in
Liberator, v. 8, Apr., 1968, pp. 6-9, and May, 1968.

2054. _____. "The Spanish-speaking Afro-Americans of the Southwest," in
Phylon, v. 27, Fall, 1966, pp. 233-46.

2055. *FOWLER, JOHN W. Spreading joy. [L. A., 1937]. [12] 50 [1] p.
illus., ports. COEB.
　　Selections from the author's historical and news column, "Spreading
joy," which appeared in the Los Angeles California eagle, the Los Angeles
California news, the Los Angeles Tribune, and other black newspapers.

2056. FRANCIS, J. H. DAVIES. "The blue and gray in California," in
California history nugget, v. 3, Oct.-Nov., 1930, pp. 92-97.
　　States that Negroes purchased their families' freedom with California
gold and mentions activities of the Rev. Darius Stokes.

2057. _____. "Building the fort with Captain Sutter, in California history
nugget, v. 3, Oct.-Nov., 1930, pp. 83-91.
　　Reports the arrival in Sacramento of a Negro cooper from Monterey
in 1841.

History and Historiography

2058. FULKS, BRYAN. Black struggle; a history of the Negro in America, by Bryan Fulks. [N. Y., Dell pub. co., c1969]. 340 p. Bibliography: pp. 327-40. CSf.
    Authored by a San Jose resident.

2059. GARDINER, HOWARD CALHOUN, 1826-1917. In pursuit of the golden dream; reminiscences of San Francisco and the northern and southern mines, 1849-1857, by Howard C. Gardiner. Ed. by Dale L. Morgan. Stoughton, Mass., Western hemisphere, inc., 1970. lxv, 390 p. illus., port., maps. CHi.
    See references to Negroes in index. No surnames are given.

2060. *HARRIS, GEORGE W. "The Negro in early America," in Colored American magazine, v. 13, Dec., 1907, pp. 456-64.
    Describes the adventures of blacks with Balboa and other early Spanish explorers and especially the activities of Esteban, York, and Jacob Dodson.

2061. HARVEY, JAMES ROSE. Negroes in Colorado. Master's thesis, Univ. of Denver, 1941. 151 p. CoHi.

2062. _____. "Negroes in Colorado," in Colorado magazine, v. 26, Apr., 1949, pp. 165-76.
    A condensation of the author's Master's thesis.

2063. HAYES, BENJAMIN IGNATIUS, 1815-1877. Pioneer notes from the diaries of Judge Benjamin Hayes, 1849-1875. L. A., Privately printed, 1929. 307 p. illus., ports., map. Available in many libraries. Rocq 2959.
    "Includes brief mention of Peter Biggs, the barber [p. 71]; Pete Middleton, coachman [p. 88]; colored cook and housekeeper for Mr. [Benjamin D.?] Wilson [p. 90]; and the presence of Negroes in emigrant parties coming to California." - Miriam Matthews.

2064. HEALD, WELDON F. "Black pathfinder of the deserts," in Crisis, v. 57, Dec., 1950, pp. 703-08.
    The adventures of Esteban in Arizona and New Mexico.

2065. HEARD, J. NORMAN. The black frontiersmen; adventures of Negroes among American Indians, 1528-1918 [by] J. Norman Heard. N. Y., John Day co. [c1969]. 128 p. illus., ports. Bibliography: pp. 121-24.
    Recounts activities of Estevanico, York, Edward Rose, James Beckwourth, and the 9th and 10th U. S. Cavalry units.

2066. HILL, DANIEL GRAFTON. The Negro in Oregon; a survey by Daniel G. Hill, Jr. ... Master's thesis, Univ. of Oregon, Eugene, 1932. 172 ℓ. OrHi.
    "Historical survey." - Miriam Matthews.

2067. _____. "The Negro in the early history of the West," in Iliff review, v. 3, Fall, 1946, pp. 132-42.

2068. Historical essays on Montana and the Northwest [in honor of Paul C. Phillips] ... Ed. by J. W. Smurr [and] K. Ross Toole. [Helena, Mont.] Western press [c1957]. 304 p. port. CU-B.

History and Historiography

Contains "Jim Crow out West," by J. W. Smurr, a study of 19th century Montana civil rights with emphasis on segregation in public schools, pp. 149-203. Credits the California supreme court's decision in Ward vs. Flood as influencing Montana attitudes.

2069. HITTELL, THEODORE HENRY, 1830-1917. History of California. S. F., Pacific press & Occidental pub. co., and N. J. Stone and co., 1885-97. 4 v. C, CHi, CL, CLU, CSf, CSmH, CU-B.
Discusses the 1849 constitutional convention's slavery discussion; testimony; founding of Downieville, 1849; Peter H. Burnett's prejudice; John Neely Johnson's attitude; and actions of the legislature. See index at end of v. 4.

2070. HOGG, THOMAS CLARK, 1935- . "Negroes and their institutions in Oregon," in Phylon, v. 30, Fall, 1969, pp. 272-85.
Essentially a history of Negroes in Oregon.

2071. HOWARD, WILLIAM DAVIS MERRY, 1819-1856. Auction. On Saturday, 12th May, will be sold at the "Leidesdorff rancho," American Fork, the horses, mares, bullocks, and other live stock, belonging to the estate of W. A. Leidesdorff, deceased, and now on said rancho. For further particulars, enquire of Messrs. S. Brannan & co., Sacramento City. [Signed] W. D. M. Howard, adm. estate, W. A. Leidesdorff, deceased, San Francisco, April 13, 1849. [S. F., 1849]. Broadside. CU-B.

2072. Illustrated history of Los Angeles county ... and biographical mention of many of its pioneers, and also of prominent citizens of to-day. Chicago, Lewis pub. co., 1889. 835 p. illus., ports. C, CBb, CCC, CHi, CL, CLSU, CLU, CMary, CO, CP, CPom, CSf, CSmH, CStb, CStmo, CU-B, Rocq 2650.
Contains "objective treatment of the Negro." - Miriam Matthews. Includes Peter Biggs, p. 110; Wesley chapel and the African Methodist Episcopal church, p. 302; Negro residents, pp. 297-304; veterans of the War with Mexico, p. 359; and Robert Owens, p. 358.

2073. JASPER, JAMES. "History of Julian area." Ms. CSdHi.
Negroes are described, pp. 170-72.

2074. JOHANESEN, HARRY. California Negro history; black's role in the old west. [Washington, D. C., Govt. print., 1968]. 15 p. C (photocopy), CHi.
A series of 10 articles which originally appeared in the San Francisco Examiner, July 22-Aug. 2, 1968, and were incorporated in the Congressional record, Oct. 3-6, 1968, under "Remarks of Hon. Thomas H. Kuchel of California."

2075. JOHANNSEN, ROBERT WALTER, 1925- . "Spectators of disunion; the Pacific northwest and the Civil war," in Pacific northwest quarterly, v. 44, July, 1953, pp. 106-14.

2076. JOHANSEN, DOROTHY O. Empire of the Columbia; a history of the Pacific northwest. By Dorothy O. Johansen and the late Charles M. Gates. 2nd ed.

History and Historiography

by Dorothy O. Johansen. N. Y., Harper and Row, 1967. 654 p. CSmH, Wa.
Contains references to Negroes in both Oregon and Washington.

2077. JOHNSTON, EFFIE ENFIELD. "Wade Johnston talks to his daughter," in
Las Calaveras, v. 18, Apr., 1970, pp. 17-28.
Contains a history of "Black pioneers" in Calaveras county, pp. 20-23,
especially informative on Philip Piper, Benjamin Buster, and the Edmington
Binum family.

2078. JOLLY, JOHN, 1823-1899. Gold Spring diary, the journal of John Jolly.
Edited and annotated by Carlo M. De Ferrari and including a brief history
of Stephen Spencer Hill, fugitive from labor. Sonora, Tuolumne county
historical society, c1966. 160 p. illus., port. CDc, CHi, CSf, CU-B.
The history of Hill, a fugitive slave, is related, pp. 126-42.
Nigger Hill, a small peak one mile north of Columbia, is named in his
honor. Further information on Hill, who arrived in California in 1849,
may be obtained by an examination of "People ex rel Hill vs. Sheriff of
the County of Tuolumne" and "Wood Tucker vs. Stephen Hill, et al.,"
Tuolumne county court, Sonora, Aug., 1854.

2079. LAPP, RUDOLPH MATTHEW, 1915- . "The Negro in gold rush California,"
in Journal of Negro history, v. 49, Apr., 1964, pp. 81-98.

2080. LARKIN, THOMAS OLIVER, 1802-1858. The Larkin papers; personal,
business, and official correspondence of Thomas Oliver Larkin, merchant
and United States consul in California. Ed. by George P. Hammond ...
Berkeley, Pub. for the Bancroft library by the Univ. of Calif. press,
1951-64. 10 v. illus.

2081. _____. _____. Index [by] Anna Marie Hager and Everett G. Hager.
Berkeley, Univ. of Calif. press, 1968. 80 p. C, CHi, CLU, CU-B.
Contains correspondence and considerable information concerning
William Alexander Leidesdorff, U. S. vice-consul at San Francisco, and
Andrés, Antonio María, and Pío Pico; also references to Negroes in Hawaii
and Oregon and the extension of slavery in the West.

2082. LAUGHLIN, FLORENCE. "Estevanico and the cities of gold," in Black
world, v. 12, Aug., 1963, pp. 19-22.

2083. LITWACK, LEON FRANK. North of slavery: the Negro in the free states,
1790-1860. Doctoral dissertation, Univ. of Calif., Berkeley, 1958. iii,
440 ℓ.

2084. _____. North of slavery; the Negro in the free states, 1790-1860.
Chicago, Univ. of Chicago press [c1961]. xi, 318 p.
"Bibliographical essay": pp. 280-303. Available in many libraries.
Places the free states in historical perspective. See the index and
the bibliographical essay for occasional references to California and
Oregon.

2085. LOWRY, RAYMOND W., ed. Contemporary communications' 1970 black history
calendar containing the names and achievements of over two hundred great

History and Historiography

Negro men and women of past and present. Raymond W. Lowry, ed. [Berkeley, Contemporary communications co., 1969]. [14] ℓ. ports. Contains little material on California and the West.

2086. MC LEOD, ALEXANDER RODERICK. -1840. The Hudson's bay company's first fur brigade to the Sacramento valley: Alexander McLeod's 1829 hunt. Introduced and edited by Doyce B. Nunis, Jr. [Fair Oaks] Sacramento book collectors club, 1968. 59 p. map. Bibliography: pp. 51-53. CHi, CSf, CSmH, CU-B.
    The transfer of George Washington from the party of Abel Stearns to that of McLeod in the Sacramento valley, 1829, is described, pp. 36-37. The Company's London records show that Washington was employed at Fort Vancouver until at least 1837, according to research notes supplied by the above editor.

2087. MC SPADDEN, HILTRUDE. Sutter and Leidesdorff in the international competition for California. Master's thesis, Stanford univ., 1935.

2088. MAHLBERG, JEAN. The history and development of the Negro community in Santa Ana, Calif. Term paper, Calif. state univ., Fullerton, 1967. 53 ℓ. charts, map. Typew. CStaB.

2089. MANSFIELD, GEORGE CAMPBELL, 1880- . History of Butte county, California, with biographical sketches of the leading men and women ... L. A., Historic record co., 1918. 1,331 p. illus., ports. C, CBb, CCC, CChiS, CHi, CL, CLSU, CLU, CO, COroB, CSS, CSf, CSj, CSmH, CSt, CU-B, Rocq 1289.
    Two documents relating to slavery in the county are textually reproduced on pp. 226-27, and the decennial Negro population, 1850-1910, is given, p. 393.

2090. MARRYAT, SAMUEL FRANCIS. Mountains and molehills, or, recollections of a burnt journal ... N. Y., Harper and brother, 1855. 393 p. illus. C, CHi, CL, CLU, CP, CPom, CSS, CSd, CSf, CSmH, Rocq 15944.
    The first U. S. edition. Vignettes of black life in California, pp. 238 and 251-52. No surnames are given.

2091. _____. Same. Reprint. in facsimile from the 1st American ed. of 1855, with intro. and notes by Marguerite Eyer Wilbur. Stanford [1952]. 393 p. illus. CBb, CChiS, CHi, CSS, CSf, CSto, CViCL, Rocq 15946.

2092. MEIER, AUGUST, 1923- . The making of black America; essays in Negro life and history. Ed. by August Meier and Elliott Rudwick. N. Y., Atheneum, 1969. xvi, 377, 507 p. CSt, CU.
    Contains "The Negro cowboy," by Philip Durham, and "The reaction of the Negro to the motion picture, Birth of a nation," by Thomas R. Cripps.

2093. MELDRUM, GEORGE WESTON. The history of the treatment of foreign and minority groups in California, 1830-1860. Doctoral dissertation, Stanford univ., Stanford, 1948. 437 ℓ.

2094. *MERIWETHER, LOUISE M. "The new face of Negro history," in Frontier, v. 17, Nov., 1965, pp. 5-7.

History and Historiography

2095. *MILLER, LOREN R., 1903-1967. "The Negro in history textbooks," in California teachers association journal, v. 61, Mar., 1965, pp. 34 and 36.

2096. [MUNRO-FRASER, J. P.]. History of Santa Clara county, California ... S. F., Alley, Bowen & co., 1881. 798 p. illus., ports., map. C, CB, CCC, CHi, CL, CLU, CO, CP, CPa, CSd, CSf, CSj, CSmH, CSt, CSto, CU-B, Rocq 13729.
   "Two mulattoes, Justo Altamirano and Maria Garcia, are included in the list of families connected with the San Francisco presidio in the year 1790 which the author has copied from the Spanish archives in San Francisco," pp. 62-63. - Miriam Matthews.

2097. MUSLADIN, WILLIAM L. An ethno-historical survey of the Sacramento region of California. Master's thesis, Calif. state univ., Sacramento, 1969. 267 ℓ.

2098. "Negro pioneers; their page in Oregon history," in Oregon native son, Jan., 1900, pp. 432-34.

2099. NEVINS, ALLAN, 1890-1971. Frémont, pathmaker of the West, by Allan Nevins. N. Y., D. Appleton-Century co., 1939. xiv, 649 p. illus., ports., maps. Available in many libraries.
   For information about Jacob Dodson and especially concerning his famous feat of horsemanship, see pp. 129, 304, and 320-21. The famous round trip ride from Los Angeles to Monterey has been described in many places. Most accounts of Frémont and his expeditions contain information about Dodson.

2100. NEWMARK, HARRIS. Sixty years in southern California, 1853-1913. N. Y., Knickerbocker press, 1916. 688 p. illus., ports. Available in many California libraries. Rocq 3221.

2101. _____. Same. 2nd ed., rev. and augmented ... N. Y., Knickerbocker press, 1926. 732 p. illus., ports. Available in many California libraries. Rocq 3222.

2102. _____. Same. 3rd ed., rev. and augmented ... Boston, Houghton, 1930. 744 p. illus., ports. Available in many California libraries. Rocq 3223.
   Accounts of Peter Biggs, pp. 137-38, Robert Owens family and George Berry, p. 138, and John Hall and Henry Buddin, p. 527.

2103. NUNIS, DOYCE BLACKMAN, 1924- . "The strangers among them," in Westways, v. 59, May, 1967, pp. 24-27.
   Describes the mining activities of non-white and non-English-speaking persons in the California gold fields.

2104. O'MAHONEY, JOSEPH. Collection of papers "containing fragments of primary sources" on Afro-American history. - E. V. Toy, University librarian. WyU.
   References are made to the Wyoming Association of colored women's clubs, 1935, and to the Casper Colored men's progressive club, 1936.

History and Historiography

2105. PARKHILL, FORBES, 1892- . Collection of papers "containing fragments of primary sources" on Afro-American history. - E. V. Toy, University librarian. WyU.

2106. PECK, ROBERT M. A letter printed in the Denver times, 1883. Typew. copy. CoHi.

2107. PERKINS, WILLIAM. Three years in California; William Perkins' journal of life at Sonora, 1849-1852. With an introduction and annotations by Dale L. Morgan & James R. Scobie. Berkeley, Univ. of Calif. press, 1964. 424 p. illus., ports., facsim. CHi, CTurS, Rocq 15394.
    Contains some information about treatment of blacks in the California mines. No surnames are given.

2108. POLLARD, LANCASTER, 1901- , comp. Synopsis of the history of the Negro in the Northwest. [1943]. Mss. [57] p., consisting of one typed and one autographed document. OrHi.

2109. "Proclamation of the mayor of Monterey, California, Shedo S. Russo; first Negro history celebration here, initiated by the Lamplighters study club," in Negro history bulletin, v. 25, Dec., 1961, p. 62.

2110. QUIMBY, GEORGE IRVING, 1913- . "Culture contact on the northwest coast, 1785-1795," in American anthropologist, v. 50, Apr., 1948, pp. 247-55.
    Chinese, Hawaiians, and Negroes.

2110a. *RHODES, ETHEL C. Negroes in Pacific coast history prior to 1865. Master's thesis, Howard univ., Washington, D. C., 1940.

2111. Richmond unified school district. Black history; supplement to U. S. history program, grades 8 and 11. [Richmond?] 1969. iv, 220 p.
    "... guide containing authentic sources of Black History to integrate readily with the U. S. History program."

2112. ROBINSON, JAMES LEE. The economic status of the free and freed Negro, 1830-1880. Master's thesis, Univ. of Calif., Berkeley, 1955. ii, 81 ℓ. tables.

2113. SANKORE, SHELBY. "Negro in California history," in Black world, v. 15, Feb., 1966, pp. 42-45.

2114. *SAVAGE, WILLIAM SHERMAN, 1890- . "The Negro pioneer in the State of of Washington," in Negro history bulletin, v. 21, Jan., 1958, pp. 93-95.

2115. *SKANKS, EVA. B. (ALLENSWORTH). "How the steamer 'Planter' ran away," in Colored American magazine, v. 6, July, 1903, pp. 513-17.
    The heroism of Robert Smalls is described by a daughter of Allen Allensworth.

2116. SNOWDEN, CLINTON A. History of Washington: the rise and progress of an American state. N. Y., Century history co., 1909. 4 v. Wa.
    Consult index in v. 4 for references to George W. Bush and to early legislation concerning Negroes.

History and Historiography

2117. STAMPP, KENNETH M., and others. "The Negro in American history textbooks," in Integrated education, v. 2, Oct.-Nov., 1964, pp. 9-26.
   A report prepared at the request of the Berkeley chapter of
C. O. R. E. and subsequently unanimously accepted by the State board of
education.

2118. THEISEN, LEE SCOTT, ed. "The fight in Lincoln, N. M., 1878, the
testimony of two Negro participants," in Arizona and the West, v. 12,
Summer, 1970, pp. 173-98.

2119. THURMAN, A. ODELL. The Negro in California before 1890. Master's
thesis, Univ. of the Pacific, Stockton, 1945. 95 p. CSto.
   Concerns the role of the Negro in Spanish, Mexican, and early U. S.
California life and the fight for civil rights.

2120. *THURMAN, SUE (BAILEY). Pioneers of Negro origin in California.
S. F., Acme pub. co., 1949. 70 p. illus., ports. C, CAna, CHi, CL,
CLob, CMS, CMary, CO, COEB, CP, CPhCL, CRic, CSd, CSf, CSfCP, CSmH, CSto,
CTurS.

2121. _____. Same. 1952 ed. CB, CChiS, CFS, CHS, CLGS, CMS, CO, CP, CSfAA,
CSfU, CSt, CU-B.
   "[These articles] first appeared ... in the San Francisco Sun-
Reporter ... 1949. Since that time the material has been considerably
revised and extended." - Foreword.

2122. TINKHAM, GEORGE HENRY. California men and events; time, 1769-1890 ...
Stockton, Record pub. co., 1915. 330 p. illus., ports.
   Fugitive slaves and Negro testimony, pp. 134-37, and admission to
public schools, pp. 224-25.
   Available in many California libraries.

2122a. *WARE, MARGUERITE EVELYN. Franco-Belgian relations, 1815-1870.
Master's thesis, Univ. of Calif., Berkeley, 1933. ii, 119 ℓ.

2123. WARREN, FRANCIS EMROY, 1844-1929. Collection of papers "containing
fragments of primary sources" on Afro-American history. - E. V. Toy,
University librarian. WyU.

2124. *WASHINGTON, NATHANIEL JASON. The historical development of the Negro
in Oklahoma. Master's thesis, Univ. of Arizona, Tucson, 1947. 113 ℓ.

2125. WEATHERWAX, JOHN MARTIN, 1900- . The founders of Los Angeles. L. A.,
Bryant foundation [1954]. 20 p. table. C, CNoS.
   An examination of the ethnic backgrounds of the founders.

2126. WEBER, FRANCIS. "California's Negro heritage," in Black world, v. 16,
Feb., 1967, pp. 87-88.
   Published originally in the Los Angeles Tidings.

2127. WILLIAMSON, JOEL RANDOLPH. The Negro in South Carolina during reconstruction, 1861-1877. Doctoral dissertation, Univ. of Calif., Berkeley,
1964. 606 ℓ.

History and Historiography

2128. WILLIS, WILLIAM LADD. History of Sacramento county, California with
    biographical sketches ... L. A., Historic record co., 1913. 1,056 p.
    illus., ports. C, CBb, CF, CHi, CL, CLU, CO, CS, CSS, CSd, CSf, CSmH,
    CU-B, Rocq 6511.
        For information on Afro-American schools and lodges, see pp. 170,
    172-73, 178-79, and 255.

2129. *WOOD, FORREST GLEN. Race demagoguery during the Civil war and re-
    construction. Doctoral dissertation, Univ. of Calif., Berkeley, 1965.
    418 ℓ. illus.

2130. *WRIGHT, RICHARD ROBERT, 1878- . "Negro companions of the Spanish
    explorers," in American anthropologist, v. 4, Apr.-June, 1902, pp. 217-28.

HOUSING, RESTRICTIVE COVENANTS, AND URBAN REDEVELOPMENT

2131. "Absolute discretion? The California controversy over fair housing
    laws," in Interracial review, v. 38, Oct., 1965, pp. 155-81, 195.
        A compilation reprinted from Research bulletin no. 7 of Sacramento
    committee for fair housing.

2132. ADLER, PATRICIA. History of the Normandie program area. Prepared for
    the Community redevelopment agency of the city of Los Angeles by Patricia
    Adler, urban historian, September 1, 1969. [L. A., 1969]. 52 [3] p.
    illus., maps. Mimeo.

2133. ALANCRAIG, HELEN SMITH. Codornices village: a study of non-segregated
    public housing in the San Francisco bay area. Master's thesis, Univ. of
    Calif., Berkeley, 1953. 1 v. tables.

2134. ALVES, RANDALL PAUL. A political analysis of the election returns of
    Proposition 14 in Sacramento county. Master's thesis, Calif. state univ.,
    Sacramento, 1965. 69 ℓ. tables.

2135. AMDUR, REUEL SEEMAN. An exploratory study of nineteen Negro families
    in the Seattle area who were first Negro residents in white neighbor-
    hoods, of their white neighbors, and of the integration process, to-
    gether with a proposed program to promote integration in Seattle.
    Master's thesis, Univ. of Washington, Seattle, 1963.

2136. American Jewish congress. California commission on law and social
    action. Three briefs on Proposition 14 in the California Supreme court.
    S. F., 1965. v.p. (Its Law commentary, v. 3, Summer, 1965). CSf.
        Housing discrimination.

2137. ASIA, BENJAMIN S. Brief of amici curiae, Benjamin S. Asia [and
    others] in the Supreme court of the state of Washington in the matter of
    the appeal of John J. O'Meara and Donna A. O'Meara, his wife, respondents,
    vs. Washington state board against discrimination, appellant, and Robert
    L. Jones, appellant-intervenor, and Raymond D. Torbenson, Richard M.
    Thatcher, and Seattle real estate board, respondents-additional

Housing, Restrictive Covenants, and Urban Redevelopment

defendants. Appeal from the Superior court of the state of Washington for King county. Seattle [1960?]. vii, 39 p. At head of title: No. 35436. CU.

2138. "Assault on the Fair housing act," in Frontier, v. 15, Feb., 1964, p. 4ff.
The activities of the Los Angeles realty board in housing segregation.

2139. BAILEY, J. "Oakland presents its case for salvaging a ghetto," in Architectural forum, v. 126, Apr., 1967, pp. 42-45.
A plan to up-grade West Oakland.

2140. BARNES, SHIRLEY M. "Elliot A. Draine - housing manager," in Opportunity, v. 25, Apr.-June, 1947, pp. 59 and 75.
About Denver housing.

2141. BARTH, ERNEST A. T., and SUE MARCH. "Research note on the subject of minority housing," in Journal of intergroup relations, v. 3, 1962, pp. 314-20.

2142. BARUCH, DOROTHY (WALTER), 1899- . "Sleep comes hard," in Nation, v. 160, Jan. 27, 1945, pp. 95-96.
Los Angeles housing.

2143. Berkeley. Citizens' committee to study discrimination in housing. Appendix to report of Citizens' committee to study discrimination in housing in Berkeley. Berkeley, 1962. 59 p. CO.

2144. _____. _____. Housing discrimination in Berkeley; a report by a Citizens' committee to the Community welfare commission. [Berkeley] 1962. 9 p. maps, tables. C, CO.
Appendices (60 p.): A. Testimony of individuals. - B. Tests for housing available to non-white persons. - C. 1. Interviews with real estate brokers. 2. Report on University housing service. - D. Census tract information. - E. Legislation and other measures in other areas. - F. Drafts of three proposed ordinances. G. Letters from citizen groups.
Letter from Mrs. Florence Casoroli, Acting executive secretary, Community welfare commission to the Mayor and City council of Berkeley (4 p.) dated Oct. 1, 1962 inserted in front.

2145. BRIGHAM, ROBERT L. Land ownership and occupancy by Negroes in Manhattan Beach, Calif. Master's thesis, Calif. state univ., Fresno, 1965.

2146. BRUNER, JOHN M. The effect of racial integration on property values and real estate practices. [L. A.] Univ. of southern Calif. Graduate school of business administration, 1970. iii, 35 p. C, CLSU.

2147. BULLOUGH, BONNIE LOUISE, 1927- . Alienation among middle class Negroes: social-psychological factors influencing housing desegregation. Doctoral dissertation, Univ. of Calif., Los Angeles, 1968. xvi, 233 ℓ. illus.

Housing, Restrictive Covenants, and Urban Redevelopment

2148. _____. Social-Psychological barriers to housing desegregation. L. A., Univ. of Calif. housing, real estate, and urban land studies programs, 1969. x, 134 p. CHS, CLU, CSS, CSfSt, CU-B.
    Based on the author's thesis, Univ. of Calif., Los Angeles.

2149. California. Governor's commission on the Rumford act. Report of the Governor's commission on the Rumford act. Approved at Commission meeting, April 6, 1967. [Sacramento] 1967. 1 v. (v.p.) CSt, CSt-Law.
    Minority report inserted at end.

2150. _____. Legislature. Assembly. Committee on governmental efficiency and economy. Fair housing in California; a staff report. [Sacramento, 1967]. v.p. tables. CSt.

2151. _____. _____. _____. _____. Rumford fair housing act: proposed bills; amendments; newspaper clippings; background material and data concerning the passage of the act, proposition 14, and subsequent amendments to the original act; and committee hearings on housing, urban redevelopment, discrimination, housing standards and financing, sales enforcement of government agency regulations, and problems of individual citizens affected. Period covered: 1959-68. 1/2 cu. ft. C-ArS.

2152. _____. _____. _____. Interim committee on governmental efficiency and economy. Fair housing in California; a staff report. Lester A. McMillan, chairman. [Sacramento] 1967. 33 [55] ℓ. CSt-Law.

2153. _____. State fair employment practice commission. Answers to questions about the California fair housing law. [n.p., 1964?]. CFS, CMS.

2154. _____. _____. A directory of fair housing in the state of California. [Sacramento] 1969. 16 p. CSt.

2155. _____. _____. Opening the door: Nine cases from FEPC files, fair housing. Sacramento [n.d.]. 2 p. CFS, CMp.

2156. _____. _____. Questions and answers about the California fair housing law. [n.p., 1964?]. CMS.

2157. _____. _____. Questions and answers about the initiative against fair housing. [n.p., 1964?]. CMS.

2158. _____. University. Berkeley. Survey research center. Housing and population tabulations from the 701 household survey of Oakland with comparison to the 1960 census. Berkeley, 1967. 110 p. map, tables. CO.
    Population and labor force characteristics including figures for non-whites.

2159. California research foundation. An analysis of the factors concerning the fair housing ordinance vote and city elections in Berkeley, California, April 2nd, 1963. L. A., 1963. 41 ℓ. form, tables (part fold.). CBSK, CSjC.

Housing, Restrictive Covenants, and Urban Redevelopment

2160. CASE, FREDERICK EWING, 1918- . The housing status of minority
families, Los Angeles, 1956, by Fred E. Case and James H. Kirk. [L. A.,
Los Angeles urban league, 1958]. iv, 78 p. maps, tables. CL, CLSU, CO.
    A joint project of the Los Angeles urban league and the Univ. of
Calif., Los Angeles.

2161. _____. Profile of the Los Angeles metropolis; its people and its
homes. Pt. 5: Minority families in the metropolis [by] Fred E. Case.
L. A., Univ. of Calif. graduate school of business administration, 1966.
47 p. (Real estate research program report no. 8). C, CLU.
    A study of black and Spanish-American family housing.

2162. _____., and others. "Reasons for home satisfaction and dissatisfaction
of minority group home owners and renters, Los Angeles, California," in
Journal of human relations, v. 6, Summer, 1958, pp. 93-99.

2163. CASSTEVENS, THOMAS W. Politics, housing, and race relations;
California's Rumford act and Proposition 14, by Thomas W. Casstevens.
Berkeley, Univ. of Calif. institute of governmental studies, 1967. vi,
97 p. Bibliographical footnotes. C, CChiS, CFS, CLSU, CNoS, CSaT, CSdS,
CSf, CSjC, CSluSP, CSrCL, CSt-Law, CU-B.

2164. _____. Politics, housing and race relations: the defeat of Berkeley's
fair housing ordinance. Berkeley, Univ. of Calif. institute of governmental studies, 1965. 117 p. CEcaC, CF, CFS, CHS, CM1G, CNoS, CPhD,
CSaT, CSbCL, CSdS, CSf, CSluSP, CStmo.

2165. COFFIN, GEORGE H. What's the issue? By George H. Coffin, III,
chairman C[alifornia] R[eal] E[state] A[ssociation] finance division,
vice chairman, CREA legislative committee. [Presentation to Compton-
Lynwood Board of realtors]. [n.p., 1964?] CMS.

2166. *COLLEY, NATHANIEL SEXTUS, 1918- and MILTON L. MCGHEE. "The
California and Washington fair housing cases," in Law in transition,
v. 22, Summer, 1962, pp. 79-92.

2167. Commission on race and housing. Where shall we live? Report. Con-
clusions from a three-year study of racial discrimination in housing
... Berkeley, Univ. of Calif. press, 1958. 77 p. CFS, CLSU, CSfSt,
CU-A.

2168. Committee for Yes on Prop. 14 to abolish Rumford forced housing act.
Some questions and answers demonstrating the need for a "yes" vote on
proposition 14. [n.p., 1964]. CMS.

2169. Council for civic unity of San Francisco. For all the people, the
right to choose a home. S. F., [1959?]. folder. CO.

2170. _____. Housing a giant; memorandum on the Willie Mays incident.
S. F., 1957. unp. CO.

Housing, Restrictive Covenants, and Urban Redevelopment

2171. CROSBY, ALEXANDER L. In these 10 cities: Charlottesville, Sledge, Phoenix, Los Angeles, Denver, Springfield, Chicago, Detroit, Waterbury [and] New York; discrimination in housing. [Written and designed by Alexander L. Crosby. Edited by Hortense W. Cabel and Maxwell S. Stewart. Prepared by the New York state committee on discrimination in housing, N. Y., Public affairs committee, 1951]. 29 p. illus., ports. CU.

2172. DENTON, JOHN H. Apartheid American style [by] John H. Denton. Berkeley, Diablo press [1967]. 164 p. CMp, CNoS, CSaT, CSf, CSjCi, CSluSP, CSrCL, CSt-Law, CU-A.
   Describes housing discrimination especially in reference to the Rumford Act and Proposition 14.

2173. _____., ed. Race and property. Berkeley, Diablo press [c1964]. vi, 159 p. Bibliography: pp. 156–57. CKenM, CMp, CPhD, CSluSP, CSrCL, CSt-Law, CSto, CU, CU-A.
   A study of California and national discrimination in housing based upon a collection of reports emanating from a Univ. of Calif. extension conference. "Government's responsibility for residential segregation," by Loren Miller, pp. 58–76.

2174. EICHLER, EDWARD P. Race & housing; an interview with Edward P. Eichler, president, Eichler homes, inc. [Santa Barbara, 1964]. 23 p. C, CHS, CLSU, CPhD, CPomCP, CU, CU-SC.
   "One of a series of interviews on the American character [by] Center for the study of democratic institutions."
   Concerns housing discrimination in California.

2175. ELEY, LYNN W., ed. The politics of fair-housing legislation; state and local case studies, ed. by Lynn W. Eley and Thomas W. Casstevens. S. F., Chandler pub. co. [c1968]. xiv, 415 p. "Suggestions for further reading": pp. 395–98. C, CNoS, CSdS, CSt.
   Includes "The defeat of Berkeley's fair-housing ordinance," and "California's Rumford act and Proposition 14," by Thomas W. Casstevens, pp. 187–284.

2176. "Fair California," in Economist, v. 219, May 14, 1966, p. 710.
   Concerns racial discrimination in San Francisco housing.

2177. FEI, JOHN CHING HAN. Rent differentiation related to segregated housing markets for racial groups – with special reference to Seattle, Washington. Master's thesis, Univ. of Washington, Seattle, 1949.

2178. GERBER, SIDNEY, –1965. Correspondence and related items regarding the State board against discrimination, the State FEPC, Fair housing listing service, and other Washington state organizations. About 10,000 items. WaU.

2179. GLAZER, NATHAN, ed. Studies in housing & minority groups, edited by Nathan Glazer and Davis McEntire. With an introd. by Nathan Glazer. Special research report to the Commission on race and housing. Berkeley, Univ. of Calif. press, 1960. xvii, 228 p. maps, tables. CFS, CHS, CKenM, CLSU, CLobS, CNoS, CSbS, CSdS, CSf, CSluSP, CSp, CSt, CU, CU-A, CU-SC, Wa.

Housing, Restrictive Covenants, and Urban Redevelopment

2180. GOLDNER, WILLIAM. New housing for Negroes: recent experience.
[Berkeley] Real estate research program, Bureau of business and economic
research, Univ. of Calif. [1958]. 29 p. tables. (Real estate research
program. Research report, 12). CLS, CLSU, CS1uSP, CSfSt, CU.
A study of California housing.

2181. Greater Modesto council of churches. Legislation and public affairs
commission. Resolution re: Rumford housing act. [Modesto?, 1964?].
CMS.

2182. GRIER, EUNICE S. Privately developed interracial housing; an analysis
of experience. [By] Eunice and George Grier. Special research report
to the Commission on race and housing. Berkeley, Univ. of Calif. press,
1960. x, 264 p. tables. Bibliography: pp. [251]-57. CCovB, CEcaC,
CFS, CHS, CKenM, CLSU, CLobS, CNoS, CSdS, CSf, CS1uSP, CSmH, CSt, CStb,
CU, CU-A, CU-SC.
Although national in scope, interracial housing in California and
Oregon is mentioned frequently.

2183. HAINES, AUBREY. "Words -- and deeds," in Frontier, v. 7, Aug., 1956,
pp. 11-12.
Restrictive covenants in Los Angeles.

2184. HARTGRAVES, ARTHUR WAYNE. A study of Proposition 14 of the 1964
California general election. Master's thesis, Univ. of the Pacific,
Stockton, 1967.

2185. HENDERSON, MARJORIE, WALTER HUNDLEY, and THELMA JACKSON. Three research studies on race and housing. Master's thesis, Univ. of Washington,
Seattle, 1963.

2186. HOLMES, BOB. "A study in subtlety: Riverside renewal," in Interracial review, v. 36, June, 1963, pp. 118-20.
Urban renewal in Riverside.

2187. Home owners' defense council, Los Angeles.* Articles of incorporation,
1945. 7 p. Typew. C-ArS.
"To abolish all racial discrimination ... and to end all ... dis-
franchisements" and to secure the right to own and occupy real property.
Directors: Purmon R. Smallwood, James D. Mitchell, Ike Thompson, Dewey
Goff, John Bowden, Truman R. Lott, Glen Hopkins, and Travis T. Lott.

2188. HUNTER, FLOYD. Excerpts from the Hunter report. Berkeley, 1964.
106 p. CBCK.
These excerpts are from the report of 118 ℓ. on housing discrimination issued by the same author in 1964.

2189. _____. Housing discrimination in Oakland, California; a study prepared for the Oakland Mayor's committee on full opportunity and the
Council of social planning, Alameda county. Berkeley, Floyd Hunter co.,
1964. 118 ℓ. fold. maps. Bibliography: ℓ. 110-18. CO, CU.

Housing, Restrictive Covenants, and Urban Redevelopment

2190. JENSEN, JOAN M. "Apartheid: Pacific coast style," in <u>Pacific his-torical review</u>, v. 38, Aug., 1969, pp. 335-40.
      Describes restrictive covenants.

2191. KAPLAN, MARSHALL. "Discrimination in California housing: the need for additional legislation," in <u>California law review</u>, v. 50, Oct., 1962, pp. 635-49.

2192. KEEN, HAROLD. "The moral dilemma of the California realtors," in <u>San Diego and Point magazine</u>, v. 16, Feb., 1964, pp. 39-41, 101-02.

2193. _____. "The Rumford act ... a deepening crisis: the moral dilemma," in <u>Los Angeles magazine</u>, v. 7, Mar., 1964, p. 46.

2194. KEOGH, JOHN F. Building and race restrictions; a review of the California cases, supplemented by other authorities, by John F. Keogh ... and M. L. White ... L. A., Title guarantee and trust co., 1931. 72 p. CNoS, CU.

2195. LAURENTI, LUIGI. Do property values go down when ...? Berkeley, Pacifica tape library A2422, 1960. [Phonotape]. Duration: 32 min. CSS.

2196. _____. Property values and race; studies in seven cities. Special report to the Commission on race and housing. Berkeley, Univ. of Calif. press, 1960. xix, 256 p. maps, tables. Bibliography: pp. [249]-52. Available in many libraries.
      Includes San Francisco, Oakland, and Portland.

2197. League of women voters of California. Capsule pros, cons -- state ballot measures, Nov. 3, 1964. CMS.
      Relates in part to the Rumford fair housing law.

2198. Letter to members of Citizens committee against segregation amendment dated Modesto, Apr. 5, 1964. CMS.
      Concerns Rumford's fair housing law.

2199. *Los Angeles urban league. Health and welfare dept. Minority housing in metropolitan Los Angeles; a summary report. L. A., 1959. 32 p. tables, maps. CL, CLS, CO.

2200. MC CLENAHAN, BESSIE AVERNE, 1885- . The changing nature of an urban residential area. Doctoral dissertation, Univ. of southern Calif., Los Angeles, 1928. v, 374 ℓ. maps., diagrs.

2201. _____. The changing urban neighborhood: from neighbor to nigh-dweller, a sociological study, by Bessie Averne McClenahan. L. A., Univ. of southern Calif. [c1929]. xi, 140 p. illus., map. "Selected biblio-graphy": pp. [117]-28. C, CL, CLSU, CLU, CSS, CSmH, Rocq 4192.

      Gives some description of residential change in Los Angeles. The author's doctoral dissertation, Univ. of southern Calif., 1928.

Housing, Restrictive Covenants, and Urban Redevelopment

2202. MC CLOSKEY, PAUL N.   Statement. By Paul N. McCloskey, Jr., 11th
   District, California, regarding fair housing Bill (H.R. 2516), April 9,
   1968. [Washington, D. C.?, 1968]. Broadside. CMp.

2203. MC ENTIRE, DAVIS. Residence and race, by Davis McEntire; final and
   comprehensive report to the Commission on race and housing. Berkeley,
   Univ. of Calif. press, 1960. xxii, 409 p. maps, diagrs., tables.
   Bibliography: pp. [381]–400. CFS, CHS, CKenM, CLSU, CNoS, CSaT, CS1uSP,
   CSmH, CStb, CU-A.
      Report of a broad study of housing problems in various urban areas
   including Los Angeles and San Francisco.

2204. MC QUISTON, JOHN MARK. Negro residential invasion in Los Angeles
   county. [L. A., Printed by McQuiston associates, 1969]. xxiv, 401 p.
   Bibliography: pp. 394–401. C, CU-B.

2205. _____. Patterns of Negro residential invasion in Los Angeles county.
   Master's thesis, Univ. of southern Calif., Los Angeles, 1968. xxiv,
   401 ℓ. illus., tables.

2206. Marin county. Human rights commission. Task force on housing.
   [San Rafael?], 1964. 85 p. CSrCL.

2207. MARINE, GENE. "The redeveloped Negro and housing in San Francisco,"
   in Frontier, v. 14, June, 1963, pp. 8–10.

2208. MAYER, WILLIAM. "Sacramento's fight for integration in public
   housing," in Crisis, v. 60, Jan., 1953, pp. 26–33 and 65.

2209. MEER, BERNARD,   –1966, and EDWARD FREEDMAN. "The impact of Negro
   neighbors on white home owners," in Social forces, v. 45, Sept., 1966,
   pp. 11–19.
      Stockton.

2210. Mid-peninsula citizens for fair housing. Equal opportunity in housing.
   Palo Alto [n.d.]. 8 p. CMp.
      (Original text courtesy of Sacramento committee for fair housing).

2211. _____. Open housing market and integrated suburbia. Palo Alto [n.d.].
   4 p. CMp.

2212. *MILLER, LOREN R., 1903–1967. "Covenants in the Bear flag state," in
   Crisis, v. 53, May, 1946, pp. 138–40 and 155.

2213. _____. "Government's role in housing equality," in Journal of intergroup relations, v. 1, Winter, 1959–60, pp. 56–61.

2214. _____. "The law and discrimination in housing," in Lawyers guild
   review, v. 20, Winter, 1960, pp. 123–36.

2215. _____. "Supreme court covenant decision -- an analysis," in Crisis,
   v. 55, Sept., 1948, pp. 265–66 and 285.

Housing, Restrictive Covenants, and Urban Redevelopment

2216. Modesto. Grace Davis high school. Panel discussion of issues involved in the proposed anti-fair housing amendment to the California
constitution. CMS.
    Adult high school local government classes, Mar. 2, 1964.

2217. Modesto committee for open housing. Minutes, June 27, 1962. CMS.

2218. MORRIS, ARVAL A., and DANIEL B. RITTER. "Racial minority housing in
Washington," in Washington law review, v. 37, 1962, pp. 131-51.

2219. MUELLER, PAUL F. C. Effects of housing discrimination on residential
segregation patterns in Sacramento 1960-1966. Prepared by Paul F. C.
Mueller for the Sacramento community integration project. [Sacramento]
1966. [15] p. C.

2220. MULKEY, LINCOLN W., plaintiff. In the Supreme court of the state of
California. Lincoln W. Mulkey, et al., plaintiffs and appellants, vs.
Neil Reitman, et al., defendants and respondents. L. A. no. 28360.
[Appellants' briefs] L. A. [1966]. 3 pts. in 1 v. Citation: 64 C.
2d 529; 50 Cal rptr. 881; 413 p. 2d 849. CSt-Law.
    Housing discrimination.

2221. _____. In the Supreme court of the state of California. Lincoln W.
Mulkey, et al., plaintiffs and appellants, vs. Neil Reitman, et al.,
defendants, respondents. L. A. no. 28360. Wilfred J. Prendergast and
Carola Eva Prendergast, cross-defendants and respondents, v. Clarence
Snyder, cross-complainant and appellant. L. A. no. 28422. [Briefs of
respondents]. L. A. [1966]. 3 pts. in 1 v. Citation: 64 C. 2d 529;
50 Cal. rptr. 881; 413 p. 2d 849. CSt-Law.

2222. NASON, MILTON. Comparative analysis of white and nonwhite home
mortgage experience based on data from the census of housing, 1950.
Master's thesis, Univ. of Calif.,   Berkeley, 1958. v, 98 ℓ.

2223. Northern California-Nevada council of churches. Board of directors.
Resolutions regarding the efforts to repeal the Rumford housing law
adopted unanimously, Nov. 1, 1963, in San Francisco. CMS.

2224. NORTHWOOD, LAWRENCE KING, 1917- . Urban desegregation: Negro
pioneers and their white neighbors [by] L. K. Northwood and Ernest A. T.
Barth. Seattle, Univ. of Washington press, 1965. xv, 131 p. map.
Bibliography: pp. 121-31. Available in many libraries.
    Results obtained from interviews obtained in 15 examples of success-
ful integration of Negro families into previously all-white neighborhoods
in Seattle.

2225. PASCAL, ANTHONY H. The analysis of residential segregation [by]
Anthony H. Pascal. Santa Monica, Rand corp., 1969. 54 p. C.
    National in scope.

2226. _____. Economics of housing segregation. Santa Monica, Rand corp.,
1965. 28 p. CSaT.

Housing, Restrictive Covenants, and Urban Redevelopment

2227. PEYTON, THOMAS ROY, plaintiff. In the Supreme court of the state of
California. Thomas Roy Peyton, M. D., plaintiff and appellant, vs.
Barrington plaza corporation, defendant and respondent. Appellant's
closing brief. Appeal from Superior court of Los Angeles county, Hon.
Maring [i.e., Martin] Katz, judge. L. A. 28449. [L. A.?, 1966?]. 27 ℓ.
Citation: 64 C. 2d 880; 50 Cal. rptr. 905; 413 p. 2d 849. CSt-Law.
    Housing discrimination.

2228. _____. In the Supreme court of the state of California. Thomas Roy
Peyton, M. D., plaintiff and appellant, vs. Barrington plaza corporation,
defendant and respondent. Appellant's opening brief. Appeal from
Superior court of Los Angeles county, Hon. Martin Katz, Judge. L. A.
no. 28449. [L. A.?, 1966?]. 21 ℓ. Citation: 64 C. 2d 880; 50 Cal.
rptr. 905; 413 p. 2d 849. CSt-Law.

2229. PRENDERGAST, WILFRED J., plaintiff. In the Superior court of the
state of California, in and for the county of Los Angeles. Wilfred J.
Prendergast and Carola Eva Prendergast, plaintiffs, vs. Clarence Snyder,
defendant. Clarence Snyder, cross-complainant, vs. Wilfred J. Prendergast and Carola Eva Prendergast, cross-defendants. Brief of defendant
and cross-complainant in support of motions and summary judgment and in
opposition to motion for preliminary injunction. No. 851,387. L. A.
[1966?]. 77, 24 ℓ. CSt-Law.
    Housing discrimination.

2230. RAGAN, ROGER L. Attitudes of white Methodist church members in selected Los Angeles metropolitan area churches toward residential segregation of the Negro. Doctoral dissertation, Southern Calif. school of
theology, Claremont, 1963. vii, 226 p.
    "About one-fourth of the subjects were tolerant of Negro residential
proximity, about half were definitely intolerant. Several factors related to a tolerant attitude were identified."

2231. RICHEY, ELINOR. "The peril of California's proposition 14," in
Black world, v. 14, Mar., 1965, pp. 40-44.

2232. ROBERTS, MYRON. "The Rumford act ... a deepening crisis: the
political dilemma," in Los Angeles, v. 7, Mar., 1964, pp. 47, 63-64.

2233. ROTHSTEIN, MIGNON E. A study of the growth of Negro population in
Los Angeles and available housing facilities between 1940 and 1946.
Master's thesis, Univ. of southern Calif., Los Angeles, 1950. x, 108 ℓ.
maps.
    A study of sociological patterns of growth of the Negro population
with focus on area of concentration, available housing, and public
housing projects.

2234. RYDALL, E. H. "California for colored folks," in Colored American
magazine, v. 12, May, 1907, pp. 386-88.
    Relates the Glendale housing difficulty of Alva Curtis Garrott,
D. D. S.

Housing, Restrictive Covenants, and Urban Redevelopment

2235. Sacramento committee for fair housing. Housing discrimination "gets clipped" in Sacramento; following the progress of the Sacramento committee for fair housing through the press. Sacramento, 1962. 8 ℓ. C.

2236. _____. Housing discrimination gets "clipped" in Sacramento; following the progress of the Sacramento committee for fair housing through the press. 1st revision. Sacramento, 1963. [24] ℓ. C

2237. SALTZMAN, JOE. "Proposition 14: appeal to prejudice," in Frontier, v. 15, Oct., 1964, pp. 5-8.

2238. San Francisco. Dept. of city planning. Minority group housing problems. S. F., 1967. 20 p. CSf.

2239. SCHMIDT, DONALD RAY. Responses of non-Negro renters and owners in Los Angeles and Orange counties to the prospect of ethnic change. Master's thesis, Univ. of southern Calif., Los Angeles, 1965. vii, 110 ℓ.

2240. Seattle. Municipal reference library. The racial restrictive covenant; an annotated bibliography ... [Seattle] 1948. 12 ℓ. CO.

2241. SHEIL, BERNARD JAMES, 1888- . Racial restrictive covenants by Most reverend Bernard J. Sheil ... and Loren Miller. With an introd. by Preston Bradley. Chicago, Chicago council against racial and religious discrimination [1946]. 31 p. illus., map. CU-B (California federation for civic unity collection).
          "Restrictive covenants versus democracy," by Loren Miller, pp. 5-23.

2242. SIGURDSON, HERBERT, and others. "Crenshaw project: an experiment in urban community development," in Sociology and social research, v. 51, July, 1967, pp. 432-44.
          Los Angeles.

2243. SMITH, WALLACE FRANCIS, 1926- . Aspects of housing demand--absorption, demolition, and differentiation. Berkeley, Center for Real estate and urban economics, Institute of urban and regional development, Univ. of Calif., 1966. 89 p. charts. (Univ. of Calif. Center for real estate and urban economics, research report, 29). CSf.
          Gives racial statistics.

2244. State employees for equality. Racial exclusion in apartment houses in downtown Sacramento. With the assistance of members of C[ongress] o[f] R[acial] E[quality] and the Sacramento committee for fair housing. [Sacramento] 1965. [3] ℓ. Survey no. 1. C.

2245. TAEUBER, KARL E. Residential segregation by color in the United States, 1940 and 1950. Doctoral dissertation, Harvard univ., Cambridge, Massachusetts, 1960.
          "Using computers and census data, the author measured and analyzed the extent of racial segregation in 188 American cities with population over 50,000." - Elizabeth W. Miller.

Housing, Restrictive Covenants, and Urban Redevelopment

2246. "Three briefs on Proposition 14 in the California Supreme court," in Law commentary, v. 3, Summer, 1965.

2247. "Townhouse design creates privacy and sense of property; Martin Luther King square," in Architectural record, v. 143, June, 1968, pp. 148-49.
San Francisco housing project.

2248. TYLER, WILLIAM HAROLD. Trade union sponsorship of interracial housing: a case study. Master's thesis, Univ. of Calif., Berkeley, 1957. v, 138 ℓ.
Concerns housing and housing discrimination in Milpitas.

2249. United San Francisco freedom movement. Committee on urban renewal. The United San Francisco freedom movement position on urban renewal and low cost housing. [S. F.], 1963. [27] ℓ. graphs, maps. C.
An adverse critical review of San Francisco urban renewal especially categorized by Negro removal in the Western addition area to other ghetto slums.

2250. U. S. Works progress administration. California. Housing survey covering portions of the city of Los Angeles, California. Conducted under the supervision of the Housing authority of the city of Los Angeles, California, and pub. by them as a report of Works projects administration project no. 65-1-07-70 ... [L. A.], 1940. 3 v. illus., maps, plans, tables. DLC.

2251. Urban league of Portland. Nonwhite neighbors and property prices in Portland, Oregon and residential attitudes toward Negroes as neighbors; two surveys. [Portland, 1956]. 24 p. CHS.
"Survey text by John Holley."

2252. VOSE, CLEMENT ELLERY, 1923- . Caucasians only: the Supreme court, the NAACP, and the restrictive covenant cases. Berkeley, Univ. of Calif. press, 1959. 296 p. illus., ports., map. Bibliographical notes. CBGTU, CEcaC, CFS, CHC, CHS, CLSU, CNoS, CPhD, CSbS, CSdS, CSfCiC, CSfSt, CSluSP, CSmH, CSt, CU-I, CU-SC.
Gives an extensive account of Barrows vs. Jackson, a Los Angeles case, in which the U. S. Supreme court ruled in 1953 "that a racial restrictive covenant may not be enforced at law by a suit for damages." The activities in this field of Loren Miller, Los Angeles attorney, are also described.

2253. WARD, MIKE. "A man buys a home," in Frontier, v. 16, June, 1962, pp. 7-9.

2254. WARSCHAW, CARMEN H. "Summary judgments; California's new fair housing law," in Southern California law review, v. 37, 1964, pp. 47-49.

2255. WEISS, MYRA TANNER. Vigilante terror in Fontana: the tragic story of O'Day H. Short and his family, by Myra Tanner Weiss, organizer, Los Angeles local, Socialist workers party. [L. A., Socialist workers party, 1946]. 20 p. illus., ports. CU-B.
Introd. by Carrie Stokes Morrison.

Housing, Restrictive Covenants, and Urban Redevelopment

Describes housing bias which resulted in the burning of Short's home
and the death of all family members.

2256. WHITE, WILLIE RAY. A descriptive study of a disadvantaged community.
Master's thesis, Sacramento state univ., 1968. 135 p.
A study of urban renewal in Sacramento.

2257. WILLIAMS, DOROTHY SLADE. Ecology of Negro communities in Los Angeles
county, 1940-1959. Doctoral dissertation, Univ. of southern Calif.,
Los Angeles, 1961. xi, 187 ℓ. illus. C (photocopy), CNoS (photocopy),
CU-A (photocopy).
"Tested hypotheses related to proportion of Negroes in the population
and existence of a spatial gradient in Negro distribution outward from
central city." Concerns real estate and housing.

2258. *WILLIAMS, FRANKLIN H.   "Jim Crow dies hard," in Crisis, v. 60, Feb.,
1953, pp. 91-93.
San Francisco housing difficulties.

2259. _____. Keepers of the wall; a survey reveals the methods by which
some real estate dealers help create and maintain California's modern
ghettos. [n.p.] 1960. 3 p.
Reprinted from Frontier, Apr., 1960.

2260. WILLIAMS, L., respondent, vs. L[ouisa] A. G. Young, appellant. Supreme
court of the state of California case no. 2628, 1861. Ms. [148] p.
C-ArS.
A suit to recover by foreclosure land purchased by Benjamin B. Young
in 1854. His widow claimed that being a Negro did not bar her homestead
rights to the land.

2261. WILSON, JOYCE R. "A-2 Brutus? Is urban renewal black removal?", in
Urban west, June, 1969, pp. 16-19.
San Francisco redevelopment agency relations with the Western addi-
tion community organization and their attitudes.

2262. WURSTER, CATHERINE BAUER. Housing and the future of cities in the
San Francisco bay area. Berkeley, Institute of governmental studies,
Univ. of Calif., 1963. v, 36 p. tables. Bibliographical footnotes.
CSf.
In part related to non-white housing.

2263. YOUNG, R. BRYCE. Oakland's changing community patterns. A report on
changes in the non-white population. Changes in the non-white owner
occupancy; comparisons based upon 1940, 1950 and 1960 census tract data.
Prepared by R. Bryce Young, intern in public affairs, Coro foundation.
Oakland, 1961. 18 ℓ. folded maps, tables. CO.

JOURNALISM

2264. BARNETT, WILHELMINA IRENE. The American Negro, 1878–1900, as portrayed in the San Francisco examiner. Master's thesis, Howard univ.,
Washington, D. C., 1948. i, 83 ℓ.

2265. BARNHILL, DONNA. The Sun Reporter: its role as a Negro weekly in the
San Francisco bay area Negro community. Master's thesis, Calif. state
univ., San Francisco, 1965. 141 ℓ. 1 fold. illus.

2266. BASS, CHARLOTTA A. (SPEARS),* 1874–1969. Forty years; memoirs from
the pages of a newspaper. L. A., Author, c1960. 198 p. illus., ports.,
map, facsim. CB, CHS, CL, CNoS, CO, CP, CSf.
    Based on "day-to-day accounts printed in the newspaper ... the
California eagle" by its editor.

2267. BRENT, JOHN ETTA. The American Negro, 1901–1907, as portrayed in the
San Francisco examiner. Master's thesis, Howard univ., Washington,
D. C., 1951. ii, 116 ℓ.

2268. BROPHY, ANNE KATHLEEN. Race, civil disorders, and the mass media.
Master's thesis, Univ. of Calif., Berkeley, 1968. 102 ℓ.

2269. *BROWN, JAMES E., 1850?- . Letters dated Jan. 24, 1892, Feb. 6, and
July, 1893, and clippings from the San Francisco Vindicator, 1891–93,
sent to Mrs. Jane (Lathrop) Stanford. In Jane Lathrop Stanford Papers.
CSt.

2270. *California. Colored citizens. State executive committee. Address
of the State executive committee to the colored people of the state of
California. Sacramento, Printed for the committee, 1859. 19 [1] p.
CU-B.
    Presents a detailed financial report of general receipts and expendi-
tures of the San Francisco Mirror of the times from Jan. 26, 1857 to
Mar. 30, 1858 when it had ceased publication. Difficulties of securing
proper and timely petitions for use in the state legislature are
described in detail. Five hundred copies of the Address were printed.
"Circular," pp. [6]–7, signed F. G. Barbadoes, C. M. Willson, Wm. H.
Hall, Committee.

2271. *California eagle publishing co., Los Angeles. Articles of incorpora-
tion, 1928. 3 p. Typew. C-ArS.
    To operate the Los Angeles California eagle. Directors: Joseph
Blackburn Bass, Mrs. Charlotta A. (Spears) Bass, John E. Prowd, Katherine
Spears, and Lewis K. Beeks.

2272. *California eagle publishing co., ltd., Los Angeles. Articles of
incorporation, 1935. 4 p. Typew. C-ArS.
    Represents a broadening of the firm's activities following the death
of Joseph Blackburn Bass. Directors: Mrs. Charlotta A. (Spears) Bass,
A. Hartley Jones, Samuel Miller Beane, Thomas L. Griffith, Jr., and Paul
Revere Williams.

Journalism

2273. *California publishing bureau and investment co., Los Angeles.
Articles of incorporation, 1901. Ms. 5 p. C-ArS.
    To purchase from J. J. Neimore and co., the Eagle publishing co., the
San Francisco sentinel, and the Fresno Fresno county banner. The major-
ity stockholder was Neimore. Others were C. H. Anderson, J. W. Coleman,
Alexander Simpson, J. D. Groves, G. W. Shields, J. D. Crawford, S. W.
Hawkins, and A. R. Wychie.

2274. COCKERHAM, WILLIAM CARL. The black athlete and the Bay area press,
1968. Master's thesis, Univ. of Calif., Berkeley, 1968. iii, 49 l.

2275. COLLIER, FRANCIS BERNARD, 1917- . Analysis of advertising copy and
advertising linage in a group of leading Negro magazines. Master's
thesis, Stanford univ., Stanford, 1955. 177 l. plates, tables.

2276. COONRADT, FREDERIC CHAPIN. The Negro news media and the Los Angeles
riots, by Frederic C. Coonradt. [L. A.] School of journalism, Univ. of
southern Calif., 1965. 49 l. CLSU, CSfSt.

2277. *DYMALLY, MERVYN MALCOLM, 1926- . The press and its relationship to
the civil rights movement. Master's thesis, Calif. state college,
Sacramento, 1969. 165 l.

2278. Elevator publishing company of San Francisco and Oakland.* Articles
of incorporation, 1885. Ms. [3] p. C-ArS.
    "To engage in and carry on the business of printing and conducting a
newspaper and doing all kinds of job printing and press work ..."
Directors: William H. Blake, Samuel W. Pollard, Richard T. Houston,
W. W. Davis, Joseph Smallwood Francis, John W. Smith, James B. Wilson,
Henry S. Peterson, James Washington, and John A. Wilds.

2279. FISHER, PAUL and RALPH L. LOWENSTEIN, eds. Race and the news media.
Freedom of information center, Univ. of Missouri, 8th annual conference,
1965. N. Y., Praeger [1967]. x, 158 p. CU-I.
    Includes article "Watts and the need for press involvement" by James
Bassett.

2280. *GORHAM, THELMA THURSTON. The Negro press; past, present & future,
a documentary research report, 1827-1967. N. Y., Negro world [1968].
40 p. CSjC.
    Contains also 1967 directory of U. S. Negro newspapers, magazines &
periodicals in 42 states. Lists California, Nevada, Oregon, and
Washington newspapers.

2281. GRAHAM, HUGH DAVIS. Tennessee editorial response to changes in the
bi-racial system, 1954-60. Doctoral dissertation, Stanford univ.,
Stanford, 1965. v, 440 l. illus.
    "Examination of editorial views (1954-60) as to whether and to what
degree the bi-racial system of education should be modified." - West,
p. 98.

2282. HOUGHTON, JEAN ANN. The establishment press and the Negro community.
Master's thesis, Univ. of Calif., Berkeley, 1968. ii, 185 l.

Journalism

2283. JERNAGIN, HOWARD EUGENE. The American Negro, 1908–1912, as portrayed in the San Francisco examiner. Master's thesis, Howard univ., Washington, D. C., 1957. 105 ℓ.

2284. JOHNSON, CLIFFORD FREDERICK. An analysis of Negro news and non-news matter appearing in four Oregon daily newspapers during the years 1931, 1936, 1941, 1945 and 1948. Master's thesis, Univ. of Oregon, Eugene, 1949.

2285. *KNOX, ELLIS ONEAL. A study of Negro periodicals in the United States. Master's thesis, Univ. of southern Calif., Los Angeles, 1928. iv, 77 ℓ.

2286. LYLE, JACK, ed. The black American and the press [by] Armistead S. Pride [and others]. Ed. by Jack Lyle. L. A., Ward Ritchie press [c1968]. xviii, 86 p. Bibliographical footnotes. Available in many libraries.
      A symposium at the Univ. of Calif., Los Angeles, which examined the effect of coverage by the news media of the "so-called Negro rebellion."

2287. MONTESANO, PHILIP MICHAEL, 1941– . Philip Alexander Bell: San Francisco black community politician of the 1860's. 19 p. Mimeo. CSf.
      Throughout his life, Bell was primarily a journalist in New York City and San Francisco.

2288. *Negro press foundation. Articles of incorporation, Los Angeles, 1949. 11 p. Typew. C-ArS.
      To establish a newspaper and printing facility; to sponsor lectures, radio programs, art exhibits; and to report the role and importance of trade unions, the evils of fascism, etc. Directors were Charlotta A. Bass, Ellis Spears, Seniel Ostrow, Ben Margolis, and Harry Rorick, Los Angeles; Paul Robeson, New York City; Dr. Edna Griffin and Brandon T. Bowlin, M. D., Pasadena; Mrs. Julian Sieroty, Beverly Hills; and Simon M. Lazarus, Tarzana.

2289. PAYNTER, JOHN H. "Joseph D. D. Rivers," in Journal of Negro history, v. 22, Apr., 1937, pp. 289–91.
      An obituary of the Denver editor.

2290. *PENN, IRVINE GARLAND, 1867–1930. The Afro-American press and its editors. With contributions by Hon. Frederick Douglass, Hon. John R. Lynch [etc.]. Springfield, Mass., Willey & co., pubs., 1891. 565 p. illus., ports., fold. facsim. CL, CLU, CSaT, CSfSt, CSmH, CSt.
      Contains description of the California Negro press and its editors, 1855–1891.

2291. _____. Same. N. Y., Arno press, 1969. CHS, CSS, CSdS, CSfSt.

2292. *[PRIDE, ARMISTEAD SCOTT, 1906–]. Negro newspapers on microfilm; a selected list. Washington, D. C., Library of congress, Photoduplication service, 1953. 8 p. CHi, CSt, CU-A, CU-B, CU-SB.
      Contains listings for California and western newspapers.

Journalism

2293. _____. A register and history of Negro newspapers in the United
States, 1827–1950. Doctoral dissertation, Northwestern univ., Evanston,
Ill., 1950. 426 ℓ. tables. CSfSt (film).
      Cites, and locates files when possible, newspapers throughout the
U. S., including the western states.

2294. PRINCE, VIRGINIA ANN. A sociological analysis of the Negro press in
Los Angeles. Master's thesis, Univ. of southern Calif., Los Angeles,
1946. vi, 147 ℓ. tables.

2295. *Richard Allen news service, Los Angeles. Articles of incorporation,
1952. Ms. 5 p. C-ArS.
      To operate a religious news service. Directors included the Rev.
Frederick D. Jordan and Vince Monroe Townsend.

2296. *WILSON, JAMES B His A. L. S. as editor of the San Francisco
Elevator to John Edward Bruce, Dec. 15, 1894. NN.

2297. WORD, CARL. "The need for black journalists," in Tuesday, v. 4,
Sept., 1968, p. 10ff.
      Describes Vista-funded projects in Oakland and in Newark, N. J.

JUVENILE LITERATURE

2298. ADAMS, RUSSELL L. Great Negroes, past and present. Illus. by Eugene
Winslow. David P. Ross, Jr., editor. Chicago, Afro-Am pub. co. [c1963].
x, 182 p. illus., maps, ports. Bibliography: pp. 178–79. COM, CSf,
CSluSP, CSt, CU-SB, WaTP.
      Contains biographical accounts of William A. Leidesdorff, Bert
Williams, Frank Silvera, Canada Lee, William Grant Still, Charles White,
and others.

2299. _____. Same. 2nd ed. 1964. C, CEcaC, CFS, CKenM, CLS, CLSU, CNoS,
CSdS, CSfCiC, CSjCi, CSmarP.

2300. ARKIN, DAVID. Black and white; a song that is a story about freedom
to go to school together. Words and drawings by David Arkin. Music by
Earl Robinson. L. A., Ward Ritchie press [1966]. 1 v. (unp.) illus.
CL, CLSU, CNoS, CSaT, CU.
      Fiction.

2301. *BONTEMPS, ARNA WENDELL, 1902–1973. Famous Negro athletes, by Arna
Bontemps. Illustrated with photographs. N. Y., Dodd, Mead & Co.
[c1964]. 155 p. ports. CNoS, CO, COM, CP, CRic, CSbCL, CSdS, CSfCiC,
CSp, CU-A.
      Includes accounts of Willie Mays, pp. 81–92, and Jackie Robinson,
pp. 57–70.

2302. *BROWN, VASHTI, and JACK BROWN. Proudly we hail. Illustrations by
Don Miller. Boston, Houghton Mifflin co., 1968. 118 p. Juvenile.
      "This book of twenty biographies, intended for fourth grade readers,

Juvenile Literature

contains short and intimate accounts of Negroes from poor and lowly backgrounds who have made significant contributions to American life and culture." Includes Sidney Poitier, Willie Mays, and others.

2303. BURT, OLIVE (WOOLEY), 1894- . Negroes in the early West. Illus. by Lorence F. Bjorklund. N. Y., Julian Messner, 1969. 96 p. CHS, CSS.

2304. California. University. Berkeley. Dept. of history. The Negro in American history textbooks; a report of a study of the treatment of Negroes in American history textbooks used in grades five and eight and in the high schools of California's public schools. [Prepared by a panel of historians from the University of California, Kenneth M. Stampp, chairman]. Sacramento, Calif. state dept. of education, 1964. iv, 25 p. Bibliographical footnotes.
Available in many California libraries.

2305. *Centennial publishers, Oakland. Learn about brave Negroes; coloring book, games & stories ... Oakland, c1963. [36] p. illus., ports. CSfAA.

2306. *COLEMAN, ANITA SCOTT. Reason for singing. Prairie City, Decker press [1948]. 49 p. NN, NUC, pre-1956.
By a resident of Los Angeles and Silver City, New Mexico.

2307. _____. The singing bells. Pictures by Claudine Nankivel. Nashville, Broadman press, c1961. unp. illus. DLC.

2308. *DUNBAR, PAUL LAURENCE, 1872-1906. A cabin tale, by Paul Laurence Dunbar. Illustrated by Metego [Sohan]. Introduction by Welvin Stroud. S. F., Julian Richardson associates [c1969]. [28] p. illus.

2309. DURHAM, PHILIP, 1912- . The adventures of the Negro cowboys, by Philip Durham and Everett L. Jones ... N. Y., Dodd, Mead. [c1965, 1966]. 143 p. illus., maps, ports. CRcS, CSf, CSto, CU-A, CU-I, Wa.
"In this volume, they recount for younger readers the most colorful of the adventures of the heroes and villains of the Negro race ..."

2310. EINSTEIN, CHARLES. Willie Mays: coast to coast giant. N. Y., Putnam [1963]. 191 p. illus. CHS, CNoS, CSf.

2311. FELTON, HAROLD W. Edward Rose, Negro trail blazer. N. Y., Dodd, Mead [c1967]. xvi, 111 p. illus., ports., maps. CSfAA.
Rose was a member of numerous early western fur trading expeditions.

2312. _____. Jim Beckwourth, Negro mountain man, by Harold W. Felton. N. Y., Dodd, Mead [1966]. xviii, 173 p. illus. Bibliography: pp. 169-70. C, CNoS, CO, CP, CSt, CStb.

2313. FREEMAN, DON. Corduroy. Story and pictures by Don Freeman. N. Y., Viking, c1968. 32 p. illus. CSf.
The author, a resident of Santa Barbara, lists 14 similar titles authored by him.

Juvenile Literature

2314. *GRAHAM, BENZELL. That big Broozer, by Benzel Graham. Illus. by
Paul Galdone. N. Y., William Morrow & co., 1959. 80 p. illus. CL.
Fiction.

2315. _____. Same. E. M. Hale co., 1965.

2316. *GRAHAM, LORENZ B., 1902- . Every man heart lay down, by Lorenz
Graham. Pictures by Colleen Browning. N. Y., Thomas Y. Crowell co.
[c1946, 1970]. [23] ℓ. illus. CL.
    Juvenile fiction authored by a Los Angeles probation officer, formerly
a resident of Seattle and Colorado. First appeared in his How God fix
Jonah.

2317. _____. How God fix Jonah ... wood engravings by Lelterio Calapai.
N. Y., Reynal, c1946. 171 p. illus. CL.
    "Stories [in verse] from the Bible ... in the idiom of the West
African native." - Introd.

2318. _____. I, Momolu, by Lorenz Graham. Illus. by John Biggers. N. Y.,
Thomas Y. Crowell [c1966]. 226 p. illus. CL, CSf.
Fiction.

2319. _____. North town [by] Lorenz Graham. N. Y., Thomas Y. Crowell co.
[c1965]. 220 p. CL, CNoS, CSf.
Fiction.

2320. _____. A road down to the sea [by] Lorenz Graham. Pictures by
Gregorio Prestopino. N. Y., Thomas Y. Crowell co. [c1946, 1970].
[23] ℓ. illus.
    Fiction. First appeared in his How God fix Jonah.

2321. _____. South town, by Lorenz Graham. Chicago, Follett pub. co.
[c1958]. 189 p. CL, CNoS, CSf.
Fiction.

2322. _____. Whose town? By Lorenz Graham. N. Y., Thomas Y. Crowell
[c1969]. 246 p. CL, CSf.
Fiction.

2323. HEAPS, WILLARD ALLISON, 1909- . Riots, U. S. A.; 1765-1965 by
Willard A. Heaps. N. Y., Seabury press [1966]. vi, 186 p. Bibliography:
pp. 174-82. CO, CSdS, CSf.
    The 1965 Los Angeles riot, pp. 163-67.

2324. HIRABAYASHI, JOANNE. "And the dark-faced child, listening." Books
about Negroes for children, by Joanne Hirabayashi and Barbara Dillon ...
[San Rafael?] School librarians' association of Marin county, 1969.
59 p.

2325. *HUGHES, LANGSTON, 1902-1967. Famous American Negroes, by Langston
Hughes. N. Y., Dodd, Mead & co. [c1954]. 147 p. illus. CLS, CLSU,
CSdS, CSf, CStb, CSuLas, WaT, WaTC, WaTP.
    Includes Ralph Bunche, Jackie Robinson, and others.

Juvenile Literature

2326. ____. Famous Negro heroes of America. Illus. by Gerald McCann.
N. Y., Dodd, Mead & co. [c1958]. 202 p. illus. CKenM, CLSU, CSf,
CSjCi, CStb, CSuLas, WaT, WaTC, WaTP.
Includes James P. Beckwourth; Esteban, discoverer of Arizona; Charles
Young; and others.

2327. ____. Same. N. Y., 1966. CNoS.

2328. ____. Famous Negro music makers, by Langston Hughes. Illus. with
photographs. N. Y., Dodd, Mead & co. [c1955]. 179 p. ports. CLSU,
CNoS, CSbCL, CSdS, CSf, CSfCiC, CStb, CU-SB, WaPu, WaT, WaTC, WaTP.
Includes biographies of Egbert Austin Williams, Bill Robinson, William
Grant Still, and Lena Horne.

2329. *JACKSON, MARY COLEMAN. Climb to the crow's nest, by Mary Coleman
Jackson. Illus. by Anthony D'Adamo. Chicago, Follett pub. co. [c1957].
80 p. CL.
By a Los Angeles resident. Also author of: Jim Beckwourth: Crow
chief.

2330. KUGELMASS, J. ALVIN. Ralph J. Bunche, fighter for peace. N. Y.,
Julian Messner [c1962]. 178 p. port. CSdS, CSf, CU-A.
For older children. Describes Bunche's life in Albuquerque, pp. 41-
46, and in Los Angeles, pp. 47-58.

2331. Los Angeles city school district. Division of instructional services.
Americans then and now. Illus. by R. Whitney Draney. [Manuscript by
Gloria S. Curtis. L. A., c1966]. 40 p. illus. CL, CLGS, CSfSt.
Vignettes of minorities in America authored by Gloria S. Curtis, a
Los Angeles black resident.

2332. ____. ____. Angelenos then and now. Illus. by Don Freeman. [Final
manuscript by Gloria S. Curtis. L. A., c1966]. 67 p. illus. CL, CLGS,
CPomCP, CSfSt.
Additional vignettes in Los Angeles.

2333. ____. ____. Californians then and now. Illus. by R. Whitney
Draney. [Manuscript by Gloria S. Curtis. L. A., c1966]. vii, 38 p.
illus. CL, CLGS, CPomCP, CSfSt.
Additional vignettes in California.

2334. LOVELL, M. MARGUERITE. Negro stories for children, a subjective
criticism. A special study in partial satisfaction for the degree of
M. A., Univ. of Calif., Berkeley, 1937. 40 ℓ.

2335. MADIAN, JON. Beautiful junk, a story of the Watts towers. With
photographs by Barbara and Lou Jacobs, Jr. Boston, Little, Brown & co.
[c1968]. 44 p. illus., ports. CNoS, COro, CP, CSf.
The story of the famous towers built by Simon Rodia and illustrated
by photographs taken in Watts about 1967.

2336. *MARVIN X. The black bird; a parable for black children, by Marvin X.
Fresno, Al Kitab sudan publication, c1968. Broadside. CU-A.

Juvenile Literature

2337. *MAYS, WILLIAM HOWARD, 1931- . Danger in center field, by Willie
    Mays and Jeff Harris. Larchmont, N. Y., Argonaut books [c1963]. 192 p.
    CSf.
        Fiction.

2338. MOLARSKY, OSMOND. Song of the empty bottles. Illustrated by Tom
    Feelings. N. Y., Henry C. Walck, inc., 1968. [51] p. illus. CNoS,
    CSf.
        Story about a boy's musical experience in a neighborhood house.

2339. *POSEY, ANITA (EDWARDS). Rings and things, and other poems, by Anita
    E. Posey. Illus. by Julie Maas. N. Y., Crowell-Collier [c1967]. 32 p.
    col. illus. CSj, NUC, pre-1956.

2340. RICHARDSON, BEN ALBERT. Great American Negroes [by] Ben Richardson.
    Rev. by William A. Fahey. Illus. by Robert Hallock. N. Y., Thomas Y.
    Crowell co. [c1956]. vi, 339 p. ports. CBea, CKenM, CLSU, CLobS,
    CNoS, CSdS, CSf, CSluSP, CU-A, CU-SB, CU-SC.
        Includes accounts of William Grant Still, Bill "Bojangles" Robinson,
    and Willie Mays. An earlier edition appeared in 1945 and is held by
    CSuLas.

2341. *ROBINSON, JOHN ROOSEVELT, 1919-1972. Breakthrough to the big
    league; the story of Jackie Robinson, by Jackie Robinson and Alfred
    Duckett. N. Y., Harper & Row [1965]. xiii, 178 p. ports. CNoS, CP,
    CSdS, CSf.

2342. *ROBINSON, LOUIE. Arthur Ashe, tennis champion, by Louie Robinson,
    Jr. Garden City, N. Y., Doubleday & co. [c1967]. 136 p. ports. CNoS,
    CPomCP, CSf.
        For older children. Includes his successes at tennis while a student
    at the Univ. of Calif., Los Angeles.

2343. SCOTT, ANN HERBERT. Big cowboy western, by Ann Herbert Scott. Pic-
    tures by Richard W. Lewis. N. Y., Lothrop, Lee & Shepard co. [c1965].
    [30] p. illus.
        Interracial juvenile by Reno resident.

2344. _____. Let's catch a monster. Illus. by H. Tom Hall. N. Y., Lothrop,
    Lee & Shepard co., c1967. [22] ℓ. illus.

2345. SHAPIRO, MILTON J. The Willie Mays story, by Milton J. Shapiro.
    N. Y., Julian Messner, inc. [c1960]. 192 p. ports. CLS, CSf.
        For older children.

2346. SHEPHERD, ELIZABETH. The discoveries of Esteban the black [by]
    Elizabeth Shepherd. Illus. with photographs and prints. With maps by
    William Steinel. N. Y., Dodd, Mead & co. [c1970]. xi, 122 p. illus.,
    maps.

2347. *SLATON, WILLIAM. Bacteria and viruses: friends or foes? By
    William and Nellie Slaton. Illus. by Delos Blackmar. Englewood Cliffs,

Juvenile Literature

N. J., Prentice-Hall, [c1965]. 64 p. illus., ports. CSf.
Authored by a Los Angeles resident.

2348. *SOUTHERN, THOMAS M., pub. and ed. The ABC picture book of eminent
Negroes past and present ... Second ed. L. A., ABC pub. co., c1951,
1959. [34] ℓ. ports.

2349. *TURNER, MORRIE. Black and white coloring book, by Morrie and Letha
Turner. Illus. by Morrie Turner. S. F., Troubador press [c1969].
[28] p. illus., ports.

2350. *WALTER, MILDRED PITTS. Lillie of Watts, a birthday discovery, by
Mildred Pitts Walter. Illus. by Leonora E. Prince. L. A., Ward Ritchie
press [c1969]. 61 p. illus. CNoS, CP.
Juvenile by a Los Angeles elementary school teacher.

2351. WARREN, MARY PHRANER. Shadow on the valley. Philadelphia, Westminster press, 1967. 189 p.
Sally Burch, a VISTA worker, finds a home with a white Oregon family.

2352. *[WILSON, FRANCES (YOUNGE)]. Our kindergarten; a. m. and p. m.
classes. [Berkeley, 1966]. 16 p. illus., ports.
Relates activities of Longfellow elementary school, Berkeley.

2353. ZEITLIN, PATTY. Castle in my city: songs for young children.
Illustrated by children in Watts, with Lucille Krasner. San Carlos,
Golden gate junior books, 1968. 43 p.
A collection of original songs for very young children, composed
while the author was teaching in one of the head start nursery schools.

LABOR

2354. ARBEITER, SOLOMON. The integration of the Negro into organized labor;
cause and effect. Master's thesis, Univ. of Calif., Berkeley, 1959.
viii, 93 ℓ.

2355. ARCHIBALD, KATHERINE. Wartime shipyard; study in social disunity
[by] Katherine Archibald. Berkeley, Univ. of Calif. press, 1947. vi,
237 p. front., plates. Available in many libraries.
Recounts labor disunity and animosity between men, women, Okies,
Negroes, and Japanese.

2356. Associated railway employees of California, Oakland.* Articles of
incorporation, 1901. 3 p. Typew. C-ArS.
A mutual benefit society. Directors: W. H. Spigner, F. P. Henry,
W. L. Vance, G. F. Howard, H. Burum, S. A. Dedrick, E. Parker, H. E.
Jackson, and Charles Jones.

2357. _____. Application for dissolution, 1918. 2 p. Typew. C-ArS.

Labor

2358. "Ban outlawed; California supreme court holds union may not refuse membership to Negroes," in Business week v. 108, Jan. 13, 1945, p. 108.

2359. "BART and the ghettos; jobs, homes, schools," in Rapid transit, an information digest from the Bay area rapid transit district," v. 11, Summer, 1969, pp. [1-6].

2360. BELLSON, FORD. "California's cotton row," in Opportunity, v. 17, Apr., 1939, pp. 114-18.
       Unionization of cotton pickers in the Bakersfield area.

2361. _____. "Labor gains on the coast," in Opportunity, v. 17, May, 1939, pp. 142-43.
       A report on integration in maritime unions on the Pacific coast.

2362. *BOICE, CARL. "Black labor is black power," in The black scholar, v. 2, Oct., 1970, pp. 29-32.
       Authored by the editor of the San Francisco People's world.

2363. *Brotherhood of sleeping car porters. [Correspondence and papers, 1927-34]. Mss. 194 pieces. CU-B.
       Contains correspondence between A. Philip Randolph and other national officers with Dad Moore and Cottrell Laurence Dellums, officers of the Pacific coast division. Information is given on strikes, "yellow dog" contracts, relations with the Pullman company, and general union business. Also contains press releases and clippings concerning the organization and its plans.

2364. California. Dept. of industrial relations. Division of apprentice-ship standards. The California plan for equal opportunity in apprentice-ship and training for minority groups. [Sacramento] 1963. CFS, Wa.

2365. _____. State agricultural society. Transactions of the California state agricultural society during the year 1872. Sacramento, State print., 1873. viii, 784 p. C, CLU, CSf, CSmH, CU, NUC, pre-1956.
       Some information about the possible and actual use of Negro labor in the growth of cotton is described in "Cotton culture in California," pp. 240-330.

2366. _____. State fair employment practice commission. Negroes and Mexican Americans in south and east Los Angeles: changes between 1960 and 1965 in population, employment, income, and family status. An analysis of a U. S. census survey of November 1965 ... S. F., 1966. 40 p. tables. Available in many libraries.
       Prepared by the Division of labor statistics and research, California Department of industrial relations.

2367. _____. _____. Same. S. F., 1968. CLS, CNoS, CStmo, CU-SC.

2368. _____. University. Berkeley. Institute of industrial relations. Public policy and discrimination in apprenticeship, by George Strauss and Sidney Ingerman. Berkeley, 1965. pp. 285-331 (Its reprint no. 260). CO.

Labor

2369. CHAVEZ, CESAR ESTRADA, 1927– . Right to work laws; a trap for
America's minorities. El derecho a trabajar; una trampa para los
minorias EE. UU., by Cesar E. Chavez and Bayard Rustin. [N. Y., A.
Philip Randolph institute; Delano, United farm workers, AFL–CIO, 1968?].
20 p. illus. CU–B.

2370. Colored chauffers [sic] association of California, inc.* Articles of
incorporation, Los Angeles, 1937. 6 p. Typew. C–ArS.
    Organized to establish a code of ethics; to discuss employment
problems; and to list positions available to members. Directors were
Oscar W. Porche, Clarence A. Armour, Roy A. Shelby, David Denton, and
Robert Bennett.

2371. *Colored east bay auto workers assoc. Articles of incorporation,
Oakland, 1929. 2 p. Typew. C–ArS.
    Organized for social purposes. Directors signing were John Sisney,
V. T. Davis, and H. E. Jackson.

2372. *Colored laborer's social club Articles of incorporation, Los
Angeles, 1919. [4] p. Typew. C–ArS.
    Organized "to advance and protect the business, moral and social
interests of its members; to care for the sick ... to protect and enforce
the civic rights of its members ..." Directors were Julius A. McAllister,
James R. Sheeley, John H. Pasco, Johnie Dale, and Hamilton Embree.

2373. *COVINGTON, FLOYD C. "Union styles: black labor in white coats," in
Opportunity, v. 9, July, 1931, pp. 208–10.
    History of local 582, Dining car cooks and waiters union, Los
Angeles, 1926–31.

2374. COX, LAWANDA (FENLASON), 1909– . Agricultural labor in the United
States, 1865–1900, with special reference to the South. Doctoral dissertation, Univ. of Calif., Berkeley, 1941. iii, 245 ℓ. maps, diagrs.

2375. EAVES, LUCILE, 1869– . ... A history of California labor legislation,
with an introductory sketch of the San Francisco labor movement, by
Lucile Eaves ... Berkeley, Univ. [of Calif.] press [c1910]. xiv,
461 p. Bibliography: pp. 444–48. (Univ. of Calif. publications in
economics, v. 2). C, CChiS, CFS, CHi, CL, CLSU, CNoS, CO, CSf, CSmH,
CStb, CU, Rocq 9261.
    The 1849 constitutional convention debate on slavery and civil
rights, 1849–63, is examined, pp. 84–104.

2376. Fair employment practice committee. Summary, findings and directives
relating to International brotherhood of boilermakers, iron shipbuilders,
welders and helpers of America, A. F. of L., Kaiser company, inc., and
the Oregon shipbuilding corporation. [n.p.], 1943. 9 p. CLSU.

2377. FRIEDMAN, RALPH. The attitudes of west coast maritime unions in
Seattle toward Negroes in the maritime industry. Master's thesis,
Washington state univ., Pullman, 1952. 250 p.

Labor

2378. GREER, SCOTT ALLEN, 1922- . The participation of ethnic minorities
in the labor unions of Los Angeles county. Doctoral dissertation, Univ.
of Calif., Los Angeles, 1952. [xiii], 413 ℓ. forms.

2379. HERZOG, JUNE. Study of the Negro defense worker in the Portland-
Vancouver area. Master's thesis, Reed college, Portland, 1944.

2380. *HOWARD, ASBURY. Free our hand! [Denver, Press and education dept.,
International union of mine, mill and smelter workers, 1951]. 19 p.
illus. CU-B.
     "An address [on Negro rights] by the regional director at Bessemer,
Alabama, for the International union of mine, mill and smelter workers,
delivered at the IUMM&SW convention, Nogales, Arizona, September 13,
1951."

2381. International longshoremen's & warehousemen's union, San Francisco.
     "We have a folder of archival material relating [to] the union's
position on minorities over the years ... We have various papers relating
to Mr. William Chester, one of our long-time Negro officers ... Most im-
portantly, there is an index to the bi-weekly Dispatcher since 1942.
This records each time a person or local was mentioned and indexes the
union's concerns under subject. All of this material would be of use to
researchers in the field of minority activities and relationships in the
West. Most of it is open to serious scholars."

2382. *IVIE, ARDIE. "Tyree, the tyro activist," in Seattle magazine, v. 6,
Dec., 1969, pp. 42-46.
     Describes Tyree Scott's leadership in the fight against the con-
struction unions.

2383. JACKSON, JOSEPH SYLVESTER. The Colored marine employees benevolent
association of the Pacific, 1921-1934; or implications of vertical
mobility for Negro stewards in Seattle. Master's thesis, Univ. of
Washington, Seattle, 1939. 105 p.

2384. *JOHNSON, CHARLES SPURGEON, 1893-1956. The Negro war worker in San
Francisco, a local self-survey. Technical staff: Charles S. Johnson,
Herman H. Long [and] Grace Jones ... A project, financed by a San Francisco citizen, administered by the Y. W. C. A., and carried out in connection with the Race relations program of the American missionary
association ... and the Julius Rosenwald fund. [S. F.?] 1944. 98 p.
Reproduced from typew. copy. C, CHS, CHi, CLGS, CLU, COEB, CU-B.

2385. _____. "Negro workers in Los Angeles industries," in Opportunity,
v. 6, Aug., 1928, pp. 234-40.

2386. LITWACK, LEON FRANK. The Negro in organized labor, 1866-1872.
Master's thesis, Univ. of Calif., Berkeley, 1952.

2387. MCWILLIAMS, CAREY, 1905- . Report on importation of Negro labor to
California, August 10, 1942. [n.p.], California Div. of immigration and
housing [1942?].

Labor

2388. MAHONEY, PATRICK J. Minority employment in the construction of BART, by Patrick J. Mahoney. [S. F.?] 1966. 37 p. tables. C, CSf.
A survey of Bay area rapid transit district policies.

2389. MARSHALL, F. RAY. The Negro and apprenticeship, by F. Ray Marshall and Vernon M. Briggs, Jr. Baltimore, Johns Hopkins press [c1967]. x, 283 p. tables. Bibliographical footnotes. CBGTU, CEcaC, CFS, CHS, CKenM, CLobS, CLSU, CNoS, COM, CPhD, CSdS, CSluSP, CSt, CU-A, CU-I, CU-SC, Wa.
A series of case studies of ten metropolitan areas including San Francisco-Oakland.

2390. MATYAS, JENNIE, 1895- . Jennie Matyas and the I. L. G. W. U. [1957]. 1 v. (film). CU-B.
Typed transcript of a tape-recorded interview conducted in 1955 for the Institute of industrial relations, Univ. of Calif., Berkeley. Contains "comments on communist infiltration, union organization on the west coast, especially in San Francisco, problems with Negro and Chinese ethnic groups ..."

2391. *[OWEN, CHANDLER]. "Negro labor and radical movments [sic] from coast to coast," in Messenger, v. 4, July, 1922, pp. 447-48.

2392. *PITTMAN, JOHN. Railroads and Negro labor. Master's thesis, Univ. of Calif., Berkeley, 1930. 92 ℓ.

2393. *PITTS, ROBERT BEDFORD, 1909- . Organized labor and the Negro in Seattle. Master's thesis, Univ. of Washington, Seattle, 1941.

2394. *PORTER, KENNETH WIGGINS. "Negro labor in the western cattle industry, 1866-1900," in Labor history, v. 10, Summer, 1969.

2395. "Postwar status of Negro workers in San Francisco area," in Monthly labor review, v. 70, June, 1950, pp. 612-17.

2396. "Racial discrimination on the jobsite: competing theories and competing forums," in UCLA law review, v. 12, May, 1965, p. 1,186.

2397. *RANDOLPH, ASA PHILIP, 1889- . "The organization tour west," in Messenger, v. 8, Apr., 1926, pp. 122-23.
His visit to Portland, Spokane, Seattle, Berkeley, and Oakland in the interest of the Brotherhood of sleeping car porters.

2398. RECORD, WILSON, 1916- . "Chico story: a black and white harvest," in Crisis, v. 58, Feb., 1951, pp. 95-101, 129-31, 133.
Agricultural labor.

2399. _____. "Negroes in the California agriculture labor force," in Social problems, v. 6, Spring, 1959, pp. 354-61.

2400. REINHARDT, RICHARD. "Discrimination and the unions," in San Francisco magazine, v. 9, Feb., 1967, pp. 26-28.

Labor

2401. STRIPP, FRED S. The relationships of the San Francisco bay area
Negro-American work with the labor unions affiliated with the A. F. L.
and the C. I. O. Doctoral dissertation, Pacific school of religion,
Berkeley, 1948. x, 305 ℓ. CU (neg. microfilm).

2402. *TATE, MERZE. "Decadence of the Hawaiian nation and proposals to
import a Negro labor force," in Journal of Negro history, v. 47, Oct.,
1962, pp. 248-63.

2403. *WILKINS, ROY, 1901- . "Collective bargaining -- California style,"
in Crisis, v. 52, Feb., 1945, pp. 41-42.
    Joseph James, employee of the Marinship corp., Sausalito, sues the
International brotherhood of boilermakers, iron shipbuilders and helpers
of America with the result that the Calif. Supreme court states that
unions cannot bar Negroes as full members if they are to maintain a
closed shop and bargain with employers.

LANGUAGE AND LANGUAGE INSTRUCTION

2404. AURBACH, JOSEPH. A phonemic and phonetic description of the speech
of selected Negro informants of south-central Los Angeles. Doctoral
dissertation, Univ. of southern Calif., Los Angeles, 1970. vii, 265 ℓ.

2405. BARANKIN, JOSEPH PAUL. The language of the ghetto as a dialectal
variant of English. Master's thesis, Calif. state univ., San Francisco,
1970. iv, 87 ℓ.

2406. BLAKELY, KAREN B. An investigation of the preference for racial
identification terms among Negro and Caucasian children. Master's
thesis, Calif. state univ., Sacramento, 1968. 93 ℓ.

2407. BOYLE, SONYA STEINER. An investigation of the effectiveness of a
language development unit for culturally deprived children. Master's
thesis, Calif. state univ., Sacramento, 1969. 84 ℓ. tables.

2408. DAVIS, CLARETHA MANNING. Helping culturally disadvantaged parents
improve the language developments of their young children. Master's
thesis, Calif. state univ., San Francisco, 1968. 73 ℓ.
    "Twenty-one Negro and two Caucasian mothers living in San Francisco
'poverty target areas' were interviewed for this study. The objectives
were to ascertain the attitudes and practices of the mothers concerning
the language development of their pre-school children and to make suggestions which would aid similar mothers in improving their children's
language development."

2409. *DE COY, ROBERT H. A Nigger's Bible. [n.p., Blawhit, 1967]. 191 p.
CRic.

2410. FARADAY, ROSALIND. A speech communication study guide for high
schools that serve disadvantaged Negroes. Master's thesis, Calif. state
univ., San Jose, 1968. vii, 136 ℓ.

Language and Language Instruction

2411. FRANKLIN, BERYLDELL CRUTCHFIELD. The reactions of Negro parents and
pupils to the teaching of standard oral English in a junior high school
of the inner city. Master's project, Mount St. Mary's college, Los
Angeles, 1967.

2412. GUSTAFSON, SUSAN LOUISE. The effectiveness of an individualized
language program on the verbal ability of preschool children with special
language needs. Master's thesis, Calif. state univ., San Francisco,
1968. 123 ℓ.
"Analyzes the effectiveness of an individualized teaching approach
on the verbal growth of preschool children having remedial language
problems. The study sample was made up of 5 San Francisco children,
4 black and one white, whose language difficulties were considered to be
primarily environmental."

2413. HIBLER, MADGE BEATRICE. A contemporary study of speech patterns of
selected Negro and white kindergarten children. Doctoral dissertation,
Univ. of southern Calif., Los Angeles, 1960. viii, 100 ℓ. illus. (part
fold.).
"Racial differences in speech patterns found significant at the 1%
level."

2414. HORLICK, NANCY JANE. Dig and be dug: an aural-oral communication
unit for teaching standard American English to speakers of Negro nonstandard dialect. Master's project, Calif. state univ., Los
Angeles, 1969.

2415. LELER, HAZEL OLIVE. Mother-child interaction and language performance
in young, disadvantaged Negro children. Doctoral dissertation, Stanford
univ., Stanford, 1970. vi, 150 ℓ. illus.

2416. MAXWELL, IDA EVELYN. Suggested program for, and problems of, the
improvement of oral language in the colored schools of New Orleans.
Master's thesis, Univ. of southern Calif., Los Angeles, 1949. iv, 160 ℓ.

2417. MILIC, BERNICE ANN. A bidialectal study of the language proficiency
of Negro and Caucasian children. Master's thesis, Calif. state univ.,
Sacramento, 1970. 35 ℓ. illus.

2418. MITCHELL, CLAUDIA L. Language behavior in a black urban community.
Doctoral dissertation, Univ. of Calif., Berkeley, 1969. iv, 164 ℓ.
CCotS.
An Oakland study.

2419. _____. Some aspects of social interaction in a black community.
Berkeley, Language – behavior research laboratory, 1968. 15 ℓ. CU.

2420. MUNSON, BEVERLY ANDREWS. Negro communication; a semantic evaluation.
Master's thesis, Calif. state univ., San Francisco, 1967. 125 ℓ.
"A semantic analysis of recent and current Negro communication with
particular references to Negro self-concepts and Negro communication
systems. Includes analyses of statements by Bruce [?] Cayton and
California's Percy Moore."

Language and Language Instruction

2421. OVERHOLD, LINDA FINK. A comparative study of certain linguistic variables obtained in samples of nonstandard Negro dialect and standard English. Master's thesis, Calif. state univ., Sacramento, 1970. 39 ℓ.

2422. PARKER, STEPHENSON ROBERT. The influence of a special course of oral language instruction upon a group of self-selected seventh-grade Negroes. Doctoral dissertation, Univ. of Calif., Berkeley, 1966. ix, 105 ℓ.

2423. RYAN, KATHLEEN E. Language and dialects in the schools. Master's thesis, Calif. state univ., San Francisco, 1969. 117 ℓ.
     "A study of the research of the disciplines of education, psychology and linguistics as it is related to language differences in the culturally deprived student population (primarily, the Urban Negro dialect). The relationship between standard English and Urban Negro dialect is discussed. The author suggests that not only an attitude change regarding the cultural conflicts involved is necessary on the part of the teacher, but also a corresponding change in practices and styles of teaching is needed to make effective teaching in the inner city schools."

2424. RYSTROM, RICHARD CARL. The effects of standard dialect training on Negro first-graders learning to read. Doctoral dissertation, Univ. of Calif., Berkeley, 1968. x, 139 ℓ.

2425. STEINMAN, MARILYN. An exploratory study of the effects of teacher-child conversation on the language growth of low-income preschool children. Master's thesis, Calif. state univ., San Francisco, 1968. 145 ℓ.
     "A study '... to test one-to-one teacher-child conversation as a factor in language growth and to explore ... the factors which appeared in the teacher's use of such an approach.' Subjects were participants in San Francisco's Mission district head start programs."

2426. WEBB, WILLIE RACHEL. Dialectal differences in the writing samples of black and white students. Master's thesis, Calif. state univ., San Francisco, 1971. v, 41 ℓ. tables.

LAW AND ORDER, CORRECTIONAL INSTITUTIONS, ETC.

2427. ALEX, NICHOLAS. Black in blue; a study of the Negro policeman ... N. Y., Appleton-Century Crofts [1969]. xxiv, 210 p. CLU, CNoS.

2428. BAYLEY, DAVID H. Minorities and the police; confrontation in America, by David H. Bayley and Harold Mendelsohn. N. Y., Free press [1968, c1969]. xii, 209 p. Bibliographical footnotes. CLSU, CSf, CSluSP.
     A study of the relationship between Denver police, Negroes, and those with Spanish surnames.

2429. B'nai B'rith. Anti-defamation league. Southern California regional office. A study of policy training programs in minority relations. Prepared ... for the Police relations committee of the Los Angeles county

Law and Order, Correctional Institutions, etc.

    conference on community relations ... L. A., 1950. 11 p. [17] ℓ. CU-B
(California federation for civic unity collection).
    Includes studies made in Denver and in Richmond and Oakland, Calif.

2430. California. Attorney-general's office. Police and minority groups,
an experiment [by] Robert W. Kenny [Attorney-general]. [Sacramento,
1946?]. 17 ℓ. CSt.

2431. _____. Dept. of corrections. Youth and adult corrections. Equality
under law ... Sacramento, 1964. 12 p. CMp.

2432. _____. Dept. of justice. Crowd control and riot prevention by
Raymond M. Momboisse. Sacramento, 1964. viii, 99 p. CMp.

2433. _____. _____. A guide to race relations for police officers: police
training bulletins. [Sacramento?], 1946. CFS.

2434. _____. Division of criminal law and enforcement. ... Guide to race
relations for peace officers ... [Sacramento, State print., 1953].
23 p. "Bibliography of selected books": pp. 21-[24]. CSt, CU, NUC,
pre-1956.
    "Report prepared [by] Emmet Daly, deputy attorney general."

2435. _____. University. University extension. Conference on law enforcement and racial and cultural tensions, October 8-10 [1964], Hotel
Claremont, Berkeley. Berkeley, c1966. 186 p. C.

2436. CARLSTRAND, ROBERT W. A comparison of Negro mobility characteristics
of probationers in Los Angeles. Master's thesis, Univ. of southern
Calif., Los Angeles, 1955. ix, 95 ℓ.

2437. CATTERALL, HELEN HONOR (TUNNICLIFF), 1870-1933. Judicial cases concern-
ing American slavery and the Negro, edited by the late Helen T. Catterall
(Mrs. Ralph C. H. Catterall), with additions by James J. Hayden ...
Washington, D. C., Carnegie institution, 1926-1937. 5 v. Publication
no. 374 of the Carnegie institution. CL, CLU, CSdS, CSf, CSmH, CSt, CU,
CU-A.

2438. _____. Same. N. Y., Octagon books, 1968. CHS, CNoS, CSS, CSaT,
CSjC, CU-I.
    "California cases" are described in v. 5, pp. 330-39. These include
In the matter of Perkins, 2 Cal. 424 (1852), Ex parte Archy, 9 Cal. 147
(1858), and Norris v. Harris, 15 Cal. 226 (1860), which relate to ownership of slaves; People v. Howard, 17 Cal. 63 (1860), relating to testimony in criminal cases; Williams v. Young, 17 Cal. 403 (1861), concerning
the ejectment from real property on the basis that the Homestead act did
not apply to Negroes; Pleasants [sic] v. N[orth] B[each] & M[ission]
R. R. co., 34 Cal. 586 (1868), and Turner v. N. B. & M. R. R. co., 34
Cal. 594 (1868), both concerning ejectment from street railways; People
v. Washington, 36 Cal. 658 (1869), pertaining to the testimony of a
Chinese against a Negro; and Ward v. Flood, 48 Cal. 36 (1874), a suit to
secure admission to the San Francisco public schools.

Law and Order, Correctional Institutions, etc.

2439. Center for the study of democratic institutions. Civil disobedience [by] Harrop A. Freeman [and others. Santa Barbara, 1966]. 32 p. Bibliography: p. 32. CSt.

2440. "Chief Parker and company; John Birch society members," in Christian century, v. 82, Oct. 27, 1965, pp. 1,308-09.

2441. Conference on law enforcement and racial and cultural tensions, Berkeley, 1964. Conference on law enforcement and racial and cultural tension, October 8-10, Hotel Claremont, Berkeley; presented by the University of California extension and the School of criminology ... Berkeley, in cooperation with the Office of the attorney general, Department of justice, state of California; editorial assistance by: Barbara Darnell. Berkeley, c1966. 186 ℓ. CSt-Law, CU.

2442. Cops and robbers; or, police in the ghetto. Berkeley, Pacifica tape library 011-1, 1968. [Phonotape] Duration: 49 min. CSS.
Four youths from the Hunters Point area of San Francisco discuss police problems. The moderator is Herb Kutchins of the San Francisco bail project.

2443. DAVIDSON, MATTHEW. "Facing a vital problem: The Negro and the police," in Black world, v. 14, Aug., 1965, pp. 21-28.
Includes Los Angeles.

2444. DEBRO, JULIUS. The Negro federal offender. Master's thesis, Calif. state univ., San Jose, 1968. x, 202 ℓ. illus.

2445. ENDORE, SAMUEL GUY, 1901- . The crime at Scottsboro, by Guy Endore. [Hollywood, Hollywood Scottsboro committee, 1938?]. 40 p. CLU, CNoS, CU-A.

2446. _____. The Sleepy lagoon mystery, by Guy Endore, illus. - Giacomo Patri. L. A., Sleepy lagoon defense committee [1944]. 48 p. illus. CLU.
Introd. by Carey McWilliams.
Cites occasional anti-black sentiment.

2447. FOGELSON, ROBERT M. "From resentment to confrontation: the police, the Negroes, and the outbreak of the nineteen-sixties riots," in Political science quarterly, v. 83, June, 1968, pp. 217-47.
Includes statements and attitudes of western Negroes. Also appeared in Social action, v. 35, Feb., 1969, pp. 6-33.

2448. GARRY, CHARLES. Can the black man get a fair trial? Berkeley, Pacifica tape library 523, 1969. [Phonotape] Duration: 45 min. CSS.
Speech of a San Francisco attorney at the annual meeting of the local chapter of the American civil liberties union, Berkeley, Feb. 27, 1969.

2449. GARTRELL, RICHARD BLAIR. Systems analysis of the Richmond, California, firearms controversy, July 1-8, 1968. Master's thesis, Calif. state univ., San Francisco, 1969. iii, 66 ℓ. illus., facsims., map.

Law and Order, Correctional Institutions, etc.

2450. GINGER, ANN FAGAN, ed. Minimizing racism in jury trials; the voir dire conducted by Charles R. Garry in People of California v. Huey P. Newton. With photographs by Dorothea Lange. Ed. by Ann Fagan Ginger. Berkeley, National lawyers guild [c1969]. xxv, 247 p. illus. CSf, CU.

2451. GOODRICH, J. "West coast crime fighter," in Black world, v. 9, Feb., 1951, pp. 62-65.

2452. GREEN, BUDDY. The Jerry Newson story, by Buddy Green and Steve Murdock. Postscript by the Reverend H. T. S. Johnson. [Berkeley, East bay civil rights congress, 1950]. 48 p. CHS, CHi, CSfAA, Rocq 799.
    Newson, an Oakland resident, was given a death sentence at San Quentin.

2453. GREENBERG, JACK, 1924- . Race relations and American law. N. Y., Columbia univ. press [c1959]. viii, 481 p. CNoS, CFS, CSf, CSt.
    Reviews laws in western and other states concerning public accommo-dations, fair employment practice, housing, civil service, school de-segregation, miscegenation, interracial adoption, etc.

2454. HERTZ, RUBY COHEN. Parole revocation: Eldridge Cleaver, a case in point. Master's thesis, Univ. of Calif., Berkeley, 1969. viii, 161 ℓ.

2455. HEYMAN, J. M. "The Chief justice, racial segregation, and the friendly critics," in California law review, v. 49, Mar., 1961, p. 104.

2456. *JACKSON, GEORGE, 1941-1971. Soledad brother; the prison letters of George Jackson. Introd. by Jean Genet. N. Y., Bantam books [c1970]. 250 p. C, CSf, CU-B.
    Letters written from Soledad prison, Salinas, 1964-70, to relatives and friends including Angela Y. Davis.

2457. JONES, LEROY VERNELL. The black police officer: a study in re-education. Master's thesis, Calif. state univ., San Francisco, 1970. v, 57 ℓ.

2458. LEMERT, EDWIN MCCARTHY, 1912- . The administration of justice to minority groups in Los Angeles county, by Edwin M. Lemert and Judy Rosenberg. Berkeley, Univ. of Calif. press, 1948. 27 p. diagr., tables. Bibliographical footnotes. CFS, CL, CLSU, CLU, CSdS, CSf, CU-B.

2459. LOHMAN, JOSEPH DEAN, 1909-1968. The police and the community: the dynamics of their relationship in a changing society, a report prepared for the President's commission on law enforcement and administration of justice [by] Joseph D. Lohman [and] Gordon E. Misner. Washington, D. C., Govt. print., 1966. 2 v. in 1. CLSU, CSd, CSdS.
    Contents: v. 1. San Diego police department; v. 2. Philadelphia police department.
    Study conducted by the School of criminology, Univ. of Calif., Berkeley.

2460. *LOMAX, ALMENA (DAVIS). "The Muslim trial in Los Angeles," in Frontier, v. 14, July, 1963, pp. 5-7.

Law and Order, Correctional Institutions, etc.

2461. MC ENTIRE, DAVIS. Police training bulletin; a guide to race relations for police officers, by Davis McEntire ... in collaboration with Robert B. Powers. [Sacramento] Dept. of justice, state of California, 1946. 38 p. CSS, CSdS, CU-B.
     On cover: "Based primarily on results of training conferences in the Richmond, California, Police department, the State department of justice, and the American council on race relations cooperating."

2462. _____., and JOSEPH E. WECKLER. "The role of police," in The annals of the American academy of political and social science, v. 244, Mar., 1946, pp. 82-89.
     Based mainly upon California law enforcement experience and using the Richmond police department as a specific example.

2463. *MC FARLAND, WALLACE. Help. I was robbed by the Bank of America; a double standard law enforcement. A study in human deception. [S. F.? Author, 196-?]. 70 p.

2464. MANES, HUGH R. A report on law enforcement and the Negro citizen in Los Angeles. Hollywood. [Privately printed, 1963?]. 1 v. v.p. C, CLSU.

2465. "Matthews and Williams: Los Angeles' new law firm," in Crisis, v. 52, Sept., 1945, p. 258.
     Biographical accounts of Charles H. Matthews and David W. Williams.

2466. *MILLER, LOREN R., 1903-1967. Of senators, supreme court justices and prior judicial experiences. N. Y., N. A. A. C. P., 1959. 5 p. DHU.

2467. *MURRAY, PAULI, 1910-   , ed. States' laws on race and color and appendices containing international documents, federal laws and regulations, local ordinances and charts. Comp. and ed. by Pauli Murray ... [Cincinnati, Woman's div. of Christian service, Board of missions and church extension, Methodist church] 1950 [i.e., 1951]. x, 746 p. forms. CSfSt.
     Contains laws effective in the 11 western states (excluding Hawaii and Alaska) and ordinances in Phoenix, Richmond, San Francisco, and Portland.

2467a. _____. Supplement, 1955. 256 p. CSfSt.
     Does not include the appendices.

2468. "Negro delinquents in public training schools in the West," in Journal of Negro education, v. 32, Summer, 1963, pp. 294-300.

2469. "Negro police officers in Los Angeles, by one of Los Angeles' Negro police officers, who, for obvious reasons remains anonymous," in Crisis, v. 41, Aug., 1934, pp. 242 and 248.

2470. O'CONNOR, GEORGE M. The Negro and the police in Los Angeles. Master's thesis, Univ. of southern Calif., Los Angeles, 1955. 237 p.

Law and Order, Correctional Institutions, etc.

2471. "Parker ... and what's next," in Los Angeles magazine, v. 10, Sept., 1965, pp. 28-29.
    Concerns William Henry Parker, Chief, Los Angeles police department.

2472. People of the state of California, appellant, vs. Albert Lee, respondent. Mss. 101 p. (1 v.) and 24 ℓ. (Supreme court case). C-ArS.
    Lee, a servant of John Charles Frémont, was accused of the murder of his wife, Maline Delphine Agnes (Pallier) Lee, 1859. Included is the transcript on appeal from the 4th Judicial district court, San Francisco, 1860, which contains the testimony of early California residents John G., and Marie A. Pallier, William Henry Yates, David W. Ruggles, Mary Marshall, Martha Bailey, Richard Houston, and others.

2473. People of the state of California, appellant, vs. George Washington, respondent. Mss. [47] p. C-ArS.
    Supreme court case no. 10,980. Washington was accused of the murder of Bill Brown in Tehama county, Mar. 13, 1883. Pleasant D. Logan was a member of the jury panel, but his service was challenged.

2474. People vs. Peter F. Ewer. Ms. [1] p. C-ArS.
    Suit no. 1472 in the Sacramento court of sessions, 1850. Ewer, the Sacramento coroner, admits his error in calling a jury of black men "who sat upon inquest and found a verdict" in the death of a black man.

2475. "Reagan on police brutality," in Nation, v. 205, Nov. 6, 1967, pp. 453-54.
    Oakland law enforcement.

2476. *REYNOLDS, RAYMOND J. In re: The Negro and crime in San Francisco; a final report submitted by R. J. Reynolds, Sept. 1, 1947 [to Edmund G. Brown, District attorney, City and county of San Francisco]. [S. F., 1947]. 12 p. Reproduced from typewritten copy. C, CHi, CSf.

2477. RISELEY, JERRY B. Papers, Toluca Lake, consisting mainly of legal briefs and transcripts, 1943-67. Mss., 4 boxes. CLU (Spec. Coll.).
    Includes cases of three Negroes, 1965-67.

2478. *RYAN, JOHN HENRY, 1866-   , and GEORGE RIDEOUT. King county legal directory. Seattle, 1902.
    Notice of publication in Seattle Republican, May 23, 1902, p. 4, col. 3.

2478a. SCHNEIDER, FRANK M. The black laws of Oregon. Master's thesis, Univ. of Santa Clara, Santa Clara, 1970.

2479. Sleepy lagoon defense committee, Los Angeles. Papers including correspondence and other records, 1942-1945. About 3,500 pieces. CLU (Spec. Coll.).
    Cites occasional anti-black sentiment in Los Angeles.

2480. _____. The sleepy lagoon case. Prepared by the Citizens' committee for the defense of Mexican-American youth. L. A., 1942. 24 [7] p. CLU, CSmH, CU-B.

Law and Order, Correctional Institutions, etc.

2481. SMITH, WILLIAM R. Police-community relations aides in Richmond, California. Berkeley, Univ. of Calif. survey research center, 1967. i, 117 ℓ. Bibliographic footnotes. CU-B.

2482. TURNER, WILLIAM W. The police establishment. N. Y., Putnam's [c1968]. 319 p.
      Police relations with Afro-American communities, as well as with other groups, are described in the cities of Los Angeles, pp. 70-106, and San Francisco, Oakland, and Berkeley, pp. 143-86.

2483. U. S. Commission on civil rights. California advisory committee. Police-minority group relations in Los Angeles and the San Francisco bay area; report of the California advisory committee to the United States commission on civil rights. [Washington, D. C.], 1963. v, 40 p. CL, CLSU, CLU.

2484. _____. Supreme court. Victory; decision of the United States Supreme court in the case of Angelo Herndon, April 1937. Full text of the majority decision setting aside the verdict in the Herndon case, by Justice Roberts; with the dissenting opinion of the minority, by Justice Van Devanter. With an introduction, by Anna Damon. S. F., Northern Calif. district, International labor defense [1937]. 30 p. Bibliographical footnotes. CU-B.
      The decision freed Herndon from a 1932 sentence of 18 to 20 years on a Georgia chain gang.

2485. *WELLS, WESLEY ROBERT. Letters from the death house. [N. Y.?, 1953]. 44 p. CHi.
      Letters describing Wells' efforts to secure clemency while at San Quentin prison.

2486. _____. My name is Wesley Robert Wells. All profit from the sale of this pamphlet will be used for the defense of Wesley Robert Wells. Foreword by Buddy Green. [S. F.?, State defense committee for Wesley Robert Wells, 1951]. 26 p. port.

2487. *WHITAKER, LEON LEROY,   -1931. Analysis of recent decisions on wills and criminal law. Doctoral dissertation, Univ. of Calif., Berkeley, 1928. 39 ℓ.

2488. WHITE, TED W. "The field of vision narrows," in Urban west, June, 1969, pp. 21-25.
      The San Francisco police department's relationship with the Negro community.

LITERATURE

ANTHOLOGIES

2489. *[ANDREWS, DONALD AND SANDRA COX, eds.]. Together. [Riverside?, 1969?]. 40 p. illus.

"Together is a collection of the literary work of black students at the University of California, Riverside during the school years, 1968-69. It is edited and produced by the UCR Black student union as the first in what is expected to become an annual event."

2490. The Black madonna writers' lab. Black American art and culture. Preston Webster, instructor. San Francisco college for women. S. F., 1968.

Poetry, plays and stories by students of the workshop.

2491. CHITTICK, VICTOR LOVITT OAKES, 1882-   , ed. Northwest harvest, a regional stocktaking. Contributions by Peter H. Odegard [and others]. N. Y., Macmillan co., 1948. xvi, 226 p. CU.

"The printed record of the Writers' Conference on the Northwest, held in Portland, Oregon, October 31, November 1 and 2, 1946, under the joint sponsorship of the Library Association of Portland and Reed College." Contains "The bitter crop," chiefly an autobiographical account, pp. 174-93, by Horace R. Cayton.

2492. *COUCH, WILLIAM, ed. New black playwrights; an anthology edited and with an introduction by William Couch, Jr. Baton Rouge, Louisiana state univ. press [1968]. xxiii, 258 p. CNoS, CSf, CU-I.

This anthology contains a short biography of Ed Bullins, p. 255, and his play, "Goin' a Buffalo; a tragifantasy," pp. 155-216.

2493. *DE COY, ROBERT H.   The beginning point, commencing a series of works toward creation of the Nigger Bible, by Robert H. de Coy ... L. A., Holloway house pub. co. [c1967]. 298 p. CHS, CKenM, CL, CNoS, CSfSt, CSfU.

2494. *GRAHAM, ARTHUR JOSEPH, 1939-   , ed. Voices from the ghetto, an anthology edited by Arthur Graham. Associate editors: Lonnie Briscoe & Isa Infante. San Diego, a Black book production, c1968. 53 p.

In English and Spanish.

2495. *HUGHES, LANGSTON, 1902-1967, ed. New Negro poets: U. S. A. Foreword by Gwendolyn Brooks. Bloomington, Ind., Indiana univ. press [1966, c1964]. 127 p. CEcaC, CFS, CKenM, CLSU, CNoS, COM, CSdS, CSf, CSfCiC, CSjCi, CU-SB, CWM, WaT, WaTC, WaTP.

Included are poems by western poets, Ray Durem (1915-1963) and Jay Wright (b. 1935).

2496. Locke high school, Los Angeles. Uhuru. [L. A.] Locke high school, 1969. [32] p.

Poetry, essays, short stories.

Anthologies

2497. *MILLER, ADAM DAVID,1922- , ed. Dices or black bones; black voices of the
seventies. Ed. with and a welcome by Adam David Miller. Illus. by Glenn
Myles. Boston, Houghton Mifflin co. [c1970]. [xv] 142 p. illus.
      Includes works of California residents Al Young, De Leon Harrison,
Sarah (Webster) Fabio, David Henderson, Patricia Parker, Miller, Glenn
Myles, and Ishmael Reed.

2498. *MURPHY, BEATRICE MURPHY, 1908-   , ed. Ebony rhythm; an anthology of
contemporary Negro verse. Freeport, N. Y., Books for libraries press,
1968 [c1948]. 162 p. CNoS, CU-I.
      Western Negro poets included are Iola M. Brister, Anita Scott Coleman,
Ylessa Dubonee, Emily Jane Greene, Dorothy Vena Johnson, Luther George
Luper, Jr., and the Rev. John Henry Owens.

2499. *MURRAY, ALMA, ed. The black hero, ed. by Alma Murray and Robert
Thomas. Photography by John Shearer ... [N. Y., Scholastic book services,
c1970]. 204 p. illus., ports.
      A literary anthology which "is a cooperative publishing effort of
the Los Angeles city schools and Scholastic book services."

2500. _____. The journey, ed. by Alma Murray and Robert Thomas. Illus. by
Diane and Leo Dillon, Tom Feelings, George Ford, and Alvin Hollingsworth
... N. Y., Scholastic book services [c1970]. 192 p. illus.
      An anthology of general essays which "is a cooperative publishing
effort of the Los Angeles city schools and Scholastic book services."

2501. *REED, ISHMAEL, 1938-   , ed. 19 necromancers from now, ed. by
Ishmael Reed. N. Y., Doubleday-Anchor, 1970. xxvi, 369 p. group port.
CSf, CSfSt, CU.
      Cover subtitle: "An anthology of original American writing for the
1970s."
      Includes the works of a number of Afro-American writers who have re-
sided in the West such as Al Young, Paul Lofty, Victor Hernandez Cruz,
Cecil Brown, and Reed.

2502. *SAAR, BETYE, 1929- . Hand book by Betye Saar. Poetry [by] Beverly
Gleaves, David Ossman [and] Pat Ryan ... [L. A., Ace letter shop, c1967].
[12] ℓ. illus.
      "Edition of 300 ..."

2503. *SEUELL, MALCHUS M., 1911- . Malchus. Poems, letters, short stories
by Malchus M. Seuell. [L. A., Allen & Allen print. co.] 1964. 86 p.
port.

2504. SJAARDEMA, EVERETT JOHN. Collection of American Negro poems, prepared
by Everett John Sjaardema, Ballona avenue school, Hawthorne, California.
[Hawthorne, 1935?]. 155 p. Typew.
      "Creative poems," pp. 130-54, were written by 7th grade pupils in the
Ballona avenue school. All other poems appear to have been authored by
non-western poets.

2505. *SPENCE, RAYMOND. Nothing black but a cadillac. N. Y., G. P. Putnam's
sons, 1969. 192 p. CNoS.

Anthologies

2506. *TROUPE, QUINCY, ed. Watts poets: a book of new poetry & essays
edited by Quincy Troupe. Moving towards Uhuru! Uhuru! Uhuru! [L. A.?]
House of respect, c1968. 90 p. CNoS.

2507. *Watts writers' workshop. From the ashes; voices of Watts. Edited
and with an introduction by Budd Schulberg. [N. Y.] New American library
[c1967]. x, 277 p. Available in many libraries.
Consists of 18 literary works authored by members of the Watts
writers' workshop.

2508. _____. Media mixed. [L. A., 1967]. [29] ℓ. illus.
"A limited edition of 100 copies."
Poetry, photography, and essays.

FOLKLORE

2509. CLAR, MIMI. "Negro beliefs," in Western folklore, v. 18, Oct., 1959,
pp. 332-34.
Mattie Jackson, Los Angeles, relates to the author a number of beliefs
she learned as a child from her mother.

2510. *MARSH, VIVIAN COSTROMA (OSBORNE), 1898- . Types and distribution of
Negro folk-lore in America. Master's thesis, Univ. of Calif., Berkeley,
1922. 53 ℓ.

2511. "Negro wakes in Los Angeles," in Western folklore, v. 3, Oct., 1944,
pp. 326-28.

2512. *SINGLETON, CALVIN. "Negro beliefs collected in Los Angeles," in
Western folklore, v. 17, Oct., 1958, pp. 277-79.
Superstitions learned by a boy from his father.

2513. WILGUS, D. K. "Mythology and folklore," a lecture given Feb. 25, 1966
for "Perspectives on the Negro in our affluent society," a lecture series
sponsored by the Associated students of Palomar college, San Marcos.
CSmarP (tape, 1200 feet).

HISTORY AND CRITICISM

2514. ABRAMSON, DORRIS E. Negro playwrights in the American theatre, 1925-
1959 [by] Doris E. Abramson. N. Y., Columbia niv. press, 1969. xii,
335 p. Bibliography: pp. [307]-17. C, CKenM, CLSU, CSdS, CSf, CSfCiC.
A study of 18 plays produced in the New York professional theater by
15 Negro authors. Includes activities of playwrights Garland Anderson,
San Francisco, and Wallace Thurman, Salt Lake City and Los Angeles.

2515. BASEY, JILL ANNE. Lorraine Hansberry's concept of responsibility.
Master's thesis, Univ. of Calif., Los Angeles, 1967. 123 ℓ.

2516. *BRIGHT, MARJORIE ELOISE. An evaluation of the contribution made by
present day Negro dramas to the American stage. Master's thesis, Univ.
of southern Calif., Los Angeles, 1932. iii, 88 ℓ. tables.

History and Criticism

2517. *BULLINS, ED, 1935–   . "The so-called western avant garde drama," in
      Liberator, v. 7, Dec., 1967, p. 16.

2518. _____. "Theatre of reality," in Black world, v. 15, Apr., 1966,
      pp. 60–66.

2519. California. University. Santa Barbara. Dept. of dramatic art.
      The black teacher and the drama; report on an Institute in repertory
      theatre. [Santa Barbara, 1968]. 25 p. C, CU-SB.

2520. COBB, I. W. A study of Negro dialects in American poetry. Master's
      thesis, Univ. of southern Calif., Los Angeles, 1941.

2521. CURTIS, MARY JULIA. A comparative analysis of the characterization of
      three male protagonists in modern American Negro drama. Master's thesis,
      Stanford univ., Stanford, 1961. iv, 97 ℓ.

2522. FARMER, GEORGE LUTHER. Majority and minority Americans: an analysis
      of best selling American fiction from 1926–1966. Doctoral dissertation,
      Univ. of southern Calif., Los Angeles, 1968. vi, 236 ℓ.

2523. FEINSTEIN, LISA DEE. Deception as a technique for survival manifested
      in recent Afro-American fiction. Master's thesis, Calif. state univ.,
      San Francisco, 1969. iv, 121 ℓ.

2524. FISCHER, RUSSELL GLENN. Invisible man as symbolic history. Master's
      thesis, Calif. state univ., San Francisco, 1970. iii, 50 ℓ.
         Based on Ralph Ellison's 1952 novel.

2525. FULFORD, ROBERT L. A comparison of ethos in speeches by Stokely
      Carmichael to predominantly white and predominantly black audiences.
      Master's thesis, Calif. state univ., Sacramento, 1968. 115 ℓ.

2526. *FULLER, HOYT WILLIAM, 1928–   . "Assembly at Asilomar: the Negro
      writer in the United States," in Black world, v. 13, Sept., 1964, pp. 42–48.

2527. *GAFFNEY, FLOYD. "Black theatre: commitment & communication," in
      The black scholar, v. 1, June, 1970, pp. 10–15.
         By an Assoc. prof. of drama, Univ. of Calif., Santa Barbara.

2528. GARTON, CHRISTIANA. The portrayal of Negro character in the American
      drama and novel. Master's thesis, Univ. of Colorado, Boulder, 1942.

2529. GILMAN, R. "White standards and Negro writing," in New republic,
      v. 158, Mar. 9, 1968, pp. 26–28ff.
         About Eldridge Cleaver.

2530. GRIFFITHS, ELEANOR WRIGHT. The critical reception of Langston Hughes'
      poetry and short stories. Master's thesis, Calif. state univ., Sacra-
      mento, 1970. 79 ℓ.

2531. HODGE, DOROTHY F. Miscegenation in the works of George W. Cable.
      Master's thesis, Calif. state univ., Sacramento, 1962. 93 ℓ.

History and Criticism

2532. JOHNSON, I. H. The American Negro as portrayed in prose literature by American authors from 1900 to 1932. Master's thesis, Univ. of southern Calif., Los Angeles, 1937.

2533. JORDAN, EDWARD STARR. The long loneliness of Richard Wright. Master's thesis, Calif. state univ., San Francisco, 1963. 136 [2] ℓ.
     An analysis of the sociological and psychological aspects of the life and work of Richard Wright.

2534. KRUMM, HELEN T. William Faulkner's Negroes; a standard by which to judge white society. Master's thesis, Calif. state univ., Sacramento, 1970. 74 ℓ.

2535. LOCEY, MARGARET LENORE. William Faulkner on race: a Southern artist confronts his heritage. Master's thesis, Calif. state univ., San Francisco, 1970. iii, 99 ℓ.

2536. *LOVELL, JOHN, 1907- . Champions of the workers in American literature of the forties. Doctoral dissertation, Univ. of Calif., Berkeley, 1938. 191 ℓ.

2537. MANGRUM, MARIANNA. The Negro in American drama. Master's thesis, Univ. of southern Calif., Los Angeles, 1934.

2538. *NANCE, ETHEL (RAY), 1899- . "The New York arts renaissance, 1924-1926," in Negro history bulletin, Apr., 1968, pp. 15-19.
     Authored by a San Francisco resident and a renaissance participant.

2539. PATTERSON, LINDSAY, comp. Anthology of the American Negro in the theatre; a critical approach. N. Y., Publishers co. [c1967]· xiv, 306 p. illus., facsims.,ports. (International library of Negro life and history). Bibliography: pp. [293]-94. CBGTU, CBea, CEcaC, CFS, CLSU, CNoS, CO, CSdS, CSf, CSjCi, CU, CU-A, CU-SB, CU-SC.
     Contains "How I became a playwright," by Garland Anderson, pp. 85-86 (reprinted from Everyman, London, May, 1928); "Porgy and Bess - a folk opera?" by Hall Johnson; and extensive information about the California stage.

2540. *PRICE, MARY ELLEN. Women in the literature of the California gold rush community. Master's thesis, Howard univ., Washington, D. C., 1941. vi, 142 ℓ.

2541. RANDOLPH, CAROLYN A. Negro poetry and poets for the intermediate grades. Master's project, Calif. state univ., Sacramento, 1969. 107 ℓ.

2542. *REARDON, WILLIAM R. The black teacher and the drama. Report on an Institute in repertory theatre operated under a grant from the U. S. office of education for potential teachers of disadvantaged youth in cooperation with the Department of dramatic art at the University of California, Santa Barbara. [Santa Barbara, Univ. of Calif., 1969?]. 1 v. unp. illus., ports. CLU.

History and Criticism

2543. REXROTH, KENNETH. "Panelizing dissent: report on conference on the
Negro writer in the United States," in <u>Nation</u>, v. 199, Sept. 7, 1964,
pp. 97-99.
    A seminar sponsored by University of California.

2544. ROSS, RONALD PATRICK. Black drama in the Federal theatre. Master's
thesis, Univ. of southern Calif., Los Angeles, 1968. v, 63 ℓ.
    The interpretation of Negro materials by black and white U. S. play-
wrights.

2545. SAHLMAN, JOYCE VIRGINIA. The white-man image in black drama. Master's
thesis, Calif. state univ., Sacramento, 1970. 67 ℓ.

2546. SCHULBERG, BUDD. "Black phoenix: an introduction," in <u>Antioch review</u>,
v. 27, Fall, 1967, pp. 277-84.
    The Watts writers workshop.

2547. SEELEY, ROBERT MARSHALL. Racial prejudices and conflicts as found in
selected American novels published between 1928 and 1949. Master's
thesis, Univ. of southern Calif., Los Angeles, 1951. vii, 198 ℓ.

2548. TIMMONS, F. ALAN. A content analysis of romance and biography story
types in Negro magazine communication. Doctoral dissertation, Univ. of
southern Calif., Los Angeles, 1958. xviii, 325 ℓ. illus.

2549. TYLER, PRISCILLA. World's literature written in English; presented
at the Conference on black literature: its value in the curriculum.
Hayward, Calif. state univ. [1969?]. 78 p. Typew. CHS.

2550. VESPER, JOAN LOUISE FRANTZ. Goal for Negro literature: the recent
critical debate and its background. Master's thesis, Stanford univ.,
Stanford, 1965. iv, 68 ℓ.

2551. WILLIAMS, BOBBYE LOUISE. A study of the Negro character in the short
story of the United States, 1920-1950. Master's thesis, Univ. of southern
Calif., Los Angeles, 1953. vi, 121 ℓ.

2552. YOUNG, JAMES OWEN. Richard Wright: a study in isolation. Master's
thesis, Univ. of southern Calif., Los Angeles, 1968. vi, 130 ℓ.

2553. ZIETLON, EDWARD ROBERT. Wright to Hansberry: the evolution of outlook in four Negro writers. Doctoral dissertation, Univ. of Washington,
Seattle, 1967.

DRAMA

2554. *ANDERSON, GARLAND. "Appearances," by Garland Anderson. [N. Y.,
1925]. [118] p. NN, NUC, pre-1956.
    Film reproduction.

Drama

2555. Bribery; or, the California senatorial election; a comedy in III acts.
[S. F., 1868]. 18 p. CLU, CSmH, CU-B, NUC, pre-1956.
    Page 16 contains a fictitious conversation between Eugene Casserly,
candidate for the U. S. Senate, and two California Negroes, Sambo and
Juba.

2556. *BULLINS, ED, 1935- . "Clara's ole man," in Drama review, v. 12, Summer, 1968, pp. 159-71.

2557. _____. How do you do; a nonsense drama. [Mill Valley] Illuminations
press [1967] c1965. 31 p. illus. CM1, CU, CU-I.
    The author "has had stories, plays, poetry and essays published in
numerous literary publications including Contact, Nexus, Ante, Wild Dog,
Illuminations, Soulbook, Negro Digest and S. F. Oracle." He arrived in
San Francisco in 1964 from Los Angeles where he had "founded the literary
magazine at Los Angeles State College [and] helped found the L. A. magazine, Ante ..." By 1967 or 1968, he was living in New York City.

2558. *EASTON, WILLIAM EDGAR, 1861- . Christophe; a tragedy in prose of
imperial Haiti, by William Edgar Easton ... Illus. by John McCullough
... L. A., Grafton pub. co. [c1911]. 122 p. illus., ports. CU, NUC,
pre-1956.
    Includes "A job for Uncle Sam" and "An hour with Harriet Tubman," by
James B. Clarke. Easton also authored "Dessalines," an historical drama
(Galveston, Tex., 1893).

2559. *GRAHAM, ARTHUR JOSEPH, 1939- . The last shine (one act). San
Diego, Author, c1969. 39 p. cover port.

2560. _____. The nationals, a black happening in three acts. San Diego,
Black book productions, c1968. 87 p.

2561. GREGORY, WAYNE. No hidin' place, a drama in one act, by Wayne
Gregory. S. F., Banner play bureau, inc., c1938. 28 p. DLC, Hatch,
p. 51.

2562. HARRIS, THOMAS WALTER. Fall of an iron horse; a play in three acts.
Master's thesis, Univ. of Calif., Los Angeles, 1959. 146 ℓ. Hatch,
p. 78.

2563. *Hiram club, Bakersfield. Dramatic recital and musical given by
Hiram club at Armory, Monday evening, November 4th, 1912. Bakersfield,
California. Bakersfield [Harris print shop], 1912. [16] p. CHi.
    Souvenir book chiefly containing advertisements.

2564. *HUFFMAN, EUGENE HENRY. Hoo-dooed. [L. A.?, 1932?].
    Produced at the Los Angeles Philharmonic auditorium. San Francisco
Spokesman, Apr. 23, 1932, p. 1, col. 3. The author stated to the compiler that the play was re-titled and copyrighted as The victory in
Chicago in the 1940's. Other plays by the same author include "Unto us
a child is born"; "The imposter in the red mausoleum"; "The lost chord";
and "St. Peter is out."

Drama

2565. HULT, RUBY EL, 1912- . "The saga of George W. Bush, unheralded
   pioneer of the Northwest territory," in Black world, v. 11, Sept., 1962,
   pp. 88-96.
      A play about a Washington state pioneer.

2566. LENNEP, JAKOB VAN, 1802-1868. Een droom van Californië; kluchtspel
   met zang, door Mr. J. Van Lennep. Amsterdam, P. Meijer Warnars, 1849.
   60 p. CHi.
      A Negro appears as one of the main characters in the dream.

2567. *MARVIN X. "Take care of business," in Drama review, v. 12, Summer,
   1968, pp. 85-92.

2568. *OWOMOYELA, OYEKAN. The slave. Master's thesis, Univ. of Calif.,
   Los Angeles, 1966. 117 l.

2569. *PAYTON, LEW, 1873- . Did Adam sin? And other stories of Negro life
   in comedy-drama and sketches, by Lew Payton. L. A., L. Payton [c1937].
   132 p. CHi, CNoS, DHU.
      Drama and fiction.

2570. *SANCHEZ, SONIA, 1935- . "The Bronx is next," in Drama review, v. 12,
   Summer, 1968, pp. 78-83.

2571. *THOMPSON, ELOISE A. (BIBB), -1928. Africannus. L. A., 1922.
   Work, p. 451.

2572. _____. Cooped up. [n.p., 1924]. Work, p. 451; Hatch, p. 41.

2573. TUOTTI, JOSEPH DOLAN. Big time Buck White, by Joseph Dolan Tuotti.
   N. Y., Grove press [c1969]. 117 p. CNoS.
      "Big Time Buck White was first performed at Budd Schulberg's Writers'
   workshop in Watts, Los Angeles. The New York premier took place on
   Dec. 8, 1968 at the Village south theatre."

ESSAYS AND SPEECHES

2574. ADOFF, ARNOLD, ed. Black on black; commentaries by Negro Americans.
   Ed. by Arnold Adoff. Foreword by Roger Mae Johnson. N. Y., Macmillan
   co. [c1968]. xvi, 236 p. CSdS, CSt.
      Contains excerpts from Bill Russell's Go up for glory, pp. 124-34
   and "Why I eulogized Malcolm X," by Ossie Davis, pp. 170-73.

2575. *BENJAMIN, ROBERT CHARLES O'HARA, 1855-1900. The Negro problem and
   the method of its solution. An address delivered at the A. M. E. Zion
   church, Portland, Oregon, June 3d, 1891, by Hon. R. C. O. Benjamin ...
   Reported in the "Oregonian" ... S. F., G. E. Watkins souvenir and
   directory pub. co., 1891. 23 p. CSt.

2576. *BROWN, PAUL, and others. Our book of soul ... Berkeley, Berkeley
   high school, west campus, 1968. 78 p. illus. CSfAA.

Essays and Speeches

Contains essays, opinion surveys, a glossary of slang, etc., prepared by Paul Brown and 17 other students of Berkeley high school, west campus.

2577. Center for the study of democratic institutions. Lyndon B. Johnson, Robert B. Weaver, Joseph P. Lyford, and John Cogley on the Negro as an American. [Santa Barbara, 1963]. 18 p. CHS, CLSU, CM1G, CPhD, CSbS, CU-SC.

2578. *CHICO, JESSIE L. (RIDLEY)   Unto us, by Jessie L. Chico. Illus. by Robert Reid. Dallas, Texas, Triangle pub. co. [c1959]. 58 p. illus. COEB.
    Essays on religion and philosophy by a Berkeley resident.

2579. _____. Same. 2nd ed., 1960.

2580. *COLEMAN, ANITA (SCOTT), 1890- . "Unfinished masterpieces," in Crisis, v. 34, Mar., 1927, pp. 14 and 24-25.
    Authored by a resident of Silver City, New Mexico and Los Angeles.

2581. FARBER, JERRY. The student as nigger; essays and stories. [North Hollywood, Contact, c1969]. 188 p. CCotS.

2582. *FITNAH, NAZZAM AL, 1944- . Sudan rajuli samia [or] black man listen, by Nazzam Al Fitnah. [S. F.?, 1970?]. 11 p. Mimeo.
    Black Muslim essays and poetry.

2583. *HIMES, CHESTER B., 1909- . "Now is the time! Here is the place!" in Opportunity, v. 20, Sept., 1942, pp. 271-73 and 284.
    An essay relating Negroes to World war II, by a Los Angeles resident.

2584. *HUBBARD, JAMES H., 1838?-1912. Orations delivered on the Emancipation and the fifteenth amendment ... S. F., Cuddy and Hughes, 1873. pam.
    Unlocated title. Notice of its printing appears in the San Francisco Elevator, Sept. 13, 1873, p. 2, col. 4.

2585. *JOHNSON, EZRA ROTHSCHILD, 1814?-1870. ... Emancipation oration by Dr. Ezra R. Johnson, and poem, by James M. Whitfield, delivered at Platt's hall, January 1, 1867, in honor of the fourth anniversary of President Lincoln's proclamation of emancipation, 1864. S. F., Pub. at the Elevator office, 1867. 32 p. C, CHi (photocopy), CSmH, CU-B.

2586. *KING, MARTIN LUTHER, 1929-1968. Martin Luther King at Stanford. Berkeley, Pacifica tape library A2043, 1967. [Phonotape]. Duration: 50 min. CSS.
    An address on the civil rights movement before the Stanford univ. student body.

2587. *LOMAX, LOUIS E.,   -1970. "Keynote," a preliminary lecture given Sept. 24, 1965 for "Perspectives on the Negro in our affluent society," a lecture series sponsored by the Associated students of Palomar college, San Marcos. CSmarP (tape, 1200 feet).
    Lomax was but a short-term resident of Los Angeles in the 1960's. For this reason, the numerous titles authored by him are not included in this bibliography.

Essays and Speeches

2588. *PHILLIPS, HILTON ALONZO, 1905- . Flames of rebellion (against en-
throned tyranny), by Hilton A. Phillips, author, scholar, historian,
heralder of the dawn of equity. [L. A., California eagle press, c1936].
viii, 237 p. port. CU.
    Prose and poetry concerning the U. S. race question.

2589. *SMITH, CARL S.   Letters from my nephew, Slim, by Carl S. Smith.
N. Y., Vantage press [c1965]. 120 p. COEB.
    Essays on civil rights and poverty, by an Oakland resident. Contains
some autobiographical information.

2590. WAGNER, HARR, 1857-1936, ed. Notable speeches by notable speakers of
the greater west ... S. F., Whitaker and Ray co., 1902. 430 p. ports.
CU-B.
    Included, pp. 323-29, is "The improvement of the colored race," a
speech delivered by Theophilus B. Morton "as his annual address as state
president of the Afro-American Leagues of California ... Fresno, July 20,
1897." Also included is a short biographical account of Morton and his
portrait.

                              FICTION

2591. *ALDRICH, GUSTAVE B.   "Coup de grace of a southern schoolmaster," in
Colored American magazine, v. 5, May, 1902, pp. 17-26.
    A short story authored by a Tacoma attorney.

2592. ANDERSON, HENRY L. No use cryin'. Introd. by the Rev. Michael
Hamilton. London, L. A., Western publishers, 1961. 208 p. DLC.
    An interracial plot.

2593. ANDERSON, WILLIAM C. The apoplectic palm tree; or, the happy happening among blacks and whites at the Greater Mount Moriah solid rock true
happiness baptist church and funeral parlor, a novel, by William C.
Anderson. N. Y., Crown publishers [1969]. 224 p. DLC, Baird 62.
    Watts locale.

2594. BAER, HOWARD, 1921- . O, huge angel. N. Y., Roy publishers [1949].
161 p. DHU, WaT, Baird 142.
    San Francisco setting involving a black seaman.

2595. *BAGLEY, JULIAN ELIHU.   "Children of chance," in Crisis, v. 29, Nov.,
1924, pp. 15-18.
    A short story by a San Francisco resident. Mr. Noah Griffin, Sr. re-
ports that Bagley was the author of Candle lighting time in Bodigley (?);
18 short childrens' stories, but a copy has not been examined.

2596. _____. "Moving pictures in an old song shop," in Opportunity, v. 5,
Dec., 1927, pp. 369-72.

2597. _____. "Niggers," in Crisis, v. 27, Nov., 1923, pp. 21-33, and Dec.,
1923, pp. 68-69.

Fiction

2598. _____. "A novelty in blue," in Crisis, v. 35, Dec., 1928, pp. 403-04 and 421-22.

2599. BALL, JOHN DUDLEY, 1911- . Cool cottontail, by John Ball. N. Y., Harper & Row [c1966]. x, 208 p. CP, CSf, CU, Baird 156.
     A mystery story by a resident of Encino in which a black Pasadena detective is the central character.

2600. _____. In the heat of the night, by John Ball. N. Y., Harper & Row, [1965]. 184 p. CO, CP, CSf.
     A mystery novel based upon a black Pasadena police officer's experience.

2601. _____. Johnny get your gun; a novel, by John Ball. Boston, Little, Brown [1969]. 227 p. DLC.
     Another mystery novel about a black detective in Pasadena.

2602. BARRETT, WILLIAM EDMUND, 1900- . The lilies of the field [by] William E. Barrett. Drawings by Burt Silverman. Garden City, N. Y., Doubleday & co. [c1962]. 92 p. CO, CP, CRic, CSf, Baird 180.
     A black army veteran helps German nuns to build a church in southern Calif.

2603. *[BECK, ROBERT]. Pimp; the story of my life, by Iceberg Slim. L. A., Holloway house pub. co. [c1969]. 317 p.
     The author, a Los Angeles resident, has also written Momma Blackwidow, and other novels.

2604. BONHAM, FRANK. Durango street, by Frank Bonham. N. Y., E. P. Dutton & co. [c1965]. 190 p. CLod, CO, CP, CPomCP, CRic, CSf, CSluSP.
     A story of Los Angeles gang life by a La Jolla resident.

2605. _____. The nitty gritty, by Frank Bonham. Illus. by Alvin Smith. N. Y., E. P. Dutton & co., inc. [c1968]. 156 p. illus., front. CNoS, CRic, CSf.

2606. *BONTEMPS, ARNA WENDELL, 1902-1973. God sends Sunday, by Arna Bontemps. N. Y., Harcourt, Brace and co. [c1931]. 199 p. DLC, NN, NUC, pre-1956.
     A story of the Watts community.

2607. *BROWN, CECIL, 1943- . The life and loves of Mr. jiveass nigger, a novel by Cecil Brown. N. Y., Farrar, Straus & Giroux [c1969]. 213 p. CSf.
     Authored by an English faculty member at the Univ. of Calif., Berkeley, and Merritt college, Oakland.

2608. *BULLINS, ED, 1935- . "Loneliest man in the universe," in Black world, v. 15, Aug., 1966, pp. 21-25.
     A short story.

2609. _____. "The storekeeper," in Black world, v. 16, May, 1967, pp. 55-58.
     A short story.

Fiction

2610. _____. "Support your local police," in Black world, v. 17, Nov.,
1967, pp. 53-58.
A short story.

2611. BUSCH, NIVEN, 1903- . They dream of home. N. Y., D. Appleton-
Century co. [1944]. 306 p. CSf, NUC, ante-1956.

2612. *CLARKE, JOHN HENRIK, 1915- , ed. American Negro short stories, ed.
by John Henrik Clarke. N. Y., Hill and Wang [c1966]. xix, 355 p. CEcaC,
CEs, CFS, CLS, CLSU, CO, CPhD, CSdS, CSf, CSfCiC, CSfGG, CSjCi, CU-SB,
WaT, WaTC.
Contains "The sky is gray," by Ernest J. Gaines, pp. 321-48.

2613. CLAY, JOSEPHINE RUSSELL. Uncle Phil. A novel ... By Mrs. John M.
Clay. Chicago, F. Tennyson Neely [c1899]. 271 p. CU (film), NUC, pre-
1956, Baird 490.
Setting in southern California. The main character is a black
servant.

2614. *COLEMAN, ANITA SCOTT, 1890- . "The brat," in Messenger, v. 8, Apr.,
1926, pp. 105-06 and 126.
A short story by a resident of Los Angeles and Silver City, New
Mexico. No attempt has been made to list here one-page short stories by
the same author appearing in various publications.

2615. _____. "Cross crossings cautiously," in Opportunity, v. 8, June,
1930, pp. 177 and 189.

2616. _____. "The eternal quest," in Opportunity, v. 9, Aug., 1931,
pp. 242-43.

2617. _____. "G'long, old white man's gal," in Messenger, v. 10, Apr.,
1928, pp. 81-2.

2618. _____. "The hand that fed," in Competitor, v. 2, Dec., 1920, pp. 259-
61.

2619. _____. "Jack arrives," in Half-century magazine, v. 8, Feb., 1920,
pp. 5 and 14.

2620. _____. "The little grey house," in Half-century magazine, v. 13,
July-Aug., 1922, pp. 17 and 19. Also Sept.-Oct., 1922, pp. 4 and 21.

2621. _____. "The Nettleby's new years," in Half-century magazine, v. 8,
Jan., 1920, pp. 5 and 14-15.

2622. _____. "Phoebe and Peter up North," in Half-century magazine, v. 6,
Feb., 1919, pp. 4 and 10.

2623. _____. "Rich man, poor man," in Half-century magazine, v. 8, May,
1920, pp. 6 and 14.

2624. _____. "Silk stockings," in Messenger, v. 8, Aug., 1926, pp. 229-31.

Fiction

2625. _____. "Three dogs and a rabbit," in Crisis, v. 31, Jan., 1926,
pp. 118-22.

2626. _____. "El Tisico," in Crisis, v. 19, Mar., 1920, pp. 252-53.

2627. _____. "Two old women a-shopping go!", in Crisis, v. 40, May, 1933,
pp. 109-10.

2628. _____. "Unfinished masterpieces," in Crisis, v. 34, Mar., 1927,
pp. 14 and 24.

2629. _____. "White folk's Nigger," in Messenger, v. 10, May-June, 1928,
pp. 104, 111, 114, 117, and 119.

2630. COOLIDGE, FAY LIDDLE. ... Black is white. N. Y., Vantage press
[c1958]. 157 p. NN.
Fictional account on "passing" in California.

2631. *DETTER, THOMAS, 1826?- . Nellie Brown, or the jealous wife,
written and published by Thomas Detter (colored) of Elko, Nevada. This
book is perfectly chaste and moral in every particular. S. F., Cuddy &
Hughes, 1871. 160 p. C, CHi, CLU, CU-B.
The first known book of fiction authored by a black person in the
West.

2632. DOBIE, CHARLES CALDWELL, 1881-1943. Less than kin; a novel, by Charles
Caldwell Dobie. N. Y., The John Day co., 1926. 405 p. CU-B.
A novel in which Mary Ellen Pleasant appears as a central character
under another name.

2633. *EDWARDS, S. W. Go now in darkness. Second edition, second printing.
Chicago, Baker press [c1965]. 353 p. illus.
Fiction by San Francisco resident.

2634. *FRENCH, MARIE LOUISE (REID),* 1894- . "The greater gift; a Christmas
story," in Crisis, v. 38, Dec., 1931, pp. 415-16.
A short story by a resident of Colorado Springs.

2635. _____. "There never fell a night so dark," in Crisis, v. 31, Dec.,
1925, pp. 73-76.

2636. *FRIERSON, EUGENE P. "An adventure in the Big Horn mountains; or,
the trials and tribulations of a recruit," in Colored American magazine,
v. 8, Apr., 1905, pp. 196-99; May, 1905, pp. 277-279; and June, 1905,
pp. 338-40.
A semi-fictional account of Tenth U. S. cavalry life in Montana.

2637. *GAINES, ERNEST J., 1933- . Bloodline, by Ernest J. Gaines. N. Y.,
Dial press, 1968. 249 p. CFS, CKenM, CO, CSbS, CSf, CSt, WaPu, WaT.
Short stories by a San Francisco and Vallejo resident.

2638. _____. Catherine Carmier. N. Y., Atheneum, 1964. 248 p. CO, CSf,
CSt, CSto.

Fiction

2639. _____. Of love and dust, a novel. N. Y., Dial, 1967. 281 p. CFS, CHS, CO, CSf, CSfCiC, CSluSP, CSt.

2640. GANT, MATTHEW. The last notch ... N. Y., Dodd [c1958]. 216 p. NN.
A New Mexico western concerning Negro slavery and crime.

2641. *GORHAM, THELMA THURSTON. "It's never too early: a trilogy," in Crisis, v. 53, Mar., 1946, pp. 82-83 and 93.
By a Berkeley resident and a former Fort Huachuca, Ariz., editor.

2642. *GRAHAM, KATHERYN (CAMPBELL). Under the cottonwood; a saga of Negro life in which history, traditions and folklore of the Negro of the last century are vividly portrayed, by Katheryn Campbell Graham. N. Y., Wendell Malliet and co. [c1941]. 262 p. CL.
Fiction by a Los Angeles author. "Dedicated to my darling daughter, Benzell."

2643. *GROSS, WERTER LIVINGSTON, 1895- . The golden recovery revealing a streamlined economic system compiled from the best authorities of the world, both ancient and modern. [Reno, Golden recovery corp., 1946]. 186 p.
Describes a modern Utopia.

2644. *GROVES, JOHN WESLEY. Pyrrhic victory; a collection of short stories. Philadelphia, United pub. [c1953]. 60 p. DHU, NN.
Includes some California locale.

2645. *HARRIS, LEON R. Run, zebra, run! A story of American race conflict, by Leon R. Harris. N. Y., Exposition press [c1959]. 260 p.
Authored by a Los Angeles resident.

2646. HENRY, WILL (pseud.). One more river to cross; the life and legend of Isom Dart [by] Will Henry. N. Y., Random house [c1967]. 236 p. CSf.
A fictional account of an ex-slave's experiences in Colorado, Texas, and Oklahoma.

2647. *HIMES, CHESTER BOMAR, 1909- ."All God's chillun got pride," in Crisis, v. 51, June, 1944, pp. 188-89 and 204.
Himes has lived at various periods of his life in Los Angeles, Oakland, and Richmond. No attempt has been made to list here a complete account of his many works written during this time.

2648. _____. "Heaven has changed," in Crisis, v. 50, Mar., 1943, pp. 78 and 83.

2649. _____. If he hollers let him go [by] Chester B. Himes. Garden City, N. Y., Doubleday, Doran & co., 1945. 249 p. CNoS, CSt.
A fictional setting in a Los Angeles World war II shipyard.

2650. _____. "In the night," in Opportunity, v. 20, Nov., 1942, pp. 334-35 and 348-49.
A short story with a Central avenue, Los Angeles locale, by an Oakland (in 1942) resident.

Fiction

2651. _____. Lonely crusade [by] Chester Himes. N. Y., Alfred A. Knopf, 1947. 398 p. CSt.
    About a black labor organizer in Los Angeles during World War II.

2652. _____. "Lunching at the Ritzmore," in Crisis, v. 49, Oct., 1942, pp. 314-15 and 331.
    Short story written while a resident of Los Angeles.

2653. _____. S'il braille, lache-la ... (If he hollers let him go). Tr. de l'américaine par Renée Vavasseur et Marcel Duhamel. Paris, A. Michel [1948]. 336 p. DHU.

2654. _____. "So softly smiling," in Crisis, v. 50, Oct., 1943, pp. 302, 314-16 and 318.

2655. _____. "Two soldiers," in Crisis, v. 50, Jan., 1943, pp. 13 and 29.

2656. HOWELL, HARRY D. Strange stories of the old deep South, by H. D. "Pop" Howell, Sr. L. A., Wetzel pub. co., inc. [c1937]. 295 p. plates. CSuLas, CU.
    "Illustrations by Thomas James Howell."
    Authored by a Los Angeles resident.

2657. HUDSON, CORDELIA J. Harmony road, by Cordelia J. Hudson. [Sacramento, 1947]. 95 p. port. C, Baird 1254.
    Fiction with an integrated plot. Sacramento at the end of World war II.

2658. *HUFFMAN, EUGENE HENRY. "Now I am civilized" [by] Eugene Henry Huffman; illus. by Herbert Rasche. L. A., Wetzel pub. co., 1930. 208 p. illus. CNoS, CU-A.
    According to the author, a revised edition was published in paperback in Los Angeles, ca. 1942-43.

2659. *JACKSON, W. WARNER. Birth of the martyr's ghost; a novel ... N. Y., Comet press books [c1957]. 167 p. NN.
    California fiction.

2660. *JENKINS, DEADERICK FRANKLIN. It was not my world, a story in black and white that's different. [L. A., Author, c1942]. 3, 104 p. CLSU, CSaT.

2661. _____. Letters to my son, by Deaderick F. Jenkins. [L. A., Deaderick F. Jenkins pub. co., c1947]. ix, 111 p. CSaT.

2662. *JOHNSON, EVELYN (ALLEN). My neighbor's island, by Evelyn Allen Johnson. N. Y., Exposition press [c1965]. 55 p. DHU.
    Authored by a director of nursing, Los Angeles.

2663. KEROUAC, JACK, 1922- . The subterraneans. N. Y., Grove press [c1958]. 111 p. CSf.
    San Francisco fiction.

Fiction

2664. *KIMBROUGH, JESSE L.   Defender of the angels: a black policeman in old Los Angeles. N. Y., Macmillan, 1969. ix, 273 p. C, CP, CSd, CSf, CU-B.
    The author's fictionalized account of his years with the Los Angeles police force. The author's The brown doughboy, also fiction, was published only in Russia.

2665. KRAUS, HENRY, 1905- . In the city was a garden; a housing project chronicle. N. Y., Renaissance press, 1951. 255 p. C, CHi, CLS, CLU, CNoS, CO, CPa, CPhD, CSbCL, CSf, CS1uSP, CSoS, CSt, CU-A, Rocq 3937.
    Fictional account based upon dwelling experience in an interracial housing project at San Pedro.

2666. LOGAN, GEORGIA SMITH. The inside view of Negro character in Native son, Invisible man, and Go tell it on the mountain. Master's thesis, Stanford univ., Stanford, 1961. ii, 135 p.

2667. *MERIWETHER, LOUISE M. Daddy was a number runner [by] Louise Meriwether. Englewood Cliffs, N. J., Prentice-Hall, inc. [c1970]. 208 p. CNoS, CSf.
    Fiction with a Harlem locale. Authored by a Los Angeles resident.

2668. MILLEN, GILMORE, 1897- . Sweet man, by Gilmore Millen. N. Y., Viking press, 1930. 299 p. CLU, CU, Baird 1752.
    Relates the rise of Central avenue, Los Angeles.

2669. PANGER, DANIEL. Ol' prophet Nat, by Daniel Panger. Winston-Salem, N. C., John F. Blair [c1967]. 159 p. illus. CSaT, CSf, CSfCiC, CSjCi.
    Fictional account of Nat Turner by a San Francisco clergyman.

2670. *PHILLIPS, JANE, 1944- . Mojo hand [by] Jane Phillips. N. Y., Trident press [c1966]. 180 p. CL.
    Fiction by a Los Angeles native.

2671. RAUCH, MABEL THOMPSON. "Perry North marches on," in Opportunity, v. 15, Jan., 1937, pp. 17-22.
    A story of black-white relationships by a Los Angeles resident.

2672. *REED, ISHMAEL, 1938- . Yellow back radio broke-down [by] Ishmael Reed. Garden City, N. Y., Doubleday, 1969. 177 p. CSf, CSt.
    Surrealist fiction about a black cowboy and his African magic. Reed, a resident of Berkeley, formerly lived in New York City where he authored The free-lance pallbearers.

2673. *RILEY, ETHEL R.   "Dark laughter," in Opportunity, v. 7, Aug., 1929, pp. 250-53.
    A short story by a San Francisco resident.

2674. SAXTON, ALEXANDER PLAISTED, 1919- . Bright web in the darkness. N. Y., St. Martin's press [c1958]. 308 p. CLU, CU-B, Baird 2206.
    Concerns San Francisco shipbuilding, trade unions, and discrimination.

Fiction

2675. Shine and the Titanic, The signifying monkey, Stackolee, and other
stories from down home. [S. F.] The More pub. co. [1970]. 22 p.

2676. *THOMAS, ALBERTA. "Gold is where you find it," in Opportunity, v. 25,
Oct.-Dec., 1947, pp. 196 and 230-31.
Short story by a Seattle resident.

2677. *THOMAS, WILL, 1905- . "Hill to climb," in Crisis, v. 53, June,
1946, pp. 173-74.

2678. *WEAVER, WERTIE CLARICE. The valley of the poor, by Wertie Clarice
Weaver. L. A., Wetzel pub. co. [c1945]. 319 p. CNoS.

2679. WILEY, HUGH, 1884- . Fo' meals a day, by Hugh Wiley. N. Y., A. A.
Knopf, 1927. 306 p. CU-B, Baird 2616.
Stories of "Wildcat," a black, with some San Francisco and Oakland
setting.

2680. _____. The prowler [by] Hugh Wiley. N. Y., A. A. Knopf, 1924. 272 p.
CU-B, Baird 2619.
More stories with the same main character in Los Angeles and San
Diego.

2681. WILLIAMS, MARGARET (pseud.). "Grazing in good pastures," in Crisis,
v. 48, Feb., 1941, pp. 42-43 and 59.
By a Denver resident.

2682. *[WRIGHT, BEATRICE ANN], 1922- . Sons of the fathers, by Martin
Kramer [pseud.]. N. Y., Macmillan [c1959]. 342 p. CLU, CU.
Fictional account of blacks in California.

2683. *YERBY, FRANK, 1916- . ... The treasure of Pleasant valley. N. Y.,
Dial press [c1955]. 348 p. CChiS, CLobS, CLSU, CSfAA, CS1uSP, CU-Λ,
WaPu, WaT, WaTC.
Fictional account of gold discovery in California.

2684. *YOUNG, AL, 1939- . Snakes, a novel, by Al Young. N. Y., Holt,
Rinehart and Winston [c1970]. 149 p. CSf.
The author is a lecturer at Stanford university. Also author of
Dancing, 1969.

2685. *YOUNG, JAMES L. Helen Duval; a French romance, by James L. Young
(colored). S. F., Bancroft co., 1891. v, 202 p. CU-B.
Author's port. on cover.

2686. _____. Same. In: Wright, Lyle Henry. American fiction, v. III,
1876-1900 (no. 6164). New Haven, Research pubs., inc. [1967-71].
Microfilm reel XYZ-Z. CU.

POETRY AND PROVERBS

No attempt has been made to list here individual short poems
appearing in periodicals.

Many white western authors make reference in their poetry to
blacks, but it is seldom that a long poem deals entirely
with the black experience. An exception is Mrs. Julia
Cooley Altrocchi's Black boat. For a study on the subject,
see "White on Black: a check list of poetry by White
Americans about the Black experience, 1708–1970," by
Conrad A. Balliet, in Bulletin of the New York public
library, v. 75, Nov., 1971, pp. 424–65.

2687. *ALI, NATHANAEL. Excerpts from the diary of a young black slowly
going mad, by Nathanael Ali. [S. F.] Shabazz pub. co. [c1970]. 44 p.

2688. ALTROCCHI, JULIA (COOLEY), 1893– . Black boat. [n.p., 194–?].
32 p. Mimeo.
"Dedicated to the memory of the two hundred and seven enlisted Negro
seamen who lost their lives at Port Chicago, California, on July 17, 1944,
at 10:19 p.m., and to the dark minority who are not yet civically, eco-
nomically, and spiritually free." Also appears in Poet lore, v. 53,
no. 4, 1947, pp. 310–47.

2689. BEECHER, JOHN, 1904– . In Egypt land. [Scottsdale, Ariz.] Rampart
press, 1960. 29 p. front. CU.
Beecher, a resident of California and Arizona for more than 20 years,
authors poetry frequently based upon Afro-American subjects. It has not
been possible to examine all of his numerous published works.

2690. _____. Land of the free; a portfolio of poems on the state of the
union, with block print decorations by Barbara Beecher. Oakland, Printed
by the Poet at the Morning star press, 1956. [23] ℓ. CLU.
"Edition limited to CCXXV copies ..."

2691. *BELL, JAMES MADISON, 1826–1902. A poem: delivered August 1st, 1862,
by J. Madison Bell at the grand festival to commemorate the emancipation
of the slaves in the District of Columbia and the emancipation of the
slaves in the British West Indian isles. S. F., B. F. Sterett, 1862.
10 p. CU-B, NUC, pre-1956.

2692. _____. A poem entitled the day and the war delivered January 1, 1864
at Platt's hall ... at the celebration of the first anniversary of
President Lincoln's emancipation proclamation. S. F., Agnew & Deffebach,
1864. 27 p. illus. C, CHi, CSmH, CU, NUC, pre-1956.
"Argument," by P. A. Bell: p. [4].
This pamphlet was published in advance of its Jan. 1 delivery, for
the pamphlet was advertised for sale in San Francisco book stores in the
San Francisco Pacific Appeal, Jan. 2, 1864, p. 3, col. 1.
CSmH holds author's inscribed copy to "Prof. C. L. Reason."

2693. _____. The poetical works of James Madison Bell ... Lansing, Mich.,
Press of Wynkoop, Hallenbeck, Crawford co. [c1901]. 208 p. ports. CHi,

Poetry and Proverbs

DHU, DLC.
"Biographical sketch of J. Madison Bell ... by Bishop B. W. Arnett":
pp. 3-14.

2694. _____. 2nd ed. [1904?, c1901]. 221 p. port.
Bell was a resident of San Francisco from 1859/60 until 1867. From
1862 to 1867, his poems appeared frequently in the San Francisco Pacific
Appeal and the San Francisco Elevator.

2695. _____. The progress of liberty, an anniversary poem delivered at the
celebration of the third anniversary of President Lincoln's emancipation
proclamation, January 1st, 1866. [S. F., 1866]. 28 p.
Notice of the publication at 50¢ per copy and a review appeared in
San Francisco Elevator, Jan. 19, 1866, p. 3, col. 4 and Feb. 2, p. 3,
col. 2.

2696. *BLACK, AUSTIN, 1928- . The tornado in my mouth; poems, by Austin
Black. N. Y., Exposition press [c1966]. 80 p. CSt.
A Los Angeles author.

2697. *BUCKNER, EVA (CARTER). Tulsa's song [and] If Lincoln could return
today ... [n.p., c1921]. 3 p. NUC, pre-1956.
Cover title.
Authored by a Los Angeles resident.

2698. *[BYER, ALDERMAN P.]. Conquest of Coomassie, an epic of the Mashanti
nation, by Aldebaran [pseud.]. With illus., by Henry M. Brooks. Long
Beach, Worth while pub. co. [c1923]. xxiv, 103 p. illus., port. NUC,
pre-1956.

2699. *CASEY, BERNIE. Look at the people [by] Bernie Casey. Illus. by the
author. Garden City, N. Y., Doubleday, 1969. 92 p. illus. CNoS.
Poems and paintings by a Los Angeles resident.

2700. *CONNER, NELLIE VICTORIA. Essence of good perfume, a book of poems.
Burbank, Ivan Deach, Jr., pub. [c1940]. xiii, 169 p. port.

2701. *CORDELL, PAUL. Lady nameless; poems. [Ijamsville, Md., The thorn,
n.d.]. [12] ℓ. CL, OrU, NUC, pre-1956.
Authored by a Los Angeles resident who has published in numerous
small literary magazines.

2702. *CORTEZ, JAYNE, 1937- . Pisstained stairs and the monkey man's wares.
[L. A., Phrase text, 1969]. [52] p. illus.

2703. *ECKELS, JON. Black right on. [S. F.] Julian Richardson associates
[c1969]. 44 p.

2704. _____. Home is where the soul is [by] Jon Eckels. Detroit, Broadside
press [c1969]. 25 p. port. CSt, CU.

2705. Etats-Unis: William Burroughs, Claude Pélieu, Bob Kaufman. Les
textes de William Burroughs et Bob Kaufman sont traduits par Mary Beach

Poetry and Proverbs

et Claude Pélieu. [Paris, Editions de l'Herne, c1967]. 306 p. illus., ports. Includes bibliographies. CSt, CU.

2706. *EVANS, BENNIE. Denim and lace and The rosary is the language of today. [L. A.?, 1950?]. 32 p.
   Contents: "Denim and lace" is poetry and prose, 11 p., and "The rosary is the language of today" is drama, 21 p.
   Title from Universal books catalog no. 164, item no. 303.

2707. *FABIO, SARAH (WEBSTER), 1928- . A mirror: a two-part volume of poems. Part I: a soul. Part II: a mirror. [S. F., Julian Richardson associates, c1969]. 29, 15 p.

2708. *GARDNER, BENJAMIN FRANKLIN, 1900- . Black. Caldwell, Idaho, Caxton printers [c1933]. 79 p. CNoS, CSmH.
   Poems, including one with a Utah locale.

2709. GILBERT, ZACK. "For Watts," in Black world, v. 15, Dec., 1965, p. 21.

2710. *GOODMAN, PAUL. "Red rocks, Denver mountain park," in Liberation, v. 5, July-Aug., 1960, p. 18.

2711. *GOODWIN, LEROY. Inside poems - but not jokes. L. A., Bean bag press, c1967. 18 p.

2712. GOODWIN, RUBY (BERKELEY), 1903- . From my kitchen window, the poems of Ruby Berkeley Goodwin. With an introduction by Margaret Widdemer ... N. Y., Wendell Malliet and co., 1942. 66 p. NN.
   Patron's edition numbered and signed by the author, a resident of Fullerton.

2713. _____. Same. [Fullerton, Printed by Orange country print. co.], 1946. 67 p. CL, CLCo, COrCL, CSmH.
   "2nd printing."

2714. _____. A gold star mother speaks ... Fullerton, Printed by Orange county print. co., 1944. [17] p. CSmH.

2715. *GREENE, EMILY JANE. In the green pastures, a book of poetry, by Emily J. Greene. L. A. [Printed by the Stockton trade press, Whittier, c1966]. 64 p.

2716. *GUILLEN, NICOLAS, 1902- . Cuba libre. Poems by Nicolas Guillen. Translated from the Spanish by Langston Hughes and Ben Frederic Carruthers. Illus. by Gar Gilbert. L. A., Ward Ritchie press, 1948. xi, 98 p. CU.

2717. *HARPER, MICHAEL S., 1938- . Dear John, Dear Coltrane; poems by Michael S. Harper. [Pittsburgh] Univ. of Pittsburgh press [c1970]. 88 p. CRic, CSf.
   The author is a member of the faculty, California state univ., Hayward.

Poetry and Proverbs

2718. *HARRISON, JERRY.   Coolhead. [S. F., c1968]. 53 p.

2719. *HOAGLAND, EVERETT.   Black velvet, by Everett Hoagland. [Pomona?, c1970]. [14] ℓ. illus.
"One half of the proceeds ... goes to the Black student union at the Claremont colleges."

2720. *JONES, EDWARD SMYTH, 1881- . The sylvan cabin. A centenary ode on the birth of Lincoln and other verse, by Edward Smyth Jones, with an introduction by William Stanley Braithwaite. Boston, Sherman, French and co., 1911. 96 p. CSmH.

2721. _____.   A centenary ode on the birth of Lincoln, with an introduction taken from the New York Times. [S. F.] Pub. by the author [Printed by Taylor & Taylor, c1915]. 17 p. illus., ports. CHi, CSmH.
"Panama-Pacific international exposition edition."

2722. _____.   Same. Chicago, Pub. by the Edward Smyth Jones pub. co., 1922. [9] ℓ. port. DHU.

2723. *KAUFMAN, BOB GARNELL, 1925- . Abomunist manifesto. [S. F., City lights books, c1959]. 1 fold. ℓ. (6 fold.). CLSU, CSf, NUC, 1942-62.

2724. _____. Golden sardine. [S. F.] City lights books [c1967]. 81 p. CLSU, CSf, CSt, CU.
"Edited by Mary Beach."
Mainly poetry.

2725. _____. Second April. [S. F., City lights books, c1959]. 1 fold. ℓ. (6 fold.). CLSU, CU, NUC, 1942-62.
Free verse.

2726. _____. Solitudes crowded with loneliness. [N. Y.] New directions [c1965]. 87 p. CFS, CL, CLCo, CLSU, CNoS, CPhCL, CRic, CSdS, CSjCL, CSt, CU.
Mainly poetry.

2727. _____. Solitudes. Textes choises et présentés par Claude Pélieu. Traduits de l'américan par M. G. Beach et Claude Pélieu. Telégramme-preface de Laurence Ferlinghetti. [Paris, Union générale d'éditions, 1966]. 104 p. CU.

2728. *LOVINGOOD, PENMAN.   Poems of a singer. Compton, The Lovingood co. [c1963]. 68 p. DHU.

2729. *MARKS, JIM.   Vibrations in sanctuary. [Palo Alto, Jamal pub. co., c1970]. 49 p. port. (cover).

2730. *MARVIN X.   Black man listen; poems and proverbs by Marvin X. Detroit, Broadside press [1970, c1969]. 28 p. CNoS.
Also available on tape.

Poetry and Proverbs

2731. _____. Fly to Allah; poems by Marvin X. Fresno, An Al Kitab Sudan pub., c1969. 24 p. port.

2732. _____. The son of man; proverbs by Marvin X. [Fresno, Pub. by Al Kitab Sudan, c1969]. 25 p. port. (cover).

2733. *MORELAND, JOHN· Only the pen was mine. [L. A., Lyric pub. co., c1966]. 25 p.

2734. *MURRELL, VIRGINIA. Burnt Icarus, by Virginia Murrell. Cover design by Maxine Kim Stussy. [Whittier, Stockton trade press, c1962]. 94 p.

2735. *NEAL, LARRY, 1937- . Black boogaloo (notes on black liberation). S. F., Journal of black poetry press, c1969. 59 p. Cover port.

2736. *PARKER, J. W. My heart's desire, by Rev. J. M. Parker, pastor of Mt. Canaan Baptist church, Oakland, California. [Oakland, 195-?]. 83 p. port (cover).

2737. *PEKTOR, IRENE MARI. Golden banners, by Irene Mari Pektor. Boston, Christopher pub. house [c1941]. ix, 211 p. DHU.

2738. _____. War - or peace? Poems by Irene Pektor. [Oceano] Harbison & Harbison [c1939]. 60 p. CLU, CSmH.

2739. *RAINS, OLLIE F. Original poems of nature and all walks of life. L. A., Privately printed, 1946. 40 p.
     Title from Universal books catalog no. 164, item no. 772.

2740. *RICKS, WILLIAM NAUNS, 1876- . The constitution. [Berkeley?] c1937.
     Broadside.

2741. _____. ... The whistle maker, and other poems, by William Nauns Ricks. [S. F., Press of Althof & Bahls, 1914]. 16 p. CSf, CSmH, CU.

2742. *SANCHEZ, SONIA, 1935- . Home coming; poems, by Sonia Sanchez. Introd. by Don L. Lee. Detroit, Broadside press [c1969]. 32 p. port. CNoS, CSt.
     By a staff member, Calif. state univ., San Francisco.

2743. _____. "Queens of the universe," in Black scholar, v. 1, Jan.-Feb., 1970, pp. 29-34.

2744. _____. We a baddddd people, by Sonia Sanchez. Introd. by Dudley Randall. Detroit, Broadside press [c1970]. 72 p. illus.

2745. *SEUELL, MALCHUS M., 1911- . The black Christ and verse by Malchus M. Seuell. [Downey, Printed by Elena Quinn, c1957]. 77 p. DHU.

2746. _____. The mad pagan and verse by Malchus M. Seuell. [Downey, Printed by Elena Quinn, c1959]. 72 p.

Poetry and Proverbs

2747. _____. Wild flower, by Malchus M. Seuell. [Detroit, Harlo press, c1965]. 30 p.

2748. *SHABAZZ, ZAKARIAH H. Portrait of a poet; poems by Zakariah H. Shabazz. [S. F., 1970, c1969]. 36 p.

2749. *[STROUD, WELVIN]. Poems by Dust. Illustrated by Metego [Sohan]. S. F., Julian Richardson associates, c1969. [12] ℓ. illus. CU-I.

2750. *THURMAN, HOWARD, 1899- . "Life seems unaware," in Black world, v. 10, July, 1961, p. 21.

2751. *TOURE', ASKIA MUHAMMAD ABU BAKR EL-. Juju (magic songs for the black nation) [by] Askia Muhammad Abu Bakr el-Toure' [and] Ben Caldwell. Chicago, Third world press [c1970]. 20 p. illus., port.
　　Contains poetry and an essay by Toure', formerly a staff member, Calif. state univ., San Francisco.

2752. *TURNER, ESTELLE (BEASLEY). Original works, by Estelle Beasley Turner. [Oakland, 1947]. 31 p. Mimeo. COEB.

2753. WEST, IRENE. The twain shall meet (a volume of race poems by an all white author), by Irene West. [L. A.?, 1943]. 52 p. COEB.

2754. *WHEATLEY, PHILLIS, 1753?-1784. Poems on various subjects, religious and moral. By Phillis Wheatley, of Boston, in New England. With memoirs, by W. A. Jackson. Denver, W. H. Lawrence & co., 1887. 149 p. port. CSmH.

2755. *WITHERS, ZACHARY. Poems after slavery ... S. F., Pacific coast appeal pub. co., 1905. 47 p.
　　See item no. 210, Catalogue no. 25 [Feb., 1965], Alta California book store, Berkeley. Purchased by Yale univ. library according to John Swingle, book store proprietor.

2756. *WYATT, FARICITA (HALL). The river must flow, by Faricita Wyatt. Berkeley, 1965. 25 p. CSfAA.
　　"Designed and printed by Lawton and Alfred Kennedy" in an edition of 500 copies.

2757. *YOUNG, AL, 1939- . Dancing; poems by Al Young. N. Y., Corinth books, 1969. 63 p. CSf.

MEDICINE AND HEALTH

2758. *BALDWIN, LOUIS FREMONT, 1863-1935. Food for the body, food for the mind and food for the soul. S. F. [191-?]. 88 p. illus., port. NUC, pre-1956.
　　Diet.

Medicine and Health

2759. _____. Food for the body, food for the mind and food for the soul.
Think right, eat right, do right, be right ... Comp. and pub. by Louis
Fremont Baldwin ... [S. F., 1924]. 88 p. port. DLC, NN, NUC, pre-1956.

2760. BRANSON, HELEN KITCHEN, 1916- . Let there be life; the contemporary
account of Edna L. Griffin, M. D. Pasadena, M. S. Sen [c1947]. 135 p.
port. CHi, CLM, CLU, NUC, pre-1956.
    This fictional account of Dr. Griffin's life was written by a
journalist who states in her preface that the true events "have been
altered only in so far as necessary to preserve the professional confi-
dence of the physicians involved."

2761. California. State board of medical examiners. Portraits and newspaper
clippings containing obituaries and other news stories of deceased
physicians, 1906-60. 18 cu. ft. Includes Afro-Americans. C-ArS.

2762. *COLLINS, DANIEL ANDREW, 1916- . Your teeth; a handbook of dental
care for the whole family [by] Daniel A. Collins. Illus. by Beresford
Weekes. Garden City, N. Y., Doubleday, 1967. xii, 224 p. illus. CSf,
WaT.
    Authored by a San Francisco dentist.

2763. *Daniel Williams hospital, Los Angeles. Articles of incorporation,
1921. [4] p. Typew. C-ArS.
    Directors: James Edward Porter, Frank A. Gordon, W. C. Gordon,
Charles S. Diggs, Claudius Ballard, Leonard Stovall, S. S. Turner,
Benjamin Arnett Jordan, and Eugene G. Johnson.

2764. *Dunbar hospital association of Los Angeles, California. Articles of
incorporation, 1923. 4 [1] p. Typew. C-ArS.
    Incorporated with capital stock of $50,000 held by its directors,
J. T. Whittaker, M. D., and R. S. Whittaker, M. D., Pasadena, and C. S.
Diggs, Los Angeles.

2765. GLASS, SUSAN. "Synanon - the integrated community," in Crisis, v. 72,
June-July, 1965, pp. 354-55.
    Activities of the organization to cure drug addiction, Santa Monica.

2766. *GOODLETT, CARLTON BENJAMIN, 1914- . "The role of the black physician," in Freedomways, v. 9, Fall, 1969, pp. 373-84.
    Portions of an address given before the National medical association
convention, San Francisco, 1969.

2767. *GRIER, WILLIAM HENRY, 1926- . Black rage, by William H. Grier and
Price M. Cobbs. Foreword by United States Senator Fred R. Harris. N. Y.,
Basic books [c1968]. viii, 213 p. Available in many libraries.
    Two San Francisco psychiatrists link racism with mental illness and
present a theory of psycho-therapy adapted specifically to the problems
of black people.

2768. HECHTER, H. H. "Longevity in racial groups differs," in California's
health, v. 22, Feb., 1965, pp. 121-22.

Medicine and Health

2769. HOLLINGER, WILLIAM H. Health of the Negro in San Francisco, California.
Master's thesis, Stanford univ., Stanford, 1948. 66 ℓ. diagrs., tables.

2770. MARRALLE, JAMES J. A case study of the patterns of influence and
action taken to obtain a hospital in southeast Los Angeles. Master's
thesis, Univ. of southern Calif., Los Angeles, 1966. 184 p.

2771. The medics. In memory of Che, the people's physician. [S. F., 1970].
27, iii p. illus. Mimeo.
A laymen's medical guide issued for use by the revolutionary movement.

2772. MONTESANO, PHILIP MICHAEL, 1941- . "The amazing Dr. Ezra Johnson,"
in Urban west, v. 1, Jan.-Feb., 1968, pp. 21-22.
Describes the career of Dr. Ezra Rothschild Johnson (1814?-1870),
New Bedford, Mass. and San Francisco businessman-physician.

2773. MORAIS, HERBERT MONTFORT, 1905-1970. The history of the Negro in
medicine, by Herbert M. Morais. N. Y., Publishers co. [c1967]. xiv,
317 p. illus., ports. (International library of Negro life and history,
v. 3). Bibliography: pp. 281-304. Available in many libraries.
Contains California and western materials throughout.

2774. *PEYTON, THOMAS ROY, 1897- . Quest for dignity; autobiography of a
Negro doctor. L. A., Warren Lewis [1950]. vii, 156 p. CGl, CHS, CHi,
CL, CLM, CLSU, CLU, CLU-C, CM1, CNoS, COrCL, CRiv, CSdS, CU-A, CVtCL,
Rocq 4305.

2775. _____. Same. L. A., Publishers western, 1963. 160 p. illus. CBaK.

2776. REED, T. EDWARD. "Research on blood groups and selection from the
child health and development studies, Oakland, California," in American
journal of human genetics, v. 19, Nov., 1967, pp. 732-46.

2777. REITZES, DIETRICH C. Negroes and medicine. Cambridge, Harvard univ.
press, 1958. xxxi, 400 p. CNoS, CU-I.
Includes chapter "The Pacific coast: Los Angeles, Calif."

2778. Rose-Netta hospital association, Los Angeles. Article of incorpora-
tion, 1942. 8 p. Typew. C-ArS.
Directors: Norris Curtiss King, Jeannette Mahoney, and Norma A.
Parks.

2779. *RUFFIN, OSOLEE (MINOR). "Jim-Crowing nurses," in Crisis, v. 37, Apr.,
1930, pp. 123 and 139-40.
Conditions at Highland hospital, Oakland.

2780. South central area welfare planning council, Los Angeles county.
Mental health survey on needs and facilities; report of the south central
area. [L. A.?] 1958. 1 v. (unpaged) tables. CU.

2781. *WASHINGTON, WILLIAM. Black contributions to health; biographical
sketches of blackmen [sic.] who have made outstanding contibutions [sic.]

Medicine and Health

in medicine and related fields. Compiled by William Washington, student, U. C., Berkeley [for] Ron Olson, health educator, San Francisco health department. [S. F.?, 1970]. [6] ℓ.

MISCEGENATION AND PASSING

2782. *BALDWIN, LOUIS FREMONT, 1863-1935. From Negro to Caucasian, or how the Ethiopian is changing his skin. A concise presentation of the manner in which many Negroes in America, who, being very fair in complexion ... have abandoned their one-time affiliation with Negroes, including their own relatives, and by mingling at first commercially or industrially, then socially with Caucasians, have ultimately been absorbed by the latter. S. F., Pilot pub. co. [c1929]. 65 p. illus., ports. CO, CSf, CSmH, NUC, pre-1956.
"Published at the request of the Society for the amalgamation of the races, New York, Paris, and London.

2783. BARNETT, LARRY D. "Interracial marriage in California," in Marriage and family living, v. 25, Nov., 1963, pp. 424-27.

2784. BURMA, JOHN HARMON, 1913- . "Interethnic marriage in Los Angeles, 1948-1959," in Social forces, v. 42, Dec., 1963, pp. 156-65.

2785. _____. "Research note on the measurement of interracial marriage," in American journal of sociology, v. 57, May, 1952, pp. 587-89.
Study made following the repeal of California's anti-miscegenation law.

2786. California. Legislature. Assembly. Twelfth session. Bill no. 51, "An act to prevent the amalgamation of different races of men in this state," 1861. Ms. [10] p. C-ArS.

2787. CONYERS, JAMES E. Selected aspects of phenomenon of Negro passing. Doctoral dissertation, Washington state univ., Pullman, 1962.
Includes attitudes of black and white college students toward passing.

2788. ERIKSSON, ELBERTA. A study of interracial marriage (black-white) in the bay area, Elberta Eriksson, Alan Mills and Barbara Phillips, joint authors. Master's thesis, Calif. state univ., Sacramento [196-?]. 156 ℓ. illus., charts, facsims.

2789. *EVERS, MYRLIE. "Why should my child marry yours?", in Ladies home journal, v. 85, Apr., 1968, pp. 80ff.

2790. FOX, THERON, ed. Mother lode race incident; letters between lodges of the I. O. O. F., regarding alleged misconduct on the part of a member. Edited and introduction by Theron Fox. San Jose [Harlan-Young press], 1966. 27 p. illus. (facsim.). CFS, CHi, CNoS, CSf, CSmH, CSto, CU-B.
"400 copies."
The charge of misconduct was lodged against a white lodge member due to his marriage with a Negro at Georgetown, El Dorado county.

Miscegenation and Passing

2791. HEER, DAVID M. "Negro-white marriage in the United States," in
Journal of marriage and the family, v. 28, Aug., 1966, pp. 262-73.
     Analyzes trends in California, Hawaii, Michigan, and Nebraska.

2792. *MILLER, JUANITA (ELLSWORTH),   -1971. "White Negroes," in Sociology
and social research, v. 12, May-June, 1928, pp. 449-54.
     "Case studies of people who at various times in their lives have
allowed people to believe that they were white." - Opportunity, Sept.,
1928. Authored by a student in the School of social welfare, Univ. of
Southern Calif.

2793. Oregon. Legislative assembly. House. [House bills. Fourth regular
session. Salem, State print., 1866]. 2 p. Or-Ar, OrU (photocopy),
Belknap 860.
     No. 1 [sic]. To prohibit amalgamation and the intermarriage of
races. Follows bill no. 1.

2794. PANUNZIO, CONSTANTINE MARIE. "Intermarriage in Los Angeles, 1924-33,"
in American journal of sociology, v. 47, Mar., 1942, pp. 690-701.
     The intermarriage of Mexicans, Japanese, Filipinos, Chinese, American
Indians, and Negroes.

2795. RILEY, L. H. "Miscegenation statutes: a re-evaluation of their constitutionality in light of changing social and political conditions," in
Southern California law review, v. 32, Fall, 1958, p. 28.

MUSIC AND DANCE

2796. ARVEY, VERNA. "Hall Johnson and his choir," in Opportunity, v. 19,
May, 1941, pp. 151 and 158-59.

2797. _____. "A Negro symphony orchestra," in Opportunity, v. 17, Sept.,
1939, pp. 267 and 286-87.

2798. _____. ... William Grant Still, by Verna Arvey, with an introduction
by John Tasker Howard. N. Y., J. Fischer & bro., 1939. 48 p. port.,
facsim. CLSU, CP, CSf, CU-B, OrP, OrU, WaS, NUC, pre-1956.

2799. BALLIETT, WHITNEY. "Jazz concerts; performance at Carnegie Hall," in
New Yorker, v. 44, May 25, 1968, p. 136ff.
     About Ray Charles.

2800. BOYKIN, CYNTHIA ANN. "Lou Rawls, a very heavy cat!", in Urban west,
v. 3, Dec., 1969, pp. 13-15.

2801. *CAYOU, DOLORES KIRTON. "The origins of modern jazz dance," in The
black scholar, v. 1, June, 1970, pp. 26-31.
     Authored by a Prof. of dance, San Francisco state college.

2802. *Cosmos social club of San Francisco. Twenty-seventh anniversary.
Presenting Roland Hayes, internationally known tenor; Lillian Block,

Music and Dance

lyric soprano. Joseph Foreman, Master of ceremonies. S. F., 1944.
Program. CSrCL.
   Club officers are listed.

2803. *DENNISTON, TIM   The American Negro and his amazing music, by Tim
   Denniston, Sr. N. Y., Vantage press [c1963]. 74 p. CNoS.
   Authored by a Los Angeles musician.

2804. EMBREE, EDWIN ROGERS, 1883-1949. 13 against the odds. N. Y., Viking,
   1946. 261 p. ports. CGl, CHS, CL, CLSU, CLobS, CPhD, CSaT, CSbS, CSf,
   CSluSP, CSmH, CSt, CStcrCL, CSto, CSuLas, CU, CU-A, CU-SB, CU-SC.
   Biography and portrait of William Grant Still, Los Angeles composer,
   pp. 196-210.

2805. _____. Same. Port Washington, N. Y., Kennikat press, 1968. CNoS,
   CSdS.

2806. EMERY, LEONORE LYNNE FANLEY, 1934- . Black dance in the United
   States, from 1619 to 1970. Doctoral dissertation, Univ. of southern
   Calif., Los Angeles, 1971. vii, 493 ℓ. CHS (photocopy).

2807. EWEN, DAVID, 1907-   , comp. American composers today, a biographical
   and critical guide. N. Y., H. W. Wilson co., 1949. 265 p. ports. NN.
   Contains a biographical account of   William Grant Still.

2808. FEATHER, LEONARD. The encyclopedia of jazz in the sixties, by Leonard
   Feather. Foreword by John Lewis. N. Y., Horizon press [c1966]. 312 p.
   ports. Bibliography: pp. [311]-12]. CSt.
   Essentially a biographical dictionary.

2809. _____. The new edition of the encyclopedia of jazz. Completely rev.,
   enl., and brought up to date. N. Y., Horizon press, 1960. 527 p. ports.
   Bibliography: pp. [524]-27. CSt.
   Essentially a biographical dictionary and includes "musicians' birth-
   places" arranged by state.

2810. *GORDON, TAYLOR, 1893- . Born to be, by Taylor Gordon; with an introduction by Muriel Draper, a foreword by Carl Van Vechten, and illustrations by [Miguel] Covarrubias. N. Y., Covici-Friede, 1929. xvi,
   236 p. col. front., plates. CLobS, CSmH, CSt, MtBC.
   Autobiography of Gordon, a White Sulphur Springs, Montana resident.

2811. HANSEN, BARRET EUGENE. Negro popular music, 1945-1953. Master's
   thesis, Univ. of Calif., Los Angeles, 1967. 169 ℓ.

2812. *HOWARD, JOSEPH H.   Drums in the Americas. N. Y., Oak publications
   [c1967]. xv, 319 p. illus., maps, music. Bibliography: pp. 294-311.
   CU.
   A major work by a foremost authority on drums, a Los Angeles resident.

2813. *JOHNSON, HALL, 1888- . The green pastures: spirituals; arranged
   for voice and piano by Hall Johnson. N. Y., Carl Fischer [c1930]. 40 p.
   CSf.

Music and Dance

2814. _____. Thirty Negro spirituals, arranged for voice and piano. N. Y.,
G. Schirmer [c1949]. 82 p. CRic.

2815. _____. Same. Zürich, Musikverlag zum Pelikan [1965] c1949. DLC.

2816. KING, CHARLES E. "Music," a lecture given Jan. 7, 1966 for "Perspectives on the Negro in our affluent society," a lecture series sponsored
by the Associated students of Palomar college, San Marcos. CSmarP (tape,
1200 feet).
    Sings several Negro spirituals and mentions related history and folk-
lore.

2817. LUKE, ORRAL STANFORD, 1903- . Differences in musical aptitude in
school children of different national and racial origin. Doctoral dissertation, Univ. of Calif., Berkeley, 1939. viii, 149 ℓ. tables, diagrs.

2818. MCADAMS, NETTIE FITZGERALD. Folk-songs of the American Negro - a
collection of unprinted texts preceded by a general survey of the traits
of Negro song, by Nettie F. McAdams. Master's thesis, Univ. of Calif.,
Berkeley, 1923. vi, 156 ℓ.

2819. *MATTHEWS, MIRIAM, 1905- . "Phylon profile, XXIII: William Grant
Still - composer," in Phylon, v. 12, Summer, 1951, pp. 106-12.

2820. MELLONS, CHARLES EDWARD. A study of the place of Negro music in the
integrated program. Master's thesis, Univ. of southern Calif., Los
Angeles, 1949. iv, 78 ℓ.

2821. *MILLSAP, RUBY JEANNE. Black ethos: source of dance. Master's
thesis, Univ. of Calif., Los Angeles, 1969.

2822. *National association of Negro musicians. [Souvenir program].
Annual convention. [L. A.?, 1967]. COEB, 44th (Los Angeles, 1967).

2823. OTIS, JOHNNY, 1921- . Listen to the lambs, by Johnny Otis. N. Y.,
W. W. Norton & co. [c1968]. 256 p. C, CNoS, CSbCL, CSf, CStb, CStmo.
    The autobiography of a Greek-American musician mainly centered in the
Watts area, Los Angeles, and in Berkeley.

2824. *Parade of youth at the piano. "The parade of youth at the piano" in
its 10th annual recital presents "Youth's musical highlights from a
decade of dreams at the opera house," War memorial opera house, San Francisco, California, Saturday, June 6, 1970 ... Patience Scales, director
... [S. F., 1970]. [35] p. illus., ports. CHi.
    Souvenir program.

2825. REISNER, ROBERT GEORGE. Bird; the legend of Charlie Parker, by
Robert George Reisner. N. Y., Bonanza books [c1962]. 256 p. illus.,
ports. Discography: pp. 241-56. CNoS, CSt.
    Eighty-one musicians and friends present recollections of Parker.
California and western experiences of Parker and others are related
throughout.

Music and Dance

2826. *SCHUYLER, PHILIPPA DUKE.   [Program, Los Angeles philharmonic auditorium, Apr. 18, 1948].   [12] p.   ports.   CSmH.

2827.   SHAW, ARNOLD.   The world of soul; black America's contribution to the pop music scene, by Arnold Shaw.   N. Y., Cowles book co., inc.   [c1970]. xiii, 306 p.   ports.   Discography: pp. 295-300.   CSf, CSt.
      Contains information about the recording industry in California as well as musicians there.

2828.   SIMPSON, RALPH RICARDO.   William Grant Still -- The man and his music. Doctoral dissertation, Michigan state univ., Lansing, 1964.   [2] 331 ℓ. illus.

2829.   SLATTERY, PAUL HAROLD.   A comparative study of the first and fourth symphonies of William Grant Still.   Master's thesis, San Jose state univ., San Jose, 1969.   12, xii, 147 p.   tables.

2830. *STILL, WILLIAM GRANT, 1895- .   Africa.   L. A., c1935.   Score, 58 p., and 60 pts.   CLU.

2831.   _____.   And they lynched him on a tree, for double mixed chorus and contralto solo, narrator and orchestra (or piano).   Poem by Katherine Garrison Chapin, music by William Grant Still.   N. Y., J. Fischer & bro. [1941].   46 p.   NN.

2832.   _____.   Bells.   L. A., Delkas music pub. co.   [1944].   Minature [sic] score, 21 p.   CLU.
      "Reproduced from manuscript copy."

2833.   _____.   Bells; two pieces for piano.   L. A., Delkas music pub. co., c1944.   2 v. in 1.   CLU.

2834.   _____.   Collection of programs, press releases, articles, etc., 1953-65.   CU-B.
      30 items.   Gift of Mrs. Still, 1965-69.

2835.   _____.   Danzas de Panama; based on Panamanian folk themes collected by Elisabeth Waldo ... for string orchestra.   N. Y., Southern music pub. co. [c1953].   Score, 32 p., and 12 pts.   CLU.

2836.   _____.   Dismal swamp, by William Grant Still.   The new music society of California, 1937.   CLU (score lacking and parts reproduced from masters in the Library's collection; some parts in manuscript), CSf (manuscript copy of parts by Works progress administration).
      Full orchestra score.

2837.   _____.   Fifty years of progress in music ... [Pittsburgh, Pittsburgh courier, 1950].   7 p.   ports.   NN.

2838.   _____.   "For finer Negro music," in Opportunity, v. 17, May, 1939, p. 137.

Music and Dance

2839. _____. From the Black belt; seven pieces for chamber orchestra ... [n.p., n.d.]. Score and 45 pts. CLU (score lacking and parts reproduced from masters in the Library's collection; some parts in manuscript).

2840. _____. In memoriam. The colored soldiers who died for democracy. L. A., Delkas [c1943]. Score, 16 p. Reproduced from manuscript copy. CLU, CSf.
    For orchestra.

2841. _____. Lenox ave., choreographic street scenes. Scenario by Verna Arvey ... N. Y., J. Fischer, c1938. Score, 41 p. CLU.
    "Lenox avenue, originally commissioned by the Columbia broadcasting system, was first presented over the radio on May 23, 1937 ... Later, transformed into a ballet, it received its first presentation by the Dance theatre group of Los Angeles on May 1, 1938, with choreography by Norma Gould."

2842. _____. "The men behind American music," in Crisis, v. 51, Jan., 1944, pp. 12-15 and 29.

2843. _____. Miniatures for flute, oboe, and piano. London, Oxford univ. press, Music dep't. [1963]. Score, 19 p., and 2 pts. CSf.

2844. _____. "The Negro musician in America," in Music educators journal, v. 56, Jan., 1970, pp. 100-01, 157-61.

2845. _____. ... Poem for orchestra. L. A., Delkas music pub. co. [1945]. Score, 40 p. CLU (reproduced from manuscript copy).

2846. _____. Seven traceries for piano. N. Y., J. Fischer, 1940. CP (also in Ms.).

2847. _____. Songs of separation. Voices and piano. N. Y., Leeds, c1949. 12 p. CLU.

2848. _____. ... Suite for violin and piano. L. A., Delkas music pub. co. [1945]. 28 p. CLU.
    "Violin part edited by Louis Kaufman."

2849. _____. Three visions for piano solo. N. Y., J. Fischer, c1936. CP.

2850. _____. Troubled island; an opera in three acts, by William Grant Still. Libretto by Langston Hughes. [193-?]. Ms. 247 p. DLC.

2851. _____. Same. N. Y., Leeds music corp., c1949. 38 p. CLU, CU-A.

2852. _____. Twelve Negro spirituals [arranged] by William Grant Still. Illustrated by Albert Barbelle ... [N. Y.] Handy bros. music co. [c1937-1948]. v. illus., ports. CP.
    Vol. 1 contains With stories of Negro life, by Ruby (Berkley) Goodwin.

2853. _____. The voice of the Lord, Psalm XXIX. Four part mixed voices with tenor solo, S. A. T. B. N. Y., M. Witmark, c1946. 10 p. CLU.
    With organ accompaniment.

Music and Dance

2854. TAMONY, PETER. Jazz: the word, and its extension to music ... S. F.,
1968. 20 p. Bibliographical notes: pp. 15-20. Mimeo.
A discussion of the origin of the word and of its relationship to
music and musicians.

2855. *THOMPSON, LEON EVERETTE. A historical and stylistic analysis of the
music of William Grant Still and a thematic catalog of his works. Doctoral dissertation, Univ. of southern Calif., Los Angeles, 1966. iv,
177 ℓ.

2856. *THURMAN, HOWARD, 1899- . Deep river; reflections on the religious
insight of certain of the Negro spirituals. Illus. by Elizabeth Orton
Jones. N. Y., Harper [1951]. 93 p. illus.

2857. _____. Same. N. Y., Kennikat press, 1955. CF, CFa, CHCL, CL, CLCo,
CLob, CMerCL, CMl, COrCL, CQCL, CRcS, CRedCL, CRic, CSluCL, CSto, CSuLas,
CYcCL.

2858. _____. Same. Rev. ed. N. Y., Harper, 1955. CNoS.

2859. _____. Same. N. Y., Kennikat press, 1969. CHS, CSt, WaT.

2860. _____. The Negro spiritual speaks of life and death; being the
Ingersoll lecture on the immortality of man, 1947 ... N. Y., Harper
[c1947]. 55 p. CCotS, CHS, CHi, CL, CLCo, CLob, CMerCL, CNoS, CSjCL,
CSt, CSuLas, CU, CU-A.
"This Ingersoll lecture is to appear in a forthcoming issue of the
Harvard Divinity School Bulletin."

2861. TILTON, CRYSTAL LEE. The Negro spiritual: its background, characteristics and function in black America. Master's thesis, Calif. state
univ., Sacramento, 1969. 144 ℓ.

2862. TOCUS, CLARENCE SPENCER. The Negro idiom in American musical composition. Master's thesis, Univ. of southern Calif., Los Angeles, 1941. vi,
143 ℓ.

2863. WONG, HERB. "Monterey festival, the jazz groove," in Urban west,
v. 2, Oct., 1968, pp. 9-10.

2864. *Woodmen minstrels   Program. [Ingelwood, 1910?]. 16 p.
Title from Universal books catalog no. 152.

2865. *YOUNG, A. S. "DOC"   The incomparable Nat King Cole; his career, his
life, his legacy. [Edited by A. S. "Doc" Young]. Collector's ed.
[Fort Worth, Tex., Sepia pub. co., c1965]. 82 p. illus., ports. NN.

POLITICS, GOVERNMENT, AND SUFFRAGE

2866. AIKEN, CHARLES J., 1901-   , ed. The Negro votes. S. F., Chandler
pub. co. [1962]. 377 p. illus. Bibliography: pp. 374-77. CEcaC, CFS,

Politics, Government, and Suffrage

CHS, CSdS, CSf, CSjCi, CS1uSP, CSt, CU, CU-A.
A study of national Negro politics and suffrage through non-western case studies, by a professor of political science, Univ. of Calif., Berkeley.

2867. BATCHELLER, HELEN M. Study of reconstruction in Mississippi and South Carolina as it touches the question of suffrage. Master's thesis, Univ. of southern Calif., Los Angeles, 1917. 94, x p.

2868. BREESE, DONALD HUBERT, 1928- . Politics in the lower South during presidential reconstruction. Doctoral dissertation, Univ. of Calif., Los Angeles, 1964. 433 ℓ.

2869. BUCKLEY, WILLIAM F. "Up from Watts," in National review, v. 21, Jan. 17, 1969, pp. 610-11.
The Bradley-Yorty mayoral campaign.

2870. California. Legislature. Sixteenth session. [Petition, San Francisco, Dec. 1, 1865, to the Senate and the Assembly from a committee of the California convention of colored citizens requesting the right of suffrage]. Ms. [1] p. CLM.
Signed by Frederick G. Barbadoes, Pres., Philip A. Bell, Sec'y., R. A. Hall, William H. Yates, Edward P. Duplex, James R. Starkey, and David W. Ruggles.

2871. *CAYTON, HORACE ROSCOE, comp. Cayton's campaign compendium of Washington, 1908. Seattle, Author [1908?]. 96 p. WaPS, WaU, NUC, pre-1956.
Contains a directory of government officials, including members of the legislature, of Washington through 1907.

2872. _____. Cayton's legislative manual, the ninth legislature of Washington, 1905. Seattle, Seattle republican, 1905. 56 p. illus., ports., tables. Wa, WaU, NUC, pre-1956.

2873. CLARK, JOSEPH EDWARD. The American critique of the democratic idea, 1919-1929. Doctoral dissertation, Stanford univ., Stanford, 1958. xi, 567 ℓ.
"Treats the critical reflection on the democratic faith found in nonfiction books, periodicals and the New York Times." - West, p. 93.

2874. COLLINS, MARY L. "Bakersfield makes history," in Crisis, v. 60, June-July, 1953, pp. 344-45.
Election of the Rev. H. H. Collins as City councilman.

2875. Colored political and social club of Los Angeles, California.*
Articles of incorporation, 1932. 5 p. Typew. C-ArS.
Organized in the Third supervisorial district of the city to stimulate the political and social interests of youth and to operate an employment service. Directors: Richard B. Whaley, Alfred W. Graham, W. A. Lightfoot, James E. Baylor, D. T. Mitchell, Ross Dean, Sidney Rowe, and J. C. McCoy.

Politics, Government, and Suffrage

2876. Communist party of the United States of America. California. State
educational commission. Guide for reporters on the National committee
resolution dealing with the Negro question. S. F., 1947. [4] ℓ. Mimeo.
CU-B.

2877. _____. _____. _____. Outline on fundamentals of Marxism for class
use or self study ... S. F. [194-?]. 35 ℓ. CU-B.
"Lesson VI - The Negro question": ℓ. 21a-23a.

2878. _____. _____. _____. State youth commission. New aspects of youth
work and organization. S. F., 1949. 7 p. Mimeo. CU-B.
Emphasizes need for black membership.

2879. DAKAN, ARTHUR WILLIAM. Electoral and population geography of south
central Los Angeles, 1932-1966. Master's thesis, Univ. of Calif.,
Los Angeles, 1970.

2880. Democratic state central committee. From the San Francisco daily
examiner, Aug. '69. Shall Negroes and Chinamen vote in California?
Read! An address by the Democratic state central committee to the
voters of California. [S. F.?, 1968]. 4 p. CHi.

2881. DVORIN, EUGENE P., ed. California politics and policies; original
essays [by] Richard Harvey [and others]. Edited by Eugene P. Dvorin and
Arthur J. Misner. Reading, Mass., Addison-Wesley pub. co. [1966].
419 p. illus. CU.
Includes bibliographies.
An essay entitled "Politics and policies of the Negro community," by
Herman T. Smith, relates to Los Angeles.

2882. DYER, BRAINERD. "One hundred years of Negro suffrage," in Pacific
historical review, v. 37, Feb., 1968, pp. 1-20.
The author's presidential address to the Pacific coast branch of the
American historical association.

2883. *DYMALLY, MERVYN MALCOLM, 1926- . Papers. CLS (Consult Library
bibliographer for use of this material).

2884. East Palo Alto. History and experience of the municipal council; a
brief history. East Palo Alto, 1968. 2 p. CMp.

2885. "Fallen Angels," in New republic, v. 160, June 9, 1969, p. 7.
Thomas Bradley's Los Angeles mayoralty campaign.

2886. GANT, CHARLES G. California Democratic council papers. 10 boxes, ca.
1960-67. CLU.
Contains 1 box (8 folders) of Negro political action association of
California materials, 1960-66.

2887. GERARD, MAURICE (pseud.). "The West coast Negro voter," in Crisis,
v. 59, Oct., 1952, pp. 497-99 and 542.

Politics, Government, and Suffrage

2888. GERMOND, JACK W. "L. A.'s about to say 'So long, Sam'!" in New
republic, v. 160, May 24, 1969, p. 10.
The mayoralty campaign of Sam Yorty and Tom Bradley.

2889. GREENE, BILL. "Stand up and be counted," in Black politician, v. 1,
Jan., 1970, pp. 28-29.
The impact of the 1970 census on the black electorate.

2889a. *GREENE, DAVID MYRON, 1936- , comp. [Material relating to the cam-
paign of Thomas Bradley for mayor of Los Angeles, 1968-1969]. Portfolio.
CU-B.
Contains speakers' manual, press releases, handbills, and clippings.

2890. HALPERIN, BERNARD SEYMOUR. Andrew Johnson, the radicals, and the
Negro, 1865-1866. Doctoral dissertation, Univ. of Calif., Berkeley,
1966. ii, 225 l.

2891. *HENDERSON, JOSEPH WHITE. The colored man and the ballot, by Joseph
White Henderson ... [Oakland] Henderson and Humphrey, proprietors,
1888. 57 p. port. (cover). DLC, NN.

2892. *HENDERSON, LENNEAL J. "Engineers of black liberation," in Black
politician, v. 1, Apr., 1970, pp. 12-16.
A study of doctoral candidates in political science by a candidate
at the Univ. of Calif., Berkeley.

2893. HEYMAN, IRA MICHAELS. "Federal remedies for voteless Negroes," in
California law review, v. 48, May, 1960, pp. 190-215.

2894. HILL, DANIEL GRAFTON. "The Negro as a political and social issue in
the Oregon country," in Journal of Negro history, v. 33, Apr., 1948,
pp. 130-45.

2895. HOBART, SUSAN GAIL. The political alienation of the urban Negro.
Master's thesis, Calif. state univ., San Francisco, 1969. 163 l.
"A study of the urban Negro's psychological proximity to the political
system. Includes a discussion of the probable effects of political
alienation which the author feels will lead to violence and revolutionary
activity."

2896. HOBBS, THADEAUS HENRY. The dynamics of Negroes in politics in the
Los Angeles metropolitan area: 1945-1956. Master's thesis, Univ. of
southern Calif., Los Angeles, 1960. vii, 189 l. illus., maps.

2897. HOUSTON, SYLVESTER R. Reapportionment in the California legislature;
effect on ethnic representation. Master's thesis, Calif. state univ.,
Sacramento, 1969. 102 l.

2898. *Independent voters. Negro representation now! [L. A., 1956?].
[20] p. illus., ports. CHi.
Strongly advocates political representation.

Politics, Government, and Suffrage

2899. *JACKSON, IDA LOUISE, 1902- . "National non-partisan council on public affairs," in Opportunity, v. 20, Nov., 1942, pp. 327-29.
    A description of the founding and activities of the Non-partisan council on public affairs, Washington, D. C., by a pioneer Oakland educator.

2900. KERBY, PHIL. "Race, television and Yorty," in Nation, v. 208, Mar. 31, 1969, pp. 403-05.
    The Bradley-Yorty campaign.

2901. _____. "Victory for a specter," in Nation, v. 208, June 16, 1969, pp. 749-50.
    The defeat of Thomas Bradley by Los Angeles mayor, Sam Yorty.

2902. KOPKIND, ANDREW. "Poverty politics in California," in New republic, v. 156, Feb. 18, 1967, pp. 19-20.

2902a. League of women voters of California. Mss. 24 boxes and 1 package. CHi.
    Minutes, correspondence, and printed materials, 1911-55. Contains some information, 1923-32, about the activities of the San Francisco colored league of women voters, the Alameda county colored league of women voters, and chapters at Bakersfield, Fresno, and Los Angeles; attempts to secure training for black nurses at Highland hospital, Oakland; and the Alameda county work of Mrs. Hettie B. Tilghman and Delilah L. Beasley.

2902b. League of women voters of San Francisco. Mss. 19 boxes and 18 v. CHi.
    Records, including minutes, correspondence, annual reports, and scrapbooks, 1911-63. Contains some information about the San Francisco colored league of women voters and its representatives, Mrs. Gregory Hobson and Mrs. Margaret J. Mabson, 1924.

2903. LEVENSON, ROSALINE. The Negro vote in California in 1952. Master's thesis, Univ. of Calif., Berkeley, 1953. viii, 197 ℓ. diagrs., tables.

2904. MARSHALL, DALE ROBERTS, 1937- . The politics of participation in poverty: a case study of the Board of economic and youth opportunities agency of greater Los Angeles. Doctoral dissertation, Univ. of Calif., Los Angeles, 1969. xii, 406 ℓ.

2905. *MATTHEWS, WILLIAM C. "The Negro bloc," in Opportunity, v. 5, Feb., 1927, pp. 49-50.
    A review of electoral successes and defeats in 1926 by a Special assistant to the U. S. attorney general, San Francisco.

2906. METCALF, ALLEN C. "A Negro congressman from Los Angeles?", in Frontier, v. 9, Apr., 1958, pp. 7-11.
    The possibility of electing a congressman by redrawing election district boundaries.

Politics, Government, and Suffrage

2907. *MILLER, ELVENA. "Making democracy work," in Crisis, v. 44, Sept., 1937, pp. 276 and 285.
    Describes a series of four Seattle lectures by William Pickens under the sponsorship of the U. S. commissioner of education.

2908. *MILLER, LOREN R., 1903-1967. "The Negro voter in the far West," in Journal of Negro education, v. 26, Summer, 1957, pp. 262-72.

2909. _____. A Negro votes. Berkeley, Pacific tape library A2420, 1959. [Phonotape]. Duration: 30 min. CSS.
    An interview on black voting philosophy especially in the Los Angeles area. Conducted by Gene Marine.

2910. _____. "One way out - Communism," in Opportunity, v. 12, July, 1934, pp. 214-17.

2911. *MORTON, THEOPHILUS B., 1849-1907. Vindication of Hon. M. M. Estee. Address delivered by T. B. Morton, president of the Afro-American league of San Francisco at its regular monthly meeting, Monday, July 2, 1894. [S. F., Valleau & Oliver, 1894]. 11 p. C, CHi.
    Advocates the election of Morris M. Estee as Republican California governor.

2912. *NATIS, FELIX. [Political announcement as candidate for Palo Alto city council, 1947]. Broadside. CPa.

2913. "The Negro as voter and officeholder, in the South, North, and West," in Journal of Negro education, v. 32, Fall, 1963, pp. 415-25.

2914. Negro non-partisan league of California. Articles of incorporation, Alameda county, 1943. 4 p. Typew. C-ArS.
    "For the purpose of improving the political, economic and social status of loyal American Negro citizens." Directors were Theodore S. Young, Daniel L. Ferneil, and John W. Oliver, Berkeley, and Thomas B. Scott and Jesse W. Ford, Oakland.

2915. Negro regular Republican club of Pasadena. Articles of incorporation, 1940. 4 p. Typew. C-ArS.
    Directors were: J. W. Coleman, Adams J. Fuller, Mrs. Pearl Fairfax, Mrs. Birdie Canado, Albert Gillem, Mrs. Mary Gillem, Herbert Mackey, Ethel Atwood, Eugene L. Flewellyn, Gertrude Wiggins, William Gilchrist, Ruby D. Langston, and David R. Clark.

2916. Negro tax payers and voters association of Pasadena. Articles of incorporation, 1914. 2 p. Typew. C-ArS.
    Purposes "are the defending, prosecuting, ascerting and perpetuating of the rights and privileges of the members ..." Directors were Abel H. Evans, J. C. C. Jaxon, Mollie C. H. Moore, William Solomon, and Maggie Perrie.

2917. Negro young Republican club of San Francisco county. Articles of incorporation, 1948. [4] p. Typew. C-ArS.

Politics, Government, and Suffrage

A political organization "to formulate and influence liberal Republican policies ..." Directors were: Estella Raye, Frank Logan, Oscar J. Hicks, George Willis, and B. B. Brown.

2918. *NYERERE, JULIUS K. Communitarian socialism. [S. F., Success print., 196-?]. [8] p. port.

2919. Oakland. Elections. 1933. Verified statement of candidates for office at the nominating municipal election to be held on Tuesday, April 18, 1933. [Oakland] 1933. [4] p. ports. CO.
Includes statement of Mamie L. Reed, candidate for school director.

2920. _____. _____. 1937. Verified statements of candidates for office at the nominating municipal election to be held on Tuesday, April 20, 1937. [Oakland] 1937. [2] p. ports. CO.
Includes statement of William M. Wilkerson, candidate for councilman.

2921. _____. _____. 1951. Verified statements of candidates for office at the nominating municipal election to be held on Tuesday, April 17, 1951. [Oakland] 1951. 4 p. ports. CO.
Includes statements of Warren L. Broussard, James Wilty, and James Jones, candidates for councilman.

2922. _____. _____. 1955. Verified statements of candidates for office at the nominating municipal election to be held on Tuesday, April 14, 1955. [Oakland] 1955. [2] p. ports. CO.
Includes statement of L. S. Odom, candidate for school director.

2923. _____. _____. 1959. Verified statements of candidates for office at the nominating municipal election to be held on Tuesday, April 21, 1959. [Oakland] 1959. 31 p. CO.
Includes statements of E. O. Lee and Thomas L. Berkley.

2924. _____. _____. 1963. Verified statements of candidates for office at the nominating municipal elections to be held on Tuesday, April 16, 1963. [Oakland] 1963. 22 p. ports. CO.
Includes statement of Atkin G. Brown.

2925. _____. _____. 1967. Verified statements of candidates for office at the nominating municipal election to be held on Tuesday, April 18, 1967. [Oakland] 1967. [24] p. ports. CO.
Includes statements of Curtis Lee Baker, Edwin D. Baker, Sr., Ralph S. Williams, Sr., and Elijah Turner.

2926. _____. _____. 1969. Verified statements of candidates for office at the nominating municipal election to be held on Tuesday, April 15, 1969. [Oakland] 1969. 14 p. ports. CO.
Includes statements of Lawrence Joyner, Charles Goody, and Electra K. Price.

2927. PATTERSON, BEEMAN COOLIDGE, 1929- . "Political action of Negroes in Los Angeles: a case study in the attainment of councilmanic representation," in Phylon, v. 30, Summer, 1969, pp. 170-83.

Politics, Government, and Suffrage

2928. _____. The politics of recognition: Negro politics in Los Angeles, 1960–1963. Doctoral dissertation, Univ. of Calif., Los Angeles, 1967. 263 ℓ. C (photocopy), CHS (photocopy), CNoS (photocopy).

2929. "Personality counts," in Economist, v. 229, Oct. 26, 1968, pp. 50, 52. Concerns Arthur Fletcher, City councilman in Pasco, Wash.

2930. PHELAN, JAMES DUVAL, 1861–1930. Correspondence and papers of a U. S. senator and San Francisco mayor, ca. 1880–1930. 131 boxes, 29 cartons, 103 volumes. CU-B. Contains occasional letters from black people regarding Democratic party politics.

2931. RANKIN, JERRY. "Reapportionment in California; more democracy and better government," in Frontier, v. 17, Dec., 1965, pp. 5–7. Contains information on Mervyn M. Dymally and William Byron Rumford.

2932. RECORD, WILSON, 1916– . The Communist party and the Negro question in the United States: a study in red and black. Master's thesis, Univ. of Calif., Berkeley, 1949. 381 ℓ.

2933. _____. The Negro and the Communist party. Chapel Hill, Univ. of North Carolina press [1951]. x, 340 p. Bibliographical references included in "Notes": pp. 317–31. CFS, CLSU, CNoS, CSaT, CSbS, CSdS, CS1uSP, CSt, CU.

2934. *RILEY, GEORGE P., 1833– . Mr. Geo. P. Riley, the eloquent colored speaker, will speak at Philharmonic hall ... April 26th, 1870. Subject-- "The colored citizen and the ballot." ... [Portland, Ore.] Geo. H. Himes, printer [1870]. Broadside. OrHi.

 Belknap 1453. In 1865, Riley was residing at New Westminster, B. C., while in 1890 he was reported at Tacoma. San Francisco Pacific appeal, June 24, 1865, p. 4, col. 4, and San Francisco Elevator, Oct. 11, 1890, p. 2, col. 3.

2935. ROBERTS, MYRON. "If it's Bradley ..." in Los Angeles, v. 14, May, 1969, pp. 26–29ff. What to expect if Thomas Bradley becomes mayor of Los Angeles.

2936. _____. "The plot to seize Los Angeles," in Los Angeles, v. 14, Jan., 1969, pp. 24–26ff. Thomas Bradley's campaign for mayor of Los Angeles.

2937. _____. "Summertime: will the livin' be easy?", in Los Angeles, v. 13, June, 1968, pp. 24–26. Thomas Bradley, William Greene, and the Los Angeles community.

2938. *RUMFORD, WILLIAM BYRON Interview of Berkeley resident in process 1971 under the auspices of the Univ. of Calif. Oral history program, Berkeley.

Politics, Government, and Suffrage

2939. RUSCO, ELMER R. Voting patterns of racial minorities in Nevada. Reno, Bureau of governmental research, Univ. of Nev., 1966. 49 p.

2940. *RYAN, JOHN HENRY, 1866- . Ryan's legislative manual, tenth session, 1907, state of Washington, historical, statistical, biographical and illustrative. J. H. Ryan, compiler ... [Tacoma] Author [c1907]. [68] p. illus., ports. DLC.
    Two other editions were published prior to 1915. Crisis, Feb., 1915, pp. 170-71.

2941. San Francisco. Elections. 1963. Declarations of candidacy including statements of qualifications of candidates ... at [the] general municipal election to be held November 5, 1963. [S. F.] 1963. 64 p. CSf.
    Includes statements of Samuel Jordan, candidate for mayor, p. 5, and Percy Moore, candidate for supervisor, p. 21.

2942. _____. _____. 1967. Declarations of candidacy including statements of qualifications of candidates ... at [the] general municipal election to be held November 7, 1967. [S. F.] 1967. 136 p. CSf.
    Includes statements of Terry A. Francois, candidate for supervisor, p. 43, and David Johnson, candidate for sheriff, p. 70.

2943. SEARS, DAVID O. "Black attitudes toward the political system in the aftermath of the Watts insurrection," in Midwest journal of political science, v. 13, Nov., 1969, pp. 515-44.

2944. SEMLER, MICHAEL HERMAN ALFRED. The failure of American pluralism: the black man in a white man's system. Master's thesis, Calif. state univ., San Francisco, 1969. 203 ℓ.
    "The study demonstrates that the Negro's ability to gain valuable resources in the society has been severely hampered by the political system itself. The author concludes that violence may be necessary for the lower status individual to bring about change in his behalf."

2945. SKOLNICK, JEROME H., 1931- . The politics of protest [by] Jerome H. Skolnick. Foreword by Price M. Cobbs and William H. Grier. N. Y., Ballantine books [c1969]. xxvii, 419 p. CNoS, CSf.
    Authored by a Univ. of Calif. professor. Discusses black militancy, white racial attitudes, judicial and police power, and anti-war and student protest.

2946. *SMITH, FORAKER. "Apolitical past and political future," in Black politician, v. 1, Apr., 1970, pp. 25-28.
    Authored by a consultant to the California state Senate Democratic caucus.

2947. TOBIAS, HENRY JACK, ed. Minorities and politics. Ed. by Henry J. Tobias and Charles E. Woodhouse. Albuquerque, Univ. of New Mexico press [c1969]. 131 p. CNoS.
    Contains "Between the tracks and the freeway: the Negro in Albuquerque," by Roger W. Banks, pp. 113-31.

Politics, Government, and Suffrage

2948. "The unsinkable Willie Brown," in Urban west, v. 2, Oct., 1968, p. 25.
An account of a California state assemblyman from San Francisco.

2949. Washington. University. A survey of racial attitudes in the Broadview
district. Seattle, 1948. Wa.

2950. *WAYMON, CARROL W. "The black politician: perceived and perceiving,"
in Black politician, v. 1, Jan., 1970, pp. 14-16.
A San Diego resident writes of the new black politician.

2951. *WHEELDIN, DONALD. "Speaking out: the blacks and Nixon," in Black
politician, v. 1, Apr., 1970, pp. 29-31.
By a teacher at California state univ., Fresno.

2952. WILLIAMS, ARTHUR JOSEPH. Political theory and the American Negro.
Master's thesis, Univ. of Calif., Berkeley, 1931. 83 ℓ.

2953. WILSON, JOYCE R. "Yvonne Brathwaite," in Urban west, v. 2, Dec., 1968,
pp. 11, 26-27.
An account of a member of the California state assembly from Baldwin
Hills.

2954. YOUNG, RICHARD. "The impact of protest leadership on Negro politicians
in San Francisco," in The western political quarterly, v. 22, Mar., 1969,
pp. 94-110.

2955. Young socialist alliance. Oakland-Berkeley local. For independent
political action in 1964. Berkeley, [1964]. 7 p. CU-B.
Aimed at securing Negro rights through political activism.

RACE RELATIONS, DISCRIMINATION, AND PREJUDICE

2956. ADAMS, BEN. Hawaii, the Aloha state; our island democracy in text and
pictures. N. Y., Hill and Wang [c1959]. 213 p. illus. NN.

2957. ADLER, PATRICIA. Paradise west: a study of Negro attitudes toward
the city of Los Angeles. Term paper, Univ. of southern Calif., 1969.
55 [6] p. Typew.

2958. "America as a racist culture": speeches given at the University of
California, Irvine, September 26, 1968. Tape (180 minutes). CU-I.
Includes "Racism in America," by John Corman; "Racism and the black
American," by Eldridge Cleaver; "Racism and Latin America," by Father
Bonpane; and "Racism and Vietnam," by Robert Scheer.

2959. American council on race relations. Intergroup relations in San
Diego; some aspects of community life in San Diego which particularly
affect minority groups, with recommendations for a program of community
action. Prepared at the joint request of the mayor, the City council,
the superintendent of schools and the Board of education of San Diego,
by Laurence I. Hewes, Jr., regional director, with the assistance of

Race Relations, Discrimination, and Prejudice

William Y. Bell, Jr. S. F., [1946]. 35 p. Bibliographical footnotes. C, CNoS, CSd, CSdS, CU, NUC, pre-1956.

2960. *AMODA, JOHN MOYIBI. Discrimination as alienation: a re-evaluation and re-interpretation of the theories of prejudice in the context of the racial problem of blacks in white America. Doctoral dissertation, Univ. of Calif., Berkeley, 1969. xix, 620 ℓ.

2961. *ANDERSON, MYRTLE BERNICE, 1897- . A plea for justice; address of Myrtle Bernice Anderson before the senior class of the Los Angeles high school. Rev. and pub. by John A. H. Eldridge ... [L. A., c1917]. 16 p. port. CSmH.
    Republished from the Chicago Defender, Jan. 20, 1917.
    Address of a high school student in answer to another student's speech attacking her race.

2962. ARVEY, VERNA. "Tolerance," in Opportunity, v. 18, Aug., 1944, p. 244.
    An essay on anti-Jewish and anti-Negro propaganda by a Los Angeles author.

2963. *ATKINS, JAMES A., 1890-1968. Human relations in Colorado; a historical record. Denver, Colorado dept. of education, 1968. 272 p. CSdS.

2964. BARUCH, DOROTHY (WALTER), 1899- . ... Glass house of prejudice. N. Y., W. Morrow and co., 1946. ix, 205 p. illus., diagr. "References and supplementary materials": pp. [185]-205. CNoS.
    Race problems in Los Angeles.

2965. BATTY, JOSEPH. Over the wilds of California; or, eight years from home. By Joseph Batty ... Ed. by Rev. John Simpson. Leeds, J. Parrott, 1867. 67 p. CU-B.
    An Englishman's experience living with a black California miner, ca. 1859, pp. 43-46.

2966. BEAVER, GENE MARVIN. The beliefs of the citizens' councils: a study in segregationist thought. Master's thesis, California state univ., Fullerton, 1968.

2967. BERNARD, WILLIAM S. "Education for tolerance," in Crisis, v. 46, Aug., 1939, pp. 239-40.
    Author describes his course in race problems at the Univ. of Colo., Boulder.

2968. "Black backlash," in Seattle magazine, v. 1, Oct., 1964, pp. 7-8.

2969. *BLAKE, J. HERMAN. "The agony and the rage," in Black world, Mar., 1967.
    Racism at the Univ. of Calif., Berkeley.

2970. BLISS, HILDE SCHEUER. Relations between the degree of prejudice and the judgements of the ethnic group membership of individuals from photographs. Master's thesis, Univ. of Calif., Berkeley, 1949. [45] ℓ. tables.

Race Relations, Discrimination, and Prejudice

2971. BOGARDUS, EMORY STEPHEN, 1882- . The survey of race relations on the
Pacific coast. L. A., Council on international relations, 1926. 14 p.
CLSU.

2972. BOND, PHYLLIS M. Discriminatory choices of pictures on the basis of
skin color by three-year-old children: a preliminary study of factors
involved in the genesis of race attitudes. Master's thesis, Univ. of
Calif., Berkeley, 1949. 51 ℓ. diagrs., tables.

2973. BONJEAN, CHARLES M. Voices that count: establishment, brown and
black influentials in San Diego county, California [by] Charles M. Bonjean [and] Wayman J. Crow. La Jolla, Western behavioral sciences institute, 1969. 1 v. (v.p.). C.

2974. BORTHWICK, J. D. Three years in California. Edinburgh, Wm. Blackwood
and sons, 1857. 384 p. illus. C, CHi, CL, CLSU, CLU, CP, CPom, CSd,
CSf, CSj, CSmH, Rocq 15706.
Attitudes toward Negroes in the mines, pp. 163-65.

2975. _____. _____. Index. Prepared under the supervision of Joseph Gaer.
Oakland, 1935. Mimeo. C, CHi, CLSU, CLU, CO, CP, CSdS, CSf, CSmH,
CU-B, CU-SB, Rocq 15707.

2976. _____. Same. Reprinted with index and foreword by Joseph A. Sullivan.
Oakland, Biobooks, 1948. 318 p. illus., map. Available in many
California libraries. Rocq 15708.

2977. _____. Same, with title: The gold hunters ... N. Y., Outing pub. co.,
1917. 361 p. Available in many California libraries. Rocq 15709.

2978. BOYLES, L. "A look at the problem through the eyes of Negroes --
Phoenix Negroes speak out," in Arizona, June 2, 1968, pp. 5-10.

2979. BRANSTEN, TOMMY. Negroes of America, by Tommy Bransten. [S. F.,
1941]. [12] p. CSt, CU-B.
"One hundred copies of this book were privately printed for Tommy
Bransten."
"This book was issued by Jane Grabhorn from the offices of the Colt
Press for Mrs. Bransten. It is an essay by a ten-year-old boy on the
question of race prejudice." - Catalogue of an exhibition of the typo-
graphic work of Jane Grabhorn, p. 27. It contains some description of
Paul Robeson and mention of his 1941 treatment in San Francisco.

2980. BRITTON, JAMES. "New heights for Logan Heights," in San Diego magazine, v. 21, Oct., 1968, pp. 66-69, 100-04.

2981. BROWN, JAMES RUSSELL. The masculine identity of the Negro male.
Master's thesis, Calif. state univ., Hayward, 1970. 54 ℓ.

2982. BRUESKE, JUDITH M. Behavior as a mechanism for the maintainance of
ethnic diversity. Master's thesis, Calif. state univ., Sacramento, 1969.
73 ℓ. map.
Includes race awareness, prejudice, and antipathy.

Race Relations, Discrimination, and Prejudice

2983. BRYAN, ELLIS. Negro-white relations in the South; an analysis of major
theories of Southerners published since 1954. Master's thesis, Univ. of
southern Calif., Los Angeles, 1960. iii, 132 ℓ.

2984. BRYAN, MELVIN. Unfinished business: the communists say, "We will
bury you," the Negroes say "We will absorb you"; what do you say? 1st ed.
Ogden, 1967. 91 p. CU-SC.

2985. BULLOUGH, BONNIE LOUISE, 1927- . "Alienation in the ghetto," in
American journal of sociology, v. 72, Mar., 1967, pp. 469-78.
Los Angeles and the San Fernando Valley.

2986. BUNNIN, NENELLE RAPPOPORT. The effect of probability feedback on
Negroes' reactions to competition with whites. Doctoral dissertation,
Univ. of Calif., Berkeley, 1968. iii, 63 ℓ.

2987. BUNZEL, PETER D. "The clubs: bastions of racial bigotry," in Seattle
magazine, v. 4, Sept., 1967, pp. 23-27, 66.
Includes information on Alfred Cowles and Carl Maxey.

2988. *BURTON, ALBERT LEE. Whole Nigger or none. [Oakland, c1964]. 256 p.
cover port. CHi, CO, CSS, CSfU.
The author expresses his views on the black-white cultural conflict.

2989. California. Dept. of parks and recreation. Cultural differences
training, course no. OT-1-B, a self-study course for supervisors [and]
public contact employees. Prepared by the Personnel and training section.
[Sacramento, 1965]. 6 v. C.
Designed to bring about a greater understanding and improved relationships among state employees and between state employees and the public.
The course is divided into five parts: 1. Race, culture, and prejudice.
2. History of minorities. 3. Population, housing, and education.
4. Employment of minorities. 5. Governor's code of fair practices.

2990. _____. Dept. of social welfare. A cultural approach toward the understanding of some of our community problems, by Dr. Joan Ablon. [Sacra-
mento?, 1965]. 11 p. C.
"Differences are frequently tolerated and respected until they
intrude on the boundaries of the values of the mainstream of society ..."

2991. _____. _____. Cultural differences: training in nondiscrimination.
[Sacramento] 1965. 2 v. in 1. illus. (Its Training aid no. 25A, 25B).
C, CLU.
A training course designed to assist county welfare departments.

2992. _____. State univ. Sacramento. A symposium on racism in America.
Sacramento state college, Sept. 27 through Oct. 4, 1968. Co-sponsored
by Cultural programs committee, inter-racial project. Comp. & ed. by
Student co-operative. Sacramento, 1969. 151 p. CSS, CSdS.

2993. _____. _____. San Diego. Afro-American workshop, Mexican-American
workshop, June 17-27, 1969. San Diego, 1969. 162 p. CSdS.

Race Relations, Discrimination, and Prejudice

2994. _____. _____. San Jose. Interracial prejudices in San Jose, California, 1950; an appraisal made by eighty students under the direction of a student committee ... San Jose, 1950. 81 p. tables. Mimeo. CO, CU-B (California federation for civic unity collection).
Study covers 11 areas of investigation including education, health and welfare, housing, labor unions, police relations, and social and fraternal organizations.

2995. _____. _____. _____. Racial prejudices in San Jose, California, as observed by a college class in race relations. [San Jose, 1948?]. 54 p. CU-B (California federation for civic unity collection).
Study covers 8 areas of investigation including employment, labor unions, housing, hotels and restaurants, recreation, health and welfare, education, and religion.

2996. California federation for civic unity. Records, 1945-56. 6 boxes (containing 150 folders) and 3 cartons. CU-B.
Includes correspondence, minutes of meetings, financial accounts, papers relating to various conferences, and miscellaneous pamphlets. Relates to racial discrimination and segregation, employment practices, and similar subjects of interest to the Federation. Includes correspondence from the Urban leagues of Los Angeles and Portland, Augustus F. Hawkins, Arizona council for civic unity, Nathaniel Colley, Los Angeles county conference on community relations, Loren Miller, Palo Alto fair play council, Wilson Record, William Byron Rumford, and the Richmond council on intergroup relations.

2997. "Cardinal McIntyre: a Ramparts special report," in Ramparts, v. 3, Nov., 1964, pp. 35-44.
Three articles on James Francis Aloysius, Cardinal McIntyre's refusal to support racial equality in southern California.

2998. CARTER, ROBERT L., 1917- . Equality [by] Robert L. Carter, Dorothy Kenyon, Peter Marcuse [and] Loren Miller. With a foreword by Charles Abrams. N. Y., Pantheon books [c1965]. xxv, 191 p. CSf.
Equality based upon quotas and preferential treatment. Miller was a Los Angeles jurist and publisher.

2999. Central Seattle community council. Records, 1946-66, including those of the Jackson street community council. 13 1/2 feet (9 cartons). WaU.

3000. Civic unity committee, Seattle. Files of the Committee, 1944-64. 25 feet. WaU.

3001. *COLEMAN, ANITA SCOTT, 1890- . "Arizona and New Mexico -- the land of esperanza," in Messenger, v. 8, Sept., 1926, pp. 275-76.
The status of blacks in these areas by a resident of Silver City, New Mexico and Los Angeles. She states that, in smaller towns, "they are as sparse as rose bushes upon the prairies."

3002. CONNER, LEONARD. A comparison of the attitudes of selected general secretaries and board presidents in the YMCA toward Negro-white relationships. Master's thesis, Univ. of southern Calif., Los Angeles, 1949. ix, 179 ℓ.

Race Relations, Discrimination, and Prejudice

3003. Council for civic unity of San Francisco. We are many people living together. [Story by Ralph Radetsky and Edward Banfield. S. F., 194-]. [16] p. illus. CU-B.

3004. _____. What to do in a changing neighborhood. S. F. [1959?]. 3 ℓ. CO.

3005. COUSINEAU, CARL ALAN. Progressivism: the Negro as an object of white reform. Master's thesis, Univ. of Calif., Davis, 1970. 125 ℓ.

3006. CROW, JOHN E. Discrimination, poverty, and the Negro; Arizona in the national context [by] John E. Crow. Tucson, Univ. of Arizona press [1968]. 53 p. illus. Includes bibliographical references. AzTeS, AzU, CBGTU, CHS, CNoS, CSS, CSaT, CSbS, CSfU, CU-A, CU-B.

3007. Culver City. Administrative office. Racial transition and Culver City, by John Greenwood. [Culver City?] 1968. v.p. C.
A study of transition with suggestions for the implementation of plans to effect certain goals.

3008. *DAVIS, FRANK MARSHALL, 1905- . "A passage to Hawaii," in Crisis, v. 57, Nov., 1949, pp. 296-301.
Racial attitudes in Hawaii.

3009. DETTERING, RICHARD WHITSON. Prejudice won't hide! Palo Alto, Palo Alto fair play council, 1960. 8 p. C.
Examples of individual prejudice have an adverse effect often worldwide.

3010. DIEGLER, JAMES D. Epilogue to progressivism: Oregon, 1920-1924. Master's thesis, Univ. of Oregon, Eugene, 1958.
Klu klux klan era.

3011. DOUGLAS, PATRICK. "New stirrings in the central area. Yeah, baby you almost got burned," in Seattle magazine, v. 4, Oct., 1967, pp. 16-22, 57-58.

3012. DOWELL, BENJAMIN FRANKLIN, 1826-1897. Letter from O. Jacobs to Dowell, Oct. 23, 1867, discussing attitude toward Negroes in Oregon. Ms. OrHi.

3013. DYKE, JEANI. "San Francisco: the Negro problem turned on its head," in Immigration and race problems, 1961, pp. 278-302. Oakland, Mills college Dept. of economics and sociology, 1961. COMC.

3014. EATON, JOSEPH W. "A California triviality," in Crisis, v. 57, May, 1950, pp. 294 and 335.
The racist tone of a mural label in the California state capitol building, Sacramento.

3015. ELLSBERG, H. "Miracle of Vallejo," in Black world, v. 9, Feb., 1951, pp. 94-97.

Race Relations, Discrimination, and Prejudice

3016. FERRY, W. H. "Two nations," in Frontier, v. 16, Sept., 1965, p. 6.

3017. FISHER, LLOYD HORACE, 1911-1953. The problems of violence: observations on race conflict in Los Angeles. [Chicago, American council on race relations, 1947]. 20 p. maps. CLU, CNoS, CU-B.
"Based on material collected by Joseph Weckler ... Laurence I. Hewes, Jr., Regional director, San Francisco."

3018. FORD, JOHN ANSON. Thirty explosive years in Los Angeles county. San Marino, The Huntington library [c1961]. 232 p. illus. CHi, CSmH, Rocq 2921.
"The problem of minority groups": pp. 129-40.

3019. FRIEDMAN, LAURENCE J., 1940- . In search of Uncle Tom; racial attitudes of the Southern leadership, 1865-1920. Doctoral dissertation, Univ. of Calif., Los Angeles, 1967. 207 ℓ.

3020. GLOCK, CHARLES Y., ed. Prejudice U. S. A. Ed. by Charles Y. Glock and Ellen Siegelman. N. Y., Praeger [c1969]. xxii, 196 p. tables. CLSU, CSdS, CSf.
Based in large part on the proceedings of a symposium held at the Univ. of Calif., Berkeley, March, 1968. Includes monographs by Jay Saunders Redding and Richard Hatcher.

3021. GORDON, ELIZABETH DE LOUIS (DAVIS). A survey of racial conflicts. Master's thesis, Ariz. state univ., Tempe, 1946. 151 ℓ. illus.

3022. *GORHAM, THELMA THURSTON. "Negroes and Japanese evacuees," in Crisis, v. 52, Nov., 1945, pp. 314-16 and 330-31.
Treats mainly of the Japanese returning to find their former homes in San Francisco's Fillmore district inhabited by blacks.

3023. GREEN, JEROME. The use of an information test about the Negro as an indirect technique for measuring attitudes, beliefs, and self-perceptions. Doctoral dissertation, Univ. of southern Calif., Los Angeles, 1954. x, 435 ℓ. illus.

3024. GRIFFIN, JOHN HOWARD, 1920- . That mountain of yes; or racism, Nazi and American. Berkeley, Pacific tape library AL1566, 1964. [Phonotape]. Duration: 117 min. CSS.
Speech at the Santa Clara writers institute, June 17, 1964. It includes a discussion of the writing of "Black like me."

3025. GRIFFITHS, KEITH S. An audit of intergroup relations in the city of Seattle. Seattle, Health and welfare council, 1950. Wa.

3026. _____. The measurement of intergroup tensions in the state of Washington and the city of Seattle: analysis of two surveys conducted under the auspices of the Washington public opinion laboratory. Doctoral dissertation, Univ. of Washington, Seattle, 1952. 218 p.

3027. GUILD, ELLA JUNE (PURCELL), 1887- . Think on these things; some black white problems as seen by a group of Negro southerners. Santa Barbara, Schauer pub. co. [c1947]. 75 p. CL, CLSU, COrCL.

Race Relations, Discrimination, and Prejudice

3028. HALPERN, MANFRED. Applying a new theory of human relations to the comparative study of racism. Denver [1970?]. 41 p. (Denver. Univ. Center on international race relations. Race and nations' monograph series, no. 1, 1969/70). CSfSt.

3029. HANSON, EARL. Los Angeles: its people and its homes, by Earl Hanson and Paul Beckett. L. A., Haynes foundation, 1944. 206 p. illus., maps (1 fold.). C, CL, CLSU, CLU, CO, CSmH, CStmo, CU-B, Rocq 3869.
 "Good general survey which includes section on minorities." - Miriam Matthews.

3030. HATTON, JOHN MERVYN. Reactions of Negroes in a biracial bargaining situation. Doctoral dissertation, Stanford univ., Stanford, 1965. vi, 52 ℓ. illus., tables.
 "Confirmed hypothesis that Negro subjects would exploit yielding whites as opposed to yielding Negroes, but would yield to demanding whites and retaliate against demanding Negroes." - West, p. 25.

3031. HAYAKAWA, SAMUEL ICHIYE, 1906- . "Psychotherapy for white folks," in Black world, v. 10, Sept., 1961, pp. 29-36.
 Reprinted from Contact.

3032. HAYES, EDWARD C. Power structure and the urban crisis: Oakland, California. Doctoral dissertation, Univ. of Calif., Berkeley, 1968. iv, 403 ℓ.

3033. HEATH, JIM F., and FREDERICK M. NUNN. "Negroes and discrimination in colonial New Mexico: Don Pedro Bautista Pino's startling statements of 1812 in perspective," in Phylon, Winter, 1970, pp. 372-78.
 Pino stated that there "was no known caste of people of African origin" in New Mexico.

3034. HELLER, JOSEPH RICHARD. The effects of racial prejudice, feedback strategy, and race on cooperative-competitive behavior. Doctoral dissertation, Univ. of Calif., Berkeley, 1966. iv, 149 ℓ.

3035. HEYWOOD, YATES. The Negro question resolved. [Salt Lake City?] 1964. 22 p. CNoS, CU-B.

3036. HONG, SUNG C. Majority perception of minority behavior and its relationship to hostility toward ethnic minorities: a test of George A. Lundberg's hypotheses. Doctoral dissertation, Univ. of Washington, Seattle, 1959.
 Negroes were included among the 18 groups studied.

3037. *HUBBARD, JOHN PURLEY. Racial equality, by J. P. Hubbard ... pastor, Beth Eden Baptist church. Oakland [192-?]. 16 p. COEB.

3038. HUEBER, D. F. "Reality or misinformation?", in Community, v. 25, May, 1966, p. 3ff.
 Concerns minorities in Spokane.

Race Relations, Discrimination, and Prejudice

3039. HUNGERFORD, THOMAS W. "An exercise in understanding," in Puget soundings, Dec., 1964, pp. 8-9.
Describes Seattle interracial home visit day.

3040. "Idle hands," in Economist, v. 221, Oct. 8, 1966, p. 153.
San Francisco race question.

3041. The Inglewood raiders; a story of the celebrated Ku klux case at Los
Angeles, and speeches to the jury. L. A., L. L. Bryson, 1923. 71 p.
Work, p. 380.

3042. Institutional racism in America. Contributors: Owen Blank [and
others]. Ed. by Louis L. Knowles and Kenneth Prewitt. With an appendix
by Harold Baron. Englewood Cliffs, N. J., Prentice-Hall [1970, c1969].
xii, 180 p. CHS.
"Based on working papers prepared for a joint program sponsored by
the Stanford chapter of the University Christian Movement and the Mid-
Peninsula Christian Ministry of East Palo Alto, Calif."

3043. Interracial committee, Tucson. A study of the Negroes of Tucson ...
Tucson, 1946. AzU.

3044. JAMES, STUART B. Race relations in literature and sociology. Doctoral
dissertation, Univ. of Washington, Seattle, 1960.

3045. JEFFRIES, VINCENT JOHN, 1936- . Cultural values and antagonism
toward Negroes. Doctoral dissertation, Univ. of Calif., Los Angeles,
1968. xx, 334 ℓ.

3046. KALVEN, HARRY, and W. H. FERRY. "Quotes for Negroes: insult or compensation?" Santa Barbara, Center for the study of democratic institutions [196-?]. Tape. 48 minutes.

3047. KATZ, MARTIN RICHARD, 1916- . Principles and techniques in changing
prejudiced attitude toward the Negro. Master's thesis, Stanford univ.,
Stanford, 1946. 125 ℓ. fold. form.

3048. KEEN, HAROLD. "It's sock it to 'em time," in San Diego magazine,
v. 20, Apr., 1968, pp. 49-52, 69, 88-89.

3049. _____. "San Diego business pitches a new ballgame," in San Diego and
Point magazine, v. 20, June, 1968, p. 44.

3050. Keesing's research report. Race relations in the USA, 1954-68.
N. Y., Charles Scribner's sons [c1970]. viii, 280 p.
Cover title: Keesing's research report no. 4.
Discusses 1967 California housing, the 1965 Los Angeles riot, and
gives occasional information about other western states.

3051. KENNARD, EDWARD D.* Essentialism and the Negro problem. Somerton,
Ariz. [Richmond, Va., The Saint Luke press, 1924]. 331 p. NN.

Race Relations, Discrimination, and Prejudice

3052. Ku klux klan. California knights. The Klan in action; a manual of leadership and organization for officers of local Klan committees. [n.p., 192-?]. 15 ℓ. Mimeo. CU-B.

3053. League of women voters of San Diego. Dimensions in discrimination. A preliminary survey of San Diego's community problems of discrimination. Introduction by Barbara Shannon. San Diego, 1965. 2 v. in 1. illus. C, CSd, CSdS, CSmarP.
        Discusses the law, employment, housing, public life, volunteer activity, and city government.

3054. LEARNED, ROY E. "Exploring racial tolerance," in Opportunity, v. 23, July-Sept., 1945, pp. 130-31.
        Authored by an elementary school principal, Sacramento.

3055. LE CONTE, JOSEPH, 1823-1901. The race problem in the South. Miami, Fla., Mnemosyne pub. inc., 1969. 350-402 p. CBGTU, CNoS, CSt.
        Reprinted from the Brooklyn ethical association's Man and the state, pub. in 1892. Authored by a faculty member, Univ. of Calif., Berkeley.

3056. *LIVINGFREE, DANIEL. The misnomer "Negro" and the abomination of racism, by Daniel Livingfree. [Tacoma, Wash., Paragon printers, 196-?]. [11] p. port. CSfAA.

3057. LIVINGSTON, LOVELESS BENJAMIN. Self-concept change of black college males as a result of a weekend black experience encounter workshop. Master's thesis, Ariz. state univ., Tempe, 1971. 103 ℓ. illus.

3058. Los Angeles committee on human relations. Minutes of monthly meetings. CL, Je10, 1946+.
        Concerns race relations in Los Angeles county.

3059. Los Angeles county. Institute on community relations. Fact manual. L. A., 1945. Mimeo.

3060. Los Angeles county committee for interracial progress. Minutes of the committee meetings. CL, My, 1944-Ap, 1946.

3061. LYFORD, JOSEPH P. Proposal for a revolution. Santa Barbara, Center for the study of democratic institutions [n.d.]. [7] p. C.
        "... the Negro cannot win equality of opportunity until American society as a whole develops some way of dealing with the rise of mass unemployment and the growing ineffectiveness of our political and educational system."

3062. *MAC BETH, HUGH E. Colored America answers the challenge of Pearl S. Buck. L. A., Author, 1942. 29 p. DHU.
        Contents: - Pearl S. Buck's open letter to the colored people of America. - Pearl S. Buck's address to the colored leadership of the U. S. A. - Colored American leadership comes into action on behalf of the entire human race, by Hugh E. Macbeth, a Los Angeles attorney.

Race Relations, Discrimination, and Prejudice

3063. MC ENTIRE,DAVIS. A study of racial attitudes in neighborhoods, in-
filtrated by non-whites, San Francisco, Oakland, and Berkeley, California,
by Davis McEntire, professor of social welfare, University of California.
[1955]. unp. CO.
"Reprinted from Northern California real estate report, second
quarter, 1955."

3064. MC MURRIN,STERLING M. The Negroes among the Mormons. [Salt Lake
City] Salt Lake City chapter of NAACP [1968]. 12 p. CU-B.
"An address given before the Annual banquet of the Salt Lake City
chapter of the National association for the advancement of colored people,
June 21, 1968."

3065. MC WILLIAMS,CAREY. "Minorities in California," in California librarian,
v. 6, Dec., 1944, pp. 47-51, 83.

3066. MANDER, LINDEN A. The Seattle civic unity committee. [Seattle], 1944.
19 p. Mimeo. Wa.

3067. MARX, GARY TRADE. Protest and prejudice; a study of belief in the
black community, by Gary T. Marx. N. Y., Harper & Row [c1967]. xxviii,
228, 27 p. tables. C, CFS, CNoS, COM, CSaT, CSdS, CSf, CU, CU-SC.
This third volume of a series, Patterns of American prejudice, part
of a Univ. of Calif. five-year study of anti-Semitism in the United
States, relates mainly to the attitudes of blacks toward their entire
environment rather than toward Jews.

3068. _____. Protest and prejudice: the climate of opinion in the Negro
American community. Doctoral dissertation, Univ. of Calif., Berkeley,
1966. v.p.

3069. *MATTHEWS, MIRIAM, 1905- . Literary activities in the field of
race relations. Master's thesis, Univ. of Chicago, 1945. iii, 85 ℓ.
NN (photocopy).
Survey of methods used by public libraries to promote racial and
cultural understanding. By a Los Angeles librarian.

3070. MEISTER, DICK. "Bureaucrats and bias," in Frontier, v. 15, Feb.,
1964, pp. 10-12.

3071. Mid-peninsula Christian ministry community house. Institutional
racism in American society: a primer ... East Palo Alto, 1968. 19 p.
CMp, CSt.

3072. *MILLER, LOREN R., 1903-1967. "Farewell to liberals: a Negro view,"
in Nation, Oct. 20, 1962, pp. 235-38.

3073. _____. "Freedom now--but what then?",in Nation, v. 196, June 29,
1963, pp. 539-42.

3074. _____. "The plight of the Negro professional man," in Opportunity,
v. 9, Aug., 1931, pp. 239-41.

Race Relations, Discrimination, and Prejudice

3075. MOLONY, REGINALD D. Rapping with whitey: an experience for improving black-white relations. Master's thesis, Calif. state univ., Hayward, 1970. vii, 98 ℓ.

3076. MORT, NANCYBELLE. A critical analysis of selected sociological writings in the field of race relations. Master's thesis, Univ. of southern Calif., Los Angeles, 1950. v, 104 ℓ.

3077. MOSK, STANLEY, 1912- . "Pattern for local unity; institute on community relations, Los Angeles county," in New republic, v. 112, May, 1945, pp. 674-75.

3078. "Mrs. Romney's quandary," in Christian century, v. 84, Feb. 8, 1967, p. 165.
    Mormon treatment of Negroes.

3079. NEWBY, IDUS ATWELL. The Negro and American racism, 1900-1930. Doctoral dissertation, Univ. of Calif., Los Angeles, 1962. 382 p.

3080. NEWHALL, R. "The Negro in Phoenix," in Phoenix point west, v. 6, Sept., 1965, pp. 15-16.

3081. _____. "We shall overcome," in Phoenix point west, v. 6, June, 1965, pp. 7-10.

3082. NORRIS, CLARENCE WINDZELL. A comparative study of selected white and Negro youth of San Antonio, Texas, with special reference to certain basic social attitudes. Doctoral dissertation, Univ. of southern Calif., Los Angeles, 1951. xvii, 332 ℓ.

3083. Oakland institute on human relations. ... seminar reports ... [Oakland, 1946]. v.p. CO.

3084. O'BRIEN, ROBERT W. "The changing cast position of the Negro in the Northwest," in Research studies, Washington state college, Pullman, v. 10, Mar., 1942, pp. 67-71.

3085. _____. "Seattle: race relations frontier, 1949; trends in race relations on the west coast - a symposium," in Common ground, v. 9, Spring, 1949, pp. 18-23.

3086. _____., and LEE M. BROOKS. "Race relations in the Pacific northwest," in Phylon, v. 7, 1st quarter, 1946, pp. 21-31.

3087. OLSEN, EDWARD G. "What shall we teach about race and racism?", in C[alifornia] T[eachers] A[ssociation] journal, v. 64, May, 1968, pp. 26-27, 30-31.

3088. PALMIERI, VICTOR H. "Business and the black revolt," in California management review, v. 11, Summer, 1969, pp. 31-36.
    Outlines four areas in which business can work to solve urban problems.

Race Relations, Discrimination, and Prejudice

3089. Palo Alto. Citizens' advisory committee on human relations.
[Report]. [Palo Alto] 1964. 25, 68 p. CSt-Law.

3090. PEPLOW, E. H. "Being a Negro is a surmountable handicap," in Arizona,
Apr. 1, 1962, pp. 12-15.

3091. PETTIT, ARTHUR G. "Mark Twain's attitude toward the Negro in the
West, 1861-1867," in Western historical quarterly, v. 1, Jan., 1970,
pp. 51-62.

3092. PIKE, JAMES ALBERT, 1913-1969. Our Christmas challenge, by the Right
reverend James A. Pike. N. Y., Sterling pub. co. [c1961]. 64 p. CHS,
CSf.
Bishop Pike writes on the philosophy of bias.

3093. *PINKNEY, ALPHONSO, 1929- . "Prejudice toward Mexican and Negro
Americans: a comparison," in Phylon, v. 24, Winter, 1963, pp. 353-59.

3094. *PITTMAN, JOHN. "Negroes challenge the jackboot in San Francisco,"
in Freedomways, v. 7, Winter, 1967, pp. 42-53.
Racism and repression.

3095. Portland city club. Committee on race relations. "The Negro in
Portland," in Portland city club bulletin, v. 26, July 20, 1945.
"An important survey." - Miriam Matthews.

3096. RAAB, EARL, ed. American race relations today. Ed. by Earl Raab.
Garden City, N. Y., Doubleday & co. [c1962]. 195 p. CEcaC, CFS, CHS,
CKenM, CLSU, CNoS, CO, CSaT, CSdS, CSf, CSluSP, CU-A, Wa.
Contains abridgements from the writings of Seymour Martin Lipset,
Morton Grodzins, Nathan Glazer, Eshref Shevsky, Charles Eric Lincoln,
and others.

3097. "The racial disturbance in Los Angeles," in Frontier, v. 13, June,
1962, pp. 3-4.

3098. The racial issue in San Diego: a report of a television program and
the reaction to it from the San Diego community. San Diego, 1965. 159 p.
C, CSd.
The report of a program offered jointly by three television stations
as a result of the August riot.

3099. "Rampages of Ku klux klan on Pacific coast," in Messenger, v. 4,
June, 1922, pp. 419-20.
Describes difficulties especially in Bakersfield and in Oregon.

3100. RAND, CHRISTOPHER. Los Angeles, the ultimate city [by] Christopher
Rand. N. Y., Oxford univ. press, 1967. 205 p. CSdS, CSf.
See pp. 124-32 and index for an analysis of race relations of the
1960's.

3101. RECORD, WILSON, 1916- . Minority groups and intergroup relations in
the San Francisco bay area. [Berkeley] Univ. of Calif. institute of

Race Relations, Discrimination, and Prejudice

governmental studies, 1963. 48 p. CChiS, CFS, CHC, CHS, CKenM, CL, CLS, CNoS, CMv, CPhD, CSf, CSluSP, CSmH, CSrCL, CSt, CSt-Law, CTurS, CU, CU-SB.

3102. *REDDICK, LAWRENCE D., ed. "Race relations on the Pacific coast," in Sociology of education, v. 19, Nov., 1945, pp. 129-206.
Contents: "The new race-relations frontier," by L. D. Reddick, pp. 129-45, and "Profiles" on "Seattle," by Robert W. O'Brien, pp. 146-57; on "Portland," by Edwin C. Berry, pp. 158-65; on "San Francisco," by Joseph James, pp. 166-78; on "Los Angeles," by Charles Bratt, pp. 179-86; a "Critical summary," by Carey McWilliams, pp. 187-97; and a "Select bibliography," by Miriam Matthews, pp. 198-206.
A special issue describing race relations and the effects of wartime migration on the Pacific coast.

3103. RICHARDSON, GRACE. "What of it?", in Messenger, v. 10, Feb., 1928, pp. 27-28.
A Berkeley artist answers an author alarmed "about the color-line and what loss of it implies."

3104. Richmond. Office of the city manager. Municipal human relations commission; a survey of programs in selected cities of the United States. Richmond, 1963. 24 l. CO.

3105. RIEFF, PHILIP. "Black and white in America." Santa Barbara Center for the study of democratic institutions [196-?]. Tape. 1 hour.

3106. RILEY, L. H. "Miscegenation statutes: a re-evaluation of their constitutionality in light of changing social and political conditions," in Southern California law review, v. 32, Fall, 1958, p. 28.

3107. RITTER, EARNESTINE. "The Negro takes strides," in California sun magazine, v. 11, Fall & Winter, 1959-60, pp. 39-41.

3108. ROSENBLUM, ABRAHAM L. Social class membership and ethnic prejudice in Cedar City. Doctoral dissertation, Univ. of southern Calif., Los Angeles, 1959. xi, 263 l.
"Prejudice varies with social class standing."

3109. RUSCO, ELMER R. "Minority groups in Nevada. Reno, Univ. of Nevada bureau of governmental research, 1966. 52 l. C.
"This report brings together some basic information about the status of racial minorities in the state in order to fill in some of the gaps in our knowledge of this area."

3110. Sacramento city-county human relations commission. Report, 1969. Sacramento, 1969. 17 p. C.
Activity, 1968-69, especially in the fields of employment, housing, and law and order.

3111. SALLEY, ROBERT LEE. Activities of the knights of the Ku klux klan in southern California: 1921-1925. Master's thesis, Univ. of southern Calif., Los Angeles, 1963. v, 199 l.

Race Relations, Discrimination, and Prejudice

3112. San Francisco. Board of supervisors. County, state and national
affairs committee. ... We must begin now--San Francisco's plan for
democratic racial relations. S. F., Bay area council against discrimination [1943?]. 11 p. CU-B.
    Advice in the area of education, employment, police relations,
housing, and the press.

3113. _____. Human relations coordinator. A human relations program for
San Francisco. [S. F.] 1964. 31 ℓ. CO.

3114. San Francisco conference on religion, race and social concerns. San
Francisco, a city in crisis: a report to the churches and synagogues.
[S. F.?, 1968?]. Ms. [565] ℓ. Photocopy of typescript. CCotS, CSaT,
CSt-Law, CU-B.
    Compiled and written by a group of young seminarians; preface by
the Rev. Eugene J. Boyle, co-chairman.
    An application of the report of the National advisory commission on
civil disorders to conditions in San Francisco contributing to racial
tension and violence in the areas of employment, education, housing,
welfare, and police and community relations.

3115. SCHUMAN, HOWARD, and BARRY GRUENBERG. "The impact of city on racial
attitudes," in American journal of sociology, v. 76, Sept., 1970, pp. 213-
61.
    A study of 15 U. S. cities including San Francisco.

3116. SCHUYLER, LAMBERT. Close that bedroom door! by Lambert and Patricia
Schuyler. Winslow, Wash., Heron house [c1957]. 188 p. CL, CSfSt.
    Concerns race relations, miscegenation, and educational segregation.

3117. *SCOTT, WILLIAM V. F. "Eliminate the 'Stokes Willies'," in Crisis,
v. 57, Jan., 1950, pp. 9-11.
    An answer to Wilson Record's "Willie Stokes at the Golden Gate."
Describes the difficulties the "Stokes Willies," members of the bottom
rung on the social structure ladder, create for others.

3118. SCOTT, WOODROW WILSON. Interpersonal relations in ethnically mixed
small work groups. Doctoral dissertation, Univ. of southern Calif.,
Los Angeles, 1959. xxii, 260 ℓ. illus.
    "Ethnically mixed [Los Angeles] factory work groups under benevolent
management reduce conflict attitudes and increase cooperative attitudes."

3119. Seattle. City council. Seminar on equal opportunities and racial
harmony. Seattle [n.d.]. 2 v. C.
    "... designed to bring together industry, labor, governmental
agencies, civil rights organizations, community groups, and the average
citizen for an honest exploration and evaluation ..."

3120. _____. Civic unity committee. History of Civic unity committee,
February 14, 1944 to January 15, 1948. [Seattle] Red feather service of
Seattle community chest, 1948. 17 p. Mimeo. Wa.

Race Relations, Discrimination, and Prejudice

3121. _____. _____. History of Seattle civic unity committee, February 1944 to January 1952. [Seattle] Red feather service of Community chest and council of Seattle and King county, 1952. 28 p. Mimeo. Wa.

3122. Seattle magazine.
    The Special issue of June, 1968 (v. 5) is entitled "White racism in Seattle" and consists of five articles: "The scarcity of decent jobs"; "Why they distrust cops"; "School integration: a skeptical view"; "How it looks from the ghetto"; and "Open housing in a closed society?"

3123. Seattle university magazine. v. 1, no. 1, Jℓ, 1968.
    The entire issue discusses racism as a national problem with deep implications in Seattle.

3124. *Seattle urban league. Seattle's racial gap. Seattle, 1968. Wa.

3125. SEVER, DAVID ARTHUR. Comparison of Negro and white attitudes in a Washington community. Master's thesis, Washington state univ., Pullman, 1967. 114 p.
    Concerns the city of Pasco.

3126. *SHAW, ALEXANDER P. Christianizing race relations as a Negro sees it [by the] Reverend A. P. Shaw, pastor, Wesley Methodist Episcopal church, Los Angeles, California. [L. A., Wetzel pub. co., c1928]. 88 p. CLCo, CU-B.
    Concerns race relations throughout the U. S.

3127. SIEGEL, STANLEY. "Incident in Pasadena," in Frontier, v. 17, Dec., 1965, pp. 11-12.
    Audience reaction to speech of Selma, Ala. sheriff.

3128. SMITH, STAN. "Compton ... a case study in gradual integration," in California sun magazine, v. 12, Fall & Winter, 1960-61, pp. 53-56.

3129. "Southern Pacific Jim-Crow," in Crisis, v. 61, Apr., 1954, pp. 219-20 and 250.
    Examples of discrimination by the Southern Pacific co., on its trains between San Francisco and Los Angeles.

3130. SPARKS, NEMMY. What is socialism, by Nemmy Sparks. L. A., Communist party of Los Angeles [1947]. 32 p. illus. CU-B.
    The Los Angeles county chairman of the Communist party mentions racial discrimination, pp. 22-23 and 31.

3131. Spokane community action council. Spokane community action anniversary report. Spokane, 1968. Wa.

3132. Stanford today, series 1, no. 24, Summer/Autumn, 1968.
    Contains four articles on race relations.

3133. STEINBERG, WARREN L. "Opportunity for Los Angeles," in Frontier, v. 16, Jan., 1965, pp. 14-16.

Race Relations, Discrimination, and Prejudice

3134. STEPHENSON, RICHARD. "Race in the cactus state," in Crisis, v. 61,
Apr., 1954, pp. 197-202.
A summary of conditions in New Mexico.

3135. STEWART, JOHN J. Mormonism and the Negro; and explanation and defense
of the doctrine of the Church of Jesus Christ of latter-day saints in
regard to Negroes and others of Negroid blood. [Logan, Utah, c1960].
54 p. CHS, CNoS, CSluSP, CU-B.
Authored by a professor of journalism, Utah state university.

3136. Survey of race relations. 40 manuscript boxes. CSt-H.
"The vast majority of material concerns the situation of Orientals in
the western United States, more particularly California. There is no
inventory for the material nor has the collection been formally processed
but a perusal of the first two boxes indicates there is material on discrimination against Afro-Americans. For example, the collection contains
a survey of housing discrimination against Orientals which includes
material on discrimination against Afro-Americans. The survey consists
of replies furnished by real estate boards of various California towns on
'how they are protecting white neighborhoods'; the period covered is the
late 1920's. There may be a vast amount of additional material concerning
Afro-Americans in the remaining 38 boxes but they could not be investigated for lack of time." - Karen Fung to James Abajian, Dec. 5, 1969.

3137. "A symposium: the Negro and the Jew," in the Burning bush, no. 3,
Summer, 1965, pp. 14-59.
Statements of 15 Jews and Negroes, mainly residents of the San Fran-
cisco bay area, about their inter-relationship.

3138. TAGGART, STEPHEN G. Mormonism's Negro policy: social and historical
origin, by Stephen G. Taggart. Salt Lake City, Univ. of Utah press
[c1970]. xiii, 82 p. CSfU.

3139. TANNER, JERALD. Joseph Smith's curse upon the Negro, by Jerald &
Sandra Tanner. Also included, Race problems as they effect the Church,
an address by Mark E. Petersen. Salt Lake City, Modern microfilm co.,
1965. 45, 7 ℓ. CU-B (photocopy).

3140. _____. The Negro in Mormon theology, by Jerald & Sandra Tanner.
[Salt Lake City, Modern microfilm co., 1967]. 58 p. CBGTU, CO, CSmH,
CU-B.
Condensed edition of some of the material which was first printed in
1965 under the same title and most of the material which appeared in
Joseph Smith's curse upon the Negro.

3141. THOMPSON, H. KEITH.
A collection, two boxes of which contain anti-Negro literature
issued in the 1950's by Mrs. Anne Smart, Larkspur; E. L. Anderson,
Sausalito; Williams publications, Santa Ana; Project big four, Laguna
Beach; The American nationalist, Inglewood; and others. Relates in part
to the Urban league, the NAACP, miscegenation, and black literature.
CSt-H.

Race Relations, Discrimination, and Prejudice

3142. *THURMAN, HOWARD, 1899– . The luminous darkness; a personal interpretation of the anatomy of segregation and the ground of hope. N. Y.,
Harper & Row, c1965. xi, 113 p. Available in many California libraries
and WaT, WaTC, WaTP.

3143. *THURMAN, WALLACE, 1902–1934. "Quoth Brigham Young: This is the
place," in Messenger, v. 8, Aug., 1926, pp. 235–36.
The status of blacks in Utah by a native of Salt Lake City.

3144. "Trends in race relations on the West coast––a symposium": "Los
Angeles, an emerging pattern," by Carey McWilliams; "The Negro in San
Francisco," by Carol Levene; [and] "Seattle: race relations frontier,
1949," by Robert O'Brien, in Common ground, v. 9, Spring, 1949, pp. 3–23.

3145. United Presbyterian church in the U. S. A. North coastal area. Toward
a witnessing community; a program to meet the crisis in race relations
... S. F., 1964. CSaT.

3146. UNRAU, HARLAN DALE. The Double V movement in Los Angeles during the
second world war: a study in Negro protest. Master's thesis, Calif.
state univ., Fullerton, 1971. 192 ℓ.
The "Double V" slogan indicated the dual fight against racism at
home and totalitarianism abroad.

3147. VAN ALSTYNE, W. W., and K. L. KARST. "State action," in Stanford law
review, v. 14, Dec., 1961, p. 3ff.
"Examination of the relation between state action and the national
interest in racial equality in all areas." – Elizabeth W. Miller.

3148. VON BRAUCHITSCH, DENNIS M. The Ku klux klan in California, 1921 to
1924. Master's thesis, Calif. state univ., Sacramento, 1967. 262 p.
facsims.

3149. WALTERS, ROBERT J. As the pendulum swings; a study of the radical
trend in the civil rights movement. [L. A., Privately printed, 1965].
214, A-[J] p. Bibliography: pp. [G-J]. CU-A.
Ink stamped: Distributed courtesy of Association for the protection
of American rights, Bell, Calif.

3150. WATKINS, MARK HANNA. "Racial situation in Denver," in Crisis, v. 52,
May, 1945, pp. 139–40.

3151. *WATTS, LEWIS G. "Racial trends in Seattle, 1958," in Crisis, v. 65,
June–July, 1958, pp. 333–38.

3152. _____. Social integration and the use of minority leadership in
Seattle, Washington," in Phylon, v. 21, Summer, 1960, pp. 136–43.

3153. WEINBERG, MEYER. "Elimination of racism ..." in Education Colorado,
Nov. 22, 1966. Denver, 1924–1927.

3154. WENKERT, ROBERT. An historical digest of Negro-white relations in
Richmond, California, by Robert Wenkert, with the assistance of John

Race Relations, Discrimination, and Prejudice

Magney [and] Fred Templeton. Rev., September, 1967. Berkeley, Survey research center, Univ. of Calif. [1967]. vii, 90 ℓ. map. Bibliographic footnotes. CSaT, CU.

3155. _____. Two weeks of racial crisis in Richmond, California, by Robert Wenkert, John Magney [and] Ann Neel. Berkeley, Survey research center, Univ. of Calif., 1967. ii, 233 ℓ. maps. Bibliographic footnotes. CHS, CU.

3156. WILDAVSKY, AARON. "The empty-headed blues: black rebellion and white reaction," in California monthly, v. 79, Jan.-Feb., 1969, pp. 19-27.

3157. WILEY, JAMES T. Race conflict as exemplified in a Washington town. Master's thesis, Washington state univ., Spokane, 1949. 225 p.
    A study of Pasco.

3158. WILLIAMS, ROBIN MURPHY, 1914- . Strangers next door: ethnic relations in American communities [by] Robin M. Williams, Jr., in collaboration with John P. Dean and Edward A. Suchman and containing adaptations of contributions from Lois R. Dean [and others]. Englewood Cliffs, N. J., Prentice-Hall [1964]. xiv, 434 p. forms, tables. Bibliographical footnotes. CEcaC, CFS, CLS, CNoS, CSbS, CSdS, CSf, CLluSP.

    Based upon studies made between 1948 and 1956 mainly in Bakersfield and three other U. S. cities.

3159. WITEBSKY, LEON IRVING. A study of the relationship of parents' and children's attitudes towards Negroes. Master's thesis, Univ. of Calif., Berkeley, 1950. 34 ℓ. diagrs., tables.

3160. WOLLENBERG, CHARLES, ed. Ethnic conflict in California history ... ed. by Charles Wollenberg. L. A., Tinnon-Brown, inc. [c1970]. ix, 215 p. C, CNoS.
    Contains "White racism and black response in California history," by Velesta Jenkins, pp. 121-33, and "Afro-Americans and Mexican-Americans: the politics of coalition," by Mervyn M. Dymally, pp. 153-71.

3161. *WOOD, FORREST GLEN. Black scare; the racist response to emancipation and reconstruction, by Forrest G. Wood. Berkeley, Univ. of Calif. press, 1968. ix, 219 p. illus. Bibliography: pp. [193]-210. C, CBGTU, CHS, CLSU, CLobS, CNoS, CPhD, CRic, CSS, CSbS, CSdS, CSf, CSfCiC, CSjC, CSt, CSluSP, CU.
    Authored by an assistant professor of history, Calif. state univ., Fresno. See index entries for California, Nevada, and Oregon.

3162. WOODBURY, NAOMI FELICIA. A legacy of intolerance; nineteenth century pro-slavery propaganda and the Mormon church today. Master's thesis, Univ. of Calif., Los Angeles, 1966. 156 ℓ.

3163. WOODMANSEE, JOHN J. An evaluation of pupil response as a measure of attitude toward Negroes. Doctoral dissertation, Univ. of Colorado, Boulder, 1965.
    "A study of pupillary dilation as an indicator of attitudes."

Race Relations, Discrimination, and Prejudice

3164. XETV (television station), San Diego. The racial issue in San Diego;
a report of a television program and the reaction to it from the San
Diego community. [San Diego, 1965]. 159 p. port. CU-B.

RANCH LIFE, INCLUDING COWBOYS

3165. BARD, FLOYD C., 1879- . Horse wrangler; sixty years in the saddle
in Wyoming and Montana, by Floyd C. Bard as told to Agnes Wright Spring.
Norman, Univ. of Okla. press [1960]. xi, 296 p. illus., ports., map.
CU, WyU.
Includes activities of some black soldiers, cowboys, and ranch cooks.

3166. BURNS, ROBERT H. "Beefmakers of the Laramie plains," in Annals of
Wyoming, v. 36, Oct., 1964, pp. 185-97.
Information on Samuel Stewart, a black cowboy, pp. 187-88.

3167. DURHAM, PHILIP, 1912- . "The Negro cowboy," in American quarterly,
v. 7, Fall, 1955, pp. 129-40, 291-301.

3168. _____. The Negro cowboys, by Philip Durham and Everett L. Jones ...
N. Y., Dodd, Mead [c1965]. 278 p. illus., maps, ports. Bibliography:
pp. 254-70. Available in many libraries.
An "account of the Negroes who became trail hands, heroes, villains,
hunted wild horses, and helped to build the new western lands."

3169. _____., and EVERETT L. JONES. "Negro cowboys," in American west, v. 1,
Fall, 1964, pp. 26-31, 87.

3170. _____. _____. "Slaves on horseback," in Pacific historical review,
v. 33, Nov., 1964, pp. 405-09.

3171. KNOX, ANDREW P. "Before Hollywood made the myth: Negro cowboys in
the old west," in Black world, v. 14, Sept., 1965, pp. 80-83.

3172. WYMAN, WALKER DEMARQUIS, 1907- . The legend of Charlie Glass, Negro
cowboy on the Colorado-Utah range, by Walker D. Wyman and John D. Hart,
including "The ballad of Charlie Glass" words and music by William L.
Clark ... River Falls, Wis., River Falls state univ. press [1970].
[10] ℓ. illus., ports.
"The legend of Charlie Glass" originally appeared in the Colorado
magazine of history, v. 46, Winter, 1969, pp. 40-54.

RELIGION AND PHILOSOPHY

3173. ADAMS, L. WASHINGTON. The enigma of peace. [S. F.] A Rolet publication printed ... by the Negro history research division. [1960?]. 65 p.
illus., port.
Cover subtitle: "A look at the peace dilemma by L. Washington Adams.

Religion **and Philosophy**

New directions toward peace could keep the future generation happy. If
you believe in goodwill and peace, this personal narrative is dedicated
to you."

3174. "African Methodist Episcopal church," in Golden notes, pub. by the
Sacramento county historical society, Jan., 1965, pp. 26-27.
A history of St. Andrew's A. M. E. church, Sacramento, 1850-83.

3175. *African Methodist Episcopal church. Bakersfield. Articles of in-
corporation, 1914. 5 p. Typew. C-ArS.
Directors were E. D. Garner, Charles Ankrum, C. B. Barton, J. W.
Price, H. E. Simpson, F. W. West, H. Caldwell, C. D. Gordon, Essex
Maddox, E. W. Winters, and W. H. Shelvy.

3176. _____. California conference. Journal of the proceedings. COEB
63rd (1928), 64th, 67th, 72nd, 75th, 78-79th, 85th, 88th, 90-91st.
Title varies: Proceedings; Official minutes.

3177. _____. _____. Journal of proceedings of the third annual convention
of the ministers and lay delegates of the African Methodist Episcopal
church. Held in Bethel church, San Francisco, from September 4th to
September 10th, 1863. S. F., B. F. Sterett, 1863. 43 [1] p. CHi (photo-
copy), CU-B.
This California conference included in area the present states of
California, Nevada, Idaho, Oregon, Washington, and the Province of
British Columbia.

3178. _____. _____. Journal of the proceedings of the third [sic] annual
session ... held in St. Andrew's church, Sacramento ... June 16th to
June 30th, 1870. S. F., Pacific appeal print. [1870]. 48 p. CBPac,
CU-B, Drury 667.

3179. _____. _____. Souvenir program ... annual session. COEB 9th [sic]
(1933); 91st (1955).
Title varies slightly.

3180. _____. _____. ... Souvenir program, semi-centennial, California
A. M. E. annual conference, August 14-19, 1917 ... [Oakland?, 1917].
[36] p. illus., ports. CU-B.
Contains "Historical sketch, by Rev. J. H. Wilson, P. E." Held at
the First African Methodist Episcopal church, Oakland.

3181. _____. _____. Women's missionary society. Annual convention
[program]. COEB 1956; 1965.

3182. _____. _____. _____. Annual reports of the officers. COEB 1964/65.

3183. _____. Colorado conference. Minutes of the eighth annual session of
the Colorado conference of the African M. E. church. Held in Helena,
Montana, October 11, 1894. Albuquerque, Pub. by order of the Conference,
J. W. Sanders, pub.; Edmund G. Rose, book and job printer [1894?]. 78p.
MtGf.

Religion and Philosophy

3184. _____. Colusa. Articles of incorporation, 1894. [5] p. Printed form filled in. C-ArS.
    Trustees: J. S. Brooks, A. W. Edwards, Wade Diggs, J. A. Reaves, and Robert McDonald.

3185. _____. Fresno. Articles of incorporation, 1891. [4] p. Printed form filled in. C-ArS.
    Trustees: A. S. Walton, Wallace Bridges, Marion Hall, James Smith, J. F. Davidson, and H. Burdett.

3186. _____. Puget Sound conference. Official minutes of the ... session ... [n.p.] ... v. DLC.

3187. _____. Sacramento. Articles of incorporation, Sacramento, 1874. Ms. [5] p. C-ArS.
    Incorporators were Abram Giles, Henry W. Dorsey, Manley Reyes, George W. Fisher, George W. Shephard, Hester Saunders, Ellen Coger [i.e., COGAR], Lucinda Ray, Henrietta Harguss, Emily Warren, Mary A. Booth, Ann Campbell, Josiah Dunlap, William S. Civells, Daniel Blue, William Greenley, Arimia Giles, Priscilla Whittaker, Eliza Postles, Maria E. Jackson, Ann Adams, Ellen Penny, Daisy Washington, Diana Brown, Elizabeth Williams, Rachel Davis, Sarah Edwards, and Martha Civell[s].

3188. _____. San Diego. Articles of incorporation, 1890. [5] p. Typew. C-ArS.
    Trustees were B. F. Newman, J. H. McReynold, Solomon Johnson, A. J. Hosman, and Cain Acker.

3189. _____. _____. Santa Barbara. Articles of incorporation, 1906. [5] p. Typew. C-ArS.
    Trustees were N. H. Hill, Jerry Mills, S. L. Wright, and W. H. Peck.

3190. _____. Southern California conference. Souvenir programme, annual session. COEB 9th (1933).

3191. *African Methodist Episcopal Zion church. Hanford. Articles of incorporation, 1892. [5] p. Printed form filled in. C-ArS.
    Trustees: Sidney A. Knox, W. W. Walker, G. W. Wood, Frank Walker, and George Johnson.

3192. _____. Los Angeles. Articles of incorporation, 1904. [6] p. Typew. C-ArS.
    Trustees: Elbert L. Leland, John B. Bowman, John Jackson, William Hurd, W. H. Shores, George Brown, Paul E. Brown, Jack Johnson, and Israel Murphy.

3193. _____. Modesto. Articles of incorporation, 1907. [5] p. Typew. C-ArS.
    Directors were Robert Williams, Laura Oby, Mrs. Tena Williams, Mary Collins, and Nick Campbell. Election officers were S. A. Knox and Lorraine Collins.

Religion and Philosophy

3194. _____. Monrovia. Articles of incorporation, 1908. [8] p. Typew.
and Ms. C-ArS.
    Trustees were   the Rev. George H. Haines, W. D. Hollins, E. L.
Adams, R. Izor, and D. Graham. Other signatories were C. E. Avatom,
Mary E. Shaw, Mrs. H. Shaw, Mrs. Daniel Graham, Martha Moore, Mrs. Alice
McQueen, Annie McQueen, and P. E. Adams.

3195. _____. Palo Alto. [Choral society program of excerpts from Nevin's
The crucified, Apr. 6, 1947]. [3] p. CPa.

3196. *African Methodist Episcopal Zion church of America.   Articles of
incorporation, San Jose, 1883. Amendment, 1945. [9] p. Ms. and typew.
C-ArS.
    Directors were   Henry Venable, William H. Davis, George Caples,
John Madden, and Howard Franklin. William H. Mitchell was pastor.

3197. *African spiritual helping hand undenominational national church.
Articles of incorporation, San Francisco, 1946. [5] p. Printed form
filled in. C-ArS.
    A branch of the principal church at Meridian, Miss., and operated in
San Francisco by the Rev. L. H. Narcisse.

3198. *Afro-American young men's Christian league association.   Articles of
incorporation, Oakland, 1909. [6] p. Typew. C-ArS.
    "... to provide for the physical, mental, and religious welfare of
the young Negro men or Afro-Americans of Oakland ..." Trustees were Z.
Withers, E. Marshall, William Butler, W. J. J. Byers, Charles E. Carpenter,
Tyler M. Davis, R. C. Gilmore, I. H. McClelland, Lawrence Sledge, and
William Gardner.

3199. *ALLEN, GEORGE R., comp. Soldiers' Bible and their life insurance,
by Geo. R. Allen. Colorado Springs, Colo., The society of the gospel
of the kingdom [c1918]. 64 p. DLC.
    Selections from the Bible, etc.

3200. ALLEN, KRING. "Integration by the cross," in Christian century, v. 75,
Aug. 20, 1958, pp. 943-45.
    Integration of McCarthy memorial Christian church, Los Angeles.

3201. *Allen temple Baptist church, Oakland.   The dedication of the new
edifice and 42nd anniversary services ... [Oakland, 1961?]. [24] p.
illus., ports. COEB.

3202. *ANDERSON, GARLAND.   Uncommon sense; the law of life in action, by
Garland Anderson ... London, L. N. Fowler & co. [1933]. 220 p. DLC.
    A philosophy of life based on curing by faith. Authored by a San
Francisco playwright.

3203. _____. Same. [N. Y., Author, 1933]. DHU.

3204. ATWOOD, ALBERT. Glimpses in pioneer life on Puget Sound. Seattle,
Denny-Coryell co., 1903. 483 p. illus., ports. CSf, CSmH, Or, OrHi,
OrU, Wa, WaSp, WaTC, WaU, NUC, pre-1956.

Religion and Philosophy

A history of the African Methodist Episcopal church, Seattle, and a
portrait of its pastor, Shepard S. Freeman, may be found, pp. 459–61.

3205. *Baptists.   California state convention.   Proceedings.   COEB 1st (1929);
1–3rd [sic] (1942–44); 6th (1948); 26th (1967).

3206. _____.   _____.   Program.   COEB 19th (1965).

3207. _____.   _____.   Union usher board.   Souvenir program.   COEB 26th
(1967).

3208. _____.   _____.   Young people's dept.   Souvenir book.   California state
Baptist convention, inc.   Young people's department presents Christian
debutantes of 1968 ... July 17, 1968 ... Los Angeles ... [L. A., 1968].
[16] p.   ports.

3209. _____.   Convention.   Minutes of a Baptist convention held with the
First Baptist church, San Francisco, Feb. 2d, 3d, and 4th, 1860.   S. F.,
Towne and Bacon, printer, 1860.   24 p.   CBBD, CU-B, Drury 202.
For information about the Third Baptist church, San Francisco, the
Second Baptist church, Stockton, Mt. Olivet Baptist church, Marysville,
and Siloam Baptist church, Sacramento, see pp. 15 and 17.

3210. _____.   General Baptist association.   Proceedings.   COEB 9th (1908);
12–16th; 18–19th; 21–23rd; 27–36th; 38th; 40–43rd; 47–48th; 56th; 58th;
61st; 63rd (1962).
Title varies: Program, minutes, constitution.

3211. _____.   National convention.   Proceedings, annual session.   COEB 59th
(Los Angeles, 1939); 79th (San Francisco, 1959); 81st (San Francisco,
1961).

3212. _____.   _____.   Woman's auxiliary.   Annual report.   COEB 11th (San
Francisco, 1959).
Title varies slightly.

3213. _____.   National Sunday school and Baptist training union conference.
Minutes.
1947 (Oakland).
1956 (Los Angeles).
Title from Universal books catalog no. 152.

3214. _____.   _____.   Souvenir program.   COEB 1947, CSfAA 18th (1962).

3215. _____.   St. John's district association of northern California.
Woman's auxiliary.   [Annual report].   COEB 1953; 1956.
Title varies slightly.

3216. _____.   Sunday school publishing board.   Report of the Sunday school
publishing board to the National Baptist convention ... S. F., 1959.
31 p.   ports.
Title from Universal books catalog no. 152.

Religion and Philosophy

3217. _____. Western Baptist association. Annual report by Dr. Horace
N. Mays, director of Christian education, and Rev. Percy Williams,
missionary-evangelist, to the sixty-seventh annual session of the
Western Baptist state convention, August 5-9, 1957. [L. A., 1957].
15 p. Mimeo.
      Title from Universal books catalog no. 152.

3218. _____. _____. First annual report of the Board of managers of the
Old folks home of the Western Baptist association, Abila, California.
[n.p., 1919?]. 50 p.
      Title from Universal books catalog no. 152.

3219. _____. _____. Minutes. 1890- . NUC, pre-1956.

3220. Beebe memorial Christian Methodist Episcopal church, Oakland.* Grand
opening, Sunday, April 17, 1966 ... [Oakland, 1966]. [44] p. illus.,
ports. COEB.
      "A brief history of Beebe memorial": pp. [6-7].

3221. *Berkeley bible and health chautauqua. Souvenir of Berkeley bible and
health chautauqua, Berkeley, California, September to November, 1929.
Songs and sermons of evangelists [Owen A.] Troy and [J. E.] Johnson ...
[Oakland?, 1929]. 16 p. illus., ports. CSfAA.

3222. *Beth Eden Baptist church, Oakland. Articles of incorporation, Oakland,
1891. Ms. [3] p. C-ArS.
      Directors were C. D. Cole, J. A. Harrod, Henry S. Peterson, Henry
Homager, and Samuel A. Jones.

3223. _____. Constitution and by-laws, Beth Eden Baptist church, 10th and
Magnolia streets, Oakland, Calif. J. P. Hubbard, minister. Adopted
Nov. 19, 1941. [Oakland, Charles Tilghman, print., 1941]. 17 p.

3224. _____. The fortieth anniversary and mortgage burning ... November 18,
19, 20, 21, 23, 24, 1930. [Oakland, 1930]. [5] p. COEB.
      "Historical sketch": p. 1.

3225. _____. Golden jubilee souvenir, 1890-1940; fiftieth anniversary of
Beth Eden Baptist church, Tenth and Magnolia streets, Oakland, California
... Berkeley, Engraved and printed by Chas. F. Tilghman & son [1940].
42 p. illus., ports. COEB.

3226. _____. Silver anniversary; the twenty-fifth anniversary of the
service of John P. and Mary E. Hubbard with the Beth Eden Baptist
church ... November 10-17, 1946. [Oakland, 1946]. 9 p. ports. COEB.

3227. * Bethel African Methodist Episcopal church, San Francisco. Bethel
A. M. E. church, 1852-1952. S. F. [1952]. 20 p. illus., ports. CHi
(photocopy).
      Contains "Bethel history," by John H. Fisher, pp. 3-8.

3228. BLOOM, JACK M. The Negro church and the movement for equality.
Master's thesis, Univ. of Calif., Berkeley, 1966. ii, 190 ℓ.

Religion and Philosophy

3229. "Cardinal McIntyre: a Ramparts special report," in Ramparts, v. 3, Nov., 1964, pp. 35-44.
   The attitude of James Francis Aloysius, Cardinal McIntyre toward racial equality in southern California.

3230. Cheyenne centennial committee, pub. The magic city of the plains; Cheyenne, 1867-1967. Cheyenne, Wyo., Cheyenne lith., inc., 1967. 123 p. illus., ports. Wy.
   Information on the founding of the African Methodist Episcopal church is given including a photograph of Mrs. Lucy Phillips (b. 1805?), pp. 37-38.

3231. Church for the fellowship of all peoples, San Francisco. ... Membership roster, 1970. [S. F.] 1970. 9 p.

3232. _____. Thumbnail history. S. F. [1968]. 3 p. Mimeo.
   A history of an integrated church, 1943-68. Founded by the Rev. Howard Thurman.

3233. Church of all faiths, Oakland.* Souvenir program ... R. Colby Thomas, minister. [Oakland, 1969]. 52 p. ports. COEB.
   "History": pp. 1-4.

3234. Church of the good shepherd (Baptist), Oakland.* Directory. [Oakland, 1963]. COEB.

3235. _____. Fifth anniversary of founding, Church of the good shepherd (Baptist), Sunday, March 11, 1962 ... [Oakland, 1962]. 4 p. illus., ports. COEB.
   "Historical sketch ...": pp. 1-2.

3236. _____. Tenth anniversary founding, 1957-1967, Church of the good shepherd (Baptist) ... [Oakland, Tilghman press, 1967]. 16 p. illus., ports. COEB.
   "Historical sketch ...": pp. 1-3.

3237. *CLARK, JOHN E. 1st battalion of the regiment. Seattle, 1907. 16 p.
   Publication is noted in the Seattle Republican, June 14, 1907, p. 3. It appears possible that the work is titled or subtitled "Religious thought: gems of truth gleaned from principal sermons recently delivered in the United States and Canada by the leading clergymen, priests, prelates, and professors of the Christian faith."

3238. CLARKE, WALTER MALCOLM. The Freedman's commission of the Protestant Episcopal church in the United States of America, 1865-1877. Master's thesis, Univ. of Calif., Berkeley, 1958. ii, 108 ℓ.

3239. *COLE, PETER K. Cole's war with ignorance and deceit, and his lecture on education delivered in the St. Cyprian church, Tuesday evening, August 11, 1857 ... S. F., Printed by J. H. Udell & R. P. Locke, 1857. 51 p. C, CHi, CSmH, CU-B.
   Preparations for the third state convention of colored citizens, San Francisco, Oct. 13, 1857, are described, pp. 1-20.

Religion and Philosophy

3240. *Cooper African Methodist Episcopal Zion church, Oakland. Souvenir program, 1898-1948; golden anniversary of the greater Cooper A. M. E. Zion church ... [Oakland, 1948]. [30] p. illus., ports. COEB.
"History of the greater Cooper A. M. E. Zion church": pp. [4-7].

3241. Counterpart, pub. Work-C[ounter] P[art]-faith-understanding. [Menlo Park], 1968. 8 p. CMp.

3242. DELAY, PETER JOSEPH, 1865- . History of Yuba and Sutter counties, California, with biographical sketches ... L. A., Historical record co., 1924. 1,328 p. illus., ports. C, CBb, CCC, CHi, CL, CLU, CMary. CO, CS, CSS, CSf, CSmH, CSt, CU-B, CYcCL, Rocq 15578.
Accounts of Marysville's African Methodist Episcopal church (est. 1854) and Mt. Olivet Baptist church (est. 1856), p. 183.

3243. "Discretion of Director of corrections not abused in refusing to grant Black Muslim prisoners rights afforded other religious groups," in UCLA law review, v. 9, Mar., 1962, p. 501.

3244. *Downs memorial Methodist church, Oakland. Downs memorial Methodist church, 1949-1965. [Souvenir program. Oakland, 1965?]. 20 p. illus., ports. COEB.

3245. _____. A living memorial to Dr. Karl Downs. Oakland [1954]. [26] p. illus., ports., plan. COEB.
Formerly the Golden gate Methodist Episcopal church.

3246. *EVERS, MYRLIE. "Black Christmas," in Ladies home journal, v. 85, Dec., 1968, pp. 83-84.

3247. FAWCETT, MARGARET GOLDSMITH. The northern Negro church - its participation in the civil rights movement. Master's thesis, Calif. state univ., San Francisco, 1969. 86 ℓ.
"An historical survey of the northern Negro church and its role in the black community. Particular emphasis is given to the Negro church in Chicago and San Francisco."

3248. *First African Methodist Episcopal church, Los Angeles. Milestones of progress: 1872, 1903, 1953; 81st anniversary of founding and 50th year at 8th and Towne ... L. A. [1953]. [25] ℓ. illus., ports.

3249. *First African Methodist Episcopal church, Oakland. Anniversary and hostess banquet celebration. CU-B 78th (1936). (photocopy).

3250. _____. Centennial ... Souvenir program. First African Methodist Episcopal church, Oakland, 1958. 40 p. illus., ports. CO, COEB.

3251. _____. ... Dedication of rebuilt sanctuary, August 19, 1969 ... and reception to one-hundred-fifth session, California annual conference, African Methodist Episcopal church ... [Oakland, 1969]. 24 p. illus., ports. COEB.
"Brief history of the California annual conference": p. 2.
"History of First African Methodist Episcopal church, Oakland, California": p. 4.

Religion and Philosophy

3252. _____. Organ – chancel – improvement. Dedication services, First
African Methodist Episcopal church, Telegraph avenue at 37th street,
Oakland, California, March 17th ... [Oakland, California voice pub. co.,
1963]. 22 p. illus., ports. COEB.
   Contains lists of church officers and committee members and some
biographical information.

3253. _____. Souvenir program, relocation service, June 20–July 4; dedication service, July 25th ... [Oakland, 1954]. 35 p. illus., ports.
COEB.

3254. First African Methodist Episcopal Zion church, San Francisco.* The
centennial year, 1852–1952 ... [S. F., 1952]. 32 p. illus., ports.
CHi (photocopy).
   Contains a history of the church entitled "Through the years."

3255. _____. Souvenir program ... dedication services ... S. F. [1960].
[32] p. illus., ports. CHi (photocopy).
   Contains a short history of the church, 1852–1960.

3256. First African Methodist Episcopal Zion church of the city of San
Francisco, appellant, vs. William H. Hillery, et al, respondents. Points
and authorites of appellant. Geo. W. Tyler, S. L. Cutter, attorneys for
appellant. S. F., Cuddy and Hughes, 1875. 2 p. No. 4832 in the Supreme
court of the state of California. C–ArS.
   A suit over possession of the church building and against the Rev.
Hillery, William J. Parker, George F. Norton, John Harris, Samuel E.
Freeman, William Harris, George Goodman, and James Hargro[ve].

3257. _____. Points and authorities of respondent. Frank G. Newlands,
counsel for respondents. [S. F., 1875]. 2 p. C–ArS.

3258. _____. Transcript on appeal. Geo. W. Tyler, S. L. Cutter, attorneys
for appellant. S. F., Cuddy and Hughes, 1875. 12 p. C–ArS.

3259. FISK, ELINOR WILLIAMS. Some of the early churches of California; a
survey by Elinor Williams Fisk and Harriet Trumbull Parsons for the
Historical activities committee of the National society of colonial dames
of America resident in the state of California. [S. F., 1968]. 23 p.
CHi.
   "Negro churches in California": pp. 11–12.

3260. *FLOWERS, SARAH. Common sense and its application in everyday life.
L. A., 1941. 204 p.

3261. _____. Same. L. A., 1953.
   Titles from Universal books catalog no. 164, items no. 326–27.

3262. _____. Metaphysical thesaurus of positive and negative words and
chronological history of the metaphysical movements from 500 B. C. to
date, by Sarah Flowers ... L. A., Author [1942]. 75 p. DLC.

Religion and Philosophy

3263. *FLUTCHER, J. E.   The dogma of the church; nature, design and general
rule of the Methodist societies [by] Rev. J. E. Flutcher. [Oakland, n.d.].
8 p. port. COEB.
       By the clergyman of Parks chapel, African Methodist Episcopal church,
Oakland.

3264. *Friendship Baptist church, Pasadena.   Articles of incorporation,
1902. Ms. 4 p. C-ArS.
       Trustees: Thomas Nixson, R. B. Scott, W. C. Dent, J. E. Iverson,
W. E. Ford, P. F. Ballard, and Henry Griffin.

3265. GRANT, CURTIS ROBERT.   The social gospel and race.   Doctoral dissertation, Stanford univ., Stanford, 1968. vii, 208 ℓ.

3266. *Gray, Henry, and Elizabeth Gray, plaintiffs and respondents, vs. the
African Methodist Episcopal Zion church of America, a corporation, defendant and appellant. Appellant's points and authorities in reply.
J. C. Black, attorney for appellants ... San Jose, Brower bros., 1888.
8 p. CU-B.
       A case in the Supreme court of the state of California over a 50 vara
lot in San Jose.

3267. _____.   Transcript on appeal. J. C. Black, for appellant. Moore &
Moore, for respondents ... San Jose, Cottle & Brower, 1885. 48 p. CU-B.

3268. GRIER, ALBERT C.   Father Divine, by Rev. Albert C. Grier.   Santa
Barbara, The red rose press [n.d.]. 28 p.

3269. HALL, MARTIN.   "What God hath wrought; experiment in church integration
in Los Angeles," in Frontier, v. 8, Sept., 1957, pp. 17-18.

3270. HENRY, HELEN ELIZABETH.   A study of attitudes and social values of
the youth of four selected Negro churches of Los Angeles ... Master's
thesis, Univ. of southern Calif., Los Angeles, 1945. vii, 108 ℓ. tables,
forms.

3271. *HILL, JOSEPH TYLER.   The influence of metaphysics upon civilization.
Master's thesis, Univ. of southern Calif., Los Angeles, 1909. 44 ℓ.

3272. HINE, LELAND D.   Baptists in California [by] Leland D. Hine.   Valley
Forge [Pa.], Judson press [c1966]. 192 p. illus., ports.
       Gives some information on Negro Baptists.

3273. Historical records survey. Illinois. Directory of Negro Baptist
churches in United States ... Prepared by Illinois historical records
survey, Division of community service programs, Work projects administration. Sponsored by the governor of Illinois. Chicago, Illinois historical records survey, Illinois public records project, 1942. 2 v.
maps. Reproduced from typew. copy. CU.
       Gives information about the Western Baptist state convention,
California; Western Baptist state convention of Colorado; Washington
Baptist state convention; and the Independent Negro Baptist churches of
Montana.

Religion and Philosophy

3274. HOGG, THOMAS CLARK, 1935- . The functions of the Negro socio-re-
ligious categories as reference groups. Master's thesis, Univ. of
Oregon, Eugene, 1963.

3275. *HORTON, ELIZA. My visions from Eliza Horton (colored lady). Oakland,
Calif., April, 1916. [Oakland?, 1916?]. [11] ℓ. COEB.
    Religious experiences in Texas, 1874-99.

3276. *HUBBARD, JOHN PURLEY. [Christianity challenged in open conflict].
Delivered as the annual sermon before the Northern California Baptist
state convention, Martinez, California, Wednesday, October 4, 1950, by
J. P. Hubbard, minister in the Beth Eden Baptist church, Oakland,
California. [Oakland?, 1950?]. 13 p. COEB.

3277. _____. Holiness as taught in the scriptures, by Rev. J. P. Hubbard,
B. D. pastor, Beth Eden Baptist church, Oakland, California. Oakland
[1922]. 6 p. port. COEB.

3277a.*HUFFMAN, EUGENE HENRY. "God is in his heaven;" a vivid description
of life in Father Divine's kingdom, by Evangelist Eugene Henry Huffman
... [Philadelphia, Hoffmano pub., c1955]. 74 p.
    Cover title.
    Authored by a Los Angeles and San Francisco resident.

3277b. _____. Now the scripture says: - a collection of the homespun
philosophy of Eugene Henry Huffman ... [L. A., Dependable printers,
c1943]. [10] ℓ.

3278. *INGLEWOOD, MARIAN. Stories from the workingman's book, by Marian
Inglewood ... Philadelphia, Dorrance and co. [1942]. 92 p. CL, CLU.
    Communism and Christianity. Authored by a Los Angeles journalist.

3279. ISAACS, JOHN BENJAMIN ST. FELIX, 1887- . An evaluation of the
literature of the African Methodist Episcopal church in the discovery
and training of leaders ... Master's thesis, Univ. of southern Calif.,
Los Angeles, 1939. v, 103 ℓ. tables, form.

3280. *JACKSON, J. H. Annual address of President J. H. Jackson delivered
at the seventy-ninth annual session of the National Baptist convention,
U. S. A., inc., September 10th, 1959, Pacific auditorium. San Francisco,
[1959]. 24 p. port. COEB.

3281. LEWIS, JOHN J. Good will among men. A San Diego publication ... by
... John J. Lewis, Minister, St. Paul Methodist church. San Diego
[1946?]. 100 p. CSd.
    Contains essays and tributes prepared for revival meetings, May 5-
17, 1956.

3282. *MC GRIFF, D. L. Withered grass; an appeal for the resurrection of
Negro Baptist churches in the great northwest, by Mr. and Mrs. D. L.
McGriff. Marysville [Printed by Reifsnider's print shop], 1946. 19 p.
port. COEB.

Religion and Philosophy

3283. MARX, GARY TRADE. "Religion: opiate or inspiration of civil rights militancy among Negroes?", in American sociological review, v. 32, Feb., 1967, pp. 64-72.
"... publication A-72 of the Survey research center, University of California, Berkeley." A general survey by a Univ. of Calif. faculty member.

3284. Methodist Episcopal church, South. Pacific conference. Minutes of the California annual conference, M. E. church, south, sixth session, held in Sacramento, November 5th-11th, 1856. S. F., Whitton, Towne & co., 1856. 26 p. CSaT (photocopy), CSmH.
Contains a pro-slavery sermon preached before the Conference.

3285. MONTESANO, PHILIP MICHAEL, 1941- . The black churches in urban San Francisco, 1860-1865; their education, civic and civil rights activities. Graduate paper, Univ. of Calif., Santa Barbara, 1968. 29 p. map, tables. CSf (photocopy).

3286. Morningstar missionary Baptist church, Los Angeles.* Thirty-eighth anniversary, 1928-1966. L. A., 1966. 56 p. illus., ports. C, CU-B.
A souvenir booklet.

3287. *MORRIS, CHARLES SATCHELL. The greatest babe ever born and other messages, by Charles Satchell Morris, II ... [n.p., 195-?]. 56 p. illus., ports. COEB.
Partly autobiographical and containing history of the Baptist church in California and biographical information on Charles Satchell (1806?-1872).

3288. *Mt. Olivet Baptist church, Marysville. Minutes and other records, 1881-1926. CHi (neg. film), CMary (film).

3289. *Mt. Zion Baptist church, San Francisco. Articles of incorporation, 1948. Ms. 5 p. C-ArS.
Directors included Samuel Johnson, Willie Colman, and Will Odoms.

3290. National united church ushers association of America, inc.* Souvenir program, forty-sixth annual convention of the National united church ushers association of America, inc., 1919-1965, July 25-31, 1965, Third Baptist church ... San Francisco ... [S. F., 1965]. 124 p. illus., ports.

3291. *North Oakland Baptist church. Souvenir program, 1913-1940; twenty-seventh anniversary of Dr. G. C. Coleman ... February 11-19, 1940. [Oakland?, 1940?] 13 p. illus., ports. COEB.
"A brief history, by Bro. F. H. Bolmer": p. 1.

3292. Oakland council of churches. Dept. of Christian human relations. Questions and answers regarding open housing. Oakland, 1959. 2 ℓ. CO.

3293. *Parks chapel African Methodist Episcopal church, Oakland. Souvenir yearbook of Parks chapel African Methodist Episcopal church, Oakland, California and welcome to the eighty-third annual session of the

Religion and Philosophy

California convention, August 26 to 31, 1947 ... [Oakland, California voice print., 1947]. 34 p. illus., ports. COEB.

3294. PLOWMAN, E. E. "Campus ministry goads strikers," in Christianity today, v. 13, Jan. 17, 1969, p. 44.
    Calif. state univ., San Francisco.

3295. PRICE, THOMAS AUBREY. Negro storefront churches in San Francisco; a study of their spatial characteristics in two selected neighborhoods. Master's thesis, Calif. state univ., San Francisco, 1969. 128 ℓ. illus., tables, 8 fold. maps.
    "'Negro storefront churches, as part of the religious-social life of black people, are one of the parts of the Negro community that must be understood before full comprehension of what it is to be black can be achieved.' The author relates his study to the income level, density, transportation and commercial activity of the districts in which these churches are prevalent."

3296. RIDOUT, LIONEL UTLEY. "The church, the Chinese, and the Negroes in California, 1849-1893," in Historical magazine of the Protestant Episcopal church, v. 28, June, 1959, pp. 115-38.
    Describes the religious activities of Peter Williams Cassey (b. 1832?) in San Francisco and San Jose and his "Phoenixian [sic] institute," San Jose.

3297. *St. Andrew's African Methodist Episcopal church of Sacramento. Articles of incorporation, 1946. 4 p. Typew. C-ArS.
    Directors were John Slaughter, Mrs. Ophelia Daniels, Willie C. Credic, W. M. Wagoner, Mrs. Alice Trigg, Charles Nicholas, Douglas McFarland, and E. F. Ridley.

3298. _____. Diamond jubilee, 1850-1925, St. Andrews church (African Methodist Episcopal) ... [Sacramento, 1925]. [8] p. illus., ports. Folder. C, CU-B.

3299. *St. Augustine's Episcopal church, Oakland. 50th anniversary and musical extravaganza ... [Oakland?, 1960]. 16 p. illus., ports. CSfAA.

3300. *St. Paul African Methodist Episcopal church, Berkeley. Annual report. COEB 1966/67-1967/68.

3301. _____. Dedication, cornerstone laying and mortgage burning ... August 9th to August 12th, 1943 ... [Berkeley, 1943]. 19 p. illus., ports. COEB.

3302. *Second African Methodist Episcopal church. Articles of incorporation, Los Angeles, 1938. 3 p. Typew. C-ArS.
    Directors were Charles Alexander Harris, pastor, Maggie E. Hicks, Olysteen Hall, Clarence L. James, John L. Lampkins, Joseph Buckner, R. E. Salisbury, Bates Mays, David Beeks, and Salena G. Jennings.

3303. *Second African Methodist Episcopal church of San Francisco. Renewal of its April 16, 1862 articles of incorporation, 1885. Ms. [3] p. C-ArS.

Religion and Philosophy

     Usually known as Bethel African Methodist Episcopal church. Officers and directors were Abraham Lee, George W. Lee, William L. Morris, John Pointer, Henry Smedley, Christopher R. Weeden, Robert C. Wilson, Robert Seymour, and F. W. Jackson.

3304. Second Baptist church, Los Angeles.* The seventh annual Spring music festival, 1970 ... [L. A., 1970]. [10] p. ports. COEB.
    Souvenir booklet.

3305. SESHACHARI, CANDADAI. Gandhi and the American scene: an intellectual history and inquiry. Doctoral dissertation, Univ. of Utah, Salt Lake City, 1964.
    "American interest in the ideas of Gandhi, with emphasis on the intellectual involvement of Reinhold Niebuhr and the practical involvement of Martin Luther King, Jr." - West, p. 86.

3306. *Shiloh Baptist church, Sacramento. 110th anniversary, 1856-1966 ... Sacramento [1966]. [110] p. illus., ports. COEB.

3307. *Shiloh Baptist church's Investigating committee, Sacramento vs. John M. Collins, J. W. Gudgel, and Humphreys Moody. Mss. [15] p. C-ArS.
    A California Supreme court suit over the repair and remodeling of the church, 1910-11. Members of the investigating committee were Mrs. Mayme Harris, James Brinson, and P. J. Clyde.

3308. *[STOKES, DARIUS P.]. A lecture upon the moral and religious elevation of the people of California delivered before the congregation of the African Methodist Episcopal church of Sacramento City, June 1853, by the Rev. Darius Stokes ... S. F., Office of the evening Journal, 1853. 18 p. CHi (photocopy), CSaT (photocopy), CSmH.

3309. TAYLOR, JOHN A. "This church in this decade"; an analysis by John A. Taylor, minister. The church for the fellowship of all peoples, San Francisco, October 8, 1969. [S. F., 1969]. 7 p. Mimeo. CSf.

3310. *Third Baptist church, San Francisco. Annual report of organizations, auxiliary and individual contributions, January-December, 1956 ... S. F., 1956. 85, 30 p. illus.

3311. _____. 1852-1952. Third Baptist church of San Francisco. Centennial booklet ... [S. F., 1952]. 152 p. illus., ports. COEB.

3312. _____. ... 1852-1962 anniversary souvenir program and honor roll, Third Baptist church ... [S. F., 1962]. [56] p. illus., ports.

3313. _____. More than a century of witnessing through spiritual involvement, Third Baptist church, Rev. F. D. Haynes, minister. [S. F., 1967]. [104] p. illus., ports. CHi.
    Souvenir book, 115th anniversary of founding.

3314. _____. Official program and dedicatory and opening services ... [S. F., 1908]. [8] p. illus., port. COEB.

Religion and Philosophy

3315. _____. Official souvenir program, Third Baptist church, seventeenth annual session, California state Baptist convention, inc. ... San Francisco, California, July 7-13, 1958 ... [S. F., 1958]. 36 p. illus., ports.

3316. _____. Third Baptist church 1969 calendar ... [S. F., 1968]. [33] p. illus., ports.

3317. *THURMAN, HOWARD, 1899- . The centering moment. N. Y., Harper & Row, [1969]. 125 p. CSf.

3318. _____. The creative encounter; an interpretation of religion and the social witness. N. Y., Harper [1954]. 153 p. CL, CLCo, CLSU, CLob, CMa, CMl, CMerCL, CPhCL, CSrCL, CSto.

3319. _____. Deep is the hunger; meditations for apostles of sensitiveness. N. Y., Harper, 1951. x, 212 p. Available in many libraries.
     An expansion of his Meditations for apostles of sensitiveness pub. in 1951.

3320. _____. "The Fellowship church of all people," in Common ground, v. 5, Spring, 1945, pp. 29-31.

3321. _____. Footprints of a dream; the story of the Church for the fellowship of all peoples. N. Y., Harper [1959]. 157 p. illus. CBaK, CF, CFa, CL, CLCo, CLob, CMl, CO, CPhCL, CRbCL, CRcS, CRic, CSbCL, CSf, CSjCL, CSluCL, CSrCL, CSt, CStcrCL, WaT.
     Doctor Thurman was pastor of this church, 1944-1954.

3322. _____. The growing edge. [N. Y.] Harper [1956]. 181 p. CL, CSf, WaT, WaTC.

3323. _____. The inward journey. N. Y., Harper [1961]. 155 p. CFa, CL, CLob, CNF, CO, COrCL, CP, CPhCL, CRic, CSf, CSjCL, CSrCL, CStrCL, CVtCL, WaT, WaTC.

3324. _____. Jesus and the disinherited. N. Y., Abington-Cokesbury press [1949]. 112 p. CF, CL, CLCo, CLSU, CLob, CP, CRic, CStcrCL, CViCL, WaT.

3325. _____. Meditations for apostles of sensitiveness. Mills college, Eucalyptus press, 1947. 6 p.ℓ., 43 [2] ℓ. CSf, CU.
     "Five hundred copies ..."

3326. _____. Same. 2d ed., 1948. 93 p. CO.

3327. _____. Meditations of the heart. N. Y., Harper [1953]. 216 p. CL, CSbCL, CSf, WaPu, WaT, WaTC.

3328. _____. Mysticism and the experience of love. Wallingford, Pa., Pendle Hill [1961]. 23 p. CLSU, WaTC.

Religion and Philosophy

3329. _____. Temptations of Jesus; five sermons given by Dean Howard Thurman in Marshal chapel, Boston university. [S. F.] Designed and printed by Lawton Kennedy, 1962. 62 p. CHi.

3330. *TROY, OWEN AUSTIN. The financial system of the Seventh-day adventist church: an evaluation of the factors entering into the adoption and practice of tithing. Doctoral dissertation, Univ. of southern Calif., Los Angeles, 1952. xii, 331 ℓ.

3331. *VASS, S. N. [Poster advertising his appearance at the Third Baptist church, San Francisco, 1913]. CHi.

3332. WACHHORST, WYN. The Catholic press views the Negro, 1945 to 1960. Master's thesis, Calif. state univ., San Jose, 1965. 281 ℓ.

3333. WALSH, MARTIN DE PORRES. The ancient black Christians, by Martin De Porres Walsh, O. P. S. F., Julian Richardson associates [c1969]. viii, 26 p. illus., ports. CSfAA.

3334. *WARD, THOMAS MYERS DECATUR, 1823-1894. [Oration delivered on the first of January in First African Methodist Episcopal Zion church]. S. F., Agnew and Deffebach, 1866.
    Unlocated title. Notice of its publication appears in the San Francisco Elevator, Feb. 2, 1866, p. 2, col. 2.

3335. *WATKINS, WALTER F. The cry of the West; the story of the mighty struggle for religious freedom in California. By Walter F. Watkins, Berkeley, California ... Oakland, Bridges print. co. [1932?]. 40 p. ports. C, COEB.
    The struggle of the Rev. Gordon C. Coleman to secure autonomy for the Negro Baptist association of northern California, 1913-25.

3336. _____. Same. S. F., R and E research associates, 1969. C, CNoS, CSt.

3337. *WEBB, JAMES MORRIS., 1874- . The black man; the father of civilization, proven by Biblical history. [Seattle, Acme press, 1910]. 49 p. illus., ports. NN.
    Contains "The regeneration of Africa," by Pivley Isaka Seme: pp. 41-49.

3338. *WILLIAMS, A. CECIL, 1929- . "Black folks are not for sale," in The black scholar, v. 2, Dec., 1970, pp. 35-42.
    The current conditions of the black church, by a San Francisco Methodist clergyman.

3339. *WISE, NAMON. The Namon Wise story, by Namon Wise. N. Y., Carlton press [c1963]. 38 p. CL.
    Religion as it effects health, by a retired Los Angeles Post office employee. Contains autobiographical information.

3340. YATES, ELIZABETH, 1905- . Howard Thurman, portrait of a practical dreamer. N. Y., John Day co. [c1964]. 249 p. port. CEcaC, CFS, CL,

Religion and Philosophy

 CLSU, CNoS, COM, CSbCL, CSbS, CSf, CSfCiC, CSluCL, CStma.
 "Chronological bibliography of works by Howard Thurman": pp. 241-42.

SLAVERY AND ANTI-SLAVERY

CALIFORNIA AND THE WEST

3341. "Admission of California," in <u>Negro history bulletin</u>, v. 14, Oct.,
1950, p. 9.

3342. American and foreign anti-slavery society. Address to the inhabitants
of New Mexico and California on the omission by Congress to provide them
with territorial government and on the social and political evils of
slavery. N. Y., The Society, 1849. 56 p. CSmH.

3343. BALDWIN, ROGER SHERMAN, 1793-1863. Speech of Hon. R. S. Baldwin of
Connecticut in favor of the admission of California into the union, and
on the territorial bills, and the bill in relation to fugitive slaves,
in connection with Mr. Bell's compromise resolutions. Delivered in
Senate of the United States, March 27 and April 3, 1850. Washington,
D. C., Printed at the Congressional globe office, 1850. 20 p. CSmH,
CU, NUC, pre-1956.

3344. _____. Speech on the bill to establish a territorial government in
Oregon, delivered in the Senate of the United States, June 5, 1848.
Washington, D. C., Congressional globe, 1848. 8 p. OrU.
 Refers to slavery provisions.

3345. Baptists. Oregon. Corvallis association. Minutes of the fifth
annual meeting of the Corvallis Baptist association, held with the
Pleasant Butte church, in Linn county, Oregon, September 6th and 7th,
1861. Corvallis, "Oregon Union" office, 1861. 8 p. OrMcL, OrP, OrU.
 Belknap 600 states that "300 copies ordered printed"; also that
"'... a charge has appeared in public print, intimating, if not alleging,
that Rev. R. C. Hill publicly taught that human slavery was an institution of Divine origin and approved in the Bible ... we have no knowledge
of his ever having taught anything of that character ...'" See also
Belknap 602.

3346. _____. _____. General association. Proceedings of the first annual
meeting of the Baptist general association, held with the Pleasant Butte
church, Linn county, Oregon, October 1st and 2d, A. D. 1858. Portland,
Printed at the office of the Oregon times, 1858. 8 p. CBBD, OrHi, OrMcL,
OrP. 500 copies ordered printed.
 Belknap 306 states, "This appears to be the first open outbreak of
the controversy among Oregon Baptists that split the church throughout
the Civil War. The Corvallis and Central associations maintained an
official position sufficiently neutral to satisfy the Southern Baptists.
The Willamette and Umpqua associations were militantly antislavery."

California and the West

3347. _____. _____. Umpqua association. Minutes of the Umpqua Baptist association. In accordance with previous understanding messengers from Table Rock, Avery's Butte and Looking Glass Baptist churches met at Looking Glass Prairie, Oct. 10th, 1863, to take into consideration the expediency of organizing a Baptist association whose characteristic feature should be non-fellowship with such churches as continued the advocacy of American slavery. [Eugene?, 1864]. 8 p. OrMcL, Belknap 675.

3348. _____. _____. Willamette association. Minutes of the thirteenth anniversary of the Willamette Baptist association, held with the church at West Union, June 22, 23 & 24, 1861. Portland, printed at the "Oregon Farmer" office, 1861. 7 p. CBBD, OrHi, OrMcL, OrP, OrU.
    Belknap 602 states that certain members declined taking seats because others had protested the reception of R. C. Hill on the ground that he had publicly taught that slavery was of divine origin.

3349. *BEASLEY, DELILAH LEONTIUM, 1871-1934. "Slavery in California," in Journal of Negro history, v. 3, Jan. 1918, pp. 33-44.

3350. BELLER, JACK. "Negro slaves in Utah," in Utah historical society quarterly, v. 2, Oct., 1929, pp. 122-26.

3351. BENNETT, HENRY, 1808-1868. Speech of Hon. Henry Bennett, of New York, on the admission of California. Delivered in the House of representatives, Monday, May 27, 1850. Washington, D. C., Printed at the Congressional globe office, 1850. 16 p. CHi.
    Also concerns slavery and the New Mexico-Texas boundary.

3352. BENTON, THOMAS HART, 1782-1858. The admission of California. Speech of Hon. T. H. Benton, of Missouri, in the Senate of the United States, April 8, 1850. On the compromise resolutions of Mr. Bell, of Tennessee, and the proposition to refer them to a select committee. [Washington, D. C.?, 1850]. 8 p. CHi.
    Speech by the father of Mrs. John C. Frémont opposing the introduction of the slavery question into the arguments on the admission of California.

3353. BERWANGER, EUGENE·HARLEY, 1929- . The frontier against slavery; western anti-Negro prejudice and slavery extension controversy. Urbana, Univ. of Ill. press, 1967. viii, 176 p. Bibliography: pp. 147-67. C, CFS, CHS, CLSU, CNoS, CPhD, CSaT, CSdS, CSfCiC, CSluSP, CSmH, CSp, CU-A, CU-B, Wa.

3354. _____. Western anti-Negro sentiment and laws, 1846-60: a factor in the slavery extension controversy. Doctoral dissertation, Univ. of Illinois, Urbana, 1964. CHi (film).

3355. _____. "Western prejudice and the extension of slavery," in Civil war history, v. 12, Sept., 1966, pp. 197-212.

3356. *BLUE, DANIEL. Petition of Daniel Blue for guardianship of the girl, Edith, being held as a slave in Sacramento county, 1864. Ms. [7] p. C-ArS.

California and the West

The Probate court issued to Blue letters of guardianship for the girl aged about 12 years.

3357. California. Constitutional convention, 1849. Report of the debates in the Convention of California, on the formation of the state constitution, in September and October, 1849. By J. Ross Browne. Washington, D. C., Printed by J. T. Towers, 1850. 479, xlvi p. C, CHi, CLSU, CLU, CSf, CSfCP, CSmH, CU, Rocq 5635.
For the extended debate on allowing slavery and free Negroes in California, see pp. 137-47 and 332-35 passim.

3358. _____. Legislature. Third session. C-ArS.
"To the honorable the senate and house of representatives of the sovereign state of California ... The undersigned ask the permission to colonize a rural district and with a population not less than two thousand of their African domestics who are prepared willingly to accompany them to their new desired homes ..."
Ms. petition introduced by Assemblyman Archibald C. Peachy, Feb. 10, 1852. 6 p. Contains signatures of residents of South Carolina and Florida including various members of the Gadsden, Adams, Weston, Hopkins, and Holmes families.

3359. _____. _____. Sixteenth session. California legislature. 16th sess., 1865-66. Constitutional amendment abolishing slavery. In legislature of California, sixteenth session, 1865 & 1866, "Joint resolution No. 1" providing for the ratification of the amendments to the Constitution of the United States ... [S. F.] Lith. by Nahl bros., L. Nagel, print. [1866]. Broadside, 30" x 23". CHi.

Shows facsimile signatures of approving members of the Legislature.

3360. _____. _____. Assembly. Fifth session. Bill no. 17, 1854, "An act amendatory to an act to amend an act respecting fugitives from labor and slaves brought to this state prior to her admission into the Union, approved April 15, 1852." Ms. [7] p. C-ArS.
States that any such persons held to labor before California's admission shall be deemed fugitives only until Apr. 15, 1855.

3361. _____. _____. _____. Ninth session. Bill no. 26, "An act concerning the recapture of slaves escaping from their owners and masters while traveling through or sojourning in this state," 1858. Ms. [5] p. C-ArS.

3362. _____. _____. Senate. Fourth session. Document no. 16 ... Majority and minority reports of the Select committee on the constitution. 31 p. C, CLU, CSf, CSfL, CSmH, CU, NUC, pre-1956.
The section on "Slavery," p. 29, states the Committee's belief that renewed "agitation of the vexed question of slavery" is groundless. This document is usually bound as an Appendix to the Journal of the Senate, 1853.

3363. _____. _____. _____. Fourteenth session. Journal of the Senate during the fourteenth session ... Sacramento, State print., 1863. 679 p.

California and the West

> C, C-ArS, CLU, CSf, CSmH, CU, NUC, pre-1956.
>   For resolutions concerning the Emancipation proclamation, see pp. 21-23.

3364. "California freedom papers," in Journal of Negro history, v. 3, Jan., 1918, pp. 45-54.
>   "These Documents were collected by Miss D[elilah] L. Beasley and M[onroe] N. Work," and consists of manumission papers, 1851-56, pp. 50-54, including those of Mrs. Biddy Mason and her children, 1856.

3365. CHRISTENSEN, J. B. "Negro slavery in Utah territory," in Phylon, v. 18, Oct., 1957, pp. 298-305.

3366. CLAY, HENRY, 1777-1852. Speech of the Hon. Henry Clay, of Kentucky, on presenting his resolutions on the subject of slavery. Delivered in Senate Feb. 5th & 6th, 1850. As reported by the National intelligencer. N. Y., Stringer and Townsend, 1850. 32 p. CLobS, CU-A.
>   Relates to the admission of California and the establishment of territorial government in the residue of territory acquired from Mexico.

3367. CLEVELAND, CHAUNCEY FITCH, 1799-1887. The California question. Speech of Hon. Chauncey F. Cleveland, of Connecticut, in the House of representatives, April 19, 1850, in Committee of the whole on the state of the union, on the president's message transmitting the constitution of California. [Washington, D. C.] Congressional globe office [1850]. 8 p. CSmH, CU-B, NUC, pre-1956.
>   Discusses the extension of slavery into California.

3368. COLE, CORNELIUS, 1822-1924. Speech of the Hon. Cornelius Cole, of California, on arming the slaves. Delivered in the House of representatives, February 18, 1864. Washington, D. C., McGill & Witherow, 1864. 15 p. CU-B, NUC, pre-1956.
>   A speech in favor of the arming.

3369. Congregational churches. Oregon. Minutes of the annual meeting of the Oregon association held at Forest Grove, Washington county, Oregon, 1858. Portland, Pacific Christian advocate press, 1858. 16 p. OrFP, OrHi.
>   Belknap 311 states: "On pp. 6-7, a strong antislavery resolution adopted by the association."

3370. _____. _____. Minutes of the Congregational association of Oregon: at their annual meeting held at Salem, Sept., 1859. Portland, Advocate press, 1859. 32 p. OrFP, OrHi, OrU.
>   Belknap 417 states: "pp. 6-7: antislavery resolutions ..."

3371. COY, OWEN COCHRAN. "Evidences of slavery in California," in Grizzly bear, v. 19, Sept., 1916, p. 4, and Oct., 1916, pp. 1-2.
>   Records the existence of manumission papers in the archives of El Dorado, Placer, and Mendocino counties.

3372. DAVENPORT, TIMOTHY W. "Slavery question in Oregon; recollections and reflections of a historical nature having special relation to the slavery

California and the West

agitation in the Oregon territory and including the political status up to the beginning of secession in 1861," in Oregon historical quarterly, v. 9, Sept., 1908, pp. 189-253; Dec., 1908, pp. 309-73.

3373. DAVIS, JEFFERSON, 1808-1889. Speech of Mr. Davis of Mississippi on the subject of slavery in the territories; delivered in the Senate of the United States, February 13 & 14, 1850. [Washington, D. C., Towers, 1850]. 32 p. CSaT, CSmH.

3373a. DE FERRARI, CARLO M. "Steven Spencer Hill, fugitive from labor," in Tuolumne county historical society Quarterly, Jan.-Mar., 1966, pp. 162-64.
    An account of Hill's legal struggles to free himself from slavery in Tuolumne county, 1853-54.

3374. DICKEY, JESSE C. Speech of Hon. Jesse C. Dickey, of Pennsylvania, in the House of representatives, in reference to the admission of California and the subject of slavery. Made in Committee of the whole, June 6, 1850. [Washington, D. C., 1850]. 7 p. DHU.

3375. DUNIWAY, CLYDE AUGUSTUS, 1866-1944. "Slavery in California after 1848," in American historical association. Annual report ... for the year 1905, v. 1, pp. 241-48.

3376. DURKEE, CHARLES, 1808-1870. Speech of Charles Durkee of Wisconsin, on the California question. Made in the House of representatives, June 10, 1850. [Washington, D. C., Printed by Buell & Blanchard, 1850]. 15 p. DHU.

3377. FOWLER, ORIN, 1791-1852. Slavery in California and New Mexico. Speech of Mr. Orin Fowler, of Massachusetts, in the House of representatives, March 11, 1850, in Committee of the whole on the state of the Union, on the President's Message communicating the Constitution of California. [Washington, D. C., Buell & Blanchard, printers, 1850]. 15 p. CBGTU, CHi, CNoS, CSaT, CSmH, CU-A, CU-B.

3378. FRANKLIN, WILLIAM E. "The Archy case: the California Supreme court refuses to free a slave," in Pacific historical review, v. 32, May, 1963, pp. 137-54.

3379. GANTNER, VALLEJO. Slavery and California. [S. F.?, 1932?]. 6 p. Typew. CHi.

3380. GENTRY, MEREDITH POINDEXTER, 1809-1866. Speech of Mr. M. P. Gentry, of Tennessee, on the admission of California. Delivered in the House of representatives, Monday, June 10, 1850. [Washington, D. C., Gideon & co., printers, 1850]. 8 p. CHi.
    Discusses the impossibility of slavery gaining a foothold in the territories acquired from Mexico.

3381. GIBBONS, RODMOND. Address to the Chamber of commerce of San Francisco, by a member. S. F., 1865. 19 p. CU-B.
    His opinions on the Crittenden compromise, the Civil war, and slavery.

California and the West

3382. GIDDINGS, JOSHUA REED, 1795-1864. Slavery in the territories. Speech of Hon. J. R. Giddings of Ohio, in the House of representatives, Monday, March 18, 1850, in Committee of the whole on the state of the Union, on the President's Message transmitting the constitution of California. [Washington, D. C., Buell & Blanchard, 1850]. 8 p. CU-A.
Makes but slight reference to California.

3383. HART, CHARLES R. D. Congressmen and the expansion of slavery into the territories: a study in attitudes, 1846-61. Doctoral dissertation, Univ. of Washington, Seattle [n.d.].

3384. HENDRICKSON, JAMES E. Joe Lane of Oregon; machine politics and the sectional crisis, 1849-1861 [by] James E. Hendrickson. New Haven, Yale univ. press, 1967. xiii, 274 p. facsim., ports. "Notes on sources": pp. 259-62. CSf, CSmH, CU, Wa.
Occasional references to anti-slavery attitudes and to Oregon blacks.

3385. HOWE, JOHN W., 1801-1873. Speech of J. W. Howe of Pennsylvania, on the California question. Made in the House of representatives, night session, June 10, 1850. [Washington, D. C., 1850]. 8 p. DHU.

3386. HUNT, AURORA. Kirby Benedict, frontier federal judge; an account of legal and judicial development in the Southwest, 1853-1874, with special reference to the Indian, slavery, social and political affairs, journalism, and a chapter on circuit riding with Abraham Lincoln in Illinois. Glendale, The A. H. Clark co., 1961. 268 p. illus., port., fold. map, facsims. Bibliography: pp. [247]-55. CU-B.
The Otero slave code and the status of slavery in New Mexico, pp. 111-18.

3387. HUNTINGTON, J. W. P. A benevolent lady opens a school. [Salem, Ore., American unionist office, 1868]. Broadside. OrU.

Belknap 1080. "A vulgar joke concerning a spelling lesson in a school for freed slaves ..."

3388. In the matter of Carter Perkins and others on habeas corpus.* Ms. [110] p. Supreme court of the state of California case no. 322, 1852. C-ArS.
To secure the release of Carter and Robert Perkins and Sandy Jones who were seized as fugitive slaves in Sacramento. Contains an affidavit of Moses A. Jackson, San Francisco.

3389. JOHANNSEN, ROBERT WALTER, 1925- . Frontier politics and the sectional conflict; the Pacific northwest on the eve of the Civil war. Seattle, University press [c1955]. xii, 240 p. maps, ports. Bibliography: pp. 221-31. CSf, Wa.
Contains a chapter on the settlers and slavery, pp. 15-50.

3390. LAPP, RUDOLPH MATTHEW, 1915- . Archy Lee; a California fugitive slave case. [S. F.] Book club of California, 1969. 67 p. illus., ports. C, CHCL, CLSU, CMary, CNoS, CP, CRcS, CSS, CSj, CSmH, CSmatC, CU-B.

California and the West

3391. LOCKLEY, FRED, 1871- . "The case of Robin Holmes vs. Nathaniel Ford,"
in Oregon historical quarterly, v. 23, June, 1922, pp. 111-37.
    Transcripts of official Polk county, Oregon records of a legal case,
1852-53, in which Robin Holmes, a former slave, sued for the freedom of
three of his children.

3391a. "Some documentary records of slavery in Oregon," in Oregon historical
quarterly, v. 17, June, 1916, pp. 107-15.

3392. LUKAS, HENRY J. California - 1850's and the slavery question.
Master's thesis, Univ. of Wisconsin, Madison, 1968.

3392a.*MC DOWELL, ALBERT. Three letters of McDowell and Prince Woodfin,
Jamestown, 1853-55, reporting their mining activities to their owners,
Charles McDowell and Nicholas Woodfin in North Carolina. Mss.
    Southern historical coll., Chapel Hill, N. C. (microfilm).

3393. MANN, HORACE, 1796-1859. Speech of Horace Mann, of Massachusetts, on
the subject of slavery in the territories, and the consequences of a
dissolution of the union. Delivered in the United States House of representatives, February 15, 1850. Boston, Redding and co., 1850. 35 p.
CU-A.

3394. MILLER, JACOB W., 1800-1862. Speech of Mr. Miller of New Jersey, on
the proposition to compromise the slavery question, and the admission of
California into the union. Delivered in the Senate of the United States,
February 21, 1850. Washington, D. C., John T. Towers, 1850. 32 p. DHU.

3395. MURPHY, HENRY CRUSE, 1810-1882. Remarks of Mr. Murphy, of New York,
delivered in the House of representatives, on the 24th of February,
1849. [n.p.], 1849. 8 p. CLobS.
    Relates to the extension of slavery to California. A partial report
of an hour-long speech.

3396. NOLLAR, CHRISTIAN. [Affidavit given before the Sacramento District
court, Oct., 1849, at the request of A. J. Thomas that "a certain black
man branded with A. on the hip ... is the property of said Nollar."].
Ms. [1] ℓ. C-ArS.

3397. Oregon (territory). Legislative assembly. House. [House bills.
Ninth regular session, Legislative assembly. Salem, Territorial print.,
1858]. 3 p. OrU (photocopy), Belknap 344.
    No. 38. To provide for the protection of slave property. Jan. 9,
1858.

3398. _____. _____. _____. Report of Judiciary committee on bill to
protect property in slaves, 10th session, 1858, House journal, pp. 129,
173-79.
    Belknap L434a lists as a lost Oregon imprint.

3399. ORR, JAMES LAWRENCE, 1822-1873. The slavery question. Speech of
Hon. J. L. Orr, of South Carolina, in the House of representatives, May
8, 1850, in Committee of the whole on the state of the Union, on the

California and the West

President's message transmitting the Constitution of California. [Washington, D. C., Printed at the Congressional globe office, 1850]. 7 p. CHi.

3400. PARISH, JOHN C. "A project for a California slave colony in 1851," in Huntington library bulletin, no. 8, Oct., 1935, pp. 171-75.
Contains a letter from James Gadsden of Charleston, S. C., to Thomas Jefferson Green, San Francisco, proposing such a plan.

3401. PETTIT, JOHN, 1807-1877. Speech on the bill to establish a territorial government in Oregon, delivered in the House of representatives, Jan. 14, 1847. Washington, D. C., Blair & Rives, 1847. 8 p. OrU.
Refers to slavery provisions.

3402. POMEROY, EARL S. "Lincoln, the thirteenth amendment and the admission of Nevada," in Pacific historical review, v. 12, Dec., 1943, pp. 362-68.
The probability that Nevada was admitted in order to secure its vote for passage of the thirteenth amendment.

3403. *Portland, Oregon. Emancipation celebration. Grand emancipation celebration and promenade concert. 1863. 1871. The colored citizens of Oregon will celebrate the 8th anniversary of the emancipation of the slaves in the United States of America, at Portland, Oregon, January 2, 1871, at the Emmet guard hall, by speaking, poems, music and other exercises ... [Portland] Geo. H. Himes, printer [1870]. [1] p. CHi, OrHi.
Committee: C. J. Graham, Frank Moore, Marcus A. Bell, Isaiah Graham, A. M. Richmond, George Washington, and William Brown.

3404. _____. _____. Great emancipation celebration. The colored people of Oregon will celebrate the sixth anniversary of the emancipation of four millions of bondsmen in the United States of America, in the city of Portland, at the County court house, January 1st, 1869, at 6 o'clock p. m. ... Oration by the Right reverend bishop Ward, of the African Methodist Episcopal mission ... [Portland] Carter & Himes, printers [1868]. 3 p. OrHi, Belknap 1185.
Mr. Belknap stated in a letter, May 8, 1971, that "The Salem Oregon Statesman reported the printing of a programme on Nov. 21, 1869 (a lost imprint), and on Dec. 28 announced plans for the celebration in some detail."

3405. POULTON, HELEN JEAN, 1920- . The attitude of Oregon toward slavery and secession, 1843-1865. Master's thesis, Univ. of Oregon, Eugene, 1946. 156 ℓ.

3406. PUTNAM, HARVEY, 1793-1855. Admission of California. Speech of Harvey Putnam, of New York, in the House of representatives, Tuesday July 30, 1850. In the Committee of the whole on the state of the Union, on the bill making appropriations for the payment of Revolutionary pensioners. [Washington, D. C., Printed at the Congressional globe office, 1850]. 8 p. CHi.
Opposes appending of slavery compromise bills to the bill admitting California to statehood.

California and the West

3407. Republican party. Oregon. Documents presented to the people of
Oregon by the Republican state committee ... Central committee. Dated,
Portland, April 25th, 1859. 24 p. Or, OrHi, OrP, OrU, WaSp.
    Belknap 487 states that the title contains "extracts from speech of
Eli Thayer of Massachusetts in the U. S. House of Representatives on
slavery in the territories (pp. 6-7); debate in the U. S. Senate, Feb.
23, 1859, on slavery in the territories (pp. 8-23). The complete text
of Thayer's speech was published on a broadside also issued by the Oregon
Republican Party in 1859 ([Belknap] no. 489."

3408. REYNOLDS, MARION HOBART. Instances of Negro slavery in California
[by] Marion Hobart Reynolds. [Cambridge, Mass., 1914]. [13] ℓ. Typew.
CU-B.

3409. ROOT, JOSEPH MOSELEY, 1817?-1889. California and New Mexico. Speech
of Hon. Joseph M. Moseley, of Ohio, in the House of representatives,
February 15, 1850, in Committee of the whole on the state of the Union,
on the resolution referring the President's Message to the appropriate
standing committees. [Washington, D. C., Printed at the Congressional
globe office, 1850]. 7 p. DHU.

3410. RYAN, WILLIAM, 1840- . Reminiscences of Ryan given in an interview
with T. F. Dawson, Aug. 23, 1921. Tells of Negro slaves in Colorado.
11 p. Typew. CoHi.

3411. RYAN, WILLIAM REDMOND. Personal adventures in upper and lower
California in 1848-49 ... London, William Shoberl, 1850. 2 v. illus.
CBb, CHi, CP, CSd, CSf, Rocq 16037.
    California's attitude toward slavery as evidenced in the 1849 con-
stitutional convention, pp. 307-10.

3412. SCALLY, WILLIAM. The question of national power over slavery in the
territories, 1846-1865. Master's thesis, Univ. of Calif., Berkeley,
1928. 188 ℓ.

3413. SEWARD, WILLIAM HENRY, 1801-1872. California, union and freedom.
Speech of William H. Seward on the admission of California. Delivered
in the Senate of the United States, March 11, 1850. [Washington, D. C.]
Printed by Buell & Blanchard [1850]. 16 p. DHU, NN.

3414. _____. Speech of the Hon. W. H. Seward on the admission of California
and the subject of slavery delivered in the United States senate on
Monday, March 11, 1850. Boston, Redding & co., 1850. 26 p. NN.

3415. _____. Speech of the Hon. Wm. H. Seward in the
States on the admission of California. <Delivered Mar. 8, 1850.>
[Washington, D. C.?, 1850]. 32 p. NN.

3416. _____. Speech of William H. Seward on the admission of California,
delivered in the Senate of the United States, March 11, 1850. Washington,
D. C., Printed and for sale by Buell & Blanchard, 1850. 46 p. DHU.

California and the West

3417. _____. The works of William H. Seward, edited by George E. Baker ...
N. Y., Redfield [c1853]. 3 v. NN.
"Freedom in the new territories": v. 1, pp. 51-110.
"Freedom in New Mexico": v. 1, pp. 119-31.

3418. SMITH, TRUMAN, 1791-1884. Speech of Mr. Smith, of Conn., on the bill
"To admit California into the Union - to establish territorial governments
for Utah and New Mexico, making proposals to Texas for the establishment
of the western and northern boundaries"; showing the responsibilities of
the late administration on account of the acquisitions which were the
result of our recent war with Mexico -- [etc.]. Delivered in the Senate
of the United States, July 8, 1850. Washington, D. C., Gideon & co.,
printers, 1850. 32 p. CHi.
Considers the effect of extending the Missouri compromise line of
36° 30' to the Pacific ocean.

3419. SPAULDING, IMOGENE. "The attitude of California to the Civil war," in
Southern California quarterly, v. 9, 1912-13, pp. 104-31.
"A well-documented article covering the effect of slavery on the
early development of the state and the loyal attitude of California to
the Union." -- Miriam Matthews.

3420. STANTON, RICHARD HENRY, 1812-1891. California and New Mexico. Speech
of Hon. R. H. Stanton, of Kentucky, in the House of representatives,
March 11, 1850. In Committee of the whole on the state of the union,
on the President's message transmitting the Constitution of California.
[Washington, D. C., Printed at the Congressional globe office, 1850].
7 p. CHi.
Favors slavery in territories acquired from Mexico.

3421. STEVENS, THADDEUS. Speech of Thaddeus Stevens, of Pennsylvania, on
the California question. Made in the House of representatives, night
session, June 10, 1850. [Washington, D. C., Buell & Blanchard, printers,
1850]. 8 p. DHU.

3422. *TATE, MERZE. "Slavery and racism as deterrents to the annexation of
Hawaii," in Journal of Negro history, v. 47, Jan., 1962, pp. 1-18.

3423. TAYLOR, PAUL S. "Foundations of California rural society," in
California historical society quarterly, v. 24, Sept., 1945, pp. 193-202.
Studies the question of early Californians: "Should California enter
the union as a slave or free state?"

3424. THAYER, ELI, 1819-1899. Fair play. Speech of Hon. Eli Thayer, Republican member of Congress from Massachusetts; delivered in the House
of representatives, February 24th, 1859. Also -- a letter from a
prominent Democrat of Oregon, Published by order of the Republican
state central committee ... [n.p., 1859?]. Broadside. OrHi, OrU.

Belknap 489 states in part: "Thayer believed that planned colonization of new lands by free men was the solution of the problem of slavery
in the territories ... 'which made him totally uninterested in congressional action about slavery in the territories' ... These views ...

California and the West

suited the situation of the new Republican Party in Oregon, to which it
was of first importance to avoid the 'smear' label of Abolitionism ..."

3425. TILTON, JAMES. "'Echo of the Dred Scott decision,' letter, Sept. 30,
1860 to H. M. McGill, Acting governor of Washington territory, regarding
British removal of a slave from a mail steamer at Victoria," in Pacific
northwest quarterly, v. 1, Oct., 1906, p. 71.

3426. WENGI, RICHARD ADOLF. Slavery in the trans-Mississippi West.
Master's thesis, Humboldt state univ., Arcata, 1964. 73 p. CU-B (photocopy).

3427. WILLIAMS, GEORGE H. "The 'Free state letter' of Judge George H.
Williams," in Oregon historical quarterly, v. 9, Sept., 1908, pp. 254-73.
The letter, entitled "Slavery in Oregon," was reprinted from The
Oregon statesman, July 28, 1857.

3428. WINANS, [JOSEPH W.], 1820-1887. In re the petition of [Charles A.]
Stovall, claimant, for the body of Archy [Lee], his alleged slave.
[Joseph W.] Winans, of counsel. Sacramento, Union presses [1858]. 22 p.
CHi, CU-B.
The Calif. supreme court case of Ex parte Archy, 9 Cal. 147 (1858).

3429. WINTHROP, ROBERT CHARLES, 1809-1894. Admission of California. Speech
of the Hon. R. C. Winthrop, of Massachusetts, on the President's message
transmitting the Constitution of California: delivered in Committee of
the whole in the House of representatives of the United States, May 8,
1850. Washington, D. C., Gideon & co., printers, 1850. 28 p. CHi,
CLobS.
Describes Southern influence in the preparation of the Constitution
which nonetheless prohibited slavery.

ELSEWHERE IN THE UNITED STATES

3430. BATES, JACK WARD. John Quincy Adams and the antislavery movement.
Doctoral dissertation, Univ. of southern Calif., Los Angeles, 1953. v,
348 ℓ.

3431. BOSKIN, JOSEPH. "The origins of American slavery: education as an
index of early differentiation," in Journal of Negro education, v. 35,
Spring, 1966, pp. 125-33.
By a Univ. of southern California historian.

3432. BRYCE-LAPORTE, ROY SIMON, 1933- . The conceptualization of the
American slave plantation as a total institution. Doctoral dissertation,
Univ. of Calif., Los Angeles, 1968. xii, 285 ℓ.

3433. CARTER, GEORGE EDWARD. The use of the "higher law" in the anti-
slavery crusade. Master's thesis, Calif. state univ., Sacramento, 1962.
117 ℓ.

Elsewhere in the U. S.

3434. DICK, ROBERT CHRISTOPHER. Rhetoric of the Negro ante-bellum protest movement. Doctoral dissertation, Stanford univ., Stanford, 1969. vii, 436 l.
Anti-slavery movement.

3435. HELWIG, ADELAIDE BERTA, 1900- . The political development of the Carolina colony, 1663-1720. Master's thesis, Univ. of Calif., Berkeley, 1924. 118, vii l.
Relates to slavery.

3436. HOWARD, WARREN S. American slavers and the federal law, 1837-1862. Berkeley, Univ. of Calif. press, 1963. xii, 336 p. illus. Bibliography: pp. [315]-24. CEcaC, CFS, CHS, CKenM, CLU, CNoS, CPhD, CSaT, CSdS, CSf, CSfCiC, CSluSP.
Authored by a southern Californian and historian, based upon his doctoral dissertation.

3437. _____. The United States government and the African slave trade, 1837-1862. Doctoral dissertation, Univ. of Calif., Los Angeles, 1959. 709 l.

3438. LE JAU, FRANCIS, 1665-1717. Carolina chronicle, 1706-1717, ed. with an introd. and notes, by Frank J. Klingberg. Berkeley, Univ. of Calif. press, 1956. vi, 220 p. illus., port. (Univ. of Calif. publications in history, v. 53). Bibliographical footnotes. CHS, CLSU, CSf, CSjC, CSluSP, CSt.
Contains the correspondence of Le Jau, an Episcopal clergyman, which provides a record of attitudes toward the colonial Negro.

3439. MC COLLEY, ROBERT MC NAIR. Gentlemen and slavery in Jefferson's Virginia. Doctoral dissertation. Univ. of Calif., Berkeley, 1960. iii, 217 l.

3440. _____. Slavery and Jefferson Virginia [by] Robert McColley. Urbana, Univ. of Illinois press, 1964. 227 p. maps. CNoS, CSdS, CSluSP, CSf, CU.
Based on his doctoral dissertation, 1960.

3441. MERKEL, BENJAMIN. The anti-slavery movement in Missouri, 1819-1865. Doctoral dissertation, Washington state univ., Pullman, 1939.

3442. MILLER, KENNETH JOHN. Some economic aspects of American Negro slavery. Master's thesis, Stanford univ., Stanford, 1950. 97, iv l. diagrs., table.

3443. MOULDS, VIRGINIA BENNETT. A study of conflicting values in the anti-slavery activity of Wendell Phillips and Horace Greeley. Master's thesis, Calif. state univ., Sacramento, 1958. 119 l.

3444. MULLIN, GERALD WALLACE. Patterns of slave behavior in eighteenth century Virginia. Doctoral dissertation, Univ. of Calif., Berkeley, 1968. viii, 565 l. maps. 2 v.

Elsewhere in the U. S.

3445. NICHOLSON, LOIS BELLE. The religious attitude of the South toward slavery and the Civil war. Master's thesis, Univ. of Calif., Berkeley, 1927.

3446. RASTEGAR, CAROL CONGRESS. The Sambo image: myth or reality. Master's thesis, Univ. of Calif., Los Angeles, 1968.
    Slavery in the South.

3447. REINERT, FREDERICK A. Lincoln's approach to the slavery controversy. Master's thesis, Univ. of southern Calif., Los Angeles, 1957. 125 ℓ.

3448. SLOCUM, WILLIAM NEILL, 1832?- . The war, and how to end it. An address to the people of California, by one of them. S. F., 1861. 38 p. CSmH, CU-B.
    Advocates the emancipation of slaves.

3449. _____. Same. 2d ed., rev. S. F., 1861. CSt, Greenwood 1560.

3450. _____. Same. 3rd ed., rev. S. F., 1861. C, CSmH, CU-B, Greenwood 1561.

3451. STAROBIN, ROBERT S. Industrial slavery in the old South, 1790-1861: a study in political economy. Doctoral dissertation, Univ. of Calif., Berkeley, 1968. vi, 547 ℓ.

3452. STONE, JACOB LEON, 1836- . Slavery and the Bible; or, slavery as seen in its punishment ... S. F., Printed by B. F. Sterett, 1863. 48 p. C, CLU, CSaT, CSmH, CU, CU-B.
    Shows that slavery, contrary to many assertions, is not advocated in the Bible.

3453. SUMNER, CHARLES, 1811-1874. Speech of the Hon. Charles Summer of Massachusetts on the barbarism of slavery, delivered in the U. S. Senate, June 4th, 1860. Also, the Republican platform. S. F., Towne & Bacon, 1860. 32 p. CHi, CU-B.

3454. WAX, DAROLD D. The Negro slave trade in colonial Pennsylvania. Doctoral dissertation, Univ. of Washington, Seattle, 1962.

3455. WEINERT, BERTRAM ALLAN. The Negro in the abolition movement. Master's thesis, Univ. of Calif., Berkeley, 1951. x, 161 ℓ. maps.

3456. ZILVERSMIT, ARTHUR. Slavery and its abolition in the northern states. Doctoral dissertation, Univ. of Calif., Berkeley, 1962. 377 ℓ.
    "Traced legal and other efforts to free the slave from colonial period to 1804." - West, p. 82.

SOCIAL AND SERVICE ORGANIZATIONS

COMMUNITY SERVICE

3457. "The Anna E. Waden branch of the San Francisco public library," in
Pioneer, v. 31, no. 1, 1969, pp. 3-7.
The publication of the Library bureau, a division of Sperry Rand
corp., describes a new library in the Hunters Point-Bayview district
and the professional philosophy of its librarian, George Alfred.

3458. *Appomatox [sic] club of Berkeley, California.   Articles of incorpora-
tion, 1933. 4 p. Typew. C-ArS.
A non-profit organization which proposed "to assist in the education,
training and entertainment of those interested in the economic and civil
conditions of the community." Directors were G. G. Grimes, D. G. Gibson,
H. Holmes, Antone D. Gautier, R. J. Powell, A. Mayes, C. Vanhook, William
Fryson, S. C. Bell, William J. Matthews, H. Reed, George Johnson, J.
Ballard, Newton C. Morgan, and T. W. Swinney.

3459. *Bay area urban league.   Annual report.   S. F., Oakland, 1925?- .

3460. *Booker T. mothers' club.   Articles of incorporation, San Francisco,
1927. 3 [1] p. Typew. C-ArS.
"To acquire, equip and conduct a day nursery ..." Directors were
Mattie Peace, Elizabeth F. Johnson, Bessie S. Hill, Cornelia Duvall,
Emma Avery, Margaret J. Mabson, Josephi[n]e Richardson, America Harris,
Almira Williams, Lulu B. Harris, and Sadie Montero.

3461. *Booker T. Washington community service center. [Annual] report.
S. F., 1926-31. 6 v. CU-B.

3462. _____. Articles of incorporation, San Francisco, 1923. [3] p. Typew.
C-ArS.
A broadly-based community service organization. Directors were Jacob
C. Peyton, Mabel Richardson, W. J. J. Byers, Mary D. Stewart, Alice Reece,
J. W. Whitfield, Ella Grubbs, Lauretta Peyton, M. Lampkins, Bertha S.
Peoples, Gregory Hobson, Albert Graves, Walter H. Sandford, Norris L.
Gaynes, and C. H. Tinsley.

3463. _____. Amendment, 1955. [4] p. Typew. C-ArS.

3464. _____. 50th anniversary, 1920-1970. [S. F., 1970]. [22] ℓ. illus.,
ports. CSfAA.

3465. _____. [Souvenir program] 30th anniversary, Booker T. Washington
community center. [S. F., 1951]. [20] p. illus., ports. COEB.
"History of Booker T. Washington center, by Mrs. Emma Scott Jones,"
pp. [5 and 7].

3466. *Booker T. Washington relief society.   Articles of incorporation, San
Francisco, 1902. 6 p. Typew. C-ArS.
"To provide homes for the homeless, poor and dependent [sic] colored
children, and to educate said children ..." Directors were Mrs. Waterloo

Community Service

B. Snelson, Mrs. Martha Wilson, Mrs. Eva Lundy, Mrs. Evaline Erskine, and Mrs. Ella S. Campbell.

3467. BORLAND, VIRGINIA. In Marin county; Marin City; a library. Study of Marin City branch, Marin county free library written for ... course in public library administration at the Univ. of Calif. School of librarian-ship. Berkeley [Printed by Marin county human rights commission], 1967. 26 p. CSrCL.

3468. CAHILL, EDVINA. "Keep the kids busy," in Crisis, v. 54, Mar., 1947, pp. 74-75 and 92.
    Junior city, a youth project in Hunters Point, San Francisco.

3469. *Colored young men and women's industrial Christian association. Articles of incorporation, San Francisco, 1919. Ms. 4 p. C-ArS.
    Organized for mutual improvement and "to secure a building and place wherein its members may secure manual, domestic, and mechanical training ..." Directors: Oval [sic] Anderson, S. L. Mash, Joseph A. Dennis, Mrs. Anna M. Martin, A. L. Lightfoot, Mrs. Tide Taylor, Albert Reed, John W. White, J. A. Foreman, R. A. Finnish, and Agnes White.

3470. Community chest and council of Seattle and King county, Washington. Review of social and economic conditions in the city of Seattle, Washing-ton as they relate to the work of the Seattle urban league. A study con-ducted by the council of social agencies with the advice and assistance of the National urban league, Department of research. March-April, 1943. [Seattle?, 1943]. 95 ℓ. tables. Typew. (carbon copy). Bibliography: ℓ. 94-95. NN.

3471. Community council of San Mateo county. Directory of agencies serving east Menlo Park and East Palo Alto. San Mateo, Community council of San Mateo county, 1963. 43 p. CMp.

3472. DAVIS, ERNEST M. "It only happens in make believe," in Crisis, v. 61, May, 1954, pp. 280-84.
    The personnel of Luke air force base, Phoenix, assist in annual Boy scounts of America summer camp.

3473. *DERRICK, JOHN A. LINCOLN, 1864?-1934. "Booker T. Washington orphanage of California," in Colored American magazine, v. 10, Mar., 1906, pp. 171-72.
    Describes a San Francisco organization founded in 1903.

3474. DONALDSON, CHARLOTTE, and GEORGE FERGUSON. Progress report on an ex-ploratory survey of the differentiation of function and role of human relations agencies and their interaction. Unpublished research project, Univ. of Washington, Seattle, 1961.

3475. Economic opportunity commission of San Diego county. Community in action; report on the war on poverty in San Diego county, 1967. 2d annual report. San Diego, 1967. 48 p. CSmarP.

3476. *Economic opportunity council, San Francisco. Western addition area community action program. Annual progress report -- program year "C",

Community Service

March, 1968 - February, 1969. [S. F., Golden's printing co., 1969]. 31 p. illus., ports. CSfAA.

3477. *Fannie Wall children's home, Oakland. [Annual report]. COEB 1959.

3478. _____. [Souvenir program] annual charity ball. COEB 1948.

3479. *Filippa Pollia foundation. Filippa pollia foundation presents Langston Hughes and Arna Bontemps ... November 30 - David Starr Jordan high school; December 1 - Manual arts high school; December 2 - Hollywood high school ... [L. A., 194-?]. Broadside. CSmH.

3480. *Home for aged and infirm colored people of California, Oakland. Annual report of the sixteenth year of the Home for aged and infirm colored people for the year ending January 1st, 1909. Home: Beulah, California. Incorporated Sept. 16, 1892. [Oakland?, 1909]. 23 p. illus. CU-B.

3481. _____. Articles of incorporation, 1892. Ms. 4 p. C-ArS. Directors: Mary E. A. Cole, Ann S. Purnell, Elenora Amos, Aremento T. Stanford, Mary Goodman, Rosa M. Lockett, Mary C. Washington, Ellen Whiting, Mary J. Humphrey, and Anna Williams, Oakland; and Harriet E. Smith, San Francisco.

3482. _____. Constitution and by-laws of the Home ... Incorporated September 16, 1892. [Oakland?] Jordan print. co. [189-?]. 16 p. CU-B.

3483. *Los Angeles urban league. Correspondence and papers relating to immigrant labor and social city planning in Los Angeles, 1944-45. 1 box containing about 200 pieces. CLU (Spec. Coll.).

3484. *Negro boys town and Negro girls town. Articles of incorporation, Los Angeles, 1941. [4] p. Typew. C-ArS. Organized to establish and maintain camps or communities for youth. Incorporated by Dr. Eva Whiting Young, E. Winston Williams, and Mrs. E. Griffine-Hinden-Butler.

3485. *Negro mothers of America. Articles of incorporation, Los Angeles, 1944. 4 p. Typew. C-ArS. "To advance the education, civic, social and economic interest of Negroes ... and to merit and demand fair treatment and representation in our city, county, state and national governmentn ..." Directors were the Mesdames Beatrice Reeves, Alta Morgan, Esther Roth, Frances Roth, Jean Atkinson, Bernard N. Roth, Gertrude Harris, Marguerite Pyles, Harriett Reeves, Jr., Regina Edmonson, J. C. Croom, and Mary Dugan.

3486. Oakland. News releases on the Oakland Interagency project. Oakland, 1963. 1 v. unp. illus. CU.

3487. _____. Associated agencies. Proposal to the Ford foundation for a program of community development with special reference to assimilation of the newcomer population. Oakland, 1961. 44 p. tables. CO.

Community Service

3488. *Phillis Wheatley, inc., Los Angeles. Articles of incorporation, 1948.
Certificate of amendments, 1951. Mss. [15] p. C-ArS.
     To provide housing and training for young girls and women. Directors:
A. J. Alexander, Mable Oliver, Mrs. Leola B. Wilson, Mrs. Grace Pollard
Dantzler, and Mrs. Lucille Howard.

3489. RHODEHAMEL, JOSEPHINE (DE WITT). "Oakland public library and America's
tenth man," in Pacific bindery talk, v. 8, June, 1936, pp. 163-65.

3490. RICHARDS, LENORA ALEXANDER. A study of the social welfare activities
of the Los Angeles urban league. Master's thesis, Univ. of southern
Calif., Los Angeles, 1941. v, 80 ℓ. tables.

3491. ROBINSON, DUANE MORRIS, 1913- . Chance to belong; story of the Los
Angeles youth project, 1943-1949. Foreword by C. Whit Pfeiffer. N. Y.,
Woman's press [1949]. xvii, 178 p. illus., maps. C, CBb, CChiS, CL,
CLS, CLU, CP, CSS, Rocq 3267.

3492. San Francisco economic opportunity council. Progress 1966; economic
opportunity council report. S. F. [n.d.]. 22 p. CMp.

3493. San Francisco youth opportunities center. An evaluation of the San
Francisco youth opportunities center, conducted by [its] Research unit.
[S. F.] 1966. 82 [1] ℓ. Bibliography: p. [83]. CU.

3494. Seattle-King county economic opportunity board. Central area motivation program: a preliminary evaluation report. Seattle, 1968. Wa.

3495. *Seattle urban league. Records, ca. 1930-65. 15 cartons. WaU.

3496. *Sojourner Truth home, Los Angeles. Some facts concerning Sojourner
Truth home, 1119 East Adams street, Los Angeles, California. [L. A.,
1913]. [3] p. illus.

3497. Sojourner Truth industrial club, Los Angeles. Articles of incorporation, 1924. Ms. 4 p. C-ArS.
     "To establish and maintain homes for young women." Among 12 directors
were Lulu Slaughter, Lucile W. Shelten, Sara Gregory Johnson, Minnie C.
Tribble, and Alethia Holcomb.

3498. _____. Golden anniversary, 1905-1954, Los Angeles, California,
October 17-21, 1954. [L. A., 1954]. [16] p. illus., ports. CL.

3499. STONE, ROBERT C. An evaluation of San Francisco's Youth opportunities
center, by Robert C. Stone, Seaton Manning, Velma Parness [and] James
Nolan. [S. F.] Institute for social research, San Francisco state
college [1965?]. 88 p. CSfAA.
     An organization in the Hunters Point district of San Francisco.

3500. TALBOT, STEVE. The East bay community action program [by] Steve
Talbot, Harold Nawy in collaboration with Martin Thimel. Produced under
the direction of Joseph D. Lohman, and Paul T. Takagi. [Berkeley] Univ.
of Calif. [1967]. 2 pts. in 1 v. Includes bibliography. CU.

Community Service

An Alameda county community planning program study "Funded by U. S.
Office of Economic Opportunity Contract."

3501. ULANSKY, GENE. "Rebels with a mission," in San Francisco magazine,
v. 10, July, 1968, pp. 76-78.
Activities of the Mission rebels, a young men's group, San Francisco.

3502. Unitarian fellowship for social justice. The Unitarian fellowship for
social justice sponsors The allied arts league presenting Langston Hughes,
Sunday, April 4, 1948 ... [L. A., 1958]. Broadside. CSmH.

3503. *Urban league of Portland, Oregon. Newsletters and other communications to members. Portland, Ore., 1945-1958. 1 v. OrU.

3504. WHITE, JAY. "Fillmore street project," in Synergy, no. 14, Feb.,
1969, pp. 23-24.
Describes means by which San Francisco public library books are made
available to those who choose only "to read books by, for and about black
people."

3505. WITCHER, KATHRYN L. The United bay area crusade and its agencies: an
assessment of UBAG and agency practices upon the delivery of social services to black people. Master's thesis, Calif. state univ., Sacramento,
1970. 72 ℓ.
San Francisco bay area.

3506. *WOOD, TED. "The Urban league in Seattle," in Opportunity, v. 18,
Apr., 1940, pp. 109-11 and 114.

3507. Young women's Christian association, Oakland. Linden branch.
[Program of] sixth annual meeting and membership dinner of the Linden
branch, Y. W. C. A., Oakland, California, February 27, 1929. [Oakland?,
1929]. 9 p. CU-B.
Contains annual report for 1928, pp. 5-9.

FRATERNAL

3508. *ABNER, E. W. D. "Fraternal insurance," in Messenger, v. 5, Nov.,
1923, pp. 867, 896, and 899.
By the Supreme commander, American woodmen, Denver.

3509. *American woodmen. Minutes ... Quadrennial meeting. DHU. 6th (1925).
A Denver-based organization.

3510. *DAVIS, A. B., pub. A souvenir of the current events [for the] week
commencing June third and ending June seventh, 1906, as pub. by A. B.
Davis, Marysville. Marysville, 1906. [16] p. ports. CHi.
Issued for a meeting of the Most worshipful sovereign grand lodge,
F. & A. M., later known as Prince Hall grand lodge, Freemasons.

Fraternal

3511. DE LEON, A. W. A. An appeal to the Free masons working under the
jurisdiction of the "National grand lodge," by A. W. A. De Leon ...
S. F. [1874?]. 12 p. NN.
   "Published in the Pacific appeal ... April 18th and 25th, 1874, and
authorized to be printed for ... Grand lodge ... of the state of
California."

3512. *Elks of the world, Improved benevolent protective order.   Grand
lodge. Annual convention program. COEB, 1956 (Los Angeles).

3513. *Freemasons.   Arizona. Grand lodge. Proceedings of the first and
second annual communication ... and Masonic grand chapter of the Eastern
star ... held at Yuma, 1920; and at Tucson, April 19, 20, 21, 1921.
[Tucson?, 1921]. 56 p. illus. NN.

3514. _____. California. Ancient Arabic order of the nobles of the mystic
shrine. Oakland. Menelik temple no. 36. Gala day ... Saturday, May 8,
1965. [Oakland, California voice pub. co., 1965]. [12] p. ports.
   Souvenir program also listing Oakland Scottish rite lodges and
officers.

3515. _____. _____. _____. _____. _____. Yearbook. CSfAA, 1966.

3516. _____. _____. Berkeley. West gate lodge no. 36. Mortgage burning
ceremony program, East gate masonic hall ... December 19, 1953.
[Berkeley, Leon Maybuce, printer, 1953?]. [32] p. illus., ports. COEB,
CU-B.

3517. _____. _____. Conventional independent grand lodge. Proceedings of
the second annual convention of ... S. F., Cuddy & Hughes, 1873. 66 p.
   Unlocated title. Notice of its printing appears in the San Francisco
Elevator, July 19, 1873, p. 3, col. 3.

3518. _____. _____. Heroines of Jericho. Grand high court. Proceedings
... Annual communication. COEB, 5th (1928); 24/25th (1949-50).
   Title varies slightly.

3519. _____. _____. Knights templars. Pacific grand commandery. Official
proceedings ... Grand annual conclave. NN (holdings not given).

3520. _____. _____. Los Angeles. Holland lodge no. 20. 10th anniversary
number ... Sept., A. D., 1921 ... [L. A.?, 1921]. 6 p. (folder). CHi.
   Gives a short history of the lodge.

3521. _____. _____. Prince Hall grand lodge. Centennial year book of the
most worshipful Prince Hall grand lodge, Free and accepted masons,
California jurisdiction. Edited and compiled by Arthur Evans. Grand
lodge history, by Clyde M. Thompson. Issued at the centennial communication of the Grand lodge held in San Francisco, California, July 17-21,
1955. [L. A.?, 1955]. 112 p. illus., ports. C, CU-B.

3522. _____. _____. _____. Masonic constitution, the landmarks of the
order and the charges of a freemason, together with the original

328

Fraternal

proclamation, the constitution, rules and code of masonic jurisprudence now in force of the ... Grand lodge ... of free and accepted masons for the state of California and its masonic jurisdiction, adopted ... June 8 ... 1911 ... amended ... June 5 ... 1912. Oakland, Bridges print. [1912]. 80 p. NN.

3523. _____. _____. _____. Official directory, Most worshipful sovereign grand lodge, state of California and jurisdiction. O. E. S. right of adoption and all Masonic bodies. [Compiled by Fred A. Houston, assisted by Lillard G. Dandridge]. [Oakland?] C. F. Tilghman [191-?]. 110 p. CU-B.

3524. _____. _____. _____. 100 years of progress, 1855-1955 ... centennial at San Francisco, Calif., July 17-21, 1955. Oakland, Prince Hall masonic digest, 1955. 19 p. illus. CHi.

3525. _____. _____. _____. Prince Hall masonic directory, most worshipful Prince Hall grand lodge, Free and accepted masons, state of California and its jurisdiction. [n.p., 1954]. 56 p. CHi, CU-B.
"Chartered ... June 19, 1855 ... named Prince Hall grand lodge July 20, 1948."

3526. _____. _____. _____. Proceedings ... Annual communication. COEB, 1905-06 (52nd), 1932, 1954; NUC, pre-1956.
Title varies slightly.

3527. _____. _____. _____. Souvenir program ... Annual communication. CHi, 1954-55; COEB, 1947 (91st), 1953, 1955, 1957, 1960, 1964; CSfAA, 1952, 1957-59, 1961; CU-B, 1948, 1951-53, 1955-63.

3528. _____. _____. _____. Order of eastern star. Golden state grand chapter. History of the Golden state grand chapter, Order of eastern star ... by Vivian Osborne Marsh ... CU-B, 1948-56, 1956-67, 1969 (4th ed.).
Title varies.

3529. _____. _____. _____. _____. _____. Proceedings. COEB, 1931 (50th), 1953/54, 1955/56-1959/60, 1961/62-1962/63.

3530. _____. _____. _____. _____. _____. Yearbook. COEB, 1966.

3531. _____. Colorado. Prince Hall grand lodge. Constitution and by-laws revised and adopted by the authority of the thirty-sixth annual communication of the Most worshipful Grand lodge, free and accepted masons for the state of Colorado and jurisdiction ... August 13-14-15 ... 1912. [Colorado Springs?, 1912]. 102 p. NN.

3532. _____. _____. _____. Proceedings ... Annual communication. NN (holdings not given).

3532a. _____. Washington (state). United grand lodge. Proceedings ... Annual communication. NN [1907-44] Note: The Schomburg collection holds an extensive group of Washington state grand lodge (white) titles which

Fraternal

contain numerous references to the controversy concerning Negro masonry
as recognized by that lodge.

3533. *Knights of Pythias.   California.   Grand lodge.   Proceedings ...
Annual session.

3534. _____. _____. _____. Official annual Thanksgiving service, Grand
lodge, Knights of Pythias and Grand court, Order of Calanthe, California
jurisdiction. Adopted July 20, 1937, at Sacramento. Compiled by Leon F.
Marsh, P. C. [n.p., 1937?]. 4 p. CU-B.

3535. _____. _____. _____. Souvenir program ... Annual session. CU-B,
1971 (60th).

3536. MURASKIN, WILLIAM ALAN, 1944- . Black Masons: the role of fraternal
orders in the creation of a middle-class black community. Doctoral dissertation, Univ. of Calif., Berkeley, 1970. 284 ℓ.

3537. _____. "Social foundations of the black community, the fraternities:
the California Masons as a test case," in Midcontinent American studies
journal, v. 11, Fall, 1970, pp. 12-33.

3538. *Odd fellows, Grand united order of, Oakland.   Occidental lodge no.
2484. Constitution, by-laws, rules of order and order of business of
Occidental lodge no. 2484, G. U. O. of O. F. S. F., J. H. Knarston,
1886. 24 p. CU-B.

3539. *Prince Hall building assoc., inc., San Francisco.   Articles of in-
corporation, 1955. Ms. 4 p. C-ArS.
     To build and operate a fraternal hall. Directors included Dero
Howard, Walter Harrison, John Wiley, Lamar Vaughn, Harry L. Gordon,
Fred Anderson, and 5 others.

3540. *Prince Hall masonic temple improvement assoc., Santa Barbara.
Articles of incorporation, 1925. Ms. 4 p. C-ArS.
     To operate a fraternal hall. Directors: B. G. Goodwin, Leon Sims,
William Boykin, Eugene Shands, and Horace Alexander.

3541. *Prince Hall masons holding assoc. of Los Angeles, California.
Articles of incorporation, 1926. Amendments, 1944 and 1951. Mss.
[32] p. C-ArS.
     To operate a fraternal hall. Among original members signing: Morgan
White, Wallace A. Clark, Thomas H. Skinner, F. G. White, William C.
Colly, J. H. Wilson, and Willis O. Tyler.

3542. *Prince Hall progressive building assoc., Los Angeles.   Articles of
incorporation, 1953. Ms. 3 p. C-ArS.
     To "operate a Masonic temple." Directors included: Frank G. White,
William C. Faulkner, John L. Thompson, and William S. Chesley.

3543. *UPTON, WILLIAM H.* Light on a dark subject, being a critical examination of objections to the legitimacy of the masonry existing among the
Negroes of America. Seattle, The Pacific mason, 1899. 137 p. DLC.

Fraternal

3544. _____. Same. 2nd ed., with a slight title change. Cambridge, Mass., 1902. CU.

SOCIAL AND BENEVOLENT

3545. *Afro-American council of America. Articles of incorporation, Los Angeles, 1912. [6] p. Typew. C-ArS.
     For general advancement and "to associate ourselves together for mutual assistance, instruction and protection." Trustees were James M. Alexander, J. D. Bowles, and George S. Brown, Los Angeles; James F. Summers, J. C. Cooper, E. H. Barrett, J. M. Bridges, G. W. Hawkins, and A. W. Cook, Oakland; G. W. Reed, Stockton; and J. H. Wilson, Riverside.

3546. *Booker T. Washington country club. Articles of incorporation, San Francisco, 1927. 3 [1] p. Typew. C-ArS.
     Directors were John H. Taylor, Ella Foster, A. R. Dobbins, William E. De Claybrook, Jr., Charles W. Edwards, Charles Phoenix, Leonard Harris, and William H. Lashley, San Francisco; Gregory Hobson, Burlingame; and W. A. Butler, Oakland.

3547. *Booker T. Washington memorial society. Articles of incorporation, Fresno, 1941. [4] p. Typew. C-Ars.
     A social, benevolent, and death benefit society. Directors were H. J. Colley, Beatrice Cooley, and Judie McNeal.

3548. *Colored entertainers club. Articles of incorporation, San Francisco, 1913. 5 p. Typew. C-ArS.
     A social and benevolent organization, the directors of which were William Powers, J. C. Harris, Nettie Compton, R. K. Brown, and William Sumner.

3549. *Colored janitor co-operative association. Articles of incorporation, San Francisco, 1927. 3 [2] p. Typew. C-ArS.
     A social and benevolent organization, the directors of which were Tony D. Johnson, James Ward, Cliff Moore, Cecil Edwards, and Siles Forest.

3550. *Colored military social club. Articles of incorporation, San Francisco, 1915. 5 p. Typew. C-ArS.
     A social and benevolent organization, the directors of which were W. A. Davis, W. H. Davis, George W. Stovall, Thomas Harding, and Frank Green.

3551. *Colored social club. Articles of incorporation, San Francisco, 1942. [3] p. Typew. C-ArS.
     A social and benevolent organization, the directors of which were William Brown, Marion Taylor, and Jim Tally.

3552. *Colored veterans service club. Articles of incorporation, San Francisco, 1927. [3] p. Typew. C-ArS.
     A social, political, and patriotic organization, the directors of

Social and Benevolent

which were Lester Mapp, E. Shropshire, A. P. Alberga, Clarence Coffin, and Alroyd Love.

3553. *Colored workingmens club.   Articles of incorporation, Los Angeles, 1913. Ms. [3] p. C-ArS.
   Organized for mutual improvement. Directors were Bradford Norman, Nalie B. Murray, John H. Hawkins, L. Garmer, and Charles S. Brown.

3554. *Colored workingmen's club.   Articles of incorporation, San Francisco, 1911. [6] p. Typew. C-ArS.
   A benevolent society, the directors of which were Lloyd V. Grey, William J. McLemore, Aaron Lewis, Charles E. Valentine, and Robert Jackson.

3555. *Exclusive men, San Francisco.   1957 cotillion presented by the Exclusive men, Mark Hopkins hotel, August 3, 1957. [S. F., 1957]. [32] p. ports. COEB.
   Contains biographies and portraits of participants.

3556. *Ladies Pacific accumulating and benevolent association of San Francisco. Incorporation papers, 1863. Ms. [7] p. C-ArS.
   Trustees were Jeremiah Burke Sanderson, James P. Dyer, Richard A. Hall, John R. Blake, Aaron F. Phillips, Andrew S. Bristol, Barney Fletcher, James Laws, and William H. Seth.

3557. *Ladies' union beneficial society of San Francisco.   Articles of incorporation, 1861. Ms. [4] p. C-ArS.
   A benevolent society. Trustees were Jeremiah B. Sanderson, Richard T. Houston, John A. Barber, Barney Fletcher, Cicero Miner, Nelson Cook, and Samuel Davis.

3558. _____. Constitution, by-laws, and act of incorporation. Organized, 1860. Incorporated February, 1861. [S. F.] Printed by B. F. Sterett [1861?] 12 p. CHi (photocopy), CU-B.

3559. *Negro incorporated aid society.   Articles of incorporation, Los Angeles, 1953. [4] p. Typew. and Ms. C-ArS.
   Organized for benevolent purposes and to promote agricultural communities and business enterprise to benefit its members. Directors were R. V. Randolph, Porter M. Mann, A. L. Wallace, M. D., M. E. Anderson, Rebecca Perkins, Johnnie Perkins, and Prentice Smith.

3560. *Negro motion picture players association.   Articles of incorporation, Los Angeles, 1939. Ms. [3] p. C-ArS.
   Organized for the mutual benefit of its members. Directors were Matilda Caldwell, Irving Smith, Alberta Clark, Ernest Wilson, Bessie Marie Reed, William J. Powell, Anna Mabry, Louise Springer, and William H. Johnson.

3561. *Negro protective fraternal society.   Articles of incorporation, San Francisco, 1908. 4 p. Typew. C-ArS.
   A benevolent society, the directors of which were Sterling P. Coffer, and R. M. Cornell, San Francisco; and Lawrence Sledge, Leroy Hayes, and Marion M. Francis of Oakland.

Social and Benevolent

3562. *Oakland literary aid society.   Articles of incorporation, 1876.   Ms.
    [5] p. C-ArS.
        Organized for literary, social, and benevolent purposes. Officers and
    directors were Henry Lancaster, Frederick Lawrence, Munford Harris,
    Cornelius Francis, John A. Wilds, Theodore Flood, and John W. Smith.

3563. *Oakland men of tomorrow.   Directory, 1967.   [Oakland, 1967].   23 p.
    COEB.
        "Historical notes on Oakland men of tomorrow, incorporated, October,
    1967, by Kenneth F. Smith, organizing founder and historian."

3564. *Progressive mutual benefit association, Los Angeles.   Articles of
    incorporation, 1920. 6 p. Typew. C-ArS.
        Directors: John H. Dixson, Jacob C. Jordan, Roy L. Loggins, William
    J. Thomas, and Ike W. Wallace.

3565. San Diego municipal employees association. Annual. CSd 1928-31.
        Contains report stating the purpose, activities, and growth of the
    Colored employees social and aid club.

3566. *San Francisco colored chauffeurs association.   Articles of incorpora-
    tion, 1923. [5] p. Typew. C-ArS.
        Directors were Isador Dennis, James B. Shorter, and W. Rice.

3567. *Veterans of foreign wars of the United States. Booker T. Washington
    post no. 3344. Articles of incorporation, Los Angeles county, 1946.
    4 [2] p. Typew. C-ArS.
        Directors were Harold A. Jameson, Henry Hyman, Ervie L. Jones,
    Kenneth C. Russ, Oliver D. Butler, Clyde Brown, M. D., Vincent I. Holman,
    Ruben B. White, Ernest D. Williams, and Harris Williams, all of Long
    Beach.

3568. *West Indian benevolent association.   Articles of incorporation, San
    Francisco, 1869. Ms. [5] p. C-ArS.
        Trustees were Robert E. Muir, William J. Simmonds [sic], James E.
    Francis, Matthew A. Phipps, Edward F. Charlton, William Smith, and Edward
    Hall. Their election was certified by John Hamilton, James Hargrove,
    and John T. Callender.

3569. *Western addition community festival.   Souvenir program, San Francisco,
    October 25 and 26, 1969 ... [S. F., 1969]. [10] p. illus., map.
        "History of the Western addition": p. [5].

                              WOMEN'S CLUBS

3570. *California council of Negro women, inc.   California council of Negro
    women, inc. 30th annual convention, May 17-18, 1969, Cabana motor hotel
    [Palo Alto. Oakland, California voice pub. co., 1969]. 28 p. ports.
        Contains biographical account of Mrs. Lillie (Donnell) Wilkerson,
    list of state officers, and several addresses.

Women's Clubs

3571. *California state association of colored women.   Constitution and by-
laws. [n.p., 1940]. 19 p. CU-B.
      "Revised by order of the El Centro state convention, June 5, 1940."

3572. _____. First annual convention of Colored women's clubs of California.
Foresters' hall, Clay St., bet. 12th and 13th, August 6-7. Oakland, 1907.
[7] p. CU-B.
      Souvenir program.

3573. _____. Journal of the annual convention. COEB, 1940 (34th)-41, 1945-
46, 1948-50, 1952-56, 1958-62, 1964-68, 1970.
      Title varies slightly. Margaret (Marlow) Nottage, longtime ed.

3574. HUNTON, A. W. "The club movement in California," in Crisis, v. 5,
Dec., 1912, pp. 90-91.
      Women's club activities in Oakland, San Francisco, Los Angeles,
Sacramento, San Jose, Bakersfield, Pasadena, etc.

3575. *Links. Oakland-Bay area chapter. Cotillion souvenir program. COEB,
1960, 1965, 1967; CSfAA, 1966.

3576. *[MAYS, IANTHA (VILLA)]. History [of] California association of
colored women's clubs, inc., 1906-1955. [Oakland, 1955?]. 34 p. COEB.

3577. *Montana federation of Negro women's clubs. State journal. Butte,
Mont., Oates and Roberts, 1921. 60 p. MtGf.
      Proceedings of the first session held at Butte, Aug. 3-5, 1921.

3578. *National association of colored women. Annual convention program.
COEB, 1952 (Los Angeles); Wa, 1948 (Seattle).
      Title varies slightly.

3579. *National council of Negro women, inc. Ninth regional conference ...
April 26-28, 1963 ... Oakland, 1963. 32 p. illus., ports. COEB.
      Souvenir booklet of Oakland meeting.

3580. _____. 20 years of endeavor; a challenge to the future. Brotherhood
luncheon, Hotel Willard, Washington, D. C., February 26, 1955. Washington, D. C., Leo Orso [1955]. Phonodisc, 2 s. NN.
      Mrs. Sue Bailey Thurman was among the speakers recorded.

SOCIOLOGY

3581. AFFLECK, MARILYN, 1932- . Reactions to marginality: a study of
mentally retarded and ethnic minorities. Doctoral dissertation, Univ. of
Calif., Los Angeles, 1966. xvii, 201 l. tables.
      A sociological study.

3582. ALLEN, DEROTHA FIELDS. The leisure time activities of a selected
group of Negro girls. Master's thesis, Univ. of southern Calif., Los
Angeles, 1949. vi, 86 l. tables.

Sociology

3583. ARRIAGA, MARY. Public welfare department and services: social
workers' length of employment and attitudes toward minority groups,
Fresno county, California. Master's thesis, Calif. state univ., Fresno,
1968.

3584. BEASLEY, JOHN AARON. A study of socioeconomic groups in relation to
the ways they differ in attitudes toward various occupational dimensions.
Doctoral dissertation, Washington state univ., Pullman, 1967. 153 p.

3585. BERRY, EDWIN C. The Negro adolescent in a white world. Portland,
Urban league [n.d.]. 4 p. DHU.
     Reprint of an address which also appeared in The social welfare re-
porter.

3586. *BILLINGSLEY, ANDREW. Black families in white America [by] Andrew
Billingsley, with the assistance of Amy Tate Billingsley. Englewood
Cliffs, N. J., Prentice-Hall [1968]. 218 p. illus., map. Bibliographi-
cal footnotes. CBea, CHS, CLSU, CNoS, CSbS, CSdS, CSfCiC, CSp, CSt,
CSuLas, CU-A, CU-I, CU-M, CU-SB.
     Authored by an educator at the Univ. of Calif., Berkeley.

3587. _____., and AMY TATE BILLINGSLEY. "Negro family life in America,"
in Social service review, v. 39, Sept., 1965, pp. 310-19.

3588. *BOND, J. MAX. "The Japanese in California," in Crisis, v. 40, June,
1933, pp. 132-33.

3589. BREWER, DAVID LESLIE, 1933- . Utah elites and Utah racial norms.
Doctoral dissertation, Univ. of Utah, Salt Lake City, 1966. vii, 180 ℓ.
forms. CBGTU (photocopy), CSaT (photocopy), CSmH (photocopy), CU-B
(photocopy).
     "Origin, status, and probable future of Utah's unique racial norms."

3590. California. State univ. San Jose. Economics dept. A racial profile
of California; senior seminar in economic research, Spring, 1968. [San
Jose, 1968]. 68 p. C.
     A study of minority composition, employment, unemployment, income,
housing, discrimination, and urban living.

3591. _____. University. Davis. Dept. of agricultural education. Family
patterns and social class [by] Mary C. Regan. Davis, 1967. 75 ℓ. C,
CU-A.
     A study of "lower class families."

3592. COSEY, LOUIS W. E. Franklin Frazier's analysis of the problems of the
Negro. Master's thesis, Univ. of southern Calif., Los Angeles, 1957.
iv, 124 ℓ.

3593. CROBAUGH, CLYDE JULIAN. The changing status of the American Negro.
Master's thesis, Stanford univ., Stanford, 1921. 143 ℓ.

3594. CROSSLEY, LUCY C. Use of services by A[id to] F[amilies with] D[e-
pendent] C[hildren] Negro mothers: a study of cultural influences on

Sociology

the attitudes of AFDC mothers of Fresno county, California. Master's thesis, Calif. state univ., Fresno, 1968.

3595. DERBYSHIRE, ROBERT L. "United States Negro identity conflict," in Sociology and social research, v. 51, July, 1967, pp. 63-67.

3596. ELDER, GLEN H. "Socialization and ascent in a racial minority," in Youth & society, v. 2, Sept., 1970, pp. 74-110.
    Based upon a study of approximately 2,000 black and white boys from grades seven through twelve in Richmond.

3597. EPPS, EDGAR G. Socio-economic status, level of aspiration, and juvenile delinquency. Doctoral dissertation, Washington state univ., Pullman, 1959.
    "Investigation of Merton's theory of delinquent behavior; included race as a variable."

3598. FARMER, GEORGE LUTHER. Afro-American attitudes and perceptions, by George L. Farmer. Culver City, West Los Angeles College, 1969. i, 97 ℓ. CLSU.

3599. _____. Afro-American problems in sociology and psychology, by George L. Farmer. L. A., Artgo pubs., 1970. xii, 196 ℓ. Bibliography: ℓ. 191-96. CLSU.
    Also includes housing.

3600. FINLEY, JARVIS M. Fertility trends and differentials in Seattle. Doctoral dissertation, Univ. of Washington, Seattle, 1958.
    "Fertility trends, 1940-1950, analyzed by various economic and educational categories and by race."

3601. FORBES, JACK DOUGLAS, 1934- . Afro-Americans in the Far West; a handbook for educators. [Berkeley, Far West laboratory for educational research and development, 1967]. 106 p. Bibliography: pp. 65-106. Available in many California libraries.
    Emphasizes the anthropological and sociological aspects of the area covered.

3602. FULWEILER, CHARLES RADCLIFFE. A preliminary investigation of the accommodation mechanism as a factor in the clinical study of the Negro adolescent. Master's thesis, Univ. of Calif., Berkeley, 1951. iv, 105 ℓ. illus., tables.

3603. GERSON, WALTER M. Social structure and mass media utilization. Doctoral dissertation, Univ. of Washington, Seattle, 1963.
    "Negro adolescents use mass media as a social agency to a greater extent than do white youth."

3604. GLASS, JOHN FRANKLIN, 1936- . Organizational dilemmas in the war on poverty: contrasts in the Neighborhood youth corps. Doctoral dissertation, Univ. of Calif., Los Angeles, 1968. xiii, 327 ℓ. illus.
    A sociological study.

Sociology

3605. HADWEN, THEODORE. "Sociology," a lecture given Oct. 8, 1965 for "Perspectives on the Negro in our affluent society," a lecture series sponsored by the Associated students of Palomar college, San Marcos. CSmarP (tape, 1200 feet).
Relates areas of racial and cultural variations of behavior, especially as they are associated with social problems.

3606. *HARE, NATHAN   "Black ecology," in The black scholar, v. 1, Apr., 1970, pp. 2-8.

3607. HARRIS, JOAN R. Ethnicity and socio-economic status as factors in patterns of child-rearing among working mothers. Master's thesis, Calif. state univ., Los Angeles, 1965.

3608. HOWARD, LEONZIE BILLY. A comparative study of Negro attitudes toward ideal, self, and others. Master's thesis, Calif. state univ., San Jose, 1956. 86 ℓ.

3609. *JAMES, JOSEPH. "Profiles: San Francisco," in Sociology of education, v. 19, Nov., 1945, pp. 166-78.

3610. JUNG, RAYMOND KAY. Leisure activities of children of different socio-economic status and from different ethnic groups. Doctoral dissertation, Univ. of Calif., Berkeley, 1963. 202 ℓ.
"Differences in leisure time activities were not pronounced, but such differences were along ethnic lines more than socio-economic divisions. Orientals, Negroes, and Caucasians were the ethnic groups studied." - West, p. 11.

3611. KLEIN, MALCOLM W. "Factors related to juvenile gang membership patterns," in Sociology and social research, v. 51, July, 1967, pp. 49-62.
Klein is a member of Youth studies center, Univ. of southern Calif., Los Angeles.

3612. LANDIS, JUDSON R., DARRYL DATWYLER, and DEAN S. DORN. "Race and social class as determinants of social distance," in Sociology and social research, v. 51, Oct., 1966, pp. 78-86.
Landis is a faculty member at California state univ., Sacramento.

3613. LEAVITT, MARGARET ELAINE. Patterns of abasement and aggression in Negro youth. Master's thesis, Univ. of Calif., Berkeley, 1949. [129] ℓ. illus., tables.

3614. LEE, LLOYD L. "A brief analysis of the role and status of the Negro in the Hawaiian community," in American sociological review, v. 13, Aug., 1948, pp. 419-37.

3615. MANESE, WILFREDO REYES. Negro-white differences in motivation. Master's thesis, Calif. state univ., San Diego, 1967. 121 ℓ.

3616. MILES, CECIL DAVID. Exploratory study of some understandings of 30 Negro male AFDC-U recipients regarding this public assistance program, by CeciJ D. Miles and Richard Louis Walthart. Master's thesis, Calif.

Sociology

    state univ., Sacramento, 1966. 86 ℓ.
      The Aid to families with dependent children program.

3617. MILLER, HERMAN PHILLIP, 1921- . Poverty and the Negro, by Herman P.
    Miller. [L. A., Institute of government and public affairs, Univ. of
    Calif., 1965?]. 30 ℓ. Bibliographical footnotes. CSfSt.

3618. MORRIS, JAMES RUSSELL. The social-economic background of Negro youth
    in California. Doctoral dissertation, Stanford univ., Stanford, 1947.
    152 ℓ. forms.

3619. _____. "Social-economic background of Negro youth in California," in
    Journal of Negro education, v. 20, no. 1, 1951, pp. 22-31.

3620. Nevada. Bureau of governmental research. Minority groups in Nevada.
    [Carson City?] 1966. 52 ℓ. tables, charts. CO.

3621. *PERRY, PETTIS. The war and the Negro people; report by Pettis Perry,
    member State committee, to Northern California conference on Negro work.
    [S. F.?, 1941]. 14 p. Mimeo. CU-B.

3622. *(PITTMAN, TAREA HALL). The operation of state and county residence
    requirements under the California indigent aid law in Contra Costa
    county. Master's thesis, Univ. of Calif., Berkeley, 1946. 76 ℓ. tables,
    forms, diagrs.

3623. ROESLER, KAREN JANE. A model for achievement motive acquisition.
    Master's thesis, Univ. of southern Calif., Los Angeles, 1969. iv, 86 ℓ.
      A study of black achievement motivation.

3624. SCHULZ, DAVID ALLEN. Variations in complete and incomplete families
    of the Negro lower-class. Doctoral dissertation, Univ. of Washington,
    Seattle, 1968. 500 p.

3625. SPECHT, HARRY, 1928- . Community development in low-income areas:
    its relevance to problems of the Negro community. [Walnut Creek, Contra
    Costa council of community services, 1966]. 49 p. Contra Costa county
    Council of community services publication no. 104. Bibliography:
    pp. 47-49. C, CO, CU-B.

3626. STEVENS, KATHLEEN H. A sociological analysis of certain intelligence
    tests given to American Negroes. Master's thesis, Univ. of southern
    Calif., Los Angeles, 1928. i, 94 ℓ. diagrs.

3627. SUDNOW, DAVID NATHAN. Passing on: the social organization of dying
    in the county hospital. Doctoral dissertation, Univ. of Calif., Berkeley,
    1966. 278 ℓ.
      "Analysis of varying meanings of dying depending on age, race and
    class status." - West, p. 9.

3628. THEIBAULT, MARY ANN. Recent trends in assimilation of nonwhites for
    selected socioeconomic factors. Master's thesis, California state univ.,
    San Jose, 1970. vi, 97 ℓ.

Sociology

3629. U. S. Bureau of labor statistics. The Negro in the West ... Some facts relating to social and economic conditions. S. F., U. S. Dept. of labor, 1965-67. 3 v. illus., maps. C (v. 3 only), CBSK, CFS, CHS, CL (v. 3 only), CLGS, CLS, CLSU (v. 3 only), CP, CPomCP (v. 1 only) CRic (v. 1 only), CSd, CSdS, CSfGG, CS1uSP, CSrCL, CSt-Law, CStmo, CU-I, CU-SB.
    Contents. - 1. The Negro worker. - 2. The Negro consumer. - 3. The Negro family.

3630. _____. _____. The Negroes in the United States; their economic and social situation. Washington, D. C., Govt. print., 1966. v, 241 p. tables, maps. Bulletin no. 1511. CFS, CSt.
    Considerable information on Los Angeles.

3631. VON HENTIG, HANS, 1887- . The criminality of the colored woman. [Boulder, Colo., 1942]. pp. 231-60. tables. (Univ. of Colorado studies. Series C, Studies in the social sciences, v. 1, no. 3). CLSU.

3632. Washington. Planning and community affairs agency. Nonwhite races, state of Washington, by Calvin F. Schmid, Charles E. Nobbe [and] Arlene E. Mitchell. Olympia, Wash., 1968. 132 p. C, Wa.
    A research report with numerous charts, graphs, and statistics.

3633. WILSON, ANITA LOUISE. Dogmatism and anti-Negro attitudes among Negroes. Master's thesis, Calif. state univ., San Jose, 1968. iv, 47 ℓ.

3634. WONG, FRANCES F. Family solidarity: a comparative study of Negro and white family cohesiveness, aid to families with dependent children, families of Madera City, Calif. Master's thesis, Calif. state univ., Fresno, 1966.

3635. YINGER, JOHN MILTON. "Integration and pluralism viewed from Hawaii," in Antioch review, v. 22, Winter, 1962-63, pp. 397-410.
    Integration of various peoples in Hawaii.

SPORTS

3636. ANACLERIO, CARL RAY. Negro sports participation and its advancement. Master's thesis, Calif. state univ., San Francisco, 1966. 85 ℓ. tables, charts.
    "Compares Negro participation in adult, amateur, and professional athletics, 1947-1966, with Negro participation during the same period in the athletic programs of an unspecified, 'large metropolitan San Francisco bay area high school'."

3637. *BROWN, JAMES NATHANIEL. Off my chest, by Jimmy Brown, with Myron Cope. Garden City, N. Y., Doubleday, 1964. 230 p. CNoS, CSbCL.
    "The former fullback of the Cleveland Browns tells of his life as a professional and his private life." - Dorothy B. Porter. Brown became a Los Angeles motion picture star.

Sports

3638. California. State athletic commission. Applications for licenses, records of investigations, newspaper clippings, etc., relating to boxers, wrestlers, referees, managers, and timekeepers, 1936-48. Includes Afro-Americans. 2/3 cu. ft. C-ArS.

3639. *CEPEDA, ORLANDO, 1938?- . My ups and down in baseball, by [Manual] Orlando Cepeda [Pennes] with Charles Einstein. N. Y., Putnam's [c1968]. 191 p. port.
   For his career as a player with the San Francisco giants, 1958-66, see pp. 39-166.

3640. CLOUD, DONALD EMERSON. A study of the change in magazine articles dealing with the Negro athlete, 1935-1941, 1947-1953. Master's thesis, Univ. of Calif., Berkeley, 1958. iii, 23 ℓ.

3641. *DE COY, ROBERT H. The big black fire, by Robert H. de Coy. L. A., Holloway house pub. co. [1969]. 312 p. CSf.
   Biography of John Alfred (Jack) Johnson (1878-1946), authored by a Los Angeles resident.

3642. *EDWARDS, HARRY, 1942- . The revolt of the black athlete [by] Harry Edwards. With a foreword by Samuel J. Skinner, Jr. N. Y., Free press [c1969]. xx, 202 p. illus., ports. C, CCotS, CHS, CLSU, CNoS, CSfU, CSjC, CSt, CU-SB.
   The Olympic games boycott, 1968, and the attitudes of black athletes.

3643. EINSTEIN, CHARLES. How to coach, manage, and play little league baseball; a commonsense instructional manual. Foreword by Willie Mays. N. Y., Simon and Schuster [1968]. 142 p. CSf.

3644. FOREMAN, THOMAS E. Discrimination against the Negro in American athletics. Master's thesis, Calif. state univ., Fresno, 1957.

3645. HANO, ARNOLD. "Amazing Willie Mays," in Black world, v. 10, Sept., 1961, pp. 20-28.
   Reprinted from Sport.

3646. HARVEY, JOHN A. The role of American Negroes in organized baseball. Doctoral dissertation, Columbia univ., Teachers college, New York City, 1961.

3647. *HENDERSON, EDWIN BANCROFT, 1883- . The black athlete; emergence and arrival, by Edwin B. Henderson and the editors of Sport magazine. N. Y., Publishers co. [c1968]. xiii, 306 p. illus., ports. (International library of Negro life and history, v. 8). Bibliography: pp. [275-97]. CBGTU, CHS, CLSU, CNoS, CSf, CSt, CU, CU-A, CU-SB.
   Contains considerable information about California but only occasional information about other western states.

3648. _____. The Negro in sports. Rev. ed. Washington, D. C., Associated pubs. [c1939]. 371 p. illus., ports. CSdS, CU.
   Includes statistics and mention of activities in California and other western states. Biographical information about Peter Jackson, Sam McVey,

Sports

John Henry Lewis, Howard P. Drew, Woodrow Wilson Strode, Walter A.
Gordon, Kenneth Washington, and others.

3649. _____. Same. Rev. ed., Washington, D. C., 1949. 507 p. CU-A.

3650. "I don't have to prove a thing," in Black world, v. 13, Mar., 1964,
pp. 12-21.
    Taken from "We are grown men playing a child's game," by Gilbert
Rogin, in Sports illustrated, Nov. 18, 1963. Concerns William Russell.

3651. KING, JOE. San Francisco giants. Introd. by George Christopher.
Pref. by Ford C. Frick. Englewood Cliffs, N. J., Prentice-Hall [1958].
177 p. illus. C, CChiS, CPa, CSbCL, CSf, CSj, CStmo, CViCL, Rocq 10069.

3652. KING, JOHN TAYLOR, 1921- . Stories of twenty-three famous Negro
Americans, by John T. King and Marcet H. King. Austin, Texas, Steck-
Vaughn, c1967. 120 p. CL.
    Includes Willie Mays.

3653. LISS, HOWARD. The Willie Mays album. N. Y., Hawthorn books, inc.,
pubs., 1966. 63 p.

3654. *LOUIS, JOE, 1914- . The Joe Louis story. N. Y., Grosset [c1953].
197 p. illus. CL, CNoS.
    "Written with the editorial aid of Chester L. Washington and Haskell
Cohen." Washington was a Los Angeles journalist.
    An earlier ed. was pub. in 1947.

3655. LOW, NAT. The Negro in sports, by Nat Low. S. F., Daily people's
world [194-?]. 31 p. illus. CU-A.
    Emphasizes California sports activities.

3656. MANN, ARTHUR WILLIAM. The Jackie Robinson story. N. Y., Grosset &
Dunlap [1951]. 224 p. CSbCL.

3657. *MARICHAL, JUAN. A pitcher's story, by Juan Marichal with Charles
Einstein. Garden City, N. Y., Doubleday [c1967]. 215 p. ports. CNoS,
CSf, CSluSP.

3658. *MAYS, WILLIAM HOWARD, 1931- . Born to play ball, by Willie Mays,
as told to Charles Einstein. N. Y., Putnam [1955]. 168 p. illus.
CHS, CSbCL, CSf.

3659. _____. My secrets of playing baseball, by Willie Mays with Howard
Liss. Photos. by David Sutton. N. Y., Viking press [1967]. 89 p.
illus. CSf, WaPu, WaT.

3660. _____. Willie Mays: my life in and out of baseball, as told to
Charles Einstein. N. Y., E. P. Dutton, 1966. 320 p. illus., ports.
CEcaC, CLSU, CNoS, CO, CSbCL, CSdS, CSluSP, WaPu.

3661. "Mays fans Mantle," in Esquire, v. 70, Aug., 1968, pp. 46-47.

Sports

3662. *MOORE, ARCHIE, 1916- . The Archie Moore story. N. Y., McGraw-Hill [c1960]. 240 p. illus. CLobS, CSd, CSf, WaT.

3663. OLSEN, JACK. The black athlete: a shameful story; the myth of integration in American sport. N. Y., Time-Life books [1968]. 223 p. CSdS, CSf, CSuLas.
    Includes information about California and Western athletics.

3664. ORR, JACK, ed. Baseball's greatest players today, ed. by Jack Orr. N. Y., Franklin Watts, inc. [c1963]. 150 p. CSf.
    Biographical accounts of players including Maury Wills, Willie Mays, Tommy Davis, Leon Wagner, Orlando Cepeda, Frank Robinson, Juan Marichal, and others. Authored by staff members of the New York world-telegram & sun.

3665. PETERSON, ROBERT. Only the ball was white, by Robert Peterson. Englewood Cliffs, N. J., Prentice-Hall, inc. [c1970]. vii, 406 p. illus., ports. CNoS, CSf.
    An appendix, pp. 257-399, gives baseball player and team statistical information. Contains some California and western material.

3666. *ROBINSON, FRANK. My life in baseball, by Frank Robinson with Al Silverman. Garden City, N. Y., Doubleday, 1968. 225 p. ports. CB, CO, CSbCL, CSf, CSto.
    A boy from Oakland's ghetto rose to become the most valuable player in both the American and National baseball leagues.

3667. *ROBINSON, JOHN ROOSEVELT, 1919-1972. Baseball has done it, by Jackie Robinson. Edited by Charles Dexter. Philadelphia, Lippincott [1964]. 216 p. CEcaC, CHS, CLU, CNoS, CO, COM, CSbCL, CSbS, CSdS, CSf, CSluSP, CU, CU-SC, WaT.
    Contains some information about his early life in Whittier and Los Angeles.

3668. _____. Jackie Robinson - my own story as told by Jackie Robinson to Wendell Smith of the Pittsburgh courier and the Chicago herald American. N. Y., Greenberg pubs., 1948. 170 p. illus., ports. DLC.

3669. _____. Wait till next year; the life story of Jackie Robinson, by Carl T. Rowan with Jackie Robinson. N. Y., Random house [1960]. 339 p. illus. COM, CSf, CSto.

3670. RODGERS, JONATHAN. "Step to an Olympic boycott," in Sports illustrated, v. 27, Dec. 4, 1967, pp. 30-31.
    Concerns a western regional black youth conference.

3671. ROEDER, BILL. Jackie Robinson. N. Y., Barnes [1950]. vi, 183 p. ports. CHS, CSbCL, CSf.

3672. *ROWAN, CARL THOMAS, 1925- . Wait till next year; the life story of Jackie Robinson, by Carl T. Rowan with Jackie Robinson. N. Y., Random house [1960]. 339 p. illus. CHS, CSf, WaPu, WaT.

Sports

3673. *RUSSELL, WILLIAM FELTON, 1934- . Go up for glory, by Bill Russell, as told to William McSweeney. N. Y., Coward-McCann [1966]. 224 p. illus., ports. CSbCL, CSf.
     The author describes his formative years in Oakland and his basketball career at the Univ. of San Francisco, pp. 17-50.

3674. *SIMPSON, ORENTHAL J. O. J.; the education of a rich rookie, by O. J. Simpson with Pete Axthelm. N. Y., The Macmillan co., c1970. 255 p. illus. CSf.

3675. SMITH, KEN. The Willie Mays story. N. Y., Greenberg, c1954. 94 p. illus., ports. CP.

3676. *WILLS, MAURY. It pays to steal [by] Maury Wills as told to Steve Gardner. Englewood Cliffs, New Jersey, Prentice-Hall [c1963]. 186 p. ports. CBea, CSto.
     Autobiography of a baseball player for the Los Angeles dodgers.

3677. *YOUNG, A. S. "DOC". Black champions of the gridiron: O. J. Simpson and Leroy Keyes, by A. S. "Doc" Young. N. Y., Harcourt, Brace & World [1969]. 120 p. illus., ports. CSf.
     Mr. Young, a Los Angeles resident, wrote to the compiler of this bibliography as follows: "I do not use any professional name, nor do I want any other used, except A. S. 'Doc' Young. My name is not 'Sturgeon' which is a fish, not the name of a person, and my birth year is not 1919." The New York public library's Schomburg collection, in common with other libraries, uses the author entry: Young, Andrew Sturgeon Nash, 1919- .

3678. _____. Great Negro baseball stars and how they made the major leagues, by A. S. "Doc" Young. N. Y., A. S. Barnes [c1953]. 248 p. illus., ports. CLU, CNoS.

3679. _____. Negro first in sports, by A. S. "Doc" Young. With illus. by Herbert Temple. Chicago, Johnson pub. co. [c1963]. xiii, 301 p. illus., tables. CFS, CHS, CNoS, COM, CPhD, CSdS, CSluSP, CU-SB.
     Gives some information about individual athletes and athletic teams in western U. S.

3680. ZIMMERMAN, PAUL BECHLER, 1903- . The Los Angeles dodgers. Preface by Walter Alston; introd. by Mayor Norris Poulson. N. Y., Coward-McCann, inc. [1960]. 221 p. illus. CSbCL, CSf, Rocq 4554.

URBAN LIFE AND HISTORY

3681. BAILEY, LESTER P. "No fairer among the fair," in Crisis, v. 63, Mar., 1956, pp. 132-35.
     Description of San Francisco.

3682. *BANNER, WARREN M. A survey of community patterns related to the program of the Seattle urban league. N. Y., National urban league, 1954. 199 p. Wa.

Urban Life and History

"Conducted for the Board of directors, Seattle urban league, by
Warren M. Banner, director, Dept. of research and community projects,
National urban league.

3683. *BARBOUR, W. MILLER, 1908- . An exploratory study of socio-economic
problems affecting the Negro-white relationship in Richmond, California,
a project of United community defense services, inc. By W. Miller
Barbour. N. Y., National urban league, 1952. vii, 73 ℓ. tables.
Bibliographical footnotes. C (photocopy), CRic.

3684. _____. A preliminary evaluation of racial minority conditions in
Tucson, Arizona and of the Tucson Urban league service council. Tucson,
Urban league service council, 1954. iv, 57 ℓ.

3685. *BILLINGSLEY, ANDREW. "Family functioning in the low-income black
community," in Social casework, v. 50, Dec., 1969, pp. 563-72.

3686. BLACKWELL, TILLIE N. An investigation of changes in non-white segregation patterns, 1950-1960. Master's thesis, Calif. state univ., San
Francisco, 1965. 82 ℓ. tables.
"A study of changes in the relative socio-economic status of non-
whites in 10 major cities, 1950-1960. The author concludes that there
is 'greater integration in areas involving secondary [i.e., jobs] as
opposed to primary [i.e., housing] interactions'."

3687. *BOND, J. MAX. The Negro in Los Angeles. Doctoral dissertation,
Univ. of southern Calif., Los Angeles, 1936. xiii, 365 ℓ. maps, tables,
diagrs. CLS (photocopy).
Social and economic conditions.

3688. BRANHAM, ETHEL. A study of independent adoptions by Negro parents in
metropolitan Los Angeles. Master's thesis, Univ. of southern Calif.,
Los Angeles, 1949. iii, 62 ℓ.

3689. BREIT, AMELIA. Problems of Negro youth in Tucson. Master's thesis,
Univ. of Arizona, Tucson, 1947.

3690. *BULLOCK, PAUL, 1924- . "Poverty in Los Angeles; facts and fantasies
about south and east Los Angeles," in Frontier, v. 17, Sept., 1966,
pp. 5-7.
Negro and Mexican areas.

3691. BURGESS, MARGARET BLAINE. A study of selected socio-cultural and
opinion differentials among Negroes and whites in Pasco, Washington
community. Master's thesis, Washington state univ., Pullman, 1949.
129 p.

3692. California. Dept. of employment. San Francisco office. The economic
status of Negroes in the San Francisco-Oakland bay area; a report based
on the 1960 census of population. [Prepared by its Research and statistics section. S. F., 1963]. 12 p. CSb, CU.

Urban Life and History

3693. _____. State univ. Sacramento. Dept. of anthropology. Research study on the felt needs of three ethnic minorities in the greater Sacramento area (Negro, Mexican-American, Chinese). Project director: Mohammad A. Rauf. Chief editor: Donna Halstead. Sacramento [1969]. 1 v. unp. maps. CSS.

3694. _____. University. Berkeley. Survey research center. Poverty and poverty programs in Oakland. A report to the Dept. of human resources of the city of Oakland. Selected results from the 701 household survey. Berkeley, 1967. 165 p. map, tables. CO.
   Including figures for ethnic composition of poor.

3695. _____. _____. Office of university relations. The city is people; a report. [Berkeley, 1967]. 12 p. illus. CLU, CU-B.
   About Los Angeles.

3696. _____. _____. University extension. Continuing education in environmental design. Survey of model cities applications in northern California. Berkeley, 1968. 61 p. tables. CO.

3697. CARMICHAEL, BENJAMIN GREEN. Hunters Point: a participant observer's view. Master's thesis, Univ. of Calif., Berkeley, 1968. 136 ℓ.

3698. CARTLAND, EARL FERNANDO. A study of the Negroes living in Pasadena. Master's thesis, Whittier college, Whittier, 1948. unp.

3699. CASIMERE, GERALD LEE. Ethnicity: as an element in the socio-economic development of minority communities. Master's thesis, Stanford univ., Stanford, 1970. iii, 47 ℓ.
   An East Palo Alto study.

3700. *CAYTON, HORACE ROSCOE, 1903-1970. "America's ten best cities for Negroes," in Black world, v. 5, Oct., 1947, pp. 4-10.
   Includes Los Angeles and San Francisco.

3701. CHING, ADELE. "San Mateo Negroes," in Problems of American communities, v. i, pp. 109-24. Oakland, Mills college Dept. of economics and sociology, 1945. COMC.

3702. COHEN, JEROME. A descriptive study of the availability and useability [sic] of social services in the south central area of Los Angeles. L. A., Univ. of Calif. institute of govt. and public affairs, c1967. 42, 6 p. map. Los Angeles riot study, MR-85. CLU, CSt-Law, CU-B.

3703. Community welfare federation of Los Angeles. Social welfare dept. The facilities for the care of dependent, semi-delinquent and delinquent Negro children in Los Angeles. A study by Agnes E. Wilson. L. A., 1925. 44 ℓ. C, CL.

3704. Coro foundation, San Francisco. The Negro community leaders in Pasadena; a social and economic survey of the northwest area in Pasadena. [S. F.] 1961. 12 p. CO.

Urban Life and History

3705. Council for civic unity of San Francisco. The San Francisco non-white population, 1950-1960. S. F. [1961?]. 15 ℓ. maps, tables. CO.

3706. COY, OWEN COCHRAN, 1884- . "The queen of the angels," in Grizzly bear, v. 49, Sept., 1931, pp. 1-2.
Describes the founding of Los Angeles and the growth of population, 1790-1800.

3707. CRIMI, JAMES E. The social status of the Negro in Pasadena, California. Master's thesis, Univ. of southern Calif., Los Angeles, 1941. 123 ℓ. maps, tables.

3708. DAY, GEORGE M. "Races and cultural cases," in Sociology and social research, v. 18, Mar.-Apr., 1934, pp. 326-39.
Study of Los Angeles minorities.

3709. DE GRAAF, LAWRENCE BROOKS. "The city of black angels: emergence of the Los Angeles ghetto, 1890-1930," in Pacific historical review, v. 39, Aug., 1970, pp. 323-52.

3710. "Denver, 'The city beautiful'--Denver, 'The city of lights'," in Colored American magazine, v. 12, May, 1907, pp. 336-38 and 382.

3711. *DU BOIS, WILLIAM EDWARD BURGHARD, 1868-1963. "Colored California," in Crisis, v. 6, Aug., 1913, pp. 182-83, 192-96.
An illustrated article describing Los Angeles, San Francisco, San Diego, Oakland, and Stockton.

3712. _____. "The great northwest," in Crisis, v. 6, Sept., 1913, pp. 234, 237-40.
An illustrated article describing Portland, Seattle, and Tacoma.

3713 EDDINGTON, NEIL ARTHUR. The urban plantation. Berkeley, Pacifica tape library A-2367, 1968. [Phonotape]. Duration: 50 min. CSS.
Eddington, who did field work for a doctorate in the Hunters Point district of San Francisco, discusses with Al Silbowitz black attitudes and the relevance of the social scientist.

3714. _____. The urban plantation: the ethnography of an oral tradition in a Negro community. Doctoral dissertation, Univ. of Calif., Berkeley, 1967. xvii, 232 ℓ.

3715. ELMAN, RICHARD M. Ill-at-ease in Compton [by] Richard M. Elman. N. Y., Pantheon books [c1967]. viii, 207 p. map (on lining papers). Available in many California libraries.
A study of urban decay in a community adjoining Watts.

3716. *ERVIN, JAMES MC FARLINE. The participation of the Negro in the community life of Los Angeles. Master's thesis, Univ. of southern Calif., Los Angeles, 1931. iv, 113 ℓ. diagrs., tables.
"Contains interviews with black and white prostitutes in Central Avenue district." - Patricia Adler.

Urban Life and History

3717. *FAUSET, JESSIE REDMON, 1884?- . "Out of the West," in Crisis, v. 27, Nov., 1923, pp. 11-18.
   An illustrated article describing Denver.

3718. FOGELSON, ROBERT M. The fragmented metropolis; Los Angeles, 1850-1930, by Robert M. Fogelson. Cambridge, Harvard Univ. press, 1967. xv, 362 p. illus., maps, tables, charts.
   Contains a description of the migration and segregation of blacks and the discrimination against them. See in index under Negroes.

3719. GILLIAM, HAROLD. The face of San Francisco. Text by Harold Gilliam. Photographs by Phil Palmer. Garden City, N. Y., Doubleday & co., [c1960]. 256 p. illus., maps (on lining papers). CSf.
   Directed mainly toward the tourist reader. Negro population is described, pp. 118-23 and 129.

3720. GITCHOFF, GEORGE THOMAS. Community response to racial tensions: an exploratory study of the street gang program in Richmond. Master's thesis, Univ. of Calif., Berkeley, 1966. ii, 115 ℓ.

3721. GOLDSMITH, RENEE LOIS. Negro youth culture and identity: the case of Hunter's Point. Master's thesis, Univ. of Calif., Berkeley, 1967. 150 ℓ. illus.
   A study made in the Hunters Point district of San Francisco.

3722. GREEN, KENNETH. An examination of some important effects of urban city planning on racial and cultural minority groups in the American racial, economic, and political context. Master's thesis, Univ. of Calif., Berkeley, 1953. v.p. tables.

3723. GRODZINS, MORTON, 1917-1964. The metropolitan area as a racial problem, 1958. [Pittsburgh, Pa.] Univ. of Pittsburgh press [1959, c1958]. 28 p. illus. CHS, CLSU, CLobS, CNoS, CSfGG.
   Describes conditions in Los Angeles.

3724. GUINN, JAMES MILLER. Historical and biographical record of Los Angeles and vicinity ... Chicago, Chapman pub. co., 1901. 940 p. illus., ports. C, CCC, CF, CFS, CHi, CL, CLSU, CO, CP, CSdS, CSf, CSfCP, CSmH, CStmo, CU-B, Rocq 2643.
   "The author gives a very satisfactory coverage of the founding of Los Angeles [pp. 30-34] and lists the eleven heads of families." - Miriam Matthews.

3725. _____. A history of California and an extended history of Los Angeles and environs ... L. A., Historic record co., 1915. 3 v. illus. C, CBb, CF, CG1, CHi, CL, CLSM, CLU, CP, CSf, CSmH, CStmo, CU-B. Rocq 2643.
   "In addition to his account of the founding of Los Angeles, the author reports [v. 1, p. 265] the presence in Los Angeles as late as 1847 of Mrs. Carmen Navarro, the mulatto wife of one of the founders." - Miriam Matthews.

Urban Life and History

3726. HALSTEAD, DONNA J. Anthropology in an urban ethnic minority community: its practical and theoretical potential. Master's thesis, Calif. state univ., Sacramento, 1970. 84 ℓ.

3727. HARDING, DOROTHY H. (HUGGINS), comp. Continuation of The annals of San Francisco ... compiled from the files of contemporary magazines and newspapers. S. F., California historical society, 1939. 124 p. illus., port. C, CBb, CCC, CChiS, CF, CFS, CHi, CL, CLSU, CLU, CLod, CMary, CP, CPa, CSaT, CSf, CSmH, CSt, CStb, CSto, CU-B, Rocq 7964.
    See index entry under Negroes. Covers the period from June 1, 1854 to Dec. 31, 1855.

3728. *HARPER, HELENA HESTER. A study of colored unmarried mothers in Los Angeles. Master's thesis, Univ. of southern Calif., Los Angeles, 1932. 61 [2] ℓ. tables.

3729. HARRIS, THERESA ELLA. Family planning practices of a selected group of black married women of child-bearing age from the Western addition of San Francisco. Master's thesis, Calif. state univ., San Francisco, 1971. vii, 84 ℓ. illus.

3730. HEITMAN, KHATANGA. An anthropological analysis and evaluation of Bay area neighborhood development foundation (BAND): a community action program. Master's thesis, Calif. state univ., San Francisco, 1968. 205 ℓ.
    "An historical and anthropoligical evaluation of BAND ... a community action consumer education project in San Francisco's Mission district and Hunter's Point communities which was funded by the Office of economic opportunity."

3731. "Hidden community; the Los Angeles Negro," in Frontier, v. 6, June, 1955, pp. 6-16.
    "Frontier special report ... [an] extensive sociological study."

3732. HIPPLER, ARTHUR EDWIN, 1935- . Family structure and social structure: matrifocality in Hunter's Point. Doctoral dissertation, Univ. of Calif., Berkeley, 1968. 275 ℓ. maps. C (photocopy).

3733. Historical society of southern California. "Commemorating the one hundred and fiftieth anniversary of the founding of Los Angeles, September 4, 1781," in its Annual publication, v. 15, part 1, 1931, pp. 1-263.
    Contains a detailed account of the founding, including "First census of Los Angeles," pp. 148-49, showing that Negroes or mulattoes comprised the majority of the first group of settlers.

3734. "The invisible wall: population statistics and housing and school conditions in the large cities," in Cascades, v. 7, Spring, 1966, pp. 26-27, 31.
    Magazine of Pacific northwest bell telephone company.

3735. JACOBS, PAUL. Prelude to riot; a view of urban America from the bottom. N. Y., Random house [1968, c1967]. x, 298 p. Available in many California libraries.
    Sponsored by the Center for the study of democratic institutions.

Urban Life and History

Concerns the relationship between government and the minority poor in Los Angeles.

3736. JAHN, JULIUS ARMIN. Principles and methods of area sampling applied to a survey of employment, housing and place of residence of white and non-white ethnic groups in Seattle, Washington, July to October, 1947. Doctoral dissertation, Univ. of Washington, Seattle, 1949. 194 p.

3737. *JOHNSON, JAMES C. "How do you define urban success? James C. Johnson, city manager, of Compton, Calif., the first non-white city manager in the nation, challenges urban America in a candid interview with Bill Foster, editor of the American city magazine," in American city, v. 84, Dec., 1969, pp. 69-71.

3738. JOHNSON, MARGARET. "The Negroes in West Berkeley," in Immigration and race problems, 1949-53, pp. 2, 865-89. Oakland, Mills college Dept. of economics and sociology, 1953. COMC.

3739. *JONES, EUGENE KINCKLE, 1885- . "Negro in community life," in National conference of social work, Proceedings, 1929, pp. 388-98. Surveys five cities, including Denver.

3740. KAISER, EVELYN LOIS. The unattached Negro woman on relief; a study of fifty unattached Negro women on relief in the Compton district office of the State relief administration of California in Los Angeles. Master's thesis, Univ. of southern Calif., Los Angeles, 1939. vi, 166 l.

3741. KASSEBAUM, PETER ARTHUR. Making out in Del Paso heights. Master's thesis, Calif. state univ., Sacramento, 1966. 100 l. illus.
Family life survey of blacks in the Del Paso heights area of Sacramento.

3742. KEEN, HAROLD. "Logan heights this summer," in San Diego and Point magazine, v. 19, Aug., 1967.

3743. _____. "Making the poverty scene," in San Diego and Point magazine, v. 18, July, 1966, pp. 53-55.

3744. _____. "San Diego's racial powder keg; the fuse is none too long," in San Diego and Point magazine, v. 16, July, 1963, pp. 66-67, 87-88, 90-93.

3745. _____. "What can I do?", in San Diego magazine, v. 20, Sept., 1968, pp. 104-08.

3746. _____. "Why CORE breaks the law," in San Diego and Point magazine, v. 17, Dec., 1964, pp. 84-86.

3747. KERNS, JAMES HARVEY. Study of social and economic conditions affecting the local Negro population made by J. Harvey Kerns, executive secretary, Division of Negro welfare of the Community chest and Council of social

Urban Life and History

agencies, Cincinnati and Hamilton county. [Oakland] Council of social
agencies and Community chest, Oakland, 1942. 31 ℓ. Mimeo. CU-B.

3748. KRAMER, RALPH M. Participation of the poor; comparative community
case studies in the war on poverty [by] Ralph M. Kramer ... Sponsored by
the Institute of governmental studies, Univ. of Calif., Berkeley.
Englewood Cliffs, N. J., Prentice-Hall, inc. [c1969]. xii, 273 p.
Bibliographical footnotes. CSf.
    Based on community case studies in San Francisco, Santa Clara county,
Oakland, Berkeley, and Contra Costa county.

3749. KREBS, OTTOLE. "The post-war Negro in San Francisco," in American
communities, 1948-49, v. 2, pp. 549-86. Oakland, Mills college Dept. of
economics and sociology, 1949. COMC.

3750. LABRIE, PETER. Urban conditions of the American Negro. Master's
thesis, Univ. of Calif., Berkeley, 1965. iii, 234 ℓ.

3751. LAYNE, JOSEPH GREGG, 1885-1952. Annals of Los Angeles from the arrival of the first white men to the Civil war, 1769-1861, by J. Gregg
Layne ... S. F., California historical society, 1935. 97 p. illus.
CBb, CHi, CL, CLSU, CLU, CO, CSf, CSmH, CU-B, Rocq 3942.
    Gives "disparaging account of the first settlers of Los Angeles,"
pp. 6-7. - Miriam Matthews.

3752. League of California cities. Los Angeles county div. Social issue
committee. Report and recommendations on poverty and race. Berkeley,
L. A., 1969. 31, 3 p. C.

3753. League of women voters of Eugene, Oregon. The Negro in Eugene.
Eugene, Ore., 1951. 8 ℓ. OrU.

3754. Life styles in the black ghetto [by] William McCord [and others].
N. Y., W. W. Norton & co. [c1969]. 334 p. Bibliography: pp. [297]-
302. CNoS, CSS, CSf.
    Contains "Watts: the revolt and after," by John Howard and William
McCord. Urban life and dissent in Oakland, San Francisco, San Diego,
Compton, and Los Angeles.

3755. LIGHT, IVAN HUBERT. Sociological aspects of self-employment and
social welfare among Chinese, Japanese, and Negroes in northern, urban
areas of the United States, 1900-1940. Doctoral dissertation, Univ. of
Calif., Berkeley, 1969. xvii, 453 ℓ.

3756. LIPSET, SEYMOUR MARTIN. Social mobility in industrial society by
Seymour Martin Lipset and Reinhard Bendix. Berkeley, Univ. of Calif.
press, 1959. xxi, 309 p. illus. Bibliographical footnotes. CSf.
    Contains an intensive study of mobility in Oakland.

3757. LORTIE, FRANCIS N. San Francisco's black community, 1870-1890:
dilemmas in the struggle for equality. Master's thesis, Calif. state
univ., San Francisco, 1970. iii, 104 ℓ. tables, fold. map.

Urban Life and History

3758. Los Angeles city board of education. Emergency education program. Historical background of Negro in Los Angeles (1935). [L. A., 1935]. 26 p. CL.

3759. "The Los Angeles Negro," in Frontier, v. 6, June, 1955, pp. 6-16.

3760. Los Angeles Times. Special issue, Feb. 12, 1909, Part III. 7 p. illus., ports.
     Gives historical and biographical information on the Los Angeles area written, except for the editor's instruction, by Negro residents there. Ed. by John Steven McGroarty.

3761. *MC DAVID, PERCY HIRAM. A social and economic survey of the community served by the Phillis Wheatley high school in Houston, Texas. Master's thesis, Univ. of southern Calif., Los Angeles, 1940. 98 ℓ. tables, form.

3762. MC WILLIAMS, CAREY, 1905- . ... Southern California country, an island on the land, by Carey McWilliams. N. Y., Duell, Sloan & Pearce [c1946]. xii, 387 p. CSf.
     "The Negroes," pp. 324-26, states their situation in Los Angeles in the early 1940's. An occasional mention is made elsewhere in the work.

3763. MARKUS, LOIS. "The problem of the Negroes in Oakland," in Problems of American communities, 1945, v. 1, pp. 141-60. Oakland, Mills college Dept. of economics and sociology, 1945. COMC.

3764. MARSTON, WILFRED GEORGE. Population redistribution and socioeconomic differentiation within Negro areas of American cities: a comparative analysis. Doctoral dissertation, Univ. of Wash., Seattle, 1966. 259 p.

3765. MARX, WESLEY. "The Negro community: a better chance," in Los Angeles, v. 3, Mar., 1962, pp. 38-41.

3766. MASON, WILLIAM M., and JAMES ANDERSON. "Los Angeles black heritage," in Museum alliance quarterly, v. 8, Winter, 1969-70, pp. 4-9.

3767. MAYER, SARAH RAFFERTY. The creation of a captive community. Master's thesis, Calif. state univ., San Francisco, 1969. v, 88 ℓ.
     Concerns two unnamed communities in western U. S.

3768. METZ, WILLIAM. "Negro segregation in Los Angeles--does it exist?", in California sun magazine, v. 12, Fall & Winter, 1960-61, pp. 49-52.

3769. *MILLER, LOREN R., 1903-1967. "The changing metro-urban complex," in Journal of intergroup relations, v. 3, Winter, 1961-62, pp. 55-64.

3770. MOGULOF, MELVIN B. "Black community development in five western model cities," in Social work, v. 15, Jan., 1970, pp. 12-18.
     An examination of the programs in predominantly black neighborhoods in Seattle, Portland, Fresno, Oakland, and Richmond (Calif.).

Urban Life and History

3771. MONTESANO, PHILIP MICHAEL, 1941- . The San Francisco black community, 1860-1865: an exception to black ghettos? Graduate paper, Univ. of Calif., Santa Barbara, 1968. 24 p. maps, tables.

3772. _____. San Francisco black people, 1860-1865; a bibliographical essay. Graduate paper, Univ. of Calif., Santa Barbara, 1968. 8 p. CSf (photocopy).

3773. _____. "Social and cultural life of the Negro community in San Francisco in the early 1860's," in Urban west, v. 1, Nov.-Dec., 1967, pp. 15-16.

3774. _____. Some aspects of the free Negro question in San Francisco, 1849-1870. Master's thesis, Univ. of San Francisco, 1967. iii, 114 p. CHi (photocopy), CSf (photocopy), CStbS (photocopy).

3775. MORRILL, RICHARD L. "The Negro ghetto: problems and alternatives," in Geographical review, July, 1965.
     Deals especially with Seattle.

3776. MOSELY, RUTH J. EDWARDS. A study of the Negro families in Los Angeles. Master's thesis, Univ. of southern Calif., Los Angeles, 1938. 115 ℓ. tables.

3777. NEWMAN, CARILANE. "Census tracts 71B, 70A, 70C, 68C, 67B and San Leandro," in Immigration and race problems, 1965, pt. 2, pp. 543-71. Oakland, Mills college Dept. of economics and sociology, 1965. COMC.

3778. Oakland. City manager. Application for planning grant model cities program. Oakland, 1967. 213 ℓ. CO.

3779. _____. Dept. of human resources. Oakland's partnership for change. Oakland, 1967. 129 p. tables. CO.

3780. "On to Denver," in Crisis, v. 30, June, 1925, pp. 65-68.
     An illus. article describing the 1925 N. A. A. C. P. annual meeting site.

3780a. RADIN, PAUL, 1883- . The racial myth, by Paul Radin ... N. Y., McGraw-Hill book co., 1934. ix, 141 p. CU.
     Authored by a professor of anthropology, Univ. of Calif., Berkeley.

3781. RAINE, DOROTHY PENTECOST. Social stratification of Negroes in Mobile, Alabama. Master's thesis, Univ. of southern Calif., L os Angeles, 1965. v, 112 ℓ. illus.

3782. REID, HIRAM ALVIN. History of Pasadena, comprising an account of the native Indian, the early Spanish, the Mexican, the American, the colony and the incorporated city ... Pasadena, Pasadena history co., 1895.
     675 p. illus., ports. C, CHi, CL, CLSU, CLU, CSf, CSmH, CU-B, Rocq 4703.
     Information is given on the African Methodist Episcopal church, p. 482; the Colored people's Baptist church, p. 486; Negro canyon, pp. 383 and 387; and on Robert Owens, p. 387.

Urban Life and History

3783. *REID, IRA DE AUGUSTINE, 1901-1968. "Negro life on the western front," in Opportunity, v. 7, Sept., 1929, pp. 275-81.
An illus. survey made at the request of the Interracial commission of Denver and limited to that city.

3784. _____. The Negro population of Denver, Colorado. Denver, Denver Interracial commission [1929]. 46 p. CSt.
An extension of his article in Opportunity, Sept., 1929.

3785. _____. Same. N. Y., 1939. DHU.

3786. REISSMAN, FRANK, and HERMINE I. POPPER. Up from poverty; new career ladders for nonprofessionals. N. Y., Harper & Row, 1968. 332 p. C.
Includes studies in public welfare in Alameda county and in police work, Richmond.

3787. ROBINSON, EFFIE MARIE. Social problems of dependent and neglected Negro children in Oakland, California. Master's thesis, Univ. of Calif., Berkeley, 1945. vi, 84 ℓ. tables, form.

3788. ROSE, TOM. The San Francisco non-white population, 1950-1960, by Tom Rose and John W. Kinch. S. F., Council for civic unity, 1961. 15 p. tables. CSf.

3789. ROY, DONALD FRANCIS. Hooverville; a study of a community of homeless men in Seattle. Master's thesis, Univ. of Washington, Seattle, 1935. 97 p.

3790. *RUMFORD, WILLIAM BYRON. Smog abatement administration with special reference to California. Master's thesis, Univ. of Calif., Berkeley, 1959. ii, 127 ℓ.

3791. SAWYER, BARBARA. "Negroes in west Oakland," in Immigration and race problems, 1949-53, pp. 2, 844-64. Oakland, Mills college Dept. of economics and sociology, 1953. COMC.

3792. SCHALLERT, EUGENE J. San Francisco report. S. F. [Univ. of San Francisco? 1965?]. 2 v. in 3. illus., maps, charts, tables. CSf.
An extensive study based upon the 1960 U. S. census. Includes information on population, housing, races, land use, and zoning. One volume is a statistical study of Roman Catholic parishes in the city.

3793. SCHEAR, RILLMOND. "How the ghetto looks from the inside," in Seattle magazine, v. 2, Nov., 1965, pp. 38-44.
Part two of a study of the Seattle Negro community.

3794. _____. "The world that whites don't know," in Seattle magazine, v. 2, Oct., 1965, pp. 14-19.

3795. SCHMID, CALVIN FISHER, 1901- . ... Social trends in Seattle, by Calvin F. Schmid ... assisted by Laura Hildreth Hoffland ... and Bradford H. Smith ... Charts delineated by the author. Seattle, Univ. of Wash. press, 1944. xi, 336 p. illus., diagrs. (Univ. of Washington

Urban Life and History

publications in the social series, v. 14). Bibliographical footnotes.
CSf, Wa.
  Minority racial groups in Seattle, an important early study, pp. 131-
51.

3796. SCHUERMAN, LEO ANTHONY. Assimilation of minority subpopulations in
Los Angeles county. Master's thesis, Univ. of southern Calif., Los
Angeles, 1969. 142 ℓ.

3797. SCHWARTZ, MARIANNE PHILIPPA. The perception of social class and
social status and its relationship to stereotyped perception as evidence
of social distance in a selected group of Negro women. Master's thesis,
Univ. of southern Calif., Los Angeles, 1964. iii, 88 ℓ. illus.
  A study of Los Angeles women.

3798. SHANNON, LYLE WILLIAM, and PATRICIA MORGAN. "Predictions of economic
absorption and cultural integration among Mexican-Americans, Negroes,
and Anglos in a northern industrial community," in Human organization,
v. 25, Summer, 1966, pp. 154-62.

3799. SHEVKY, ESHREF. The social areas of Los Angeles, analysis and typology,
by Eshref Shevky and Marilyn Williams. Berkeley, Pub. for the John
Randolph Haynes and Dora Haynes foundation by the Univ. of Calif. press,
1949. xvi, 172 p. maps (part fold., part col.), diagrs., tables.
Bibliography: pp. 163-66. Available in many California libraries. Rocq
4385.

3800. SIGURDSON, HERBERT, and others. "Crenshaw project: an experiment in
urban community development," in Sociology and social research, v. 51,
July, 1967, pp. 434-44.
  Los Angeles.

3801. SMITH, CHARLES V. Social change in certain aspects of adjustment of
the Negro in Seattle, Washington. Doctoral dissertation, Washington
state univ., Pullman, 1951.

3802. SPECHT, HARRY, 1928- . "Community development in low-income Negro
areas," in Social work, v. 11, Oct., 1966, pp. 78-89.
  "Observations and insights reported here are based on experiences
with the Richmond community development project, which is financed by
the Office of economic opportunity."

3803. STEGNER, WALLACE EARLE, 1909- . "Changes in the black ghetto: East
Palo Alto," in Saturday review, v. 53, Aug. 1, 1970, p. 12ff.

3804. *TAYLOR, DORA JONES. Broken homes as a factor in the maladjustment of
delinquent Negro boys in Los Angeles. Master's thesis, Univ. of southern
Calif., Los Angeles, 1936. 61 ℓ.

3805. TERRELL, HENRY SZOLD. The fiscal impact of Negroes on central cities.
Doctoral dissertation, Stanford univ., Stanford, 1969. vii, 151 ℓ.

Urban Life and History

3806. THOMPSON, WAYNE EDWARD. "Developing a city's human resources," in
Public management, v. 45, Apr., 1963, pp. 74-78.
     Oakland.

3807. _____. "People problem," in National civic review, v. 51, Sept., 1962,
pp. 424-28.
     Oakland.

3808. _____. "Quit treating symptoms," in National civic review, v. 53,
Sept., 1964, pp. 423-28.
     Oakland.

3809. *THOMPSON, WILLIE   Enemy of the poor; a report of the war on poverty
in San Francisco. By Willie Thompson. Dedicated to those who died in
the Watts revolt, Los Angeles, California, August, 1965 ... [S. F., 1965].
36 p.

3810. ULANSKY, GENE. "Glimmer in the ghetto," in San Francisco magazine,
v. 9, Dec., 1967, pp. 40-41.

3811. U. S. Economic development administration. An analysis of surveys,
plans and studies undertaken in south central Los Angeles, California
[by] Development research associates. Washington, D. C. [1970]. 1 v.
(v.p.). C.
     Period covered: 1960-69. An appendix gives an inventory of studies
and reports located and reviewed.

3812. University of southern Calif., Los Angeles. Youth studies center.
Delinquency prevention training project. Training series for social
agencies. L. A., 1965. 8 v. CLSU, CSdS.

3813. WALLIS, MARIE POPE. A study of dependency in one hundred cases taken
from files of Bureau of county welfare, Catholic welfare bureau, Los
Angeles county relief administration (Torrance and Watts districts).
Master's thesis, Univ. of southern Calif., Los Angeles, 1935. iii,
81 ℓ. maps, tables.

3814. WATSON, HOMER K. ... Causes of delinquency among fifty Negro boys,
by Homer K. Watson, A. B. L. A. Southern California sociological society,
Univ. of southern California [1919]. 12 p. Studies in sociology; sociological monograph, no. 14, v. 4; no. 2, Dec., 1919. C, CL, CSt.

3815. _____. A study of the causes of delinquency among fifty Negro boys
assigned to special schools in Los Angeles. Master's thesis, Univ. of
southern Calif., Los Angeles, 1923. 68 ℓ.

3816. Welfare planning council, Los Angeles region. Research dept. Profile
north and south by Lloyd Street. L. A., 1962. 23 ℓ. Working paper
no. 43. C.
     Economic and social conditions in a local area.

Urban Life and History

3817. WHITE, PERSIS, and SARAH HAYNE. "Marin City, a social problem to Marin county," in Immigration and race problems, 1954, pp. 316-35. Oakland, Mills college Dept. of economics and sociology, 1954. COMC.

3818. WHITE, VIVIAN ELIZABETH. The social contributions of a welfare center for Negro girls in the city of Los Angeles, California ... Master's thesis, Univ. of southern Calif., Los Angeles, 1947. 127 ℓ. tables, forms.

3819. WHITE, WILLIE RAY. A descriptive study of a disadvantaged community. Master's thesis, Calif. state univ., Sacramento, 1968. 135 ℓ.
    A Sacramento study.

3820. *WILLIAMS, FRANKLIN H. "The Bakersfield community," in Crisis, v. 58, Apr., 1951, pp. 231-33.

3821. _____. "Sunshine and Jim crow," in Crisis, v. 61, Apr., 1954, pp. 205-06.
    Description of ghetto and Jim crow life in Las Vegas, Nevada.

3822. WILLIAMS, MARCUS ASIE. The class structure of a minority group in a valley city. Master's thesis, Univ. of the Pacific, Stockton, 1956. 49 p.

3823. WILSON, AGNES E. The facilities for the care of dependent semi-delinquent and delinquent Negro children in Los Angeles, a study by Agnes E. Wilson, Research division, Social welfare department. Made at the request of the Budget committee of the Community welfare federation. February-March, 1925. [L. A., 1925?]. 44 p. C, CL.

3824. WORKMAN, BOYLE. Boyle Workman's city that grew as told to Caroline Walker ... L. A., Southland pub. co., 1935 [i.e., 1936]. 430 p. illus., port. C, CBb, CHi, CL, CLSU, CLU, CPom, CSd, CSmH, CStmo, CU-B, Rocq 4541.
    Contains brief mention of Negroes in Los Angeles, pp. 102, 114-15.

3825. Workshop on change in an interracial community, Burbank junior high, Berkeley, 1962. Berkeley unified school district, Council of social planning, Berkeley area [and] Berkeley community welfare commission: co-sponsored workshop on change in an interracial community; housing, employment, education, March 16 and 17, 1962, Burbank junior high. [Berkeley] 1962. 51 p. maps, tables. CU.

3826. YANCY, JAMES WALTER. The Negro of Tucson, past and present. Master's thesis, Univ. of Arizona, Tucson, 1933.

MISCELLANEOUS

3827. *BENJAMIN, ROBERT CHARLES O'HARA, 1855-1900. Don't; a book for girls. By R. C. O. Benjamin, lawyer, author and journalist. Life is what you make it. S. F., Valleau & Peterson, 1891. 76 p. CSmH.

Miscellaneous

Gives advice to girls and young women on their conduct and
language.

3828. *BENSON, J. J. "San Bernardino, California," in Alexander's magazine,
v. 3, Dec. 15, 1906, pp. 111-13.
An illus., promotional article.

3829. *BONTEMPS, ARNA WENDELL, 1902-1973. Anyplace but here [by] Arna Bontemps and Jack Conroy. N. Y., Hill and Wang [1968, c1966]. viii, 372 p.
"A selected list of references and sources": pp. 349-60. Available in
many libraries.
A revised and expanded version of They seek a city. Information is
given on western housing, pp. 315-20, and on western pioneers, and the
Watts riot, pp. 257-77.

3830. _____. They seek a city [by] Arna Bontemps and Jack Conroy. Garden
City, N. Y., Doubleday, Doran & co., 1945. xvii, 265 p. Available in
many libraries.
See index for location of information about California, John C.
Frémont, Biddy Mason, Oregon, San Francisco, Jeremiah B. Sanderson,
Washington (state), etc.

3831. BOWERS, GEORGE B. "Will Imperial Valley become a land of opportunity
for Negro citizens?", in Southern workman, v. 59, July, 1930, pp. 305-13.
Gives accounts by valley residents.

3832. California. Governor, 1967- . (Ronald Reagan). "to every man the
right to live, to work, to be himself, and to become whatever thing his
manhood and his vision can combine to make him." [Sacramento, 1968?].
[21] p. C.
A formulation of administration attitude toward the plight of
minority groups.

3833. *CATALOGNE, GERARD DE. ... Les nostalgies de San Francisco. [Port-
au-Prince, H. Deschamps, 1945?]. 85 p. illus. DLC, NN.

3834. *DEAN, ALVANO. Solution of the Riccati equation. Vandenberg air
force base, Air force systems command, 1966. 91 p. CL.
Differential equations.

3835. *FERGUSON, LLOYD NOEL, 1918- . Absorption spectra of some linear
conjugated compounds. Doctoral dissertation, Univ. of Calif., Berkeley,
1943. 46 ℓ. tables, diagrs.
Author of numerous titles in the field of chemical research.

3836. FRANKLIN, RAYMOND S. The relative economic status of the Negro male:
an econometric study. Doctoral dissertation, Univ. of Calif., Berkeley,
1966. vi, 144 ℓ.

3837. *GIER, JOSEPH THOMAS, 1910- . Nocturnal measurement of roadway illumination due to automobile headlamps. Master's thesis, Univ. of Calif.,
Berkeley, 1940. 32 ℓ. illus., tables (part fold.), diagrs. (part fold.).

Miscellaneous

3838. *GRIFFIN, A. D. "The Lewis and Clark centennial exposition," in
Voice of the Negro, v. 2, Sept., 1905, pp. 628-31.
The editor of the Portland New age sets forth the advantages of the
exposition and of the Pacific northwest.

3839. HAEHN, JAMES O. "Racial minorities in northern California," in North
state review, v. 1, May, 1964, pp. 22-26.
Reasons are given for the relatively low percentage of black residents
in the area.

3840. *HAN[D]COCK, CLIFFORD C. "Alaska, or life in the frozen region," in
Colored American magazine, v. 6, Aug., 1903, pp. 553-61.
Authored by a Seattle resident.

3841. HAYAKAWA, SAMUEL ICHIYE, 1906- . "The semantics of being Negro," in
Review of general semantics, v. 10, 1953, pp. 163-75.

3842. *HAYES, ROBERT LEE, 1933- . The black American travel guide, by Bob
Hayes. [S. F.] Straight arrow books [c1971]. 302 p.
Authored by the chief of a San Francisco travel association. Includes
extensive information for tourists in Hawaii, Las Vegas, Los Angeles,
Reno, Lake Tahoe, San Diego, and San Francisco.

3843. HOLMES, SAMUEL JACKSON, 1868- . "The biological trend of the Negro,"
in University of California chronicle, v. 32, Jan., 1930, pp. 38-70.

3844. _____. The Negroes' struggle for survival, a study in human ecology,
by S. J. Holmes ... Berkeley, Univ. of Calif. press, 1937. xii, 296 p.
illus., maps, tables, diagrs. "References": pp. 263-90. CHS, CL, CLSU,
CLU, CLobS, CSbS, CSf, CSjC, CSluSP, CSt, CU, CU-SB.

3845. _____. Same. Port Washington, N. Y., Kennikat press [1966, c1965].
CEcaC, CFS, CNoS, CSaT, CSdS, CSfCiC, CSt, CU-SC.
A statistical treatment by a Univ. of Calif. professor of anthropology.

3846. *HUFFMAN, EUGENE HENRY. Hee! Haw! Haw! A compilation of original
humor, by Eugene Henry Huffman. [L. A., Dependable printers, c1938].
16 p. port.

3847. HUNTINGTON, COLLIS POTTER, 1821-1909. Remarks of C. P. Huntington
at the Hampton normal and agricultural institute, Hampton, Va., January 1,
1900, on "The future of the Negro." [n.p., 1900?]. 12 p. CSt.
Huntington was one of the original "Big four" partners in the construction of the Central Pacific railroad.

3848. *International library of Negro life and history. N. Y., Publishers
co. [c1967, c1968]. 10 v. illus., ports. Available in many libraries.
Includes information on biography, medicine, theatre, music, art,
literature, athletics, and civil rights relating to California and the
West.

Miscellaneous

3849. JACKSON, GEORGE. Contributions made to the American civilization by Negro Americans. Master's thesis, Ariz. state univ., Tempe, 1947. 75 l.

3850. *JOHNSON, GEORGE MARION, 1900- . The uniform taxation of interstate and intrastate sales. J. S. D. thesis, Univ. of Calif., Berkeley, 1936. 163 l.

3851. JOHNSON, REGINALD A. The west coast and the Negro. [n.p., 1944]. 24 p. Wa.

3852. *JOHNSTON, C. GRANVILLE. Training manual and horseman's guide. S. F., 1871. 59 p.
    Notice of publication, San Francisco Pacific appeal, Dec. 9, 1871, p. 2, col. 5. Unlocated title.

3853. KENNY, ROBERT WALKER. Papers and correspondence, 1920-47. 41 boxes, 16 cartons. CU-B.
    Consists chiefly of his correspondence as Attorney general of California, 1942-46. Contains 6 letters of Edward A. Bailey, 1943, as President of the San Diego NAACP; 3 letters of Mrs. Charlotta A. Bass, Los Angeles, 1943-46; 17 letters from the NAACP, 1944-46; 2 letters from the National Negro Congress, 1939-45; 4 letters of William R. Brown, 1944, as President of the United Negroes of California and concerning the Homer Turner case; 2 letters of Mrs. Frances Albrier, 1944; 2 letters of Walter Arthur Gordon, 1944-46; 2 letters of Loren Miller, 1943-44; 1 letter of Paul Robeson, 1946; 5 letters of Ernest J. Torregano, 1943-46; 2 letters from the Urban league of Los Angeles, 1944-46; 5 letters of Leon H. Washington, Los Angeles, 1944-46; and others.

3854. LORENZINI, AUGUST PETER, 1922- . A study of the patterns of communication used by fifty Negro and fifty Spanish-named residents of Phoenix, Arizona. Doctoral dissertation, Univ. of Denver, Denver, 1963. AzU.
    "Differences in the channels of communication within a group and between groups."

3855. LYONS, HELEN SCOTT. A critical analysis into the cultural contribution of the Afro-American descendant to society. Master's thesis, Univ. of southern Calif., 1939. 142 l.

3856. MACDONALD, ALAN. Communicating with middle and upper class Negroes, with particular emphasis on media attitudes of generalized influentials. Doctoral dissertation, Univ. of Oregon, Eugene, 1967. 240 p.

3857. MAILER, NORMAN, 1923- . The white Negro. [S. F.] City lights books [c1957]. 1 v. unp. CU.
    "Originally published in Dissent."

3858. MICHELSON, STEPHAN EDWARD. Income of racial minorities. Doctoral dissertation, Stanford univ., Stanford, 1968. viii, 217 l. illus.

Miscellaneous

3859. MIGHTY, JULIA GAINES. "Negroes in Alaska," in Black world, v. 13, Nov., 1963, pp. 35-44.

3860. MILLER, FLOYD. "Angel of Hunters Point," in Reader's digest, v. 93, Oct., 1968, pp. 81-85.
    Concerns a wife's reaction to the death of her husband, Martin Whitted, San Francisco.

3861. The Negro in American history. [Mortimer J. Adler, ed.] [Chicago] Encyclopedia Britannica educational corp. [c1969]. 3 v. illus., facsims., maps, ports. CSf.
    Vol. I, Black Americans, 1928-1968, contains an excerpt from Black rage, by William H. Grier and Price M. Cobbs; "The Black Muslims," by Louis E. Lomax; and "Uncle Tom in Hollywood," a description of discrimination in the motion picture industry, by Loren Miller.

3862. Negroes in California. Pamphlet box of 20th century miscellaneous announcements, form letters, pamphlets, and broadsides. CU-B.

3863. *OWEN, CHANDLER. "From coast to coast," in Messenger, v. 4, Apr., 1922, pp. 407-10. Continued as "Through the Northwest and up the Pacific coast," June, 1922, pp. 424-25.
    The co-editor of Messenger describes his speaking tour, giving a detailed account of visits to Denver, Los Angeles, and Pasadena and lesser descriptions of San Francisco, Oakland, Sacramento, Seattle, Tacoma, and Spokane.

3864. Palo Alto Ravenswood post. Idea, beginning, failure, renewal; counterpart. Palo Alto, 1969. 8 p. CMp.
    Reprint of 3 articles appearing in the Ravenswood post, Dec. 25, 1968-Jan. 15, 1969.

3865. "Racial studies: academy states position on call for new research," in Science, v. 158, Nov. 17, 1967, pp. 892-93.
    The argument of William Shockley, Stanford univ., for an expansion of research on the relative effects of heredity and environment on human intelligence and performance.

3866. RITTER, EARNESTINE. "The Negro takes strides," in California sun magazine, v. 11, Fall & Winter, 1959-60, pp. 39-41.

3867. ROBERSON, ROBERT L. Changing economic status of the American Negro. Master's thesis, Univ. of southern Calif., Los Angeles, 1943. xiii, 130 l.

3868. SINGERMAN, MATILIE. A comparison of the opinion of the Negro leaders in World war I and World war II. Master's thesis, Stanford univ., Stanford, 1945. 104 l.

3869. *SMITH, CARL S. Letters from my nephew, Slim, by Carl S. Smith. N. Y., Vantage press [c1965]. 120 p. COEB.
    An Oakland resident presents an economic formula for improving the lot of the underprivileged. Contains some autobiographical information.

Miscellaneous

3870. STONE, WILLIAM JAMES. The influence of race and socio-economic status on physical performance. Doctoral dissertation, Univ. of Calif., Berkeley, 1966. iv, 60 ℓ. diagrs.

3871. *STRATTEN, JAMES EDWARD, 1912- . "The future of the young Negro in America," in California school boards, v. 27, May, 1968, pp. 10-13.

3872. STURDIVANT, ARTHUR. The poor pay more. Doctoral dissertation, Univ. of southern Calif., Los Angeles, 1967.
    Los Angeles.

3873. SULLIVAN, NOEL, 1890-1956. Papers and correspondence, ca. 1911-56. 135 boxes (boxes 131-32 are sealed). CU-B.
    Carton 3 contains manuscripts of short stories, poems, and plays some of which were submitted by the authors for an auction to raise money for the Scottsboro boys in 1934. Langston Hughes is represented. Carton 5 contains newspaper clippings, articles, announcements, programs, etc., some of which relate to Richmond Barthe, Roland Hayes, Langston Hughes, Dorothy Maynor, and the NAACP. Cartons 9 and 10 contain photographs, some of which show Paul Robeson, Jr., Ethel Waters, Marian Anderson, Dorothy Maynor, Paul Robeson, Roland Hayes, and Langston Hughes. There are 3 letters of Richmond Barthe, 1943-44; 101 letters of Roland Hayes, 1925-56; 179 letters of Langston Hughes, 1932-56; 9 letters of Alain Locke, 1927-50; 46 letters of Dorothy Maynor, 1942-56; 2 letters of Etta Moten, 1934-37; 3 letters of Paul Robeson, 1931; 2 letters of Mrs. Eslanda Cardoza (Goode) Robeson, 1931; 3 letters of William Grant Still, 1941-49; and others.

3874. *THURMAN, SUE (BAILEY). "How far from here to Mexico," in Crisis, v. 42, Sept., 1935, pp. 267 and 274.
    Advice on black travel.

3875. UHLENBERG, PETER. Minorities in California's population. [n.p., 1969]. 13 p. C.
    A demographic study essentially based on the 1960 U. S. census.

3876. *WAMBLE, THELMA, 1916- . Look over my shoulder, by Thelma Wamble. N. Y., Vantage press [c1969]. 109 p.
    A Los Angeles resident's tribute to Pres. John F. Kennedy.

3877. *WASHINGTON, BOOKER TALIAFERRO, 1856-1915. Invitation to his address at the Mechanics' pavilion, San Francisco, Jan. 8 [1903], Mayor Eugene E. Schmitz, presiding, and Benjamin Ide Wheeler making the introduction. [2] ℓ. CHi.

3878. *WATKINS, BEN, ed. We also serve; 10 per cent of a nation working and fighting for victory. [Oakland, Charles F. Tilghman, 1944]. 65 p. illus., ports.
    Describes World War II activities in the Oakland area.

3879. *WHITE, JOSEPH. "Guidelines for black psychologists," in The black scholar, v. 1, Mar., 1970, pp. 52-57.
    Authored by the Director of black studies, Univ. of Calif., Irvine.

Miscellaneous

3880. *WHITELAW, CHARLES S. Life is only a journey. L. A., 1964.
Title from Universal books catalog no. 164, item no. 948.

3881. *WILLIAMS, JOHN ALFRED, 1925- . This is my country too [by] John A.
Williams. N. Y., New American library [c1964]. ix, 158 p. CEcaC, CFS,
CNoS, CRic, CSf, WaT, WaTC, WaTP.
Describes an automobile trip throughout the U. S. Includes his ex-
periences in western states, pp. 97-123.

3882. WINSELL, KEITH ANDREW. Conflict in Negro leadership. Master's
thesis, Calif. state univ., San Francisco, 1965. 214 ℓ.
"An historical survey of American Negro leadership, concentrating on
Booker T. Washington, W. E. B. Du Bois, and Marcus Garvey. Not a
biography [sic], this thesis highlights the relationship between leaders
(as members of an elite) and the contemporary social scene."

3883. WOLTERS, RAYMOND REILLY. The Negro and the New deal economic recovery
program. Doctoral dissertation, Univ. of Calif., Berkeley, 1967.
442 ℓ.

PERIODICALS AND NEWSPAPERS

Special credit for the implementation of this section is
due Armistead Scott Pride, Lincoln Univ., Jefferson City,
Mo., and Lawrence Brooks de Graaf, California state
Univ., Fullerton.

It is probable that many more black publications existed
for short periods of time, and it hoped that this
section will encourage both their discovery and
collection.

Dates enclosed in brackets represent broken files.

Names of individual newspapers and periodicals appearing in
the following two subject categories are not separately
listed in the index to this volume.

PERIODICALS

3884. A. M. E. guide. Los Angeles.

3885. Action report. San Francisco. Ag28, 1970-
Interracial. Pub. by the Mayor's office of youth affairs.

3886. Alameda county human relations commission newsletter. Oakland.
Ap, 1966?- m.

Periodicals

3887. Aldebaran review. [Berkeley?] 1968?-   ir. CU, no. 1+.
    A revolutionary interracial literary magazine.

3888. American civil liberties union-news. San Francisco. 1936-
    CLU, 1951+; CSt, Ja, 1946+.
        Pub. by the Northern California branch, American civil liberties
    union.

3889. American commoner. San Francisco. Mr15, 1924-   w ? CU-B, Mr15,
    1924.
        "Formerly The American criterion. Established in 1896."
        Ed. by Louis Fremont Baldwin. Issued by The commoner pub. co., Oscar
    Hudson, Pres., Titus Alexander, Vice-pres., William J. McLemore, field
    sec'y.

3890. American woodmen informer. Denver. 1950?- q. DHU, [1960+].
        Official organ of the Supreme camp, American woodmen. Laurence W.
    Lightner, ed. Also listed as Lawrence H. Lightner.

3891. Ante. Los Angeles. Summer, 1964-[Winter?] 1968//. ir. CLSU, Com-
    plete; CU, Complete.
        An interracial literary magazine.

3892. Antinarcissus; surrealist conquest. San Francisco. Summer, 1969- q.
    CU, Summer, 1969.
        Interracial literary magazine, ed. and pub. by Stephen Schwartz.

3893. Archon. Oakland. 1931?-   bi-annual. DHU [1938+].
        Official organ of Zeta Phi Beta sorority.

3894. Arizona council for civic unity. Fact sheets. S, 1950-
    AzU, S-O, 1950 (no. 1-5).

3895. Ball & chain review. Berkeley, Albany. 0, 1969-v. 1, no. 8, 1970//.
    m. CLU, Complete; CSt, no. 3, 6/7; CU, complete.
        Pub. by Black journalists, an organization of media workers in the
    San Francisco bay area.

3896. Baptist herald. Oakland. N7, 1915-   w. COEB, N7-D26, 1915;
    Ja2, 23, 1916.
        Official organ of the Beth Eden Baptist church. Errol Marshall, ed.

3897. Bay area scoop. San Francisco, 1969?-   w. CSf, Ap17, My8, 1969.
        The San Francisco edition of Scoop, Los Angeles.

3898. Bayviewer. Berkeley. Je, 1967-   m, b-m, ir. CU, My, 1968+.
        Lennie Anderson, ed.

3899. Bessie Coleman aero news. Phoenix. My, 1930-   m. DHU, My, 1930.
        William J. Powell, ed.

3900. Black business review. Oakland. Je, 1969+   m. CO, Je, 1969+.
        Pub. by Black achievement research.

Periodicals

3901. Black cobra. Sacramento. 1967?-   m. CU-A, My, 1969.

3902. Black dialogue. San Francisco. 1965-   q. CLU, 1965+; CU, Winter,
   1966+; CU-A, 1969+.
      Political and literary. In 1969, Black dialogue had moved to
   New York City.

3903. Black family. Berkeley. F, 1971-   w? CU-A, Mr2, 1971.
      Pub. by the Black studies student assoc., Univ. of Calif., Berkeley.

3904. Black fire. San Francisco. 1968-   w, m. CSf, D9, 1968; Ja16,
   1969; CU-A, F, 1969.
      Organ of the Black students union, Calif. state univ., San Francisco.

3905. Black graphics international, a magazine of the arts in the third
   world. San Francisco. 1969-   q.
      In 1970, Black graphics international had moved to Detroit.

3906. Black guards organ. San Francisco. F, 1970-   m? CU-A, Jℓ, 1970.
      Pub. by the African descendants peoples republic provisional govern-
   ment sometimes known as the African descendants nationalist independence
   partition party.

3907. Black panther. Emeryville, San Francisco. 1967-   w. C, Ja, 1970+;
   CFS, Ap25, 1967; Ja15, 25, 1969; N28, 1970-Ja29, F20, 1971; CL, S13,
   1969+; CLS, 1968+; CLSU, Ag23-30, O11, 1969; Ap 6, 1970; CLU, v. 2, no. 1
   (1968)+; CRcS, 1969+; CSdS, 1969+; CSf, [Ja4, 1969+]; CSt-H, [S14, 1968+];
   CU, S, 1968+; CU-A, 1969+; CU-SB, 1968+.
      Pub. by the Black panther party.

3908. Black panther community newsletter. w? Je16, 1969-   CLU, Je16,
   1969+.
      Issued by the Black panther party, Southern California chapter.

3909. Black panther party. Ministry of information. Bulletin. San Francisco. 1967?-   ir.

3910. Black politician, a journal of current political thought. Los Angeles.
   Jℓ, 1969+   q. CL, Jℓ, 1969+; CLU, Jℓ, 1969+; CSS, Ja, 1970+; CSt, O,
   1969+; CU, Jℓ, 1969+.
      Pub. by the Urban affairs institute, Los Angeles. Mervyn M. Dymally,
   Lynne Bennett, Judy Ann Miller, and Marie D. Brown, eds.

3911. Black politics; a journal of liberation. Berkeley. Ja, 1968-
   m, b-m. CFS, Ja, 1969+; CLU, Ja, 1968+; CSf, Summer, S-O, 1968 (v. 2,
   nos. 13-14); CSt-H, F-Ap, 1969; CU, F, 1968; CU-A, 1969+.

3912. Black power. San Francisco. v. 1, 1967?-   CSf, v. 1, no. 13.
      "Published by: House of Umoja."

3913. Black scholar. San Francisco and Sausalito. N, 1969+   m., except
   July and Aug. CHS, N, 1969+; CLU, N, 1969+; CSS, N, 1969+; CSbS, Mr,
   1970+; CSf, N, 1969+; CSjC, N, 1969+; CSt, N, 1969+; CU, Ja, 1970+.

Periodicals

Pub. by the Black world foundation and Nathan Hare; Robert Chrisman, ed. Subtitle: Journal of black studies and research.

3914. Black student union news service. Hayward. 023, 1969–   s-m. CLU, N, 1969+; CSf, D11, 1969.
Pub. by The black student union of California state univ., Hayward.

3915. Black theatre. New York City. 1969–   b-m. CLU, no. 2+; CSf, nos. 2, 3; CU, no. 1+; CU-SB, 1969+.
Pub. by the New Amsterdam theatre. Lists Los Angeles, San Francisco, and Oakland correspondents.

3916. Black unity. Berkeley. D, 1969–   w.
A Muslim-oriented publication.

3917. Black view. Seattle. D, 1970–   m.

3918. Black voice. Los Angeles. w. S, 1968–   CL, 024, 1968 (v. 1, no. 6); CLS, Je, 1968-Ja, 1969.
Pub. by Black perspective for the Los Angeles black congress. Don Wheeldin, ed.

3919. Breakthrough. San Francisco. Mr, 1969+   b-m, m. CU, Complete.

3920. Broadway. Los Angeles. 194-?–   m.

3921. Bronze California. Los Angeles. S, 1963–   b-m, m. CLU, [196-?]; COEB, S, 1963; CSfAA, Ap, Je, D, 1964; Je, 1965.
Lincoln C. Hilburn, ed.

3922. Bronze tattler. Los Angeles. 194-?–   m, b-m. NN, S-O, 1941.

3923. Budget. San Francisco. 1894-?   w.
Typewritten and issued to members of the Assembly club, a social organization, in 1894 and perhaps other years. See Theophilus B. Morton, Vindication of Hon. M. M. Estee ... (S. F., 1894), p. 8.

3924. California. State fair employment practice commission. Fair practices news. San Francisco. Jl, 1960-O, 1966//. CU, Complete.
Title varies: Fair employment newsletter.

3925. California. Transportation-employment project. South central and east Los Angeles transportation-employment project. Progress report. Los Angeles. no. 1, O, 1966–   q. CLS, (no. 1+); CO, (nos. 4-10).

3926. California cactus. Los Angeles. 1909?–   m, ir. DHU, v. 1, no. 4 (1910-11).
C. A. Butler, ed.

3927. Campus core-lator. Berkeley. 1964–   q. CLU (Special Coll.), Spring, 1965.
Pub. by the Berkeley campus chapter of the Congress of racial equality.

Periodicals

3927a. Cayton's monthly. Seattle. F, 1921-   m.
    Follows Seattle CAYTON's weekly.
    Horace R. Cayton, ed.

3928. Change! Oakland. 1967+ CBSK, no s. 1-2.
    Pub. by the Unitarian-Universalist project east bay, inc.

3929. Christian register. Oakland. Mr, 1923-   m, w. CU-B, My, S, N4,
    D23; Ja13, 27, F17-Mr9, 23-Ap 13, 1924; Ap12, 1925.
    Pub. by First African Methodist Episcopal church.

3930. Chronicle. Oakland. ca. 1925+   w.
    Pub. of the Beth Eden Baptist church containing its calendar, social
news, etc.

3931. Clarion. Los Angeles. 192-?-

3932. Cloud's children's pictorial. Los Angeles. 0, 1936?-   m. CLU,
    (George P. Johnson Coll.), 0, 1936.
        Frank H. Cloud, pub.; William C. Edwards, managing ed.; Floyd C.
Covington, ed. Pub. and distributed free by Cloud's photographic studios.

3933. Coastlines. Los Angeles, Santa Monica. Spring, 1955-1964//.   q, ir.
    CL, 1955-64; CLSU, Complete; CSt, 1964-65; CU, Spring, 1955-64 (no. 1-22).
    Merged into Genesis west.
    An interracial literary magazine.

3934. Colleague. Los Angeles. 1954-   q.
        Pub. by the Los Angeles branch, National urban league. CLU, 1961 (nos.
    1, 3, 4); 1963 (nos. 2, 3); 1964 (no. 4); 1965 (no. 2).

3935. Colored citizen. Bakersfield. N1, 1914-   m.
        The announcement of a new national publication ed. by J. Gordon
McPherson appears in the Bakersfield COLORED citizen, Oct. 17, 1914,
p. 2, col. 2.

3936. Combination. Oakland. 1963?-   m. COEB, F, 1964; Ap, My, Jℓ, 1967;
    CSfAA, S, 1968.
        Pub. by "the Bay area studio/printing co."; Brackeen McCarty, pub.;
George Walther, ed.

3937. Community reporter. Los Angeles. 1949?-   ir. CLU, 1966+; NN, Je9,
    N25, 1949; F10, My24, Jℓ14, 1950; Ja26, 1951.
        Pub. by the Los Angeles county conference on community relations.

3937a. Compassionate review and world youth crusader. San Francisco. Ap,
    1966-   ir.
        Pub. in the "interests of the Church of Our Lord's Most Tender Com-
passion ... United African Appeal, Inc., and World Youth." Eugene H.
Huffman, ed.

3938. Contact. Sausalito. 1958-Mr, 1965//.   q, b-m. CL, v. 1-4; CLSU,
    1958-0, 1964; CSmH, 1958-S, 1961 (nos. 1-9); CU, 1958-F/Mr, 1965.

Periodicals

"Incorporating Western review, the San Francisco collection of new writing, art & ideas." An interracial literary magazine.

3939. Council for civic unity, San Francisco. Committee on civil rights inventory. A civil rights inventory of San Francisco, 1958–   CU, 1958+.

3940. Craftsmen aero-news. Los Angeles. Ja, 1937–1938//.   m. CHU, Ja, Je–Jℓ, 1937; Ja, Mr–Ap, Ag, 1938.
     A trade journal pub. by craftsmen of Black wings, inc. Mrs. Zola Benjamin, ed.

3941. Criterion. Oakland. Mr, 1941–   m. COEB, My, 1941.
     Louis H. Campbell, ed.

3942. Cure: citizens united for racial equality. San Diego. CSdS, 1969+.

3943. Dare. Los Angeles. 1965–   q. DHU, Jℓ/Ag, 1965.

3944. Deserted times. San Francisco. 1968?–   "10 issues" per year.
     CU, v. 1 (n.d.); Ag, 32(!) [1968?].
     A literary magazine.

3945. Dust. El Cerrito. 1964–   q. CLU, v. 2, no. 1 (Spring/Summer, 1965)+; CU, v. 1, no. 2 (Summer, 1964)+.
     Interracial; literary.

3946. Ebon. San Francisco. Ja, 1970–
     Pub. by the San Francisco comic book co.
     Chronicles the adventures of Ebon, a "superman."

3947. Echo. Pasadena. 192–?   w. CU-B, My31, 1925.
     "Official organ of the First A. M. E. church, Pasadena, California."

3948. Education corps newsletter. Greenbrae. O, 1969–   b–m. CSf, D, 1969 (photocopy); CSrCL, O, 1969+.

3949. Elegant. Los Angeles. 1964–1968//?   m. COEB, v. 1, no. 6 (1964); F, 1965; CSfAA, F [Ap], 1964.
     A fashion magazine ed. and pub. by John R. Daniels; Roy Walden, ed., 1965ff.

3950. Equalizer. Los Angeles. Ja, 1968–   m. CLU, My, 1969+.
     Pub. gratis by National equalizer enterprises "to serve as a direct line of communication between employers and potential employees."

3950a. Essence. Boulder, Colo. My, 1970–   m.
     Ida Lewis, Gordon Parks, Marcia Gillespie, and Barbara Kerr, eds.

3951. Fair lady magazine. Oakland.

3952. Fair play. Seattle. 1950?–   q. DHU, N–D, 1953.
     Pub. by Seattle Civic unity committee.

Periodicals

3953. Fair practices news. San Francisco. Jℓ/Ag, 1960+   b-m. CLSU,
       1960+; CU,Jℓ -Ag, 1960+.
            Issued by the California state fair employment practice commission.
       Title varies: Jℓ/Ag, 1960-Jℓ/Ag, 1963, Fair employment newsletter.

3954. Falcon. Oakland. 1960-   m? DHU, N, 1960.
       Thomas Nash, ed.

3955. Family savings and loan association community newsletter. Los Angeles.
       0, 1967-   m.

3956. Femme. Los Angeles. 1954-1962//?   m.
            Pub. in the interest of Negro women by Libby Clark. Alternate
       title: Femne.

3957. Flash. Los Angeles. Ja12, 1929-   w. CLU, (George P. Johnson
       Coll.), D31, 1929; Ja13, 25, 1930; DHU, S, 1929.
            A news magazine. D. E. Taylor, pub. Fay (Jackson) Robinson and
       James W. McGregor, eds.

3958. Golden pen. Los Angeles. 1970?-   m.
            "Published monthly by the Public Relations Office for employees and
       associates of Golden State Mutual Life Insurance Company ..." John
       Green, ed.

3959. Golden state mutual messenger. Los Angeles. Je, 1930-   q, m.
       COEB, 0, 1939; Ja, Ap, 1940; Ja, 1941; Ap-My, Jℓ, S-0, D, 1942; Ja,
       Spring, 1943; 0, 1945 (20th anniversary); F-Mr, Jℓ-Ag (25th anniversary),
       1950.
            Pub. by the Golden state mutual life insurance co. Title varies:
       Golden state news; Golden state mutual insurance company bulletin; etc.
       Eds. have included Helen F. Chappell and Verna A. Hickman.

3960. The grapevine. San Mateo. 196-?-   m.
       Pub. by San Mateo community service center.

3961. Grok. San Francisco. 1967?-   ir. CSf, v. 1, no. 3; CU, v. 1,
       no. 3 [n.d.].
            An interracial literary magazine.

3962. Guiding star. Los Angeles, San Diego, Berkeley, etc. 1930-   q, ir.
       COEB, Jℓ, 1960; My, 1963.
            "Official organ of the Golden state grand chapter, Order of eastern
       star, Prince Hall rite of adoption, California and its jurisdiction."
       Among the editors were Ruth A. Green and Jessie Spigners.

3963. Hamitic review. Los Angeles. Mr, 1935-   m. CLU, (George P.
       Johnson Coll.), Ap, 1935.
            Elmo L. Dinkins, ed.; Lillian Dinkins and Thelma Daniels, assoc. eds.

3964. Hollywood-Wilshire fair housing council news. Los Angeles. Je6,
       1969?-   w? CLU, (Spec. Coll.), Je13, 1969.

Periodicals

3965. Hunters Point-Bayview community health service news. San Francisco.
     1969-   b-m. COEB, Ag/S, 1969; D, 1969/Ja, 1970; D, 1970/Ja, 1971.
        Lillian Fortier, ed.

3966. Impulse. Seattle. 1964?-   m. CSfAA, v. 1, no. 2.
        Fitzgerald Beaver, ed.

3967. The integrator. Los Angeles. 1968-   q.
        Pub. by Crenshaw neighbors, inc. Devoted to the activities of inter-
     racial communities in the United States.

3968. Interracial progress. Portland, Ore. 1952-   m. OrU, Ag, 1952-Je,
     1957.
        Pub. by the Urban league of Portland.

3969. Ivy leaf. Berkeley. 1922-   q.
        A sorority publication. Thelma T. Gorham was ed. in 1949.

3969a. Journal advocate. Berkeley. Dl, 1956-   m.? COEB, Dl, 1956.
        "Published in the interest of progress by the East Bay Cities
     Business League, Inc." Madison Harvey, ed.

3970. Journal of black poetry. San Francisco. Spring, 1966+   q, ir.
     CHS, 1968+; CL, Fall, 1968+; CLU, Spring, 1966+; COM, 1966+; CRcS, 1969+;
     CSdS, 1968+; CSf, Winter, 1967/68+; CSfAA, Summer, 1967; Spring, 1969;
     CSluSP, 1969+; CSt, 1967+; CU, Spring, 1969+; CU-A, 1969+; CU-SB, [1966-].
        Joe Goncalves, ed.

3971. Journal of black studies. Beverly Hills. S, 1970-   q. CLU, S,
     1970+; CU, S, 1970+.
        Ed. by Arthur L. Smith at the Afro-American studies center, Univ. of
     Calif., Los Angeles.

3972. Journal of the new African literature and the arts. Stanford.
     Spring, 1966+   semi-annual, q. CL, Spring, 1966-Fall, 1967; COM,
     Spring, 1966+; CSf, Fall, 1966+; CSt, Spring, 1966+; CU, Spring, 1966+.

3973. Lampost. San Francisco. My, 1969+   m, ir. CSf, Fall/Winter, 1969.
        Pub. by Youth for service.

3974. Liberator. Los Angeles. 1899-191-?//.   m, b-m, w. CL, F (v. 1,
     no. 17)-D, 1901; Mr-D, 1902.
        Pub. by Jefferson Lewis Edmonds (d. 1914).

3975. Lou Jones newsletter. San Mateo. 1959+   m. CSf, My, 1965; Ap-My,
     Jl, S, N-D, 1967; [Ja, 1968+].
        Pub. monthly by Intergroup relations association of northern
     California. Louis W. Jones, executive director.

3976. Lunar visitor. San Francisco. Ja, 1862-   m. CU-B, F, 1862.
        A literary magazine edited by John Jamison Moore (ca. 1818-1883),
     pastor of the First African Methodist Episcopal Zion church, San Fran-
     cisco.

Periodicals

3977. Mafundi potential. Los Angeles. F, 1970-   m.
Pub. by the Mafundi institute.

3978. Marin City memo. Marin City. 1966?-   s-m, m. CSf, N-D, 1969;
CSrCL, v. 1, no. 9+.
Pub. by the Southern Marin economic opportunity council. Ed. by
Doretha Mitchell.

3979. Messenger. Los Angeles. 1940?-   m, b-m. DHU, v. 11, no. 1-7
(1950); v. 12, no. 1-3 (1951).
Pub. by the Golden state mutual life insurance company.

3980. Mid-peninsula citizens for fair housing. Newsletter. Palo Alto.
1965?-   CMp, Ap2-018, 1968; Ag5, 1969.

3981. Militant. [Denver?] 1937?-   w. CoHi, (James Atkins Coll.),S20,
018-25, D13, 27, 1965; Ja3-10, 24-31, F21-My9, 23, Je20-27, Jℓ25, 1966.

3982. Minaret. San Francisco. 1970-   m.
Pub. by Muhammad's mosque number 26.

3983. Movement. San Francisco. F, 1965-1970//.   m. CLU, v. 4, no. 1
(1968)-v. 6, no. 1 (1970); CRcS, 1969+; CSaT, 1965+; CSf, My, 1969; CSt,
My, 1965+; CU, 1968+; CU-I, 1966+; CU-SB, 1969+.
Pub. by the Student nonviolent coordinating committee of California.

3984. NAACP bulletin. Oakland. 194-?-   q. COEB, Ja-Ap, 0, 1950.
Pub. by the Alameda county branch, National association for the
advancement of colored people. Lewis A. Baskervill, ed.

3985. NAACP freedom journal. Stanford univ. branch. Stanford. Ja, 1953?-
m. CPa, My-Jℓ, N, 1967; N, 1968; Ja-Ag, 1969.

3986. National Baptist extension advocate. Los Angeles. 1925?-   m.
DHU, D, 1932.
Official organ of the National Baptist extension board of America,
the California Baptist state convention, and the Masonic brotherhood.

3987. National lever. Los Angeles. Jℓ, 1915-
A "new magazine." - Los Angeles New age, Aug. 6, 1915, p. 4, col. 4.

3988. Neighborhood legal news. San Francisco. v. 1, 1968+   w. CU, v. 1+.
A "part of the Western addition law office community education
project, a school-community involvement program."

3989. New day informer. Oakland. S, 1924-1929//? m. COEB, N, 1924.
Clifford Ernest Ware (1885-1950), ed. Vivian Osborne Marsh, women's
ed.

3990. New lady. Hayward. Ja, 1966-   m. COEB, O-N, 1969; F, 1970;
CSfAA, Ja, 1966; DHU, Ja-F, 1966; S, 1969-Ap/My, 1970.
Pub. by Mecco enterprises, inc., David H. Wellington, general manager,
W. Warner Beckett, pub., and Edward N. Evans, Jr., ed.

Periodicals

3991. New tide. Los Angeles. S, 1934?-   m.
       Carl Bulosan, ed.

3992. News edition. Los Angeles. D, 1934-   m.
       Edward Grubbs and Sewilla Pollard, pubs.; Gertrude L. Jones, ed.

3993. News from Bay area council against discrimination. San Francisco.
       194-?-My, 1944//.   m. CU, D, 1942-My, 1944.

3994. News letter. San Francisco. 196-?-   m? DHU, My, 1970.
       Pub. by Plan of action for challenging times, inc.

3995. Nigger uprising. Pasadena. N, 1968?-   m. CL, N, 1968 (v. 2,
       no. 10)+.
       Follows Uprising.

3996. Nommo. Los Angeles. 1968?-   m. CLU, D4, 1968+.
       "Published once every month during the school year except during
       summer, vacation and examination periods, by the ASUCLA communications
       board for the Black students union," Univ. of Calif.

3997. Now, inc. Los Angeles. 1943-   s-m. CL, Jℓ, 1943-S, 1946 (v. 1-4).
       "Interracial publication" - Miriam Matthews.

3998. O. E. D. C. Reporter. Oakland. O, 1965-   m? CO, O,
       1965-Jℓ, 1968.
       Pub. by the Oakland economic development council.

3999. Open forum. Los Angeles. D6, 1924-   b-w, m. CLU, D6, 1924-1964
       (film); CSt, D6, 1924-D29, 1934; Ja6-D22, 1945; Ja5, 1946-Mr/Ap, 1953.
       Official organ of the American civil liberties union, Southern
       California branch.

4000. Outlet. Los Angeles. S, 1924-   m. CLU, (George P. Johnson Coll.)
       S-D, 1924; Ja, 1925.
       H. Wallace Thurman, ed.

4001. Pacific northwest bulletin. Seattle. 194-?-1948//?   s-m.
       P. S. Barnett, ed., 1945-48.

4002. Pastime. San Francisco? 1967-   m? CSfAA, My, 1967.
       L. S. Jamerson, Jr., pub.; Reginald Major, ed.

4003. Peace guide. Los Angeles.
       Cited by Beasley, p. 256.

4004. Phase II; journal of black art renaissance. Berkeley. Spring, 1970-
       q.
       Pub. by the Black heritage class, Univ. of Calif. Sarah (Webster)
       Fabio, ed.

4005. Plain talking. Los Angeles. Je, 1931-   m. DHU, Je, 1931.
       Artis N. Ward, ed.

Periodicals

4006. Prince Hall masonic digest. Oakland. Jℓ, 1951–   q, ir.   CHi, Jℓ,
1951–N, 1959; F, Ag, 1961–S, 1962; F, 1966; F, 1967; [Ag?] 1968; COEB,
[1951–1968]; CU, Jℓ, 1951–Ap, 1966.
    "Official publication of the Prince Hall grand lodge of free and
accepted masons of California and its jurisdiction." Preceded by
Western light. Royal E. Towns, ed.

4007. Progress. Portland, Ore. 195–?–   b–m.
    Pub. by the Urban league of Portland.

4008. Pulse. El Rito, N. M. 1970–   ir.
    A political–literary, interracial publication by Illuminations press,
Norm Moser, ed.

4009. Quarterly bibliography on cultural differences. Sacramento.   Jℓ,
1964–   q. C, Jℓ, 1964+.
    Comp. and pub. by the California state library, Sacramento.

4010. Rage magazine. Denver. 1970–   w.   DHU, Jℓ3, 1970.

4011. Railroad men's guide. 191–?–
    Founded by William J. McLemore – San Francisco Western appeal,
Oct. 5, 1921, p. 2, col. 1.

4012. Richmond neighborhood courier. Richmond.   – 196–? //.

4013. Roots in revolt. San Francisco. Mr, 1968?–   m, b–m. CU, Ap/My,
1968+.
    Pub. by the Black community research and communication project.
"Dedicated to the outpouring of ... information for the development of
the politically aware Black community."

4014. San Francisco African American historical and cultural society.
California history series. San Francisco. 1965–   m, q, ir. CHi,
Ja, 1966; Ag, 1966; Ap, 1968; Je, 1968; CSf, S, 1965+; CSfAA, S, 1965+;
CSj, S, 1965+; CSjC, No. 9 (1966)+; CSmH, S, 1965–D, 1967; CSt, S, 1965+.
    Formerly the San Francisco Negro historical and cultural society.
Ethel (Ray) Nance, ed. Contains monographs authored mainly by James
Abajian, John H. Dorsey, Price M. Cobbs, James A. Fisher, Philip M.
Montesano, James W. Pilton, and John H. Telfer.

4015. Scoop. Los Angeles. v. 1, 1967+   w.
    Emphasizes entertainment industry news. A San Francisco edition,
Bay area scoop, was issued early in 1969.

4016. Score. Seattle. My, 1960–Jℓ, 1961//. Wa, Complete.

4017. Sepia Hollywood. Los Angeles. Je, 1945–1950//? CLU, (George P.
Johnson Coll.) O, 1945; DHU, N, 1946; NN, Ja, 1946; Ap, 1947.
    Entertainment industry–oriented. Mrs. Lillian Cumber, ed.; Clarence
Rhodes and Gerald Cumber, pubs.

Periodicals

4018. Shrewd. Los Angeles. 1968-   b-m. COEB, Ap, 1969; CU, Ap, 1969.
Frank Childress, ed. and pub.

4019. Silhouette pictorial. Los Angeles. Ap, 1938-195-?// CLU, (George P.
Johnson Coll.) F, Ap-My, 1939; Jℓ, 1940; DHU, N, 1938; Mr, Je, 1940; NN,
Mr-Ap, 1939; Ja, S, 1940.
Ed. and pub. by Edward Grubbs.

4020. Skills center news letter. Oakland. N/D, 1969-   b-m. COEB, N/D,
1969.
Edith M. Austin, ed. Pub. by the East bay skills center.

4021. Soledad brothers news letter. San Francisco. 1970-   m?

4022. Soul. Los Angeles. 1965+ b-w. CLS, Mr3, 1969+.
Entertainment industry-oriented; Ken Jones, ed. and pub.

4023. Soul illustrated. Los Angeles. Je, 1968-   b-m. DHU, D, 1969; Jℓ,
0, 1970.
Entertainment industry-oriented; Ken Jones, ed. and pub.

4024. Soulbook, the quarterly journal of revolutionary Afroamerica.
Berkeley. 1964?-   q, ir. CFS, Spring/Summer, 1969; Fall/Winter,
1970; CLU, 1967+; CSdS, 1969+; CSfAA, Spring, 1965; Winter, 1965/66;
CU, Fall, 1965+.

4025. Stanford research institute. Research memorandum. Menlo Park. 1967-
CSt-Law, no. 1+; CU, no. 1+.
Prepared for: San Francisco unified school district [to study
alternative means by which racial imbalance in San Francisco's public
schools might be diminished].

4026. Student nonviolent coordinating committee. San Francisco regional
office. Key mailing list, KLM1-454; My15, 1965-Jℓ23, 1967//. CSt, N,
1966-Jℓ, 1967; CU, My15, 1965-Ap16, 1967 (no. 1-386); My14-Jℓ23, 1967
(no. 400-54).

4027. Syndrome. Oakland. 1967?-   b-m. CLU, v. 4, no. 1 (S-0, 1969)+;
CSt, v. 3, no. 4; v. 7, no. 1 (1970); CU, v. 4, no. 1+; DHU, Mr/Ap,
1967; S/0, 1969.
"Cultural motivation publications, inc."

4028. This is L. A.: L. A.'s only sepia magazine. Los Angeles. Ap, 1960-
m.
Benton P. Steptoe, pub.; Bill Robertson and Earl Anthony, eds.

4029. Topic. Los Angeles. 196-?-   m.
Pub. by the Press and publications service, U. S. information agency,
for distribution in Africa. Dennis Askey, Jeff Stansbury, Jacques
Fidao, and Howard Smethen, eds.

4030. Tribune: a magazine of report and opinion. Los Angeles. 1964-
1965//. b-m. DHU, Mr15, 1965.
Almena (Davis) Lomax, ed.

Periodicals

4031. Uhuru. Oakland. Ja, 1968?–   m, b–m. CSf, D, 1968 (v. 2, no. 1);
    CU, Ap–My, 1968; D/Ja 196–? (v. 1, no. 8–9, 12).
        Political and literary.

4032. Uprising. Pasadena. Ja, 1967?–   m. CL, Ja–S, 1968; CSf, F, 1968.
    "An Ashanti publication." Followed by Nigger uprising.

4033. Urban light. Los Angeles. Je, 1931–Ja, 1935//.   m, q, ir. CL,
    Complete; CLSU, Ja–D, 1931; Mr–S, 1932; Ja, 1933; Ja, 1934; Ja, 1935.
        Pub. by the Los Angeles branch of the National urban league. Floyd
    C. Covington, ed.

4034. Urban west. San Francisco. S–O, 1967–   b–m. CL, 1968+; CLS, 1967+;
    CLU, Ja, 1970+; COM, 1967+; CSbS, 1969+; CSdCiC, Ja–F, 1969+; CSf, S–O,
    1967+; CSfAA, S–O, 1967; S–O, 1968; O, 1969; Ap, 1970; CSj, N–D, 1968+;
    CSrCL, S–O, 1967+; CSt, 1967+; CU, 1967+; CU–SB, My–Je, 1968+; WaT, My–
    Je, 1968–; WaTC, N–D, 1967– .
        John C. Bee, Jr., ed.

4035. Val Verde news. Los Angeles. Ap, 1954–   m.
        Pub. by the Val Verde improvement Assoc. Frank D. Godden, chairman,
    bulletin committee.

4036. Voice of Watts. Los Angeles. O, 1968–   m.

4037. WACO organizer. San Francisco. 1967?–   m.
        Pub. by the Western addition community organization.

4038. Washington. State board against discrimination. Quarterly news-
    letter. [Olympia?] 1967?–   q. CU, Ag, 1958+; WaU, Fall, 1967+.

4039. We, a monthly calendar of bay area events. Oakland. Mr, 1958–   m.
    COEB, Mr, 1959.

4040. We not they. San Rafael. Jℓ19, 1968+   ir. CSf, Ag–D, 1969;
    CSrCL, Jℓ19, 1968+.
        Newsletter of the Marin county human rights commission.

4041. Western Christian recorder. Los Angeles. 1900–1947//.   s–m, w.
    COEB, S12, 1940.
        Pub. by the African Methodist Episcopal church. J. H. Wilson, ed.
    in 1930's–194–?

4042. Western informant, the modern magazine. Los Angeles. 0, 1936–1938//.
    m. CLU, (George P. Johnson Coll.) Mr, 1937; CU, v. 1, no. 1–8; DHU,
    [1937–1938]; NN, O–N, 1936.
        Followed by the Los Angeles AFRO–TEMPO.
        Mattie Mae Stafford, ed.–pub.; Goler V. Banks, assoc. ed.

4043. Western light. Santa Monica. 1939–   CHi, v. 1, no. 1 [n.d.].
        "Official organ, Most worshipful sovereign grand lodge of free and
    accepted masons of California and its jurisdiction." Succeeded by
    Prince Hall masonic digest.

Periodicals

4044. Western star of Zion. Redding. Ap, 1902-   m?
     Official organ of African Methodist Episcopal church on the Pacific
coast. Ed. by the Rev. H. L. McKinney. Associate ed., the Rev. E. H.
Brown. Receipt of first issue noted, San Francisco PACIFIC coast appeal,
Apr. 19, 1902, p. 4, col. 1.

4045. Western states review. Los Angeles. 1928?-   m. DHU, Ag, 1928.
     Thomas W. Gaither, ed. "A magazine devoted to the advancement of
the colored people."

4046. Wildcat. San Francisco. Ag, 1970-   m.
     Interracial and revolutionary.

4047. Woman's journal. Oakland, Los Angeles. 194-?-   annual? COEB, 1942;
CU-B, [1944]-45.
     Organ of the California association of colored women's clubs.

4048. Woodmen banner. Denver. q.
     Pub. by the Supreme camp of the American woodmen.

NEWSPAPERS

ALASKA

4049. Anchorage ALASKA spotlight. w. 1952+.
     Giles Trammel, ed. 1952-55; George C. Anderson, ed. and pub. 1952+.

ARIZONA

4050. Nogales BULLET. w. 1921?-   CLU,(George P. Johnson Coll.) D24,
1926.
     "Published by the 25th Infantry without expense to the government."

4051. Phoenix ARIZONA gleam. w. 1936-1946//?

4052. Phoenix ARIZONA informant. w. 1957+.
     Founded by Charles R. Campbell and Walter Powell. Sometimes pub. as
the Phoenix informant.

4053. Phoenix ARIZONA sun. w. 1942-1960//? Az, Jℓ7-14, 1944; My17, 31,
Je21, Jℓ12, S13-D18, 1958; F4-21, 1960.
     D. F. Benson, ed.

4054. Phoenix ARIZONA tribune. w. 1958+. Az, Jℓ, 1958+; AzTeS, S, 1967+.
     Founded by Edward Banks and later ed. and pub. by his widow, Mrs.
Eloise L. H. Banks.

4055. Phoenix INDEX. w. 1936-1939//?

4056. Phoenix TRIBUNE. w, m. 1918-1946//? Az, Ja, 1919-1929; Apl, 1946;
AzU, 1920-1922; [1923-1931].
     Arthur R. Smith, ed.

Newspapers

Arizona (cont.)

4057. Phoenix WESTERN dispatch. w. 1924-1929//.
        W. W. Jones, ed.

4058. Tucson ARIZONA times. w. 0, 1925-1934//? CLU, (George P. Johnson
        Coll.) 029, N19, 1926.
        Louis J. Washington, ed.

4059. Tucson ARIZONA's Negro journal. w. 1942-1943//?

4060. Tucson INTER-STATE review. w. 1920?-1933//?
        E. J. Richardson, ed.

4061. Tucson SPOKESMAN. w. 192-?-
        George B. Cruikshank, ed.

CALIFORNIA

4062. Albany BLACK times. m. 1970-
        Theodore Walker, ed.

4063. Bakersfield COLORED citizen. w. Ap18, 1914-1915//? C, Ap 18-031,
        1914.
            J. Gordon McPherson, ed. Contains local news columns from Allensworth
        and Vallejo.

4064. Bakersfield colored citizen. San Joaquin valley industrial edition of
        the Bakersfield colored citizen. [Bakersfield, 1914]. 12 p.
            Issue of Sept. 26, 1914.
            Its issue of 10,000 copies is described in the Bakersfield COLORED
        citizen, Sept. 5, 1914, p. 2, cols. 2-3.

4065. Bakersfield OUTLOOK. w. 196-?-
        Elorise N. James, ed. and pub.

4066. Berkeley POST. w. 1963-   C, 1964-1968 (film of San Francisco ed.
        on order, 1971); CSt, Jℓ24, 1969+ (Oakland ed.); CU, N2, 1966+ (Oakland
        ed.).
            Thomas L. Berkley, ed. and pub. Other editions pub. in Oakland,
        Richmond, San Francisco, and Seaside.

4066a. Chula Vista STAR news - The voice. w. 196-?-
        Rowland K. Reblee, ed.

4067. Compton METROPOLITAN gazette. w. 1966+
        Hillard Hamm, ed. and pub.

4068. Compton TRI-CITY news. w. 1959?-
        Essentially a throwaway paper in the Compton-Watts-Willowbrook areas.

4069. Compton WESTERN advocate. w. 196-?-
        Robert Douglas, ed.

Newspapers

<u>California</u> (cont.)

4070.   Fresno CALIFORNIA advocate. w. **Ja**, 1968+ CF, My8, 1969+
        Lesly H. Kimber, ed. and pub.

4071.   Fresno FRESNO county banner. w. 189-?-
        Pub. by John J. Neimore and co., in 1901.

4072.   Fresno PEOPLE'S paper; black free press. w? 1970-

4073.   Los Angeles ADVOCATE. w. 1888-
        John J. Neimore, ed.

4074.   Los Angeles AFRO American. w.? 191-?-

4075.   Los Angeles AFRO-TEMPO. w. 1939-1943//.
        Follows Western informant, the modern magazine.

4076.   Los Angeles AMERICAN news. 1956?-1960//?
        Follows Los Angeles NEIGHBORHOOD news.
        James Erwing, Jr., ed. and James Erwing, Sr., pub.

4077.   Los Angeles BEAM. w? 194-?-

4078.   Los Angeles BRONZEVILLE news. w. N, 1943-   CLM, Ja22, 1944 (v. 1,
        no. 10).
        George Garner, ed.

4079.   Los Angeles CALIFORNIA courier. w. 196-?-

4080.   Los Angeles CALIFORNIA eagle. w. 1891?-1966//?   C, Ag29, 1915*;
        N12, 1953; S2, 1954. (newsprint) 07, 1943-Λp26, 1951. (film); CL, D23,
        1927 (holiday ed.); CLM, S5, 1903; D15, 1906; CLU, [Ja31, 1914-Ap26,
        1951] Ja3, 1952-D9, 1954; D23, 1954- D10, 1964. (film); CU, D13, 1913;
        Ja31, Je20, Ag22-S12, 03-24, N21-D5, 26, 1914; Ja16-23, F6, 20-27, Mr13-
        My29, Je19, Jℓ3-Ag28, S11-25; 09-N27, D11-18, 1915; Ja1-8, F12, 26-Ap8,
        29-My13, 27, Ag19, 1916; 025, N8, 29, 1919; Ja1-8, Ap2, My28, Je10-Jℓ2,
        16, Ag12, 26, 01, N26, D24, 1921; Ja7-14, 28, F11-18, Mr4-25, 1922; F14,
        1924; Ja1-8, My7, 1926; F4-11, 014, D23, 1927; Je22, Jℓ13, 1928; F22,
        Mr8-15, Ap5, My3, S27-04, 1929; Mr14-21, 1930. (film) Ja1-Je17, Jℓ1-D30,
        1948; 1949-1953. (newsprint); OrU, D, 1955; N8, 1956; F21, My2, 1957;
        1958-59; [1960].
            Possibly follows the Los Angeles OWL. Absorbed the Los Angeles
        CALIFORNIA news, <u>ca</u>. 1936. Title varies: Los Angeles eagle before 1913;
        Los Angeles CALIFORNIA eagle, 1913-My3, 1951; Los Angeles new California
        eagle, My10, 1951ff.
            Founded by John J., and Ida B. Neimore; Robert R. McKinney, ed. 1906;
        Charlotta A. (Spears) Bass, ed. and pub. 1912-51; Loren Miller, ed. and
        pub. 1951-64; Grace Simons, ed. 1957-64; A. S. Young, ed. and James L.
        Tolbert, pub. 1964-66. Contains local news columns from Allensworth,
        Bakersfield, Calexico, El Centro, Fresno, Hanford, Needles, Pasadena,
        Sacramento, San Diego, Santa Barbara, and Santa Monica.

(*) A spurious issue which announced the sinking of the British navy and

Newspapers

California (cont.)

which was confiscated by the Los Angeles police department. Los Angeles Examiner, Aug. 30, 1915, p. 1, col. 4.

4081. Los Angeles CALIFORNIA news. w. N, 1929-1936//? CF1S, F27, Mr6-Jℓ24, Ag7-D25, 1930; Ja1-Ap2, 16, 30-O29, N12, 26, D10-23, 1931; Ja7-Mr3, 24-Ap21, My5, 19-Je23, Ag4-O27, D8, 1932; F2-23, Mr2, 16-Ag17, 31-D28, 1933; Ja11-My17, 31-Jℓ19, Ag2-23, S6-D27, 1934; Ja4-My3, 1935. (film).
    Est. by David Eugene Taylor. Editors included Loren Miller, John Prowd, Fay M. Jackson, and Commodore Wynn. Merged with Los Angeles CALIFORNIA eagle, ca. 1936. Contains local news columns from Bakersfield, Blythe, El Centro, Fresno, La Jolla, Marysville, Modesto, Monrovia, Oroville, Pasadena, Sacramento, San Diego, Santa Barbara, Val Verde, Victorville, and Fort Huachuca, Ariz.

4082. Los Angeles CENTRAL avenue news. w. Je17, 1910-1911//? C, N, 1910-My19, 1911.
    L. B. Shook, ed.; Sadie Ward, ed. after Ap21, 1911. Appears to be a white newspaper in a changing neighborhood.

4083. Los Angeles CENTRAL news. w. 1961+
    The Sept. 15, 1966 issue announced the purchase from Larry Hews by Chester L. Washington. Serves southeast Los Angeles. Essentially a throwaway newspaper.

4084. Los Angeles CITIZENS advocate. w. 1916-1923//. CU, D11, 18, 1920; Ja1-F19, Mr5-My21, Je18-Jℓ2, 16-30, 1921. (film).
    Charles Alexander, ed.

4085. Los Angeles CRITERION. w. 1940-
    James Stevens, ed.

4086. Los Angeles DEFENDER. w. 1916-1919//.
    J. Gordon McPherson, ed.

4087. Los Angeles EASTSIDE news. w. My18, 1933-Ag20, 1936//.
    Followed by Los Angeles SENTINEL.

4088. Los Angeles ENTERPRISE. w. Je28, 1902-1915//?
    Thomas A. Greene, ed. Not to be confused with a publication with the same name issued by the Veterans hospital, Sawtelle.

4089. Los Angeles FIRST word. w. 1943?-1946//?

4090. Los Angeles GRAPHIC. w. 1939-
    Follows Los Angeles ILLUSTRATED reflector.

4091. Los Angeles GUARDIAN. w.

4092. Los Angeles HERALD American. w? 193-?-

Newspapers

California (cont.)

4093. Los Angeles HERALD-DISPATCH. w. 1952+   C, F9, 04, D13, 1956; CF1S,
     1966+; CLS, Ag, 1968+; CLU, Mr, 1967+.
          John Lee and E. Pat Alexander, eds.; S. Alexander, pub. At various
     times published the following additional editions: Pacoima, Watts-
     Willowbrook, and national.

4094. Los Angeles ILLUSTRATED journal. w. Ag16, 1956-   CLU, (George P.
     Johnson Coll.) Ag16, 04, 1956.
          Dora H. Moore, pub.

4095. Los Angeles ILLUSTRATED reflector. w. 1937-   CLU, (George P.
     Johnson Coll.) Je30, 1937.
          Followed by Los Angeles GRAPHIC. Frederick L. Buford, ed.

4096. Los Angeles METROPOLITAN gazette. w? 1966?-

4097. Los Angeles MILITANT. w. 1944-1946//?

4098. Los Angeles NEIGHBORHOOD news. w, s-w. 1930-1956//? CLU, Je6-Ag8,
     1946.
          James Erwing, Jr., ed. and James Erwing, Sr. pub. Title varies:
     Housewives' news; East side advertisements.

4099. Los Angeles NEW age dispatch. w. 1904-1948//?   CF1S, 025, 1922;
     CLU, (George P. Johnson Coll.) F25, Ap5, 22, 1921; Jℓ2, 1937; CU, Je26,
     Ag28-S25, 09-30, N13-20, D4-25, 1914; Ja1-F19, Mr5-12, 26-Ap16, 30-Ag20,
     S3, 17-022, N5-D17, 31, 1915; Ja7-Mr10, 1916; Ag2, 1918; My23, 1919;
     My14, N5-19, 1920; Ja14, Mr4, Je10-24, Jℓ22, Ag12-26, S23, N11-D9, 30,
     1921; Ja6, 1922. (film); NN, Ja1-8, 1937.
          Title varies slightly. Acquired the Los Angeles WESTERN dispatch.
     Founded by T. L. Brooks and ed., ca. 1912-48, by Frederick Madison
     Roberts as the Los Angeles new age. Contains local news columns from
     Allensworth, Pasadena, San Bernardino, and San Diego.

4100. Los Angeles NEW era. w. 1939?-
          Est. by Vada Somerville.

4101. Los Angeles NEWS. w. 196-?-

4102. Los Angeles NEWS-GUARDIAN. w. 1937-1944//. CF1S, Je1, 1939.
          Est. by Vada Somerville.

4103. Los Angeles NOW. s-m. 1944-1946//.
          Follows Los Angeles WAR worker.

4104. Los Angeles OBSERVER. w. Jℓ7, 1888-   CLM, 013-20, 1888; COEB, 020,
     1888. (photocopy); CSfAA, 020, 1888. (photocopy); CU-B, 020, 1888. (photo-
     copy).
          Robert Charles O'Hara Benjamin, ed., see San Francisco ELEVATOR,
     Sept. 8, 1888. Thomas Pearson, ed. Oct., 1888. Other managers and
     editors included William S. Sampson, Tilghman Brown, Mrs. H. M. Spiller,
     and John J. Neimore.

Newspapers

California (cont.)

4105. Los Angeles OPEN city. w. 196-?-
       Directed toward minority readership.

4106. Los Angeles OWL. w. M48, 1879-1891//?
       Possibly an apocryphal publication. Said to have been followed by
the Los Angeles CALIFORNIA eagle.
       John J. Neimore, ed.

4107. Los Angeles PACIFIC defender. m, w. S5, 1923-1937//?   CLU, (George
P. Johnson Coll.) S5, 13, 1923; My29, Je5, 1924; O15, 1925; N4, 1926;
Je16, Jℓ21, 1927; Mr8, 1928; CU-B, O22, 1925.
       Merged with Los Angeles CALIFORNIA news. Fred C. Williams, ed.;
James M. Alexander, assoc. ed.

4108. Los Angeles PACIFIC enterprise. w. Ja29, 1927-   CLU, (George P.
Johnson Coll.) Ja29-F12, 26, Mr12, 1927.
       William A. Venerable, ed.

4109. Los Angeles POST. w. 1915-
       A white newspaper of which Buber Brown (d. 1916) was editor.

4110. Los Angeles POSTAGE stamp. w? 191-?-

4111. Los Angeles RECORD. w. 1944+
       Founded by C. Erwin and J. Morris as a throwaway. Eds. included
Mrs Lillian Cumber and William Kimbell; Jim Goodson, pub. in 1967.

4112. Los Angeles REFLECTOR. w. 193-?-

4113. Los Angeles SEARCHLIGHT. w. 1896-
       Shepard S. Freeman, ed. ca. 1905.

4114. Los Angeles SENTINEL. w. My 18, 1933-   C, 1946+.(film); CF1S,
1934-0, 1940; D, 1945+; CL, Mr21, 1946+.(film); CLM, My3, 1945; CLS,
1967+; CLU, Mr21, 1946+.(film); CSdS, 1946+; CSt, 1946+.(film).
       Leon H. Washington, ed. and pub. 1933+; Loren Miller, ed. 1940-47.

4115. Los Angeles SOUTH end news. w. ca. 1930-
       David Desseau, pub. A throwaway appearing in three editions includ-
ing the Florence Messenger and the Compton Westside bee.

4116. Los Angeles SOUTHERN California guide. w. 1891-1895//. KHi, Ja16-
23, 1892.
       John J. Neimore and George E. Watkins, proprietors.

4117. Los Angeles SOUTHWEST news. w. 1953-
       The Sept. 15, 1966 issue announced purchase from Larry Hews by
Chester L. Washington. Serves southwest Los Angeles. Essentially a
throwaway newspaper.

4118. Los Angeles SPARK. w. 196-?-

Newspapers

<u>California</u> (cont.)

4119. Los Angeles SPOTLIGHT. w. 1944?-1946//?
       Pub. by Eddie Burbridge.

4120. Los Angeles SUBURBAN home and Watts news. w. 1914-1925//?   CU,
       My9-16, 30-Jℓ25, 1918.
          Pub. as Los Angeles suburban home, 1914-My2, 1918. Follows the Los
       Angeles WATTS news.
          Eds. and pubs. include P. H. Ludolph, C. A. Wellsher, W. S. Ward,
       J. W. Mayer, and Lewis A. Kirkpatrick. Title varies: Suburban home and
       news; Suburban home (1924-25). Probably a white newspaper.

4121. Los Angeles TATTLER. w? 1939?-1944//?
          Est. by Mrs. Lillian Cumber. Entertainment industry-oriented.
       Discontinued upon issuance of Sepia Hollywood.

4122. Los Angeles TELLER. w. 1944?-1946//?
          Entertainment industry-oriented.

4123. Los Angeles TOWN talk. w. S19, 1930-   CLU, (George P. Johnson
       Coll.) N21, 1930.
          Loren Miller, ed.; Leon H. Washington, bus. mgr.

4124. Los Angeles TRIBUNE. w. 1940-1960//?   C, Mr16, 1946-D, 1956.
       (film); CLU, D6, 1943-D, 1947; Ja-Je, Ag, 1949-D, 1957.
          Lucius W. Lomax, Jr. ed. and pub.; Almena (Davis) Lomax, ed. De
       Graaf states that it was founded as the Los Angeles Interfaith churchman.

4125. Los Angeles UNITED pictorial review. w. Mr16, 1965+
          George Scott, Jr., pub.; Fritz Baskett, ed.

4126. Los Angeles VALVLRDIAN· voice of the hills. m. Ja, 1940-
          Harry Ted Daily, ed.

4127. Los Angeles WAR worker. s m? Jℓ1, 1943-
          Followed by Los Angeles NOW.
          William Cummings, pub.

4128. Los Angeles WATTS advertiser-review. w. 1908-1940//?   CL, Ap, 1938.
       (25th anniversary progress ed.).
          Pub. as Watts advertiser, 1908-Ap12, 1928. Acquired Los Angeles
       WATTS review, ca. 1929.
          P. F. Adelsbach, ed. (1915); C. H. Turner, ed. (1916); W. L. Lefavor,
       ed. (1919-25); A. D. Lefavor, ed. (1926-29); Joseph L. Asbury, ed. (1930);
       Berle Dean Maxson, ed. (1931-32); and Mrs. Berle Dean Maxson, ed. (1933-
       40). Editorial dates are approximate. Probably a white newspaper.

4129. Los Angeles WATTS herald. w. 1923-192-//?
          Oscar E. Winburn, ed. Probably a white newspaper.

4130. Los Angeles WATTS news. w. 1906-My3, 1918//.   CU, Ag23, 1917-My3,
       1918.

Newspapers

<u>California</u> (cont.)

United with Suburban home to form the Los Angeles SUBURBAN home and Watts news, May 9, 1918.
    A. A. King and Peebles Shoaff, eds. Probably a white newspaper.

4131. Los Angeles WATTS observer. w. 1913-1920//?
    Y. C. Brown and A. H. Knutson, eds. Probably a white newspaper.

4132. Los Angeles WATTS review. w. 1915-1929//?
    S. S. Bellesfield, ed. Probably a white newspaper.

4133. Los Angeles WATTS star-review. w? 192-?-
    Ed. by H. A. Howard and Mrs. Fostina Johnson.

4134. Los Angeles WESTERN clarion. w. Ja, 1926?-   CLU, (George P. Johnson Coll.) Jℓ9, 1927 (v. 2, no. 27).
    E. T. Hubbard, ed.

4135. Los Angeles WESTERN dispatch. w. O6, 1921-1922//?   CLU, (George P. Johnson Coll.) D1, 1921; Ja12-19, 1922; CU, O6, 27, N17, D8-13, 1921.
    Est. by W. M. Austin, John A. Somerville, Willis O. Tyler, and J. C. Banks. Louis S. Tenette, ed. Merged to become the Los Angeles NEW age dispatch.

4136. Los Angeles WESTERN record. w? Ag3, 1936-
    E. Winston Williams, ed.

4137. Los Angeles WLCAC news. w? 196-?-   CLU, 1967+
    A throwaway publication issued by the Watts labor community action committee.

4138. Oakland BEACON. d, w, t-w. Jℓ, 1945-1947//?
    Founded by Amos White and later purchased by Claude O. Allen and Matt Crawford.

4139. Oakland CALIFORNIA voice. w. F, 1919+   C, Mr21, 1952; Ap28, 1961. (newsprint) My5, 1961+ (film); CLU, (George P. Johnson Coll.) Ja22, Ap23, 1921; D3, 1926; COEB, O13, 1922; Je5, 1942; CSdS, 1969+; CU, O2, 1921; Ja7, 1922; D18, 1925; Ag6, 1926; Mr4, My6, 1927; Ja25, F15, 1929; Ap18, My23, Jℓ4, 1930; S2-D30, 1938; Ja6-F17, 1939; Je6, Ag1-N28, 1941; Mr6, 1942; Jℓ16, 1943; Ja27, 1950; Mr30-D28, 1951; 1952 (complete); Ja2-Ag7, 21-D25, 1953; 1954-1966. (negative film); 1967+ (newsprint).
    Errol Marshall, ed. 1919-27; Elbert Allen Daly, ed. and pub. 1927-71; L. H. Campbell, ed. 1964. Absorbed Oakland SUNSHINE.

4140. Oakland FLATLANDS. w, b-w. Mr12, 1966-1969//?   C, Mr26, 1966+; CO, [Mr12, 1966-N18, 1968]; CSaT, 1966+.
    Gerry Leo, ed.

4141. Oakland GOLDEN state. w. 192-?-

Newspapers

California (cont.)

4142. Oakland HERALD. w. 1943–
    James E. Jones, ed.

4143. Oakland ILLUSTRATED guide. w. 1892–1896//. C, 027, 1894.
    "Official organ of the Afro-American league of Alameda county."
    George E. Watkins, manager.

4144. Oakland INDEPENDENT. w. 1929–1931//? CU, 019, D14, 1929; Mr15,
    My10–17, 1930. (negative film).
    Follows the Oakland WESTERN American. Followed by the San Francisco
    SPOKESMAN.
        Mrs. A. A. Martin, pub.; George C. Martin, ed.; and Vivian Osborne
    Marsh, women's ed. Purchased by Byron O'Reilly, Feb., 1931. Contains
    local news columns from San Mateo and Vallejo.

4145. Oakland LIGHT. w. 1944?–1945//?
    Amos White, ed.

4146. Oakland SUNSHINE. w. 1897–1923//. C, N13, 1909; CLU, (George P.
    Johnson Coll.) Mr12, 1921; COEB, Je21, 1902; Ap 29, 1906; Jℓ1, 1916; N23,
    D7, 21, 1918; CU, D21, 1907; S11, 1909; D27 (holiday ed.), 1913; Mr20–27,
    My29–Jℓ3, 17–S4, 18–N13, D11, 1915; Mr25, Jℓ22, D30, 1916; D18, 1920;
    F25, 1922. (negative film).
        Est. by John A. Wilds with J. W. Green, ed. Later purchased by James
    Monroe Bridges with James B. Wilson as political ed.; Errol Marshall,
    manager in 1909; Gordon C. Coleman, ed. 1918–21. Merged with Oakland
    CALIFORNIA voice. Contains local news columns from Allensworth, Bakers-
    field, Fowler, Hanford, Los Angeles, Modesto, Pacific Grove, Sacramento,
    San Francisco, San Jose, Stockton, and Woodland.

4147. Oakland TIMES. w. S29, 1923–1924//? CU, S29, 1923.
    S. De Witt Moss, ed. and pub.; Charles F. Tilghman, assoc. ed.

4148. Oakland WESTERN American. w. My28, 1926–Ag3, 1929//. CLU, (George
    P. Johnson Coll.) Ja28, F11, 25–Mr6, 25, 1927; CU, My28, Je 25, Jℓ30–01,
    29, N26, D17, 1926; Ja7, 21–Je3, 24–Jℓ1, 15–Ag19, D2, 1927; Ja6–13, F24,
    Mr9–16, Ap6, Jℓ13, Ag24–S14, 28–N9, 30–D14, 1928; Ja4, 1929. (negative
    film).
        S. De Witt Moss, ed. 1926–28. Charles F. Tilghman, pub.; Henry J.
    Meadows and Byron O'Reilly, eds. 1928–29; and Vivian Osborne Marsh,
    women's ed. Contains local news columns from Chico, Fresno, Los Angeles,
    Modesto, Pittsburg, Richmond, Sacramento, San Francisco, San Jose, San
    Mateo, Portland, Ore., and Ogden, Utah.

4149. Oakland WESTERN outlook. w. S, 1894–1929//. CLU, (George P.
    Johnson Coll.) My 28, 1927; CU, Je3, 1911; N7, 28, D12–26, 1914; Ja2–9,
    23–30, F13–My1, 15–29, Je12–19, Jℓ3, 24–S4, 25–D18, 1915; Ja1–15, 29–F5,
    Mr11, Jℓ22, 1916; 022, 1921; Mr25, Ap22–29, 1922; F20, My15, Je12, Ag21,
    D18, 1926; Ja1–8, F12, Je11, D10, 24, 1927; Ja21, F4, 18–25, Mr10–17,
    Ap14, 28–My26, 1928. (negative film); CU-B, Ja4, 1896; N3, 1900.
        Founded by Joseph S. Francis, Walter G. Maddox, and John Lincoln

Newspapers

California (cont.)

Derrick. In 1926, Derrick and Jesse E. Wysinger were eds. and proprietors. San Francisco and Los Angeles sometimes were included on the masthead. Occasionally separate editions were published in these cities. Contains local news columns from Marysville, Portland, Ore., Red Bluff, Woodland, Fresno, San Jose, Sacramento, and Phoenix, Ariz. Titles varies.

4150. Palo Alto COMMUNITY bulletin. w. 1968-

4151. Palo Alto EXPLANATORY globe. w. 196-?- CPa, Mr13, 1968.

4152. Palo Alto PENINSULA bulletin weekly. w. N16, 1967- CPa, F1, 1968; CSf, O3-N7, D12-26, 1968; Ja2, 16-My31, Je21-Ag2, 16-S20, O4-N1, 29-D27, 1969; CSt, N16, 1967+.

4153. Palo Alto RAVENSWOOD post. w. 1953+ CRcS, Ja6, 1960-Je25, 1969. (film), Jℓ2, 1969+ (newsprint).
    Clarence A. Burley, pub. to 1966; Richard W. Nowells, pub. 1966+. Eds. included Phyllis Walker, William G. Godfrey, David Goodwin, James Horne, Albert Negri, Andrea Couture, Carolyn Hamann, and Don M. Wilson.

4154. Pasadena CROWN city press. w. 1956-196-?//. C, My23, 1957.
    J. Robert Smith, ed. 1958.

4155. Pasadena EAGLE. w. 1968- CLS, 1968+.

4156. Pasadena EQUALIZER. CP, [1968].

4157. Pasadena INFORMER. w. 1930?-
    Barney Durham, associate ed., 1930.

4158. Pomona FREEWALK gazette. m. O, 1962- CPom, O, 1962; Je, 1965; O, 1965.

4159. Pomona INLANDS report. m. D, 1961- CPom, D, 1961.

4160. Richmond NEWS. s-m. 1945?-1946//?

4161. Riverside REPORTER. w. 1969-
    Reginald Strickland, pub.

4162. Sacramento AMERICAN. w. 1944-1947//?

4163. Sacramento FORUM. b-w. Ap2, 1906- C, Ap2, 1906.
    J. Gordon McPherson, ed., Robert J. Fletcher, assoc. ed. Contains a local news column from Woodland.

4164. Sacramento OBSERVER. b-w, w. 1962+ C, N22, 1962-F21, 1963. (newsprint) F28, 1963+ (film); CS, Ja31, 1969+; CU, Ap25-N28, D12, 1968+.
    William H. Lee, ed. and pub.

Newspapers

California (cont.)

4165. Sacramento OUTLOOK. s-m. 1942-1967//?
    J. T. Muse and Geno Gladden, eds.

4166. Sacramento WESTERN review. m. 1914-1925//?   COEB, Jℓ28, 1917; CU,
    Jel, 1919.
    John M. Collins, ed.

4167. San Bernardino AMERICAN. w. My, 1969+
    Sam Martin, Sr., pub.

4168. San Bernardino PRECINCT reporter. w. 1966-
    Art Townsend, ed. and pub.

4169. San Bernardino TRI-COUNTY bulletin. w. 1945-
    J. Robert Smith, ed.

4170. San Diego COMET. w. Mr15, 1946-
    Julius W. Holder, ed.

4171. San Diego EAGLE. w. 1922-1925//.   CLU, (George P. Johnson Coll.)
    Jel4, 1924.
    Charlotta A. (Spears) Bass, pub.; Joseph B. Bass, ed.

4172. San Diego INFORMER. b-w, s-m. 1934-1948//.   CSd, Je17, 1935.
    E. Parker, ed. 1934-39; W. L. McDonald and E. A. Dorsey, eds. 1940;
    Lillian Moore, ed. 1943-48; Clifford Ernest Ware, pub. 1934-48.

4173. San Diego LEDGER. w? 192-?-
    Edward Kimber, pub.

4174. San Diego LIGHT house. w. 1939-Mr, 1968//.   CSd, [Ja11-N15] D,
    1967; Ja, 1958-D, 1961; Ja, 1964-Mr, 1968; CSdS, 1967+.
    N. M. Young, ed. and pub.

4175. San Diego NEW idea. w. 1921-1926//.   CSd, F24, 1923.
    F. T. Anderson, pres.; G. W. Woodbey and J. B. Wilkins, eds.

4176. San Diego SOUTHEAST San Diego reporter and shopper. w. Jℓ30-Ag14,
    1969//.   CSd, Complete.

4177. San Diego SOUTHERN California informant. w. 189-?-

4178. San Diego VIEWPOINT. w. Je5-Jℓ17, 1969//.   CSd, Je5-Jℓ17, 1969.
    Followed by San Diego VOICE and viewpoint, Jℓ23, 1969.
    Earl Davis, ed.

4179. San Diego VOICE. w. 1961-Jℓ17, 1969//.   CSd, My5-O20, 1966; Mr23,
    1967-F27, 1968; Ag7, 1968-Jℓ17, 1969.
    Followed by San Diego VOICE and viewpoint, Jℓ23, 1969.
    Resumed publication under new owner, Wendell Reid, on Feb. 28, 1963.
    - San Diego Union, Mar. 21, 1963, p. 31, col. 1. Earl Davis, ed., 1968.

Newspapers

<u>California</u> (cont.)

4180. San Diego VOICE and viewpoint. w. Jℓ23, 1969+   CSd, Jℓ23, 1969+; CSdS, 1969+.
    Published as the San Diego VOICE and the San Diego VIEWPOINT prior to Jℓ23, 1969. A. H. Graham, pub.; Earl Davis, ed.

4181. San Francisco CALIFORNIA independent. w. Ja, 1903–
    Richard F. Douglas, ed.

4182. San Francisco CITIZEN. w. 1888–1890//?

4183. San Francisco ELEVATOR. w. Ap7, 1865–Ag, 1904//.   C, O30, 1868; CHi, (film of CU–B holdings); COEB, Ap8, 1870; CSf, Ag13, 27, N5, D17, 1869; F11, Mr18, 1870; Je15, N30, D14–21, 1872; Ja25–F1, 15, Mr15, 1873; CSmH, My6, 1876; CSt, (film of CU–B holdings); CStoPM, Mr8, 1873; CU–B, Ap7–D29, 1865; Ja5–Mr30, O26, 1866; Jℓ5, Ag16–D27, 1867; 1868 (complete); Ja1–Jℓ2, 16, 30, Ag13–S3, 17, O15, 29–D3, 17–31, 1869; F11–25, Mr11–25, Ap15–22, My6, 27–Jℓ8, D2, 1870; O18 (special issue), D29, 1871; Ap27–Je22, Jℓ20–Ag3, 24–31, S14–21, O5, 19–D28, 1872; Ja4–Jℓ5, 19–D27, 1873; Ja10–F7, 21–My16, 30–D26, 1874; Ag28, 1875; Mr17, 21–Ap7, 1877; D3, 1881; My2, 1885; Jℓ3, S11, 1886; O11–18, 1890; Je18, 1892; Je11, 1898. (negative film); KHi, S8, 1888; MWA, My4, 1865; Ja11, Je21, 1867; N, O13. 1865. Absorbed by the San Francisco PACIFIC coast appeal, Aug. 20, 1904.
    Est. by Philip Alexander Bell (1809–1889), well–known civil rights advocate and ed. N. Y. <u>Colored American</u>, 1837–40. William Ector and James B. Wilson were among later editors of the ELEVATOR.

4184. San Francisco FILLMORE shopping guide. w. 1950–
    Followed by the San Francisco INDEPENDENT.
    Donald Vincent Welcher, ed.

4185. San Francisco FREE lance. w ? 191–?–
    Founded by William J. McLemore. San Francisco <u>Western appeal</u>, Oct. 5, 1921, p. 2, col. 1.

4186. San Francisco GOLDEN state news. w. 194–?//.

4187. San Francisco GRAPHIC. w. Ja–Je, 1949//.

4188. San Francisco HUNTER'S Point beacon. s–m. S1, 1943–O1, 1945//.
    CSf, S1–D1, 1943; Ja6, 1944–O1, 1945.
    Although a white newspaper, it is a source reflecting the transforma-tion from a World War II interracial housing project area to a poverty area heavily populated by Afro–Americans.

4189. San Francisco INDEPENDENT. w. 195–?–
    Donald Vincent Welcher and Daryle Lewis, eds.

4190. San Francisco MIRROR of the times. w. O, 1856–Mr, 1858//.   C, Ag2, D12, 1857; CHi, Ag2, D12, 1857. (negative photocopy).
    Jonas Holland Townsend, ed.

Newspapers

<u>California</u> (cont.)

4191. San Francisco PACIFIC appeal. w, ir. Ap5, 1862-1880//?   C, Jℓ11,
1863; CHi, (film of CU-B holdings). Jℓ30, 1864. (newsprint); CLU, (film
of CU-B holdings); CSf, (film of CU-B holdings); CSmH, Ap 24, 1875;
CU-B, Ap5, 1862-Mr26, 1864; Je24, 1865; Jℓ6, Ag10-S14, 28-05, 19-26, N9,
23-D7, 21-28, 1867; Ja25-Ag29, 1868; S3-015, N5, 19-D3, 31, 1870; Ja7,
Ap15, My13, 27-Je3, Jℓ1, 22, Ag12, 26-S2, 23-07, N4, 18-25, D6-16, 1871;
Ja6-Je22, Jℓ6-20, Ag3-N16, 30-D7, 21-28, 1872; Ja4-Je7, 21-D27, 1873;
Ja3-24, F7-Je6, 20-27, Jℓ11-S26, 010-31, N14-D26, 1874; Ja2-Ag7, 21-D11,
25, 1875; Ja1-15, 29-Jℓ15, 29-Ag5, 26-S30, 014-N25, D9-23, 1876; Ja13,
F3-17, Mr3-31, Ap21-Jℓ14, 28-Ag25, S15-06, 27, N10-D15, 29, 1877; Ja5,
19-Ap6, 20, My4-Je8, Jℓ6, 20, Ag3-17, 31, S14, 05-N9, 30-D14, 28, 1878;
Ja4, F8-Mr1, 15, 29-My10, 24-Jℓ5, 025, N8-15, 1879; F28, My1, 22, Je12,
1880. (negative film).
        Publication suspended S5, 1868-Ag27, 1870.
        Est. by Peter Anderson. Philip A. Bell, ed. 1862; Peter Anderson,
ed. 1862ff. In 1879, pub. by William H. Carter with G. W. Jackson,
General agent.

4192. _____. Ap5-D27, 1862. Reprint. S. F., R & E research associates,
1969. C, CSd, CSf, CSfAA.

4193. San Francisco PACIFIC coast appeal. b-w, m, ir. 1898-1925//.   C,
N16-D21, 1901; Ja4-18, F15, Ap5-D6, 1902; Ja2-S5, 03, 31-D19, 1903; Ja2-
Jℓ16, Ag20, S17-029, N12-D24, 1904; D26, 1906. (Cataloged as a periodi-
cal).
        Title varies: San Francisco Pacific coast appeal and San Francisco
Elevator, Aug. 20, 1904- . George E. Watkins and James B. Wilson,
eds., William H. Blake, associate ed.; Frank D. Myers, ed. in 1924. Ab-
sorbed San Francisco ELEVATOR, 1904. Contains local news columns from
Bakersfield, Chico, Fowler, Fresno, Hanford, Marysville, Modesto, Palo
Alto, Pasadena, Paso Robles, Redding, San Jose, San Mateo, Stockton,
Visalia, and Woodland.

4194. San Francisco PACIFIC times. w. Mr15, 1912-   COEB, My31, 1912.
        N. S. Russell, ed. Contains local news columns from Bakersfield,
San Jose, and North Yakima, Wash.

4195. San Francisco PEOPLES advocate. b-w. Ja5, 1944-   CU-B, F12, 1944;
NN, Ja5, 24, 1944.
        Angelo Herndon, ed.-in-chief; William H. McClendon and Walter Cran-
shaw, Jr., eds.

4196. San Francisco REPORTER. s-m. Mr, 1900-
        Publication reported, Seattle REPUBLICAN, Apr. 6, 1900, p. 1, col. 4.

4197. San Francisco REPORTER. w. 1942-   COEB, S6, 1947.
        Followed by the San Francisco SUN-REPORTER.
        H. I. Fontellio-Nanton, ed.

4198. San Francisco SENTINEL. w. 1890-   CU-B, S20, D6-13, 1890.
        Robert Charles O'Hara Benjamin and Augustus A. Collins, eds. and

Newspapers

<u>California</u> (cont.)

managers. Pub. by J. J. Neimore and co., in 1901. Contains local news
columns from Colusa, Fresno, Marysville, Pasadena, Sacramento, San Jose,
and Stockton.

4199. San Francisco SPOKESMAN. w. 010, 1931-   C, Ja13, 1933-Ag16, 1935;
CU, F13-Mr26, Ap9-D15, 29, 1932; Ja6-Ap6, 20-Ag3, S7-D28, 1933; Ja4-Mr1,
15-D28, 1934; F11-Je14, 28-Ag16, 1935. (film).
Follows San Francisco WESTERN appeal and Oakland INDEPENDENT.
John Pittman and Mason Roberson, eds.; Gladys (Wysinger) Crawford,
managing ed.; and Vivian Osborne Marsh, women's ed. Contains local news
columns from Bakersfield; Carmel; Fresno; Loyalton; McCloud; Modesto;
Monterey; Mountain View; Palo Alto; Redding; Sacramento; Calif. state
univ., San Francisco; San Jose; San Mateo; Stockton; Vallejo; and Weed.

4200. San Francisco SPOKESMAN. w. 196-?-
Robert Simms, ed. Sometimes referred to as the Hunter's Point
spokesman.

4201. San Francisco SUN. w. 1947-
S. Wendell Green, ed., Frank Laurent, pub. Followed by the San
Francisco SUN-REPORTER.

4202. San Francisco SUN-REPORTER. w. 1945+   C, Mr22, 025, D13, 1952;
Je6, 20, Jℓ4, 25, S26-031, N14, 1953; Ap17, 1954; Je16, S1, 06, 1956;
My25, Jℓ13, S28, 012, 1957; Ja11-18, F22, 1958; My 23, 1959; COEB, S6,
1947; CSt, D6, 1969+; CU, Mr17-D29, 1951; 1952-1958; Ja3-N21, D5-26,
1959; 1960-1961; Ja6-S8, 22-N24, D8-29, 1962; Ja5-Je22, Jℓ6-13, 27-026,
N9-D28, 1963; Ja4-Je27, Jℓ11-D26, 1964; Ja2-Ag14, 28-D25, 1965. (film)
1966+ (newsprint).
Follows San Francisco SUN and San Francisco REPORTER.
Carlton B. Goodlett, pub. Daniel A. Collins, joint pub. <u>ca.</u> 1957-
59; Frances B. Glover and Jay C. Williams, ed. 1950's; Thomas C. Fleming,
ed. 1970. Contained a local news column from Fresno in 1947.

4203. San Francisco TRIBUNE. w. 194-?-

4204. San Francisco VINDICATOR. w. Ag23, 1884-1906//. C, S20, 1884; Ag15,
1885; Ag6, 1892; S15, 027, 1894; CHi, 07, 1896. (newsprint) N17, 1888;
F9-16, 1889. (film); CU, N17, 1888; F9-16, 1889. (film); CU-B, My2, 16,
Je11, 25, Jℓ30, Ag13, 1887. (film); KHi, N17, 1888; F9-16, 1889.
James E. Brown and George Washington Dennis, Jr., eds.

4205. San Francisco WEST coast star. w. 194-?-

4206. San Francisco WESTERN appeal. s-m. 1918-1933//?   CU, 014, 1920;
Je8-22, Ag17-D21, 1921; Ja4, F1-Mr8, Ap8-My3, Je6, S20, 1922; D16, 1925;
F3, Ag20, 01, D17, 1926; Ja21, F25, Mr18-Ap1, My6, 1927. (negative film).
Ed. by George E. Watkins who stated, Oct. 14, 1920, that this paper
"has no connection with 'The Pacific Coast Appeal'. Neither is its
editor in any way associated with F. D. Myers." Contains local news
columns from Madera, Modesto, Merced, Hollister, Pittsburg, Redding,

Newspapers

California (cont.)

Stockton, McCloud, Bakersfield, San Jose, Richmond, Oroville, Fresno, Allensworth, and Sacramento.

4207. San Jose FORUM. w. Mr14, 1908-   C, Mr21-Ap18, My2, 16-Je6, 20, 27, 1908.
       J. Gordon McPherson, ed. "We shall hereafter publish the Forum in magazine form, and we invite any of our literary inclined friends to send us spicey articles for publication, not over 500 words. We are in search of promising Western writers." - San Jose FORUM, June 20, 1908, p. 6, col. 1. Includes local news columns from Marysville, Pacific Grove, Hollister, Sacramento, Woodland, Fresno, and Goldfield, Nev.

4208. Santa Monica BAY cities informer. w. 194-?-

4209. Stockton CALIFORNIA echo. w. S12, 1962-   CSto, N7, 1962; D11, 1963.

4210. Stockton CALIFORNIA Negro press. m. 194-?-   CSto, O, 1952 (v. 7, no. 15).

4211. Stockton GUIDE. w. 1944-1947//?

4212. Stockton PROGRESSOR. w. My24, 1969-   CSto, My24, 1969+; CStoC, 1969+.
       Title varies: San Joaquin progressor.

COLORADO

4213. The State historical society of Colorado holds four boxes of unlisted newspapers in its James A. Atkins Papers. The Colorado years covered in the collection are 1950-68, and the newspapers represented are the "Denver Blade, Denver Inquirer, Service Record, The Militant, The Call."

4214. Colorado Springs COLORADO advance. 1906-1917//.
       E. B. Butler, ed.

4215. Colorado Springs COLORED dispatch. w. 1900-1913//.
       Porter S. Simpson, ed.

4216. Colorado Springs EAGLE. w. 1912-1913//.
       Mrs. Julia Embry, ed.

4217. Colorado Springs LIGHT. w. 1908-1912//?
       Frederick Madison Roberts, ed.

4218. Colorado Springs VOICE of Colorado. w. 1912?-1914//?

4219. Colorado Springs WESTERN enterprise. w. 1896-1912//.   DLC, Ja6, 27, 1900; NN, Ja6, 27, 1900.
       J. L. Fleming, John Henry Jackson, Charles S. Muse, and Eugene Parker Booze, eds. at various periods.

Newspapers

Colorado (cont.)

4220. Denver AFRICAN advocate. w. Mr, 1890-1891//.

4221. Denver AFRO-AMERICAN. w. 1889-1890//.

4222. Denver ARGUS. w. 1886-1888//.

4223. Denver BLADE. w, s-m. Ag31, 1961-1970//?   CoD, Ag31, 1961+;
       CoHi, Ag31, 1961+.
            Joe Brown, ed. and pub.

4224. Denver COLORADO exponent. w. 1889-

4225. Denver COLORADO statesman. w. 1894-1961//.   CLU, (George P.
       Johnson Coll.) Ja8, 1927; CoD, Mr1, 1940-S15, 1956; CoHi, O29, 1904-Ap17,
       1954; DLC, Ja27, 1900.
            Joseph D. D. Rivers (1856-1937) and E. V. Dorsey, eds.

4226. Denver EXPONENT. w. 1892-1895//?
            Absorbed by the Denver STATESMAN.
            A. R. Wilson, ed.

4227. Denver FIVE pointer. w. 1944?-1946//?

4228. Denver INDEPENDENT. w. 1910-1913//?
            Thomas Campbell, ed.

4229. Denver INQUIRER. w. Ag7, 1952-   CoHi, (James Atkins Coll.) Ag7,
       28, S11, 25-O2, 23-N6, 20-D26, 1952: Ja23-F6, 20-Mr27, Ap10, 24. My8-
       Je12, 26, Jℓ17-24, Ag14-28, S11-O23, N13, 27-D11, 25, 1953; Ja1-8, 29-
       Ap2, 23-Je18, Jℓ2-9, S10-17, O15, 1954.

4229a. Denver weekly NEWS. w. D, 1970?-
            Cosmo Harris, ed.

4230. Denver STAR. w. N23, 1912-1967//?   CoD, Ap13, 1940-F8, 1963; CoHi,
       N23, 1912-O26, 1918. (James Atkins Coll.) D1-8, 1961; Ja5, Ag31, 1962;
       CoU, Je29, 1962+.
            Follows Denver STATESMAN.
            Editors included Charles S. Muse, Wendell A. Peters, and George G.
       Ross.

4231. Denver STATESMAN. w. 1889-N16, 1912//.   CoHi, Ja13, 1905-N16,
       1912; DLC, Ja27, 1900.
            Followed by Denver STAR. Absorbed Denver EXPONENT. Title varies:
       Denver Statesman-exponent, 1895-96.
            Edwin H. Hackley, Chester Arthur Franklin, and G. F. Franklin, eds.

4232. Denver TIMES speaker. s-w. 190-?-
            J. S. Sharp, ed. See notice in Butte NEW age, Aug. 9, 1902, p. 4,
       col. 1.

Newspapers

Colorado (cont.)

4233. La Junta MEGAPHONE. w. 1913-1915//.
T. L. Cate, ed.

4234. Pueblo COLORADO eagle. w. 1910-1914//.
Followed by the Pueblo COLORADO times-eagle.

4235. Pueblo COLORADO times-eagle. w. 1904-1914//.
A consolidation of the Pueblo Colorado times and the Pueblo COLORADO
eagle.
M. B. Brooks, pub., and H. Franklin Bray, ed.

4236. Pueblo RELIGIOUS world. w. 1906?-1908//.

4237. Pueblo RISING sun. w. 1919-1923//.
Thomas L. Cate, ed.

4238. Pueblo TIMES. w. 1894-1895//?
O. L. Boyd, ed.

4239. Pueblo TRIBUNE. w. 1898-1900//.

4240. Pueblo TRIBUNE-PRESS. w. 1895-1904//.
O. L. Boyd, ed.

4241. Pueblo WESTERN ideal. w. 1919?-1960//.
M. O. Seymour, ed.

4242. Trinidad LEADER. w. 1911-1915//?

MONTANA

4243. Butte NEW age. w. My30, 1902-F7, 1903//?   MtHi, My30-Ag9, 23-D27,
1902; Ja3-17, 31-F7, 1903.
Chris. Dorsey, Charles F. Smith, and John W. Duncan, eds. Contains
local news columns from Anaconda, Great Falls, and Helena; Ogden and
Salt Lake City, Utah; Oakland and San Francisco, Calif.; Spokane, Wash.;
and Boise, Idaho Springs, and Pocatello, Idaho.

4244. Fort Harrison KNOCKER. w. 1902-
Publication reported in the Butte NEW age, Dec. 6, 1902, p. 1, col. 4.
It doubtless carried news of the activities of the large number of black
soldiers stationed at the Fort.

4245. Helena COLORED citizen. w. S3, 1894-D15, 1894//.
MtHi, S3-N5, 1894. (film).
James Presley Ball, Jr., ed. Politically motivated. Contains local
news columns from Billings and Seattle, Wash.

4246. Helena MONTANA plaindealer. w, m, ir. Mr16, 1906-S8, 1911//.
MtHi, Mr16-D22, 1906; Ja4-D20, 1907; Ja10-Jl31, S11, 09-D19, 1908; Ja15-
Ag28, 029-N26, 1909; Ja29-028, D9, 1910; Ja27-S3, 1911. (film).

Newspapers

Montana (cont.)

      Joseph Blackburn Bass, ed. Contains local news columns from Anaconda, Billings, Bozeman, Butte, Great Falls, Havre, and Seattle.

4247. Helena REPORTER. s-m. 1899?-1901//?   DLC, Fl, 1900.

NEVADA

4248. Las Vegas VOICE. w. 1963+   NvHi, [O3, 1963-Je19, 1969].
      Charles I. West, pub.

NEW MEXICO

4249. Albuquerque AMERICAN. w. 1896?-
      J. M. Griffin and William H. Joyce, eds. and pubs.

4250. Albuquerque NEW age. w. 1911-1915//?
      Edward Thornton Ellsworth, ed.

4251. Albuquerque SOUTHWEST review. w. 1921-1930//.   CLU, (George P.
    Johnson Coll.) Jℓ30, 1927; NmU, 1925-1927.
      S. W. Henry, ed.

4252. Albuquerque WESTERN star. w. 1940-1941//.

4253. Las Cruces WESTERN voice. w. Jℓ, 1938-1940//.

OREGON

4254. Portland ADVOCATE. w. S3, 1903-1937//.   OrP, My5, 1923-D2, 1933.
    (film); OrU, [Jℓ27, 1906-D2, 1933] (film).
      Est. by McCants Stewart and Edward D. Cannady, ed., who was succeeded about 1932 by his widow, later Mrs. Beatrice (Cannady) Franklin.

4254a. Portland CHALLENGER. w. 195-?-   OrU, [N28, 1952-Ag7, 1953].

4255. Portland CLARION defender. w. 1953-   OrP, D16, 1965+.

4256. Portland INQUIRER. w. Jℓ12, 1944-   OrU, Jℓ12, 1944-Mr22, 1946.
    (film).

4257. Portland NEW age. w. Ap, 1896-1907//.   OrHi, Ja-Mr26, 1904.;
    OrP, [1905-1907]; OrU, [N25, 1899-My4, 1907] (film).
      Adolphus D. Griffin, ed. Contains local news columns from Everett, Seattle, Spokane, Tacoma, and Walla Walla, Wash., and Great Falls and Helena, Mont.

4258. Portland the NEWSPAPER. b-w. N13, 1969+   OrP, N13, 1969+.

4259. Portland NORTHWEST clarion. w. 1944-

Newspapers

Oregon (cont.)

4260. Portland NORTHWEST defender. w. Ja25, 1962–S15, 1965//.   OrP,
       [Ja25, 1962–S15, 1965//].

4261. Portland OBSERVER. w. 1901?–1903//?

4262. Portland OBSERVER. w. 1943?–195–?//   OrU, [Je29, 1943–Jℓ, 1950]
       (film).
           Sometimes issued as the Portland People's observer.

4262a. Portland OBSERVER. w. 1970+   OrU, [01, 1970+].
           Alfred L. Henderson, ed. and pub.

4263. Portland OREGON advance times. w. F1, 1968–N7, 1968//.   OrP,
       Complete.

4263a. Portland OREGON mirror. w. 196–?–   OrU, [Mr21–Je27, 1962] (film).

4263b. Portland PORTLAND observer. w. D16, 1938–1950//.   OrHi, [1938–1950];
       OrP, Complete. (film); OrU, [D16, 1938–My25, 1939] (film).

4264. Portland TIMES. w. 1909–1924//.
           Founded by William J. McLemore – San Francisco Western appeal, Oct.
       5, 1921, p. 2, col. 1. J. A. Merriman, ed. before 1922.

UTAH

4265. Ogden EAGLE. s–m, w. 1946–1947//.

4266. Salt Lake City BROADAXE. Ag3, 1895–1931//.
           Julius F. Taylor, ed. Removed to Chicago in 1897. Title varies:
       Salt Lake City broad ax [sic].

4267. Salt Lake City TRI–CITY oracle. w. 1902–1903//.

4268. Salt Lake City UTAH plain dealer. w. 1895–1909//.
           William W. Taylor, ed. A biographical account of James Finley Wilson
       in Who's who in colored America (1929 ed.) credits Wilson and W. L. [sic]
       Taylor as having founded the paper.

WASHINGTON

4269. Everett RISING sun. w. 191–?–

4270. Seattle AFRO–AMERICAN journal. w. 1967+

4271. Seattle BEE. w. 189–?–1900//.
           Daniel Webster Griffin, ed.

4272. Seattle BEE. w. Ja, 1906–
           Walter Griffin, ed.

Newspapers

<u>Washington</u> (cont.)

4273. Seattle BUILDER. w.   -1954//.

4274. Seattle CAYTON'S weekly. w. 1916-1921//.   Wa, Jℓ14, 1917-D18,
    1920; F-Mr, 1921; WaU, [Jℓ, 1917-Mr, 1921] (film).
        Became Cayton's monthly in F, 1921.
        Horace R. Cayton, ed.

4275. Seattle FACTS. w. 1962+   WaU, 1962+.
        Sometimes pub. as the Seattle Facts news. Also pub. a Tacoma
    edition. Fitzgerald Beaver, ed. and pub.

4275a. Seattle MEDIUM. w. 1970-
        Christopher H. Bennett, ed. and pub.

4276. Seattle NORTHWEST enterprise. w. 1920?-1962//?   CU, Ja14-Ap22,
    My6, 27-Je3, S23, 1927; Wa, F, 1937-D, 1952; WaPS, 08, 1926; 1927+;
    WaU, Je15, 1933-Ap4, 1952. (film).
        Pub. as the Seattle Enterprise, 1920-30. William H. Wilson, ed.
    1920; C. R. Anderson, ed. 1937-38; J. O. Lewis, ed. 1939-40; E. I.
    Robinson, ed. and pub. 1941-50; Martin Phillips, pub. 1951.

4277. Seattle NORTHWEST herald. w. 1943-1946//.   WaU, Ja2-D25, 1945.

4278. Seattle NORTHWEST illuminator. w. 1898-
        George E. Watkins, ed.

4279. Seattle OBSERVER. w. 1964-1966//.   WaU, Mr-D, 1964.

4280. Seattle PACIFIC leader. w? 195-?-   WaU, Ja, 1954; N, 1956.

4281. Seattle PROGRESSIVE herald. w, m. 1933-   WaU, Mr, N, 1933.

4282. Seattle PUGET sound observer. m, w. 1954?-1966//.   WaU, S-O, 1954;
    Mr, 1957-D, 1958.

4283. Seattle REPUBLICAN. w. F26, 1894-1917//?   DLC, Ja19, 1900; Wa,
    [Ja4, 1896-D27, 1907] (film) Ja3, 1908-Ja, 1909; Je25, 1909-My2, 1913.
    (newsprint); WaU, [Ja4, 1896-D27, 1907].
        Horace Roscoe Cayton, ed.; Susie (Revels) Cayton, associate ed.
    Contains local news columns from Roslyn and Spokane.

4284. _____. The Seattle Republican greater Seattle ed. [Seattle, 1903].
    28 p. illus., ports., map. v. 10, no. 28, Dec. 25, 1903. DLC.

4285. _____. Northwest Negro progress number. Seattle, 1907. 78 p.
    illus., ports.
        A special souvenir edition advertised in the Seattle <u>Republican</u>,
    Nov.-Dec., 1907.

Newspapers

Washington (cont.)

4286. Seattle SEARCHLIGHT. w. Jℓ, 1905-1925//? WaS, [My, 1919-1920].
       Editors included Shepard S. Freeman, Samuel Brown, Joseph A. Clark,
   Wesley C. Peoples, and Samuel P. De Bow.

4287. Seattle STANDARD. w. 1891-1902//.
       Britain Oxendine, Horace Roscoe Cayton, and I. Israel Walker, eds.
   Title varies: Seattle Washington standard.

4288. Seattle TRUMPET. m. 1966+

4289. Seattle WESTERN sun. w. 1898-1900//.

4290. Seattle WORLD. w. 1898-1903//. DLC, Ja4, 1899.
       Daniel Webster Griffin, ed.

4291. Spokane CITIZEN. w. 1908-1913//.
       Charles S. Parker and Charles S. Barrows, eds. and pubs.

4292. Spokane FORUM. m. 1908-1912//.

4293. Spokane NORTHWEST echo. w. 1896?-
       A. D. Griffin and C. A. Lucas, eds.

4294. Spokane NORTHWEST review-bulletin. b-w. 1936-

4295. Spokane STAR. w. Ap12, 1946-

4296. Spokane VOICE of the west. w. 1913?-1915//?

4297. Tacoma Sunday morning ECHO. w. 1907-1912//?
       Gustave B. Aldrich, ed. A religious publication.

4298. Tacoma FORUM. w. Jℓ, 1903-1920//? Wa, Ap, 1907-1915; WaT, Ja,
   1904; D22, 1906; Ap6, 1907-D25, 1915.
       John H., and Ella E. Ryan, eds.

4299. Tacoma JOURNAL reporter. w. Je30, 1967+ WaT, Je30, 1967+.
       Follows the Tacoma REPORTER.

4300. Tacoma PACIFIC northwest review. s-m. 1936?-1949//?
       George M. Francis, pub.

4301. Tacoma REPORTER. w. Je17, 1966-Je23-1967//. WaT, Complete.
       Followed by the Tacoma JOURNAL reporter.

MISCELLANEOUS

4302. Pittsburgh, Pa. COURIER. w. 1910- CHi, Jℓ3, 1943; Ja12, 1946.
       Published a Pacific coast ed. during World war II and to 195-?
   Contains local news columns from Berkeley, Denver, Ogden, and probably
   other cities.

Index

Pagination in underlined type reflects major subject headings in
  this bibliography.
The State designation is not used after any California place name
  nor is it used after place names of obvious location, e.g.,
  Albuquerque, Denver, Seattle, etc.
Individual titles shown in the Periodicals and in the Newspapers
  sections are not separately listed in the index.

A

Abajian, James de T., 4014
Abbott, Lenwood, 932, 934
Abila: Old folks home of the
  Western Baptist assoc., 3218
Ablon, Joan, 2990
Abner, E. W. D., 3508
Abnormal children: education, 1744
Abolition movement, 3430-56 passim
Abraham Lincoln high school, San
  Francisco, 839
Abrams, Charles, 2998
Abramson, Doris E., 2514
Acker, Cain, 3188
Adams, Ann, 3187
Adams, Ben, 2956
Adams, E. L. (Monrovia, 1908), 3194
Adams, Elizabeth Laura: auto-
  biography, 275-77
Adams, John Quincy (Los Angeles),
  1301
Adams, John Quincy (U. S. Pres.),
  3430
Adams, L. Washington, 3173
Adams, Mary Elizabeth: scrapbooks,
  482
Adams, Ovid P., 565
Adams, P. E., 3194
Adams, Ron, 127
Adams, Russell L., 2298-99
Adams, Thomas, 930
Adams family: slaveholders, 3358

Adams state college, Alamosa, Colo.
  See Colorado: Adams state college.
  Alamosa.
Addison (Wallace), books, Los Angeles:
  sales catalogs, 145-49
Addresses. See Literature: essays
  and speeches; Speeches and lectures
Adelsbach, P. F., 4128
Adkins, W. B., 23, 1158
Adler, Mortimer J., 3861
Adler, Patricia, 150, 669, 2132, 2957
AD NIP party. See African descendants
  nationalist independence partition
  party
Adoff, Arnold, 2574
Adoption: laws, 2453. See also
  Children: adoption
Adult education: 486, 1708-09, 1719,
  1791
Advertising: periodicals, 2275
Aeronautical engineering, 312
Aeronautics. See Air pilots; Airplane
  industry
A. F. D. C. See Aid to families with
  dependent children
Affleck, Marilyn, 3581
Africa: art, 73-109 passim; as it
  relates to U. S., 1-22; Mashanti
  nation, 2698; migration to, 1188;
  missionary work in, 832; source
  materials on, 7, 190; U. S. In-
  formation agency, 4029. See also

Africa: (cont.)
    individual countries, e. g.,
    Angola; Liberia
African American historical and
    cultural society, San Fran-
    cisco. See San Francisco
    African American historical
    and cultural society
African bibliographic center:
    bibliography, 151
African communities league. See
    Universal Negro improvement
    assoc. and African communi-
    ties league
African descendants nationalist
    independence partition party,
    San Francisco: manifesto,
    831; publication, 3906
African Methodist Episcopal church:
    A. M. E. guide, 3884; Colorado
    conference, 3183; encyclo-
    paedia, 481; in Bakersfield,
    3175; in Cheyenne, Wyo., 3230;
    in Colusa, 3184; in Fresno,
    3185; in Marysville, 3242; in
    Sacramento, 3187; in San
    Diego, 3188; in Santa Barbara,
    3189; in Seattle, 3204;
    literature evaluation, 3279;
    Puget Sound conference, 3186;
    Southern California confer-
    ence, 3190; Western Christian
    recorder, 4041; Western star
    of Zion, 4044
--California conference: history,
    3251; proceedings, 3176-78;
    souvenir programs, 3179-80;
    Women's missionary society,
    3181-82
African Methodist Episcopal Zion
    church: in Hanford, 3191; in
    Los Angeles, 3192; in Modesto,
    3193; in Monrovia, 3194; in
    Palo Alto, 3195; Western star
    of Zion, 4044
African Methodist Episcopal Zion
    church of America, San Jose,
    3196, 3266-67
African mission and industrial
    assoc. of Los Angeles, 832
African spiritual helping hand
    undenominational national
    church, San Francisco, 3197
African studies. See Black
    studies programs

Afro-American colonization co. of
    Mexico, San Diego, 1159
Afro-American congress: letters, 891
Afro-American co-operative assoc.,
    San Francisco, 926
Afro-American cooperative cleaning and
    dyeing plant, Los Angeles, 927
Afro-American cooperative laundry co.,
    Ocean Park, 928
Afro-American council commercial co.,
    Los Angeles, 929
Afro-American council of America,
    Los Angeles, 3545
Afro-American institute, San Francisco,
    1, 556
Afro-American investment co., Watts,
    930
Afro-American league of Alameda
    county, 4143
Afro-American league of San Francisco:
    history, 833; program, 834;
    speech, 2911
Afro-American real estate assoc. and
    employment bureau of Calif.,
    Oakland, 931
Afro-American state league of Calif.:
    articles of incorporation, 835;
    first meeting, 833; Fresno meeting,
    918
Afro-American young men's Christian
    league assoc., Oakland, 3198
Agger, Robert E., 1322
Agriculture: Calif. migratory workers,
    1181a; labor, 2374, 2398-99; Negro
    incorporated aid society, 3559;
    U. S. census, 1297. See also
    Cowboys; Hides and tallow trade;
    Ranch life; and under names of
    agricultural products, e. g.,
    Cotton; Vegetable gardening; etc.
Aguirre Beltrán, Gonzalo, 2005
Aid to families with dependent
    children, 3616; Fresno county,
    3594; Madera, 3634
Aiken, Charles J., 2866
Ainsworth, Edward Maddin, 671
Air pilots, 452, 469
Air pollution, 3790
Airplane industry: Bessie Coleman
    aero news, 3899; Craftsmen aero-
    news, 3940; employment, 1910-11
Akolo, J. B., 133
Alabama: schools, 1483; Tuskegee
    institute, 1480. See also under
    individual geographical locality,

Alabama: (cont.)
e. g., Selma, Ala.
Alameda county: Council of social
planning, 2188-89; directories,
1245, 1248, 1264-65; National
assoc. for the advancement of
colored people, 3984; Negro
non-partisan league of Calif.,
2914; public welfare, 3786.
See also San Francisco bay
area
Alameda county colored league of
women voters, 2902a
Alameda county human relations
commission newsletter, Oakland,
3886
Alancraig, Helen Smith, 2133
Alaska, 3859; description (1903),
3840; historic sites, 2047;
newspaper, 4049; Tootsie Wade,
307
Albany: newspaper, 4062
Alberga, Aurelius P., 3552
Albina corp., Portland, Ore., 457
Albrier, Frances, 3853
Albritton, Theodore, 971
Albuquerque: biographies of
residents, 310, 2330; civil
rights, 1094; National assoc.
for the advancement of
colored people, 653; news-
papers, 4249-52; politics,
2947
Alcoholics anonymous, Northern
Calif. assoc. of, 520a
Aldebaran (pseud.) See Byer,
Alderman P.
Aldrich, Gustave B., 2591, 4297
Alex, Nicholas, 2427
Alexander, A. J., 3488
Alexander, Charles, 29-30, 278,
4084
Alexander, E. Pat, 4093
Alexander, Emmet Gerald, 1471
Alexander, Frank A., 1174
Alexander, Horace, 3540
Alexander, James Beauchamp, 1230
Alexander, James Hanks: 1888
manuscript itinerary, 483
Alexander, James M., 929, 3545,
4107
Alexander, James Milo: papers,
483
Alexander, Ruth, 1574
Alexander, S., 4093

Alexander, Titus, 524, 946, 3889;
papers, 483
Alfred, George, 3457
Ali, Nathanael, 2687
Al Kitab Sudan publications, Fresno,
2336, 2731-32
Allen, A. L. (Reno), 936
Allen, A. L. (San Diego), 1175-76
Allen, Claude O., 4138
Allen, Derotha Fields, 3582
Allen, Gary, 672, 836-37
Allen, George R., 3199
Allen, Kring, 3200
Allen, La Mar, 1615
Allen, M. D., 1159, 1175-76
Allen (Richard) news service,
Los Angeles, 2295
Allen, Robert Lee, 1016
Allen temple Baptist church,
Oakland, 3201
Allensworth, Allen: biographical
accounts, 422, 474-75; biography,
278
Allensworth, Eva B. See Skanks, Mrs.
Harrie Byron (Eva B. Allensworth)
Allensworth, 1160-61; description
(1912), 1213; history, 1182;
land co., 1200-02; local news
columns, 4063, 4080, 4099, 4146,
4206; state historic park plans,
1169, 2030; water supply, 1209.
See also Historic sites
Allensworth city water co., 932
Allensworth land co., 933
Allensworth rural water co., 934
Alston, Charles, 127
Alta California (province): ethnic
groups (1793), 2005; governor's
biography, 413; Presidio of San
Francisco, 2096; residents become
U. S. citizens, 2024; U. S. con-
sul's letters, 418
Alta California bookstore, Albany:
sales catalog, 152
Altamirano, Justo, 2096
Altman, Robert A., 1631
Altrocchi, Mrs. Rudolph (Julia Cooley),
2688
Alves, Randall Paul, 2134
Amador county: petitions of residents,
1046, 1052
Amdur, Reuel Seeman, 2135
A. M. E. guide, Los Angeles, 3884
American and foreign anti-slavery
society, 3342

American assoc. of university
    professors: Univ. of Ore.,
    1616
American civil liberties union:
    Berkeley, 2448; Northern
    Calif., 1017-18; Southern
    Calif., 673, 838, 1323, 3999
American civil liberties union-
    news, San Francisco, 3888
American council of learned so-
    cieties: Committee on Negro
    studies, 205
American council on education:
    Denver meeting (1951), 1629
American council on race relations,
    2461, 2959
American criterion, San Francisco,
    3889
American freedman's union com-
    mission: San Francisco
    meeting, 2006
American Jewish congress: Calif.
    commission on law and social
    action, 2136
American missionary assoc.:
    archives, 2007; race rela-
    tions program, 2384
American nationalist,
    Inglewood, 3141
American oil co., 2008-09
American river college library,
    Sacramento: library
    holdings, 153
American woodmen, 2864, 3508-09,
    3890, 4048
Ametjian, Armistre, 1510
Amoda, John Moyibi, 2960
Amos, Elenora, 3481
Amos, Emma, 133
Anaclerio, Carl Ray, 3636
Anaconda, Mont.: local news
    columns, 4243, 4246
Anderson, Bernard E., 1832-33
Anderson, Chester H., 2273
Anderson, Clarence R., 4276
Anderson, Donald George, 1324
Anderson, E. L., 3141
Anderson, Eddie "Rochester," 961
Anderson, F. T., 4175
Anderson, Fred, 3539
Anderson, Garland, 364, 1948-49,
    1968, 2514, 2539, 2554,
    3202-03; letter, 528
Anderson, George C., 4049
Anderson, Henry L., 2592

Anderson, James, 3766
Anderson, Jervis, 566
Anderson, Lennie, 3898
Anderson, M. E., 3559
Anderson, M. Margaret, 1696
Anderson, Marian, 3873
Anderson, Myrtle Bernice, 2961
Anderson, Orval, 3469
Anderson, P. J., 929
Anderson, Peter, 4191
Anderson, Rosa Claudette: autobiog-
    raphy, 279
Anderson, Talmadge, 935
Anderson, Wilhelmina, 994
Anderson, William C., 2593
Anderson, Winslow, 231
Andrews, Benny, 108, 129
Andrews, Donald, 2489
Andrews, J. H., 832
Andrews, Mrs. J. H., 832
Angel, Myron, 2010-12
Angelou, Maya: autobiography, 280
Angola, 2, 11-16
Ankrum, Charles, 3175
Ante, Los Angeles, 2557, 3891
Anthony, Earl Leon, 567, 4028
Anthropology, 3601, 3726, 3730, 3780a,
    3843-45
Appomattox club of Berkeley, 3458
Apprenticeships: labor, 1141
Aptheker, Herbert, 674, 2013
Arbeiter, Solomon, 2354
Archbald, John, 1058
Archibald, Katherine, 2355
Architects: Watts, 676. See also
    Williams, Paul Revere
Archives. See Manuscripts
Arithmetic. See Mathematics
Arizona: census (1870-80), 1299;
    early exploration, 374, 432, 449,
    470, 2060, 2064-65, 2082, 2326-27,
    2346; economic conditions, 3006;
    Freemasons, 3513; historic sites,
    2047; laws, statutes, etc., 2467-
    67a; lumber industry, 1889; news-
    papers, 4050-61; race relations,
    3001; steel industry, 1923; U. S.
    army in, 23-66 passim; university,
    1623; Wham robbery, Howard county,
    45. See also Southwest
--Fort Huachuca: black soldiers at,
    65; local news columns, 4081;
    nurses at, 65; USO shows, 40;
    WAC's experiences, 51
--public schools, 1735; adult, 1709;

public schools (cont.)
   Maricopa county, 1717;
   primary, 1540; segregation,
   1325, 1467
Arizona council for civic unity,
   2996, 3894; school study,
   1325
Arkansas: schools, 1615
Arkin, David, 2300
Arlen, David, 1986
Armed services, 23-68, 3165; Black
   Muslims in, 564; Civil war
   equality, 1096; Colored military social club, San Francisco, 3550; Colored veterans
   service club, San Francisco,
   3552; Custer's interpreter,
   329, 381; Fort Du Chesne,
   Utah, 483; Fort Harrison,
   Mont. Knocker, 4244; Fort
   Washakie, Wyo., 483; Luke air
   force base, Phoenix, 3472;
   memoirs of Henry Ossian
   Flipper, 336; Ninth cavalry,
   27, 483, 2065; Tenth cavalry,
   27, 2065, 2636; tests, 1915;
   Twenty-fifth infantry, 4050;
   Veterans of foreign wars of
   the U. S., 3567. See also
   Civil war; Fort Huachuca,
   Ariz.; Modoc war; U. S. Army;
   War with Mexico; World war I;
   World war II
Armour, Clarence A., 2370
Armstrong, Calvin: interview,
   484
Armstrong, Hubert C., 1671
Armstrong, Vernon Lee, 1326
Arnold, Ralph, 133
Arriaga, Mary, 3583
Arrowhead allied arts council, 69
Art, 69-144, 3848; bibliography,
   247; Black graphics inter-
   national, a magazine of the
   arts in the third world,
   3905; Calif. state capitol
   mural, 3014; cartoons, 290;
   exhibit catalogs, 69-110
   passim; exhibits, 2288;
   Frederic Remington with 10th
   cavalry, 53-54; primary and
   pre-school, 1571; Watts
   towers, 789, 2335
Artists: works in permanent
   collections, 118-44

Art-west associated/north, inc.:
   exhibit catalog, 103
Arvey, Verna. See Still, Mrs. William
   Grant (Verna Arvey)
Asbury, Joseph L., 4128
Ashanti publications, Pasadena, 4032
Ashberry, Nettie J.: papers, 485
Ashburne, Alexander P., 941
Ashe, Arthur: biography, 2342
Ashley, William H., 2014
Asia, Benjamin S., 2137
Asilomar: writers' conference, 2526
Askey, Dennis, 4029
Assembly club, San Francisco, 3923
Associated railway employees of
   Calif., Oakland, 2356-57
Association for the protection of
   American rights, Bell, 3149
Association for the study of Negro
   life and history: Los Angeles
   branch, 2015
Athletics. See Sports
Atkins, James A., 2963; papers (1920-
   68), 486, 4213
Atkinson, Jean, 3485
Atlanta, Ga.: Clark college, 1478
Attaway, H., 972
Attitude, 3163, 3608
Atwood, Albert, 3204
Atwood, Ethel, 2915
Aurbach, Joseph, 2404
Austin, Edith M., 4020
Austin, Lettie Jane, 1472
Austin, W. M., 4135
Australia: gold rush, 1204
Autobiographies, 279-476 passim, 486;
   bibliography, 194. For auto-
   biographies connected with indi-
   vidual fields of interest, see
   under appropriate subject headings,
   e. g., Medicine; Music; etc.
Automobiles: Colored chauffeurs
   assoc. of Los Angeles, 2370;
   Colored east bay auto workers
   assoc., Oakland, 2371; headlight
   illumination, 3837; San Francisco
   colored chauffeurs assoc., 3566;
   U. S. tour, 3881
Avatom, C. E., 3194
Avery, Emma, 3460
Aviation. See Air pilots; Airplane
   industry
Axthelm, Pete, 3674
Ayer, John Edwin, 282
Ayers, James J., 1058

B

Babow, Irving Paul, 1019–22
Bacon, Jacob, 1058
Badal, Alden W., 1712
Baer, Howard, 2594
Bagley, Julian Elihu, 2595–98
Bailey, Calvin: biographical
    account, 463
Bailey, Edward A., 3853
Bailey, J., 2139
Bailey, Lester P., 3681
Bailey, Martha, 2472
Bailey, Richard C., 406
Bailey, William, 1023
Baird, Newton D., 154
Baja California: land co., 963
Baker, Barbara, 226
Baker, Charles, 972
Baker, Curtis Lee, 2925
Baker, Edwin D., Sr., 2925
Baker, George. See Divine, Morgan
    J. (assumed name)
Bakers and bakeries, 563. See also
    Cookery; Dining car cooks and
    waiters
Bakersfield: African Methodist Epis-
    copal church, 3175; City council,
    2874; Colored league of women
    voters, 2902a; cotton workers'
    unionization, 2360; directory,
    1267; Hiram club, 2563; Ku
    klux klan, 3099; local news
    columns, 4080–81, 4146, 4193–94,
    4199, 4206; newspapers, 4063–65;
    Prince Hall no. 5 credit union,
    983; race relations, 3158; urban
    life, 3820; women's clubs, 3574
Bakersfield Colored citizen, 524
Bakewell, Dennis C., 163–64
Baldwin, James, 2666
Baldwin, Louis Fremont, 2758–59,
    2782, 3889
Baldwin, Roger Sherman, 3343–44
Ball, James Presley, Jr., 4245
Ball, John Dudley, 2599–2601
Ball, Joseph W., 928
Ball, N. A. Haven, 1057
Ballard, Claudius, 2763
Ballard, J., 3458
Ballard, P. F., 3264
Balliett, Whitney, 2799
Bancroft, Hubert Howe, 450–51
B. A. N. D. See Bay area neighbor-
    hood development foundation

Banfield, Edward, 3003
Bank of America, San Francisco, 2463;
    employment practices, 1834, 1852,
    1908
Banks, Edward, 4054
Banks, Mrs. Edward (Eloise L. H.),
    4054
Banks, Goler V., 4042
Banks, Henry A., 839
Banks, J. C., 4135
Banks, Robert: biographical account,
    460–61
Banks, Roger W., 2947
Banks, Walden, 952
Banks and banking: Bank of America,
    San Francisco, 1834, 1852, 1908,
    2463; employment, 1939; Ethiopia
    co-operative business assoc.,
    Oakland, 952; Family savings and
    loan assoc., Los Angeles, 81, 3955;
    home mortgages, 2222; Trans-bay
    federal savings and loan assoc.,
    San Francisco, 991. See also
    Credit unions
Banner, Warren M., 3682
Banning, Magnolia Lowe, 1672
Baptists: church directory, 3273;
    convention (1860), 3209; General
    Baptist assoc., 3210; in Calif.,
    3272, 3287; Independent Negro
    Baptist churches of Montana, 3273;
    in Northwest, 3282; National con-
    ventions, 3211–12, 3280; National
    Sunday school and Baptist training
    union conference, 3213–14; National
    united church ushers assoc. of
    America, 3290; Northern Calif.
    Baptist state convention, 3276,
    3335–36; Oregon, 3345–48; St. John's
    district assoc. of northern Calif.,
    3215; Sunday school publishing
    board, 3216; Washington Baptist
    state convention, 3273; Western
    Baptist assoc., 3217–19; Western
    Baptist state convention of Colo-
    rado, 3273. See also under geo-
    graphical locality, e.g., San Fran-
    cisco: Third Baptist church;
    Pasadena: Baptist church; etc.
--Calif. state conventions: official
    publication, 3986; proceedings,
    3205; programs, 3206, 3315; Union
    usher board, 3207; Young people's
    dept., 3208
Barankin, Joseph Paul, 2405

Barbadoes, Frederick G., 973, 1039, 2270, 2870; eulogy, 506

Barbados: Codrington plantation, 998, 1010; history, 1006
Barbelle, Albert, 2852
Barber, John Augustus, 3557
Barbour, J. Pius, 583
Barbour, W. Miller, 3683–84
Bard, Floyd C., 3165
Barnes, Medill McCormick, 1327
Barnes, Shirley M., 2140
Barnett, Don, 2
Barnett, Larry D., 2783
Barnett, Powell S., 4001; reminiscences, 487
Barnett, Wilhelmina Irene, 2264
Barnhill, Donna, 2265
Baron, Harold, 3042
Barr, Roberta Byrd, 399
Barrett, Enoch H., 835, 951, 3545
Barrett, Samuel, 840–44
Barrett, William Edmund, 2602
Barrington plaza corp., Los Angeles, 2227–28
Barrow, Joe Louis, 3654
Barrow, William, 24
Barrows, Charles S., 4291
Barrows vs. Jackson, 2252
Barth, Ernest A. T., 2141, 2224
Barthé, Richmond, 127, 3873
Bartlett, Virginia Stivers, 283
Bartling, Peter Ralph, 1024
Barton, C. B., 3175
Barton, Rebecca (Chalmers), 452
Baruch, Dorothy (Walter), 2142, 2964
Baruch, Ruth-Marion, 99, 570
Bascom, William, 73
Baseball. See Sports
Basey, Jill Anne, 2515
Baskervill, Lewis A., 3984
Baskett, Fritz, 4125
Bass, Joseph Blackburn, 946, 1236, 2271–72, 4080, 4171, 4246
Bass, Mrs. Joseph Blackburn (Charlotta A. Spears), 2017, 2266, 2271–72, 2288, 3853, 4080, 4171
Bassett, James, 2279
Batcheller, Helen M., 2867
Bates, Jack Ward, 3430
Batie, Henry, 929
Batteau, Elgie Adelaide, 25
Battista, Daniel Joseph, 1025
Battu, Zoe A., 284

Batty, Joseph, 2965
Bay area. See San Francisco bay area
Bay area council against discrimination, San Francisco, 1026, 3112, 3993
Bay area crusade, 3505
Bay area neighborhood development foundation, 3730
Bay area rapid transit district, 2359, 2388
Bay area studio/printing co., Oakland, 3936
Bay area urban league, 1835
Bay cities investment co., Oakland, 936
Bayley, David H., 2428
Baylor, James E., 2875
Bazaar, Mona, 571, 846
Beach, Mary G., 2705, 2724, 2727
Beal, I., 835
Beals, Henry Channing, 1058
Bean, Benjamin W., 1027
Bean, Edwin F., 1237
Bean, Walton Elbert, 2016
Beane, Junior, 981
Beane, Samuel Miller, 2272
Bearden, Romare, 120
Beasley, Delilah Leontium, 242, 2017–19, 2902a, 3349, 3364; biographical accounts, 317, 458; correspondence, 488
Beasley, John Aaron, 3584
Beasley, Miles, 958
Beattie, George William, 453–54
Beauty culture. See Cosmetics
Beaver, Fitzgerald, 3966, 4275
Beaver, Gene Marvin, 2966
Beavers, Louise, 1950; biographical account, 436
Beck, Nicholas, 650
Beck, Robert, 2603
Becker, William L., 1846
Beckett, Paul, 3029
Beckett, W. Warner, 3990
Beckford, Felix, 914
Beckwourth, James Pierson, 178, 297, 332, 362, 978, 2014, 2041, 2065; autobiography, 285; biographical accounts, 344, 357, 380, 393, 470, 2326–27; biographies, 396, 420, 2312, 2329; incident, 322–23
Beckwourth pass, 297
Becnel, Milton Joseph, 1673
Bee, John C., Jr., 4034
Beebe memorial Christian Methodist

Beebe (cont.)
    Episcopal church, Oakland, 3220
Beecher, John, 2689-90
Beeks, David, 3302
Beeks, Lewis K., 927, 946, 2271
Behavior. See Etiquette
Belafonte, Harold (Harry), 113-14,
    1995
Belanger, Laurence L., 1617
Belasco, David, 1994
Belden, David, 1055
Belden, Rachel: biographical
    account, 462
Belknap, George Nicholas, 155
Bell, Horace, 286, 2020
Bell, Howard Holman, 1028-29, 2021
Bell, James Madison: biographical
    account, 455; poems, 2691-95
Bell, Marcus A., 996, 1045, 3403
Bell, Philip Alexander, 2870, 4183,
    4191; biographical accounts,
    460-61, 2287
Bell, S. C., 3458
Bell, Thomas, 355
Bell, Wendell, 997
Bell, William Y., Jr., 2959
Bell: Association for the protec-
    tion of American rights, 3149
Beller, Jack, 3350
Bellesfield, S. S., 4132
Bellevue, Wash.: account of
    pioneer, 407
Bellow, Cleveland, 133
Bellson, Ford, 2360-61
Bendix, Reinhard, 3756
Benedict, Kirby, 3386
Benevolent societies, 3545-68 passim;
    Old folks home of the Western
    Baptist assoc., Abila, 3218.
    See also Community service organ-
    izations; Social clubs
Benjamin, Robert Charles O'Hara,
    288, 1030, 2575, 3827, 4104,
    4198; biographical accounts,
    287, 474-75
Benjamin, Zola, 3940
Bennett, Christopher H., 4275a
Bennett, Henry, 3351
Bennett, J. Harry, 998
Bennett, Lynne, 3910
Bennett, Robert, 2370
Benson, D. F., 4053
Benson, J. J., 3828
Benton, Thomas Hart, 3352
Bergman, G. M., 289

Bergman, Mort N., 2022
Bergman, Peter M., 2022
Berkeley, Ellen P., 676
Berkeley: American civil liberties
    union, 2448; Appomattox club, 3458;
    Berkeley high school, 2576; black
    power rally, 836; Brotherhood of
    sleeping car porters, 2397;
    Citizens' committee to study dis-
    crimination in housing, 2143-44;
    Conference on law enforcement and
    racial and cultural tensions, 2441;
    Congress of racial equality, 2117,
    3927; Council of social planning,
    1877; directory, 1267; East bay
    cities business league, 3969a,
    economic conditions, 3748;
    elections (1963), 2159; employment,
    3825; Fire dept., 1836; Freemasons,
    3516; housing, 2143-44, 2159, 2164,
    2175, 3825; local news columns,
    4302; Longfellow elementary school,
    2352; Nation of Islam (Black
    Muslims), 3916; National assoc. for
    the advancement of colored people,
    659; newspaper, 4066;
    Personnel dept. employment study,
    1836; Police dept., 1836, 2482;
    politics, 2164; race relations,
    2164; riots, 837, 890; St. Paul
    African Methodist Episcopal church,
    3300-01; unemployment, 1877, 1879,
    1947; urban life, 3738; Workshop
    on change in an interracial com-
    munity, 3825; Workshop on wasted
    manpower, 1947; Young socialist
    alliance, 2955. See also Alameda
    county; California: University.
    Berkeley; San Francisco bay area
--Public schools, 1674, 1756, 3825;
    buildings, 1695; primary and pre-
    school, 1523; secondary, 1597;
    segregation, 1328-36, 1369-70,
    1374, 1379, 1382-83, 1388, 1402-03,
    1427, 1433, 1443, 1450, 1452-55,
    1457, 1470
Berkeley bible and health chautauqua,
    Berkeley, 3221
Berkeley community welfare commission,
    3825
Berkeley conference on black power and
    its challenges, 847, 849
Berkeley interracial committee, 2023
Berkes, Ross N., 3
Berkley, Ruby. See Goodwin, Ruby
    (Berkley)

Berkley, Thomas L., 966, 2923, 4066
Bernard, William S., 2967
Bernstein, Irving, 1841–42
Bernstein, Saul, 848
Berrigan, Philip F., 572
Berry, Edwin C., 1675, 3102, 3585
Berry, George, 2102
Berry, Lanny, 1680
Berwanger, Eugene Harley, 1031, 3353–55
Beth Eden Baptist church, Oakland, 3222–26, 3896, 3930
Bethel African Methodist Episcopal church, San Francisco, 3177, 3227, 3303
Better, Norman Michael, 1837
Beulah, Calif. See Home for aged and infirm colored people of Calif., Oakland
Bevel, James, 849
Beverley, Stanley Y., 980
Bianchi, Eugene C., 677
Bibb, Eloise A. See Thompson, Mrs. Noah Davis (Eloise A. Bibb)
Bible, 3199; slavery in, 3452
Bibliographies, 7, 98, 145–274, 2240, 2324, 3102
Bidleman, Joseph B., 1058
Bigelow, John, 26
Biggers, John, 2318
Biggs, Peter, 286, 2020, 2063, 2072, 2100–02
Biggs, Susan D., 994
Billings, Frederick, 1058; speech, 2006
Billings, Mont.: local news columns, 4245, 4246
Billingsley, Amy Tate, 3586–87
Billingsley, Andrew, 1618, 3586–87, 3685
Bimini baths, Los Angeles, 1109
Binder, Carol Timberlake, 1032
Binum, Edmington: family, 2077
Biographies, 275–481, 486, 3760, 3848; bibliography, 194. For biographies connected with in- dividual fields of interest, see under appropriate subject headings, e.g., Medicine; Music; etc.
Birch (John) society, 2440
Birmingham, Ala., 817
"Birth of a nation." See Motion pictures
Bjorklund, Jaunita H., 1302

Bjorklund, Lorence F., 2303
Black, Austin, 2696
Black, John C., 3266
Black achievement research, pubs., Oakland, 3900
"Black Billy Sunday." See McPherson, J. Gordon
Black book productions, San Diego, 2494, 2560
Black community research and communi- cation project, San Francisco, 4013
"Black Harris." See Harris, Moses
Black madonna writers' lab, San Fran- cisco college for women, 2490
"Black Mary." See Fields, Mary
Black movement, 556–925, 762, 2945, 3545; and education, 1679; and religion, 3283; journalistic treat- ment, 2277; periodical publications, 3887–4046 passim; relations with business, 3088. See also Benevo- lent societies; Pan-Africanism; Social clubs
Black Muslims. See Nation of Islam
Black panther party, 565–639; photo- graphs by Pirkle Jones, 99, 570; program, 852; publications, 3907– 09
"Black Patti." See Jones, Sissieretta
Black perspective for the Los Angeles black congress: publication, 3918
"Black steward." See Light, Allen B.
Black student unions, 639a–49, 1643, 1657, 2719; publications, 3903–04, 3996
Black studies programs: colleges and universities, 4, 1618, 1626, 1639, 1643, 1657, 1659, 1669; curricula, 640, 1653, 1824–25; handbook, 1720–21; in San Diego, 1815; Journal of black studies, 3971; Nation of Islam, 1742; primary schools, 1556; secondary schools, 1592, 1599; syllabus, 1716. See also History: teaching of
Black world foundation: publication, 3913
Blackman's art gallery, San Francisco, 72
Blackmar, Delos, 2347
Blackmon, Bernard H., 1473
Blackwell, Tillie N., 3686
Blake, Charles Thompson, 1058

Blake, Dudley Arthur, 1511
Blake, J. Herman, 2969
Blake, John R., 3556
Blake, William H., 2278, 4193
Blakely, Karen B., 2406
Blank, Dennis M., 290
Blank, Owen, 3042
Blankenship, Georgiana (Mitchell), 291
Blauner, Robert, 679, 714, 1838
Blevins, Clifton, 850
Bliss, Hilde Scheuer, 2970
Block, Lillian, 2802
Bloom, Jack M., 3228
Bloomer, Hiram G., 1058
Blossom, Herbert Henry, 1619
Blount, George Winfield, 1033
Blount, Mildred Eliza, 423; biographical account, 463
Blue, Daniel, 3187, 3356
Blythe: local news columns, 4081
B'nai B'rith. Anti-defamation league: Southern Calif. regional office, 2429
Board of economic and youth opportunities agency of greater Los Angeles, 2904
Bogardus, Emory Stephen, 2971
Boghossian, Alexander, 127
Boice, Carl, 2362
Boise, Ida.: local news columns, 4243
Bolivar, Simon, 1004
Bolivar, William T., 992
Bolmer, F. H., 3291
Bolner, James, 1676
Bolton, Ina Alexander, 1620
Bolton, Barron & co., San Francisco, 1058
Bond, Horace Mann, 1034
Bond, J. Max, 3588, 3687
Bond, Julian, 634
Bond, Marjorie H., 1677
Bond, Phyllis M., 2972
Bonham, Frank, 2604-05
Bonjean, Charles M., 2973
Bonner, Thomas D., 285
Bonpane, Father, 2958
Bontemps, Arna Wendell, 292-93, 2301, 2606, 3479, 3829-30
Book stores. See Addison (Wallace), books, Los Angeles; Alta California bookstore, Albany; Universal books, Hollywood
Booker T. luncheon club, Richmond, 937

Booker T. mothers' club, San Francisco, 3460
Booker T. Washington apts., Los Angeles, 938
Booker T. Washington community service center, San Francisco, 540a, 3461-65
Booker T. Washington country club, San Francisco, 3546
Booker T. Washington memorial society, Fresno, 3547
Booker T. Washington relief society, San Francisco, 3466, 3473
Bookertee film co., Los Angeles, 939, 1976
Boone, F. Theressa, 1621
Booth, Mary A., 3187
Booth, Robert E., 156
Booze, Eugene Parker, 4219
Borland, Virginia, 3467
Borthwick, J. D., 2974-77
Boskin, Joseph, 680-82, 851, 896, 3431
Bosqui, Edward, 1058
Boulder county, Colo.: mining, 517
Boulder dam: employment discrimination, 1888, 1909
Bowdon, John, 2187
Bowen, Don R., 881
Bowers (Charles H.) memorial museum, Santa Ana: art holdings, 124
Bowers, George B., 3831
Bowles, J. D., 3545
Bowlin, Brandon Alexander Theophilus, 2288
Bowling: discrimination, 1095
Bowman, John B., 3192
Bowser, Frederick Park, 999
Boxing: account of Isaac Isaacs, 294. See also Sports
Boy scouts of America, Phoenix, 3472
Boyar, Burt, 1959
Boyar, Jane, 1959
Boyd, G. F., 1512
Boyd, Malcolm, 683
Boyd, O. L., 4238, 4240
Boyd, Willis Dolmond, 1162
Boydston, Eleanor Ruth Hertz, 1513
Boykin, Cynthia Ann, 1622, 2800
Boykin, Leander L., 1678
Boykin, William, 3540
Boyle, Eugene J., 3114
Boyle, Sonya Steiner, 2407
Boyles, L., 2978
Bozeman, Mont.: local news columns, 4246

Bracey, John H., 852
Bracy, James, 853
Braden, Anne, 1035
Bradford, Amory, 854
Bradford, James Lovelle, 1514
Bradford, Viola, 1623
Bradley, Preston, 2241
Bradley, Thomas: mayoral campaign
   (1969), 2869, 2885, 2888,
   2889a, 2900-01, 2935-37
Braithwaite, William Stanley,
   2720
Branch, Harrison, 133
Brand, Lillian, 1515
Brandon, Brumsic, 133
Branham, Ethel, 3688
Brann, James, 1624
Branson, Helen Kitchen, 2760
Bransten, Tommy, 2979
Branton, Leo, Jr., 1989
Brathwaite, Yvonne W. See
   Burke, Yvonne W. (Brathwaite)
Brawley, Benjamin Griffith, 455
Bray, H. Franklin, 4235
Bray, Thomas: biography, 382
Brazear, John, 978
Brazil: slavery, 1001
Breese, Donald Hubert, 2868
Breit, Amelia, 3689
Brell, Harry, 855
Brent, John Etta, 2267
Brewer, David Leslie, 3589
Brewer, William Henry, 2024
Bridges, James Monroe, 968, 992,
   3545, 4146
Bridges, Wallace, 3185
Bridges printing co., Oakland, 3335,
   3522
Briggs, Vernon M., Jr., 2389
Brigham, Robert L., 2145
Bright, Marjorie Eloise, 2516
Brimmer, Andrew Felton, 1839
Brinker, Leola Elizabeth, 1516
Brinson, James, 3307
Briscoe, Lonnie, 2494
Brister, Iola M., 2498
Bristol, Andrew S., 3556
Bristol, Sherlock, 294
British Columbia: African Methodist
   Episcopal church (1863), 3177;
   migration to, 1186-87, 1198,
   1203; slave at Victoria, 3425
Britt, Arthur L., 132
Britton, James, 2980
Britton, Sylvester, 133

Britton, W. H., 930
Broderick, Francis L., 295-96
Brodt, John H., 1058
Bromwich, Rose Meyer, 1517
Bronson, Charles E. A., 928
Bronson, Joseph, 929
Bronson, Lewis W., 928
Brookings, O. E., 929
Brooks, Clarence A., 962
Brooks, Dudley A., 962
Brooks, Gwendolyn, 2495
Brooks, J. S., 3184
Brooks, Jacqueline, 297
Brooks, M. B., 4235
Brooks, T. L., 4099
Brophy, Anne Kathleen, 2268
Brotherhood of sleeping car porters:
   Pacific coast division, 2397;
   papers, 2363
Brotherhood, U. S. A., 1677
Broun, Heywood, 1994
Broussard, Warren L., 2921
Brown, Atkin G., 2924
Brown, B. B., 2917
Brown, Bill (Tehama county), 2473
Brown, Buber, 4109
Brown, Cecil, 2501, 2607
Brown, Charles S., 3553
Brown, Charlotte L., 1036
Brown, Clara: biography, 298
Brown, Clyde, 3567
Brown, Diana, 3187
Brown, E. H. (Fresno), 1174
Brown, E. H. (Redding), 4044
Brown, Earl, 28
Brown, Edmund G., 2476
Brown, F. J., 1238
Brown, George, 486
Brown, George (Los Angeles, 1904),
   3192
Brown, George S., 3545
Brown, Grafton Tyler, 123, 133, 143
Brown, Hattie D., 994
Brown, Jack, 2302
Brown, James E., 2269, 4204
Brown, Mrs. James E., 1036
Brown, James Nathaniel "Jimmy," 3636
Brown, James Russell, 2981
Brown, Joe, 4223
Brown, Marie D., 3910
Brown, Minta (Palmer), 1679
Brown, Paul, 2576
Brown, Paul E., 3192
Brown, R. K., 3548
Brown, Rebecca Danice, 1303

Brown, Reuben Henry, 1474
Brown, Roscoe C., 233
Brown, Samuel, 4286
Brown, Thaddeus A., 926
Brown, Tilghman, 4104
Brown, Vashti, 2302
Brown, Warren Henry, 157
Brown, William (Portland, Ore.),
    996, 3403
Brown, William (San Francisco),
    3551
Brown, William R., 3853
Brown, Willie, 2948
Brown, Y. C., 4131
Browne, John Ross, 3357
Brownell, Jean B., 158
Browning, Colleen, 2316
Browning, William H., 939
Bruce, John Edward, 2296
Brueske, Judith M., 2982
Bruff, Joseph Goldsborough,
    2025-26
Bruner, John M., 2146
Bruÿn, Kathleen, 298
Bryan, Ellis, 2983
Bryan, Melvin, 2984
Bryant, Edwin, 299
Bryant, G. E., 967
Bryant, Ira Babington, 1475
Bryant, Sam, 944
Bryce-Laporte, Roy Simón, 3432
Buchanan, O. Lee, 1547
Buck, P. D., 946
Buck, Pearl Sydenstricker), 3062
Buckbee, Edna Bryan, 300, 456
Buckley, William F., 577-78, 2869
Buckner, Eva (Carter), 2697
Buckner, Joseph, 3302
Buddin, Henry, 2102
Buddress, Loren A. N., 856
Buffalo soldiers. See Armed
    services: ninth cavalry, etc.;
    and under geographical locali-
    ties, e.g., Fort Huachuca,
    Ariz.; Fort Harrison, Mont.;
    etc.
Buford, Curtycinc J., 1518
Buford, Frederick L., 4095
Buggs, John A., 684
Building industry. See
    Construction industry
Bukunin, Mikhail Alexandrovich,
    569
Bullen, Marion Prosper, 940
Bullins, Ed , 1951, 2492, 2517-18,

2556-57, 2608-10
Bullock, James, 1680
Bullock, Paul, 685-87, 1681, 1840-42,
    3690
Bullough, Bonnie Louise, 2147-48,
    2985
Bulosan, Carl, 3991
Bunche, Ralph Johnson: autobiographi-
    cal account, 301; biography,
    2330; biographical account, 2325;
    speech, 1625
Buniff, Egbert D. N., 1000
Bunnin, Nenelle Rappoport, 2986
Bunzel, John H., 1626
Bunzel, Peter D., 2987
Burbank, David, 1058
Burbank: Lockheed aircraft corp.,
    311
Burbridge, Edward, 4119
Burch, Edward Alexander, 1843
Burch, Pauline, 2027
Burch, Samuel Townsend: family, 2027
Burckel, Christian E., 478
Burdett, H., 3185
Burdett, Samuel, 1037
Burgess, Margaret Blaine, 3691
Burke, Nelson S., 1730
Burke, William Lee, 1952
Burke, Yvonne W. (Brathwaite), 2953
Burkes, Eugene Alexander, 133
Burley, Clarence A., 4153
Burma, John Harmon, 2784-85
Burnett, Calvin, 133
Burnett, Peter Hardeman, 2028-29;
    black exclusion advocate, 1163,
    2069
Burnett, Wellington Cleveland,
    1135-36
Burns, Eugene A., 133
Burns, Robert H., 3166
Burris, Samuel D., 1045;
    biographical account, 429-30
Burroughs, Margaret, 133
Burroughs, William, 2705
Burt, McKinley, 457
Burt, Olive (Wooley), 2303
Burton, Albert Lee, 2988
Burton, Mary Lillian, 1627
Burton, Philip L.: correspondence
    (1950-62), 489
Burum, H., 2356
Busch, Niven, 2611
Bush, George Washington, 229-31, 309,
    389, 439, 442, 2116; biographical
    accounts, 282, 348, 398, 470,

Bush, George Washington (cont.)
1211; biography, 433; drama
about, 2565; family activities,
291, 352; research notes on, 544.
See also Washington, George
Bush, John S., 316
Bush, Robert L., 1519
Bush, William Owen, 316, 398
Business, 926-96, 1891, 3088, 3755;
Black business review, 3900;
census information, 1297; con-
tractors' operations, 1897;
directories, 1251, 1271-72a, 1294;
East bay cities business league,
3969a; in Watts, 775; National
Negro business league, 852,
968; Negro incorporated aid
society, Los Angeles, 3559;
Plan of action for challenging
times (PACT), San Francisco,
977, 1271, 3994. See also
Economics; Industry; Occupa-
tions; etc.
Busing. See Education:
segregation
Buskin, Martin, 1682
Buster, Benjamin, 2077
Butler, C. A., 3926
Butler, Charles E., 1955
Butler, E. B., 4214
Butler, Mrs. E. (Griffine)
(Hinden), 3484
Butler, John Harold, 1683
Butler, Oliver D., 3567
Butler, Vivian Leola, 1684
Butler, Walter Archibald, 992,
3546
Butler, William Wesley, 3198
Butte county: petition of resi-
dents, 1047; population
tables, 2089
Butte, Mont.: directory, 1236;
local news columns, 4246;
newspaper, 4243
Byer, Alderman P., 2698
Byers, W. J. J., 3198, 3462
Byrd, William H., 1045
Byrne, William S., 1240

C

Cable, George W., 2531
Cable cars, 440
Caddle, Benjamin, 1159, 1175-76
Cadoo, Foyer, 133

Cadwalader, George, 1057
Cagle, Mabelle Clair, 1575
Cahill, Edvina, 3468
Calanthe, Order of, 3534
Calapai, Lelterio, 2317
Calaveras county: Joiner family,
386; pioneers, 2077
Caldwell, Ben, 2751
Caldwell, H., 3175
Caldwell, Matilda, 3560
Caldwell, Wallace F., 1038
Caldendar of events, 2085
Calexico: local news columns, 4080
California: admission, 184, 3341-
3429 passim; airplane industry,
1911; as fiction locale, 2613,
2630, 2632, 2644, 2659, 2682-83;
Attorney-general's office, 2430,
2441; biographies of residents,
468; Bureau of criminal identification and investigation, 558;
Bureau of criminal statistics,
688; censuses, 1206, 1296-97,
1168, 1241; civil rights statutes,
1089; Civil war attitude, 3419;
Colored citizens' conventions,
1028-29, 1039-42, 2870; Colored
citizens' state executive committee, 1360, 2270; Commission on
discrimination in teacher employment, 1685-86; constitution
(1849), 2375, 3357, 3399, 3411;
Coordinating council for higher
education, 1628; Democratic state
central committee (1869), 2880;
Dept. of corrections, 2431; Dept.
of education, 1338-44, 1686-93;
Dept. of employment, 1844, 1946,
3692; Dept. of industrial relations, 2364; Dept. of justice,
1043, 2432-33, 2441, 2461; Dept.
of parks and recreation, 2030,
2989; Dept. of social welfare,
2990-91; Director of corrections,
3243; directory of northern Calif.,
1245; directory of residents
(1850-67), 1291; Division of
criminal law and enforcement, 2434;
elections (1952), 2903; Freedmen's
missionary committee, 2007; gold
rush, 1091-92, 2039, 2042-46,
2059, 2078-79, 2090-91, 2103,
2107, 2540, 2566, 2683, 2965,
2974-77; Governor's commission on
the Los Angeles riots, 689-92,

California (cont.)
707, 713-14, 719, 730, 745, 751,
768, 786-87, 795, 816, 896; historic sites, 2047; history, 2007-
2128 passim; Insurance industry
committee, 693; laws, statutes,
etc., 1044, 2467-67a; lumber
industry, 1889; migration to
Vancouver island, 1186-87, 1198,
1203; National guard, 694, 1096;
newspapers, 4062-4212; petroleum
industry, 1894; racial minorities, 3839; residents before
1848, 450-51; San Luis Obispo
state polytechnic college
library holdings, 175; State
agricultural society, 2365;
State athletic commission archives, 3638; State board of
cosmetology, 1850; State board
of medical examiners archives,
2761; state capitol building
mural, 3014; State justice
dept., 1155; State personnel
board, 1864; state prisons, 308,
540a, 2456; steel industry, 1923;
Technical advisory committee on
testing, 1865; Transportation-
employment project, Los Angeles,
3925. See also Alta California
(province); Pacific coast
--Legislature, 2069; Emancipation
proclamation resolutions, 3363;
opposes black residence, 1164-
67; petitions to, 1045-60, 2870;
ratifies 13th amendment, 3359;
reapportionment, 2897, 2931;
right of testimony bills, etc.,
1045-63
--State fair employment practice
commission, 1851-63, 1881, 1942,
2153-57; history, 1940; Los
Angeles survey, 2366-67; newsletters, 3924, 3953; Oakland
schools survey, 1694
--State library: publication,
4009
--State library. Administrative-
legislative reference service:
bibliography, 173
--State library. Law library:
housing bibliography, 174
--State univ. Fresno: library
holdings, 159
--State univ. Hayward: library

holdings, 160; Black student
union, 3914
--State univ. Long Beach: library
holdings, 161
--State univ. Los Angeles: Black
students union, 644; library
holdings, 162
--State univ. Northridge: library
holdings, 163-64; student revolt,
641
--State univ. Sacramento: Dept. of
anthropology, 3693; library
holdings, 165-66; racism symposium, 2992
--State univ. San Bernardino:
library holdings, 167-69
--State univ. San Diego: ethnic
workshop, 2993; library holdings,
170
--State univ. San Francisco, 643;
Black students union, 639b, 649,
1657, 3904; black studies program, 1626, 1657, 1659; local
news columns, 4199; student revolt, 642, 645, 647, 1632, 1635,
1637, 1646, 1657, 3294
--State univ. San Jose, 1624; art
holdings, 119; library holdings,
171-72; minorities study, 3590;
race prejudice studies, 2994-95
--University. Berkeley; African art
committee, 120; art holdings,
120; black studies program, 1618,
3903, 4004; College and university
self-study institute, 1631;
Congress of racial equality,
3927; Dept. of history, 2031;
Eldridge Cleaver at, 600, 603,
1656; Institute of governmental
studies, 1866; Institute of industrial relations, 2368; Lowie
museum of anthropology, 73;
racism at, 2969; School of
criminology, 2441, 2459; School
of education, 1576-77, 1695;
Student and alumni placement
center, 1870; student revolt, 642,
890, 1650, 1661; Survey research
center, 1345, 1867, 2158, 3694
--University. Davis: Dept. of agricultural education, 3591;
library holdings, 176
--University. Irvine: speeches,
2958
--University. Los Angeles: Afro-

California (cont.)
American studies center, 3971;
Angela Davis at, 899-900; art
galleries, 74; art holdings,
121; Black panthers and Ron
Karenga at, 622; Black students
union, 3996; Bunche hall, 1625;
Educational opportunities program, 1617, 1630; Institute of
industrial relations, 1868-69;
segregation, 1636; Office of
human relations, 3695
--University. Riverside: Black
student union, 639a, 2489
--University. Santa Barbara: Dept.
of dramatic art, 2519; library
holdings, 177
--University. University extension, 2435, 3696
California assoc. of colored
women's clubs, 3576, 4047
California cocoanut pulverizing
co., San Francisco, 941
California college of arts and
crafts, Oakland: art holdings,
122
California commission of immigration and housing, 1170
California council of Negro
women, 3570
California eagle publishing co.,
Los Angeles, 902, 1242, 2271-
73, 2588
California elementary school principals' assoc., 1696
California federation for civic
unity: archives, 2996
California historical society,
San Francisco: art holdings,
123; Quarterly index, 178
California library assoc.:
bibliography, 179
California publishing bureau and
investment co., Los Angeles,
2273
California real estate assoc.,
2165
California research foundation,
2159
California state assoc. of colored
women, 3571-73
California voice press, Oakland,
1248, 3252, 3293, 3570
Calkin, Milo, 1058
Callahan, Ed, 1229

Callender, John T., 951, 3568
Callender's minstrels, 2002
Callis, Albert G., 2045
Calvert, Robert, 1870
Campa, Arthur Leon, 1629
Campbell, Ann, 3187
Campbell, Basil: biographical
accounts, 358, 390
Campbell, Charles R., 4052
Campbell, Ella S., 3466
Campbell, Louis H., 3941, 4139
Campbell, Nick, 3193
Campbell, Thomas, 4228
Canado, Birdie, 2915
Canal zone: schools, 1008
Candee, Beatrice, 942
Canevaro, G., 933
Cannady, Camille, 1989
Cannady, Edward D., 4254
Cannady, Mrs. Edward D. (Beatrice),
4254
Cannon, Terry, 579
Cantine, Garrett A., 1045
Caples, George, 3196
Cappelluzzo, Emma M., 1520
Caribbean, 997-1015 passim
Carlson, Oliver, 1171
Carlstrand, Robert W., 2436
Carmel: local news columns, 4199
Carmichael, Benjamin Green, 3697
Carmichael, Stokely, 587, 847, 2525.
See also Student nonviolent
coordinating committee
Carollo, Dorothy B., 1521
Carpenter, Charles E., 3198
Carpentier, Horace Walpole, 1058
Carraway, Arthur, 118, 133
Carroll, John Alexander, 64
Carroll, Joseph F., 936
Carroll, Sarah J., 1114, 1130
Carroll, William, 2032
Carruthers, Ben Frederic, 2716
Carson City, Nev.: Freemasons, 2010
Carter, Emmet, 928
Carter, George Edward, 3433
Carter, Kate B., 2033
Carter, Phil, 1953
Carter, Randolph Warren: corres-
pondence, etc., 490
Carter, Robert L., 2998
Carter, Thomas E., 944
Carter, Thomas P., 1347
Carter, Yvonne, 133
Carter, William, 127
Carter, William H., 4191

Cartland, Earl Fernando, 3698
Cartoonist, 290
Casal, James, 1065
Case, Frederick Ewing, 2160-62
Caselli, Ron, 254
Casey, Bernie, 108, 135, 2699
Cashen, George R., 835, 951
Cashin, Hershel V., 29-30
Casimere, Gerald Lee, 3699
Casper, Wyo.: Colored men's pro-
    gressive club, 2104
Casserly, Eugene, 2555
Cassey, Peter Williams, 1058, 3296
Casstevens, Thomas W., 2163-64
Castles, Jean I., 2034
Catalogne, Gérard de, 3833
Cate, Thomas L., 4233, 4237
Catlin, Amos Parmalee, 304
Catterall, Mrs. Ralph C. H. (Helen
    Honor Tunnicliff), 2437-38
Cattle industry. See Ranch life
Caughey, John Walton, 1349-52
Caughey, Mrs. John Walton (LaRee),
    1066, 1349, 1352
Cavin, E. M., 1238
Cayou, Dolores Kirton, 2801
Cayton, Bruce [i.e., Horace?],
    2420
Cayton, Horace Roscoe, Jr.:
    article by, 3700; autobi-
    ographies, 305, 2491; bio-
    graphical accounts, 292-93,
    414; death, 333
Cayton, Horace Roscoe, Sr., 306,
    2871-72, 3927a, 4274, 4283,
    4287
Cayton, Mrs. Horace Roscoe, Sr.
    (Susie Sumner Revels), 4283
Cayton's year book, 306
Census. See U. S. Bureau of the
    census; and under name of in-
    dividual states, e.g.,
    California: census
Centennial publishers, Oakland,
    2305
Center for the study of democratic
    institutions, Santa Barbara,
    2439, 2577, 3735
Center on urban and minority
    affairs, Los Angeles, 1243
Central casting corp., Los Angeles,
    1955
Central City, Colo., 298
Central Seattle community council:
    archives, 2999

Centralia, Wash.: biographical
    accounts of founder, 366, 370,
    397, 402, 410, 416, 424, 470
Century City: peace march, 838
Cepeda, Orlando, 3639, 3664
Cervantes, Alfonso J., 858
Chabot college library: holdings,
    180
Chamberlain, Roderick, 1871
Chamberlin, William Henry, 2035
Chambers, R. L., 1353
Chapin, Katherine Garrison, 2831
Chapman, Abraham, 181
Chappell, Helen F., 3959
Charles, Ray, 2799
Charleys Butte: origin of name, 326
Charlton, Edward F., 3568
Chavez, Cesar Estrada, 2369
Cheek, William F., 2036
Cheltenham, Eugene, 133
Chemical industry: employment, 1918
Chemistry, 3835; curriculum, 1714
Chesley, William S., 3542
Chester, William H., 2381
Chevallier, Cadet, 978
Cheyenne, Wyo.: African Methodist
    Episcopal church, 3230; hotel,
    405; World war II soldiers at,
    66
Chicago: World's Columbian ex-
    position, 303
Chicanos. See Mexican-Americans
Chico, Jessie L. (Ridley), 2578-79
Chico: agricultural labor, 2398;
    local news columns, 4148, 4193
Child guidance. See Education:
    counseling and guidance
Child welfare. See Juvenile welfare
Children: adoption, 3688; leisure
    activities, 3610
Children, abnormal: education, 1744
Children's aid. See Community
    service organizations
Children's homes. See Orphanages
Children's literature. See
    Juvenile literature
Childress, Frank, 4018
Chinese: (1785-95), 2110; housing,
    3136; in Calif., 3296; in Sacra-
    mento area, 3693; labor unions,
    2390; miscegenation, 2794; suf-
    frage, 2880; testimony right,
    1110-11, 2437-38; urban life,
    3755
Ching, Adele, 3701

Chinn, Marie, 945
Chisom, Harvey, 979
Chittick, Victor Lovitt Oakes, 2491
Chrisman, Bertrand, 952
Chrisman, Robert, 859, 3913
Christensen, J. B., 3365
Christmas, 3246
Christy, Wilford L., 1354
Chudhuri, Arun K., 1954
Chula Vista: newspaper, 4066a
Chung, Inso, 160
Church for the fellowship of all
    peoples, San Francisco, 3231-32,
    3309, 3320-21
Church of all faiths, Oakland, 3233
Church of Jesus Christ of latter-day
    saints. See Mormons
Church of our Lord's most tender
    compassion, San Francisco,
    3937a
Church of the good shepherd
    (Baptist), Oakland, 3234-36
Churches. See Religion and under
    the names of individual churches
    by geographical locality, e.g.,
    Oakland: St. Augustine's Epis-
    copal church; San Francisco:
    First African Methodist Epis-
    copal Zion church; etc.
Churchman, James, 1055
Cisco, Aaron, 1045
Citizens' advisory committee on
    Oakland school needs, 1355
Citizens interracial committee,
    San Diego, 1872
City, G. W., 946
City college of San Francisco, 839
City planning. See Urban planning
Civells, Martha, 3187
Civells, William S., 3187
Civic unity committee, Seattle:
    archives, 3000
Civil disobedience. See Riots
Civil rights, 1016-1157, 2016, 2119,
    2589, 3848; Bay area council
    against discrimination, San
    Francisco, 3993; church ac-
    tivity, 3285; Colored laborer's
    social club, Los Angeles, 2372;
    Council for civic unity, San
    Francisco, 3939; in California
    (1849-63), 2375; in Los Angeles,
    895; in Montana, 2068; Marin
    county human rights commission,
    1099, 2206, 4040; Nation of

Islam religious rights, 3243;
    public accommodations, 2453; re-
    ligious participation, 3247. See
    also Education: segregation;
    Ejectment; Employment: discrimina-
    tion; Homestead law; Housing;
    Restrictive covenants; Washington:
    State board against discrimination;
    etc.
Civil service. See Employment:
    civil service
Civil war, 3381; arming slaves, 3368;
    army cooks, 1096; Calif. attitude,
    3419; Pacific northwest, 2075;
    race demagoguery, 2129; Southern
    religious attitude, 3445; termina-
    tion means, 3448-50; troops, 31.
    See also Armed services; Recon-
    struction; Secession
Claiborne, M. C., 2023
Clamorgan, Jacques: biographical
    account, 344
Clar, Mimi, 2509
Claremont: Scripps college art
    gallery exhibit, 108
Claremont colleges: Black student
    union, 2719
Clark, Alberta, 3560
Clark, Alice M., 1356
Clark, C., 307
Clark, Claude, 75, 133
Clark, Claude Lockhart, 75
Clark, Claude Rockingham, 78
Clark, David R., 2915
Clark, James H., 929
Clark, John E., 3237
Clark, Joseph A., 4286
Clark, Joseph Edward, 2873
Clark, Libby, 3956
Clark, Sandra Jean, 1630
Clark, Wallace A., 3541
Clark, William L., 3172
Clark, William Richard, 1699
Clarke, James B., 2558
Clarke, John Henrik, 2612
Clarke, Maxine Adams, 1068
Clarke, Tobin, 257
Clarke, Walter Malcolm, 3238
Clawson, Marion, 1172
Clay, Henry, 3366
Clay, Josephine Russell, 2613
Cleaning: Los Angeles cooperative,
    927. See also Laundry; Soap
    industry
Cleaver, Eldridge, 308, 566-639 passim,

Cleaver, Eldridge (cont.)
1656, 2454, 2529, 2958
Cleaver, Lowell Henry, 1700
Clemens, Samuel Langhorne, 3091
Clendenen, Clarence Clemens, 5-6, 10
Cleveland, Chauncey Fitch, 3367
Clothing trade: Oakland store, 993
Cloud, Donald Emerson, 3640
Cloud, Frank H., 3932
Clubs. See Benevolent societies;
Fraternal organizations; Greek
letter societies; Social clubs;
Women's clubs
Clyde, P. J., 3307
Coal mines and mining: Green river
coal co., 990
Cobb, I. W., 2520
Cobb, Willie Lenox, 1476, 1578
Cobbs, Price Mashaw, 695, 2767,
2945, 3861, 4014
Cockerham, William Carl, 2274
Codornices village, 2133
Coffer, Sterling P., 3561
Coffey, Alvin Aaron: biographical
accounts, 308a, 470; overland
trip, 1194
Coffin, Bessie B., 994
Coffin, Clarence, 3552
Coffin, George H., 2165
Coffin, Samuel A., 994
Coffroth, James Wood, 1112
Cogar, Ellen, 3187
Cogley, John, 2577
Cohan, George M., 1994
Cohen, David K., 1357
Cohen, Jerome, 3702
Cohen, Jerry, 696
Cohen, Nathan Edward, 697-700
Cohen, William, 1388
Coker, George Cicero, 943
Colbert, Robert E., 1173
Cole, C. D., 3222
Cole, Cornelius, 2006, 2038, 3368
Cole, Johnnetta B., 860
Cole, Martin, 2037
Cole, Mary E. A., 3481
Cole, Nat "King": biographical
account, 1993; biography, 2865
Cole, Peter K., 3239
Cole, V. M., 946
Coleman, Anita Scott, 2306-07,
2498, 2580, 2614-29, 3001
Coleman, Bessie, 3899
Coleman, Gordon C., 3335-36, 4146
Coleman, Hoyd W., 133

Coleman, J. W. (1940), 2915
Coleman, James S., 1388, 1701
Coleman, John Wesley, 2273
Coles, Nathaniel Adams. See Cole,
Nat "King"
Coles, Robert, 594
College and university self-study
institute (1970), 1631
College of Marin, 839
College of San Mateo, 1663
Colleges. See Education: colleges
and universities
Colley, Nathaniel Sextus, 2166, 2996
Collier, Francis Bernard, 2275
Collier, Mary E., 928
Collins, Augustus A., 4198
Collins, Charles, 1244
Collins, Daniel Andrew, 2762, 4202
Collins, H. H., 2874
Collins, Henry M., 950; biographical
account, 460-61
Collins, John M., 3307, 4166
Collins, Lorraine, 3193
Collins, Mary (Modesto), 3193
Collins, Mary L., 2874
Collins, Robert, 5, 7
Collins, William E., 1874
Collins family, 371
Colly, William C., 3541
Colman, Willie, 3289
Coloma: Sutter's mill, 520
Colonization, 1159-1218 passim; Calif.
slave colony, 3358, 3400. See
also Allensworth; Cooperative
societies; Deerfield, Colo.;
Liberia; Mexico; Migration; etc.
Colorado, 2106; Adams state college
bibliography, 182; African Methodist Episcopal church, 3183;
American missionary assoc. archives, 2007; as fiction locale,
2646; census (1870-80), 1299;
civil rights (1859-67), 1103;
civil rights statutes, 1089;
colleges and universities, 1629;
cowboys, 3172; Freemasons, 3531-
32; gold rush, 1225; historic
sites, 2047; history, 2051, 2061-
62; James A. Atkins papers (1950-
68), 486; laws, statutes, etc.,
2467-67a; mines, 517, 1931; newspaper bibliography, 228; newspapers, 4213-42; pioneer residents,
555; race relations, 2963; slavery,
3410; steel industry, 1923;

Colorado (cont.)
    University, 2967; Western Baptist
    state convention, 3273
Colorado committee for equal em-
    ployment opportunities, 1873
Colorado magazine: index to, 255-56
Colorado Springs: newspapers, 4214-
    19; reminiscence of, 1975
Colored-American employees' assoc.,
    San Francisco, 1874
Colored business men's assoc. of
    Stockton, 944
Colored chauffeurs assoc. of Calif.,
    Los Angeles, 2370
Colored citizens' conventions,
    Calif. See California:
    Colored citizens' conventions
Colored colonization assoc. of
    Fresno county, 1174
Colored colonization co., San
    Diego, 1175
Colored Democratic league of
    southern Calif., 524
Colored east bay auto workers
    assoc., Oakland, 2371
Colored employees social and aid
    club, San Diego, 3565
Colored entertainers club, San
    Francisco, 3548
Colored janitor co-operative assoc.,
    San Francisco, 3549
Colored laborer's social club,
    Los Angeles, 2372
Colored marine employees benevolent
    assoc. of the Pacific, 2383
Colored men's progressive club,
    Casper, Wyo., 2104
Colored Mexican colonization co.,
    San Diego, 1176
Colored military social club, San
    Francisco, 3550
Colored political and social club
    of Los Angeles, 2875
Colored social club, San Francisco,
    3551
Colored veterans service club,
    San Francisco, 3552
Colored women's federation of
    Washington (state): papers
    (1889-1966), 485
Colored workers assoc., Los Angeles
    (1933), 945
Colored workers' assoc., Los Angeles
    (1922), 861
Colored workingmens club, Los Angeles,
    3553

Colored workingmen's club, San Fran-
    cisco, 3554
Colored young men and women's in-
    dustrial Christian assoc., San
    Francisco, 3469
Coltrane, John, 2717
Columbia broadcasting system, 701-02
Colusa: African Methodist Episcopal
    church, 3184; directory, 1263;
    local news columns, 4198
Colvig, Richard, 183
Comic books, 3946
Commercial council of Los Angeles,
    946
Commission on race and housing, 2167
Commoner publishing co., San Fran-
    cisco, 3889
Communism, 2910, 3278; street riots,
    837; U. S. guerrilla warfare,
    879
Communist party, 1069, 2932-33; and
    Angela Davis, 898-900; in
    Calif., 1069-72, 2876-78; labor
    union infiltration, 2390
Communist party of Los Angeles, 3130
Community chest and council of
    Seattle and King county, Wash.,
    3470
Community council of San Mateo county,
    3471
Community health workers, San
    Francisco, 1247
Community service organizations,
    3457-3507; Old folks home of
    the western Baptist assoc., Abila,
    3218; San Francisco bay area
    directory, 1272a. See also
    Benevolent societies; Social clubs
Community welfare federation of Los
    Angeles, 3703
Compton, Nettie, 3548
Compton: City manager, 3737; direc-
    tories, 1300; newspapers, 4067-
    69; public welfare, 3740; racial
    dissent, 1765; schools, 1442,
    1605; urban life, 3715
Compton-Lynwood board of realtors,
    2165
Compton Westside bee, 4115
Conference on law enforcement and
    racial and cultural tensions,
    Berkeley, 2441
Congregational churches: Oregon,
    3369-70
Congress of racial equality, 1097;
    dispute with Bank of America, 1834;

Congress of racial equality (cont.)
dissertation on, 894; in
Berkeley, 2117, 3927; in Los
Angeles, 1358; in Sacramento,
2244; in San Diego, 3746; in
Seattle, 309; Western regional
office, 862
Conner, Leonard, 3002
Conner, Nellie Victoria, 2700
Conner, Veda N., 310
Conot, Robert E., 703-04
Conrad, Earl, 1958
Conroy, Jack, 3829-30
Construction industry: in Oakland,
1897; labor unions, 2382
Contra Costa council of community
services. 1838, 3625
Contra Costa county: directory,
1264; economic conditions, 3748;
public welfare residence laws,
3622. See also San Francisco
bay area
Conventions: (1830-61), 1028-29.
See also California: Colored
citizens' conventions
Conyers, James E., 2787
Cook, A. W., 3545
Cook, J. C., 914
Cook, J. E., 947
Cook, Nelson, 3557
Cook, Texas, 861
Cookery, 1229-35; Civil war cooks,
1096. See also Bakers and
bakeries; Dining car cooks
and waiters
Coolbrith, Ina Donna, 362
Cooley, Beatrice, 3547
Cooley, H. J., 3547
Coolidge, Fay Liddle, 2630
Coon, Henry Perrin, 1058
Coonradt, Frederic Chapin, 2276
Cooper, Bella Taylor: papers, 491
Cooper, Clare C., 1875
Cooper, Elijah, 946
Cooper, Elizabeth Keyser, 1702
Cooper, Felix B.: papers, 492
Cooper, J. C., 3545
Cooper, Leonard, 78
Cooper, Ralph, 964
Cooper African Methodist Episcopal
Zion church, Oakland, 3240
Cooperative societies, 926-83
passim; San Francisco bay area
directory, 1272a. See also
Colonization; Credit unions

Cope, Myron, 3637
Corbo, James, 1359
Cordell, Paul, 2701
C. O. R. E. See Congress of racial
equality
Corman, John, 2958
Cornell, R. M., 3561
Cornish, Dudley T., 31
Cornish, Henry C., 1045
Coro foundation, 1876, 3704
Corporation law: stockholder's
rights, 959
Corsaro, Richard J., 1703
Cortez, Jayne, 2702
Cosby, Bill, 1974
Cosey, Louis W., 3592
Cosmetics: Calif. state board of
cosmetology, 1850; East bay cos-
metologists assoc., 949
Cosmos social club of San Francisco,
2802
Costain, Dave, 705
Costa Rica: history, 1000
Cotton culture: Calif., 1218, 2365;
unionization, 2360
Couch, William, Jr., 2492
Council for civic unity, San Francisco,
1019, 2169-70, 3003-04, 3705;
publication, 3939
Council of social planning, Alameda
county, 2188-89
Council of social planning,
Berkeley, 1877
Counseling. See Education:
counseling and guidance
Counterpart, Menlo Park, 3241
Cours. See Law and order
Cousineau, Carl Alan, 3005
Couture, Andrea, 4153
Cover, Robert, 595
Covington, Floyd C., 311-13, 1955,
2373, 3932, 4033; biographical
account, 463
Cowan, Robert Granniss, 184
Cowboys, 2092, 2309, 2343, 3165-72;
death of Charles Summers, 326;
fictional account, 2672; Nat
Love, 377-78. See also Agri-
culture; Hides and tallow trade;
Ranch life
Cowdery, Jabez Franklin, 1360
Cowles, Alfred, 2987
Cox, Alexander, 1159, 1175
Cox, Earnest Sevier, 1177
Cox, LaWanda (Fenlason), 2374

Cox, Sandra, 2489
Coy, Owen Cochran, 2039, 3371, 3706
Coyne, John R., 596
Crabb, Riley Hansard, 706
Cragwell, John F., 314
Craighill, Karilyn (Frampton), 1704
Crain, Robert L., 1361
Craine, James Forrester, 1878
Crane, Warren Eugene, 314
Crane, William W., Jr., 1119,
    1133-34, 1136
Cranshaw, Walter, Jr., 4195
Crawford, Gladys Gwendolyn
    (Wysinger), 4199
Crawford, J. D., 2273
Crawford, Matt, 4138
Credic, Willie C., 3297
Credit unions: Ethiopia credit
    union, Oakland, 953; Prince
    Hall bay counties credit union,
    979; Prince Hall credit union,
    Riverside, 980; Prince Hall
    no. 2 credit union, Los
    Angeles, 981; Prince Hall
    no. 3 credit union, Vallejo,
    982; Prince Hall no. 5 credit
    union, Bakersfield, 983. See
    also Banks and banking;
    Cooperative societies
Cremer, Marva, 133
Crenshaw neighbors, inc., Los
    Angeles, 3967
Crime and criminals. See
    California: University.
    Berkeley: School of criminology;
    Law and order
Crimi, James E., 3707
Cripps, Thomas R., 1956, 2092
Cristóbal, Juan, 493
Crittenden (John J.) compromise,
    3381
Crobaugh, Clyde Julian, 3593
Crocker, Edwin Bryant, 512
Cromwell, John, 1045
Croom, Mrs. J. C., 3485
Crosby, Alexander L., 2171
Crosby, Harry Lillis "Bing", 1957
Cross, Mrs. Joseph, 928
Crossley, Lucy C., 3594
Crouchett, Laurence, 185
Crow, John E., 3006
Crow, Wayman J., 2973
Cruikshank, George B., 4061
Crumal, Glena, 1579
Crumbly, Floyd H., 315

Crump, Spencer, 707
Cruz, Victor Hernandez, 2501
Cuba: biography of Nicolás Guillèn,
    1002; race war (1912), 1011
Cuffe, Paul: descendant, 320
Cultural exchange center of Los
    Angeles, 77, 107
Culver City: race relations, 3007
Cumber, Gerald, 4017
Cumber, Lillian, 4017, 4111, 4121
Cummings, William, 4127
Cummins, Thomas J., 1632
Cureton, Minnie Edith, 2040
Curry, Willa Clothilde, 1304
Curtis, Mrs. Austin Maurice
    (Namahyoke Gertrude Sockum):
    biographical account, 458
Curtis, Gloria S., 2331-33
Curtis, Mary Julia, 2521
Custer, George Armstrong: inter-
    preter for, 329, 381
Cutter, Samuel L., 3256, 3258
Cyr, Helen, 226

D

D'Adamo, Anthony, 2329
Daily, Harry Ted, 4126
Dakan, Arthur William, 2879
Dale, Harrison Clifford, 2041
Dale, Johnie, 2372
Dallas, Texas: schools, 1473
Daly, Elbert Allen, 4139
Daly, Emmet, 2434
Damon, Anna, 2484
Dance and dancing, 2821; history,
    2806; jazz, 2801; pre-school,
    1553
Dance theatre group, Los Angeles,
    2841
Dandridge, Dorothy: biography, 1958
Dandridge, Lillard G., 3523
Daniels, Hazel Burton, 1580
Daniels, John R., 3949
Daniels, Ophelia, 3297
Daniels, Thelma, 3963
Dannette, Sylvia G. L., 458
Dantzler, Grace Pollard, 3488
Darden, Charles S., 946
Darnell, Barbara, 2441
Data analysis: in Watts, 813
Datwyler, Darryl, 3612
Dauterive, Verna Blanche, 1362
Davenport, Timothy W., 3372
Davidson, Basil, 8

Davidson, Douglas, 1618
Davidson, J. F., 3185
Davidson, Matthew, 2443
Davis, A. B., 3510
Davis, Allen, 965
Davis, Angela Yvonne, 863, 887,
    892, 898-900, 2456
Davis, C. A., 914
Davis, Claretha Manning, 2408
Davis, Claude J., 952
Davis, Earl, 4178-80
Davis, Elizabeth Lindsay, 317
Davis, Ernest M., 3472
Davis, Frank Marshall, 3008
Davis, Jefferson, 3373
Davis, Lenwood G., 185a
Davis, Ossie, 2574
Davis, Rachel, 3187
Davis, Sammy, Jr., 1959; biographi-
    cal account, 1993
Davis, Samuel, 3557
Davis, Samuel Post, 318
Davis, Tommy, 3664
Davis, Tyler M., 3198
Davis, V. T., 2371
Davis, W. A., 3550
Davis, W. H., 3550
Davis, W. W., 2278
Davis, Walker, 1176
Davis, William, 861
Davis, William H. (Los Angeles),
    981
Davis, William H. (San Jose), 3196
Davis: Calif. univ. library
    holdings, 176
Davison, Berlinda. See Mabson,
    Mrs. Edward D. (Berlinda
    Davison)
Davy, Marguerite Ross, 319
Dawson, Aide L., 936
Dawson, Helaine, 1705
Dawson, Leon, 1874
Day, George M., 3708
Day, Thomas, 1058
Day, William H., 20
Deadwood Dick. See Love, Nat
Deaf: mental abilities, 1527
Dean, Alvano, 3834
Dean, Corinne Coloytha, 1706
Dean, Harry: autobiography, 320
Dean, John P., 3158
Dean, Lois R., 3158
Dean, Ross, 2875
Death: Los Angeles wakes, 2511;
    public welfare patients, 3627

De Barry, Clyde Edward, 1322, 1707
De Bow, Samuel P., 473, 4286;
    papers, 494
Debrow, Julius, 2444
Decker, Peter, 2042
Declair, Philip, 830
De Claybrook, William E., 958
De Claybrook, William E., Jr., 3546
de Coy, Robert H., 459, 2409, 2493,
    3641
Dedrick, Simon A., 988, 2356
Deerfield, Colo., 1178
Dees, Robert, 243
De Ferrari, Carlo M., 2078, 3373a
de Ford, Miriam Allen (Mrs. Maynard
    Shipley), 321
de Graaf, Lawrence Brooks, 1179, 3709
Delano, Alonzo, 322-23, 1055
Delano: street riots, 837
Delany, Cassandria McKoin: bio-
    graphical account, 462
Delany, Daniel, 462
Delany, Martin Robison, 460-61
Delany, Rachel: biographical
    account, 462
Delany, William: biographical
    account, 462
Delay, Peter Joseph, 3242
De Leon, A. W. A., 3511
Delinquency. See Juvenile delinquency
Dellefield, Calvin J., 1708
Dellums, Cottrell Laurence: corres-
    pondence, 2363; papers, 496;
    taped interview, 495
Del Paso heights school district,
    Sacramento, 1395
Democratic party: Calif., 524;
    (1869), 2880
Demography. See U. S. Bureau of
    the census
Dennis, Abraham Lincoln, 926
Dennis, George Washington, Jr., 4204
Dennis, Isador, 3566
Dennis, Joseph A., 931, 3469
Denniston, Tim, Sr., 2803
Dent, W. C., 3264
Dentistry, 2762; Los Angeles, 426-
    27, 538
Denton, David, 2370
Denton, John H., 2172-73
Denver: American woodmen, 3508-09,
    3890, 4048; as poetry locale,
    2710; banks and banking, 1939;
    described (1922), 3863; hotels,
    405; housing, 2140, 2171;

Denver (cont.)
Interracial commission, 3783-85;
letter (1861), 1225; local news
columns, 4302; newspapers, 4220-
32; Police dept., 2428-29; Pub-
lic schools, 1327, 1363, 1459,
1790; race relations, 3150,
3153; urban life, 3710, 3717,
3739, 3780, 3783-85; World war
II soldiers at, 66
Denver art museum, 88-89
Depression, business. See
Economic conditions
Derbigny, Irving Antony, 1633
Derbyshire, Robert L., 1634, 3595
Derrick, John A. Lincoln, 835, 992,
3473, 4149
de Saisset art gallery & museum,
Santa Clara univ., 142
Desegregation. See Segregation
Desseau, David, 4115
Detter, Thomas, 2631
Dettering, Richard Whitson, 3009
Deutsch & Shea, inc., 186
Devers, Anderson, 984
Dewson, W. W., 992
Dexter, Charles, 3667
de Young (M. H.) memorial museum,
San Francisco: exhibit
catalog, 100
Diablo valley college, Pleasant
Hill: library holdings, 187
Dibble, Alford B., 1055
Dickey, Jesse C., 3374
Dickey, Lloyd Duquesne, 1709
Dickinson, James K., 835, 951
Didion, Joan, 597, 1635
Diegler, James D., 3010
Dietrich, Dr., 2043
Diggs, Charles S., 2763-64
Diggs, Wade, 3184
Dillon, Diane, 2500
Dillon, Leo, 2500
Dillon, Mrs. Richard (Barbara),
2324
Dining car cooks and waiters
union, Los Angeles, 2373
Dining car waiters, 1937
Dinkins, Elmo L., 3963
Dinkins, Lillian, 3963
Dinks, Moses, 456
Directories: 1236-1300 passim,
3523, 3525, 3563; fair housing,
2154; legal, 2478; newspapers,
2292-93; newspapers and

periodicals, 2280. See also
under names of cities, e.g.,
Butte, Mont.: directories; Los
Angeles: directories; etc.
Disciples of Christ: schools, 1758
Discography. See Music
Discrimination. See Civil rights;
Housing; Race relations; etc.
Divine, Morgan J. "Father", 3268,
3277a
Dixon, William H.: papers, 497
Dixson, John H., 3564
Dizard, Jan E., 1879
Dobbins, A. R., 3546
Dobie, Charles Caldwell, 324, 2632
Dobson, Griffin, 1045
Dodge, Henry Lee, 1058
Dodson, Dan W., 1341, 1365
Dodson, Jacob, 289, 2060, 2099;
biographical accounts, 360, 470
Donaldson, Charlotte, 3474
Dones, Sidney P., 939
Donner, Christopher Silvester, 1001
Doram, E. A., 930
Dorman, Isaiah, 329, 381; biographi-
cal account, 471
Dorn, Dean S., 3612
Dorsen, Norman, 634
Dorsey, Chris, 4243
Dorsey, E. A., 4172
Dorsey, E. V., 4225
Dorsey, George W., 965
Dorsey, Henry W., 3187
Dorsey, John Henry, 4014
Dosier, Mrs. Andrew (Mary Johnson):
biographical account, 395
Dotson, Alporta, 1477
Douglas, Helen Gahagan (Mrs. Melvyn
Douglas), 32; her secretary, 338
Douglas, Jesse S., 1180
Douglas, Patrick, 325, 598, 3011
Douglas, Richard F., 4181
Douglas, Robert, 4069
Douglass, Emory, 569
Douglass, Frederick, 303, 2290-91
Douglass (Frederick) cooperative
realty company of San Francisco,
958
Douglass house foundation, Los
Angeles, 734
Dove, Pearlie C., 1478
Dover, Cedric, 78-80
Dow, Joseph E., 981
Dowell, Benjamin Franklin, 3012
Downie, William, 2045-46

Downieville, 2045, 2069
Downs, Karl E., 463, 3245
Downs memorial Methodist church,
    Oakland, 3244-45
Doyle, Helen (MacKnight), 326
Draine, Elliot A., 2140
Drake, Cisco, 327
Drake, E. Maylon, 1880
Drama: high schools, 1586; Watts
    workshop, 734, 773. See also
    Literature: drama; Theater
Draney, R. Whitney, 2331, 2333
Draper, Harold, 1075
Draper, Leo, 967
Drew, Howard P., 3648
Drotning, Phillip T., 464, 2047
Drug addiction, 2765
Drug industry, 1882
Drums. See Music
Drury, Clifford Merrill, 189
Dry cleaning. See Cleaning
Du Bois (W. E. B.) clubs of America:
    founding convention, 917
Du Bois, William Edward Burghardt,
    652, 1994, 3711-12, 3882; bio-
    graphical account, 347; bi-
    ography, 295-96
Duchouquette, François, 978
Duckett, Alfred, 2341
Duckett, Thomas J., 930
Duffy, John F., 1881
Dugan, Mary, 3485
Duggar, Andrew S., 936
Duignan, Peter James, 5-7, 9-10,
    190
Dunayevskaya, Raya, 890
Dunbar, Paul Laurence, 2308
Dunbar hospital assoc. of Los
    Angeles, 2764
Dunbar hotel, Los Angeles, 652
Duncan, Albert E., 946
Duncan, C. P., 835
Duncan, John W., 1236, 4243
Duncan, T. Roger, 1366
Duncan, William L., 1058
Duniway, Clyde Augustus, 3375
Duniway, David Cushing, 1181
Dunlap, Josiah, 3187
Dunn, Eugenia V., 133
Dunnaway, Edwin E., 1710
Dunne, John Gregory, 710-11
Duplex, Edward P., 2870
Du Pont, Phyllis McLean, 1522
Durem, Ray, 2495
Durham, Barney, 4157

Durham, Philip, 2309, 3167-70
Durkee, Charles, 3376
Dust (pseud.). See Stroud, Welvin
Duvall, Cornelia, 3460
Du Valliere, Max, 945
Dvorin, Eugene P., 2881
Dwinelle, John Whipple, 1566-68
Dyck, Henry Otto, 1367
Dyer, Brainerd, 2882
Dyer, James P., 973, 3556
Dyke, Jeani, 3013
Dymally, Mervyn Malcolm, 1169, 1243,
    1368, 1697, 2048, 2931, 3160,
    3910; papers, 2883; thesis, 2277

E

Eades, James H., 975
Eames, Ninetta, 328
Eason, Charles Lewis, 864
Eason, Newell D., 948
East bay area: National assoc. of
    Negro business and professional
    women's clubs, 1264
East bay cities business league,
    Berkeley, 3969a
East bay civil rights congress, 2452
East bay community action program,
    3500
East bay cosmetologists assoc., 949
East bay guidance council, Oakland,
    1305-06
East bay skills center, Oakland,
    4020
East Palo Alto: directory, 3471;
    Mid-peninsula Christian community
    house, 3071; Mid-peninsula
    Christian movement, 3042; Munici-
    pal council, 2884; urban life,
    3699, 3803. See also Palo Alto
Eastern star, Order of. See Free-
    masons. California: Order of
    eastern star
Easton, William Edgar, 2558
Eaton, Joseph W., 3014
Eaves, Lucile, 2375
Ebony, 191
Echols, Jack W., 1479
Eckels, Jon, 2703-04
Economic conditions, 2589, 3617,
    3629-30, 3685, 3786, 3798, 3836,
    3858, 3867, 3883; (1830-80),
    2112; in Ariz., 3006; in Calif.,
    2902, 3590; in Los Angeles,
    2366-67, 2904, 3690, 3816, 3872;

Economic conditions (cont.)
in Los Angeles county, 3752;
in Oakland, 3747; in Richmond,
3802; in San Diego, 3743; in
San Francisco, 3809; in San
Francisco bay area, 3748; in
Seattle, 3470, 3789; in Watts,
678-823 passim; Neighborhood
youth corps, 3604; San Francisco
bay area poverty programs di-
rectory, 1272a; slavery, 3442.
See also Sociology; Urban life
Economic opportunity commission of
San Diego county, 3475
Economic opportunity council, San
Francisco, 3476, 3492
Economics, 935-95 passim;
bibliography, 182. See also
Business; Property
Ector, William, 4183
Eddington, Neil Arthur, 3713-14
Edmerson, Estelle, 1961
Edmonds, George, 343
Edmonds, Jefferson Lewis, 928, 3974
Edmonds, Susie E., 928
Edmonson, Regina, 3485
Edmonston, Samuel, 1159, 1175-76
Education: 1301-1831, 2989, 3061;
(ante 1880), 1818, 2013, 3239;
(1960), 1858-60; adult, 486,
1708-09, 1719, 1791; and
slavery, 3431; bibliographies,
221, 226-27, 238, 254; Calif.
directories, 1272a, 1290; church
activity, 3285; civil rights,
1087; Congress of racial
equality, 862; counseling and
guidance, 1301-20, 1607, 1627,
1655; Education corps newsletter,
3948; Equal opportunity program,
1617, 1630, 1660; handbook,
3601; health programs, 1652,
1673; history instruction, 1639,
1697-98, 1719, 1796-97, 2031,
2048, 2095, 2111, 2117; in Canal
Zone, 1008; in Missouri, 1474;
in Pacific northwest, 3734; in
San Francisco, 1026; in South,
1367, 1471-1509, 1615, 1627,
1633, 1652; in Watts, 689, 805,
828; industrial arts, 1537, 1741,
1886, 3469; musical aptitudes,
2817; Phoenixonian institute,
San Jose, 3296; physical, 1652;
race relation instruction, 3087;

segregation, 1321-1470, 1564-68,
1636, 1774, 1800-01, 2013, 2032,
2068, 2122, 2281, 2453, 3116,
3122; study of attitudes, 3163;
truancy, 1700; visual art guide,
75. See also Employment:
teachers; and under geographical
locality, e.g., San Jose: Public
schools; Seattle: Public schools;
etc.
--colleges and universities, 1615-70;
African students at, 22; African
studies, 4; Arkansas, 1615; black
movement, 839; black workshop,
3057; counseling and guidance,
1302-03, 1313; doctoral research
bibliography (1933-66), 269;
drama instruction, 2519, 2542;
Georgia, 1478, 1503; in South,
1487, 1500, 1507, 1583; media
guide, 186; placement list, 1932;
South Carolina, 1501; state-supported, 1486; Texas, 1479, 1492;
Texas southern univ., 1504. See
also Black student unions; Black
studies programs; and under names
of individual colleges and universities.
--history, 1733-34; Calif., 1718,
1773, 1814; Pacific coast, 1798;
San Francisco (1850-60), 1823
--primary and pre-school, 1510-73,
2352; Kansas City, 1474; language
instruction, 112, 1536, 1559,
2408, 2411-13, 2422, 2424-25;
music, 2353; poetry anthology,
2504; poetry instruction, 2541;
resource books, 253; sculpture
program, 90; drawings and language
relationship, 112; South, 1491;
Texas, 1506
--secondary, 1574-1614; athletics instruction, 3636; bibliographies,
227, 267; counseling, 1310, 1312,
1318; language instruction, 2411;
Louisiana, 1481, 1498; North
Carolina, 1493; resource books,
227, 2111; speech guide, 2410;
Texas, 1472-73, 1475-76, 1488,
1490, 1496, 1499, 3761
Edwards, A. W., 3184
Edwards, Calvin, 980
Edwards, Cecil, 3549
Edwards, Charles W., 3546
Edwards, Harry, 640, 3642

Edwards, Mel, 131
Edwards, S. W., 2633
Edwards, Sarah, 3187
Edwards, Thomas Bentley, 1369
Edwards, William C., 3932
Ege, Robert J., 329
Egerton, John, 1636
Eichler, Edward P., 2174
Einstein, Charles, 2310, 3639, 3643,
    3657-58, 3660
Ejectment: in San Francisco, 1036,
    1115-19, 1133-36, 2437-38
Ekberg, Dennis, 1307
El Camino college: library
    holdings, 192
El Centro: directory, 1267; edu-
    cator's reminiscences, 476;
    local news columns, 4080-81
Elder, Glen H., 3596
El Dorado county: directory, 1270;
    petition of residents, 1053;
    slavery, 3371
Electric power industry: employment
    in, 1832
Elementary education. See Educa-
    tion: primary and pre-school
Elevator publishing co. of San
    Francisco and Oakland, 2278
Elevator silver mining co., San
    Francisco, 950
Eley, Lynn W., 2175
Elinson, Howard, 886
Elioff, Ione Hill, 1523
Elko, Nev.: resident, 2631
Elks of the world, Improved
    benevolent protective order,
    3512
Ellensburg, Wash.: interview of
    resident, 537
Ellery, Epes, 1058
Elliott, Merle Hugh, 1712
Ellis, Judith, 1076
Ellis, Margretta, 653
Ellis, Robert, 1962
Ellis, William Russell, 1713
Ellison, Ralph, 2524, 2666
Ellison, William Henry, 400
Ellsberg, H., 3015
Ellsworth, Edward Thornton, 4250
Ellsworth, Juanita (Mrs. Loren R.
    Miller), 2792
Elman, Richard M., 3715
el-Sayeh, Hussein Bayoumi, 1480
Emancipation proclamation: British
    West Indies, 2691; District of

Columbia, 2691
--United States, 3161, 3363, 3448-50;
    in Portland, Ore., 3403-04;
    oration on, 2584; poetry, 2692,
    2695
Embers family, 453-54
Embree, Edwin Rogers, 2804-05
Embree, Hamilton, 2372
Embry, Julia, 4216
Emery, Leonore Lynne Fanley, 2806
Emigration. See Migration
Emory (pseud.). See Douglass, Emory
Employment, 486, 1832-1947, 2989, 3061,
    3584, 3590; Afro-American real
    estate assoc. and employment
    bureau of Calif., Oakland, 931;
    agencies, 931, 1874; airplane in-
    dustry, 1910-11; Bank of America,
    1834, 1852, 1908; bibliographies,
    202, 1866; Boulder dam, 1888,
    1909; Calif. federation for civic
    unity archives, 2996; chemical
    industry, 1918; college graduates,
    1870; Congress of racial equality,
    862; cosmetology, 1850; discrimina-
    tion, 1832-1947 passim; drug manu-
    facturing, 1882; electronics,
    1921; fair employment practices,
    1839-1943 passim, 2453; fire
    depts., 1836; hotels, 1895; in
    Berkeley, 3825; in Colorado, 486,
    1873; in Oakland, 2158; in Pasa-
    dena, 1854; in Sacramento, 3110;
    in San Diego, 1855, 1872, 3053,
    3565; in San Francisco, 1026,
    1874, 1917, 1922, 1927-30, 3112,
    3114; in Seattle, 1945, 3119,
    3122; insurance industry, 1883;
    lumber and lumbering, 1889; meat
    industry, 1884; paper industry,
    1912; petroleum industry, 1894;
    police depts., 1836; serial publica-
    tion, 3950; public utilities, 1832-
    33; rubber tire industry, 1913;
    shipping, 1885; steel industry,
    1923; street railways, 1920;
    tests, 1864-65, 1915. See also
    Labor; Unemployment
--civil service, 1866, 1902, 1907,
    2453; Calif., 1845-49, 1864,
    1896, 2989
--job and on-job training, 1713, 1722,
    1835; in Menlo Park, 1914; in
    San Francisco, 1921; retraining,
    1926

Employment (cont.)
--teachers, 1685-86, 1792, 1794;
    in Los Angeles county, 1880;
    in Mass., 1699; in Oakland,
    1694; secondary, 1837; turn-
    over, 1725
Endore, Samuel Guy, 1077, 2445-46
English. See Language and language
    instruction; Slang
Enterprise Rochedale co., Oakland,
    951
Entertainment industry, 1948-2004;
    Colored entertainers club, San
    Francisco, 3548; Los Angeles
    Tattler, 4121; Los Angeles
    Teller, 4122; Sepia Hollywood,
    4017; Soul, 4022; Soul illus-
    trated, 4023; We, a monthly
    calendar of bay area events,
    4039. See also Motion pictures;
    Music; Theater; etc.
Environmental design. See Urban
    life; Urban redevelopment
E. O. P. See Equal opportunity
    programs
Epps, Edgar G., 1581, 3597
Epting, Marion A., 119, 121, 134
Equal opportunity programs: in
    education, 1617, 1630, 1660
Eriksson, Elberta, 2788
Erroll, Leon, 1994
Erskine, Evaline, 3466
Ervin, James McFarline, 3716
Erwin, C., 4111
Erwing, James, Jr., 4076, 4098
Erwing, James, Sr., 4076, 4098
Essays. See Literature: essays
    and speeches
Essentialism, 3051
Essien, Joseph Efiong, 1714
Esteban (explorer), 374, 449, 2060,
    2064-65, 2082; biographical
    accounts, 470, 2326-27; bi-
    ographies, 432, 2346
Estee, Morris M., 2911
Ethiopia co-operative business
    assoc., Oakland, 952-53
Ethiopia credit union, Oakland, 953
Etiquette: for young women, 3827
Eubanks, Jonathan, 133
Eugene, Ore.: League of women
    voters, 3753; National assoc.
    for the advancement of colored
    people, 654; urban life, 3753
Evans, Abel H., 2916

Evans, Arthur, 3521
Evans, Bennie, 2706
Evans, Edward N., Jr., 3990
Evans, John Thomas, 444-47
Everett, Wash.: local news columns,
    4257; newspaper, 4269
Evers, Mrs. Medgar (Myrlie), 331,
    3246; article by, 2789; auto-
    biography, 330
Eversley, Fredric, 133
Ewen, David, 2807
Ewer, Peter F., 2474
Ewer, Warren Baxter, 1055
Ewing, Belle C., 332
Exclusive men, San Francisco, 3555
Exhibits: art exhibit catalogs,
    69-110 passim; Negro pageant
    movement, Los Angeles, 1990. See
    also Chicago: World's Columbian
    exposition; Philadelphia: U. S.
    centennial exhibition; Portland:
    Lewis and Clark centennial ex-
    position
Ex parte Archy. See Lee, Archy
Explorers, Spanish, 449, 2060, 2130
Expositions. See Exhibits

F

Fabio, Sarah (Webster), 2497, 2707,
    4004
Fabré, Michel, 333
Fahey, William A., 2340
Fair employment practice commissions.
    See California: state fair em-
    ployment practice commission;
    Employment: fair employment
    practices; Washington (state):
    State fair employment practice
    commission
Fair employment practice committee,
    2376
Fair employment practices, 1839-1943
    passim, 2453
Fairfax, Pearl, 2915
Faith cure, 3202-03, 3339
Family life. See Aid to families
    with dependent children; So-
    ciology; Urban life; etc.
Family planning, 3729
Family savings and loan assoc., Los
    Angeles, 81, 3955
Fannie Wall children's home, Oakland,
    3477-78
Faraday, Rosalind, 2410

Farber, Jerry, 2581
Farmer, George Luther, 1715-16, 2522, 3598-99
Farrell, Joseph Richard, 1002
Fascism: Negro press foundation, Los Angeles, 2288
Faulk, Henry Daniel, 1481
Faulkner, William, 2534-35
Faulkner, William C., 3542
Fauset, Jessie Redmond, 1994, 3717
Favors, Kathryne, 1371
Favors-Curtis, Juanita Gwendolyn, 1717
Fawcett, Margaret Goldsmith, 3247
Fax, Elton Clay, 82
Feather, Leonard, 2808-09
Federal theater project, 2544
Federal writers' project: Calif., 1181a, 2049-50; Colo., 555, 2051
Feeble minded, 3581
Feeley, Malcolm, 1388
Feelings, Tom, 2338, 2500
Fei, John Ching Han, 2177
Feinstein, Lisa Dee, 2523
Feldman, F. L., 896
Felton, Harold W., 2311-12
Ferguson, Charles, 133
Ferguson, George, 3474
Ferguson, Ira Lunan: auto-biography, 334
Ferguson, Lloyd Noel, 3835
Ferguson, R. H., 1238
Ferguson, Xenophon F., 1003
Ferlinghetti, Laurence, 2727
Ferneil, Daniel L., 2914
Ferrell, Dennis, 954
Ferrier, William Warren, 1718
Ferry, W. H., 3016, 3046
Fertility: Seattle trends, 3600
Fiction. See Literature: fiction
Fiction locale. See under geo-graphical locality, e.g., California: as fiction locale; Pasadena: as fiction locale; etc.
Fidao, Jacques, 4029
Fields, Mary: biographical accounts, 345, 470
Fields, Riley, 1045
Fields, W. C., 1994
Fields, William L., 975
Fifteenth amendment: Calif., 1064, 1083; oration, 2584; Oregon, 229-30; Southern opposition, 1033. See also Suffrage
Filipinos: miscegenation, 2794;

secondary education, 1589-90
Filippa Pollia foundation, Los Angeles, 3479
Fillmore district, San Francisco. See Western addition area, San Francisco
Fillmore shopping guide, San Francisco, 4184
Fine arts gallery of San Diego: art holdings, 126
Fine arts patrons of Newport harbor, Newport Beach: art holdings, 125
Finley, Jarvis M., 3600
Finley, Leighton, 33
Finnie, Richard, 955
Finnish, R. A., 3469
Firearms: controversy, 2449
Fire departments. See under name of individual locality, e.g., Berkeley: Fire dept.
First African Methodist Episcopal church, Los Angeles, 3248
First African Methodist Episcopal church, Oakland, 3249-53; publication, 3929
First African Methodist Episcopal church, Pasadena, 3782; publication, 3947
First African Methodist Episcopal Zion church, San Francisco (sometime Starr King A. M. E. Zion church), 3254-58, 3334
Fischer, Russell Glenn, 2524
Fisher, Barbara Ester, 34
Fisher, George W., 3187
Fisher, James Adolphus, 1078, 2052, 4014
Fisher, John (pioneer), 1211
Fisher, John H. (San Francisco, 1952), 3227
Fisher, Lloyd Horace, 3017
Fisher, Paul, 2279
Fishing: (1847), 514
Fisk, Elinor Williams, 3259
Fitch, Henry Delano, 498
Fitnah, Nazzam Al, 2582
Flake family, 453-54
Fleishman, Stanley, 1079
Fleming, G. James, 335, 478
Fleming, J. L., 4219
Fleming, Karl, 729
Fleming, Thomas C., 4202
Flesher, Lorna, 193
Fletcher, Arthur, 2929
Fletcher, Barney, 3556-57

Fletcher, Charles Henry, 1893
Fletcher, F. Marion, 1882
Fletcher, Linda Pickthorne, 1883
Fletcher, Minans H., 994
Fletcher, Robert J., 941, 4163
Fletcher, Mrs. Robert J. (Anna Madah Hyers): biographical account, 458
Flewellyn, Eugene L., 2915
Flipper, Henry Ossian: auto-biography, 336
Flippin, Robert Browning, 540a
Flood, Noah F.: judicial case, 1564-68, 2437-38
Flood, Theodore, 3562
Florence Messenger, 4115
Florida: schools, 1489
Flory, Ishmael P., 337
Flowers, Allen Elmer: family papers, 499
Flowers, Charles E., 956
Flowers, Sarah, 3260-62
Fluellen, Joel, 1989
Flutcher, J. E., 3263
Fogel, Walter A., 1884
Fogelson, Robert M., 713-14, 866-67, 3718
Foley, James, 1182
Folger, Benjamin F., 1057
Folk songs. See Music
Folkes, Robert: legal case, 1105
Folklore, 2509-13, 2816
Folsom, Joseph Libby, 394
Folsom: history, 421
Folsom state prison, 308
Foner, Philip Sheldon, 599
Fontana: housing bias, 2255
Fontellio-Nanton, H. I., 4197
Food. See Cookery
Forbes, Alexander, 1058
Forbes, Jack Douglas, 1720-21, 2053-54, 3601
Ford, Barney L.: biographical account, 471; biography, 405
Ford, George, 2500
Ford, Jesse W., 2914
Ford, John Anson, 3018
Ford, John Major, 576
Ford, Nathaniel, 3391; family, 2027
Ford, W. E., 3264
Ford, William F., 926
Foreman, J. A., 3469
Foreman, Joseph, 2802
Foreman, Thomas E., 3644

Forest, Siles, 3549
Forman, Doyle, 133
Forman, Robert, 516
Fort, Edward Bernard, 1372
Fort Du Chesne, Utah, 483
Fort Harrison, Mont.: newspaper, 4244
Fort Huachuca, Ariz.: local news columns, 4081; nurses, 65; soldiers, 66; USO shows, 40; WAC's experiences, 51
Fort Washakie, Wyo., 483
Fortier, Lillian, 3965
Foster, Ella, 3546
Foster, G. W., 1373
Foundations. See under individual name, e.g., Jeans (Anna T.) foundation; Rosenwald (Julius) fund; Simril-Curry-Moore scholar-ship foundation; Slater (John F.) fund; etc.
Fountain, Oliver, 965
Fourteenth amendment: Calif., 1121; Ore., 229-30
Fowler, James M., 1159, 1175-76
Fowler, John W., 2055
Fowler, Marvin E. See Marvin X (assumed name)
Fowler, Orin, 3377
Fowler: local news columns, 4146, 4193
Fox, Theron, 2790
France, Edward Everett, 1183
Francis, Abner Hunt: biographical account, 460-61
Francis, Cornelius, 3562
Francis, George M., 4300
Francis, J. H. Davies, 2056-57
Francis, James Eugene, 3568
Francis, John A., 965
Francis, Joseph Smallwood, 2278, 4149
Francis, Marion M., 3561
Francis, Robert Coleman, 957, 1885
Francois, Terry Arthur, 868, 2942
Frank, Frank Hillel, 1722
Frankel, Benjamin Adam, 1004
Franklin, Beatrice (Cannady), 4254
Franklin, Beryldell Crutchfield, 2411
Franklin, Chester Arthur, 4231
Franklin, G. F., 4231
Franklin, Howard, 3196
Franklin, John Hope, 1341
Franklin, Raymond S., 3836
Franklin, Ruth, 715

Franklin, William E., 3378

Fraser, Clara: taped interview, 500

Fraternal organizations: American woodmen, 3508-09, 3890, 4048; elks of the world, Improved benevolent protective order, 3512; in San Jose, 2994; Knights of Pythias, 3533-35; odd fellows, Grand united order of, 3538; odd fellows, Independent order of, 2790; Pacific coast membership lists, 473. See also Freemasons; Greek letter societies; Social clubs

Frazier, Edward Franklin, 3592

Free speech: at Berkeley, 890

Freedman, Edward, 2209

Freedman, Mervin B., 1637

Freedman: fictional account, 2646

Freedman's commission of the Protestant Episcopal church, 3238

Freedmen, 2038; (1790-1860), 2083-84; (1830-80), 2112; in Calif., 2016, 3357; in Ore., 3387

Freedmen's missionary committee of Calif., 2007

Freedom of speech: at Berkeley, 890

Freeman, Don, 2313, 2332

Freeman, Harrop Arthur, 2439

Freeman, Leah, 165

Freeman, Samuel E., 3526

Freeman, Shepard S., 3204, 4113, 4286

Freeman, Walter, 965

Freemasons, 3543-44; dissertation, 3536. See also Prince Hall

Freemasons. Arizona: Grand lodge proceedings, 3513

Freemasons. California, 3537; Ancient Arabic order of the nobles of the mystic shrine, Oakland, 3514-15; Berkeley, 3516; Conventional independent grand lodge, 3517; Heroines of Jericho, 3518; Knights templars, 3519; Los Angeles, 3520; publication, 3986; Sacramento, 2128; Scottish rite, Oakland, 3514

Freemasons. California. Order of eastern star: directory, 3523; history, 3528; official organ of, 3962; proceedings, 3529; yearbook, 3530

Freemasons. California. Prince Hall grand lodge: centennial history, 3521, 3524; constitution, 3522; directories, 3523, 3525; Marysville meeting, 3510; official publications, 4006, 4043; proceedings, 3526; sourvenir programs, 3527

--Colorado. Prince Hall grand lodge: constitution, 3531; proceedings, 3532

--Nevada: Carson City lodge, 2010

--Washington (state): United grand lodge, 3532a

Freeways: illumination by auto headlights, 3837; cause of segregation, 1404

Frelow, Robert Dean, 1582

Fremont, John Charles, 360, 2099, 2472, 3830

French, Gerald Dean, 1525

French, Marie Louise (Reid), 2634-35

Fresno: African Methodist Episcopal church, 3185; Al Kitab Sudan publications, 2336, 2731-32; Booker T. Washington memorial society, 3547; Calif. state univ. library holdings, 159; Colored league of women voters, 2902a; directory, 1267; local news columns, 4080-81, 4148-49, 4193, 4198-99, 4202, 4206-07; model cities program, 3770; newspapers, 4070-72; urban life, 3770

--Public schools: compensatory education, 1723; primary and preschool, 1563; secondary, 1602; segregation, 1389

Fresno county: Colored colonization assoc., 1174; public welfare, 3583, 3594

Fresno Fresno county banner, 2273

Freudenthal, Daniel K., 1374

Friedman, Laurence J., 3019

Friedman, Ralph, 1963, 2377

Friendship Baptist church, Pasadena, 3264

Frierson, Eugene P., 2636

Friis, Leo J., 1080

Fritchman, Stephen Hole, 716

Fry, Kenneth B., 1358

Fryson, William, 3458

Fugitive slaves. See Slavery

Fulford, Robert L., 2525

Fulks, Bryan, 2058

Fuller, Adams J., 2915
Fuller, Hoyt William, 83, 2526
Fuller, Juanita Boykin, 194
Fuller, Varden, 1219
Fuller, William Parmer, 1057
Fulweiler, Charles Radcliffe, 3602
Funeral rites and customs, 2511
Fur trade, 978, 2014, 2041. See
    also Beckwourth, James Pierson;
    Clamorgan, Jacques; Harris,
    Moses; Light, Allen B.; Ranne,
    Peter; etc.
Furgatch, Leon, 338

G

Gabel, Hortense W., 2171
Gadsden, James, 1218, 3400; family,
    3358
Gaffney, Floyd, 2527
Gafford, Alice (Taylor), 81, 124,
    127
Gage, R. P., 932, 934
Gail, G., 832
Gaines, Ernest J., 2612, 2637-39
Gaither, Thomas W., 4045
Galdone, Paul, 2314
Gandhi, Mohandas Karamchand, 3305
Gant, Charles G.: papers, 2886
Gant, Harry, 962
Gant, Matthew, 2640
Gantner, Vallejo, 3379
García, María, 2096
Gardiner, Howard Calhoun, 2059
Gardner, A. J., 937
Gardner, Benjamin Franklin, 2708
Gardner, David P., 600
Gardner, Steve, 3676
Gardner, William, 3198
Garfield, John, 1964
Garmer, L., 3553
Garner, E. D., 3175
Garner, George, 4078
Garrison, Lillian Joy, 84
Garrott, Alva Curtis, 2234
Garry, Charles R., 2448, 2450
Garton, Christiana, 2528
Gartrell, Richard Blair, 2449
Garvey, Marcus Mosiah, 885, 3882.
    See also Universal Negro im-
    provement assoc. and African
    communities league
Gas industry: employment in, 1832.
    See also Petroleum industry
Gass, Gertrude Zemon, 1926

Gautier, Antone D., 3458
Gaynes, Norris L., 3462
Gayton, John Thomas: family, 325;
    papers, 501
Geismar, Maxwell, 308
Genet, Jean, 2456
Gentry, Meredith Poindexter, 3380
Gentry, Walter, 936
Georgetown, 2790
Georgia: Atlanta univ., 1503; Clark
    college, 1478; schools, 1485
Gerard, Maurice (pseud.), 2887
Gerber, Sidney, 2178
Gerberding, Christian Otto, 1058
Geriatrics. See Longevity
Germond, Jack W., 2888
Gerner, Henry L., 1081
Gerson, Walter M., 3603
Gibb, Daniel, 1058
Gibbons, Henry, 1058
Gibbons, Rodmond, 3381
Gibbs, Mifflin Wistar: autobiography,
    339-40; biographical accounts,
    359, 471, 474-75; letter, 2013
Gibson, D. G., 3458
Gibson, Lucinda (Ray), 3187
Giddings, Joshua Reed, 3382
Gier, Joseph Thomas, 3837
Gilbert, Gar, 2716
Gilbert, Zack, 2709
Gilchrist, William, 2915
Giles, Abram, 3187
Giles, Arimia, 3187
Giles, Hermann Harry, 1375
Gillem, Albert, 2915
Gillem, Mary, 2915
Gillespie, Marcia, 3950a
Gilliam, Harold, 3719
Gillis, William Robert, 1249
Gilman, R., 2529
Gilman, Thomas, 456
Gilmore, R. C., 3198
Ginger, Ann Fagan, 2450
Gitchoff, George Thomas, 3720
Gitelson, Alfred E., 1376
Gladden, Geno, 4165
Glasgow, Douglas Graham, 717
Glass, Alvin W., 938
Glass, Charlie, 3172
Glass, Edward L. N., 35
Glass, John Franklin, 3604
Glass, Susan, 2765
Glazer, Nathan, 2179, 3096
Gleaves, Beverly, 2502
Glendale: housing discrimination, 2234

Glick, Ronald, 869-70
Glock, Charles Y., 3020
Glover, Frances B., 4202
Glover, Robert, 133
Godden, Frank D., 4035
Godfrey, H. H., 968
Godfrey, William G., 4153
Goff, Dewey, 2187
Golden gate Methodist Episcopal
    church, Oakland, 3245
Golden state mutual life insurance
    co., Los Angeles, 113, 940, 987,
    1638, 1933; employment and
    training practices, 1892; fine
    arts holdings, 85-87, 127;
    serial publications, 3958-59,
    3979
Goldfield, Nev.: local news
    columns, 4207
Goldner, William, 2180
Goldsmith, Renee Lois, 3721
Goldsmith, W. P., 1055
Goldstein, Lillian Faidar, 1526
Goncalves, Joe, 3970
Good, Donnie D., 36
Gooden, John Eddie, 1482
Goodlett, Carlton Benjamin, 1527,
    2766, 4202; papers, 502
Goodman, George, 3256
Goodman, George W., 718
Goodman, Mary, 3481
Goodman, Paul, 2710
Goodrich, J., 2451
Goodson, Jim, 4111
Goodwin, B. G., 3540
Goodwin, Cardinal Leonidas, 1082
Goodwin, David, 4153
Goodwin, Leroy, 2711
Goodwin, Ruby (Berkley), 2852;
    autobiography, 341; poems,
    2712-14
Goodwin, Terenz: taped interview,
    503
Goody, Charles, 2926
Gordon, C. D., 3175
Gordon, Elizabeth De Louis
    (Davis), 3021
Gordon, Frank A., 2763
Gordon, Harry L., 3539
Gordon, Russell T., 133
Gordon, Taylor, 342, 452, 2810
Gordon, W. C., 2763
Gordon, Walter Arthur: bio-
    graphical accounts, 337, 3648;
    dissertation, 959; letters,

3853; taped interview, 504
Gordon, William, 1045
Gorham, Thelma Thurston, 2280, 2641,
    3022, 3969
Gould, Norma, 2841
Government: bibliography of publica-
    tions (1960-70), 193; San Fran-
    cisco bay area directory, 1272a
Graham, A. H., 4180
Graham, Alfred W., 2875
Graham, Arthur Joseph, 2494, 2559-60
Graham, B. H., 946
Graham, Benzell, 2314-15, 2642
Graham, Charles J., 3403
Graham, D., 3194
Graham, Mrs. Daniel, 3194
Graham, Hugh Davis, 2281
Graham, Isaiah, 3403
Graham, Katheryn (Campbell), 2642
Graham, Lorenz B., 2316-22
Graham, Luelva Broussard, 1308
Granberg, W. J., 960, 1639
Grand united order of odd fellows,
    3538
Grant, Curtis Robert, 3265
Grant, Doris, 1528
Grant, Eva H., 1724
Grant, George, 946
Grant, M. Earl: biographical account,
    463
Grass Valley: directory, 1240;
    public schools, 1818
Grasses, James, 527
Graves, Albert, 3462
Graves, Jackson Alpheus, 343
Gray, E. B., 936
Gray, Elizabeth, 3266-67
Gray, Elizabeth Bayne, 1005
Gray, Henry, 3266-67
Gray, Matthias, 1058
Gray, William Theodore, 1483
Great Falls, Mont.: local news
    columns, 4243, 4246, 4257
Greek letter societies: sorority
    publications, 3893, 3969. See
    also Benevolent societies;
    Fraternal organizations; etc.
Greeley, Horace, 3443
Green, Andrew, 978
Green, Buddy, 2452, 2486
Green, Dick, 978
Green, E. R., 952
Green, Frank, 3550
Green, J. W., 4146
Green, Jerome, 3023

Green, John, 3958
Green, Kenneth, 3722
Green, Robert, 953
Green, Rose, 127
Green, Ruth A., 3962
Green, S. Wendell, 4201
Green, Thomas Jefferson, 3400
Green river coal company, 990
Greenberg, Jack, 2453
Greene, Bill, 2889
Greene, David Myron, 2889a
Greene, Donald, 133
Greene, Emily Jane, 2715
Greene, Michael, 133
Greene, Thomas Augustus, 313, 4088
Greene, William, 2937
Greenley, William, 3187
Greenwood, John, 3007
Greenwood, Robert, 154
Greer, Scott Allen, 2378
Gregory, Dick, 1974
Gregory, Thomas, 1176
Gregory, Wayne, 2561
Grey, Lloyd V., 3554
Grier, Albert C., 3268
Grier, Eunice S., 2182
Grier, William Henry, 2767, 2945, 3861
Griffin, Adolphus D., 1250, 3838, 4257, 4293
Griffin, Daniel Webster, 4271, 4290
Griffin, Edna La Flore, 2288, 2760
Griffin, Henry, 3264
Griffin, J. M., 4249
Griffin, John Howard, 3024
Griffin, Ples Andrew, 1377
Griffin, Walter, 4272
Griffith, Thomas L., Jr., 2272
Griffiths, Eleanor Wright, 2530
Griffiths, Keith S., 3025-26
Grigly, Thomas, 1159
Grigsby, J. Eugene, 78
Grimes, G. G., 3458
Grimes, Leola: taped interview, 505
Grimké, Francis James, 506
Grimm, L. E., 933
Grissom, Thomas William, 1886
Grocery trade: Negro alliance grocery co., 965
Grodzins, Morton, 3096, 3723
Groff, Patrick J., 1725
Grose, William, 497
Gross, Robert George, 973
Gross, Werter Livingston, 2643

Gross, William, 497, 1045; family papers, 507
Groves, J. D., 2273
Groves, John Wesley, 2644
Grubbs, Albert, 1112
Grubbs, Edward, 3992, 4019
Grubbs, Ella, 3462
Gruenberg, Barry, 3115
Grunwald, Joan H., 1529
Gudgel, J. W., 3307
Guidance. See Education: counseling and guidance
Guild, Ella June (Purcell), 3027
Guillén, Nicolás, 1002, 2716
Guinn, James Miller, 3724-25
Gunsky, Frederic R., 1378, 1726
Gurian, Marlene, 1266
Gustafson, Susan Louise, 2412
Gwin, William McKendree, 1064
Gwynn, Douglas Bruce, 1887

H

Hacker, Frederick J., 719
Hackett, James Alexander, 835, 951
Hackett, Mattie (Nance), 1727
Hackett, Sylvester R., 951
Hackley, Edwin H., 4231
Hadsell, Virginia T., 1379
Hadwen, Theodore, 3605
Haehn, James O., 3839
Hafen, Leroy R., 344
Hager, Don J., 1380
Hager, John Sharpenstein, 1064, 1083
Haight, Fletcher Mathew, 1058
Haight-Ashbury settlement house art project, San Francisco, 112
Haine, Joseph, 1058
Haines, Aubrey, 2183
Haines, George H., 3194
Haiti: history, 1005; migration from Calif., 1029; U. S. relations with, 1015
Haley, Fred T., 1381
Hall, Charles Edward, 1222-23
Hall, Edward, 3568
Hall, H. Tom, 2344
Hall, John, 2102
Hall, Marion, 3185
Hall, Martin, 3269
Hall, Olysteen, 3302
Hall, Richard A., 2870, 3556
Hall, William Henry, 2270
Halliburton, Cecil D., 1965
Hallie Q. Brown index, 201

Hallock, Robert, 2340

Halperin, Bernard Seymour, 2890

Halpern, Betty, 1383

Halpern, Manfred, 3028

Halpern, Ray, 1382–83

Halpin, James, 1966

Halstead, Donna J., 3693, 3726

Hamann, Carolyn, 4153

Hamilton, John, 3568

Hamilton, Michael, 2592

Hamilton, W. H. (San Diego), 1159, 1176

Hamilton, Walter, 1888

Hamilton, William H. (San Francisco), 1045

Hamm, Hillard, 4067

Hammers, Ronald, 133

Hammons, David, 133

Hampton, Claudia Hudley, 1384

Hampton institute, 3847

Hancock, Allen C., 1583

Handcock, Clifford C., 3840

Hanford, Cornelius Holgate, 37

Hanford: African Methodist Episcopal Zion church, 3191; local news columns, 4080, 4146, 4193; rubber tire industry, 1913

Hannah, Helen Wallis, 1309

Hannon, Michael, 720

Hano, Arnold, 3645

Hansberry, Lorraine, 2515, 2553

Hansen, Barret Eugene, 2811

Hanson, Earl, 3029

Harden, Marvin, 76, 120, 138, 144

Harding, Mrs. George Laban (Dorothy H. Huggins), 3727

Harding, Nathaniel R., 975

Harding, Thomas, 3550

Hardwick, Leon, 970

Hare, Nathan, 871, 1640, 1659, 3606, 3913

Hargrove, James, 3256, 3568

Harguss, Henrietta (Thompson), 3187

Harlan, Hugh, 2049

Harlem, 871; as fiction locale, 2667. See also New York City

Harper, Helena Hester, 3728

Harper, Michael S., 2717

Harper, William H., 1045

Harrell, Hugh, 133

Harrell, Jerry D., 654

Harris, America, 3460

Harris, B. F., 972

Harris, "Black". See Harris, Moses

Harris, Charles Alexander, 3302

Harris, Claiborne H., 941

Harris, Cosmo, 4229a

Harris, Elizabeth, 994

Harris, Ellsworth C., 981

Harris, Florence, 1584

Harris, George W., 2060

Harris, Gertrude, 3485

Harris, Howard, 944

Harris, J. C., 3548

Harris, Jeff, 2337

Harris, Joan R., 3607

Harris, John, 3256

Harris, Leon R., 2645

Harris, Leonard, 3546

Harris, Lulu B., 3460

Harris, Mark, 345

Harris, Mayme, 3307

Harris, Michael, 601

Harris, Morgan, 1641

Harris, Moses, 2028; biographical account, 344

Harris, Munford, 3562

Harris, Scotland, 133

Harris, Sheldon, 641

Harris, Theresa Ella, 3729

Harris, Thomas Walter, 2562

Harris, William, 3256

Harrison, De Leon, 2497

Harrison, Gloria, 655

Harrison, Jerry, 2718

Harrison, Nathaniel: biographical accounts, 283, 346, 361, 434, 448

Harrison, Walter, 3539

Harrod, J. A., 3222

Hart, Beula: taped interview, 508

Hart, Charles R. D., 3383

Hart, John D., 3172

Hart, John Fraser, 1184

Hartgraves, Arthur Wayne, 2184

Harvey, James Rose, 2061–62

Harvey, John A., 3646

Harvey, Madison, 3969a

Harvey, Richard, 2881

Harvey, Roy, 11

Harwood, Jim, 1229

Hatch, James Vernon, 195

Hatch, Robert H., 1585

Hatcher, Richard, 3020

Hathman, John L., 1238

Hats, women's: designer, 423

Hatton, John Mervyn, 3030

Haughey, John C., 602

Havre, Mont.: local news columns, 4246

Hawaii, 2080-81, 2956; historic sites, 2047; Honolulu attorney, 540a; integration, 3635; labor, 2402; miscegenation, 2791; public schools, 540a, 1816; race relations, 3008, 3422, 3614; slavery, 3422; steel industry, 1923; tourism, 3842

Hawaiians: (1785-95), 2110; (1847-48), 514

Hawkins, Augustus F., 2996

Hawkins, Eugene, 133

Hawkins, George W., 3545

Hawkins, John H., 3553

Hawkins, Leland Stanford, 1874, 1888

Hawkins, S. W., 931, 968, 2273

Hawthorne: Ballona avenue school, 2504

Hayakawa, Samuel Ichiyé, 3031, 3841

Hayden, Palmer, 133

Hayes, Benjamin Ignatius, 2063

Hayes, Edward C., 3032

Hayes, Leroy, 3561

Hayes, Olen, 969

Hayes, Robert Lee, 3842

Hayes, Roland, 2802, 3873

Hayne, Sarah, 3817

Haynie, Wilbur, 125, 134, 136

Hays, Mitzi Pitts, 1728

Hayward: Chabot college library holdings, 180; Mecco enterprises, inc., 3990

--Calif. state univ.: Black students union, 3914; library holdings, 160

Hazard, Ben, 133

Head, Robert W., 963

Heald, Weldon F., 2064

Health. See Medicine and health; Public health

Heaps, Willard Allison, 2323

Heard, J. Norman, 2065

Hearst, Bennie: taped interview, 509

Heath, Jim F., 3033

Hechter, H. H., 2768

Heer, David M., 2791

Heffernon, Andrew William, 1310

Heitman, Khatanga, 3730

Helena, Mont.: African Methodist Episcopal church, 3183; local news columns, 4243, 4257; newspapers, 4245-47

Helix, Daniel Clare, 1385

Heller, Joseph Richard, 3034

Heller, Paul, 196

Hell's angels: in Los Angeles, 829

Heltsley, Diane Victoria, 1586

Helwig, Adelaide Berta, 1006, 3435

Henderson, Alfred L., 4262a

Henderson, Archie Maree, 1185

Henderson, D. J., 915

Henderson, David, 2497

Henderson, Edwin Bancroft, 3647-49

Henderson, Joseph White, 2891

Henderson, Lenneal J., 347, 2892

Henderson, Leroy W., 133

Henderson, Marjorie, 2185

Henderson, Nelson, 968

Henderson, William Mike, 133

Hendrick, Irving G., 1386, 1441

Hendricks, Harry G., 1484

Hendrickson, James E., 3384

Henehan, Anne, 721, 725

Heningburg, Alphonse M., 1084

Hennessey, Erin, 1643

Henry, F. P., 2356

Henry, Francis, 348

Henry, Helen Elizabeth, 3270

Henry, S. W., 4251

Henry, Will (pseud.), 2646

Herberg, Will, 722

Heredity and environment. See Sociology

Herman, Melvin, 793

Herndon, Angelo, 4195; judicial case, 2484

Herndon, James, 1587-88

Heroines of Jericho, 3518

Herrick, William Francis, 1058

Herskovits, Melville Jean, 88-89

Hertz, Ruby Cohen, 2454

Herzog, June, 2379

Hester, B. L., 967

Hewes, Laurence I., Jr., 2959, 3017

Hewitt, Mary Jane C., 872

Hews, Larry, 4083, 4117

Heyman, Ira Michaels, 1388, 1821, 2893

Heyman, J. M., 2455

Heywood, Yates, 3035

Hibler, Madge Beatrice, 2413

Hickerson, Nathaniel, 1347, 1387, 1589-90

Hickman, Mrs. Paul Edward (Verna Alvis Wright), 3959

Hicks, Estelle (Bell): autobiography, 349

Hicks, Leon, 133

Hicks, Maggie E., 3302
Hicks, Oscar J., 2917
Hides and tallow trade (1843), 514.
    See also Agriculture; Cowboys;
    Ranch life
Highland hospital, Oakland, 2779,
    2902a
Hightower, Jack, 969
Highways. See Freeways
Hilburn, Lincoln C., 3921
Hill, Beatrice M., 1730
Hill, Bessie S., 3460
Hill, Daniel Grafton, 2066-67,
    2894
Hill, Herbert, 1922
Hill, Herman, 969
Hill, James, 945
Hill, Joseph Tyler, 3271
Hill, Laurence Landreth, 350-51
Hill, N. H., 3189
Hill, R. C., 3345, 3348
Hill, Roscoe, 1388
Hill, Roy L., 465, 873
Hill, Stephen Spencer, 2078,
    3373a
Hillery, William H., 3256-58
Himes, Chester B., 874-75, 2583,
    2647-55
Hine, Leland D., 3272
Hines, Harvey K., 352
Hippler, Arthur Edwin, 3732
Hirabayashi, Joanne, 2324
Hiram club, Bakersfield, 2563
Hispanic America, 999-1013
    passim
Historical records survey: Baptist
    church directory, 3273
Historical society of southern
    Calif., Los Angeles, 3733
Historic sites, 2008-09, 2047
History, 2005-2130, 3601, 3829-30;
    African, 8-9; bibliography,
    196; Calif., 1763, 2006-2128
    passim; Calif. bibliographies,
    209, 244; Calif. race relations,
    3160; Calif. historical murals,
    86; Mormon Negro policy, 3138;
    of education, 1718, 1733-34,
    1773, 1798, 1814, 1823; resource
    books, 1796-97, 2013, 2111, 3861;
    teaching of, 1639, 1697-98,
    1719, 1796-97, 2031, 2048, 2095,
    2111, 2117; textbooks, 2331-33.
    See also under geographical
    locality, e.g., Los Angeles:

history; San Francisco: history;
    etc.
Hitch, Charles, 603
Hittell, John Shertzer, 1058
Hittell, Theodore Henry, 1058, 2069
Hoagland, Everett, 2719
Hoard, Jessie D., 861
Hoard, Sophie Ann, 861
Hobart, Susan Gail, 2895
Hobbs, Thadeaus Henry, 2896
Hobson, Gregory, 3462, 3546
Hobson, Mrs. Gregory, 2902b
Hodge, Dorothy F., 2531
Hodge, Jacqueline G., 1389
Hodge, M., 914
Hoffland, Laura Hildreth, 3795
Hogg, Thomas Clark, 2070, 3274
Hohn, F. R., 1390, 1591
Holbrook, C. H., 1057
Holbrook, Charles E., 1058
Holcomb, Alethia, 3497
Holden, David, 931
Holder, Julius W., 4170
Holdredge, Helen (O'Donnell), 353-54,
    1230; research notes, 510
Holisi, Clyde, 876
Holland, A. F., 1174
Holland, H. R., 1045
Holley, John, 2251
Hollinger, William H., 2769
Hollingsworth, Alvin, 2500
Hollins, W. D., 3194
Hollister: local news columns,
    4206-07
Hollowdyce, A. B., 1175
Hollowell, Ellis Chandler, 356
Hollywood. See Los Angeles
Hollywood Scottsboro committee, 2445
Hollywood-Wilshire fair housing
    council, Los Angeles, 3964
Holman, Vincent I., 3567
Holmes, Bob, 2186
Holmes, H., 3458
Holmes, Robin: judicial case, 3391
Holmes, Samuel Jackson, 3843-45
Holmes family, 3358
Holyoke, S. J., 565
Homager, Henry, 3222
Home for aged and infirm colored
    people of Calif., Oakland,
    3480-82
Home owners' defense council, Los
    Angeles, 2187
Homestead law: judicial case, 2260,
    2437-38; exception made, 1151

Homitz, Wallace, 850
Honeybuss, Claude C., 1990
Hong, Sung C., 3036
Hooker, Forrestine Cooper, 34
Hooper, Elvoyce, 133
Hooper, William, 1058
Hopkins, Donald, 1085
Hopkins, Glen, 2187
Hopkins, Starling James, 980
Hopkins family, 3358
Horlick, Nancy Jane, 2414
Horne, Frank Smith, 1485
Horne, James, 4153
Horne, Lena, 2328
Hornitos: Washington mining co.,
    993a
Horowitz, Benjamin, 113
Horowitz, Harold, 1388
Horse training, 3852
Horsemanship. See Dodson, Jacob
Horton, Eliza, 3275
Hosman, A. J., 3188
Hospitals. See Medicine and health
Hotels: biography of Barney L.
    Ford, 405; employment, 1895;
    in San Francisco, 1074, 1125,
    1895; in San Jose, 2995. See
    also names of individual hotels
    under geographical locality,
    e.g., Los Angeles: Somerville
    hotel; San Francisco: City
    hotel
Houghton, Jean Ann, 2282
House of Umoja: publication, 3912
Houseworth, Thomas, 1058
Housing, 486, 1710, 2131-2263, 2989,
    3050, 3122, 3136, 3590, 3599,
    3829; bibliographies, 174, 211;
    Congress of racial equality
    papers, 862; fictional account,
    2665; Hollywood-Wilshire fair
    housing council news, 3964; in
    San Francisco bay area, 2133;
    Mid-peninsula citizens for fair
    housing newsletter, Palo Alto,
    3980; Rumford Calif. fair
    housing act, 2131-2254 passim.
    See also Restrictive covenants;
    Urban redevelopment; and under
    geographical locality, e.g.,
    Los Angeles: housing
Houston, Frederick A., 3523
Houston, Norman Oliver, 946
Houston, Richard T., 973, 2278,
    2472, 3557

Houston, Sylvester R., 2897
Houston, Tex.: freedom ride, 1097-
    98; riot, 881; urban life, 3761
Howard, People vs. (judicial case),
    2437-38
Howard, Ashbury, 2380
Howard, Dero J., 979, 3539
Howard, G. F., 2356
Howard, H. A., 4133
Howard, John, 881, 1765-66
Howard, John C., 1889
Howard, John Robert, 559
Howard, Joseph H., 2812
Howard, Leonzie Billy, 3608
Howard, Lucille, 3488
Howard, Michael, 1045
Howard, W. L., 968
Howard, Warren S., 3436-37
Howard, William Davis Merry, 2071
Howard univ., Washington, D. C.:
    art holdings, 128; library
    holdings, 197-98
Howay, Frederic William, 1186-87
Howden, Edward, 857, 1019
Howe, John W., 3385
Howell, Harry D., 2656
Howell, John Bernard, 90
Howell, Raymond, 133
Howell, Thomas James, 2656
Howison, Victorinne Hall, 1530
Hubbard, E. T., 4134
Hubbard, James H., 2584
Hubbard, John Purley, 1086, 3037,
    3226, 3276-77
Hudson, Barbara, 1866
Hudson, Cordelia J., 2657
Hudson, Luther Martin, 968
Hudson, Oscar, 3889
Hueber, D. F., 3038
Huffman, Eugene Henry, 876a, 1188,
    2564, 2658, 3277a-b, 3846, 3937a
Huggins, Dorothy H. See Harding,
    Mrs. George Laban (Dorothy H.
    Huggins)
Hughes, Langston, 1696, 1968-69,
    2325-28, 2495, 2530, 2716, 2850-
    51, 3479, 3502, 3873
Hughes, Lloyd Harris, 1007
Hughes, Ruth Carol, 1087
Hughes, William Edward, 1731
Huls, H. K., 933
Hult, Ruby El, 2565
Hultgren, Ruth Davis, 1531
Human relations agencies. See
    Community service organizations

Humiston, Thomas Frederic, 1642
Humor, 3846. See also Comic books
Humphrey, Dwight H., 199
Humphrey, Margo, 133
Humphrey, Mary J., 3481
Hundley, Walter, 2185
Hungerford, Thomas W., 3039
Hunsaker, Jane Chandler: papers, 511
Hunt, Aurora, 3386
Hunt, Curtis N., 966
Hunt, Ollie T., 966
Hunt, Richard (artist), 127, 133
Hunt, Richard (news commentator), 701
Hunter, Floyd, 2188-89
Hunter, Robert G., 1970
Hunters Point-Bayview community health service, San Francisco, 3965
Hunter's Point beacon, 4188
Hunters Point district, San Francisco. See San Francisco: Hunters Point
Hunter's Point spokesman, San Francisco, 4200
Huntington, Collis Potter, 3847
Huntington, J. W. P., 3387
Hunton, A. W., 3574
Hurd, William, 3192
Hutchinson, William H., 357
Hydes, Foster, 830
Hyers, Anna Madah (Mrs. Robert J. Fletcher): biographical account, 458
Hyers, Emma Louise: biographical account, 458
Hyman, Henry, 3567

I

I. B. P. O. E. W. See Elks of the world, Improved benevolent protective order
Iceberg Slim (pseud.). See Beck, Robert
Idaho: African Methodist Episcopal church (1863), 3177; census (1870-80), 1299; directory, 1269; historic sites, 2047; laws, statutes, etc., 2467-67a; lumber industry, 1889
Idaho Springs, Ida.: local news columns, 4243
Identity. See Sociology

Ikard, Bose: biographical account, 470
Iliff, John G., 200
I. L. W. U. See International long-shoremen's & warehousemen's union
Immaculate heart college, Los Angeles, 1643
Immigration. See Migration
Imperial Valley, 3831
Improved benevolent protective order, elks of the world. See Elks of the world, Improved benevolent protective order
Ince, John E., 950
Independent voters, Los Angeles, 2898
Index to selected periodicals, 201
Indians: blacks among, 2065; Calif. (1847), 514; miscegenation, 2794
Industrial arts. See Education: industrial arts
Industry, 948, 1832-1939 passim. See also Labor and under names of individual industries, e.g., Drug industry; Insurance; etc.
Infante, Isa, 2494
Inger, Morton, 1361
Ingerman, Sidney, 2368
Inghram, Dorothy, 1391
Inglewood, Marian, 3278
Inglewood: American nationalist, 3141; library exhibit, 93; public schools, 1682; Woodmen minstrels, 2864
Inglewood raiders (Ku klux klan), 3041
Ingraham, George, 835, 951
Institute of labor and industrial relations, Univ. of Michigan-Wayne state univ.: employment bibliography, 202
Institute on community relations, Los Angeles county, 3059, 3077
Insurance, 956; American woodmen, 3508; in U. S., 954, 1883; in Watts, 693. See also Golden state mutual life insurance co., Los Angeles
Integration. See Segregation
Intergroup relations assoc. of northern Calif., 3975
Intermarriage. See Miscegenation
International brotherhood of boiler-makers, iron shipbuilders, welders and helpers of America, 2376, 2403
International ladies garment workers union, 2390

International library of Negro life
and history, 3848
International longshoremen's &
warehousemen's union, San
Francisco, 2381
International union of mine, mill
and smelter workers, 2380
Interracial committee, Tucson, 3043
Interracial council for business
opportunity, Los Angeles, 1251
Inventors, 312, 457
Irvine: Calif. univ., 2958
Isaacs, Edith Juliet (Rich), 1971
Isaacs, Isaac, 294
Isaacs, John Benjamin St. Felix,
3279
Isenberg, Irwin, 725
I. U. M. M. & S. W. See Inter-
national union of mine, mill
and smelter workers
Iverson, J. E., 3264
Ivie, Ardie, 2382
Izor, R., 3194

J

Jackmon, Owendell, 967
Jackson, Callie D., 994
Jackson, F. W., 3303
Jackson, Fay M., 3957, 4081
Jackson, George (Arizona), 3849
Jackson, George (Soledad prison),
2456
Jackson, George W., 4191
Jackson, Giles B., 891
Jackson, H. E., 2356, 2371
Jackson, Ida Louise: article by,
2899; reminiscences, 476, 541;
thesis, 1732
Jackson, J. H., 3280
Jackson, James W., 38
Jackson, John, 3192
Jackson, John Henry, 1733-34, 4219
Jackson, Joseph Sylvester, 1311,
2383
Jackson, Lillie, 1231
Jackson, M. B., 726
Jackson, Maria E., 3187
Jackson, Mary Coleman, 2329
Jackson, Mattie, 2509
Jackson, Miles M., 203
Jackson, Moses A., 3388
Jackson, Peter, 3648
Jackson, Robert, 3554
Jackson, Sametta Wallace, 359

Jackson, Thelma, 2185
Jackson, Thomas Conrad, 1735
Jackson, W. A., 2754
Jackson, W. Warner, 2659
Jackson, Wilfred P., 1736
Jackson, William (artist), 133
Jackson, William (Oakland, 1927), 914
Jacobs, Alma (Smith), 259
Jacobs, Barbara, 2335
Jacobs, Lou, Jr., 2335
Jacobs, O., 3012
Jacobs, Paul, 604, 1890, 1922, 3735
Jahn, Julius Armin, 3736
Jamaica: history, 1003; political
leaders, 997; slave laws, 1012
Jamerson, L. S., Jr., 4002
James, Clarence L., 3302
James, Elorise N., 4065
James, Joseph (Marinship employee),
2403
James, Joseph (San Francisco author),
3102, 3609
James, Laura M., 361
James, Stuart B., 3044
James, Wilmer, 133
Jameson, Harold A., 3567
Jamestown: mining, 3392a
Japanese: in Calif., 3588; in San
Francisco, 3022; in Watts, 749;
miscegenation, 2794; shipyard
labor, 2355; urban life, 3755
Jarrard, Raymond Dennis, 1737
Jarrette, Alfred Q., 560
Jasper, James, 2073
Jaxon, J. C. C., 2916
Jazz. See Music
Jeans (Anna T.) foundation, 1683
Jefferson, Thomas J., 952
Jeffries, Vincent John, 759-60, 3045
Jenkins, Deaderick Franklin, 2660-61
Jenkins, Valesta, 3160
Jenness, Mary, 466-67
Jennings, Elijah: biographical
account, 358
Jennings, Salena G., 3302
Jensen, Arthur Robert, 1392
Jensen, Joan M., 2190
Jernagin, Howard Eugene, 2283
Jerome, Victor Jeremy, 1972-73
Jews: Anti-defamation league, Los
Angeles, 2429; in San Francisco
bay area, 3137; in schools, 1702;
race relations, 2962; Westside
Jewish community center, Los
Angeles, 144

Job training. See Employment:
    job and on-job training
Johanesen, Harry, 2074
Johannsen, Robert Walter, 2075,
    3389
Johansen, Dorothy O., 2076
John Birch society, 2440
Johns, William N., 133
Johnson, Andrew, 2890
Johnson, Barbara Child, 1532
Johnson, Brooks, 1974
Johnson, Charles Spurgeon, 2384-85
Johnson, Clifford Frederick, 2284
Johnson, Daniel, 127
Johnson, David, 2942
Johnson, Elizabeth F., 3460
Johnson, Emma, 861
Johnson, Eugene G., 2763
Johnson, Evelyn (Allen), 2662
Johnson, Ezra Rothschild, 2585,
    2772
Johnson, Fostina, 4133
Johnson, George (Berkeley), 3458
Johnson, George (Hanford), 3191
Johnson, George Marion, 3850;
    biographical account, 428
Johnson, George Perry: Lincoln
    motion picture co., 962, 1975;
    memorabilia collection, 1976;
    taped interview, 1975
Johnson, H. T. S., 2452
Johnson, Hall, 2539, 2796, 2813-15
Johnson, Hycinthia L., 1739
Johnson, I. H., 2532
Johnson, Mrs. Ivan (Dorothy P.
    Vena), 1738, 2498
Johnson, J. E., 3221
Johnson, Jack (boxer). See
    Johnson, John Alfred
Johnson, Jack (Los Angeles, 1904),
    3192
Johnson, James, 1159, 1175-76
Johnson, James C., 3737
Johnson, James Weldon, 364-65; San
    Francisco experiences, 363
Johnson, John Alfred "Jack", 3641
Johnson, John B., 984
Johnson, John R., 984
Johnson, John Neely, 2069
Johnson, Joseph, 914
Johnson, Laurence, 1008
Johnson, Lyndon Baines, 2577
Johnson, Margaret, 3738
Johnson, Marie Edwards, 92
Johnson, Mayme Evelyn Lawlah, 1740

Johnson, Melvin G., 133
Johnson, Milo Perry, 1741
Johnson, Milton, 133
Johnson, Noble M., 962, 1976
Johnson, Peter, 351
Johnson, Ralph H., 980
Johnson, Reginald A., 3851
Johnson, Roger Mae, 2574
Johnson, Samuel, 3289
Johnson, Sara Gregory, 3497
Johnson, Sargent Claude, 71, 78, 126,
    128, 133, 139, 140; biographical
    information, 455
Johnson, Solomon, 1175, 3188
Johnson, Tony D., 3549
Johnson, William H. (actor), 3560
Johnson, William H. (artist), 133
Johnson county (Wyo.) war, 47
Johnston, A. L., 946
Johnston, Andrew V., 1533
Johnston, C. Granville, 3852
Johnston, Effie Enfield, 2077
Johnston, Ralph, 1639
Johnston, William E., 1486
Joiner, Benjamin: family, 386
Jolly, John, 2078
Jones, A. Hartley, 946, 2272
Jones, Alvin Henry, 1312
Jones, Arlynne L., 1644
Jones, B. Marion, 972
Jones, Bobby, 1742
Jones, C. T., 946
Jones, Carrie W., 994
Jones, Charles, 2356
Jones, Edward Smyth, 2720-22
Jones, Elizabeth Orton, 2856-59
Jones, Emma Scott, 3465
Jones, Ervie L., 3567
Jones, Eugene Kinckle, 3739
Jones, Everett L., 2309, 3168-70
Jones, Gertrude L., 3992
Jones, Grace, 2384
Jones, Harold P., 1305
Jones, Henry Leon, 1891
Jones, Henry W., 993
Jones, Jack, 727-28
Jones, James (Oakland), 2921
Jones, James E., 4142
Jones, James L., 1892
Jones, Ken, 4022-23
Jones, Leroy Vernell, 2457
Jones, Lillian, 1893
Jones, Louis W., 3975
Jones, Martin C., 1313
Jones, Martin H., 1313

Jones, Pirkle, 99, 570
Jones, Reginald L., 311
Jones, Robert, 1978
Jones, Robert L., 2137
Jones, Samuel A., 3222
Jones, Sandy, 3388
Jones, Sissieretta, 2002
Jones, W. J., 4057
Jordan, Benjamin Arnett, 2763
Jordan, Edward Starr, 2533
Jordan, Frederick Douglass, 2295
Jordan, George: biographical
    account, 470
Jordan, Jack, 127, 133
Jordan, Jackson, 1151
Jordan, Jacob C., 3564
Jordan, Samuel, 2941
Jordan, William D., 930
Jordan high school, Los Angeles,
    828
Jourdan, Jackson, 1113
Journalism, 2264-97; athletic
    coverage, 3640; bibliography
    of newspapers, 157; in Sacra-
    mento, 2236; in San Francisco,
    1026, 3112; middle class in-
    fluentials, 3856; Pacific coast
    news bureau, 1975; Richard
    Allen news service, 2295; Roman
    Catholic press, 3332. See also
    Newspapers; Periodicals; Tele-
    vision
Journalists, 465
Joyce, William H., 4249
Joyner, Lawrence, 2926
Juarez, Lynne Marie, 1743
Judah, Benjamin Wyth, 1045
Julian (San Diego county): history,
    2073
Jung, Raymond Kay, 3610
Junior city, San Francisco, 3468
Jury trials, 2450
Justice, David Blair, 877
Juvenile delinquency, 1780, 2468,
    3597, 3689; in Los Angeles,
    864, 3703, 3804, 3812, 3814-
    15; in Seattle, 1581; in Watts,
    746; street gangs, 3611, 3720
Juvenile literature, 1738, 2298-
    2353, 2595; bibliography, 203;
    history and criticism, 2334;
    reading method, 1799
Juvenile studies. See Education;
    Sociology
Juvenile welfare: in Fresno county,

3594; in Oakland, 3787; in San
    Francisco, 3885

K

Kahl, Sue Ann, 1592
Kahn, Roselle, 459
Kaiser, Evelyn Lois, 3740
Kaiser center, Oakland: exhibit
    catalog, 103
Kaiser co., inc., 2376
Kalven, Harry, 3046
Kansas City, Mo.: schools, 1474
Kaplan, John, 1388; research notes,
    1770
Kaplan, Marshall, 2191
Karenga, Ron, 622, 876
Karolevitz, B., 366
Karst, K. L., 3147
Kassebaum, Peter Arthur, 3741
Katz, Lilian Gonshaw, 1534
Katz, Martin (Los Angeles), 2227-28
Katz, Martin Richard (Stanford), 3047
Kaufman, Bob Garnell, 2705, 2723-27
Kaufman, Louis, 2848
Keeler, Kathleen F. R., 1744
Keen, Harold, 367, 961, 1088, 1593,
    2192-93, 3048-49, 3742-46
Keesing's research report, 3050
Kelley, Estelle F., 204
Kelley, James Hugh, 926
Kelly, J. Wells, 1252-54
Kendall, Robert, 1745-46
Kennard, Edward D., 3051
Kennedy, John Fitzgerald, 3876
Kennedy, Louise Venable, 245-46
Kennedy, T. H., 878
Kenny, Robert Walker, 2430; papers,
    3853
Kent, Carl A., 936
Kenyon, Dorothy, 2998
Keogh, John F., 2194
Kerby, Phil, 730-31, 1393, 2900-01
Keridt, Leonard, 1394
Kern county: resident interviewed,
    406
Kerner (Otto) report, 909-13, 3114
Kerns, James Harvey, 3747
Kerouac, Jack, 2663
Kerr, Adelaide, 93
Kerr, Barbara, 3950a
Kerrigan, Jean M., 1535
Keveli, Hamaji Udumu, 605
Keyes, Leroy, 3677
Khan, Taki Mohammad, 1645

Kievman, Elaine Larson, 1536
Kilbourn, Charlotte, 1189
Killens, John Oliver, 1979
Killick, Victor W., 1190
Kimbell, William, 4111
Kimber, Edward, 4173
Kimber, Lesly H., 4070
Kimbrough, Jesse L., 2664
Kimtex corp., 732
Kinch, John W., 3788
King, A. A., 4130
King, Carl B., 1894
King, Celestus, 971
King, Charles E., 2816
King, Ella, 914
King, James Ferguson, 1009
King, Joe, 3651
King, John Taylor, 3652
King, Louis Devoid, 1537
King, Martin Luther, Jr., 733, 1032,
    1455, 3305; biography, 388;
    speech, 2586
King (Martin Luther, Jr.) square,
    San Francisco, 2247
King, Norris Curtiss, 2778
King, Thomas Sim, 1058
King, Thomas Starr. See First
    African Methodist Episcopal
    Zion church, San Francisco;
    Starr King elementary school,
    San Francisco
Kinney, Richard, 133
Kirk, J. H. (Oakland), 972
Kirk, James H. (Los Angeles), 2160
Kirk, Sherri, 176
Kirkpatrick, Lewis A., 4120
Kirschman, Richard, 734, 1646
Klein, Malcolm W., 3611
Klingberg, Frank Joseph, 1010
Knapp, Dale L., 1747
Knight, Charles L., 1487
Knight, Henry: biographical
    account, 460-61
Knights of Pythias, 3533-35
Knights templars, Calif., 3519
Knowles, Louis L., 3042
Knox, Andrew P., 3171
Knox, Ellis Oneal, 1647, 2285
Knox, Sidney A., 3191, 3193
Knutson, A. H., 4131
Koenigsberg, Sylvia, 1266
Konvitz, Milton Ridvas, 1089
Kopkind, Andrew, 735-37, 2902
Kossow, Henry H., 1395
Koziara, Edward C., 1895

Koziara, Karen S., 1895
Kramer, Martin (pseud.). See
    Wright, Beatrice Ann
Kramer, Ralph M., 3748
Kraus, Henry, 2665
Krebs, Ottole, 3749
Kroepsch, Robert H., 1669
Kroger, Marie N., 1464, 1612
Kronenberger, Louis, 1982
Krumm, Helen T., 2534
Ku klux klan: Calif. knights manual,
    3052; in Bakersfield, 3099; in
    Calif., 3148; in Los Angeles,
    3041; in Ore., 3010, 3099; in
    southern Calif., 3111; on Pacific
    coast, 3099
Kuchel, Thomas H., 2074
Kuffman, Dorothy, 1232
Kugelmass, J. Alvin, 2330
Kurth, Myrtle, 1594
Kutchins, Herb, 2442
Kuzma, Kay Judeen, 1538
Kyburz, Samuel, 1057

                    L

Labor, 486, 2354-2403, 3278, 3629;
    apprenticeships, 1141; Assoc.
    railway employees of Calif.,
    2356-57; Brotherhood of sleeping
    car porters, 2363; Colored janitor
    co-operative assoc., San Francisco,
    3549; colored marine employees
    benevolent assoc. of the Pacific,
    2383; Colored workingmens club,
    Los Angeles, 3553; Colored work-
    ingmen's club, San Francisco,
    3554; Dining car cooks and waiters
    union, 2373; dining car waiters,
    1937; in literature, 2536, 2651,
    2674; in Los Angeles, 2385, 3118,
    3483; in Milpitas, 2248; in San
    Jose, 2994-95; in Seattle, 2377,
    2382, 2393, 3119; International
    brotherhood of boilermakers, iron
    shipbuilders, welders and helpers
    of America, 2376, 2403; Inter-
    national ladies garment workers
    union, 2390; International long-
    shoremen's & warehousemen's union,
    San Francisco, 2381; International
    union of mine, mill and smelter
    workers, 2380; mobility, 3756;
    Negro motion picture players
    assoc., 3560; news organ, 2288;

Labor (cont.)
  oil painting, 84; Pacific coast
  membership lists, 473; railroads,
  2392; San Francisco bay area
  directory, 1272a; Watts labor
  community action committee, 4137.
  See also Employment; Professions;
  and under geographical locality,
  e.g., San Francisco: labor
Labor unions. See Labor
Labrie, Peter, 3750
Ladies Pacific accumulating and
  benevolent assoc. of San Fran-
  cisco, 3556
Ladies' union beneficial society of
  San Francisco, 3557-58
La Grone, Herbert (Hobart?) Lee, 310
Laguna Beach: Project big four, 3141
Laidley, James, 1058
La Jolla: local news columns, 4081
La Jolla art center: exhibit
  catalog, 94
La Jolla museum of art: art
  holdings, 129; exhibit
  catalog, 110
La Junta, Colo.: newpaper, 4233
Lake Tahoe: tourism, 3842
Lamoreaux, Lillian A., 1748
Lampkin, Daisy E., 656
Lampkin, James C., 930
Lampkins, John L., 3302
Lampkins, M., 3462
Lamplighters study club, Monterey,
  2109
Lancaster, Henry, 3562
Lancha Plana: mining, 973
Land. See Homestead law; Housing;
  Real estate business; Restrictive
  covenants; etc.
Landeway, John R.: family, 546
Landis, Judson R., 3612
Lane, Doyle, 133
Lane, H. B., 1488
Laney, L. M., 1090
Lang art gallery, Scripps college,
  108
Lange, Dorothea, 2450
Langer, Leonard H., 1749
Langston, Ruby D., 2915
Language and language instruction,
  2404-26; dialects, 2520; for
  young women, 3827; in Phoenix,
  3854; primary and pre-school,
  112, 1536, 1559, 2408, 2412-13,
  2424-25; secondary school, 2411,

2422; slang, 2576. See also
Speech
Lanier, Raphael O'Hara, 1489
Lapp, Rudolph Matthew, 368, 1091-92,
  2079, 3390
Lardner, Ring, 1994
Larieau, Peter, 982
Larkin, Thomas Oliver, 418, 2080-81
Larsen, Cecil Evva, 1595
Las Cruces, New Mexico: newspaper,
  4253
Las Vegas, Nev.: entertainment in-
  dustry, 1959; newspaper, 4248;
  tourism, 3842; urban life, 3821
Lash, John S., 1980
Lashley, William H., 3546
Laskey, Robert Lemuel, 1750
Latimore, Charles, 969
Lauderdale, Jack, 969
Laughlin, Florence, 2082
Laundry: Ocean Park cooperative, 928.
  See also Cleaning; Soap industry
Laurence, Paul, 1751
Laurent, Frank, 4201
Laurenti, Luigi, 2195-96
Law and order, 540a, 2427-88, 2945;
  bibliography, 207; Black guards
  organ, 3906; Black panther party
  and, 571-634 passim; Calif. residence law, 1031; Calif. state
  prisons, 308, 2456; civil rights
  statutes, 1031-1155 passim;
  criminal women, 3631; education
  laws, 1338, 1362, 1668, 1697-98,
  1779, 1814; garnishment, 1027; in
  South, 1030; jury trials, 2450;
  labor legislation, 2375; Neighborhood legal news, San Francisco,
  3988; New Mexico fight, 2118;
  para-military groups, 558; police,
  486, 776, 781, 805, 2427-88
  passim; right to work laws, 2369;
  San Francisco bay area directory,
  1272a; slavery laws, 3354; Soledad
  brothers news letter, 4021;
  Western addition law office community education project, San
  Francisco, 3988. See also Education: segregation; Housing;
  Lynching; Testimony, right of;
  and under geographical locality,
  e.g., California: State fair employment practice commission; Los
  Angeles: police; San Francisco:
  ordinances, etc.; San Francisco:

Law and order (cont.)
    Police dept.; wasnington:
    State board against discrimina-
    tion; etc.
Law and society assoc., 1321
Lawrence, Frederick, 3562
Lawrence, George C., 1058
Lawrence, Jacob, 120
Lawrence, Paul Frederick, 1596,
    1658, 1752
Laws, C. C. X., 931
Laws, James, 3556
Layne, Janice L., 1753
Layne, Joseph Gregg, 3751
Lazarus, Simon M., 2288
League of Calif. cities, 1896, 3752
League of women voters: Calif.,
    2197, 2902a-b; Eugene, Ore.,
    3753; San Diego, 3053
Leard, Robert Benson, 1191
Learned, Roy E., 3054
Leary, Mary Ellen, 606
Leather work, 423
Leavitt, Margaret Elaine, 3613
Leckie, William H., 39
Le Conte, Joseph, 3055
Lee, Abraham, 3303
Lee, Albert, 2472
Lee, Archy: judicial case, 2437-38,
    3378, 3390, 3428; petition, 512
Lee, Arthur P., 931
Lee, Canada, 2298-99
Lee, Chauncey, 40
Lee, Daniel, 369-70
Lee, Don L., 2742
Lee, Douglas William, 1754
Lee, E. O., 2923
Lee, George W., 3303
Lee, Irvin H., 41-42
Lee, John, 4093
Lee, Lloyd L., 3614
Lee, Ulysses Grant, 43
Lee, William H., 4164
Lee-Smith, Hughie, 127
Lefavor, A. D., 4128
Lefavor, W. L., 4128
Leggett, James J., 928
Leidesdorff, William Alexander, 178,
    299, 409, 418, 421, 2080-81;
    biographical accounts, 321,
    394, 417, 470, 2087, 2298-99;
    biography, 387; estate, 302,
    304, 2071; papers, 513-15; San
    Francisco city treasurer, 532-33
Leighton, Amanda, 371

Leighton, George R., 28
Leisure. See Parks and recreation;
    Recreation
Le Jau, Francis, 3438
Leland, Elbert L., 3192
Leler, Hazel Olive, 2415
Lemert, Edwin McCarthy, 2458
Lenard (artist), 133
Lennep, Jakob van, 2566
Leo, Gerry, 4140
Leon, Wilmer Joseph, 1897
Leonard, Robert: family business,
    960
Lester, Peter, 1058, 2013
Levene, Carol, 3144
Levenson, Rosaline, 2903
Lewinson, Paul, 205
Lewis, Aaron, 3554
Lewis, Daryle, 4189
Lewis, Edmonia, 101, 141
Lewis, Edna, 740
Lewis, Ida, 3950a
Lewis, J. O., 4276
Lewis, John (Sacramento, 1850), 516
Lewis, John (1966), 2808
Lewis, John Henry, 3648
Lewis, John J., 3281
Lewis, Junius R.: correspondence, 517
Lewis, Lloyd, 1981
Lewis, Mary S., 1539
Lewis, Oscar, 372
Lewis, Richard W., 2343
Lewis, Samella S., 95, 108, 133
Lewis and Clark centennial exposition,
    Portland, 3838
Liberalism: white, 1076
Liberation support movement, 2, 11-16
Liberia: founding, 1181; migration
    to, 1216
Librarians: biography of Miriam
    Matthews, 281
Libraries: art exhibits, 93, 101; in
    Los Angeles, 206-07, 758; in Marin
    City, 3647; in Oakland, 3489; in
    Phoenix schools, 1424; in San
    Francisco, 3457, 3504; race re-
    lations activities, 3069
Library holdings. See Bibliographies
Light, Allen B., 178, 400, 403, 435,
    498, 517a; biographical account,
    373
Light, Ivan Hubert, 3755
Lightfoot, A. L., 3469
Lightfoot, W. A., 2875
Lightner, Laurence W., 3890

Lightner, Lawrence H., 3890
Lilly, Anthony, 1174
Lincoln, Abraham, 3402; and slavery,
    3447; black policy, 1177
Lincoln, Charles Eric, 561, 3096
Lincoln motion picture co., Los
    Angeles, 962, 1975
Linguistics. See Language and
    language instruction
Links: Oakland-Bay area chapter,
    3575
Lippett, Francis J., 1058
Lipset, Seymour Martin, 3096, 3756
Liss, Howard, 3653
Literature, 2489-2757, 3141, 3848;
    anthologies, 2489-2508; biblio-
    graphies, 181, 204; folklore,
    2509-13, 2816; history and
    criticism, 181, 2334, 2514-53,
    2873; humor, 3846; Oakland
    literary aid society, 3562;
    periodical publications, 3887-
    4046 passim; race relations,
    3044, 3069
--drama, 2554-73, 2706; anthologies,
    240, 2490-2507 passim; biblio-
    graphies, 240, 261; history and
    criticism, 2514-45 passim
--essays and speeches, 2574-90,
    2751, 3281; anthologies, 2489-
    2508 passim
--fiction, 2591-2685; bibliographies,
    154, 261, 270-71
--poetry, 2582, 2585, 2588, 2687-
    2757; African, 15-16; antholo-
    gies, 2489-2508 passim; biblio-
    graphies of poets, 235-36, 252;
    Calif. bibliography, 261; history
    and criticism, 2520, 2530, 2541;
    Journal of black poetry, 3970;
    Nation of Islam (Black Muslims),
    2582
--short stories, 2581, 2591-2681
    passim; anthologies, 2489-
    2507 passim; history and
    criticism, 2551
Literature, juvenile. See
    Juvenile literature
Little, Malcolm. See Malcolm X
    (assumed name)
Little Rock, Ark., 1120, 1122
Littlejohn, J. N., 963
Litwack, Leon Frank, 2083-84, 2386
Livingfree, Daniel, 3056
Livingston, Loveless Benjamin, 3057

Lloyd, Kent Murdock, 1093, 1898
Locey, Margaret Lenore, 2535
Locke, Alain Leroy, 1696, 3873
Locke high school, Los Angeles:
    publication, 2496
Lockett, Rosa M., 3481
Lockheed aircraft corp., Burbank, 311
Lockley, Fred, 3391-91a
Lockwood, Lee, 607
Loftus, William, 1200
Lofty, Paul, 2501
Logan, Frank, 2917
Logan, Georgia Smith, 2666
Logan, Pleasant D., 2473
Logan, Rayford W., 374, 449
Logging industry, 1889
Loggins, Roy L., 3564
Lohman, Joseph Dean, 1654, 1755-57,
    2459, 3500
Lomax, Louis E., 3861; lecture, 2587
Lomax, Lucius W., Jr., 4124
Lomax, Mrs. Lucius W., Jr. (Almena
    Davis), 562, 2460, 4030, 4124
Lompoc: Vandenberg air force base,
    564
Long, George, 1094
Long, Herman H., 2384
Long, John Cornelius, 1758
Long Beach: Calif. state univ.
    library holdings, 161; chemical
    industry, 1918; directory, 1267
Long Beach museum of art: art
    holdings, 130
Longevity, 2768
Lopez, Leo, 1759
Loren, Eugene L., 741
Lorenzini, August Peter, 3854
Lortie, Francis N., 3757
Los Angeles, 656, 2016; African Metho-
    dist Episcopal Zion church, 3192;
    African mission and industrial
    assoc., 832; Afro-American co-
    operative cleaning and dyeing
    plant, 927; Afro American council
    commercial co., 929; Afro-
    American council of America, 3545;
    Anti-defamation league, 2429;
    architecture, 106; as fiction
    locale, 2604, 2649-51, 2664, 2668,
    2680; banks and banking, 1939;
    Barrington plaza corp., 2227-28;
    Bimini baths, 1109; biographies
    of residents, 3760; Black
    congress meeting, 923; Board of
    education, 1397, 1760-62, 3758;

Los Angeles (cont.)
book store catalogs, 145-49, 262; Booker T. Washington apts., 938; Bookertee film co., 939, 1976; Calif. eagle pub. co., 902, 1242, 2271-73, 2558; Calif. publishing bureau and investment co., 2273; census (1850), 1295; Central casting corp., 1955; chemical industry, 1918; child adoption, 3688; church integration, 3269; churches, 3270; Citizens' committee for the defense of Mexican-American youth, 2480; City council police, fire and civil defense committee, 742; City planning commission, 743; civil rights, 895, 1066, 1075, 1138; Colored chauffeurs assoc., 2370; Colored laborer's social club, 2372; Colored league of women voters, 2902a; Colored political and social club, 2875; Colored workers' assoc. (1922), 861; Colored workers assoc. (1933), 945; Colored workingmens club, 3553; Commercial council of Los Angeles, 946; Communist party, 3130; Community redevelopment agency, 2132; Community welfare federation, 3703; Congress of racial equality, 1358; Council of social agencies, 1899; Crenshaw district, 2242; Crenshaw neighbors, inc., 3967; Cultural exchange center of, 77, 107; Dance theater group, 2841; Daniel Williams hospital, 2763; described (1922), 3863; Dining car cooks and waiters union, 2373; directories, 1238, 1242, 1250, 1267; District attorney's office, 745; Double V movement, 3146; Douglass house foundation, 734; drug industry, 1882; Dunbar hospital assoc., 2764; economic conditions, 3630, 3687, 3690, 3735, 3816, 3872; elections, 2869, 2879, 2885, 2888, 2889a, 2900-01, 2909; elks of the world, Improved benevolent protective order, 3512; employment, 2366-67; entertainment industry, 1950-2001 passim; family life, 3776; Family savings and loan assoc., 81, 3955; Filippa Pollia foundation,

3479; Fire dept., 1128; First African Methodist Episcopal church, 2072, 3248; folklore, 2509, 2512; founding, 2125, 3706, 3724-25, 3733, 3751; Golden state mutual life insurance co., 85-87, 113, 127, 940, 987, 1638, 1892, 1933, 3958-59, 3979; Hell's angels, 829; Historical society of southern Calif., 3733; history, 97, 1179, 2049, 2063, 2072, 3687, 3709, 3758, 3760, 3766; Hollywood-Wilshire fair housing council, 3964; Home owners' defense council, 2187; hotel employment, 1895; housing, 1170, 2132-2257 passim; Housing authority of, 2250; housing of women, 3488, 3497; illiteracy, 1826; Immaculate heart college, 1643; Independent voters, 2898; journalism, 2266-95 passim; juvenile delinquency, 864, 3703, 3804, 3812, 3814-15; Ku klux klan, 3041; labor, 2385, 3118, 3483; language, 2404; librarian, 281; Lincoln motion picture co., 962, 1975; local news columns, 4146, 4148; Locke high school, 2496; Los Angeles high school, 2961; Lower Calif. Mexican land & development co., 963; McCarthy memorial Christian church, 3200; Mafundi institute, 3977; medicine and health, 2763-80 passim; Methodist church, 2230; migration to, 1179, 1226, 2233, 3718; Million dollar productions, inc., 964, 1976; miscegenation, 2784, 2794; Morningstar missionary Baptist church, 3286; motion picture industry, 1950-2001 passim; Nation of Islam (Black Muslims), 560-62; National assoc. for the advancement of colored people, 650-52, 658, 660, 667, 1987-88; National committee to free Angela Davis, 887; National Negro congress, 888; National urban league, 2160, 2199, 2996, 3483, 3490, 3853, 3934, 4053; Negro art theatre, 1989; Negro boys town and Negro girls town, 3484; Negro business assoc., 967; Negro business men's assoc. of southern Calif., 969; Negro consumers' agency, 970; Negro

Los Angeles (cont.)
consumer's and producer's assoc.,
971; Negro culinary art club,
1233; Negro incorporated aid
society, 3559; Negro mothers of
America, 3485; Negro motion picture players assoc., 3560; Negro
pageant movement, 1990; Negro
press foundation, 2288; Negro
social register, inc., 1266;
newspapers, 4073-4137; Normandie
area, 2132; opinion survey, 1766;
Otis art institute, 134; Our
authors study club, 2015; Paramount pictures corp. library
collection, 104; People's auditorium co., 975; Phillis Wheatley,
inc., 3488; Pico boulevard, 327;
Police commission, 538; Police
dept., 670-825 passim, 1154, 2440,
2443, 2464, 2469-71, 2482-83,
2664; politics, 538, 796, 798-
800, 805, 2881, 2896, 2904, 2906,
2927-28; poverty, 1869; Prince
Hall masons holding assoc., 3541;
Prince Hall no. 2 credit union,
981; Prince Hall progressive
building assoc., 3542; probation,
2436; Probation dept., 746; Progressive mutual benefit assoc.,
3564; Public library, 206-07,
758; public welfare, 3813, 3816;
race relations, 2957-3146 passim,
3937, 3967; racial dissent, 1765;
real estate business, 2257; restrictive covenants, 2183; Richard
Allen news service, 2295; riot
(1943), 875, 880; riots bibliography, 207; Rose-Netta hospital
assoc., 2778; rubber tire industry, 1913; Second African
Methodist Episcopal church,
3302; Second Baptist church,
3304; Sleepy lagoon defense committee, 2446, 2479-80; social
conditions, 3483, 3630, 3687;
social services, 3702; Socialist
workers party, 783, 2255; Sojourner Truth home, 3496; Sojourner Truth industrial club,
3497-98; Somerville hotel, 652;
South central and east Los Angeles transportation-employment
project, 1935-36, 3925; Stolper
galleries of primitive arts, 94;
street transportation, 668, 675,
1935-36; tourism, 3842; unemployment, 1869, 1890, 1906;
Unitarian fellowship for social
justice, 3502; Universal books
sales catalogs, 262; Universal
Negro improvement assoc. and
African communities league, 830,
922; unmarried mothers, 3728;
Urban affairs institute, 3910;
urban life, 3483, 3695-3824 passim;
urban redevelopment, 2132, 2242;
vegetable market, 986; Welfare
planning council, 3816; Wesley
chapel, 2072; West side investment
assoc., 994; Western student movement, 1828; Westside Jewish community center, 144; women, 3574,
3797, 3818; World war II, 3146;
Young men's Christian assoc.,
313. See also California: University. Los Angeles; Watts
--Calif. state univ.: Black students
union, 644; library holdings, 162
--employment, 1899-1900; agencies,
1890; employers' experience, 1919;
FEPC hearings, 1924; government,
1907; in bus transportation, 1935-
36; in manufacturing, 1843
--Public schools, 1681, 1689, 1719,
1745-46, 1760-63, 1805, 1808,
1829; adult education, 1791;
counseling, 1308; history of,
1414, 1763; history textbooks,
2331-33; industrial arts, 1741;
literary anthologies, 2499-2500;
primary, 1515; secondary, 828,
1301, 1308, 1591, 1595, 1606,
1608, 1611; segregation, 1323,
1349-52, 1356, 1358, 1376, 1390,
1393, 1397, 1406, 1410, 1414,
1440
--Univ. of southern Calif.: (1903-07),
538; library holdings, 263;
slavery collection, 199
Los Angeles California eagle, 2266,
2271. See also California eagle
publishing co., Los Angeles
Los Angeles committee for fair play in
bowling, 1095
Los Angeles committee on human relations, 3058
Los Angeles county: administration of
justice, 2458; Board of economic
and youth opportunities agency of

Los Angeles county (cont.)
    greater Los Angeles, 2904; economic conditions, 3752; employment ordinance, 1900; history, 2072; housing integration, 2239; Institute on community relations, 3059, 3077; labor unions, 2378; League of Calif. cities, 3752; public welfare, 3813; race relations, 3018, 3058-60; South central area welfare planning council, 2780; teacher employment, 1880; urban life, 3796; Veterans of foreign wars of the U. S., 3567
Los Angeles county committee for interracial progress, 3060
Los Angeles county conference on community relations, 2429, 2996, 3937
Los Angeles county museum of art: art holdings, 131; exhibit catalogs, 96, 109
Los Angeles county museum of natural history: exhibit catalog, 97
Los Angeles dodgers, 3680
Los Angeles Herald-dispatch, 561
Los Angeles Interfaith churchman, 4124
Los Angeles New age dispatch, 4099. See also New age pub. co., Los Angeles
Los Angeles realty board, 2138
Los Angeles Times, 751, 3760
Los Angeles Western outlook, 4149
Los Angeles youth project, 3491
Lott, Mabel Smith, 1490
Lott, Travis T., 2187
Lott, Truman R., 2187
Louie, James W., 1901
Louis, Joe, 3654
Louisiana: schools, 1481. See also New Orleans: schools
L'Ouverture, Toussaint: biography, 288
Lovdjieff, Crist, 608
Love, Alroyd, 3552
Love, Nat: autobiography, 377-78
Love, Ruth B., 1314-16
Lovell, John, 2536
Lovell, M. Marguerite, 2334
Lovingood, Penman, 379, 2728
Lovingood, Reuben Shannon: biography, 379

Low, Nat, 3655
Lowenstein, Ralph L., 2279
Lower Calif. Mexican land & development co., Los Angeles, 963
Lowry, Raymond W., 2085
Loya, Theresa, 1618
Loyalton: local news columns, 4199
Lucas, Charles A., 4293
Lucas, Eugene, 1246
Luce, Phillip Abbott, 609, 879
Ludolph, P. H., 4120
Lukas, Henry J., 3392
Luke, Orral Stanford, 2817
Luke air force base, Phoenix, 3472
Lumber and lumbering, 1889
Lundberg, George A.: hypotheses, 3036
Lundy, Eva, 3466
Luper, Luther George, Jr., 2498
Lyford, Joseph P., 2577, 3061
Lyle, Jack, 2286
Lynch, John Roy, 2290-91; biography, 356
Lynching, 1037, 1086
Lyons, Helen Scott, 3855

Mc

McAdams, Nettie Fitzgerald, 2818
McAdoo, Benjamin: correspondence, 518
McAllister, Julius A., 2372
McAteer, J. Eugene, 1398-99
McAteer act, 1776
Macbeth, Hugh E., 963, 3062
McCall, Olalee, 1491
McCambe, Eliza: correspondence, 519
McCarthy memorial Christian church, Los Angeles, 3200
McCarty, Brackeen, 3936
McClellan, William Circe, 1540
McClelland, I. H., 3198
McClenahan, Bessie Averne, 2200-01
McClendon, William H., 4195
McCloskey, Paul N., 2202
McCloud: local news columns, 4199, 4206
McClure, Galen, 380
McClymonds high school, Oakland, 1576-77
McColley, Robert McNair, 3439-40
McConahay, John B., 801-02
McCone, John A., 1764
McCone (John A.) commission. See California: Governor's commission

McCone (John A.) (cont.)
    on the Los Angeles riots
McConnell, Roland C., 381
McCord, William M., 752, 881, 1765-66
McCormick, Stephen J., 1255-56
McCoy, Edward A., 981
McCoy, J. C., 2875
McCreary, Eugene, 1597
McCullough, G., 133
McCullough, John, 2558
McCullough, John G., 1096, 1117
McCullough, Samuel Clyde, 382
McDavid, Percy Hiram, 3761
MacDonald, Alan, 3856
McDonald, Emanuel B.: autobiography, 383
McDonald, Franklin Randolph, 1767
McDonald, Jack Arthur, 1492
McDonald, Robert, 3184
McDonald, Sam, 383
McDonald, Vernon Sugg, 384
McDonald, W. L. (San Diego), 4172
McDonald, Walter L. (Riverside), 980
McDowell, Albert, 3392a
McDowell, B. L., 967
McDowell, Leona Baber, 1598
McElroy, John W., 930
McEntire, Davis, 2179, 2203, 2461-62, 3063
McEvoy, James, 642
McFarland, Douglas, 3297
McFarland, Wallace, 2463
McGaughy, Verl, 983
McGee, Du Bois, 980
McGhee, Milton L., 2166
McGregor, James W., 3957
McGriff, D. L., 3282
McGroarty, John Steven, 3760
McGrory, Mary, 753
McGue, D. B., 385
McIntosh, Mary Susan, 1192
McIntyre, James Francis Aloysius, Cardinal, 2997
McKenney, J. Wilson, 1400
McKinney, H. L., 4044
McKinney, Robert R., 4080
McKune, John H., 512
McLane, Louis, 1058
McLatchy, Patrick, 208
McLean, Sandra, 98
McLemore, William J., 3554, 3889, 4011, 4185, 4264
McLeod, Alexander Roderick, 2086

McManus, John T., 1982
McMillan, Lester A., 2152
McMillian, Cecille Vandel, 386
McMurrin, Sterling M., 3064
McNeal, Judie, 3547
McNeil, James, 133
McNeil, William, 133
McNichols, Steven E., 1097-98
McPherson, J. Gordon, 3935, 4063, 4086, 4163, 4207; letters, 524
McQueen, Alice, 3194
McQueen, Annie, 3194
McQuiston, John Mark, 2204-05
McReynold, J. H., 3188
McSpadden, Hiltrude, 2087
McSweeny, William, 3673
McVey, Sam, 3648
McVey, Wayne W., 1212
McWilliams, Carey, 754, 880, 2387, 3065, 3102, 3144, 3762
McWorter, Gerald A., 1361

M

Maas, Julie, 2339
Mabry, Anna, 3560
Mabson, Mrs. Edward D. (Berlinda Davison), 1768
Mabson, Margaret J., 2902b, 3460
Mackey, Herbert, 2915
Macklin, Anderson, 133
Macon, Robert A., 965
Macondray & co., San Francisco, 1058
Madden, John, 3196
Maddox, Essex, 3175
Maddox, Walter G., 4149
Madera: family life, 3634; local news columns, 4206
Madian, Jon, 2335
Madkin, Norma Hillary, 1769
Mafundi institute, Los Angeles, 3977
Magazines. See Periodicals
Magney, John, 3154-55
Magubane, Bernard, 17
Mahlberg, Jean, 2088
Mahoney, Jeannette, 2778
Mahoney, Patrick J., 2388
Mailer, Norman, 3857
Major, Reginald W., 1401, 4002
Malcolm X (assumed name), 2574
Malcolm X unity house, San Francisco. See Afro-American institute
Management development training act program, Oakland, 1307
Mandelbaum, David Goodman, 44

Mander, Linden A., 3066
Manes, Hugh R., 2464
Manese, Wilfredo Reyes, 3615
Mangrum, Marianna, 2537
Manhattan Beach: housing, 2145
Manley, Albert Edmond, 1493
Mann, Arthur William, 3656
Mann, Horace, 3393
Mann, Margery, 99
Mann, Porter M., 3559
Manning, Harvey, 1648
Manning, James Francis, 387
Manning, Seaton Wesley, 3499
Mansfield, George Campbell, 2089
Manumission. See Slavery
Manuscripts, 60, 483-553 passim,
    660, 663-64, 862, 891, 993a,
    1013, 1850, 2104-05, 2038,
    2123, 2178, 2883, 2886, 2902a-b,
    2996, 2999-3000, 3136, 3483,
    3495, 3638, 3853, 3873
Mapp, Lester, 3552
Marascuilo, Leonard A., 1402-03
March, Sue, 2141
Marcuse, Peter, 2998
Margolis, Ben, 2288
Marichal, Juan, 3657, 3664
Marin City: education program,
    1680, 1750; public library,
    3467; settlement of, 955;
    Southern Marin economic oppor-
    tunity council, 3978; urban
    life, 3817
Marin county: College of Marin,
    830; housing, 2206; Human
    rights commission, 1099, 2206,
    4040. See also San Francisco
    bay area
Marine, Gene, 610-13, 2207, 2909
Marinship corp., Sausalito, 2403;
    history of, 955
Mariposa county: petition of resi-
    dents, 1054; Washington mining
    co., 993a
Maritime workers. See Shipping
Markey, Beatrice, 1128, 1902
Marks, Jim, 2729
Markus, Lois, 3763
Marralle, James J., 2770
Marryat, Samuel Francis, 2090-91
Marsh, Leon Frederic, 3534
Marsh, Mrs. Leon Frederic (Vivian
    Costroma Osborne), 2510, 3528,
    3989, 4144, 4148, 4199
Marshak, Marianne, 1541

Marshall, Dale Roberts, 2904
Marshall, Ellen, 968
Marshall, Errol, 968, 972, 3198, 3896,
    4139, 4146
Marshall, F. Ray, 2389
Marshall, Mary, 2472
Marshall, Otto Miller, 45
Marshall, Rachelle, 1404
Marston, Wilfred George, 3764
Martin, Mrs. A. A., 4144
Martin, Anna M., 3469
Martin, George C., 4144
Martin, Sam, Sr., 4167
Martin, W. T., 927
Martyn, Kenneth A., 689, 1649
Marvin X (assumed name), 1951, 2336,
    2567, 2730-32
Marx, Gary Trade, 3067-68, 3283
Marx, Wesley, 755, 3765
Marysville: African Methodist Epis-
    copal church, 3242; City council
    Minutes index, 1257; directories,
    1258-63; Freemasons, 3510; local
    news columns, 4081, 4149, 4193,
    4198, 4207; Mt. Olivet Baptist
    church, 3209, 3242, 3288; public
    schools (1863), 1688; Rare ripe
    gold and silver mining co., 984
Mash, S. L., 528, 3469
Mason, Biddy, 1211, 3364, 3830
Mason, Phillip Lindsay, 133
Mason, William M., 97, 3766
Masotti, Louis H., 881
Mastronarde, Linda, 756
Mathematics: equations, 3834; primary
    and pre-school, 1561
Matheson, Mark J., 1045
Matlock, Harold Lloyd, 983
Matthews, Charles Hearde, 2465
Matthews, Jim, 388
Matthews, Miriam, 209, 2819, 3069,
    3102; biography, 281
Matthews, William C., 2905
Matthews, William J., 3458
Matyas, Jennie, 2390
Matzen, Stanley Paul, 1542
Maxey, Carl, 2987
Maxson, Berle Dean, 4128
Maxson, Mrs. Berle Dean, 4128
Maxwell, Ida Evelyn, 2416
May, Lieut., 1027
May, Henry F., 1650
May, S. B. W., 946
Mayer, J. W., 4120
Mayer, Martin, 1771

Mayer, Sarah Rafferty, 3767
Mayer, William, 2208
Mayers, Richard, 1341
Mayes, A., 3458
Maynor, Dorothy, 3873
Mays, Bates, 3302
Mays, Horace N., 3217
Mays, Iantha (Villa), 3576
Mays, William Howard "Willie", 2170,
    2337, 3643, 3645, 3661; bio-
    graphical accounts, 2301-02,
    2340, 2345, 3652, 3664; bio-
    graphies, 2310, 3653, 3658-60,
    3675
Meadows, Henry J., 4148
Meat industry and trade, 1884
Mecco enterprises, inc., Hayward,
    3990
Meckler, Zane, 1405, 1772
Media. See Newspapers; Television;
    etc.
Medicine and health, 2758-81, 3848;
    county hospitals, 3627; Hunters
    Point-Bayview community health
    service news, 3965; in Angola,
    15; in juvenile literature,
    2347; San Francisco bay area
    directory, 1272a; Watts riot,
    682. See also Psychiatry;
    Public health
Meeker, Ezra 389
Meer, Bernard, 2209
Meier, August, 852, 2092
Meister, Dick, 882-83, 3070
Meldrum, George Weston, 2093
Mellons, Charles Edward, 2820
Meltzer, Milton, 1968
Mendelsohn, Harold, 2428
Mendocino county: account of
    Nathaniel Smith, 328; slavery,
    3371
Menlo Park: Counterpart, 3241;
    directory, 3471; Opportunities
    industrialization center west,
    1914; public schools, 1529
Menlo Park Ravenswood post. See
    Palo Alto Ravenswood post
Mental health. See Medicine and
    health; Psychiatry; Psychology
Mental retardation. See Children,
    abnormal
Meo, Yvonne, 133
Merced: local news columns, 4206
Meredith, James C., 1067
Meriwether, Louise M., 757, 2094, 2667

Merkel, Benjamin, 3441
Merrill, Annis, 1058
Merriman, J. A., 4264
Merritt college, Oakland, 1622;
    library guide, 210
Messner, Stephen D., 211
Metaphysics, 3262, 3271
Metcalf, Allen C., 2906
Metego. See Sohan, Metego
Methodist church, 3263; housing
    attitude, 2230
Methodist Episcopal church, South:
    Pacific conference, 3284
Metz, William, 1406
Mexican-Americans: 3798;
    bibliographies, 159, 163, 167-69,
    171-72, 221, 243; college and
    university education, 163;
    employment in state govern-
    ment (Calif.), 1847-48,
    1864; in Sacramento area, 3693;
    in schools, 1702, 1769; in Urban
    league training project, 1921;
    language patterns, 3854; literary
    anthology, 2494; miscegenation,
    2794; police relationships, 2428;
    primary and pre-school education,
    1526, 1538, 1551, 1554, 1569-70;
    race relations, 2973, 3093;
    right to work laws, 2369; San
    Diego workshop, 2993. See also
    Race relations
--Los Angeles, 2366-67, 3690; housing,
    2161; schools, 1689; Sleepy
    lagoon case, 2446, 2479-90
Mexico: Afro-American colonization
    company of Mexico, San Diego,
    1159; Colored colonization co.,
    San Diego, 1175; Colored Mexican
    colonization co., San Diego, 1176;
    history (1519-1810), 2005; Lower
    Calif. Mexican land & development
    co., Los Angeles, 963; migration
    from, 1196; reform laws, 1007;
    Sonora archives, 1013; tourism,
    3874. See also Alta California
    (province); War with Mexico
Mezz, Sheila Mayers, 1599
M. H. de Young memorial museum, San
    Francisco: exhibit catalog, 100
Michelson, Stephan Edward, 3858
Michigan. University. See Institute
    of labor and industrial relations,
    Univ. of Michigan-Wayne state
    univ.

Middleton, Pete, 2063
Middleton, William J., 18
Mid-peninsula Christian ministry
    community house, East Palo Alto,
    3071
Mid-peninsula Christian ministry of
    East Palo Alto, 3042
Mid-peninsula citizens for fair
    housing, Palo Alto, 2210-11,
    3980
Mighty, Julia Gaines, 3859
Migration: 1158-1228, 2387; agri-
    cultural workers, 1181a; biblio-
    graphies, 245-46; Calif. resi-
    dence law, 1031; Los Angeles
    company promotes, 946; to Haiti,
    1029; to Liberia, 1216; to Los
    Angeles, 1179, 1226, 2233, 3718;
    to Oakland, 3487; to Pacific
    coast, 3102; to San Francisco,
    1193, 1205, 3117; Washington
    (state) policy, 1150. See
    also Colonization; U. S. Bureau
    of the census
Miles, Cecil David, 3616
Milic, Bernice Ann, 2417
Mill Valley: public schools, 1369
Millen, Gilmore, 2668
Miller, Adam David, 2497
Miller, Albert, 1058
Miller, Don, 2302
Miller, Earl, 76
Miller, Elizabeth W., 212
Miller, Elvena, 2907
Miller, Floyd, 3860
Miller, George R., 944
Miller, Guy, 78
Miller, Herman Phillip, 3617
Miller, Jacob W., 3394
Miller, Judy Ann, 3910
Miller, Kenneth Johh, 3442
Miller, Loren R.: articles by, 886,
    1154, 1651, 1903, 1983-84, 2095,
    2173, 2212-15, 2241, 2466, 2908,
    2910, 2998, 3072-74, 3769, 3861;
    book publication, 1100; corres-
    pondence, 2996, 3853; newspapers
    edited by, 4080-81, 4114, 4123;
    obituaries, 375-76, 392; taped
    interview, 2909
Miller, Mrs. Loren R. (Juanita
    Ellsworth), 2792
Miller, Maggie Ullery, 884
Millerton: hotel waiter, 2024
Millinery: designer, 423

Million dollar productions, inc.,
    Los Angeles, 964, 1676
Mills, Alan, 2788
Mills, Jerry, 3189
Mills, P'illa, 127
Mills college: Black students union,
    646, 648
Millsap, Ruby Jeanne, 2821
Milpitas: housing, 2248
Miner, Cicero, 3557
Mines: census information, 1297;
    Elevator mining co., 950; in
    Boulder county, Colo., 5171, in
    Calif., 445-47, 1931; in Colo.,
    1931; in Tuolumne county, 456,
    3392a; in Utah, 1931; in White
    Pine county, Nev., 950; Inter-
    national union of mine, mill and
    smelter workers, 2380; Nil des-
    perandum mining co., San Francisco,
    973; Rare ripe gold and silver
    mining co., Marysville, 984;
    Washington mining co., Hornitos,
    993a. See also Australia: gold
    rush; California: gold rush; Coal
    mines and mining; Colorado: gold
    rush; Sutter's mill, Coloma
Mingori, Lynn Bosley, 1773
Mining engineer, 312
Minke, Karl Alfred, 1101
Minnie, Jicky (pseud.). See Phillips,
    Jane
Minor, Billy J., 1317
Minor, Richard H., 973
Minstrelsy: in Inglewood, 2864; in
    San Francisco, 2002
Miscegenation, 2531, 2783-95 passim,
    3116, 3141; laws, 1044, 2453.
    2786, 2793, 2795. See also Passing
Misner, Arthur J., 2881
Misner, Gordon E., 2459
Mission rebels, San Francisco, 3501
Mississippi: reconstruction, 2867
Missouri: abolition movement, 3441;
    schools, 1474
Missouri compromise: extension to
    Pacific ocean, 3418
Mitchell, Arlene E., 3632
Mitchell, Claudia I., 2418-19
Mitchell, D. T., 2875
Mitchell, Doretha, 3978
Mitchell, Earl L., 980
Mitchell, Harry, 932, 934
Mitchell, James D., 2187
Mitchell, James P., 1905

Mitchell, Marilyn, 1193
Mitchell, Robert M., 975
Mitchell, William H., 3196
Mobile, Ala., 3781
Model cities program, 3770; in
    northern Calif., 3696; in
    Oakland, 3770, 3778; in Wash-
    ington (state), 490
Modeste, H. H., 968
Modeste, Nettie, 968
Modesto: African Methodist Episcopal
    Zion church, 3193; Citizens com-
    mittee against segregation
    amendment, 2198; Grace Davis
    high school, 2216; Greater
    Modesto council of churches,
    2181; Human rights commission,
    1102; local news columns, 4081,
    4146, 4148, 4193, 4199, 4206
Modesto committee for open housing,
    2217
Modoc war, 445-47
Mogulof, Melvin B., 3770
Molarsky, Osmond, 2338
Molony, Reginald D., 3075
Momboisse, Raymond M., 2432
 Monget, Patricia Ann, 1543
Monroe, Arthur, 142
Monroe, George: biographical
    accounts, 437, 471
Monroe, Pearley: taped interview,
    520
Monroe Meadow: origin of name, 437
Monrovia: (1934), 656; African
    Methodist Episcopal Zion Church,
    3194; local news column, 4081
Montana: as fiction locale, 2636;
    bibliography (1800-1945), 259;
    census (1870-80), 1299; historic
    sites, 2047; history, 2068; In-
    dependent Negro Baptist churches,
    3273; laws, statutes, etc.,
    2467-67a; lumber industry,
    1889; newspapers, 4273-47;
    ranch life, 3165; tenth
    cavalry operations, 27, 2065.
    See also under individual place
    name, e.g., Anaconda, White
    Sulphur Springs, etc.
Montana federation of Negro women's
    clubs, 3577
Montana, the magazine of western
    history: index, 208
Monterey: jazz festival, 2863; local
    news columns, 4199; Negro history

celebration, 2109
Montero, Sadie, 3460
Montesano, Philip Michael, 101, 1194,
    2287, 2772, 3285, 3771-74, 4014
Montesano, Randy, 616
Montgomery, Evangeline J., 133
Montgomery, Jay Howard, 312
Montgomery, L., 1159, 1175-76
Moody, Humphreys, 3307
Moon, Harry [Henry Lee Moon?], 486
Moon, Henry Lee, 392
Moore, Archie, 3662
Moore, Cliff, 3549
Moore, Dad, 2363
Moore, Dora H., 4094
Moore, E. T., 758
Moore, Frank, 3403
Moore, George, 967
Moore, H. C., 3267
Moore, J. H., 3267
Moore, John Jamison, 2006, 3976
Moore, Lillian, 4172
Moore, Martha, 3194
Moore, Mollie C. H., 2916
Moore, Percy, 2420, 2941
Moore dry dock co., Oakland, 1893
Moorman, Madison Berryman, 1195
Morais, Herbert Montfort, 2773
Moran, James Anne (religious), 1544
More book store, San Francisco, 213
More publishing co., San Francisco,
    2675
Moreland, John, 2733
Morgan, Alta, 3485
Morgan, Charles, 393
Morgan, Earnest: taped interview,
    521
Morgan, John Edward, 394
Morgan, Newton C., 3458
Morgan, Norma, 133
Morgan, Patricia, 3798
Morgan Hill: head start program, 1531
Mormons: race relations, 3064, 3078,
    3135, 3138-40, 3143, 3162; San
    Bernardino migration, 453-54.
    See also Utah
Morningstar missionary Baptist church,
    Los Angeles, 3286
Morrill, Richard L., 3775
Morrill, Sibley S., 102
Morris, Arval A., 2218
Morris, Charles Satchell, 3287
Morris, Greg, 734
Morris, J., 4111
Morris, James Russell, 3618-19

Morris, Richard Thacker, 759-60
Morris, William L., 3303
Morrison, Carrie Stokes, 2255
Morrison, Ernest (Sunshine Sammy), 1999
Morrow, W. L., 1239
Morse, John F., 1057
Mort, Nancybelle, 3076
Mortgages, home, 2222
Mortimer, John Clarence, 950
Morton, Theophilus B., 918, 926, 2590, 2911
Mosely, Ruth J. Edwards, 3776
Moser, Norm, 4008
Moses, Robert, 890
Moses, Wellington Delaney, 1045
Mosk, Stanley, 3077
Moss, Jeffery Alan, 1774
Moss, Phoebe Eleanor, 885
Moss, S. De Witt, 4147-48
Moten, Etta, 3873
Mothers for equal education bookstore, Palo Alto, 1545
Mothershead, Harmon, 1103
Motion pictures, 1950-2001 passim, 2092; Bookertee film co., Los Angeles, 939, 1976; Central casting corp., 1955; Lincoln motion picture co., Los Angeles, 962, 1975; Los Angeles theater, 975; Louise Beavers, 436; Million Dollar productions, inc., Los Angeles, 964, 1976; Negro motion picture players assoc., 3560; Paramount pictures' library collection, 104. See also Entertainment industry; Theater
Motivation. See Psychology
Moulds, Virginia Bennett, 3443
Mt. Olivet Baptist church, Marysville, 3209, 3242, 3288
Mt. San Antonio college, Walnut: library holdings, 214
Mt. Zion Baptist church, San Francisco, 3289
Mountain men. See Fur trade
Mountain View: local news columns, 4199
Movimento popular de libertação de Angola. See Angola
Moynihan, Daniel Patrick, 1906
Mtume, James, 876
Mueller, Paul F. C., 2219
Muir, Robert E., 3568

Mulherin, Kathy, 617
Mulkey, Lincoln W., 2220-21
Muller, William G., 46
Mullin, Gerald Wallace, 3444
Mumey, Nolie, 396
Mumford, Arnett William, 1652
Munro-Fraser, J. P., 2096
Munson, Beverly Andrews, 2420
Muraskin, William Alan, 3536-37
Murdock, Steve, 2452
Murphy, Beatrice M., 2498
Murphy, Henry Cruse, 3395
Murphy, Israel, 3192
Murphy, Raymond John, 761, 886
Murphy, S. Jackson, 1600
Murphy, William S., 696
Murray, Alma, 2499-2500
Murray, George, 576, 618
Murray, Lloyd, 982
Murray, Nalie B., 3553
Murray, Pauli, 2467-67a
Murray, Robert A., 47
Murrell, Virginia, 2734
Muse, Benjamin, 762
Muse, Charles S., 4219, 4230
Muse, Clarence E., 1985-86; biographical account, 411
Muse, J. T., 4165
Museums: art exhibits, 73-110 passim; art holdings, 118-144
Music, 2796-2685, 3848; bibliographies, 166, 183, 241; hymnology, 241; in motion pictures, 1998; juvenile, 2338, 2353; recording co., 966; vocational course in, 1736. See also Entertainment industry
Musical revues, comedies, etc.: bibliography, 195
Musicians: biographical accounts, 2328
Musladin, William L., 2097
Muslims. See Nation of Islam
Myers, Frank D., 4193, 4206
Myles, Glenn, 2497
Mythology. See Folklore

N

N. A. A. C. P. See National assoc. for the advancement of colored people
Nace, William (pseud.). See Ricks, William Nauns
Nahl brothers, San Francisco, 3359
Nakayama, Antonio, 1196

Nance, Ethel (Ray), 2538, 4014
Nankivel, Claudine, 2307
Nankivell, John H., 48
Nanton, H. I. _See_ Fontellio-Nanton, H. I.
Narcisse, John, 981
Narcisse, L. H., 3197
Nash, Thomas, 3954
Nason, Milton, 2222
Nation of Islam, 556-64; educational system, 1742; essays and poetry, 2582; publications, 3916, 3982, 4093; religious rights, 3243; Richmond, Calif. bakery, 563
National assoc. for African-American education, 1653
National assoc. for the advancement of colored people, 650-67, 1129, 2252, 3141, 3873; Alameda county, 3984; Albuquerque, 653; Berkeley, 659; Denver, 3780; Eugene, Ore., 654; Los Angeles, 650-52, 658, 660, 667, 1987-88; Northern Calif., 200, 661; Oakland, 662; Portland, Ore., 1104-05; Salt Lake City, 3064; San Diego, 3853; San Francisco, 647; Seattle, 663; Stanford univ., 3985; Tacoma, 485; Vancouver, Wash., 664; West coast region, 200, 665-66; Washington (state), 489
National assoc. of colored women, 3578
National assoc. of Negro business and professional women's clubs: East bay area (Calif.), 1264
National assoc. of Negro musicians, 2822
National broadcasting system, 701
National committee to free Angela Davis, Los Angeles, 887
National council of Negro women, 1235, 3579-80
National equalizer enterprises, 3950
National institute of mental health, 1539
National Negro business league: editorial, 852; in Oakland, 968
National Negro congress, 3853; in Los Angeles, 888
National society of colonial dames resident in the state of Calif., 3259
National Sunday school and Baptist training union conference, 3213-14
National united church ushers assoc. of America, 3290
National urban league, 1084, 3141; Los Angeles, 2160, 2199, 2996, 3483, 3490, 3853, 3934, 4033; Oakland, 1835; Portland, Ore., 2251, 2996, 3503, 3968, 4007; San Francisco, 1835, 1921; San Francisco bay area, 3459; Seattle, 1311, 1932, 3124, 3470, 3495, 3506, 3682; Tucson, 3684
Natis, Felix, 2912
Navarro, Carmen, 3725
Nawy, Harold, 3500
Neal, Larry, 2735
Needham, Walter E., 1495
Needles: local news columns, 4080
Neff, Ted, 1407
Negri, Albert, 4153
Negro alliance grocery co., San Francisco, 965
Negro America transcribed, inc., Alameda county, 966
Negro art theatre, Los Angeles, 1989
Negro bibliographic and research center, Washington, D. C., 216
Negro boys town and Negro girls town, Los Angeles, 3484
Negro business assoc., Los Angeles, 967
Negro business league, Oakland, 968
Negro business men's assoc. of southern Calif., Los Angeles, 969
Negro Canyon (Pasadena), 3782
Negro citizens and taxpayers league, Portland, Ore., 889
Negro consumers' agency, Los Angeles, 970
Negro consumer's and producer's assoc., Los Angeles, 971
Negro culinary art club of Los Angeles, 1233
Negro development and exposition company of the United States, 891
Negro handbook, 215
Negro in print, 216
Negro incorporated aid society, Los Angeles, 3559
Negro mothers of America, Los Angeles, 3485
Negro motion picture players assoc., Los Angeles, 3560

Negro national political and pro-
tective league, Oakland, 972
Negro non-partisan league of
Calif., Alameda county, 2914
Negro pageant movement, Los Angeles,
1990
Negro political action assoc. of
Calif., 2886
Negro press foundation, Los Angeles,
2288
Negro protective fraternal society,
San Francisco, 3561
Negro regular Republican club of
Pasadena, 2915
Negro social register, inc., Los
Angeles, 1266
Negro tax payers and voters assoc.
of Pasadena, 2916
Negro year book, 217
Negro young Republican club of San
Francisco county, 2917
Neighborhood youth corps: in
Calif., 1730
Neimore, John J., 2273, 4071, 4073,
4080, 4104, 4106, 4116, 4198
Neimore, Mrs. John J. (Ida B.),
4080
Nein, Robert M., 399
Nelson, C. W. H., 965
Nelson, Clara, 994
Nelson, Dennis Denmark, 49-50
Nelson, Eugene Curry, 946; bio-
graphical account, 404
Nelson, Henry T., 994
Nelson, London, 1775
Nevada: admission, 3402; African
Methodist Episcopal church
(1863), 3177; Bureau of governmental research, 3620; census
(1870-80), 1299; churches, 2010;
directories, 1244, 1249, 1252-54;
elections, 2939; Elevator silver
mining co., 950; emancipation
and reconstruction, 3161; experiences of James Williams,
445-47; first Western fiction,
2631; historic sites, 2047;
laws, statutes, etc., 2467-67a;
minority groups, 3620; newspaper,
4248; Northern Calif.-Nevada
council of churches, 2223;
public schools, 2010; race relations, 3109. See also under
individual place name, e.g.,
Goldfield, Las Vegas, etc.

Nevada county: directories, 1237,
1240; petition of residents, 1055
Nevins, Allan, 763, 2099
New age publishing co., Los Angeles,
1267
New Granada (viceroyalty): slavery,
1009
New Mexico: as fiction locale, 2640;
census (1850-80), 1296; colleges
and universities, 1629; early exploration, 374, 432, 449, 470,
2060, 2064-65; fight at Lincoln,
2118; historic sites, 2047; laws,
statutes, etc., 2467-67a; newspapers, 4249-53; race relations,
3001, 3134, (1812) 3033; slavery,
3342, 3351, 3377, 3386, 3409,
3417, 3420; Spanish speaking
blacks, 2054; territorial government, 3418; U. S. army in, 23-68
passim; University art holdings,
132. See also Southwest
--public schools, 1353, 1375, 1812;
segregation, 1467
New Orleans, La.: schools, 1477,
1498, 2416
New York City: literary renaissance,
2538; Public library Schomburg
collection, 201, 218-19. See also
Harlem
New York City Colored American, 4183
New York Times, 2873
New York times index, 220
Newby, Idus Atwell, 3079
Newcom, Grethel C., 1379
Newhall, R., 3080-81
Newlands, Francis Griffith, 3257
Newman, B. F., 3188
Newman, Carilane, 3777
Newman, Kathryn Leah, 1546
Newmark, Harris, 2100-2102
Newport Beach: Fine art patrons of
Newport harbor, 125
News agencies, 1975, 2295
News & letters, 890
News media. See Journalism; Periodi-
cals; Radio broadcasting; Tele-
vision
Newson, Jerry, 2452
Newspapers: 4049-4302; directories
of, 188, 1272a, 2290-93; guides
to, 186, 228; social utilization,
3603. See also Journalism; News
agencies; Periodicals
Newton, Huey P., 571, 584, 618-19,

Newton, Huey P. (cont.)
623, 633, 852, 2450
Nice, Evert C., 1318
N. I. C. E. See Nurseries in
cross-cultural education
Nicholas, Charles, 3297
Nichols, Margaret S., 221
Nichols, Ruby Marion, 1496
Nicholson, Lois Belle, 3445
Nickerson, William, Jr.:
biographical account, 463
Nidever, George: biographies, 400,
435
Niebuhr, Reinhold, 3305
Nigger Hill (near Columbia), 2078
Nil desperandum mining co., San
Francisco, 973
Ninth cavalry. See Armed services:
ninth cavalry
Nixon, Richard Milhous, 2951
Nixson, Thomas, 3264
Nobbe, Charles E., 3632
Noble, Peter, 1991-92
Nogales, Ariz.: labor union
meeting, 2380; newspaper, 4050
Nolan, James, 3499
Nolan, Nichols, 60
Nollar, Christian, 3396
Non-partisan council on public
affairs, Washington, D. C.,
2899
Non-partisan league. See Negro
non-partisan league of Calif.
Non-violence: Martin Luther King,
Jr., and, 1032
Noone, George, 226
Norcross, Daniel, 1058
Norman, Bradford, 3553
Norris, Clarence Windzell, 3082
Norris vs. Harris (Judicial case),
2438
North, George E., 1547
North Carolina: (1663-1720), 3435;
schools, 1493
North Oakland Baptist church, 3291
Northern Calif. conference on
Negro work, 3621
Northern U. S.: slavery abolition
in, 3456
Northridge: Calif. state univ.,
163-64, 641
Northrup, Herbert Roof, 1910-13
Northwest. See Pacific northwest
Northwood, Lawrence King, 2224
Norton, George F., 3256

Nottage, Margaret (Marlow), 3573
Novack, George, 817
Nowells, Richard W., 4153
Nunis, Doyce Blackman, 2086, 2103
Nunn, Frederick M., 3033
Nurseries in cross-cultural education
project (NICE), San Francisco,
1544, 1546
Nurses and nursing: Oakland, 2779,
2902a; Namahyoke S. Curtis, 458
Nutrition. See Medicine and health
Nyerere, Julius K., 2918
Nygreen, Glen T., 401

O

O. A. A. U. See Organization of
Afro-American unity
Oakland: Afro-American real estate
assoc. and employment bureau of
Calif., 931; Afro-American young
men's Christian league assoc.,
3198; Allen temple Baptist church,
3201; Ancient Arabic order of the
nobles of the mystic shrine, 3514-
15; as fictional locale, 2679;
Associated agencies, 3487; Associated railway employees of
Calif., 2356-57; Bay cities investment co., 936; Beebe memorial
Christian Methodist Episcopal
church, 3220; Beth Eden Baptist
church, 3222-26, 3896, 3930;
Black panther party, 612; Bridges
printing co., 3335, 3522; Brotherhood of sleeping car porters,
2397; building contractors, 1897;
Calif. college of arts and crafts,
122; Calif. voice press, 1248,
3252, 3293, 3570; Church of all
faiths, 3233; Church of the good
shepherd (Baptist), 3234-36; City
manager, 3778; civil rights hearings, 1139; Colored east bay auto
workers assoc., 2371; construction
industry, 1897; cookery, 1232;
Cooper African Methodist Episcopal
Zion church, 3240; Council of
social agencies and community
chest, 3747; Dept. of human resources, 3694, 3779; described
(1922), 3863; directories, 1245,
1248, 1267; Downs memorial Methodist church, 3244-45; East bay
guidance council, 1305-06; East

Oakland (cont.)
bay skills center, 4020; economic conditions, 3694, 3747-48; elections, 2919-26; Enterprise Rochedale co., 951; Ethiopia co-operative business assoc., 952; Ethiopia credit union, 953; Fannie Wall children's home, 3477-78; Federal writers' project, 1181a; First African Methodist Episcopal church, 3250-53, 3929; first black teacher, 476; Golden gate Methodist Episcopal church, 3245; Highland hospital, 2779, 2902a; Home for aged and infirm colored people of Calif., 3480-82; housing, 2139-2263 passim; Interagency project, 1408, 3486; journalism, 2278, 2297; juvenile welfare, 3787; Kaiser co., inc., 2376; labor, 2389; Links, 3575; local new columns, 4243; Management development training act program, 1307; medicine and health, 2776, 2779; Merritt college, 210, 1622; migrants, 3487; model cities program, 3770, 3778; Moore dry dock co., 1893; National assoc. for the advancement of colored people, 662; National urban league, 1835; Negro business league, 968; Negro national political and protective league, 972; newspapers, 4066, 4138-49; North Oakland Baptist church, 3291; odd fellows, Grand united order of, 3538; opinion survey, 1766; Parks chapel African Methodist Episcopal church, 3293; Police dept., 612, 2429, 2475, 2482; population change, 2263; property values, 2196; race relations, 3032, 3083; racial dissent, 854, 881, 1765; restaurant, 988; St. Augustine's Episcopal church, 3299; Scottish rite, 3514; social mobility, 3756; Tilghman (Charles F., Jr.) press, 665-66, 1245, 1265, 3223, 3225, 3236, 3523, 3878; unemployment, 1867, 1938, 1946; United hall assoc., 992; Universal Negro improvement assoc. and African communities league, 914; urban life, 3711, 3747, 3756, 3763, 3770, 3778-79, 3791, 3806-08; urban redevelopment, 1576-77; West Oakland district, 3791; women's clubs, 3574; World war II activities, 3878; Young socialist alliance, 2955; Young women's Christian assoc., 3507. See also Mills college; San Francisco bay area
--Public library, 3489; bibliographies, 222-25, 242
--Public schools, 226-27, 1777-78, 1821; library and audio-visual materials, 226; secondary, 1576-77, 1592, 1601; segregation, 1342, 1355, 1408-09, 1712; teacher employment, 1694
Oakland city college workshop on cultural diversity, 1654
Oakland council of churches, 3292
Oakland economic development council, 3998
Oakland institute of human relations, 3083
Oakland literary aid society, 3562
Oakland men of tomorrow: directory, 3563
Oakland museum: art holdings, 133; exhibit catalog, 103
Oberschall, Anthony R., 767
O'Brien, Kenneth Bostwick, 1779
O'Brien, Robert W., 402, 1198, 3084-86, 3102, 3144
O'Brien, William Jess, 1780
O'Bryan, W. H., 932, 934, 1200
Oby, Laura, 3193
Occupations. See Employment; Labor
Ocean Park: Afro-American cooperative laundry co., 928
O'Connor, George M., 2470
Odd fellows, Grand united order of, 3538
Odd fellows, Independent order of, 2790
Odegard, Peter H., 2491
Odom, L. S., 2922
Odoms, Will, 3289
Oehlerts, Donald E., 228
Ogden, Adele, 403
Ogden, Utah: local news columns, 4148, 4243, 4302; newspaper, 4265; World war II soldiers at, 66
Ohles, John F., 1781
Oklahoma: as fiction locale, 2646;

Oklahoma (cont.)
    black advancement in, 884;
    history, 2124; vocational edu-
    cation, 1886
Olayinka, Moses Siyanbola, 1655
Old folks home of the Western Baptist
    assoc., Abila, 3218
Oliver, John W., 2914
Oliver, Mable, 3488
Olney, John N., 1058
Olsen, Edward G., 3087
Olsen, Jack, 3663
Olson, E., 1410
Olympic games: (1968), 3642, 3670
O'Mahoney, Joseph, 2104
O'Meara, John J., 2137
On-the-job training. See Employment:
    job and on-job training
Opportunities industrialization
    center west, Menlo Park, 1914
Orange county: housing integration,
    2239
Order of Calanthe, 3534
Oregon, 2080-81, 2083-84, 3830;
    African Methodist Episcopal
    church (1863), 3177; Baptists,
    3345-48; bibliographies, 155,
    158, 185a; biographies of resi-
    dents, 2027; census, 1180, 1296;
    civil rights legislation, 1089,
    1104, 1107, 1199; colleges and
    universities, 1616; Congrega-
    tional churches, 3369-70; de-
    portation of black, 1224; direc-
    tories, 1267, 1269; emancipation
    proclamation, 3161; historic
    sites, 2047; history, 2066, 2070,
    2098, 2110a; housing, 2182;
    journalism (1931-48), 2284; Ku
    klux klan, 3010, 3099; laws,
    statutes, etc., 2467-67a, 2478a;
    lumber industry, 1889; misce-
    genation law, 2793; newspapers,
    4254-64; politics, 2894; race re-
    lations (1867), 3012; reconstruc-
    tion reaction, 3161; Republican
    party, 3407; slavery, 3345-48,
    3369-70, 3372, 3384, 3391-91a,
    3397-98, 3401, 3405, 3427; steel
    industry, 1923; suffrage, 2934.
    See also Pacific northwest;
    Pacific coast
--Legislative assembly, 2028; poll
    tax act, 1107
--University. Eugene: National

assoc. for the advancement of
    colored people, 654
Oregon historical society: index to
    its Quarterly, 229-30
Oregon shipbuilding corp., 2376
Oregon spectator: index, 231
O'Reilly, Byron, 4144, 4148
Organization of Afro-American unity:
    West coast, 893
Oroville: local news columns, 4081,
    4206
Orpaz, Yitshak, 769
Orphanages: Booker T. Washington re-
    lief society, San Francisco,
    3466, 3473; Fannie Wall children's
    home, Oakland, 3477-78
Orr, Jack, 3664
Orr, James Lawrence, 3399
Orr, Samuel Marshall, 1915
Orrick, William H., Jr., 647, 1657
Osborne, A., 929
Ossman, David, 2502
Ostrov, Gordon I., 1602
Ostrow, Seniel, 2288
Otero slave code, New Mexico, 3386
Otis, Johnny, 2823
Otis art institute, Los Angeles:
    art holdings, 134
Otter hunting. See Fur trade
Our authors study club, Los Angeles,
    2015
Outterbridge, John Wilfred, 108, 133
Overhold, Linda Fink, 2421
Overland journeys to the Pacific
    (1849), 1194; (1850), 1195. See
    also California: gold rush;
    Voyages to the Pacific
Overstreet, Joe, 133
Owen, Chandler, 404, 2391, 3863
Owens, Christopher Columbus, 1782
Owens, Edward Douglas, 930
Owens, G., 1268
Owens, George, 1269
Owens, John Henry, 2498
Owens, Robert, Sr., 522, 2072, 3782;
    family, 2100-02
Owens, Robert Curry: autobiography,
    522; biographical accounts, 315,
    365
Owens valley: death of early resi-
    dent, 326
Owomoyela, Oyekan, 2568
Oxendine, Britain, 4287

P

Pacific coast: history of education, 1798; maritime unions, 2361; medicine and health, 2777; race relations, 2971, 3102. See also Pacific northwest

Pacific coast appeal publishing co., San Francisco, 974, 2755

Pacific coast news bureau, Los Angeles, 1975

Pacific farming co., Alpaugh, 1200-02

Pacific Grove: local news columns, 4146, 4207

Pacific northwest, 2068; Baptists, 3282; Civil war, 2075; history, 1185, 1210, 2076, 2108, 2110; housing, 3734; race relations, 3084, 3086; schools, 3734; slavery, 3389. See also Pacific coast

Pacific parachute co., San Diego, 961

Pacion, Stanley, 621

Pacoima: newspaper, 4093

P. A. C. T. See Plan of action for challenging times

Paden, Mrs. William Guy (Irene Dakin), 1195

Page, Donald, 771

Pallier, John Giraud, 1045, 2472

Pallier, Mrs. John Giraud (Marie A.), 2472

Palm Springs desert museum: art holdings, 135

Palmer, J. W., 932, 934

Palmieri, Victor H., 3088

Palo Alto: African Methodist Episcopal Zion church, 3195; Citizens' advisory committee on human relations, 3089; City council candidate, 2912; local news columns, 4193, 4199; Midpeninsula citizens for fair housing, 2210-11; Mothers for equal education bookstore, 1545; newspapers, 4150-53; race relations, 3089. See also East Palo Alto; Stanford univ.

--Public schools: primary and preschool, 1524, 1528; secondary, 1234; segregation, 1404

Palo Alto fair play council, 2996, 3009

Palo Alto Ravenswood post, 3864

Palomar college, San Marcos: lectures, 3, 1751, 2513, 2587, 2816, 3605

Palomar mountain. See Harrison, Nathaniel

Pan-Africanism, 18, 885. See also Black movement

Pandex of the press, 318

Panger, Daniel, 2669

Panunzio, Constantine Marie, 2794

Paper industry: employment, 1912

Parade of youth at the piano, San Francisco, 2824

Paramount pictures corp., Los Angeles: library, 104

Pardee, George Cooper, 891

Parish, John C., 3400

Parker, Charles S., 4291

Parker, Charlie, 2825

Parker, E. (Oakland), 2356

Parker, E. (San Diego), 4172

Parker, J. W., 2736

Parker, Leroy, 133

Parker, Michael, 772

Parker, Patricia, 2497

Parker, Pauline E., 1603

Parker, Roy, 944

Parker, Stephenson Robert, 2422

Parker, William Henry, 2440, 2471

Parker, William J., 3256

Parkhill, Forbes, 405, 2105

Parks, Gordon, 3950a

Parks, Norma A., 2778

Parks and recreation, 2030, 2989; in Berkeley, 1332. See also Recreation

Parks chapel African Methodist Episcopal church, Oakland, 3293

Parmee, Leila K., 1783

Parness, Velma, 3499

Parole: revocation, 2454. See also Probation

Parrott, Wanda Sue, 105

Parsons, Edgar W., 1108

Parsons, Harriet Trumbull, 3259

Parsons, Levi, 1058

Pasadena, 656; as fiction locale, 2599-2601; Baptist church, 3782; city employment practices, 1854; community leaders, 3704; described (1933), 3863; directory, 1267; First African Methodist Episcopal church, 3782, 3947; Friendship Baptist church, 3264; local news columns, 4080-81, 4099, 4193, 4198; medical practice, 2760;

Pasadena (cont.)
Negro canyon, 3782; Negro regular Republican club, 2915; Negro tax payers and voters assoc., 2916; newspapers, 4154-57; public library bibliography, 232; race relations, 3127; urban life, 3698, 3707, 3782; women's clubs, 3574
--Public schools: secondary, 1594; segregation, 1388, 1439
Pasadena art museum: art holdings, 136
Pascal, Anthony H., 2225-26
Pasco, John H., 2372
Pasco, Wash.: City council, 2929; high school, 1613; race relations, 3125, 3157, 3691
Pasnick, Ray, 1411
Paso Robles: local news columns, 4193
Passing, 2782, 2787, 2792; fictional account, 2630. See also Miscegenation
Patri, Giacomo, 2446
Patterson, Beeman Coolidge, 2927-28
Patterson, Edgar James: taped interview, 523
Patterson, Frank Sanders, 967
Patterson, Lindsay, 2539
Patterson, S. D., 967
Patterson, William Lorenzo, 405a, 1874
Pawley, Thomas D., 240
Payne, Eileen, 1548
Paynter, John H., 2289
Payton, Lew, 1990, 2569
Peace, Glenda, 176
Peace, Mattie, 3460
Peace, 3173
Pearl, Charles E., 946
Pearson, C. E., 950
Pearson, H. H., 950
Pearson, Thomas, 4104
Peck, James, 1109
Peck, Robert M., 2106
Peck, W. H., 3189
Pektor, Irene Mari, 2737-38
Pélieu, Claude, 2705, 2727
Pendel, Mary Helen, 1643
Peneton, Solomon, 1045
Penfield, Kathleen, 1403
Penn, Irvine Garland, 2290-91
Penn, Nolan, 1604-05
Pennes, Manual Orlando Cepeda. See

Cepeda, Orlando
Pennsylvania: slave trade in, 3454
Penny, Ellen, 3187
People vs. Albert Lee, 2472
People vs. George Washington (Nevada City), 1110-11, 2437-38; (Tehama county), 2473
People vs. Howard, 2437-38
People's auditorium co., Los Angeles, 975
Peoples, Bertha S., 3462
Peoples, Wesley C., 4286
Peplow, E. H., 3090
Pepsi-cola scholarship board, 1658
Periodicals, 3884-4048; advertising, 2275; athletic coverage, 3640; directory of, 188; guide to, 186; literary analyses, 2548, 2873; social utilization, 3603; study of, 2285. See also Journalism; News agencies; Newspapers
Perkins, Carter: judicial case, 2437-38, 3388
Perkins, Johnnie, 3559
Perkins, Rebecca, 3559
Perkins, Robert, 2437-38, 3388
Perkins, William, 2107
Perkins, In the matter of (judicial case), 2437-38, 3388
Perpener, John O., 1497
Perrie, Maggie, 2916
Perry, A., 972
Perry, Lincoln (Stepin Fetchit), 1960
Perry, Mary Ellen, 1659
Perry, Pettis, 3621
Personality. See Sociology
Peru: slavery in, 999
Peters, Gene Raymond, 893
Peters, Wendell A., 4230
Petersen, Mark E., 3139
Peterson, Caleb, 970
Peterson, Carl Daniel, 1660
Peterson, Henry S., 2278, 3222
Peterson, Mozart Ernest, 1784
Peterson, Robert, 3665
Petras, James, 1661
Petroleum industry: employment, 1894. See also Gas industry
Pettigrew, Thomas F., 212
Pettit, Arthur G., 3091
Pettit, John, 3401
Pettit, Tom, 701
Petty, Edwin Louis, 986
Peyton, Jacob C., 3462
Peyton, Lauretta, 3462

Peyton, Thomas Roy, 2227–28, 2774–75
Pfeiffer, C. Whit, 3491
Pharmaceutical industry, 1882
Phelan, James Duval: papers, 524
Phelps, Frederick E., 52
Philadelphia, Pa.: Police dept.,
    2459; U. S. centennial ex-
    hibition, 941
Phillips, Aaron F., 3556
Phillips, Barbara, 2788
Phillips, Hilton Alonzo, 1785,
    2588
Phillips, James Richard, 941
Phillips, Jane, 2670
Phillips, Lucy, 3230
Phillips, Martin, 4276
Phillips, Wendell, 3443
Phillis Wheatley, inc., Los
    Angeles, 3488
Philosophy, 3173, 3239, 3260–61
Phipps, Matthew A., 3568
Phoenix, Charles, 3546
Phoenix: banks and banking, 1939;
    Boy Scouts of America, 3472;
    civil rights hearings, 1140;
    housing, 2171; language patterns,
    3854; local news columns, 4149;
    Luke air force base, 3472;
    newspapers, 4051–57; ordinances,
    etc., 2467–67a; race relations,
    2978, 3080–81; riot, 909–13
--Public schools, 1727; libraries,
    1424; primary and pre-school,
    1547
Phoenix art museum: art holdings,
    137
Phoenixonian institute, San Jose,
    3296
Phonograph records. See Music
Photography, 2508; periodical, 3932
Physical education, 1652
Physical performance, 3870
Pickens, William, 2907
Pico, Pío de Jesús, 327, 2037;
    biographies, 413, 425
Pico boulevard, Los Angeles, 327
Pico family, 438, 2080–81; papers,
    525
Pierce, Joseph, 976
Pierce county, Wash.: bibliography
    of library holdings, 258
Pike, James Albert, 3092
Pilson, Victor, 682
Pilton, James William, 1203, 4014
Pimsleur, Joel L., 890

Pinkney, Alphonso, 3093
Pinkney, William Henry: interview
    with, 406
Piper, Philip, 2077
Pippin, Horace, 131
Pitter, Edward A., 473
Pittman, John, 19, 1917, 2392, 3094,
    4199
Pittman, Mrs. William R. (Tarea Hall):
    taped interview, 526; thesis,
    3622
Pitts, J. C., 1606
Pitts, Lucia Mae, 51
Pitts, Robert Bedford, 431, 2393
Pitts, Wilson D., 979
Pittsburg: local news columns, 4148,
    4206
Pittsburgh, Pa. Courier: Pacific
    coast edition, 4302
Pivnick, Isadore, 1809
Pixley, Frank Morrison, 1058
Place names. See Beckwourth pass;
    Charleys Butte; Monroe Meadow;
    Nigger Hill; Negro Canyon; Pico
    boulevard, Los Angeles
Placer county: petition, 1056;
    slavery, 3371
Placerville: directory, 1270
Plan of action for challenging times,
    San Francisco: publications,
    977, 1271, 3994
Planning, city: 3722; in San Fran-
    cisco, 3792; schools, 1337
Platt, Elizabeth Frazier, 1549
Platt, William J., 1412
Pleasant, Mary Ellen (Mrs. John James
    Pleasant), 300; autobiography,
    318; biographical accounts, 372,
    1230; biographies, 353–55; eject-
    ment suit, 1115–19, 2437–38;
    fictional account, 2632; letters,
    527; memorial services, 408; re-
    lationship with Thomas and Theresa
    Bell, 324; research notes on, 510
Pleasant Hill: Diablo valley college
    library holdings, 187
Ploski, Harry A., 233
Plowman, E. E., 3294
Poal, Susie E., 994
Pocatello, Ida.: local news columns,
    4243
Poe, Elizabeth, 774, 1413
Poetry. See Literature: poetry
Poets: bibliographies, 235–36, 252
Pointer, John, 3303

Poitier, Sidney, 734; biographical
    account, 1993, 2302
Police. See Law and order: police
Politics, 2866-2955, 3061, 3160;
    (1860) 2032; attitudes of African
    students, 22; Black dialogue,
    3902; Black politician, a journal
    of current political thought,
    3910; Black politics, a journal
    of liberation, 3911; directories,
    1243, 1272a; fair employment
    practice commissions, 1924;
    housing, 2163-64, 2175; in
    Berkeley, 2164; in 1868 drama,
    2555; in Los Angeles, 538, 796,
    798-800, 805, 2881, 2896, 2904,
    2906, 2927-28; in San Francisco,
    2287, 3552; liberals, 3072;
    Negro national political and
    protective league, Oakland, 972;
    Pulse, 4008; Uhuru, 4031. See
    also Suffrage
Poll tax, 1107, 2013
Pollard, Lancaster, 2108
Pollard, Samuel W., 2278
Pollard, Sewilla, 3992
Polos, Nicholas C., 1414
Pomeroy, Earl S., 3402
Pomona: newspapers, 4158-59
Pontiflet, James H., 914
Pool, Samuel H., 994
Pope, Alvin, 133
Popkin, Frances, 964
Popkin, Harry M., 964
Popkin, Leo C., 964
Popper, Hermine I., 3786
Population. See Migration; U. S.
    Bureau of the census
Porche, Oscar W., 2370
Port Chicago: as poetry locale,
    2688
Porter, James Amos, 113
Porter, Mrs. James Amos (Dorothy
    Burnett), 234-37
Porter, James Edward, 2763
Porter, Kenneth W., 978, 2394
Portland, Ore.: African Methodist
    Episcopal Zion church, 2575;
    Albina corp., 457; attorney,
    540a; biography of Abner H.
    Francis, 460-61; Brotherhood
    of sleeping car porters, 2397;
    Committee on race and education,
    1415; directories, 1255-56;
    Emancipation proclamation

celebrations, 3403-04; Flowers
    family papers, 499; housing dis-
    crimination, 2251; labor, 2379;
    Lewis and Clark centennial ex-
    position, 3838; Library assoc.
    of Portland and Reed college,
    2491; local news columns, 4148-
    49; model cities program, 3770;
    National assoc. for the advancement
    of colored people, 1104-05;
    National urban league, 2251, 2996,
    3503, 3968, 4007; Negro citizens
    and taxpayers league, 889; news-
    papers, 4254-64; ordinances,
    etc., 2467-67a; property values,
    2196, 2251; race relations, 3095,
    3102; urban life, 3712, 3770;
    Workingman's joint stock assoc.,
    996
--Public schools, 1512, 1675; segre-
    gation, 552, 1322, 1415, 1459
Portland (Ore.) city club, 3095
Portland (Ore.) People's observer,
    4262
Portugues, Stephen Howard, 1550
Posey, Mrs. Leroy Kadell, Jr. (Anita
    Edwards), 2339
Postles, Eliza, 3187
Potrero hill nursery school, San
    Francisco, 1553
Potter, Elizabeth (Gray), 409
Potter, William H., 1114, 1130
Potts, A. L., 927
Potts, Alfred M., 238
Potts, E. Daniel, 1204
Poulton, Helen Jean, 3405
Poverty. See Economic conditions
Powell, Caesar, 975
Powell, Ingeborg Breitner, 894
Powell, R. J., 3458
Powell, Walter, 4052
Powell, William J., 452, 469, 3560,
    3899
Powers, Robert B., 2461
Powers, William, 3548
Pozovich, Gregory J., 1551
Pratt, Ed, 865
Prejudice. See Race relations
Pre-emption law: exception made,
    1151; judicial case, 2260,
    2437-38
Prendergast, Wilfred J., 2221, 2229
Prentice, Mrs. B. E., 946
Presbyterian church: north coastal
    area, 3145

Pre-school education. See Education: primary and pre-school

Press. See Journalism; News agencies; Newspapers; Periodicals

Prestopino, Gregorio, 2320

Prewitt, Kenneth, 3042

Price, Electra K., 2926

Price, J. W., 3175

Price, Leslie, 133

Price, Mary Ellen, 2540

Price, Rita M., 1786

Price, Thomas Aubrey, 3295

Pride, Armistead Scott, 2286, 2292-93

Primary education. See Education: primary and pre-school

Primary source materials. See Manuscripts; Newspapers; Periodicals

Prince, Leonora E., 2350

Prince, Virginia Ann, 2294

Prince Hall bay counties credit union, Alameda county, 979

Prince Hall building assoc., San Francisco, 3539

Prince Hall credit union, Riverside, 980

Prince Hall grand lodge. See Freemasons. California: Prince Hall grand lodge; Freemasons. Colorado: Prince Hall grand lodge

Prince Hall masonic temple improvement assoc., Santa Barbara, 3540

Prince Hall masons holding assoc., Los Angeles, 3541

Prince Hall no. 2 credit union, Los Angeles, 981

Prince Hall no. 3 credit union, Vallejo, 982

Prince Hall no. 5 credit union, Bakersfield, 983

Prince Hall progressive building assoc., Los Angeles, 3542

Printing: Los Angeles (1949), 2288. See also Newspapers; Periodicals

Printing and publishing. See under names of individual presses, e.g., Al Kitab Sudan publications, Fresno; Bridges printing co., Oakland; California eagle pub. co., Los Angeles; California voice press, Oakland; More pub. co., San Francisco; New age pub.

co., Los Angeles; Pacific coast appeal pub. co., San Francisco; Richardson (Julian) associates, San Francisco; Seattle Republican; Success pub. co., San Francisco; Tilghman (Charles F.) press, Oakland

Prisons: Calif., 308, 540a, 2456. See also Law and order

Probation: Los Angeles, 746, 2436. See also Parole

Produce gardening: in Seattle, 960

Produce markets: in Los Angeles, 986

Professions, 3074. See also Law; Medicine; etc.

Progressive mutual benefit assoc., Los Angeles, 3564

Project big four, Laguna Beach, 3141

Property, 2131-2263 passim; in ghettos, 782. See also Business; Economics; Real estate business

Proposition 14. See Housing: Rumford Calif. fair housing act

Prosser, William Farrand, 410

Prostitution: in Los Angeles, 3716

Protestant Episcopal church: Freedman's commission, 3238; in San Francisco and San Jose, 3296

Prowd, John E., 2271, 4081

Psychiatry: and racism, 2767; bibliography, 173; National institute of mental health, 1539; Watts riot analyzed, 793. See also Medicine and health

Psychology, 3583-3633 passim, 3879; autobiography of I. L. Ferguson, 334; educational, 1811; of black revolution, 853. See also Attitude

Public accommodations. See Civil rights; Hotels; Restaurants; etc.

Public health: Hunters Point-Bayview community health service news, 3965; Menlo Park, 1914; Negro college programs, 1652; San Francisco agencies, 1247; San Jose, 2994-95; Watts agencies, 715. See also Medicine and health

Public housing. See Housing

Public utilities: employment in, 1832-33

Public welfare: Aid to families with dependent children, 3594, 3616, 3634; county hospitals, 3627; in Alameda county, 3786; in Compton,

Public welfare (cont.)
3740; in Contra Costa county,
3622; in Fresno county, 3583,
3594; in Los Angeles, 3816; in
Los Angeles county, 3813, 3816;
in San Francisco, 3114; in San
Jose, 2994-95; in Watts, 715,
804
Pueblo, Colo.: newspapers, 4234-41
Puget Sound observer, Seattle, 4282
Puget Sound univ., Tacoma, 1639
Purifoy, Noah, 108, 133
Purnell, Ann S., 3481
Purnell, William Whipper, 972
Pusey, Mavis, 133
Putnam, Harvey, 3406
Pyburn, Don, 133
Pyles, Marguerite, 3485

Q

Quay, William Howard, 1918
Queen, William, 1045
Quimby, George Irving, 2110
Quinn, Alfred Thomas, 1416

R

Raab, Earl, 3096
Rabé, William, 1058
Race relations, 486, 2163, 2956-3164,
3590, 3851; American council on,
2461; American missionary assoc.
correspondence, 2007; athletics,
3642, 3644, 3663, 3670; attitudes
toward Africa, 17; bibliography,
200; blacks vs. blacks, 3633;
Calif. gold rush, 2039; colleges
and universities, 1616-70 passim;
police officers' guide, 2434;
public schools, 1753; Rosenwald
(Julius) fund, 1672. See also
Education; Entertainment; Housing;
under names of geographical localities, e.g., Phoenix: race
relations; and under names of
ethnic groups, e.g., Mexican-
Americans; etc.
Rachiele, Leo D., 1552
Racial dissent, 556-925; Los Angeles
(1960s), 538; Watts riot, 668-
829
Rader, Tonja Evetts, 1553
Radetsky, Ralph, 3003
Radicals and radicalism. See Black

movement; Black panther party;
Communist party; Socialist workers
party; Third world liberation
front; etc.
Radio broadcasting: (1922-53), 1961;
guide to, 186; in Los Angeles,
2288; in Seattle, 1966; social
utilization, 3603; Watts commentary,
726. See also Television
Ragan, Roger L., 2230
Railroads: Associated railway employees of Calif., Oakland, 2356-57;
Brotherhood of sleeping car por-
ters, 2363; Dining car cooks and
waiters union, Los Angeles, 2373;
dining car waiters, 1937; labor,
2392; Pennsylvania railroad, 943;
Railroad men's guide, 4011;
Southern Pacific co., 1937, 3129
Raine, Dorothy Pentecost, 3781
Raine, Walter Jerome, 775-76
Rainey, Douglas L., 1272-72a
Rains, Ollie F., 2739
Ranch life, 3165-72; autobiography of
Nat Love, 377-78; fictional ac-
count, 2640; labor (1866-1900),
2394. See also Agriculture; Cow-
boys; Hides and tallow trade
Rand, Christopher, 3100
Randall, Albert G., 1058
Randall, Dudley, 2744
Randals, Edwyna Henrietta, 1554
Randolph, Asa Philip, 2363, 2397
Randolph (Asa Philip) institute,
New York, 2369
Randolph, Carolyn A., 2541
Randolph, R. V., 3559
Rankin, Jerry, 2931
Ranne, Peter, 2041
Ransford, Harry Edward, 777, 895
Rapier, Richard G., 1195
Rare ripe gold and silver mining co.,
Marysville, 984
Rasche, Herbert, 2658
Rasmussen, Louis J., 1273
Rastegar, Carol Congress, 3446
Ratterman, Breen, 1607
Rau, John L., 970
Rauch, Lawrence Lee, 411
Rauch, Mabel Thompson, 2671
Rauf, Mohammad A., 3693
Ravenswood city school district in-
structional materials center, 239
Ravenswood high school, East Palo Alto,
1234

Rawitscher, Audrey, 896

Rawls, Lou, 2800

Ray, Emma J. (Smith): autobiography, 412

Ray, Mrs. Henry (Mary Johnson): biographical account, 395

Ray, L. P.: autobiography, 412

Ray, Lucinda, 3187

Raye, Estella, 2917

Reagan, Ronald, 2475, 3832

Real estate business, 2137-2259 passim; Afro-American real estate assoc. and employment bureau of Calif., Oakland, 931; Allensworth land co., 933; Colored colonization assoc. of Fresno county, 1174; Colored colonization co., San Diego, 1175; Colored Mexican colonization co., San Diego, 1176; Colored workers assoc., Los Angeles, 945; Frederick Douglass cooperative realty company of San Francisco, 958; home mortgages, 2222; in Calif., 2259, 3136; in Los Angeles, 2257; Lower Calif. Mexican land & development co., 963; Pacific farming co., Alpaugh, 1200-02; Workingman's joint stock assoc. of Portland, Ore., 996. See also Homestead law; Housing; Property; Restrictive covenants

Reardon, William R., 240, 2542

Reasons, George, 470-71

Reaves, J. A., 3184

Reblee, Rowland K., 4066a

Reconstruction, 2867-68, 2890, 3161. See also Civil war; Freedmen; and under individual state, e.g., Mississippi: reconstruction

Record, Jane Cassels, 1120

Record, Wilson, 897, 1120, 1205, 1319, 1417-20, 1787, 2398-99, 2932-33, 2996, 3101, 3117

Recording, musical. See Music

Recreation, 1332, 2030; child activities, 3610; in San Jose, 2995; in Watts, 805. See also Parks and recreation

Red Bluff: local news columns, 4149

Reddick, Lawrence D., 3102

Redding, Jay Saunders, 3020

Redding: local news columns, 4193, 4199, 4206

Reece, Alice, 3462

Reed, Albert, 3469

Reed, Bessie Marie, 3560

Reed, G. W., 3545

Reed, H., 3458

Reed, Ishmael, 2497, 2501, 2672

Reed, Mamie L., 2919

Reed, T. Edward, 2776

Reese, Arthur L., 319

Reese, James Marshall, 1045

Reeve, Frank D., 52

Reeves, Beatrice, 3485

Reeves, H. A., 929

Reeves, Harriett, 3485

Regan, John T., 1121

Regan, Mary C., 3591

Reich, Kenneth, 898

Reid, Hiram Alvin, 3782

Reid, Ira De Augustine, 3783-85

Reid, Robert, 2578-79

Reid, Wendell, 4179

Reiner, Burton A., 97

Reinert, Frederick A., 3447

Reinhardt, Richard, 2400

Reisner, Robert George, 2825

Reissman, Frank, 3786

Reitman, Neil, 2220-21

Reitnouer, Minnie Grage, 1498

Reitzes, Dietrich C., 2777

Religion, 3173-3340; American missionary assoc., 2007; biographical dictionaries, 480-81; Calif. bibliography, 189; denominational schools, 1647, 1782; directory of San Francisco bay area churches, 1272a; essays on, 2578-79; in San Jose, 2995; in Watts, 805; in Yuba county, 2035; Northern California-Nevada council of churches, 2223; Pacific coast membership lists, 473; Southern attitudes, 3445; U. S. census, 1297. See also under name of individual sects, e.g., African Methodist Episcopal church; Baptists; etc.; and under names of individual churches by geographical locality, e.g., San Francisco: First African Methodist Episcopal Zion church; Oakland: St. Augustine's Episcopal church; etc.

Beller, Theodore Lee, 1788

Rembar, Charles, 634

Remington, Frederic, 53-54

Reneau, Henry, 832

Reneau, M., 832
Reno: school segregation, 1459; tourism, 3842
Republican party: in Oregon, 3407; in Pasadena, 2915; in San Francisco, 2917
Resource books, 1796-97, 2013, 2111, 3861
Resource materials. See Bibliographies; Manuscripts; Newspapers; Periodicals; etc.
Restaurants: in Oakland, 988; in San Jose, 2995
Restrictive covenants, 2131-2259 passim; bibliography, 2240. See also Housing; Real estate business
Revels, Hiram Rhoades: biography, 443
Revels, Susie Sumner. See Cayton, Mrs. Horace Roscoe, Sr. (Susie Sumner Revels)
Revitt, Paul Joseph, 241
Revolutionary movements. See Black movement; Black panther party; Communist party; Nation of Islam; Socialist workers party; Third world liberation front; etc.
Rexroth, Kenneth, 2543
Reyes, Manley, 3187
Reynolds, Marion Hobart, 3408
Reynolds, Raymond J., 2476
Reynolds, William H., 1919
Rhetoric. See Literature: essays and speeches; Speeches and lectures
Rhodehamel, Josephine (De Witt), 242, 3489
Rhodes, Clarence, 4017
Rhodes, Ethel C., 2110a
Rice, C. H., 952
Rice, Hallie Evelyn, 413
Rice, W., 3566
Richard Allen news service, Los Angeles, 2295
Richards, Eugene Scott, 1206-08, 1789
Richards, Lenora Alexander, 3490
Richards, Marion, 243
Richardson, Adeline (Claff), 1608
Richardson, Ben Albert, 2340
Richardson, E. J., 4060
Richardson, Grace, 3103
Richardson, H. L., 972

Richardson, Josephine, 3460
Richardson (Julian) associates, San Francisco, 2308, 2703, 2707, 2749, 3333
Richardson, Mabel, 3462
Richey, Elinor, 2231
Richmond, A. M., 3403
Richmond, Alexander, 1920
Richmond: Booker T. luncheon club, 937; employment, 1838; firearms controversy, 2449; local news columns, 4148, 4206; model cities program, 3770; Nation of Islam bakery, 563; newspapers, 4066, 4160; ordinances, etc., 2467-67a; Police dept., 2429, 2461-62, 2481, 3786; public schools, 1345, 1468, 3596; race relations, 3104, 3154-55, 3683; street gang program, 3720; Unified school district, 2111; urban life, 3770, 3802
Richmond community development project, 3802
Richmond council on intergroup relations, 2996
Ricks, J. Thomas, 1045
Ricks, William Nauns, 2740-41
Riddle, John, 133
Rideout, George, 2478
Ridley, E. F., 3297
Ridout, Lionel Utley, 3296
Rieff, Philip, 3105
Rigby, Gerald, 1122
Rigg, Dorothy Mae, 424
Riker, James H., 1045
Riker, Mrs. James H. (Charlotte L. Brown), 1036
Riker, Samuel, 1921
Riles, Wilson Camanza, 1421-23
Riley, Ethel R., 2673
Riley, George P., 996, 2934
Riley, L. H., 2795
Riordan, Marguerite, 1790
Riots, 680-82, 851, 858, 866, 875, 877, 880-81, 896, 2323, 2439; bibliography, 207; in Los Angeles (1943), 875, 880; in San Francisco (1966), 848, 857, 909-13; journalism, 2268; prevention, 2432. See also Watts: riot (1965)
Riseley, Jerry B., 2477
Risher, Howard W., Jr., 1894
Ritchey, Bert, 367
Ritter, Daniel B., 2218
Ritter, Earnestine, 3107

Rivers, John C., 835, 926
Rivers, Joseph D. D., 2289, 4225
Riverside: Calif. univ. Black
    student union, 639a, 2489;
    directory, 1267; newspaper,
    4161; Prince Hall credit union,
    980; public schools segregation,
    1344, 1364, 1369, 1386; urban
    renewal, 2186
Robbins, Charles F., 1058
Roberson, Alberta Carl, 1499
Roberson, Mason, 4199
Robeson, Paul, 2288, 2979, 3853,
    3873
Roberson, Robert L., 3867
Roberts, Andrew J., 963
Roberts, Frederick Madison, 4099,
    4217
Roberts, Myron, 780, 899, 2232,
    2935-37
Roberts, S. V., 900
Robertson, Bill, 4028
Robertson, Cornelia Jones, 284
Robertson, Florence (Kenney), 1791
Robeson, Mrs. Paul (Eslanda
    Cardoza Goode), 3873
Robeson, Paul, Jr., 3873
Robinson, Bill "Bojangles": bio-
    graphical accounts, 2328, 2340
Robinson, Charles D., 979
Robinson, Duane Morris, 3491
Robinson, E. I., 4276
Robinson, Earl, 2300
Robinson, Effie Marie, 3787
Robinson, Fay M. (Jackson), 3957,
    4081
Robinson, Frank, 3664, 3666
Robinson, H., 832
Robinson, Ida, 832
Robinson, Isaiah, 971
Robinson, James Lee, 2112
Robinson, John Roosevelt "Jackie":
    autobiographies, 2341, 3667-68;
    biographical accounts, 470,
    2301, 2325; biographies, 3656,
    3669, 3671-72
Robinson, Louie, 781, 1209, 2342
Robinson, Louis George, 927;
    biography, 419
Robinson, Preston, 832
Robinson, Roygene, 923
Robinson, W. A., 1424
Robinson, Wilhelmina S., 472
Robinson, William "Bojangles": bio-
    graphical accounts, 2328, 2340

Robison, Joseph, 782
Rochelle, Charles Edward, 1662
Rocq, Mrs. Pierre F. (Margaret
    Miller), 244
Rodda, Albert S., 1368
Rodgers, Jonathan, 3670
Rodia, Simon, 789, 2335
Roeder, Bill, 3671
Roelof-Lanner, T. V., 107
Roeser, Veronica A., 1425
Roesler, Karen Jane, 3623
Rogers, Charles D., 133
Rogers, Moses L., 993a, 1211
Rogers, Ray, 622
Rogers, Wanda J., 1555
Rogin, Gilbert, 3650
Rollins, Charlemae Hill, 1993
Rollins, Henry, 133
Rolph, James: papers, 528
Roman Catholic church, 2997, 3332;
    in Los Angeles county, 3813;
    in San Francisco, 3792
Romney, Mrs. George (Lenore La
    Fount), 3078
Root, Joseph Moseley, 3409
Rorick, Harry, 2288
Rose, Edward, 978, 2065, 2311
Rose, Julius K., 1058
Rose, Tom, 3788
Roseberg, Judy, 2458
Rosebury, Celia, 623
Rosenberg, Harry E., 1792
Rosenblum, Abraham L., 3108
Rose-Netta hospital assoc., Los
    Angeles, 2778
Rosenfels, Isabelle G., 1613
Rosenthal, Simon, 1055
Rosenwald (Julius) fund, 1672, 2384
Rosenwein, Sam, 1079
Roslyn, Wash.: local news columns,
    4283
Ross, Andrew, 937
Ross, Arthur Max, 1922
Ross, Charlene, 1266
Ross, David P., Jr., 2298
Ross, Frank Alexander, 245-46
Ross, George G., 4230
Ross, James R., 952
Ross, Ronald Patrick, 2544
Rossa, Della, 783
Roston, James A., Jr.: taped
    interview, 529
Roston, James A., Sr.: papers, 530
Rotero, C., 972
Roth, Mrs. Bernard N., 3485

Roth, Esther, 3485
Roth, Frances, 3485
Rothe, Anna, 414
Rothstein, Mignon E., 2233
Rousseve, Ronald J., 1793
Rowan, Carl Thomas, 3669, 3672
Rowan, Richard L., 1923
Rowe, Robert N., 1427
Rowe, Sidney, 2875
Rowell, Bruce Frederick: biographi-
    cal account, 401
Rowland, Donald Winslow, 1011
Rowland, Mabel, 1994
Roy, Donald Francis, 3789
Royce, Josiah, 1055
Rubber tire industry: employment,
    1913
Rubin, Arnold, 109
Rubin, Marvin, 1841-42
Ruchames, Louis, 1924
Rudwick, Elliott, 852
Ruffin, Osolee [Osceola?] (Minor),
    2779
Ruggles, David Wright, 2472, 2870
Rumford, William Byron, 2931; cor-
    respondence, 2996; oral history
    of, 2938; reminiscences, 476;
    thesis, 3790
Rumford (William Byron) fair housing
    act, 2131-2254 passim
Rusco, Elmer R., 2939, 3109
Rusmore, Jay Theodore, 1925
Russ, Kenneth C., 3567
Russell, Charles: taped interview,
    531
Russell, Clayton D., 971
Russell, Harold, 967
Russell, N. S., 4194
Russell, William Felton "Bill",
    2574, 3650, 3673
Rust, Ben, 1794
Rustin, Bayard, 714, 784-88, 2369
Rutherford, Gemel B. H., 835
Rutledge, Aaron L., 1926
Ryan, James A., 994
Ryan, John Henry, 2478, 2940, 4298
Ryan, Mrs. John Henry (Ella E.),
    4298
Ryan, Kathleen E., 2423
Ryan, Pat, 2502
Ryan, William, 3410
Ryan, William Redmond, 3411
Rydall, E. H., 2234
Rystrom, Richard Carl, 2424

S

Saar, Betye, 76, 108, 131, 133, 2502
Sackett, Charles, 1114
Sacramento: (1841), 2057; African
    Methodist Episcopal church, 3187;
    American river college library
    holdings, 153; as fiction locale,
    2657; Calif. state univ., 165-66,
    2992, 3693; Congress of racial
    equality, 2244; described (1922),
    3863; directories, 1267, 1274-81,
    1283; experiences of James
    Williams, 444-47; family life,
    3741; Freemasons, 2128; housing,
    2134-2256 passim, 3110; journalism,
    2236; law and order, 3110; local
    news columns, 4080-81, 4146, 4148-
    49, 4198-99, 4206-07; newspapers,
    4162-66; 1850 jury, 2474; pro-
    slavery sermon, 3284; race rela-
    tions, 3110; regional history,
    2097; St. Andrew's African Metho-
    dist Episcopal church, 1040, 3174,
    3178, 3297-98, 3308; Shiloh
    Baptist church, 3306-07; Siloam
    Baptist church, 3209; slavery,
    512, 2437-38, 3378, 3388, 3390,
    3396, 3428; State employees for
    equality, 2244; urban life, 3693,
    3741; urban redevelopment, 2256;
    women's clubs, 3574. See also
    entries under California relating
    to state administrative activities
    in Sacramento
--Public schools, 2128; (1854-59),
    1818; (1863), 1688; segregation,
    1326, 1369, 1372, 1395
Sacramento city-county human relations
    commission, 3110
Sacramento committee for fair housing,
    2131, 2235-36, 2244
Sacramento community integration
    project, 2219
Sacramento county: petitions of
    residents, 1048, 1057; Rumford
    fair housing act, 2134; slavery,
    3356; suffrage, 1282
Sacramento observer, 1283
Sacramento valley: (1829), 2086;
    business, 974
Sahlman, Joyce Virginia, 2545
St. Andrew's African Methodist Episco-
    pal church, Sacramento, 1040, 3174,
    3178, 3297-98, 3308

St. Augustine's Episcopal church, Oakland, 3299

St. Cyprian church, San Francisco, 3239

St. James, Edward Antonine, 983

St. John's district assoc. of northern Calif., 3215

St. Paul African Methodist Episcopal church, Berkeley, 3300-01

Salata, Dorothy H., 1266

Sales tax, 3850

Salinas: rubber tire industry, 1913; Soledad state prison, 2456

Salisbury, R. E., 3302

Salley, Robert Lee, 3111

Salmon Falls: public schools, 2032

Salt Lake City: local news columns, 4243; National assoc. for the advancement of colored people, 3064; newspapers, 4266-68; school segregation, 1459

Saltzman, Joe, 2237

Sample, Henry, 928

Sampson, William S., 4104

Sams, Jessie (Bennett), 415

Samuels, Gertrude, 624

San Anselmo: San Francisco theological seminary, 1126

San Antonio, Tex.: 3082

San Bernardino: description, 3828; directory, 1267; local news columns, 4099; newspapers, 4167-69; residents in 1850s, 453-54

--Public schools: segregation, 1369, 1391, 1432

--State univ. library holdings, 167-69

San Diego, 656, 850; accommodations discrimination, 1065; African Methodist Episcopal church, 3188; Afro-American colonization company of Mexico, 1159; as fiction locale, 2680; Black book productions, 2494, 2560; black movement, 903; Calif. state univ., 170, 2993; Citizens interracial committee, 1872; civil service, 1855, 3565; Colored colonization co., 1175; Colored employees social and aid club, 3565; Colored Mexican colonization co., 1176; Congress of racial equality, 3746; directories, 1239, 1246, 1267, 1872;

employment, 1855, 3053; employment directory, 1872; Fine arts gallery of, 126; housing, 3053; Jewish community center, 138; League of women voters, 3053; local news columns, 4080-81, 4099; Logan heights, 2980; National assoc. for the advancement of colored people, 3853; newspapers, 4170-80; Pacific parachute co., 961; Police dept., 2459; race relations, 2959, 3048-49, 3053, 3098, 3164, 3942; racial dissent, 1765; segregation, 1088; Station XETV, 3164; tourism, 3842; urban life, 3711, 3742-46

--Public schools, 1530, 1815; art bibliography, 247; secondary, 1587-88, 1593; segregation, 1425, 1428-29

San Diego county: Economic opportunity commission, 3475; history of Julian, 2073; race relations, 2973

San Diego municipal employees assoc., 3565

San Fernando valley: race relations, 2985

San Fernando valley state univ., Northridge, 163-64, 641

San Francisco: 1850s, 339-40; 1870s, 320; Abraham Lincoln high school, 839; African American historical and cultural society, 118, 408, 4014; African descendants nationalist independent partition party, 831; African spiritual helping hand undenominational national church, 3197; Afro-American cooperative assoc., 926; Afro-American institute, 556; Afro-American league, 833-34, 2911; American freedman's union commission, 2006; as fiction locale, 2594, 2632, 2663, 2674, 2679; autobiography of psychologist, 334; Bank of America, 1834, 1852, 1908; banks and banking, 1939; Bay view elementary school, 1535; Bethel African Methodist Episcopal church, 3177, 3227, 3303; Black community research and communication project, 4013; Blackman's art gallery, 72; Board of education, 1430-31, 1795; Board of supervisors, 1927, 3112; Booker T. mothers' club, 3460;

San Francisco (cont.)
Booker T. Washington community service center, 540a, 3461-65; Booker T. Washington country club, 3546; Booker T. Washington relief society, 3466, 3473; Broadway grammar school, 1564-68; cable cars, 440; Calif. historical society, 123; California historical society quarterly index, 178; Chamber of commerce (1865), 3381; children, abnormal, 1744; Church for the fellowship of all peoples, 3231-32, 3309, 3320-21; Church of our Lord's most tender compassion, 3937a; churches, 3247, 3285, 3295; City college of, 839; City hotel, 514; Colored-American employees' assoc., 1874; Colored citizens' convention (1857), 3239; Colored entertainers club, 3548; Colored janitor co-operative assoc., 3549; Colored military social club, 3550; Colored social club, 3551; Colored veterans service club, 3552; Colored workingmen's club, 3554; Colored young men and women's industrial Christian assoc., 3469; Commission on equal employment opportunity, 1928; Cosmos social club, 2802; Council for civic unity, 1019, 2169-70, 3003-04, 3705, 3939; crime, 2476; Dept. of city planning, 2238; described (1922), 3863; de Young (M. H.) memorial museum exhibit catalog, 100; directories, 1247, 1267, 1271, 1284-88, 1294, 1535; economic conditions, 3748, 3809; Economic opportunity council, 3476, 3492; elections, 2941-42; Elevator publishing co., 2278; Elevator silver mining co., 950; Emancipation proclamation celebrations, 2584, 2692, 2695; entertainment industry, 1951-2003 passim; Exclusive men, 3555; family planning, 3729; First African Methodist Episcopal Zion church, 3254-58, 3334; First Unitarian church, 629-30; Frederick Douglass cooperative realty co., 958; ghetto nationalism, 882; Haight-Ashbury

settlement house art project, 112; history (1849-70) 3774, (1854-55) 3727, (1860-65) 3771-73, (1870-90) 3757; hotels, 1074, 1125, 1895; housing, 540a, 1019, 1026, 2169-2261 passim, 3112, 3114, 3792; Human relations coordinator, 3113; Human rights commission, 1123-24, 1929; International longshoremen's & warehousemen's union, 2381; James Weldon Johnson in, 363; journalism, 2264-96 passim; Julian Richardson associates, 2308, 2703, 2707, 2749, 3333; labor and labor movement, 2375, 2384, 2389-90, 2395, 2401; Ladies Pacific accumulating and benevolent assoc., 3556; Ladies' union beneficial society, 3557-58; leadership in, 921; local news columns, 4146, 4148, 4243; Martin Luther King square, 2247; Mayor's office of youth affairs, 3885; medicine and health, 2769, 2772, 3965; migration to, 1193, 1205, 3117; minstrelsy, 2002; Mission rebels, 3501; More book store, 213; More publishing co., 2675; Mt. Zion Baptist church, 3289; municipal railway employment, 1920; Nation of Islam (Black Muslims), 3982; National assoc. for the advancement of colored people, 657; National urban league, 1835, 1921; Negro alliance grocery co., 965; Negro protective fraternal society, 3561; Negro young Republican club of San Francisco county, 2917; newspapers, 4066, 4181-4206; Nil desperandum mining co., 973; North Beach and mission railroad co., 1036, 1115-19, 1133-36, 2437-38; Nurseries in cross-cultural education, 1544, 1546; ordinances, etc., 1927, 1930, 2467-67a; Pacific coast appeal publishing co., 974, 2755; Parade of youth at the piano, 2824; Plan of action for challenging times, inc. (PACT), 977, 1271, 3994; Police dept., 1026, 2442, 2482-83, 2488, 3112, 3114; politics, 2954; poll tax, 2013; Potrero hill nursery school, 1553; Presidio of, 2096; Prince Hall building assoc., 3539;

San Francisco (cont.)
property values, 2196; Protestant
Episcopal church, 3296; public
welfare, 3114; race relations,
1922, 3013, 3040, 3094, 3102,
3113-15, 3144; racial dissent,
1765; recollections of, 3833;
Republican party, 2917; riot
(1966), 848, 857, 909-13; Roman
Catholic church, 3792; St. Cyprian
church, 3239; shoe store, 339-40;
Society of Calif. pioneers, 143,
308a; Starr King elementary
school, 90; street railway ejectment, 1036, 1115-19, 1133-36;
Success publishing co., 1294,
2918; theater, 1948-2003 passim;
Third Baptist church, 3209, 3310-
16, 3331; tourism, 3842; town
journal (1847-48), 532-33; Trans-
bay federal savings and loan
assoc., 991; unemployment, 1876;
United African appeal, 876a,
3937a; United nations conference,
1034, 1084; United San Francisco
freedom movement, 2249; urban life,
3681-3810 passim; urban planning,
3792; urban redevelopment, 2238,
2247, 2249, 2261; West Indian
benevolent assoc., 3568; Western
addition area, 1539, 1544, 2249,
3022, 3476, 3729, 4184; Western
addition community festival,
3569; Western addition community
organization, 2261, 4037;
Western addition law office community education project, 3988;
women's clubs, 3574; World war
II labor, 2384; Youth for service,
3973
--Calif. state univ., 643; Black
students union, 639b, 649, 1657,
3904; black studies program,
1626, 1657, 1659; local news
columns, 4199; student revolt,
642, 645, 647, 1632, 1635, 1637,
1646, 1657, 3294
--civil rights: hearings, 1139;
march, 1127; religious stand,
3247
--employment, 1026, 1874, 1917, 1922;
Commission on equal employment
opportunity, 1928; FEPC ordinances,
1927, 1930; Human rights commission, 1929

--Hunters Point, 3697, 3713-14, 3860;
Bay area neighborhood development
foundation, 3730; directory, 1535;
family structure, 3732; Hunters
Point-Bayview community health
service, 3965; Hunters Point-Bayview library, 3457; Hunter's
Point beacon, 4188; Junior city,
3468; police relations, 2442;
youth, 3721; Youth opportunities
center, 1705, 3493, 3499
--Public library: Anna E. Waden
branch, 3457; bibliography, 248;
Fillmore St. project, 3504
--Public schools, 1770, 3112, 3114,
4025; (1854-59), 1818; (1862),
1813; (1863), 1688; primary and
pre-school, 1539, 1544, 1546, 1553,
2408, 2412, 2425; segregation,
1361, 1365, 1388, 1401, 1430-31,
1446-47, 1463, 1564-68, 2437-38;
teaching guide, 1556
San Francisco African American historical and cultural society, 118,
408; California history series,
4014
San Francisco bay area: artists of,
102; business survey (1928), 957;
directories, 1272-72a; economic
conditions, 3692; education, 1768;
employment testing, 1925; food and
restaurants, 1231; housing, 2133-
2262 passim; labor unions, 2401;
migration to, 1183; miscegenation,
2788; National assoc. for the advancement of colored people, 656;
National urban league, 3459;
police, 2483; public schools,
1788, 3636; race relations, 3101,
3137; secondary education, 1582,
1586, 1589-90. See also Bay area
San Francisco college for women:
Black madonna writers' lab, 2490
San Francisco colored chauffeurs
assoc., 3566
San Francisco colored league of women
voters, 2902a-b
San Francisco comic book co., 3946
San Francisco conference on religion,
race and social concerns, 3114
San Francisco Elevator, 1039, 2278,
2296, 2585
San Francisco Examiner (1878-1900),
2264; (1901-07), 2267; (1908-12),
2283

San Francisco giants, 3639, 3651
San Francisco maritime museum: art holdings, 139
San Francisco mime troupe, 1968
San Francisco Mirror of the times, 2270
San Francisco museum of art: art holdings, 140
San Francisco Negro historical and cultural society. See San Francisco African American historical and cultural society
San Francisco Outlook, 4149
San Francisco Pacific coast appeal, 4193, 4206. See also Pacific coast appeal pub. co., San Francisco
San Francisco daily People's world, 1920
San Francisco Sentinel, 2273
San Francisco Sun-reporter, 2265
San Francisco theological seminary, San Anselmo, 1126
San Francisco Vindicator (1891-93), 2269
San Francisco Western outlook, 4149
San Francisco youth opportunities center. See San Francisco: Hunters Point Youth opportunities center
San Joaquin progressor, 4212
San Joaquin valley: business, 974
San Jose: African Methodist Episcopal Zion church of America, 3196, 3266-67; churches, 2995; directory, 1289; fraternal organizations, 2994; hotels and restaurants, 2995; housing, 2994-95; labor unions, 2994-95; local news columns, 4146, 4148-49, 4193-94, 4198-99, 4206; newspaper, 4207; Phoenixonian institute, 3296; police relations, 2994-95; public health and welfare, 2994-95; Public library art holdings, 101, 141; public schools, 1688, 1822, 2994-95; race relations, 2994-95; social clubs, 2994; women's clubs, 3574
--State univ., 1624; art holdings, 119; library holdings, 171-72; race relations studies, 2994-95
San Leandro: urban life, 3777
San Luis Obispo: State polytechnic college library holdings, 175

San Marcos: Palomar college, 3, 1751, 2513, 2587, 2816, 3605
San Mateo: College of San Mateo, 1663; directory, 1267; Intergroup relations assoc. of northern Calif., 3975; kindergarten study, 1548; local news columns, 4144, 4148, 4193, 4199; urban life, 3701
San Mateo community service center, 3960
San Mateo county: Community council, 3471. See also San Francisco bay area
San Mateo county library system: bibliography, 249
San Mateo school district: bibliography, 250
San Pedro: as fiction locale, 2665
San Quentin state prison, 540a
Sanchez, Sonia, 2570, 2742-44
Sanders, Charles D., 1500
Sanders, Stanley, 790-91
Sanderson, Jeremiah Burke, 3556-57, 3830; biographical account, 368
Sandford, Paul L., 1501
Sandford, Walter H., 3462
Sands, Joseph R., 926
Sankore, Shelby, 2113
Santa Ana: Bowers (Charles H.) memorial museum, 124; history, 2088; Williams publications, 3141
Santa Barbara: African Methodist Episcopal church, 3189; baptism (1819), 493; Calif. univ. library holdings, 177; Center for the study of democratic institutions, 2439, 2577, 3737; directory, 1267; local news columns, 4080-81; Prince Hall masonic temple improvement assoc., 3540; public schools, 1748
Santa Clara county: economic conditions, 3748
Santa Clara univ., Santa Clara: art holdings, 142
Santa Clara writers institute (1964), 3024
Santa Cruz: school bequest, 1775
Santa Monica, 656; directory, 1267; local news columns, 4080: newspaper, 4208; Synanon, 2765
Satchell, Charles, 3287
Satchell, Ernest, 133
Satterwhite, Betty S., 1290

Satterwhite, Frank J., 1290
Satterwhite, Mildred McKinley, 1664
Saunders, Cornelia: taped interview, 534
Saunders, Hester, 3187
Saunders, Raymond, 76, 122
Saunders, Robert: taped interview, 535
Sausalito: Marinship corp., 955, 2403; School district, 1369, 1573, 1750
Savage, William Sherman, 416-18, 1210-11, 1798, 1931, 2114
Savio, Mario, 890
Sawyer, Barbara, 3791
Saxton, Alexander Plaisted, 2674
Sayre, Nora, 625-26, 792
Scales, Patience, 2824
Scally, William, 3412
Schallert, Eugene J., 3792
Schanche, Don A., 627-28
Schatz, Walter, 251
Schear, Rillmond, 3793-94
Scheer, Robert, 582, 2958
Scheville, James, 1127
Schmid, Calvin Fisher, 1212, 3632, 3795
Schmidt, Donald Ray, 2239
Schneider, Frank M., 2478a
Scholefield, Harry B., 629-30
Schomburg, Arthur Alfonso, 252
Schomburg (Arthur Alfonso) collection, New York public library: index of periodicals, 201; library holdings, 218-19
Schreiber, Flora Rheta, 793
Schuerman, Leo Anthony, 3796
Schulberg, Budd, 763, 794, 2507, 2546
Schulz, David Allen, 3624
Schuman, Howard, 3115
Schuyler, Lambert, 3116
Schuyler, Patricia, 3116
Schuyler, Philippa Duke, 2826
Schwab, Heidi, 901
Schwartz, M. L., 733
Schwartz, Marianne Philippa, 3797
Schwartz, Paulette, 616
Schwartz, Ruth Evelyn, 1434
Schwartz, Stephen, 3892
Scoble, Harry M., 795-96
Scoop, Los Angeles: San Francisco bay area edition, 3897
Scott, Ann Herbert, 2343-44
Scott, George, Jr., 4125

Scott, Horatio L., 20
Scott, John R., 963
Scott, Johnie, 1435
Scott, R. B., 3264
Scott, Thomas B., 2914
Scott, Tyree, 2382
Scott, William V. F., 3117
Scott, Woodrow Wilson, 3118
Scottish rite, Oakland, 3514
Scottsboro case, 2445, 3873
Screen, Frank F., 930
Scripps college. Lang art gallery: exhibit catalog, 108
Scruggs, Baxter S., 419
S. D. S. See Students for a democratic society
Seale, Bobby, 604, 631-35
Seales, Daniel, 1045
Searchlight pub. co., Seattle, 473
Sears, David O., 798-803
Seaside: newspaper, 4066
Seattle: African Methodist Episcopal church, 3204; autobiographies of residents, 412; banks and banking, 1939; barber, 314; biographies of residents, 306, 395, 399, 401, 487, 865; Broadview district, 2949; Brotherhood of sleeping car porters, 2397; Central Seattle community council archives, 2999; City council, 3119; Civic unity committee, 1945, 3000, 3066, 3120-21, 3952; Colored marine employees benevolent assoc. of the Pacific, 2383; Community chest and council, 3470; described (1922), 3863; economic conditions, 3470, 3789; employment, 1945, 3119, 3122, 3736; fertility trends, 3600; Gayton family, 325; housing, 2137, 3736; housing integration, 2135, 2177, 2224, 3122; industry, 3119; Jackson street community council archives, 2999; labor unions, 2377, 2382, 2393; local news columns, 4245-46, 4257; minority races, 1212; model cities program, 3770; Municipal reference library bibliography, 2240; National assoc. for the advancement of colored people, 663; Nation of Islam (Black Muslims), 557; National urban league, 1311, 1932, 3124, 3470, 3495, 3506, 3682; newspapers, 4270-90; Pickens lecture, 2907; Police dept., 3122;

Seattle (cont.)
    primary source materials on,
    482-554 passim; race relations,
    2968, 2987, 3011, 3025-26, 3039,
    3066, 3085, 3102, 3119-24, 3144,
    3151-52, 3952; radio broadcastings,
    1966; servicemen's recreation, 55;
    social conditions, 3470; truck
    farm, 960; urban life, 3470,
    3712, 3770, 3775, 3793-95, 3801;
    World war I servicemen, 37
--Public schools: bibliography,
    253; counseling, 1311; secondary,
    1581, 1609; segregation, 1436-38,
    1459, 3122
Seattle-King county (Wash.): legal
    directory, 2478
Seattle-King county (Wash.) economic
    opportunity board, 3494
Seattle-King county (Wash.) health
    and welfare council, 55
Seattle real estate board, 2137
Seattle Republican, 2872
Seattle searchlight. See Searchlight
    pub. co.
Secession: Ore. reaction, 231, 3405.
    See also Civil war
Second African Methodist Episcopal
    church, Los Angeles, 3302
Second African Methodist Episcopal
    church, San Francisco. See
    Bethel African Methodist Epis-
    copal church, San Francisco
Second Baptist church, Los Angeles,
    3304
Second Baptist church, Stockton,
    3209
Sedgwick, Marshall, 1045
Seeley, Robert Marshall, 2547
Segregation: armed services, 56;
    in San Diego, 1088. See also
    Civil rights; Education: segre-
    gation; Ejectment; Housing;
    Restrictive covenants; etc.
Seguie, George, 835
Seidenbaum, Art, 1440
Sekoto, C., 133
Selby, Anne, 804
Selby, Earl, 804
Selma, Ala., 695; freedom march,
    1077, 1126; sheriff speaks,
    3127
Semantics, 3841
Seme, Pivley Isaka, 3337
Semler, Michael Herman Alfred, 2944

Sentiment maker, 1213
Serial publications. See Newspapers;
    Periodicals
Sermons. See Religion; Speeches and
    lectures
Seshachari, Candadai, 3305
Seth, William H., 3556
Settle, D. C., 969
Seuell, Malchus M., 2503, 2745-47
Seventh-day adventist church, 3330
Sever, David Arthur, 3125
Seward, William Henry: speeches,
    3413-17
Seymour, M. O., 4241
Seymour, Robert, 3303
Shabazz, Nasser Ahmad, 831
Shabazz, Zakariah H., 2748
Shaffer, Anatole, 1838
Shamley, Elijah, 994
Shamley, Lewis, 994
Shands, Eugene, 3540
Shannon, Barbara, 3053
Shannon, Lyle William, 3798
Shapiro, Milton J., 2345
Sharp, J. S., 4232
Shasta county: homestead law suit,
    2260; petition of residents, 1049
Shattuck, David Olcott, 1058
Shaw, Alexander P., 3126
Shaw, Arnold, 1995, 2827
Shaw, Mrs. H., 3194
Shaw, James, 849
Shaw, Mary E., 3194
Shearer, John, 2499
Sheeley, James R., 2372
Sheil, Bernard James, 2241
Shelby, Roy A., 2370
Shelten, Lucile W., 3497
Shelvy, W. H., 3175
Shepard, Betty, 420
Shephard, George W., 3187
Shepherd, Elizabeth, 2346
Sherman, Jimmie, 806
Sherman, William Tecumseh, 1058
Sherwood, Frank Persons, 1128
Shevsky, Eshref, 3096, 3799
Shew, Jacob, 1057
Shields, G. W., 2273
Shikomba, Madeline, 1799
Shiloh Baptist church, Sacramento,
    3306-07
Shipley, Mrs. Maynard (Miriam Allen
    de Ford), 321
Shippey, Mervyn G., 1800-01
Shipping, 1885; autobiography, 320;

Shipping (cont.)
  Calif. (1844-48), 514; Colored
  marine employees benevolent
  assoc. of the Pacific, 2383;
  fictional accounts, 2649, 2674;
  International brotherhood of
  boilermakers, iron shipbuilders,
  welders and helpers of America,
  2376, 2403; International longshoremen's & warehousemen's
  union, San Francisco, 2381; labor
  unions, 473, 2355, 2361, 2377;
  Marinship corp., Sausalito, 955;
  Oakland welder, 1893; Ore. ship-
  building corp., 2376; passenger
  lists, 1273; whaling captain, 536
Shoaff, Peebles, 4130
Shockley, William, 3865
Shook, L. B., 4082
Shores, W. H., 3192
Shorey, William T., 536, 926, 951
Short, O'Day H., 2255
Short stories. See Literature:
  short stories
Shorter, James B., 3566
Shrine, Ancient Arabic order of the
  nobles of, Oakland, 3514-15
Shropshire, E., 3552
Sieber, Roy, 109
Siegel, Jay, 1214
Siegel, Stanley, 3127
Siegelman, Ellen, 3020
Sieroty, Mrs. Julian, 2288
Sierra county: petition of resi-
  dents, 1059
Sigurdson, Herbert, 2242
Silberman, Charles Eliot, 807
Silberstein, Ruth Leibowitz, 1558
Silbowitz, Al, 3713
Silk, Kenneth R., 1129
Sills, Thomas, 131, 137
Siloam Baptist church, Sacramento,
  3209
Silver mines. See Mines
Silvera, Frank, 2298-99
Silverman, Al, 3666
Silverthorn, William A., 1610
Simmons, Edward S., 996
Simmons, Joseph, 979
Simmons, William J. (author),
  474-75
Simmons, William J. (San Francisco,
  1869), 3568
Simms, Robert, 4200
Simonds, Olive B., 1559

Simons, Grace, 4080
Simpson, Alexander, 2273
Simpson, Alice Fisher, 421
Simpson, Dorothy, 1866
Simpson, H. E., 3175
Simpson, Orenthal J., 3674, 3677
Simpson, Porter S., 4215
Simpson, Ralph Ricardo, 2828
Simril-Curry-Moore scholarship
  foundation, 1802
Sims, Leon, 3540
Singer, Harry, 1441
Singerman, Matilie, 3868
Singh, Surendra Pratap, 1803
Singleton, Calvin, 2512
Singleton, Richard C., 1219
Singleton, Robert, 1681, 1804
Siracusa, Ernest V., 1291
Siskiyou county: petition of resi-
  dents, 1050
Sisney, John, 2371
Sjaardema, Everett John, 2504
Skanks, Mrs. Harrie Byron (Eva B.
  Allensworth), 2115
Skinner, James R., 930
Skinner, Samuel J., Jr., 3642
Skinner, Thomas H., 3541
Skolnick, Jerome H., 2945
Slang: glossary, 2576
Slaten, Minnie, 945
Slater (John F.) fund, 1683
Slater, Van, 133
Slaton, Nellie, 2347
Slaton, William, 2347
Slattery, Paul Harold, 2829
Slaughter, Jesse, 941
Slaughter, John, 3297
Slaughter, Lula, 3497
Slavery, 3341-3456; African trade, 10,
  21, 3436-37; bibliography, 199;
  British West Indies emancipation,
  2691; fictional account, 2640; in
  Brazil, 1001; in Jamaica, 1012;
  in Mexico, 1013; in New Granada
  (viceroyalty), 1009; in Ore., 229-
  31; in Peru, 999; in Tuolumne
  county, 3373a, 3392a; in West
  Indies, 1014; judicial cases,
  2437-38; pro-slavery sentiments,
  3162, 3284; speeches, 3342-3429
  passim, 3434, 3448-50, 3453. See
  also Abolition movement; Emancipation; Freedmen; Underground
  railroad
--California, 2016, 2020, 2056, 3341-

Slavery (cont.)
--California (cont.)
   3429 passim; Butte county, 2089;
   constitutional convention (1849),
   2069, 2375; fugitive slaves,
   2078, 2122, 3390; laws, 1044;
   plantation projected, 1218
--California and the West, 2080-81;
   Congressional speeches on, 184
Sledge, Lawrence, 992, 3198, 3561
Sleepy lagoon case, Los Angeles,
   2446, 2479-80
Sloan, Blanding, 1986
Slocum, William Neill, 3448-50
Small, Charles H., 830
Small, Kathleen Edwards, 422
Smalls, Robert, 2115
Smallwood, Purmon R., 2187
Smallwood, William, 423; biographical
   account, 463
Smart, Anne, 3141
Smedley, Henry, 3303
Smethen, Howard, 4029
Smith, Alma. See Jacobs, Alma
   (Smith)
Smith, Alvin, 2605
Smith, Annie Isabelle, 1806
Smith, Arthur L., 3971
Smith, Arthur R., 4056
Smith, Bradford H., 3795
Smith, Brenda Joyce, 1807
Smith, Carl S., 2589
Smith, Charles F., 4243
Smith, Charles V., 3801
Smith, Edward: taped interview, 537
Smith, Foraker, 2946
Smith, Frank E., 133
Smith, Garret, 1933
Smith, Grant, 946
Smith, Harriet E., 3481
Smith, Henry M., 952
Smith, Herman T., 2881
Smith, Herndon, 424
Smith, Hughie. See Lee-Smith, Hughie
Smith, Irving, 3560
Smith, J. Robert, 986, 4154, 4169
Smith, J. Thomas, 962
Smith, James, 3185
Smith, John W., 2278, 3562
Smith, Ken, 3675
Smith, Kenneth F., 3563
Smith, L. B., 1502
Smith, Marian Elizabeth, 425
Smith, Nathaniel, 328
Smith, Norvell, 1622

Smith, Prentice, 3559
Smith, Robert Worthington, 1012
Smith, Skippy, 961
Smith, Stan, 1442
Smith, Stanley Hugh, 1934
Smith, Thomas Lynn, 1215
Smith, Truman, 3418
Smith, Wallace Francis, 2243
Smith, Wendell, 3668
Smith, William (San Francisco) 3568
Smith, William (Santa Barbara, 1819),
   493
Smith, William E., 133
Smith, William M., 941
Smith, William R., 2481
Smith, William Thomas, 987, 1996
Smog, 3790
Smurr, J. W., 2068
Snellinge, Rolland. See Toure, Askia
   Muhammad Abu Bakr el = (assumed
   name)
Snelson, Mrs. Floyd Grant (Waterloo
   Bullock), 3466
Snook, George A., 1058
Snowden, Clinton A., 2116
Snowden, Sylvia, 133
Snyder, Clarence, 2221, 2229
Snyder, David L., 1130
Snyder, Patricia O., 1631
Soap industry: California cocoanut
   pulverizing co., 941. See also
   Cleaning; Laundry
Soares, Laura, 133
Sobel, Lester A., 1131
Social and service organizations,
   3457-3580
Social clubs, 3545-68 passim, 3923;
   Colored east bay auto workers
   assoc., Oakland, 2371; Colored
   laborer's social club, Los Angeles,
   2372; Colored political and social
   club of Los Angeles, 2875; Cosmos
   social club, San Francisco, 2802;
   Hiram club, Bakersfield, 2563; in
   San Jose, 2994; in Seattle (white),
   2987; Negro social register, inc.,
   Los Angeles, 1266. See also
   Benevolent societies; Community
   service organizations; Fraternal
   organizations
Social clubs (white), 2987
Social gospel, 3265
Social welfare. See Public welfare
Social workers: in Watts, 740
Socialist workers party, 783, 2255.

Socialist...(cont.)
See also Young socialist alliance
Society for the amalgamation of
races, 2782
Society of Calif. pioneers, San
Francisco, 143, 308a
Sociology, 3581-3635, 3865; analysis
of writings, 3076; bibliographies,
173, 182. See also Economic
conditions; Public welfare;
Social and service organizations;
Urban life; etc.
Soderstrom, Mary McGowan, 1443
Sohan, Metégo, 565, 2308, 2749
Sojourner Truth home, Los Angeles,
3496
Sojourner Truth industrial club,
Los Angeles, 3497-98
Solano county: directory, 1264
Soledad state prison, Salinas, 2456
Soliman, Abd Ellatif, 902
Sollen, Robert H., 808
Solomon, Benjamin, 1444
Solomon, William, 2916
Somerville, Bill, 1665
Somerville, John Alexander: auto-
biography, 426-27; founds news-
paper, 4135; taped interview,
538
Somerville, Mrs. John Alexander (Vada
J. Watson), 4100, 4102; taped
interview, 538
Somerville (John Alexander) hotel,
Los Angeles, 652
Sonoma county: Office of education
ethnic bibliography, 254
Sonora, 2107; Sugg family, 384
Sonora, Mexico: parish archives,
1013
Sons of Watts improvement assoc.,
717
Sororities. See Greek letter
societies
Source materials. See Bibliographies;
History; resource books; Manu-
scripts; Newspapers; Periodicals;
etc.
South. See Southern U. S.
South America, 999, 1001, 1004
South Carolina: history, 2127,
3435, 3438; reconstruction,
2867; schools, 1501
South central and east Los Angeles
transportation-employment
project, 1935-36, 3925

South central area welfare planning
council, Los Angeles county, 2780
Southern, Thomas M., 2348
Southern Calif. guide, Los Angeles,
4116
Southern Calif. informant, 4177
Southern Marin economic opportunity
council, 3978
Southern Pacific co.: dining car
waiters, 1937; discrimination
policies, 3129
Southern U. S.: law and order, 1030;
race relations, 2983, 3019, 3055;
slavery, 3431-51 passim. See also
under name of geographical local-
ity, e.g., Alabama; New Orleans;
etc.
Southwest: Spanish-speaking blacks,
2054
Spanish explorers, 449, 2060, 2130.
See also Esteban (explorer)
Sparks, Nemmy, 3130
Sparrow, Glen, 1445
Spaulding, Imogene, 3419
Spearman, Elihu: taped interview,
539
Spearman, Mrs. Elihu (Vivian):
taped interview, 540
Spears, Charlotta A. See Bass, Mrs.
Joseph Blackburn (Charlotta A.
Spears)
Spears, Ellis, 2288
Spears, Harold, 1809
Spears, Katherine, 2271
Specht, Harry, 3625, 3802
Speech: stuttering, 1807. See also
Language and language instruction
Speeches and lectures: 3, 1751, 2513,
2525, 2575-90 passim, 2816, 2889a,
2958, 3024, 3239, 3276, 3308,
3329, 3334, 3605; abolition move-
ment, 3434. See also Cleaver,
Eldridge; Literature: essays and
speeches
Spence, Raymond, 2505
Spigner, W. H., 2356
Spigners, Jessie, 3962
Spikes, Richard B.: biographical
account, 457
Spiller, Mrs. H. M., 4104
Spindler, George D., 1810
Spinks, William C., 1997
Spirituals. See Music
Spokane: Brotherhood of sleeping car
porters, 2397; described (1922),

Spokane (cont.)
   3863; local news columns, 4243,
   4257, 4283; newspapers, 4291-96;
   race relations, 3038
Spokane community action council,
   3131
Sports, 3636-80, 3848; biographical
   accounts, 2301-45 passim; boxing
   of Isaac Isaacs, 294; discrimina-
   tion in bowling, 1095; in Watts,
   805; journalistic treatment, 2274
Spraings, Violet E., 1811
Spriggs, Haroldie K., 1812
Spring, Agnes Wright, 3165
Springer, Louise, 3560
Sprott, Talmadge, 734
Stafford, Mattie Mae, 4042
Stage. See Entertainment industry;
   Motion pictures; Theater
Stagecoach drivers, 328, 437
Stampp, Kenneth M., 2031, 2117
Stanford, Aremento T., 3481
Stanford, Leland, 1057
Stanford, Mrs. Leland (Jane
   Lathrop), 2269
Stanford brothers, San Francisco,
   1058
Stanford research institute, 1446-
   47, 1938
Stanford univ.: National assoc. for
   the advancement of colored people,
   3985; reminiscences of, 383;
   speech of Martin Luther King,
   Jr., 2586; student revolt, 642
Stansbury, Jeff, 4029
Stanton, Richard Henry, 3420
Stanton, Robert, 930
Starkey, James Rylander, 2870;
   letters, 1216
Starobin, Robert S., 3451
Starr, Abraham Dubois, 1057
Starr King African Methodist Episcopal
   Zion church. See First African
   Methodist Episcopal Zion church,
   San Francisco
Starr King elementary school, San
   Francisco, 90
State employees for equality,
   Sacramento, 2244
State historical society of Colorado:
   index to its Colorado magazine,
   255-56
Station XETV, San Diego, 3164
Statistics. See Data analysis
Stauffer, Henry, 428

Stearns, Abel, 2086
Stebbins, Horatio, 2006
Steel, Ronald, 636
Steel industry: employment, 1923
Steffgen, Kent H., 1132
Stegner, Wallace Earle, 3803
Steinberg, Warren L., 3133
Steinel, William, 2346
Steinfield, Melvin, 903
Steinman, Marilyn, 2425
Stephenson, Richard, 3134
Stepin Fetchit (pseud.). See Perry,
   Lincoln
Steptoe, Benton P, 4028
Stevens, James, 4085
Stevens, Kathleen H., 3626
Stevens, Thaddeus, 3421
Stewart, Carlotta, 540a
Stewart, Evelyn S., 1455
Stewart, Gilchrist, 540a
Stewart, John J., 3135
Stewart, McCants, 540a, 4254
Stewart, Mary D., 3462
Stewart, Maxwell S., 2171
Stewart, Samuel, 3166
Stewart, Thomas McCants, 540a
Still, John Hamilton, 1058
Still, William, 429-30
Still, William Grant: analysis of
   compositions, 2829; articles by,
   1998, 2837-38, 2842, 2844; bio-
   graphical accounts, 455, 463, 471,
   2298-99, 2328, 2340, 2798, 2804-
   05, 2807, 2819; biography, 2828;
   letters, 3873; musical composi-
   tions, 2830-53 passim
Still, Mrs. William Grant (Verna
   Arvey), 70-71, 281, 2796-98, 2841,
   2962
Stillman, Richard Joseph, 56
Stocker, J., 1448
Stockton: Colored business men's
   assoc., 944; directories, 1292-93;
   discrimination, 1101; local news
   columns, 4146, 4193, 4198-99,
   4206; newspapers, 4209-12; public
   schools (1863), 1688; Second
   Baptist church, 3209; urban life,
   3711
Stockton and San Joaquin county public
   library: library holdings, 257
Stokes, Darius P., 2056, 3308
Stokes, Elizabeth (pseud.). See
   Coleman, Anita Scott
Stolper galleries of primitive arts,
   Los Angeles, 94

Stone, Irving, 476, 541
Stone, Jacob Leon, 3452
Stone, Robert C., 3499
Stone, William James, 3870
Stout, Bill, 702
Stovall, Charles A., 3428
Stovall, George W., 3550
Stovall, Leonard, 2763
Strather, Abraham, 926, 931
Stratten, James Edward, 1724, 3871
Straughter, Otis, 983
Strauss, George, 1922, 2368
Strickland, Reginald, 4161
Stripp, Fred S., 2401
Strode, Woodrow Wilson, 3648
Strong, Eva: taped interview, 542
Stroud, Welvin, 2308, 2749
Strunk, Gordon B., 431
Student nonviolent coordinating
    committee, 619, 847; Calif.
    publication, 3983; San Francisco
    regional office, 4026. See also
    Carmichael, Stokely
Students for a democratic society:
    Berkeley, 847, 849
Studio Watts workshop, Watts, 105
Sturdivant, Arthur, 3872
Stussy, Maxine Kim, 2734
Stuttering, 1807
Success publishing co., San Fran-
    cisco, 1294, 2918
Suchman, Edward A., 3158
Sudan, Omar Mali (assumed name).
    See Hoagland, Everett
Sudnow, David Nathan, 3627
Suffrage, 2866-67, 2870, 2880, 2882,
    2934; poll tax, 1107, 2013;
    Sacramento county, 1282. See
    also Fifteenth amendment;
    Politics
Sugg family, 384
Sullivan, Neil Vincent, 1370, 1379,
    1449-57
Sullivan, Noel, 3873
Summers, Charles: death, 326
Summers, James F., 835, 931, 951,
    3545
Summersette, John Fred, 1503
Sumner, Charles, 3453
Sumner, William, 3548
"Sunshine Sammy" (pseud.). See
    Morrison, Ernest
Survey of race relations, 3136
Sutter, John Augustus, 2087
Sutter (John Augustus) mill,

Coloma, 520
Sutton, David, 3659
Swaim, Lawrence, 637-38
Swanston, David, 645
Swett, H., 1217
Swett, John, 1414, 1813-14
Swinerton, George W., 1057
Swinney, T. W., 3458
Synanon, Santa Monica, 2765
Szabo, Andrew, 170
Szanto, George H., 639

T

Tabachnick, Benjamin Robert, 1560
Tacoma: described (1922), 3863;
    local news columns, 4257; National
    assoc., for the advancement of
    colored people, 485; newspapers,
    4275, 4297-4301; public school
    segregation, 1381; Univ. of Puget
    Sound, 1639; urban life, 3712
Tacoma area urban coalition: biblio-
    graphy of Pierce county library
    holdings, 258
Taeuber, Karl E., 2245
Taggart, Stephen G., 3138
Tahoe, Lake: tourism, 3842
Takagi, Paul T., 1755-56, 3500
Takaki, Ronald Toshiyuki, 21
Talbot, Steve, 3500
Tally, Jim, 3551
Tamalpais high school, Marin county,
    839
Tamony, Peter, 2854
Tanner, Henry Ossawa, 131
Tanner, Jerald, 3139-40
Tanner, Sandra, 3139-40
Tarquinio, Cheryl, 1815
Tate, Merze, 1816, 2402, 3422
Taxation: poll tax, 1107, 2013;
    sales, 3850
Taylor, Annie H., 994
Taylor, Archie, 247
Taylor, Charles: taped interview,
    543
Taylor, David Eugene, 3957, 4081
Taylor, Dora Jones, 3804
Taylor, Ethel Alexandrie, 1561
Taylor, John (Colorado): biographical
    account, 385
Taylor, John (San Francisco), 958
Taylor, John A., 3309
Taylor, John H., 3546
Taylor, Marion, 3551

Taylor, Paul S., 3423
Taylor, Mrs. Tide, 3469
Taylor, W. L., 4268
Taylor, William W., 4268
Taylor, Walter J., 979
Taylor, William C., 810
Taylor, Willis P., 936
Teilhet, Jehanne, 110
Teiser, Ruth, 563
Telephone industry: employment in, 1832
Television: Los Angeles election, 2900; news bias, 710; San Diego racial study, 3164; social utilization, 3603; treatment of race and riots, 2268, 3098; Watts riot, 701-02, 710, 2276, 3098. See also Columbia broadcasting system; National broadcasting system; Radio broadcasting
Telfer, John H., 4014
Temple, Herbert, 3679
Templeton, Fred, 3154
Tenette, Louis S., 4135
Ten Houten, Diana L., 813
Tennessee: journalism (1954-60), 2281
Tenth cavalry. See Armed services: Tenth cavalry
Teodori, Massimo, 904
Terrell, Henry Szold, 3805
Terrell, John Upton, 432
Terry, Juanita: biographical account, 338
Tessema, Memo, 133
Testimony, right of: in Calif., 1045-63, 1078, 1112-14, 1130, 2069, 2122, 2437-38; in Sacramento, 2474; legislative bills, 1061-62. See also Law and order
Tests, 1767, 3023; armed services, 1915; employment, 1864-65, 1915, 1921, 1925; intelligence, 1326, 1552, 1554, 1704, 1786, 1806, 3626; Leiter scale, 1706; literacy, 1073; Oseretsky, 1807; Rorschach, 1749
Texas: as fiction locale, 2646; religion, 3275; schools, 1472-1509 passim. See also under individual geographical locality, e.g., Houston; San Antonio
Thacker, M. Eva, 1218
Thayer, Eli, 3407, 3424

Theater, 1948-2004 passim, 3848; bibliography, 195; history and criticism, 2514-45 passim; periodical, 3915. See also Drama; Entertainment industry; Literature: drama; Motion pictures
Theibault, Mary Ann, 3628
Theisen, Lee Scott, 2118
Theodore, Terry, 2000
Thieblot, Armand J., 1939
Thimel, Martin, 3500
Third Baptist church, San Francisco, 3209, 3310-16, 3331
Third world liberation front, 643
Thirteenth amendment, 2038, 3359, 3402
Thomas, A. J., 3396
Thomas, Alberta, 2676
Thomas, Ariel Eaton, 646
Thomas, Ethel, 1990
Thomas, James A., 929
Thomas, Oliver S., 975
Thomas, Paul F., 433, 544
Thomas, Robert, 2499-2500
Thomas, Robert Colby, 3233
Thomas, Will, 2677
Thomas, William J., 3564
Thompson, Amelia Ellen (Brown), 1817
Thompson, Clyde M., 3521
Thompson, Erwin Normore, 57-58
Thompson, H. Keith, 3141
Thompson, Ian M., 1669
Thompson, Ike, 2187
Thompson, J. M., 965
Thompson, John L., 3542
Thompson, Leon Everette, 2855
Thompson, Lucille W. (Smith), 259
Thompson, Nanette C., 434
Thompson, Noah Davis, 111, 922, 946, 989
Thompson, Mrs. Noah Davis (Eloise A. Bibb), 2571-72
Thompson, Virginia, 435
Thompson, W. J. D., 953, 1248
Thompson, Warren Simpson, 1219
Thompson, Wayne Edward, 3806-08
Thompson, William Neely, 1058
Thompson, Willie, 3809
Thorndale, C. William, 990
Thorne, Kathleen, 172
Thorne, Richard, 905
Thornsley, Jerome Russell, 1458
Thornton, Peter B., 1504
Thurman, A. Odell, 2119
Thurman, H. Wallace. See Thurman, Wallace

Thurman, Howard: articles by, 873, 1666, 2750, 3320; biographical accounts, 335, 466-67; biography, 3340; books by, 906, 2856-60, 3142, 3317-19, 3321-29
Thurman, Mrs. Howard (Sue Bailey), 1235, 2120-21, 3580, 3874
Thurman, Wallace, 2514, 3143, 4000
Tilghman, Charles F., Jr., 4147-48
Tilghman (Charles F., Jr.) press, Oakland and Berkeley, 665-66, 1245, 1265, 3223, 3225, 3236, 3523, 3878
Tilghman, Mrs. Charles F., Sr. (Hettie B. Jones), 992, 2902a
Tilghman, Robert, 1045
Tilton, Crystal Lee, 2861
Tilton, James, 3425
Timmons, F. Alan, 2548
Tinkham, George Henry, 2122
Tinsley, Charles Henry, 3462
Tipton, William, 835, 931
Tishman, Paul: art collection, 109
Titcomb, John H., 1058
Tobias, Henry Jack, 2947
Tobriner, Michael Charles, 1940
Tocus, Clarence Spencer, 2862
Tolbert, James L., 4080
Toluca Lake, 2477
Tomlinson, Tommy Mack, 803, 812-14, 881, 907
Toole, K. Ross, 2068
Torrance: public welfare, 3813
Torregano, Ernest J., 3853
Toure, Askia Muhammad Abu Bakr el- (assumed name), 852, 2751
Tourism. See Travel guides
Towns, Royal E., 4006
Townsend, Art, 4168
Townsend, Chauncey, 436
Townsend, Jonas Holland, 1818, 2013, 4190
Townsend, Vince Monroe, 2295
Trammel, Giles, 4049
Trans-bay federal savings and loan assoc., San Francisco, 991
Transport a child foundation, Los Angeles, 1440
Transportation. See Ejectment; Freeways; Los Angeles: street railways; Railroads; etc.
Trapping. See Fur trade
Travel guides, 2008-09, 2047, 3842, 3874, 3881
Travels. See Explorers; Overland

journeys to the Pacific; Voyages to the Pacific
Treat, J. R., 1200
Tretten, Rudie Weber, 1819
Tribble, Minnie C., 3497
Trigg, Alice, 3297
Trillingham, C. C., 1820
Trinidad, Colo.: newspaper, 4242
Troupe, Quincy, 2506
Troy, Owen A.: evangelist, 3221
Troy, Owen Austin: dissertation, 3330
Troy, Theodore W., 963
Truck farming, 960, 986
Truehill, Charles S., 952
Truman, Ben Cummings, 437
Trumbo, Dalton, 2001
Truth (Sojourner) home, Los Angeles, 3496
Truth (Sojourner) industrial club, Los Angeles, 3497-98
Tucson, Ariz.: history, 3826; Inter-racial committee, 3043; National urban league, 3684; newspapers, 4058-61; public schools, 1580, 1771, 1830; race relations, 3684; urban life, 3826; youth problems, 3689
Tulare: public schools, 1579
Tuolumne county: mining, 456; slavery, 3373a-3392a; Sugg family, 384
Tuotti, Joseph Dolan, 2573
Turchin, Leah Lillian, 1320
Turner, C. H., 4128
Turner, Elijah, 2925
Turner, Emma Jane: judicial suit, 1133-36, 2437-38
Turner, Estelle (Beasley), 2752
Turner, Frederick Jackson: safety-valve theory, 1227-28, 2040
Turner, Homer, 3853
Turner, Letha, 2349
Turner, Morris, 290, 2349
Turner, Nat: fictional account, 2669
Turner, S. S., 2763
Turner, William W., 2482
Tuskegee normal and industrial institute, 1480
Twain, Mark, 3091
Twenty-fifth infantry. See Armed services
Twenty-fourth infantry. See Armed services
Tyler, George W., 1118-19, 3256, 3258

Tyler, Helen, 438
Tyler, Priscilla, 2549
Tyler, William Harold, 2248
Tyler, Willis O., 3541, 4135
Tyrrell, Frank Edward, 1562

U

Uhlenberg, Peter, 3875
Ulansky, Gene, 3501, 3810
Underground railroad, 429-30, 444-47.
    See also Abolition movement;
    Freedmen; Slavery
Underhill, Jacob, 1058
Underwood, William H.: papers, 545
Unemployment, 1844-1947 passim. See
    also Employment
U. N. I. A. See Universal Negro
    improvement assoc. and African
    communities league
Unions. See Labor
Unitarian church, Los Angeles, 716,
    3502
Unitarian church, San Francisco,
    629-30
Unitarian fellowship for social
    justice, Los Angeles, 3502
Unitarian-Universalist project
    east bay, Oakland: publica-
    tion, 3928
United African appeal, San Fran-
    cisco, 876a, 3937a
United bay area crusade, 3505
United community defense services,
    3683
United hall assoc., Oakland, 992
United nations conference, San
    Francisco, 1034, 1084
United Negroes of Calif., 3853
United Presbyterian church in
    the U. S. A.: North coastal
    area, 3145
United San Francisco freedom
    movement, 2249
U. S. Adjutant general's office,
    59; Area redevelopment adminis-
    tration, 1869, 1941; Army
    military division of the
    Missouri, 60; bibliographies
    (1960-70), 193; Bureau of labor
    statistics, 3629-30; Bureau of
    the census, 260, (1790-1915)
    1220-21, (1850-80) 1295-99,
    (1920-32) 1222-23, (1960) 1197,
    (1970) 1144, 2889; Economic

development administration, 3811;
    House un-American activities com-
    mittee, 1035; Information agency
    Topic, 4029; National advisory
    commission on civil disorders,
    909-13, 3114; National archives,
    205; National commission on the
    causes and prevention of violence,
    647, 1657; Office of economic op-
    portunity, 3500, 3802; Office of
    education, 1563, 1822; Supreme
    court, 1100, 2484. See also
    Armed services; Federal theater
    project; Fifteenth amendment;
    Fourteenth amendment; Historical
    records survey; Model cities pro-
    gram; Thirteenth amendment;
    Writers' program; etc., and under
    individual wars, e.g., Civil war,
    War with Mexico, World war I, and
    World war II
--Commission on civil rights, 908,
    1137, 1141, 1770; Calif. advisory
    commission reports, 816, 1142;
    Los Angeles hearing, 1138; Los
    Angeles-San Francisco bay area
    police, 2483; Oakland hearing,
    1139; Oakland schools, 1821;
    Phoenix hearing, 1140; San Fran-
    cisco hearing, 1139; school
    segregation, 1459.
--Works progress administration
    (Calif.): bibliography of litera-
    ture, 261; Los Angeles housing
    survey, 2250; San Francisco
    theater history, 2002; West Indian
    slavery, 1014
Universal bakery, Richmond, 563
Universal books, Hollywood: sales
    catalogs, 262
Universal Negro improvement assoc. and
    African communities league:
    Calif. representative, 915; in
    Los Angeles, 830, 922; in Oakland,
    914. See also Garvey, Marcus
    Mosiah
Universities. See Education:
    colleges and universities
Univ. of southern Calif., Los Angeles:
    (1903-07), 538; library holdings,
    263; slavery collection biblio-
    graphy, 199; Youth studies center,
    3812
Unrau, Harlan Dale, 3146
Upton, William H., 3543-44

Urban affairs institute, Los Angeles: publication, 3910

Urban history, 3687-3826 passim; intracity migration, 1214

Urban league. See National urban league

Urban life, 3681-3826 passim; in Calif., 3590. See also Community service organizations; Economic conditions; Education; Employment; Housing; Public health; Sociology; etc.; and under names of individual cities, e.g., Los Angeles: urban life; Seattle: urban life

Urban planning, 3722; in San Francisco, 3792; schools, 1337

Urban redevelopment, 1576-77, 2132-2262 passim. See also Housing

Ury, Claude, 1307

Utah: as poetry locale, 2708; census (1850-80), 1296; colleges and universities, 1629; cowboys, 3172; directory, 1268; Fort Du Chesne, 483; historic sites, 2047; history, 2033; laws, statutes, etc., 2467-67a; mines, 1931; newspapers, 4265-68; race relations, 3143, 3589; slavery, 3350, 3365; steel industry, 1923; territorial government, 3418. See also Mormons and under individual geographical localities, e.g., Ogden, Salt Lake City, etc.

V

Valentine, Charles E., 3554

Valleau, John, 1460

Vallejo, 3015; (1934), 656; directory, 1267; local news columns, 4063, 4144, 4199; Prince Hall no. 3 credit union, 982; school segregation, 1461

Val Verde: local news columns, 4081

Val Verde improvement assoc., 4035

Valverdian: voice of the hills, Los Angeles, 4126

Van, Melvin. See Van Peebles, Melvin

Van Alstyne, W. W., 3147

Vance, William L., 988, 2356

Vancouver, Wash.: labor, 2379;

National assoc. for the advancement of colored people, 664

Vandenberg air force base, Lompoc, 564

Vanderpool, Jacob, 1224

Van Dyke, Duane John, 1942

Vanecko, James J., 1361

Vanhook, C., 3458

Van Lowe, Blossom Lorraine, 1530

Van Peebles, Melvin, 440

Vanport City, 1189

Vass, S. N., 3331

Vassault, Ferdinand, 1058

Vassel, David E., 914

Vaudeville. See Entertainment industry

Vaughn, Lamar, 3539

Vaughn, Royce H., 133

Vaughner, Philip B., 981

Veatch, Laurelyn Lovett, 22

Vegetable gardening: in Seattle, 960

Vegetable markets: in Los Angeles, 986

Vena, Dorothy P. See Johnson, Mrs. Ivan (Dorothy P. Vena)

Venable, Elizabeth (Landeway): letter, 546

Venable, Henry, 3196

Venediger, David J., 1272

Venerable, William A., 4108

Venezuela: history, 1004

Venice: biography of Arthur L. Reese, 319; directory, 1267

Vernon, Robert, 817

Vesper, Joan Louise Frantz, 2550

Veterans of foreign wars of the U. S., Los Angeles county, 3567

Victoria, B. C. See British Columbia

Victorville: local news columns, 4081

Vietnam war: Century City march, 838

Vines, Dwight Delbert, 1143

Virginia: slavery, 3439-40, 3444

Visalia: local news columns, 4193; school history, 1800-01

Vischer, Edward, 1058

Vocational education, 1537, 1741, 1886, 3469. See also Employment: job and on-job training

Vollmer, Howard Mason, 1667

Von Brauchitsch, Dennis M., 3148

von Hentig, Hans, 3631

Vosburg, Fitz James, 984

Vose, Clement Ellery, 2252

Voyages to the Pacific, 320; (1851) 444-47; passenger lists, 1273.

Voyages to the Pacific (cont.)
See also California: gold rush;
Overland journeys to the Pacific

W

Wachhorst, Wyn, 3332
W. A. C. O. See Western addition
community organization, San
Francisco
Waco, Tex.: residents invest in
Calif. land, 1174
Waddy, Ruth G., 95, 133
Wade, Tootsie, 307
Wagner, Charles D., 938
Wagner, Harr, 918
Wagner, Leon, 3664
Wagner, Marvin G., 938
Wagoner, Henry Oscar: biographical
account, 441; letter, 1225
Wagoner, W. M., 3297
Wagstaff, Thomas, 919
Waite, Edwin G., 1055
Waiters, 1937, 2373
Walden, Roy, 3949
Waldie, Helen Bullock, 1823
Waldo, Elisabeth, 2835
Walker, Eugene, 890
Walker, Frank, 3191
Walker, George W., 2003
Walker, I. Israel, 4287
Walker, Jesse William, 994
Walker, Joseph M., 927
Walker, Larry, 133
Walker, Oliver, 1611
Walker, Paul, 1668
Walker, Phyllis, 4153
Walker, Theodore, 4062
Walker, W. W., 3191
Wall (Fannie) children's home,
Oakland, 3477-78
Wallace, A. J., 1174
Wallace, A. L., 3559
Wallace, Ike W., 3564
Waller, Ben C., 969
Waller, E., 963
Wallis, Marie Pope, 3813
Walnut: Mt. San Antonio college
library holdings, 214
Walsh, Martin De Porres, 3333
Walter, Mildred Pitts, 2350
Walters, Robert J., 3149
Walthart, Richard Louis, 3616
Walther, George, 3936
Walton, A. S., 3185

Walton, Sidney F., 1144, 1653,
1824-25
Wamble, Thelma, 3876
War with Mexico: veterans, 2072.
See also Mexico
Ward, Andrew J., 1564-68, 2068,
2437-38
Ward, Artis N., 4005
Ward, Bertha, 937
Ward, C. H., 61
Ward, James, 3549
Ward, Mary Frances, 1564-68, 2068,
2437-38
Ward, Mike, 2253
Ward, Sadie, 4082
Ward, Thomas Myers Decatur, 3334,
3404
Ward, W. S., 4120
Ward vs. Flood (judicial case), 1564-
68, 2068, 2437-38
Warden, Donald, 1462
Ware, Clifford Ernest, 3989, 4172
Ware, Marguerite Evelyn, 2122a
Ware, Waymon: taped interview, 547
Warren, Earl, 2455
Warren, Emily, 3187
Warren, Francis Emroy, 2123
Warren, Mary Phraner, 2351
Warschaw, Mrs. Louis (Carmen Harvey),
2254
Washington, Booker Taliaferro, 1480,
3877, 3882. See also Booker T.;
Bookertee; etc.
Washington, Chester L., 3654, 4083,
4117
Washington, Daisy, 3187
Washington, George (Centralia, Wash.):
biographical accounts, 366, 370,
397, 402, 410, 416, 424, 470
Washington, George (Nevada City),
1110-11, 2437-38
Washington, George (Portland, Ore.),
3403
Washington, George (Sacramento valley,
1829), 2086
Washington, George (Tehama county),
2473
Washington, George. See also Bush,
George Washington
Washington, Hazel (Mrs. Roscoe
Washington), 423, 463
Washington, James (artist), 78, 133
Washington, James (San Francisco),
2278

Washington, James (Washington state), 548

Washington, Kenneth, 3648-49

Washington, Leon H., 3853, 4114, 4123

Washington, Louis J., 4058

Washington, Mary C., 3481

Washington, Nathaniel Jason, 2124

Washington, Timothy, 131

Washington, William (Berkeley, 1970), 2781

Washington, William (San Francisco, 1852), 1045

Washington (state): African Methodist Episcopal church (1863), 3177; airplane industry, 1911; Baptist state convention, 3273; biographies of residents, 473; census (1860-80), 1298; civil rights statutes, 1089; Colored women's federation of, 485; directories, 1267, 1269; employment, 1943-45; employment discrimination, 1934; Fair housing listing service, 2178; Freemasons, 3532a; Green river coal co., 990; historic sites, 2047; history, 2114, 3829-30; housing, 2218; laws, statutes, etc., 2467-67a; legislative manuals, 2871-72, 2940; lumber industry, 1889; Model cities program, 490; National assoc. for the advancement of colored people, 489; newspapers, 4269-4301; non-white races, 3632; papers and reminiscences of residents, 482-554 passim; Planning and community affairs agency, 3632; race relations, 3026; State commission on the causes and prevention of civil disorders, 920; State fair employment practice commission, 1093, 2178; steel industry, 1923; unemployment directory, 1932. See also Pacific coast; Pacific northwest

--Legislative assembly, 442, 2116; pre-emption law, 1151; residence act, 1150

--State board against discrimination, 489-90, 1146-49, 1613, 1943-44, 2137, 2178; annual report, 1145; news letter, 4038

--State library: bibliographies, 265-66; holdings, 264

--University: Institute of labor economics, 1945; race relations, 1648, 2949

Washington mining co., Hornitos, 993a

Washington standard, Seattle, 4287

Wasserman, Susan Arnesty, 1569

Waters, Ethel, 3873

Watkins, April Johnson, 112

Watkins, Ben, 3878

Watkins, George E., 477, 2575; newspaper editor, 4116, 4143, 4193, 4206, 4278

Watkins, Jocelyn Henderson, 1505

Watkins, Mark Hanna, 3150

Watkins, Pauline Melonee, 1506

Watkins, Ted, 755

Watkins, Walter F., 3335-36

Watson, Homer K., 3814-15

Watsonville: public schools, 1574

Watts, Lewis G., 3151-52

Watts, 2823, 668-829; (1970), 826; Afro-American investment co., 930; as fiction locale, 2593, 2906; directories, 1300; festival, 827; history, 770, 818; juvenile art, 2353; literary anthologies, 2506-08; newspapers, 2279, 4068, 4080, 4082, 4093, 4120, 4128-33; Operation bootstrap, 985; poem, 2709; public schools, 1435, 1781, 1827; public welfare, 3813; race relations, 805; small business, 995; Urban workshop, 105, 676, 734; Voice of Watts, 4036. See also Los Angeles

--riot (1965), 668-829, 837, 848, 877, 881, 895, 909-13, 916, 1765, 1820, 2323, 3050, 3829; newspaper coverage, 2276, 2286; television coverage, 701-02, 710, 2276, 3098

Watts Advertiser-review, 818

Watts industrial park, 457

Watts labor community action committee, 4137

Watts towers, 789, 2335

Watts writers' workshop, 2546, 2573; literary anthologies, 2507-08

Waugh, John C., 725

Wax, Darold D., 3454

Waymon, Carrol W., 2950

Weatherwax, John Martin, 2125

Weaver, Robert B., 2577

Weaver, Valerie Whittemore, 1152

Weaver, Wertie Clarice, 2678

Webb, James Morris, 3337

Webb, Ulysses Sigel, 1121
Webb, Willie Rachel, 2426
Weber, Francis, 2126
Webster, Argow, 822
Webster, Preston, 2490
Webster, Staten Wentford, 1463-64, 1612
Weckler, Joseph E., 2462, 3017
Weed: local news columns, 4199
Weeden, Christopher R., 3303
Weekes, Beresford, 2762
Weinberg, Carl, 1827
Weinberg, Meyer, 267, 1388, 1465, 3153
Weinberger, Andrew D., 1153
Weinert, Bertram Allan, 3455
Weir, Mrs. James S. (Victoria S. Dickinson), 540a
Weiss, Myra Tanner, 2255
Welcher, Donald Vincent, 4184, 4189
Welfare. See Public welfare
Welfare planning council, Los Angeles region, 3816
Wellington, David H., 3990
Wellman, David: article by, 1946
Wellman, David Thomas: thesis, 921
Wells, Gerald: papers, 549
Wells, Wesley Robert, 2485-86
Wellsher, C. A., 4120
Welsch, Erwin K., 268
Wengi, Richard Adolf, 3426
Wenkert, Robert, 3154-55
Wert, Robert J., 648
Wesley chapel, Los Angeles, 2072
West, Charles I., 4248
West, Earle H., 269
West, F. W., 3175
West, Irene, 2753
West Indian benevolent assoc., San Francisco, 3568
West Indies: slavery, 1014
West side investment assoc., Los Angeles, 994
Western addition area, San Francisco, 1539, 1544, 2249, 3022, 3476, 3729, 4184
Western addition area community action program, San Francisco, 3476
Western addition community festival, San Francisco, 3569
Western addition community organization, San Francisco, 2261, 4037
Western addition law office community education project, San Francisco, 3988
Western interstate commission for higher education, 1631, 1669
Western student movement, Los Angeles, 1828
Westin, Alan F., 1154
Weston family, 3358
Westside Jewish community center, Los Angeles: art holdings, 144
Whaley, Richard B., 2875
Wham robbery, 45
Wharfield, Harold B., 62-64
Wheatley, Phillis, 2754
Wheatley (Phillis) inc., Los Angeles, 3488
Wheeldin, Donald, 824, 2951, 3918
Wheeler, Benjamin Ide, 3877
Wheeler, Gerald Everett, 443
Whitacre, Robert Huntley, 1015
Whitaker, Hazel Gottschalk, 1829
Whitaker, Leon Leroy, 2487
White, Aaron, 1045
White, Agnes, 3469
White, Amos, 4138, 4145
White, Charles Wilbert, 78, 82-83, 91, 113-14, 117, 120, 127, 130-31, 133, 2298-99
White, Clarence, 979
White, Ernst: taped interview, 550
White, Forester F., 835
White, Frank G., 3541-42
White, Jay, 3504
White, John W., 3469
White, Joseph, 1646, 3879
White, M. L., 2194
White, Mamie V., 945
White, Milton, 564
White, Morgan I., 3541
White, Persis, 3817
White, Ruben B., 3567
White, Ted W., 2488
White, Vivian Elizabeth, 3818
White, Willie Ray, 2256
White Pine county, Nev.: Elevator silver mining co., 950
White Sulphur Springs, Mont., 342, 2810
Whitelaw, Charles S., 3880
Whiteman, Maxwell, 270-71
Whitfield, J. W., 3462
Whitfield, James Monroe, 2585; biographical information, 455
Whiting, Ellen, 3481
Whitley, George W., 929, 994
Whitley, Maggie J., 994

Whitman, Winslow, 1613
Whittaker, J. T., 2764
Whittaker, Priscilla, 3187
Whittaker, Richard Salinthus, 2764
Whitted, Martin, 3860
Whitton, Abel, 1058
Who's who. See Autobiographies;
    Biographies
Wicker, Tom, 910-11
Wickliffe, Gustavus Woodson, 939
Widdemer, Margaret, 2712-13
Wiggins, Gertrude, 2915
Wiggins, Samuel Paul, 1466, 1507
Wildavsky, Aaron, 3156
Wilds, John A., 2278, 3562, 4146
Wiley, Hugh, 2679-80
Wiley, J. M., 984
Wiley, James T., 3157
Wiley, John, 3539
Wilgus, D. K., 2513
Wilkerson, Lillie (Donnell), 3570
Wilkerson, William M. (Oakland),
    2930
Wilkerson, William McKinley
    (Bakersfield), 983
Wilkins, Charles, 2045
Wilkins, J. B., 4175
Wilkins, Roy, 65-66, 2403
Wilkinson, Frank, 825
Williams, A. Cecil, 3338
Williams, Alfred C., 975
Williams, Almira, 3460
Williams, Anna, 3481
Williams, Arthur Joseph, 2952
Williams, Bert. See Williams,
    Egbert Austin
Williams, Bobbye Louise, 2551
Williams, Charlotte Anne, 1570
Williams, (Daniel) hospital, Los
    Angeles, 2763
Williams, David W., 2465
Williams, Dorothy Slade, 2257
Williams, E. Winston, 3484, 4136
Williams, Egbert Austin: bio-
    graphical accounts, 455, 470,
    1968, 1971, 1981, 1993-94, 1997,
    2002-03, 2298-99, 2328
Williams, Elizabeth, 3187
Williams, Ernest D., 3567
Williams, Ethel L., 480
Williams, Franklin H., 1155, 2258-
    59, 3820-21
Williams, Fred C., 4107
Williams, George H., 3427
Williams, Georgia Mae, 1614

Williams, Harris, 3567
Williams, James: autobiography,
    444-47
Williams, James Henry, 1508-09
Williams, Jay C., 4202
Williams, John Alfred, 3881
Williams, Joseph Johnson, 1571
Williams, Kelly, 1248
Williams, L. (Shasta county), 2260
Williams, LePage, 1874
Williams, Marcus Asie, 3822
Williams, Margaret (pseud.), 2681
Williams, Marilyn, 3799
Williams, Paul Revere, 115-16, 946,
    2272; biographical accounts,
    106, 111, 455, 463, 471
Williams, Percy, 3217
Williams, R. L. (Oakland), 936
Williams, Ralph S., Sr., 2925
Williams, Robert, 3193
Williams, Robert L. (author, 1956),
    1226
Williams, Robin Murphy, 1467, 3158
Williams, Simon, 1174
Williams, Tena, 3193
Williams, Thomas L., 941
Williams, Mrs. Tobe, 968
Williams, William James, 995
Williams publications, Santa Ana,
    3141
Williams vs. Young (judicial case),
    2260, 2437-38
Williamson, Joel Randolph, 2127
Williford, Stanley O., 826
Willis, George, 2917
Willis, William Ladd, 2128
Willkie, Wendell, 667
Willowbrook: newspapers, 4068, 4093
Wills, Maury, 3664, 3676
Willson, C. M., 2270
Wilson, A. R., 4226
Wilson, Agnes E., 3703, 3823
Wilson, Alan Bond, 1345, 1468
Wilson, Anita Louise, 3633
Wilson, Benjamin D., 2063
Wilson, Charles Henry, 67
Wilson, Charles M., 2270
Wilson, Don M., 4153
Wilson, Ed, 1159, 1175
Wilson, Ernest, 3560
Wilson, Frances (Younge), 2352
Wilson, Fred R., 133
Wilson, Israel C., 926
Wilson, J. H. (Los Angeles), 3541,
    4041

Wilson, J. H. (Oakland), 3180
Wilson, J. H. (Riverside), 3545
Wilson, James B., 931, 2278, 2296, 4146, 4183, 4193
Wilson, James Finley, 4268
Wilson, Joyce R., 827, 923, 2261, 2953
Wilson, Leola B., 3488
Wilson, Martha, 3466
Wilson, Robert C., 3303
Wilson, William H., 4276
Wilty, James, 2921
Winans, Joseph W., 3428
Winburn, Oscar E., 4129
Wingert, Paul S., 100
Winsell, Keith Andrew, 3882
Winslow, Eugene, 2298
Winters, E. W., 3175
Winthrop, Robert Charles, 3429
Wirt, Frederick M., 1369
Wise, Namon, 3339
Witcher, Kathryn L., 3505
Witebsky, Leon Irving, 3159
Withers, Geraldine, 992
Withers, Zachary, 1156, 2004, 2755, 3198
Woffert, Liola: taped interview, 551
Wogaman, Thomas D., 1457, 1469
Wolfe, Evelyn, 117
Wollenberg, Charles, 3160
Wolters, Raymond Reilly, 3883
Woman's auxiliary, Baptist national convention, 3212
Woman's auxiliary, St. John's district assoc. of northern Calif., 3215
Women: and child rearing, 3607; criminology, 3631; etiquette manual, 3827; family planning, 3729; in Calif. gold rush literature, 2540; in college, 1620; in Los Angeles, 3574, 3797, 3818; in World war II, 51, 65, 942; Los Angeles housing, 3488, 3497; National assoc. of Negro business and professional women's clubs, 1264; National council of Negro women, 1235, 3579-80; periodical publication, 3956; public welfare, 3740; social status, 3797; unmarried mothers, 3728. See also League of women voters; Young women's Christian assoc.; etc.

Women's clubs, 3570-80; Calif. assoc. of colored women's clubs, 3576, 4047; Colored women's federation of Washington (state), 485; National assoc. of Negro business and professional women's clubs, 1264; National council of Negro women, 1235, 3579-80; Wyoming assoc. of colored women's clubs, 2104
Wong, Frances F., 3634
Wong, Herb, 2863
Wood, Catherine M., 448
Wood, Forrest Glen, 2129, 3161
Wood, G. W., 3191
Wood, Ted, 3506
Wood, Thomas Alexander: autobiography, 552
Woodard, Beulah E. (Mrs. Brady Woodard), 70, 127
Woodbey, G. W., 4175
Woodbury, Naomi Felicia, 3162
Woodfin, Prince, 3392a
Woodhouse, Charles E., 2947
Woodland: high school building, 1600; local news columns, 4146, 4149, 4163, 4193, 4207
Woodmansee, John J., 3163
Woodmen, American, 3508-09, 3890, 4048
Woodmen minstrels, 2864
Woodring, P., 649
Woodruff, Hale, 127
Woods, Annie, 928
Woods, Enoch A., 966
Woodson, Fred Patterson: papers and interview, 553
Woodward, Elon A., 59
Woodworth, Frederick A., 1058
Woodworth, Mrs. Selim E., 1117
Woolfolk, George Ruble, 1227-28
Word, Carl, 2297
Work, Lena Brown, 828
Work, Monroe Nathan, 272-74, 3364
Workingman's joint stock assoc. of Portland, Ore., 996
Workman, Boyle, 3824
World war I: black participation, 67; civilian leadership, 3868; mobilization, 38; reminiscences of John A. Somerville, 538; Seattle servicemen, 37; spurious newspaper extra, 4080. See also Armed services
World war II: Africa, 19; soldiers in

World war II (cont.)
   West, 66; civilian labor segregation, 888; civilian leadership, 3868; Double V movement,
   Los Angeles, 3146; employment
   of black troops, 43; essay, 2583;
   gold star mother, 2714; in fiction, 2649, 2651; Los Angeles
   War worker, 4127; Marinship
   corp., Sausalito, 955; migration, 1172-1226 passim; Oakland
   activities, 3878; Port Chicago
   disaster, 2688; Portland-Van-
   couver (Wash.) labor, 2379;
   report to Northern Calif. conference on Negro work, 3621;
   San Francsico labor, 2384; shipyard labor, 2355; women in industry, 942. See also Armed
   services; Fort Huachuca, Ariz.
World's fairs. See Chicago:
   World's Columbian exposition;
   Philadelphia: U. S. centennial
   exhibition; Portland: Lewis
   and Clark centennial exposition
Worthy, William, 570
Wrestling. See Sports
Wright, Beatrice Ann, 2682
Wright, Crispus A., 971
Wright, George: taped interview,
   554
Wright, Jay, 2495
Wright, Jerome Wendell, 924
Wright, Lyle Henry, 2686
Wright, Richard, 2533, 2552-53,
   2666
Wright, Richard Robert, 449, 481,
   2130
Wright, S. J., 1640
Wright, S. L., 3189
Wright, William, 1045
Writers' program: Calif., 1181a,
   2049-50; Colo., 555, 2051
Wurster, Catherine Bauer, 2262
Wyatt, Faricita (Hall), 2756
Wychie, A. R., 2273
Wylley, John A., 926, 965
Wyman, Walker Demarquis, 3172
Wynn, Commodore, 468, 4081
Wyoming, 2105, 2153; census (1870-
   80), 1299; colleges and uni-
   versities, 1629; Fort Washakie,
   483; historic sites, 2047;
   Johnson county war, 47; laws,
   statutes, etc., 2467-67a; ranch

life, 3165-66. See also under
   individual place name, e.g.,
   Casper, Cheyenne, etc.
Wyoming assoc. of colored women's
   clubs, 2104
Wysham, George M., 1045
Wysinger, Gladys Gwendolyn. See
   Crawford, Gladys Gwendolyn
   (Wysinger)
Wysinger, Jesse E., 4149
Wysinger vs. Cruikshank (judicial
   case), 1800-01

            X, Y, Z

XETV (television station), San Diego,
   3164

Yablon, Roberta Seifert, 1572
Yabroff, Lawrence Jonas, 1573
Yakima, Wash.: local news columns
   from North Yakima, 4194
Yates, Charles E., 133
Yates, Elizabeth, 3340
Yates, William Henry, 2472, 2870
Yeargans, Hartwell, 133
Yerby, Frank, 2683
Yinger, John Milton, 3635
Yoder, Edwin M., 925
Yolo county: biographical accounts
   of Basil Campbell and Elijah
   Jennings, 358, and of Basil Camp-
   bell, 390; schools, 1519
York (explorer), 978, 2060, 2065;
   biographical account, 470
Yorty, Samuel William, 671, 805;
   mayoral campaign (1969), 2869,
   2888, 2900-01, 2935-37
Yosemite Valley, 437
Young, A. S. "Doc", 2865, 3677-79,
   4080
Young, Al, 2497, 2501, 2684, 2757
Young, Benjamin B., 2260
Young, Charles, 2326-27
Young, Mrs. Benjamin F. (Eva Whiting),
   3484
Young, James L., 2685-86
Young, James Owen, 2552
Young, James Walter, 3826
Young, Karl, 68
Young, Kenneth Evans, 1670
Young, Louisa A. G., 2260, 2437-38
Young, N. M., 4174
Young, R. Bryce, 2263
Young, Richard, 2954

Young, Theodore S., 2914
Young, Woodrow, 966
Young men's Christian assoc.:
    administrative attitudes, 3002;
    in Los Angeles, 313
Young socialist alliance, 2955.
    See also Socialist workers party
Young women's Christian assoc.,
    Oakland, 3507; San Francisco,
    2384
Youth. See Community service
    organizations; Education;
    Sociology; Urban life; etc.
Youth for service, San Francisco,
    3973
Youth guidance. See Education:
    counseling and guidance
Yuba City: directory, 1263
Yuba county: history, 2035;
    petitions of residents, 1051,
    1060

Zanders, Ida O. Williams, 1830
Zeitlin, Patty, 2353
Zeta Phi Beta sorority, 3893
Zietlon, Edward Robert, 2553
Zilversmit, Arthur, 3456
Zimbabwe African people's union, 13
Zimbleman, Ernest August, 1831
Zimmerman, Paul Bechler, 3680
Zimpel, Lloyd, 1157
Zoot suit riots, Los Angeles,
    875, 880